Introduction to Electronic Commerce

Introduction to Electronic Commerce 3/e

Efraim Turban
University of Hawaii

David King
JDA Software Group, Inc.

Judy Lang
Lang Associates

with contributions from

Linda Lai
Macau Polytechnic University, China

Carol Pollard
Appalachian State University

Deborrah C. Turban
University of Santo Tomas, Philippines

Linda Volonino
Canisius College

Ivan C. Seballos II
La Salle Lipa, Philippines

Prentice Hall
Boston Columbus Indianapolis New York San Francisco Upper Saddle River
Amsterdam Cape Town Dubai London Madrid Milan Munich Paris
Montreal Toronto Delhi Mexico City Sao Paulo Sydney
Hong Kong Seoul Singapore Taipei Tokyo

Editorial Director: Sally Yagan
Editor in Chief: Eric Svendsen
Executive Editor: Bob Horan
Editorial Project Manager: Kelly Loftus
Director of Marketing: Patrice Lumumba Jones
Senior Marketing Manager: Anne Fahlgren
Senior Managing Editor: Judy Leale
Production Project Manager: Ann Pulido
Senior Operations Supervisor: Arnold Vila
Operations Specialist: Ilene Kahn
Creative Director: Christy Mahon
Senior Art Director/Design Supervisor: Janet Slowik

Interior Designer: Jill Little
Cover Designer: Janet Slowik
Cover Illustration: John Bleck
Manager, Rights and Permissions: Karen Sanatar
Media Project Manager: Lisa Rinaldi
Media Editor: Denise Vaughn
Full-Service Project Management: BookMasters, Inc./Sharon Anderson
Composition: Integra
Printer/Binder: Edwards Brothers
Cover Printer: Lehigh-Phoenix Color/Hagerstown
Text Font: 10/12 ACaslon Regular

Credits and acknowledgments borrowed from other sources and reproduced, with permission, in this textbook appear on appropriate page within text.

Microsoft® and Windows® are registered trademarks of the Microsoft Corporation in the U.S.A. and other countries. Screen shots and icons reprinted with permission from the Microsoft Corporation. This book is not sponsored or endorsed by or affiliated with the Microsoft Corporation.

Library of Congress Cataloging-in-Publication Data

Introduction to electronic commerce / Efraim Turban ... [et al.]. — 3rd ed.
  p. cm.
  Prev. ed. published under author: Efraim Turban.
  Includes bibliographical references and index.
  ISBN-13: 978-0-13-610923-5
  ISBN-10: 0-13-610923-3
  1. Electronic commerce. I. Turban, Efraim. II. Turban, Efraim. Introduction to electronic commerce.
  HF5548.32.T87 2011
  658.8'72—dc22

2010006664

10 9 8 7 6 5 4 3 2 1

Prentice Hall
is an intprint of

www.pearsonhighered.com

ISBN-13: 978-0-13-610923-5
ISBN-10:   0-13-610923-3

Dedicated to all those who are interested
in learning about electronic commerce.

Contents in Brief

www.pearsonhighered.com/turban

Contents

Part 3 Business-to-Business E-Commerce   169

Part 4 Other EC Models and Applications   253

Part 5 EC Support Services   329

Online Chapter

Part 7 Applications and Site Development

Online Chapter Files

Preface

The global economic crisis of 2009–2010 forced organizations to reduce expenses in an environment of reduced economic activities. One of the most popular cost-reduction activities is conducting more business online. Actually, we are experiencing one of the most important changes to our daily lives—the move to an Internet-based society. Internet World Stats (internetworldstats.com) reported in December 2009 that more than 74 percent of the North American population (almost 341 million) surf the Internet. More interesting is the fact that more than 90 percent of people between the ages of 5 and 17 surf the Internet on a regular basis. According to Pew/Internet, in 2008 the biggest increase in generational use of the Internet occurred in the 70 to 75 age category, with a 45 percent increase in older people going online (reported by *Marketing Charts* 2009). It is clear that these percentages will continue to increase, and similar trends exist in most other countries. As a result, much has changed at home, school, work, and in the government—and even in our leisure activities. Some of these changes are spreading around the globe. Others are just beginning in some countries. These trends facilitate the conduct of business online, which is known as electronic commerce, or in its broader scope as e-business.

Electronic commerce (EC) describes the manner in which transactions take place over networks, mostly the Internet. It is the process of electronically buying and selling goods, services, and information. Certain EC applications—such as buying and selling stocks and airline tickets on the Internet—are growing very rapidly, exceeding non-Internet trades. But EC is not just about buying and selling; it is also about electronically communicating, collaborating, and discovering information. It is about e-learning, e-government, social networks, and much more. Electronic commerce has an impact on a significant portion of the world, including developing countries, affecting businesses, professions, and, of course, people.

WHAT'S NEW IN THIS EDITION?

The following are the major changes in this edition.

▶ **New Contributors.** We welcome Deborrah C. Turban who brings expertise in several e-business areas and Ivan C. Seballos II who created a number of our exhibits.

▶ **New Appendix.** A new appendix (Appendix A) describing e-supply chains in general as related to EC has been added.

▶ **Consolidation.** In order to reduce the size of the book, we eliminated two chapters by combining topics and moving material to online files. Old Chapter 6 about supply chains, collaborative commerce, and corporate portals is an example of this. Supply chains and their management is now an online appendix (Appendix A), collaborative commerce is now in Chapter 6, and portals are introduced in Chapter 2.

CHAPTERS WITH MAJOR CHANGES

- Chapter 1 now includes social networks, green computing, new business models, and other leading-edge topics.
- Chapter 2 has been expanded to include both traditional EC and Web 2.0 mechanisms.
- Chapter 4 includes new coverage of advertising models and strategies related to social networks.
- Chapter 9 on security has been completely rewritten and reorganized, moving from a generic view of security to an e-commerce orientation.
- Online Chapters 13 and 14 were merged into new Online Chapter 12.

CHAPTERS WITH LESS SIGNIFICANT CHANGES

All data in the chapters were updated. More than 25 percent of all cases have been replaced. About 50 percent of all end-of-chapter material has been updated and/or expanded. Managerial Issues were updated as were figures and tables. Duplications were eliminated and explanations of exhibits have been made more understandable. New topics were added in many of the sections to reflect the Web 2.0 revolution.

ONLINE FILES

The online files were updated and reorganized. Many new files have been added.

THE IMPORTANCE OF EC

The impact of EC is not just in the creation of Web-based businesses. It is the building of a new industrial order. Such a revolution brings a myriad of opportunities as well as risks. Beginning in 2005, we have witnessed the emergence of the second generation of the Web—Web 2.0, which expanded the boundaries of e-commerce from trading, information search, and collaboration with a business orientation to what is known as social commerce, which is driven by social computing technologies that were designed for individual use (such as blogs, wikis, file sharing, discussion groups, and social networks). As indicated earlier, organizations are attempting to increase the effectiveness and efficiency of their operations using e-commerce, including social commerce.

Forrester Research reports that the easy connections that social computing has given us have made a major impact not only on the social structure that exists outside the business world, but also on the global economy. Because of the pervasiveness of social computing, Forrester suggests that individuals share information with each other more often, rather than obtaining this information from institutional sources like mainstream media outlets and corporations. For a company to survive, Forrester suggests that its marketing initiatives must fundamentally change from a top-down information flow to one where communities and social computing initiatives are made a part of its products and services (reported by Blacharski 2006).

In revising *Introduction to Electronic Commerce*, we paid great attention to these developments. The reason is that so-called "social computing" is changing not only our lives and the way we do business, but also the fields of information technology and e-commerce itself.

The purpose of this book is to describe what EC is—how it is being conducted and managed—as well as to assess its major opportunities, limitations, issues, and risks—both in the traditional and social-computing business environments. It is written from a managerial perspective. And because EC is an interdisciplinary topic, it should be of interest to managers and professionals in any functional area of business, and in all industries. People in government, education, health services, and other areas also will benefit from learning about EC.

Today, EC and e-business are going through a period of consolidation in which enthusiasm for new technologies and ideas is accompanied by careful attention to strategy, implementation, and profitability. Most of all, people recognize that e-business has three parts; it is not just about technology, it is also about commerce and people.

This book is written by experienced authors and contributors who share academic as well as real-world practices. It is a concise text that can be used in one-semester or one-quarter courses. It also can be used to supplement a text on Internet fundamentals, management information systems (MIS), or marketing.

FEATURES OF THIS BOOK

Several features are unique to this book.

MANAGERIAL ORIENTATION

Electronic commerce can be approached from two major view points: technological and managerial. This text uses the second approach. Most of the presentations are about EC applications and implementation. However, we do recognize the importance of the technology; therefore, we present the essentials of security in Chapter 9 and the essentials of infrastructure and application development in Online Chapter 12, which is located on the book's Web site (pearsonhighered.com/turban). We also provide some detailed technology material in the files, appendices, and a tutorial on the book's Web site. Managerial issues are also provided at the end of each chapter.

REAL-WORLD ORIENTATION

Extensive, vivid examples from large corporations, small businesses, governments, and not-for-profit agencies from all over the world make concepts come alive. These examples show students the capabilities of EC, its cost and justification, and the innovative ways real corporations are using EC in their operations. Examples cover both large and small (SME) companies.

SOLID THEORETICAL BACKGROUND

Throughout the book, we present the theoretical foundations necessary for understanding EC, ranging from consumer behavior to the theory of marketing and competition. Furthermore, we provide Web site resources, many exercises, and extensive references to supplement the theoretical presentations.

MOST CURRENT CUTTING-EDGE TOPICS

The book presents the most current topics related to EC, as evidenced by the many 2008 to 2009 citations. Topics such as social networking, e-learning, e-government, e-strategy, Web-based supply chain systems, collaborative commerce, mobile commerce, and EC economics are presented from the theoretical point of view as well as from the application side.

INTEGRATED SYSTEMS

In contrast to other books that highlight isolated Internet-based systems, we emphasize those systems that support the enterprise and supply chain management. Intra- and interorganizational systems are highlighted as are the latest innovations in global EC and in Web-based applications.

GLOBAL PERSPECTIVE

The importance of global competition, partnerships, and trade is increasing rapidly. EC facilitates export and import, the management of multinational companies, and electronic trading around the globe. International examples are provided throughout the book including many from developing countries.

ONLINE SUPPORT

More than 100 files are available online to supplement text material. These include files on generic topics such as data mining and intranets, cases, technically oriented text, and much more.

USER-FRIENDLINESS

While covering all major EC topics, this book is clear, simple, and well organized. It provides all the basic definitions of terms as well as logical conceptual support. Furthermore, the book is easy to understand and is full of interesting real-world examples and "war stories" that keep readers' interest at a high level. Relevant review questions are provided at the end of each section so the reader can pause to review and digest the new material.

ORGANIZATION OF THE BOOK

The book is divided into 11 chapters grouped into 6 parts. One additional chapter (12), two appendices, and one tutorial are available as online supplements.

PART 1—INTRODUCTION TO E-COMMERCE AND E-MARKETPLACES

In Part 1, we provide an overview of today's business environment as well as the fundamentals of EC, some of its terminology (Chapter 1), and a discussion of electronic markets and their mechanisms (Chapter 2).

PART 2—INTERNET CONSUMER RETAILING

In Part 2, we describe EC B2C applications in two chapters. Chapter 3 addresses e-tailing and electronic service industries (e.g., travel, e-banking). Chapter 4 deals with online consumer behavior, market research, and online advertising.

PART 3—BUSINESS-TO-BUSINESS E-COMMERCE

In Part 3, we examine the one-to-many B2B models (Chapter 5), including auctions, many-to-many models, and exchanges. Chapter 6 describes several interesting applications such as e-government, e-learning, consumer-to-consumer EC, and collaborative commerce.

PART 4—OTHER EC MODELS AND APPLICATIONS

Chapter 7 covers the topics of Web 2.0 and social networks. Chapter 8 explores the emerging applications in the world of wireless EC (m-commerce and l-commerce).

PART 5—EC SUPPORT SERVICES

Chapter 9, the first chapter of Part 5, begins with a discussion of the need to protect business transactions, consumers and their privacy, as well as the merchants and intellectual property. It also describes various types of computer fraud and crime, and discusses how to minimize these risks through appropriate security programs. Chapter 10 describes a major EC support service—electronic payments. Order fulfillment, another key support service, is covered in Online File W10.1.

PART 6—EC STRATEGY AND IMPLEMENTATION

Chapter 11 discusses strategic issues in implementing and deploying EC. The chapter also presents global EC and EC for small businesses. It also deals with legal, ethical, and societal issues.

PART 7—APPLICATIONS AND SITE DEVELOPMENT

Online Chapter 12 is unique; it describes the justification of EC systems as well as how to build an *Internet company* and a *Webstore* from scratch. It takes the reader through all the necessary steps and provides guidelines for success. Finally, the chapter discusses EC applications development, including the emerging concepts of Web services, SaaS, and SOA.

HOW THIS BOOK DIFFERS FROM
ELECTRONIC COMMERCE 2010

This book was derived in part from *Electronic Commerce 2010* by Efraim Turban et al., Pearson Prentice Hall 2010. The major differences are:

▶ This book is much smaller (552 pages versus 792 pages; 12 chapters versus 18 chapters).
▶ *EC 2010* is designed for one or two semesters; this book is designed for one quarter or semester.
▶ *EC 2010* is designed for upper undergraduate and graduate levels.
▶ *EC 2010* has a strong strategy and research orientation with twice as many references.
▶ In many places, more technical details, examples, and discussions are available in *EC 2010*.
▶ Several chapters were eliminated in this book (e.g., auctions) or combined (e.g., payments and order fulfillment is one chapter instead of two).
▶ This book includes some simplified cases and examples.
▶ This book is more up-to-date (2011 versus 2010).

LEARNING AIDS

The text offers a number of learning aids for the student:

- **Chapter Outlines.** A listing of the main headings ("Content") at the beginning of each chapter provides a quick overview of the major topics covered.

- **Learning Objectives.** Learning objectives at the beginning of each chapter help students focus their efforts and alert them to the important concepts to be discussed.

- **Opening Cases.** Each chapter opens with a real-world example that illustrates the importance of EC to modern corporations. These cases were carefully chosen to call attention to the major topics covered in the chapters. Following each vignette, a short section titled "What We Can Learn" links the important issues in the vignette to the subject matter of the chapter.

- **EC Application Cases.** In-chapter cases highlight real-world problems encountered by organizations as they develop and implement EC. Questions follow each case to help direct student attention to the implications of the case material.

- **Insights and Additions.** Topics sometimes require additional elaboration or demonstration. Insights and Additions boxes provide an eye-catching repository for such content.

- **Exhibits.** Numerous attractive exhibits (both illustrations and tables) extend and supplement the text discussion. Many are available online.

- **Review Questions.** Each section ends with a series of review questions about that section. These questions are intended to help students summarize the concepts introduced and to digest the essentials of each section before moving on to another topic.

- **Marginal Glossary and Key Terms.** Each Key Term is defined in the margin when it first appears. In addition, an alphabetical list of key terms appears at the end of each chapter with a page reference to the location in the chapter where the term is discussed.

- **Managerial Issues.** At the end of every chapter, we explore some of the special concerns managers face as they adapt to doing business in cyberspace. These issues are framed as questions to maximize readers' active engagement with them.

- **Chapter Summary.** The chapter summary is linked one-to-one with the learning objectives introduced at the beginning of each chapter.

- **End-of-Chapter Exercises.** Different types of questions measure students' comprehension and their ability to apply knowledge. Questions for Discussion by Individual Students and Topics for Class Discussion are intended to develop critical-thinking skills. Internet Exercises are challenging assignments that require students to surf the Internet and apply what they have learned. More than 250 hands-on exercises send students to interesting Web sites to conduct research, investigate an application, download demos, or learn about state-of-the-art technology. The Team Assignments and Projects exercises are challenging group projects designed to foster teamwork.

- **Closing Cases.** Each chapter ends with a real-world case, which is presented in somewhat more depth than the in-chapter EC Application Cases. Questions follow each case relating the case to many of the topics covered in the chapter.

SUPPLEMENTARY MATERIALS

The following support materials are also available.

- **Online Instructor's Resource Center** (pearsonhighered.com/turban). This convenient online *Instructor's Resource Center* includes all the supplements: Instructor's Manual, Test Item File, TestGen, PowerPoint Lecture Notes, and Image Library (text art).
- **Instructor's Manual.** Written by Jon Outland, the Instructor's Manual includes answers to all review and discussion questions, exercises, and case questions.
- **Test Item File.** Written by Lisa Miller is an extensive set of multiple-choice, true/false, and essay questions for each chapter. The Test Item File contains questions tagged to the AACSB Assurance of Learning Standards. It is available in Microsoft Word, **TestGen**, and WebCT- and Blackboard-ready test banks.
- **PowerPoint Lecture Notes.** Created by Judy Lang, these are oriented toward text-learning objectives.
- **Companion Web site** (pearsonhighered.com/turban). The book is supported by a Companion Web site that includes:
  - An online chapter (Chapter 12).
  - Two appendices: Appendix A on e-commerce and supply chains, and Appendix B on e-CRM.
  - An interactive tutorial on preparing an e-business plan.
  - All the Internet Exercises from the end of each chapter in the text are provided on the Web site for convenient student use.

MATERIALS FOR YOUR ONLINE COURSE

Prentice Hall supports adopters using online courses by providing files ready for upload into Blackboard course management systems for our testing, quizzing, and other supplements. Please contact your local Pearson Prentice Hall representative for further information on your particular course.

ACKNOWLEDGMENTS

Many individuals helped us create this text. Faculty feedback was solicited via reviews and through individual interviews. We are grateful to the following faculty for their contributions.

- Linda Volonino of Canisius College contributed some material used in Chapters 9 and 11.
- Linda Lai of the Macau Polytechnic University of China contributed some material used in Chapter 3.
- Carol Pollard of Appalachian State University contributed some material used in Online Chapter 12, available on the book's Web site.
- Deborrah C. Turban (University of Santo Tomas, Philippines) contributed material to several chapters via her Internet search efforts.
- Ivan C. Seballos II contributed the creation of some of the new exhibits in the text.

We thank the many students of San Yat—Sun University in Taiwan for their help in searches and diagramming. We thank Daphne Turban, Sarah Miller, and all these people for their dedication and superb performance shown throughout this revision.

We also recognize the various organizations and corporations that provided us with permissions to reproduce material. Special thanks go to Dion Hinchcliffe for allowing us to use his figures.

Thanks also to the Pearson Prentice Hall team that helped us from the inception of the project to its completion under the leadership of Executive Editor Bob Horan. The dedicated staff includes Editorial Project Manager Kelly Loftus, Editorial Assistant Jason Calcano, Production Project Manager Ann Pulido, Senior Managing Editor Judy Leale, and Media Project Manager Lisa Rinaldi.

REVIEWERS

We wish to thank the faculty who participated in reviews of this text and our other EC titles.

Michelle August, Moraine Valley Community College

Bandula Jayatilaka, Binghamton University

Parag Kosalge, Grand Valley State University

Deborah LaBelle, Nazareth College

Deanne Mulholland, Iowa Western Community College

Mohammed M. Nadeem, National University

Daniel Shen, SUNY New Paltz

Elizabeth Sigman, Georgetown University

Elliot B. Sloane, Villanova University

Rolf Wigand, University of Arkansas at Little Rock

REFERENCES

Blacharski, D. "How Social Computing Is Changing the World." *ITWorld.com*, February 27, 2006. itworld.com/nls_itinsights_social_060301?page=0%2C0 (accessed December 2009).

Internet World Stats. "Internet Usage Statistics: The Big Picture." December 2009. internetworldstats.com/stats.htm (accessed December 2009).

Marketing Charts. "Old and Young Use the Internet Differently." marketingcharts.com/interactive/generations-online-use-internet-differently-8145/pew-internet-generations-percentage-onlinegenerations-by-age-january-2009jpg (accessed December 2009).

Introduction to
Electronic Commerce

CHAPTER **1**

OVERVIEW OF ELECTRONIC COMMERCE

Content

Learning Objectives

Upon completion of this chapter, you will be able to:

1. Define electronic commerce (EC) and describe its various categories.

2. Describe and discuss the content and framework of EC.

3. Describe the major types of EC transactions.

4. Discuss e-commerce 2.0.

5. Understand the elements of the digital world.

6. Describe the drivers of EC as they relate to business pressures and organizational responses.

7. Describe some EC business models.

8. Describe the benefits and limitations of EC to organizations, consumers, and society.

ZAPPOS WOWs THEIR CUSTOMERS

Zappos.com Inc. ("Zappos.com"; *zappos.com*) is an online retailer with one of the largest selection of shoes anywhere—online or offline.

The Opportunity

Nick Swinmurn founded the company in 1999 after spending a day at a San Francisco mall looking for a pair of shoes and returning home empty-handed. If one store had the right style, it did not have the right color; the next store had the right color, but it did not have the correct size. Nick tried to locate the shoes he wanted online, but after a frustrating day of browsing, he discovered that he was unable to find what he wanted online.

Swinmurn discovered that there was no major online retailer that specialized in shoes. So, he decided to create a Web site that offered the very best selection in shoes in terms of brands, styles, colors, sizes, and widths.

The Solution

The company's strategy was to offer such a huge selection that the customers would say WOW! And by 2009 this selection exceeded 3.3 million items (from 1,200 vendors)—unmatchable by any online or offline store.

The company's initial business model was to sell only online, and only shoes. This model has evolved to also sell several related products ranging from jewelry to clothes and to also sell via a few physical outlets.

Believing that the speed at which a customer receives an online purchase plays a very important role in customer retention, Zappos constructed huge warehouses containing everything it sells.

In order to ensure fast order fulfillment, the company worked with Arup, a global firm of designers, engineers, planners, and business consultants providing a diverse range of professional services to its suppliers; designers; and other business partners around the globe. For example, the logistics designers worked with the Zappos warehouse automation team to design a world-class "direct-to-customer" fulfillment system. The high-speed material handling system (from FKI Logistex) is fully automated and housed in a Shepherdsville, Kentucky, 800,000 square foot warehouse. The system allows rapid delivery to customers no matter where they are located. The company offers free shipping with domestic orders, and often delivers the next day.

The Zappos shopping experience also features extensive Web site search options and clear views of every product (see photo on next page). Unlike most other online retailers, Zappos does not offer an item for sale unless it is physically available in its warehouse. Once the last size or color of a shoe is shipped out, it is no longer offered on the Web site. The moment a new style, size, or color is available in the warehouse, it instantly pops up on the Web site. This "live inventory" is made possible by a full-service photo lab in the fulfillment center, where digital photographs of each item are taken from a variety of angles and immediately uploaded to Zappos.com. The photo lab even includes a studio to shoot live human models for certain shoes, apparel, and accessories.

The company's culture is also a key to the success of the business. Without dedicated and excited employees, the company becomes an adequate company, not the best.

The culture has matured over the life of the company to include ten (10) core values from which the company developed the culture, brand, and business strategies. These values are shown in Online File W1.1.

Zappos also realized that, along with the best selection, customer service is a key success factor. Therefore, Zappos operates under the theory that providing an excellent shopping experience (instead of maximizing profits) will be followed by sales growth.

The company's "WOW" philosophy of customer experiences and the huge selection are supplemented by 365-day free returns and 24/7 customer service. Until 2008, it also included 110 percent price protection and free overnight shipping on every order.

The company uses EC mechanisms such as blogs, Tweets, discussion forums, e-newsletters, user-contributed videos, and more to create a community of loyal buyers and foster its relationship with its customers.

The employees are members of an enterprise social network, and the mechanisms listed in the customers' community, as well as other features of social networks, are used to keep employees happy and, therefore, more productive. Employees are well trained to work as individuals, as well as in teams. The company provides EC mechanisms to foster individual and team work.

Doing business online requires a security system to protect customers' and vendors' data. Zappos provides encryption and other security measures to protect customer data.

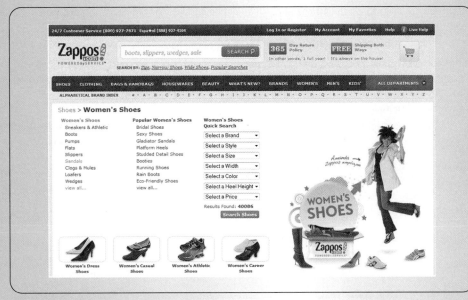

Source: *zappos.com/shoes*. Used with permission.

The Results

Gross merchandise sales started at "almost nothing" in 1999 and doubled every year to reach more than $1 billion in 2008. The total number of employees grew from 3 in 1999 to over 1,500 in 2009.

By focusing on service and product selection that WOWs the customers, employees, vendors, and investors, Zappos is on its way to fulfilling its vision that one day 30 percent of all retail transactions in the United States of shoes and related items will be online; and people will buy from the company with the best service and the best selection—Zappos will be that company.

In July 2009, Amazon.com "acquired" Zappos. However, the Zappos brand will continue to be separate from the Amazon.com brand. Zappos will have access to many of Amazon.com's resources, but will continue to build the brand and culture just as it has in the past. The Zappos mission remains the same: delivering happiness to all stakeholders, including employees, customers, and vendors. Zappos plans to continue to maintain its relationships with its vendors, and Amazon.com will continue to maintain its relationships it has with its own vendors.

Sources: *zappos.com* (accessed July 2009), *FKI Logistex* (2007), *Logistics Online* (2008), Taylor (2008), *Wall Street Journal* (2009), and *en.wikipedia.org/wiki/Zappos.com* (accessed November 2009).

WHAT WE CAN LEARN . . .

The Zappos case illustrates a story of a very successful start-up company that is doing business almost exclusively online. Doing business electronically is one of the major activities of e-commerce (EC), the subject of this book. Selling online is a popular and very competitive activity. In this case, a business is selling to individual customers in what is known as business-to-customer (B2C). The case demonstrates several of the topics that you will learn in Chapter 1 and throughout the book. These are:

a. You need to have the right idea, capitalizing on the capabilities of online business.

b. These capabilities include the ability to offer a very large number of products such that no single company in the physical world can even come close to your inventory. You can do it because your customer base is huge, and people can buy from anywhere at any time. You can also do it with less cost since you do not need physical stores.

c. Every company needs a business model that describes how the company operates, how it generates sales, and how it provides value to the customers and eventually profits to its owners. This model is a part of EC strategy and can be changed over time.

d. In online businesses customers cannot see the physical product, store, or sellers. Therefore, a good business needs to provide services such as superb customer care, a good return policy, detailed information about the products including a superb visual presentation of each product, and trust in the brand.

e. In a regular store you pay and pick up the merchandize. In an online business the product is shipped to you. Therefore, order fulfillment needs to be very efficient and timely.

f. A major strategy to engage both customers and employees is to use social networking within the company's Web site(s).

g. Finally, an online business is a business first, and it must use all basic and critical success factors of a business, such as having a business strategy, operating an effective supply chain, having financial viability, providing a superb relationship with its business partners, notably the suppliers; and, perhaps most important, being innovative, creative, and open-minded in order to maintain a strategic advantage.

The Zappos case covers major topics related to B2C and doing business online in general. These topics are discussed throughout the book. Chapter 1 provides an introduction to the field and an overview of the book. The chapter also covers the drivers, benefits, and limitations of EC.

1.1   ELECTRONIC COMMERCE: DEFINITIONS AND CONCEPTS

Let's begin by looking at what the management guru Peter Drucker had to say about EC:

> *The truly revolutionary impact of the Internet Revolution is just beginning to be felt. But it is not "information" that fuels this impact. It is not "artificial intelligence." It is not the effect of computers and data processing on decision making, policymaking, or strategy. It is something that practically no one foresaw or, indeed even talked about 10 or 15 years ago; e-commerce—that is, the explosive emergence of the Internet as a major, perhaps eventually the major, worldwide distribution channel for goods, for services, and, surprisingly, for managerial and professional jobs. This is profoundly changing economics, markets and industry structure, products and services and their flow; consumer segmentation, consumer values and consumer behavior; jobs and labor markets. But the impact may be even greater on societies and politics, and above all, on the way we see the world and ourselves in it. (Drucker 2002, pp. 3–4)*

electronic commerce (EC)
The process of buying, selling, or exchanging products, services, or information via computer.

e-business
A broader definition of EC that includes not just the buying and selling of goods and services, but also servicing customers, collaborating with business partners, and conducting electronic transactions within an organization.

DEFINING ELECTRONIC COMMERCE

Electronic commerce (EC) is the process of buying, selling, transferring, or exchanging products, services, and/or information via computer networks, mostly the Internet and intranets. EC is often confused with e-business. For an overview, see en.wikipedia.org/wiki/E-commerce.

DEFINING E-BUSINESS

Some people view the term *commerce* as describing only buying and selling transactions conducted between business partners. If this definition of commerce is used, the term *electronic commerce* would be fairly narrow. Thus, many use the term *e-business* instead. **E-business** refers to a broader definition of EC, not just the buying and selling of goods and services, but also servicing customers, collaborating with business partners, conducting e-learning, and conducting electronic transactions within an organization. However, others view e-business as comprising those activities that do not involve buying or selling over the Internet, such as collaboration and intrabusiness activities; that is, it is a *complement* of the narrowly defined e-commerce. In this book, we use the broadest meaning of electronic commerce, which is basically equivalent to the broadest definition of e-business. The two terms will be used interchangeably throughout the text.

MAJOR EC CONCEPTS

Several other concepts are frequently used in conjunction with EC. The major ones are as follow.

Pure Versus Partial EC

EC can take several forms depending on the degree of digitization (the transformation from physical to digital) of (1) the product (service) sold, (2) the process (e.g., ordering, payment, fulfillment), and (3) the delivery method. The possible configurations of these three dimensions (Exhibit 1.1) determine different levels of EC. A product may be physical or digital, the process may be physical or digital, and the delivery method may be physical or digital. These alternatives create eight cubes, each of which has three dimensions. In traditional commerce, all three dimensions of the cube are physical (lower-left cube); in pure EC, all dimensions are digital (upper-right cube). All other cubes include a mix of digital and physical dimensions.

If there is at least one digital dimension, we consider the situation EC, but only partial EC. For example, purchasing a computer from Dell's Web site or a book from Amazon.com is partial EC, because the merchandise is physically delivered. However, buying an e-book from Amazon.com or a software product from Buy.com is pure EC, because the product, payment, and delivery to the buyer are all digital.

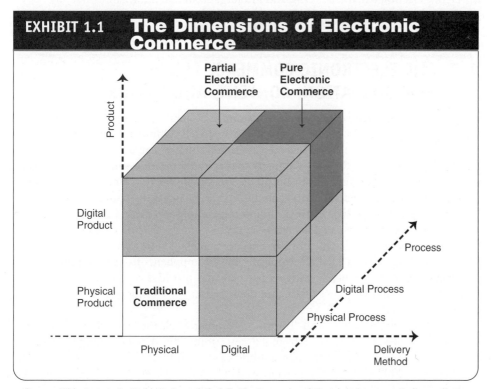

EXHIBIT 1.1 The Dimensions of Electronic Commerce

Source: Whinston, A. B., Stahl, D. O., and Choi, S. *The Economics of Electronic Commerce*. Indianapolis, IN: Macmillan Technical Publishing, 1997. Used with permission of authors.

brick-and-mortar (old economy) organizations
Old-economy organizations (corporations) that perform their primary business offline, selling physical products by means of physical agents.

virtual (pure-play) organizations
Organizations that conduct their business activities solely online.

click-and-mortar (click-and-brick) organizations
Organizations that conduct some e-commerce activities, usually as an additional marketing channel.

electronic market (e-marketplace)
An online marketplace where buyers and sellers meet to exchange goods, services, money, or information.

intranet
An internal corporate or government network that uses Internet tools, such as Web browsers, and Internet protocols.

extranet
A network that uses the Internet to link multiple intranets.

EC Organizations

Purely physical organizations (companies) are referred to as **brick-and-mortar (old economy) organizations,** whereas companies that are engaged only in EC are considered **virtual,** or **pure-play, organizations**. **Click-and-mortar (click-and-brick) organizations** are those that conduct some EC activities, usually as an additional marketing channel. Gradually, many brick-and-mortar companies are changing to click-and-mortar ones (see the application case about Mary Kay in Online File W1.2).

ELECTRONIC MARKETS AND NETWORKS

EC can be conducted in an **electronic market (e-marketplace)** where buyers and sellers meet online to exchange goods, services, money, or information. Any individual can also open a market selling products or services online. Electronic markets are connected to sellers and buyers via the Internet or to its counterpart within organizations, an *intranet*. An **intranet** is a corporate or government network that uses Internet tools, such as Web browsers, and Internet protocols. Another computer environment is an **extranet,** a network that uses the Internet to link multiple intranets in a secure manner.

Section 1.1 ▶ REVIEW QUESTIONS

1. Define EC and e-business.
2. Distinguish between pure and partial EC.
3. Define click-and-mortar and pure-play organizations.
4. Define electronic markets, IOSs, and intraorganizational information systems.
5. Define intranets and extranets.

1.2 THE ELECTRONIC COMMERCE FIELD: CLASSIFICATION, CONTENT, AND HISTORY

The EC field is diversified so some classification can help. A good example how EC is done over these networks can be seen in the case of Dell (Online File W1.3).

The Dell case demonstrates several ways that businesses can use EC to improve the bottom line. Dell is not the only company that is doing business online. Thousands of other companies, from retailers to hospitals, are moving in this direction. In general, selling and buying electronically can be either business-to-consumer (B2C) or business-to-business (B2B). In B2C, online transactions are made between businesses and individual consumers, such as when a person purchases a pair of shoes at zappos.com or a computer at dell.com. In B2B, businesses make online transactions with other businesses, such as when Dell electronically buys components from its suppliers. Dell also collaborates electronically with its partners and provides customer service online (e-CRM). Several other types of EC are described in the closing case, and others will be described soon.

According to the U.S. Census Bureau, e-commerce sales accounted for 3.2 percent of total retail sales in 2007, rising from 2.8 percent in 2006. The percentage was flat in 2008. Forrester estimates that retail e-commerce sales will increase to 6 percent of total retail sales in 2009 and 2010, 7 percent in 2011, and 8 percent in 2011 (reported by Todé 2009).

These activities comprise the essence of EC. However, EC can be explained better by viewing the following framework.

AN EC FRAMEWORK

The EC field is a diverse one, involving many activities, organizational units, and technologies (e.g., see Khosrow-Pour 2006). Therefore, a framework that describes its contents is useful. Exhibit 1.2 introduces one such framework.

As can be seen in the exhibit, there are many EC applications (top of exhibit), some of which were illustrated in Online File W1.3 about Dell; others will be shown throughout the book (see also en.wikipedia.org/wiki/E-commerce). To execute these applications, companies need the right information, infrastructure, and support services.

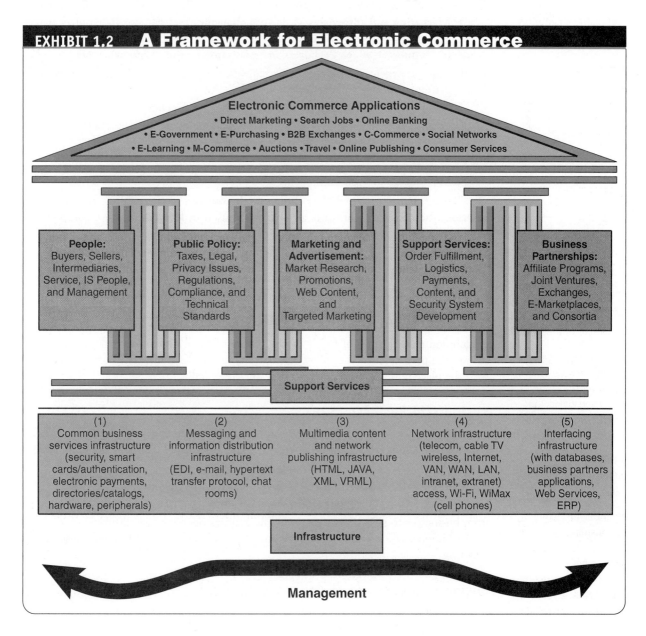

EXHIBIT 1.2   A Framework for Electronic Commerce

Electronic Commerce Applications
• Direct Marketing • Search Jobs • Online Banking
• E-Government • E-Purchasing • B2B Exchanges • C-Commerce • Social Networks
• E-Learning • M-Commerce • Auctions • Travel • Online Publishing • Consumer Services

| **People:** Buyers, Sellers, Intermediaries, Service, IS People, and Management | **Public Policy:** Taxes, Legal, Privacy Issues, Regulations, Compliance, and Technical Standards | **Marketing and Advertisement:** Market Research, Promotions, Web Content, and Targeted Marketing | **Support Services:** Order Fulfillment, Logistics, Payments, Content, and Security System Development | **Business Partnerships:** Affiliate Programs, Joint Ventures, Exchanges, E-Marketplaces, and Consortia |

Support Services

| (1) Common business services infrastructure (security, smart cards/authentication, electronic payments, directories/catalogs, hardware, peripherals) | (2) Messaging and information distribution infrastructure (EDI, e-mail, hypertext transfer protocol, chat rooms) | (3) Multimedia content and network publishing infrastructure (HTML, JAVA, XML, VRML) | (4) Network infrastructure (telecom, cable TV wireless, Internet, VAN, WAN, LAN, intranet, extranet) access, Wi-Fi, WiMax (cell phones) | (5) Interfacing infrastructure (with databases, business partners applications, Web Services, ERP) |

Infrastructure

Management

Exhibit 1.2 shows that EC applications are supported by infrastructure and by the following five support areas (shown as pillars in the exhibit):

> **People.** Sellers, buyers, intermediaries, information systems and technology specialists, other employees, and any other participants comprise an important support area.
> **Public policy.** Legal and other policy and regulatory issues, such as privacy protection and taxation, which are determined by governments. Included as part of public policy is the issue of technical standards, which are established by government and/or industry-mandated policy-making groups. Compliance with regulations is an important issue.
> **Marketing and advertising.** Like any other business, EC usually requires the support of marketing and advertising. This is especially important in B2C online transactions, in which the buyers and sellers usually do not know each other.
> **Support services.** Many services are needed to support EC. These range from content creation to payments to order delivery.
> **Business partnerships.** Joint ventures, exchanges, and business partnerships of various types are common in EC. These occur frequently throughout the *supply chain* (i.e., the interactions between a company and its suppliers, customers, and other partners).

The infrastructure for EC is shown at the bottom of the exhibit. *Infrastructure* describes the hardware, software, and networks used in EC. All of these components require good *management practices*. This means that companies need to plan, organize, motivate, devise strategy, and restructure processes, as needed, to optimize the business use of EC models and strategies.

CLASSIFICATION OF EC BY THE NATURE OF THE TRANSACTIONS AND THE RELATIONSHIPS AMONG PARTICIPANTS

A common classification of EC is by the nature of the transactions or the relationship among the participants. The following major types of EC transactions are listed below with the place in the book where that they are presented.

Business-to-Business (B2B)

All the participants in **business-to-business (B2B)** e-commerce are either businesses or other organizations. Today, over 85 percent of EC volume is B2B (Mockler et al. 2006).

Business-to-Consumer (B2C)

Business-to-consumer (B2C) EC includes retail transactions of products or services from businesses to individual shoppers. The Zappos opening case illustrates B2C. The typical shopper at Zappos or Amazon.com is an individual. This EC type is also called **e-tailing**.

Business-to-Business-to-Consumer (B2B2C)

In **business-to-business-to-consumer (B2B2C)** EC, a business provides some product or service to a client business. The client business maintains its own customers, who may

business-to-business (B2B)
E-commerce model in which all of the participants are businesses or other organizations.

business-to-consumer (B2C)
E-commerce model in which businesses sell to individual shoppers.

e-tailing
Online retailing, usually B2C.

business-to-business-to-consumer (B2B2C)
E-commerce model in which a business provides some product or service to a client business that maintains its own customers.

be its own employees, to whom the product or service is provided. An example is Godiva (see Case 1.1 p. 10). The company sells chocolates directly to business customers. Those businesses may then give the chocolates as gifts to employees or to other businesses. Godiva may mail the chocolate directly to the recipients (with compliments of . . .). An interesting example of B2B2C can be found at wishlist.com.au.

Consumer-to-Business (C2B)

The **consumer-to-business (C2B)** category includes individuals who use the Internet to sell products or services to organizations and individuals who seek vendors to bid on products or services for them. Priceline.com is a well known organizer of C2B travel service transactions.

Intrabusiness EC

The **intrabusiness EC** category includes all internal EC organizational activities that involve the exchange of goods, services, or information among various units and individuals in that organization. Activities can range from selling corporate products to one's employees, to online training, and to collaborative design efforts.

Business-to-Employees (B2E)

The **business-to-employees (B2E)** category is a subset of the intrabusiness category in which an organization delivers services, information, or products to individual employees. A major category of employees is *mobile employees*, such as field representatives. EC support to such employees is also called *business-to-mobile employees (B2ME)*. The Mary Kay application case (Online File W1.2) also demonstrates B2E.

Consumer-to-Consumer (C2C)

In the **consumer-to-consumer (C2C)** category (see Chapter 6), consumers transact directly with other consumers. Examples of C2C include individuals selling residential property, cars, and so on in online classified ads. EBay's auctions are mostly C2C. The advertising of personal services over the Internet and the online selling of knowledge and expertise are other examples of C2C.

Collaborative Commerce

When individuals or groups communicate or collaborate online, they may be engaged in **collaborative commerce,** or **c-commerce.** For example, business partners in different locations may design a product together (see the Boeing case at Online File W1.4).

E-Learning

In **e-learning,** training or formal education is provided online. E-learning is used heavily by organizations for training and retraining employees (called *e-training*). It is also practiced at virtual universities.

E-Government

In **e-government** EC, a government entity buys or provides goods, services, or information from or to businesses (G2B) or from or to individual citizens (G2C) (see Chapter 6).

Many examples of the various types of EC transactions will be presented throughout this book.

---

consumer-to-business (C2B)
E-commerce model in which individuals use the Internet to sell products or services to organizations or individuals who seek sellers to bid on products or services they need.

intrabusiness EC
E-commerce category that includes all internal organizational activities that involve the exchange of goods, services, or information among various units and individuals in an organization.

business-to-employees (B2E)
E-commerce model in which an organization delivers services, information, or products to its individual employees.

consumer-to-consumer (C2C)
E-commerce model in which consumers sell directly to other consumers.

collaborative commerce (c-commerce)
E-commerce model in which individuals or groups communicate or collaborate online.

e-learning
The online delivery of information for purposes of training or education.

CASE 1.1
EC Application
WANT TO BUY CHOCOLATE ONLINE? TRY GODIVA.COM

The Business Opportunity

The demand for high-quality chocolate has been increasing rapidly since the early 1990s. Several local and global companies are competing in this market. Godiva Chocolatier is a well-known international company based in New York whose stores can be found in hundreds of malls worldwide. The company was looking for ways to increase its sales. It had the courage to try online sales as early as 1994. The company was a pioneering first mover online that exploited an opportunity years before its competitors.

The Project

Teaming with Fry Multimedia (an e-commerce pioneer), Godiva.com (*godiva.com*) was created as a division of Godiva Chocolatier. The objective was to sell online both to individuals (B2C) and to businesses (B2B). Because its online activities began in 1994, the Godiva.com story parallels the dynamic growth of e-commerce. Godiva.com went through difficult times—testing e-commerce technologies as they appeared; failing at times, but maintaining its commitment to online selling; and, finally, becoming the fastest-growing division of Godiva, outpacing projections. Godiva.com embodies a true success story. Here we present some of the milestones it encountered.

The major driving factors in 1994 were Internet user groups of chocolate lovers, who were talking about Godiva and to whom the company hoped to sell its product online. Like other pioneers, Godiva had to build its Web site from scratch without EC-building tools. A partnership was made with *Chocolatier Magazine,* allowing Godiva.com to showcase articles and recipes from the magazine on its site in exchange for providing an online magazine subscription form for e-shoppers. The recognition of the importance of relevant content was correct, as was the need for fresh content. The delivery of games and puzzles, which was considered necessary to attract people to EC sites, was found to be a failure. People were coming to learn about chocolate and Godiva and to buy—not to play games. Another concept that failed was the attempt to make the Web site look like the physical store. It was found that different marketing channels should look different from one another.

Godiva.com is a user-friendly place to shop. Its major features include electronic catalogs, some of which are constructed for special occasions (e.g., Mother's Day and Father's Day); a store locator (how to find the nearest physical store and events at stores close to you); a shopping cart to make it easy to collect items to buy; e-cards; a gift selector and a gift finder; custom photographs of the products; a search engine by product, price, and other criteria; instructions on how to shop online (take the tour); a chocolate guide that shows you exactly what is inside each box; a place to click for live assistance or for a paper catalog; and the ability to create an address list for shipping gifts to friends or employees. The site also features "My Account," a personalized place where customers can access their order history, account, order status, and so on; general content about chocolate (and recipes); and tools for making shipping and payment arrangements.

Godiva.com sells both to individuals and to corporations. For corporations, incentive programs are offered, including address lists of employees or customers to whom the chocolate is to be sent—an example of the B2B2C EC model.

Godiva.com continues to add features to stay ahead of the competition. The site is now accessible using wireless technologies. For example, the store locator is available to wireless phone users, and Palm Pilot users can download mailing lists. There is an the app available to iPhone users that allows them fast access to Godiva's best sellers, express checkout, product descriptions with color images, and contact list for billing and shipping information.

The Results

Godiva.com's online sales have been growing at a double-digit rate every year, outpacing the company's "old economy" divisions, as well as the online stores of competitors.

Sources: Compiled from Reda (2004) and from *godiva.com* (accessed November 2009).

Questions

1. Identify the B2B and B2C transactions in this case.
2. Why did Godiva decide to sell online? List the EC drivers in this case.
3. Visit godiva.com. How user-friendly is the site?
4. Describe B2B2C at Godiva.

A BRIEF HISTORY OF EC

EC applications were first developed in the early 1970s with innovations such as *electronic funds transfer (EFT)* (see en.wikipedia.org/wiki/Guide_to_E-payments), whereby funds could be routed electronically from one organization to another. However, the use of these applications was limited to large corporations, financial institutions, and a few other daring businesses. Then came *electronic data interchange (EDI),* a technology used to electronically transfer routine documents, which later expanded from financial transactions to other types of transactions (see Chapter 5 for more on EDI). EDI enlarged the pool of participating companies from financial institutions to manufacturers, retailers, services, and many other types of businesses. Such systems were called *interorganizational system (IOS)* applications, and their strategic value to businesses has been widely recognized. More new EC applications followed, ranging from travel reservation systems to stock trading.

The Internet began life as an experiment by the U.S. government in 1969, and its initial users were a largely technical audience of government agencies and academic researchers and scientists. Some of them started to place personal classifieds on the Internet. A major milestone in the development of EC was the introduction of the World Wide Web in the early 1990s. This allowed companies to have presence on the Internet with both text and photos. When the Internet became commercialized and users began flocking to participate in the World Wide Web in the early 1990s, the term *electronic commerce* was coined. EC applications rapidly expanded. A large number of so-called dot-coms, or *Internet start-ups*, also appeared. One reason for this rapid expansion was the development of new networks, protocols, and EC software. The other reason was the increase in competition and other business pressures (see discussion in Section 1.5).

Since 1995, Internet users have witnessed the development of many innovative applications. Almost every medium- and large-sized organization in the world now has a Web site, and most large U.S. corporations have comprehensive portals through which employees, business partners, and the public can access corporate information. Many of these sites contain tens of thousands of pages and links. In 1999, the emphasis of EC shifted from B2C to B2B, and in 2001 from B2B to B2E, c-commerce, e-government, e-learning, and m-commerce. In 2005, social networks started to receive quite a bit of attention, as did m-commerce and wireless applications. Given the nature of technology and Internet usage, EC will undoubtedly continue to grow, shift, and change. More and more EC successes are emerging. For a comprehensive ready-reference guide to EC including statistics, trends, and in-depth profiles of over 400 companies, see Plunkett (2006) and en.wikipedia.org/wiki/E-commerce.

While looking at the history of EC, one must keep in mind the following:

The Interdisciplinary Nature of EC

Because EC is a new field, it is just now developing its theoretical and scientific foundations. From just a brief overview of the EC framework and classification, you can probably see that EC is related to several different disciplines. The major academic EC disciplines include the following: *accounting, business law, computer science, consumer behavior, economics, engineering, finance, human resource management, management, management information systems, marketing, public administration,* and *robotics.*

The Google Revolution

During its early years, EC was impacted by companies such as Amazon.com, eBay, AOL, and Yahoo! However, since 2001 no other company has probably had more of an impact on EC than Google. Google related Web searches to targeted advertisements

e-government
E-commerce model in which a government entity buys or provides goods, services, or information from or to businesses or individual citizens.

much better than its competitors did. Today, Google is much more than just a search engine; it employs many innovative EC models, is involved in many EC joint ventures, and impacts both organizational activities and individual lives. For more details, see Vise and Malseed (2006).

EC Failures

Starting in 1999, a large number of EC companies, especially e-tailing and B2B exchanges, began to fail (see disobey.com/ghostsites). Well-known B2C failures include eToys, Xpeditor, MarchFirst, Drkoop, Webvan, and Boo. Well-known B2B failures include Chemdex, Ventro, and Verticalnet. (Incidentally, the history of these pioneering companies is documented in David Kirch's "The Business Plan Archive" [businessplanarchive.org]). A survey by *Strategic Direction* (2005) found that 62 percent of dot-coms lacked financial skills, and 50 percent had little experience with marketing. Similarly, many companies failed to ensure they had the inventory and distribution setup to meet the fluctuating demand for their products. The reasons for these and other EC failures are discussed in Chapters 3, 5, and 12. In 2008, many start-ups related to Web 2.0 started to collapse (per blogs.cioinsight.com/knowitall/content001/startup_deathwatch_20.html).

Does the large number of failures mean that EC's days are numbered? Absolutely not! First, the dot-com failure rate is declining sharply. Second, the EC field is basically experiencing consolidation as companies test different business models and organizational structures. Third, some pure EC companies, including giants such as Amazon.com, are expanding operations and generating increased sales. Finally, the click-and-mortar model seems to work very well especially in e-tailing (e.g., Sears, Walmart, Target, and Best Buy).

EC Successes

The last few years have seen the rise of extremely successful virtual EC companies such as eBay, Google, Yahoo!, Amazon.com, VeriSign, AOL, and E-Trade. Click-and-mortar companies such as Cisco, Walmart online, General Electric, IBM, Intel, and Schwab also have seen great success. Additional success stories include start-ups such as Alloy.com (a young-adults-oriented portal), Blue Nile, Ticketmaster, Zappos, Expedia, and Campusfood (see Online File W1.5).

THE FUTURE OF EC

Today's predictions about the future size of EC, provided by respected analysts such as AMR Research, Jupiter Media, Emarketer.com, and Forrester, vary. For a list of sites that provide statistics on EC see Chapter 3, Exhibit 3.1. For example, according to Forrester, online retail (B2C) spending will increase from $141 billion in 2008 to $229 billion in 2013 (reported by Todé 2009). In 2008, 80 percent of Generation X (Internet users ages 33 to 44) shop online. Of Generation Y (users ages 18 to 32) 71 percent shop online. Interest in online shopping is considerably lower among the youngest and oldest groups; 38 percent of online teens buy products online, as do 56 percent of Internet users ages 64 to 72, and 47 percent ages 73 and older (reported by Jones and Fox 2009).

The number of Internet users worldwide was estimated at over 1.5 billion in 2008 (Schonfeld 2009). According to IDC's Digital Marketplace Model and Forecast, 50 percent of all Internet users will shop online by 2009 (*IDC* 2008). EC growth will come not only from B2C, but also from B2B and from newer applications such as e-government, e-learning, B2E, and c-commerce. Overall, the growth of the field will continue to be strong into the foreseeable future. Despite the failures of individual companies and initiatives, the total volume of EC has been growing every year.

The rising price of petroleum, along with repercussions of the 2008–2009 financial meltdown, should motivate people to shop from home and look for bargains online where price comparison is easy and fast.

Finally, EC is now entering its second phase of life as illustrated next.

Section 1.2 ▶ REVIEW QUESTIONS

1. List the major components of the EC framework.
2. List the major transactional types of EC.
3. Describe the major landmarks in EC history.
4. List some EC successes and failures.
5. Summarize the future of EC.

1.3   E-COMMERCE 2.0: FROM WEB 2.0 TO ENTERPRISE SOCIAL NETWORKING AND VIRTUAL WORLDS

The first generation of EC involved mainly trading, e-services, and corporate-sponsored collaboration. We are moving now into the second generation of EC, which we call e-commerce 2.0. It is based on Web 2.0 tools, social networks, and virtual worlds, the result of social computing.

SOCIAL COMPUTING

Social computing is computing that is concerned with the intersection of social behavior and information systems. It is performed with a set of tools that includes blogs, mashups, instant messaging, social network services, discussion forums, wikis, social bookmarking and other *social software,* and marketplaces. Whereas traditional computing systems concentrate on supporting organizational activities and business processes and zero in on cost reduction and increases in productivity, social computing concentrates on improving collaboration and interaction among people and on user-generated content. It is a shift from traditional top-down management communication to a bottom-up strategy where individuals in communities become a major organizational power. In social computing and commerce, people can collaborate online, get advice from one another and from trusted experts, and find goods and services they really like.

Example. Advances in social computing are affecting travel decisions and arrangements. Travelers share information and warn others of bad experiences at sites such as tripadvisor.com.

The premise of social computing is to make socially produced information available to all. This information may be provided directly, as when systems show the number of users who have rated a book or a movie (e.g., at amazon.com and netflix.com). Or, the information may be provided indirectly, as is the case with Google's page rank algorithms, which sequence search results based on the number of page hits. In all of these cases, information that is produced by individuals is available to all, usually for free. Social computing is largely supported by Web 2.0 tools.

WEB 2.0

The term **Web 2.0** was coined by O'Reilly Media in 2004 to refer to a supposed second generation of Internet-based services that let people generate and control content and

social computing
An approach aimed at making the human–computer interface more natural.

Web 2.0
The second generation of Internet-based services that lets people collaborate and share information online in new ways, such as social networking sites, wikis, communication tools, and folksonomies.

collaborate and share information online in perceived new ways, such as social networking sites, wikis, communication tools, and folksonomies. O'Reilly Media, in collaboration with MediaLive International, used the phrase as a title for a series of conferences. Since then, it has become a popular, ill-defined, and often criticized buzzword in the technical and marketing communities.

O'Reilly (2005) divided Web 2.0 into the following four levels:

▶ Level 3 applications, the most "Web 2.0" oriented, exist only on the Internet, deriving their effectiveness from interhuman connections and from the network effects that Web 2.0 makes possible and growing in effectiveness as people make more use of them. O'Reilly offered eBay, Craigslist, Wikipedia, del.icio.us, Skype, Dodgeball, and AdSense as examples of level 3 applications.

▶ Level 2 applications can operate offline but gain advantages from going online. O'Reilly cited Flickr as an example, which benefits from its shared photo database and from its community-generated tag database.

▶ Level 1 applications operate offline but gain features online. O'Reilly pointed to Writely (now Google Docs & Spreadsheets) and iTunes (because of its music store portion) as examples.

▶ Level 0 applications work as well offline as online. O'Reilly offered the examples of MapQuest, Yahoo! Local, and Google Maps.

For more information on Web 2.0, see en.wikipedia.org/wiki/WEB_2.0. The major characteristics of Web 2.0 are presented in Online File W1.6. The major tools of Web 2.0 are described in Chapter 2, and the applications are described in most chapters. Also, browse Don Hinchcliffe's Web 2.0 blog at web2.socialcomputingjournal.com for Web 2.0 definitions, explanations, and applications.

SOCIAL NETWORKS AND SOCIAL NETWORK SERVICES

The most interesting e-commerce application in recent years has been the emergence of social and enterprise social networks. Originating from online communities (Chapter 7), these networks are growing rapidly and providing for many new EC initiatives, revenue models, and business models.

A **social network** is a social structure composed of nodes (which are generally individuals or organizations) that are tied by one or more specific types of interdependency, such as values, visions, ideas, financial exchange, friendship, kinship, dislike, conflict, or trade. The structures are often very complex.

In its simplest form, a social network can be described as a map of all relevant ties (connection) between the nodes. The network can also be used to determine the social capital of individual participants. These concepts are often displayed in a social network diagram, where nodes are the points and ties are the lines.

Participants in a *social network* congregate on a Web site where they can create their own homepage for free and on which they can write blogs and wikis; post pictures, videos, or music; share ideas; and link to other Web locations they find to be interesting. Social networkers chat using instant messaging and Twitter, and tag the content they post with their own key words, which makes the content searchable and facilitates the conduct of people-to-people transactions. In effect, in a social network there are *online communities* of people with similar interests.

Social Network Services

Social network services (SNSs), such as MySpace and Facebook, provide a Web space for people to build their homepages, which they then host for free, and they also provide basic communication and other support tools for conducting different activities in the

social network
A category of Internet applications that help connect friends, business partners, or individuals with specific interests by providing free services such as photos presentation, e-mail, blogging, and so on using a variety of tools.

social network service (SNS)
A service that builds online communities by providing an online space for people to build free homepages and that provides basic communication and support tools for conducting different activities in the social network.

social network. These activities are referred to as *social networking*. Social networks are people oriented. For example, a 15-year-old Filipino singer named Pempengco thought her music career was doomed after she lost a local singing competition in 2006, but YouTube gave her a "cyber" of a lifetime when a video clip of her singing Jennifer Holliday's "And I'm Telling You I Am Not Going" caught the attention of TV host Ellen DeGeneres and Grammy Award–winning producer David Foster. Initially, social networks were used for only social activities. Today corporations are starting to have an interest in the business aspects of social networks (e.g., see linkedin.com, a network that connects businesses by industry, functions, geography, and areas of interest). For more on social networking, see De Jonge (2008) and en.wikipedia.org/wiki/Social_networking.

Finally, we define **social networking** as the execution of any activity, such as blogging, in a social network.

The following are examples of representative social network services:

▶ Facebook.com: Facilitates socialization for people of all ages.
▶ YouTube.com and Metacafe.com: Users can upload and view video clips.
▶ Flickr.com: Users share and comment on photos.
▶ Friendster.com: Provides a platform to find friends and make contacts.
▶ Hi5.com: A popular global social network.
▶ Cyworld.nate.com: Asia's largest social networking Web site.
▶ Habbo.com: Entertaining country-specific sites for kids and adults.
▶ MySpace.com: The most visited social network Web site (see Case 1.2, pp. 17–18).

Representative Capabilities and Services Provided by Social Network Sites.
Social network sites provide many capabilities and services such as:

> ▶ Users can construct a Web page that they can use to present themselves to the larger community.
> ▶ Users can create a circle of friends who are linked together.
> ▶ The site provides discussion forums (by group, by topic).
> ▶ Photo, video, and document viewing and sharing (streaming videos, user-supplied videos) are supported.
> ▶ Wikis can be used to jointly create documents.
> ▶ Blogs can be used for discussion, dissemination of information, and much more.
> ▶ The site offers community e-mail and instant messaging (IM) capabilities.
> ▶ Experts can be made available to answer member queries.
> ▶ Consumers can rate and comment on products.
> ▶ The site provides an e-newsletter.
> ▶ Online voting may be available to poll member opinions.
> ▶ The site supports conference (group) chatting, combined with photo sharing.
> ▶ Message and bulletin board services are available for posting information to groups and anyone on the Web site.
> ▶ The site provides storage for content, including photos, videos, and music.
> ▶ Users can bookmark self-created content.
> ▶ Users can find other networks, friends, or topics of interest.

Not all networks have all these capabilities, but some have even more.

social networking
The creation or sponsoring of a social network service and any activity, such as blogging, done in a social network (external or internal).

BUSINESS-ORIENTED SOCIAL NETWORKS

business-oriented networks
Social networks whose primary objective is to facilitate business.

Business-oriented networks are social networks whose primary objective is to facilitate business. The prime example here is linkedin.com, which provides business connections and enables job finding and recruiting. Another example is YUB. Yub.com is a huge online shopping mall with about 6 million items. Users can also hang out at Yub.com with friends and meet others who are looking for discounts and bargains. Yet another example is craigslist.org, the classified ad super site, which offers many social-oriented features (see Chapter 2). Businesses are increasingly using business social networks as a means of growing their circle of business contacts and promoting themselves online. Because businesses are expanding globally, social networks make it easier to keep in touch with other contacts around the world. Specific cross-border EC platforms and business partnering networks now make globalization accessible even for small and medium-sized companies and for individuals.

Example of a Business-Oriented Social Network

Originating in Germany, Xing.com (xing.com) is a business network that attracts millions of executives, sales representatives, and job seekers from many countries, mostly in Europe. The site offers secure services in 16 languages. Users can visit the site to:

- Establish new business contacts.
- Systematically expand and manage their contacts' networks.
- Market themselves to employers in a professional business context.
- Identify experts and receive advice on any topic.
- Organize meetings and events.
- Control the level of privacy and ensure that their personal data are protected.

For more on Xing.com, take the site's "Guided Tour." Services also are available for mobile device users.

With Web 2.0 tools, companies can engage users on a one-to-one basis in a way that old media, from flat Web sites to Super Bowl ads, was never able to accomplish. More direct communication is achieved by offering more ways for consumers to engage and interact. For example, a company can:

- Encourage consumers to rate and comment on products.
- Allow consumers to create their own topic areas and build communities (forums) around shared interests possibly related to a company's products.
- Hire bloggers or staff editors who can lead more company-formatted essays and discussions that allow, but are not driven by, customer comments.
- Provide incentives such as sweepstakes and contests for customers to get involved in new product (service) design and marketing campaigns.
- Encourage user-made videos about products/services and offer prizes for winning video ads. Capitalize on streaming videos.
- Provide interesting stories in e-newsletters.

ENTERPRISE SOCIAL NETWORKS

Business-oriented social networks can be public, such as LinkedIn.com. As such, they are owned and managed by an independent company. Another type of business-oriented social network is private, owned by corporations and operated inside them. These are known as *enterprise social networks*.

CASE 1.2
EC Application
MYSPACE: A WORLD'S POPULAR SOCIAL NETWORKING WEB SITE

An Overview
MySpace is an interactive social network of user-submitted blogs, profiles, groups, photos, MP3s, videos, and an internal e-mail system. It has become an increasingly influential part of contemporary pop culture. The site claims to have over 100 million members (the world's fourth most popular English-language Web site) and draws 500,000 new members each week.

MySpace is also used by some independent musicians and filmmakers who upload songs and short films on their profiles. These songs and films can also be embedded in other profiles, an interconnectedness that adds to MySpace's appeal.

Contents of a MySpace Profile
Each member's profile contains two "blurbs": "About Me" and "Who I'd Like to Meet." Profiles also can contain optional sections about personal features such as marital status, physical appearance, and income. Profiles also contain a blog with standard fields for content, emotion, and media. Users can also upload images and videos to their MySpace page.

Users can choose a certain number of friends to be displayed on their profile in the "Top Friends" area. In 2006, MySpace allowed up to 24 friends to be displayed. The "Comments" area allows the user's friends to leave comments. MySpace users can delete comments or require all comments to be approved before posting. The site gives users some flexibility to modify their user pages, and "MySpace editors" are available to help.

The Major Capabilities of MySpace
MySpace has many capabilities and more are being added constantly. Here are some representative examples:

- Instant messenger (MySpace IM)
- Groups
- MySpace TV for video sharing
- MySpace Mobile for accessing MySpace with mobile devices
- MySpace News to display RSS feeds submitted by users
- MySpace classifieds for person-to-person advertising

Other capabilities include MySpace Books, MySpace Horoscopes, MySpace Jobs, and MySpace Movies.

MySpace Celebrities
MySpace has led to the emergence of MySpace celebrities—popular individuals who have attracted hundreds of thousands of "friends," leading to coverage in other media.

Some of these individuals have remained only Internet celebrities; others have been able to jump to television, magazines, and radio.

Major Issues Surrounding MySpace
The following are several major issues surrounding MySpace use.

Accessibility
Sometimes there are accessibility problems on users' profiles, because the site is set up so that anyone can customize the layout and colors of their profile page with virtually no restrictions. Poorly constructed MySpace profiles may freeze up Web browsers. Also, new features, such as song and video sharing through streaming media, and the huge number of MySpace users joining daily mean that more users are online for longer periods; this increase in usage slows down the MySpace servers at peak times.

Potential Damage to Students
The *Chicago Tribune*'s RedEye printed an article concerning MySpace and an individual's search for employment. The author argued that young college graduates compromise their chances of starting careers because of the content they post on their accounts. For example, an employer may not hire a highly qualified candidate because the candidate maintains an account that suggests overly "exuberant" behavior.

Security and Safety
MySpace allows registering users to be as young as 14. Profiles of users with ages set to 14 to 15 years are automatically private. Users whose ages are set at 16 or over do have the option to restrict their profiles, as well as the option of merely allowing certain personal data to be restricted to people other than those on their "friends list." The full profiles of users under age 18 are restricted to direct MySpace friends only.

MySpace Music
In September 2008, MySpace launched a joint venture with Universal, Sony BMG, and Warner Music called MySpace Music, a digital music service that enables MySpace users to listen to any song from the catalog of the participating media companies for free (but with on-screen ads).

Globalization and Competition
In 2006, News Corporation took MySpace to China, where it is spreading rapidly (in Chinese, of course). MySpace is available in many countries and languages.

(continued)

Other Issues
Other issues affecting MySpace are musicians' rights and the user agreement, social and cultural issues, and legal issues.

Competition and Income Source on MySpace
When News Corporation purchased MySpace in July 2005 for $580 million, many questioned the wisdom of paying so much for a site with no income and questionable advertisement revenue sources. However, in August 2006 Google paid MySpace more than the entire purchase sum for allowing Google to place its search and advertising on MySpace pages. This is helpful to MySpace, too, because now its users do not have to leave the site to conduct a Google search.

MySpace's major competitors are Facebook, Xanga, Wayn, and Friendster.

Sources: Compiled from Hupfer (2007), Sellers (2006), and *en.wikipedia.org/wiki/MySpace* (accessed August 2009).

Questions

1. Why does MySpace attract so many visitors?
2. List the major issues faced by the company.
3. What are the benefits to MySpace and Google from their collaboration?
4. Visit *myspace.com* and review some features not discussed in this case. Prepare a report.

Example of an Enterprise Social Network

Carnival Cruise Lines sponsors a social networking site (carnivalconnections.com) to attract cruise fans. Visitors use the site to exchange opinions, organize groups for trips, and much more. It cost the company $300,000 to set up the site, but Carnival anticipates that the cost will be covered by increased business. For details, see Fass (2006).

VIRTUAL WORLDS AND SECOND LIFE

virtual world
A user-defined world in which people can interact, play, and do business. The most publicized virtual world is Second Life.

A special class of social networking is the *virtual world*. A **virtual world,** also known as a *metaverse*, is a 3D computer-based simulated environment built and owned by its residents. In addition to creating buildings, people can create and share cars, clothes, and many other items. Community members inhabit virtual spaces and interact via *avatars*. These avatars are usually depicted as textual, 2D, or 3D graphical presentations, although other forms are possible. The essentials of virtual worlds and the prime example, Second Life (secondlife.com), are presented in Chapter 2.

Until 2007, virtual worlds were most often limited to 3D games, including massively multiplayer online games. More recently, they have become a new way for people to socialize, and even do business. For example, there.com focuses more on social networking activities, such as chatting, creating avatars, interacting, playing, and meeting people.

How Students Make Money in a Virtual World

According to Alter (2008), the research firm Gartner Media estimates that by 2011 as many as 80 percent of all Internet users worldwide will have avatars, making animated online persons as common as e-mail and screen names are today. This means that there will be many jobs available to provide support to virtual worlds.

However, you do not have to wait until 2011 to make money in virtual worlds. If you cannot get a summer (or other) job, try a job in a virtual world. With summer jobs in short supply, more young people are pursuing money-making opportunities in virtual worlds. According to Alter (2008), a new breed of young entrepreneurs is honing their computer skills to capitalize on the growing demand for virtual goods and services.

Alter provides examples of six young and successful entrepreneurs:

> ▶ Mike Mikula, age 17, uses graphic design tools to build virtual buildings. His avatar in Teen Second Life, Mike Denneny, helps him to earn $4,000 a month as a builder and renovator of sites on Second Life.
>
> ▶ Ariella Furman, age 21, earns $2,000 to $4,000 a month using her avatar Ariella Languish in Second Life. She is a machinima, a filmmaker who works exclusively in Second Life. She directs avatars using a virtual producer and works in the virtual world for companies like IBM and Nestlé.
>
> ▶ John Eikenberry, age 25, earns $2,000 to $4,000 a month building Second Life neighborhoods, creating malls, coffee shops, and an auditorium over 16 landscaped acres called regions. His avatar is Lordfly Digeridoo in Second Life.
>
> ▶ Kristina Koch, age 17, is a character designer. Her avatar in Teen Second Life, Silver Bu, earns $600 to $800 a month using Second Life tools to add effects, such as shadows, to avatars. She and her boyfriend also design and sell virtual fairy wings and wizard's robes to dress avatars.
>
> ▶ Mike Everest, age 18, is a virtual hunter and trader, selling the skins of what he hunts. He also learned how to transform virtual ore into virtual weapons, which he sells. His avatar in the virtual world of Entropia Universe, Ogulak Da Basher, earns $200 to $1,000 a month. He is the family's primary money maker, and he was able to finance his brother's college education.
>
> ▶ Twins Andy and Michael Ortman, age 19, are inventors. Their avatars in Teen Second Life, Alpha Zaius and Ming Chen, earn about $2,500 a month each. The engineering majors work for Deep Think Labs, a virtual world development company based in Australia. They program Open Simulator, which allows companies and individuals to hold private meetings and training sessions in virtual environments similar to Second Life.

THE MAJOR TOOLS OF WEB 2.0

Web 2.0 uses dozens of tools such as wikis, RSS feeds, blogs, and microblogs (e.g., Twitter). These are described in Chapters 2 and 7. In 2009, Twitter became a major tool of Web 2.0 with diversified business applications.

The Essentials of Twitter for Business

Twitter is a communications platform that helps businesses and their customers. As a business, you can use it to quickly share information with people interested in your company, gather real-time market intelligence, and customer feedback, and build relationships with customers, partners, and other people who care about your company. As an individual user, you can use Twitter to tell a company (or anyone else) that you've had a great—or disappointing—experience with their business, offer product ideas, and learn about great offers.

Twitter connects you to your customers right now, in a way that was never before possible. For example, let's say you work for a custom bike company. If you run a Twitter search for your brand, you may find people posting messages about how happy they are that your bike lets them ride in the French Alps—giving you a chance to share tips about cyclist-friendly cafés along their route.

Others may post minor equipment complaints or desired features that they would never bother to contact you about—providing you with invaluable customer feedback that you can respond to right away or use for future planning. Still others may twitter about serious problems with your bikes—letting you offer customer service that can turn around a bad situation.

The Major Benefits of Twitter. One of Twitter's key benefits is that it gives you the chance to communicate informally and casually with customers on their terms, creating friendly relationships along the way—tough for corporations to do in most other communication mediums. The conversational nature of twittering lets you build relationships with customers, partners, and other people important to your business. Beyond transactions, Twitter gives your constituents direct access to your employees and a way to contribute to your company; as marketers say, it shrinks the emotional distance between your company and your customers. Plus, the platform lends itself to integration with your existing communication channels and strategies.

Example.   Suppose you run a big retail Web site. In addition to learning more about what your customers want, you can provide exclusive Twitter coupon codes, link to key posts on your blog, share tips for shopping online, and announce specials at store locations. And you can take things a step further by occasionally posting messages about fun, quirky events at your company, providing a small but valuable connection with the people in your company. For examples see business.twitter.com/twitter101 and click on best practices and case studies.

Section 1.3 ▶ REVIEW QUESTIONS

1. Define social computing and list its characteristics.
2. Define Web 2.0 and list its attributes.
3. Define social networks.
4. Describe the capabilities of social network services (SNSs).
5. Describe MySpace. Why is it so popular?
6. What is an enterprise social network?
7. Define virtual worlds and list their characteristics.
8. Describe some ways for students with computer skills to make money from virtual worlds.
9. Describe how Twitter can help businesses.

1.4   THE DIGITAL WORLD: ECONOMY, ENTERPRISES, AND SOCIETY

digital economy
An economy that is based on digital technologies, including digital communication networks, computers, software, and other related information technologies; also called the *Internet economy,* the *new economy,* or the *Web economy.*

The digital revolution is upon us. We see it every day at home and work, in businesses, schools, hospitals, on the roads, in entertainment and even in wars. Next, we describe three elements of the digital world: economy, enterprises, and society.

THE DIGITAL ECONOMY

The **digital economy** refers to an economy that is based on digital technologies, including digital communication networks (the Internet, intranets, extranets, and VANs), computers, software, and other related information technologies. The digital economy is sometimes called the *Internet economy,* the *new economy,* or the *Web economy.* This platform displays the following characteristics:

- ▶ A vast array of digitizable products—databases, news and information, books, magazines, TV and radio programming, movies, electronic games, musical CDs, and software—are delivered over a digital infrastructure anytime, anywhere in the world. We are moving from analog to digital; even the media is getting digital (TVs as of February 2009).
- ▶ Consumers and firms conduct financial transactions digitally through digital currencies that are carried via networked computers and mobile devices.
- ▶ Microprocessors and networking capabilities are embedded in physical goods such as home appliances and automobiles.
- ▶ Information is transformed into a commodity.
- ▶ Knowledge is codified.
- ▶ Work and production are organized in new and innovative ways.

The term *digital economy* also refers to the convergence of computing and communications technologies on the Internet and other networks and the resulting flow of information and technology that is stimulating EC and vast organizational changes. This convergence enables all types of information (data, audio, video, etc.) to be stored, processed, and transmitted over networks to many destinations worldwide.

Exhibit 1.3 describes the major characteristics of the digital economy. The digital revolution accelerates EC mainly by providing competitive advantage to organizations. The digital revolution also enables many innovations, and new ones appear almost daily. The digital revolution provides the necessary technologies for EC and creates major changes in the business environment, as described in Section 1.5.

EXHIBIT 1.3 Major Characteristics of the Digital Economy

Area	Description
Globalization	Global communication and collaboration; global electronic marketplaces and competition.
Digital system	From TV to telephones and instrumentation, analog systems are being converted to digital ones.
Speed	A move to real-time transactions, thanks to digitized documents, products, and services. Many business processes are expedited by 90 percent or more.
Information overload and intelligent search	Although the amount of information generated is accelerating, intelligent search tools can help users find what they need.
Markets	Markets are moving online. Physical marketplaces are being replaced by electronic markets; new markets are being created, increasing competition.
Digitization	Music, books, pictures, videos, and more are digitized for fast and inexpensive distribution.
Business models and processes	New and improved business models and processes provide opportunities to new companies and industries. Cyberintermediation and no intermediation are on the rise.
Innovation	Digital and Internet-based innovations continue at a rapid pace. More patents are being granted than ever before.
Obsolescence	The fast pace of innovation creates a high rate of obsolescence.
Opportunities	Opportunities abound in almost all aspects of life and operations.
Fraud	Criminals employ a slew of innovative schemes on the Internet. Cybercons are everywhere.
Wars	Conventional wars are changing to cyberwars.
Organizations	Organizations are moving to digital enterprises.

digital enterprise
A new business model that uses IT in a fundamental way to accomplish one or more of three basic objectives: reach and engage customers more effectively, boost employee productivity, and improve operating efficiency. It uses converged communication and computing technology in a way that improves business processes.

THE DIGITAL ENTERPRISE

The term *digital enterprise* has a number of definitions. It usually refers to an enterprise, such as Dell, Amazon.com, Google, or Ticketmaster, that uses computers and information systems to automate most of its business processes. The **digital enterprise** is a new business model that uses IT in a fundamental way to accomplish one or more of three basic objectives: (1) reach and engage customers more effectively, (2) boost employee productivity, and (3) improve operating efficiency. It uses converged communication and computing technology in a way that improves business processes. The major characteristics of a digital enterprise are provided in Exhibit 1.4, where they are compared with those of a traditional enterprise.

A digital enterprise uses networks of computers to facilitate the following:

▶ All internal communication is done via an intranet, which is the counterpart of the Internet inside the company.

▶ All business partners are reached via the Internet, or via a secured Internet, called an extranet, or via value-added private communication lines.

The vast majority of EC is done on computers connected to these networks. Many companies employ a **corporate portal,** which is a gateway for customers, employees, and partners to reach corporate information and to communicate with the company.

The major concern of many companies today is how to transform themselves into digital enterprises so that they can take part in the digital economy. For example, Harrington (2006) describes why and how, as a CEO, he transformed the Thomson Corp. from a traditional $8 billion publishing business into an electronic information

corporate portal
A major gateway through which employees, business partners, and the public can enter a corporate Web site.

EXHIBIT 1.4 **The Digital Versus Brick-and-Mortar Company**	
Brick-and-Mortar Organizations	**Digital Organizations (Enterprises)**
Selling in physical stores	Selling online
Selling tangible goods	Selling digital goods as well
Internal inventory/production planning	Online collaborative inventory forecasting
Paper catalogs	Smart electronic catalogs
Physical marketplace	Electronic marketplace
Use of telephone, fax, VANs, and traditional EDI	Use of computers, smart phones, the Internet and extranets
Physical auctions, infrequently	Online auctions, everywhere, any time
Broker-based services, transactions	Electronic infomediaries, value-added services
Paper-based billing	Electronic billing
Paper-based tendering	Electronic tendering (reverse auctions)
Push production, starting with demand forecasting	Pull production, starting with an order (build-to-order)
Mass production (standard products)	Mass customization, build-to-order
Physical-based commission marketing	Affiliated, virtual marketing
Word-of-mouth, slow and limited advertisement	Explosive viral marketing, in particular in social networks
Linear supply chains	Hub-based supply chains
Large amount of capital needed for mass production	Less capital needed for build-to-order; payments can be collected before production starts
Large fixed cost required for plant operation	Small fixed cost required for plant operation
Customers' value proposition is frequently a mismatch (cost > value)	Perfect match of customers' value proposition (cost <= value)

services provider and publisher for professionals in targeted markets. In five years, revenue increased over 20 percent and profit increased by more than 65 percent.

Note that the term *enterprise* refers to any kind of organization, small or large. An enterprise can be a manufacturing plant, a hospital, a university, or even a city. They are all moving toward being digitized.

THE DIGITAL SOCIETY

The final, and perhaps most important, element of the *digital world* is people and the way they live and interact. Clearly, the digital society has changed contemporary life with regard to almost any activity we can think of—work, play, shopping, entertainment, travel, medical care, education, and much more. Almost every day new digital applications are developed. Just think about your digital camera, your digital TV, your digital car, and almost anything else. It is only natural that people are utilizing EC at an accelerating rate. Let's take a look at some examples:

▶ Kaboodle.com makes it easy to shop online with friends. You can share recommendations and discover new products and services from your community friends. Shopping at Kaboodle can be fun. You can discover many useful things from people with similar tastes and styles and discuss with them certain vendors and products. You can even enrich your life with a wish list.

▶ As of 2008, high school girls were able to solicit feedback from their friends regarding 70 different prom dresses that were displayed by Sears on Facebook. This enabled Sears to extend the shopping experience into the social sphere.

▶ As of 2009, users can use *social smart phones* (e.g., the Android handset from Motorola) to connect quickly and easily to mobile features in networks such as Facebook and MySpace. For example, users can communicate directly in messages with network friends who are on their phone contact lists.

▶ According to Farivar (2004), VIP patrons of the Baja Beach Club in Barcelona, Spain, can have RFID chips, which are the size of a grain of rice, implanted into their upper arms, allowing them to charge drinks to a bar tab when they raise their arm toward the RFID reader. The RFID is a tiny tag that contains a processor and antenna; it can communicate wirelessly with a detecting unit in a reader over a short distance (see Online File W1.7 and Loebbecke 2006). "You don't call someone crazy for getting a tattoo," says Conrad Chase, director of Baja Beach Clubs International. "Why would they be crazy for getting this?"

▶ Dryers and washers in college dorms are hooked to the Web. Students can punch a code into their cell phones or sign in at esuds.net and check the availability of laundry machines. Furthermore, they can receive e-mail alerts when their wash and dry cycles are complete. Once in the laundry room, a student activates the system by swiping a student ID card or keying in a PIN number. The system automatically injects premeasured amounts of detergent and fabric softener, at the right cycle time.

▶ Using his blog site (oneredpaperclip.blogspot.com), Kyle MacDonald of Canada was able to trade a red paper clip into a three-bedroom house. He started by advertising in the barter section of craigslist.org that he wanted something bigger or better for one red paper clip. In the first iteration, he received a fish-shaped pen, and he posted on Craigslist again and again.

Following many iterations and publicity on TV, after one year, he traded for a house (MacDonald 2007).

▶ Camera-equipped cell phones are used in Finland as health and fitness advisors. A supermarket shopper using the technology can snap an image of the bar code on a packet of food. The phone forwards the code number to a central computer, which sends back information on the item's ingredients and nutritional value. The computer also calculates how much exercise the shopper will have to do to burn off the calories based on the shopper's height, weight, age, and other factors.

▶ Doggyspace.com allows dog lovers from around the globe to come together. You can build a page and a profile and post a video or photos to show off your dog, creating a social experience around the pets you care about. The site offers medical and other advice. Like in any other social network, people can create groups of friends with whom to share their doggy experiences.

▶ A remote medical monitoring system can help with early diagnosis of heart failure. A person stands on a special bathroom scale that can wirelessly transmit data to a clinician's screen. A computer analyzes the weight change and triggers an alarm for a suspected anomaly that predicts possible trouble. The medical technician then calls the person to discuss medication, the need to see a doctor, and so forth. The system keeps patients healthier and cuts health care costs.

▶ Similar remote monitoring devices are used to treat children with asthma, adults with mental disorders, patients with diabetes, and more. Some systems allow for real-time audio and video consultation with a physician. A unique system sells an electronic pill box that records whether and when patients take their medicine. Interested? Try Health Buddy from Health Hero Network (healthhero.com/about/about_health_hero.html) and visit the eWeek Health Care Center (eweek.com/c/s/Health-Care-IT) for the latest news, views, and analysis of technology's impact on health care.

▶ Online dating and matching services are becoming more popular. Companies such as eHarmony, Match.com, JDate, and Yahoo! Personals, are leading hundreds of other companies worldwide that are making matches. For example, Match.com has begun offering free profile and photo tips via an online video with Jay Manuel, of the television show *America's Next Top Model.* The company also sells services for $2 to $6 a month that offer advice on dating and ways to make profiles and photographs stand out. Match.com views online dating as the candidates being on stage and being viewed by thousands of prospects. It suggests spending some time backstage getting ready. Several companies can help you to get ready, mostly for free (e.g., dating-profile.com and e-cyrano.com).

▶ Bicycle computers (by Bridgestone Cycle Co.) can automatically keep track of your travel distance, speed, time, and calorie consumption. Travel data are stored for 30 days, and you can transmit it to your computer. A community Web site allows you to share experiences. You can also find people to ride around the world with. Interested? See emeters.jp/try.html.

Additional examples of the digital world in everyday life are provided in Online File W1.8.

One of the most interesting phenomena of the digital society is the changes in the way that politicians interact with the public. This topic will be discussed in

Chapter 6. However, as an example, note the extensive use of EC made by President Barack Obama. For example, Obama purchased Internet ads featured in 18 video games through Microsoft's Xbox Live Service. His objective was to target young adult males, who are difficult to reach through traditional campaign advertising. For other innovative and pioneering EC initiatives used by President Obama, see Online File W1.9. It is estimated that these activities netted him at least 2 percent of the vote. Some claim that without such tactics Obama would have lost the election (Needle 2008).

Section 1.4 ▶ REVIEW QUESTIONS

1. Define the digital revolution and list its components.
2. List the characteristics of the digital economy.
3. Define a digital enterprise.
4. Compare traditional and digital enterprises.
5. Describe the digital society.
6. Visit doggyspace.com and dogtoys.com. Compare the two sites and relate their contents to the digital society.

1.5 ELECTRONIC COMMERCE DRIVERS AND THE CHANGING BUSINESS ENVIRONMENT

EC is driven by many technological, economic, and social factors. These are frequently related to global competition and rapid changes in the business environment.

THE DRIVERS OF EC AND ITS GROWTH

EC initiatives play an increasing role in supporting innovations and strategies that help companies to compete and flourish, especially companies that want to introduce changes rather than respond to them. What makes EC suitable for such a role is a *set of capabilities* and *developments*; the major capabilities and developments are summarized in Exhibit 1.5.

The essentials of the capabilities that drive EC are the ability to:

> ▶ Provide efficient and effective business transactions.
> ▶ Provide global reach for selling, buying, or finding business partners.
> ▶ Conduct business anytime, from anywhere, in a convenient way. For example, there are more than 250 million wireless subscribers in the United States (Burns 2007).
> ▶ Disseminate information rapidly, frequently in real time (e.g., the Beijing Olympics).
> ▶ Compare prices.
> ▶ Customize products and personalize services.
> ▶ Use rich media in advertisement, entertainment, and social networking.
> ▶ Receive experts' and other users' advice quickly.
> ▶ Collaborate in different ways, both internally and externally.
> ▶ Share information and knowledge.

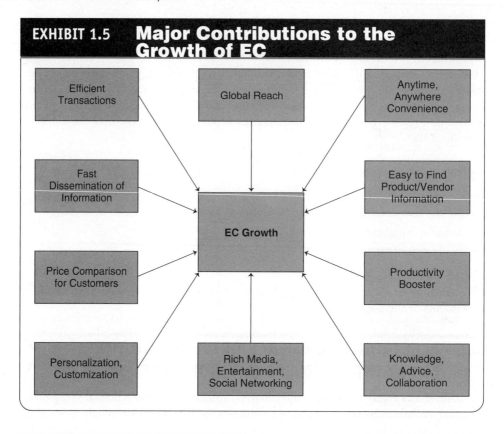

EXHIBIT 1.5   Major Contributions to the Growth of EC

- Increase productivity and performance, reduce costs, and compress time (e.g., by having smarter applications).
- Easily and quickly find information about vendors, products, and competitors.

Because EC technology is improving over time and decreasing in cost, its comparative advantage is increasing, further contributing to the growth of EC. EC growth is related to the changing business environment.

The Changing Business Environment

Economic, legal, societal, and technological factors have created a highly competitive business environment in which customers are becoming more powerful. These environmental factors can change quickly, vigorously, and sometimes in an unpredictable manner. Companies need to react quickly to both the problems and the opportunities resulting from this new business environment.

Because the pace of change and the level of uncertainty are expected to accelerate, organizations are operating under increasing pressures to produce more products, faster, and with fewer resources. For example, the financial/economic crisis of 2008–2009 has resulted in many companies going out of business or being acquired by other companies. It has also presented the opportunity for large banks to buy even larger ones. These business environment changes impact the manner in which companies operate, and many firms have restructured themselves and their information systems, as well as their EC model.

Let's see how all of these impact organizational performance.

PERFORMANCE, BUSINESS PRESSURES, AND ORGANIZATIONAL RESPONSES

Most people, sports teams, and organizations are trying to improve their *performance*. For some, it is a challenge; for others, it is a requirement for survival. Yet for others it is the key to improved life, profitability, or reputation.

Most organizations measure their performance periodically, comparing it to some metrics and to the organization's mission, objectives, and plans. Unfortunately, in business, performance often depends not only on what you do but also on what others are doing, as well as on forces of nature. In the business world, we refer to such events, in totality, as the *business environment*. Such an environment may create significant pressures that can impact performance in uncontrollable, or sometimes even in unpredictable, ways.

The Business Environment and Performance Impact Model

The model shown in Exhibit 1.6 illustrates how the business environment (left) creates pressures, problems, and opportunities that drive what organizations are doing in their business processes (the "Our Company" circle). Other drivers are the organization's mission, goals, strategy, and plans. Business processes include competencies, activities, and responses to the environmental pressures that we call *critical response activities* or *solutions*. The business processes and activities result in measurable performance, which provides solutions to problems/opportunities, as well as feedback as to the attainment of the mission, strategy, goals, and plans.

Notice that in the exhibit EC and IT provide support to organizations' activities and to the resultant performance, countering the business pressures. We will demonstrate this cyclical process throughout the book. Now, let's examine the two major components of the model: business pressures and organizational responses.

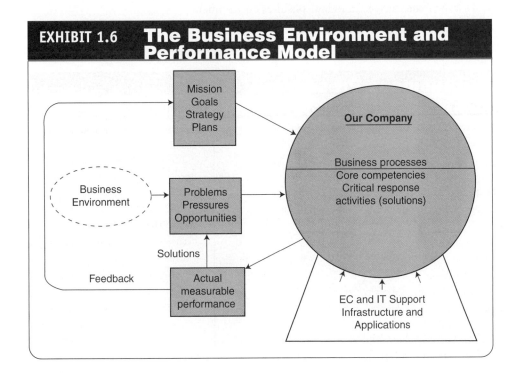

EXHIBIT 1.6   The Business Environment and Performance Model

Business Pressures

In this text, business pressures are divided into the following categories: market (economic), societal, and technological. The main types of business pressures in each category are listed in Exhibit 1.7. (Note that some of the business environment conditions create opportunities.)

Organizational Response Strategies

How can organizations operate in such an environment? How can they deal with the threats and the opportunities? To begin with, many traditional strategies are still useful in today's environment. However, because some traditional response activities may *not* work in today's turbulent and competitive business environment, many of the old solutions need to be modified, supplemented, or discarded. Alternatively, new responses can be devised. Critical response activities can take place in some or all organizational processes, from the daily processing of payroll and order entry to strategic activities such as the acquisition of a company. Responses can also occur in the supply chain, as demonstrated by the cases of Boeing (Online File W1.4) and Dell (Online File W1.3). A response activity can be a reaction to a specific pressure already in existence, or it can be an initiative that will defend an organization against future pressures. It can also be an activity that exploits an opportunity created by changing conditions.

Many response activities can be greatly facilitated by EC, and this fuels the growth of the field. In some cases, EC is the *only* solution to certain business pressures. Representative EC-supported response activities are provided in Exhibit 1.8 and in Online File W1.10.

Section 1.5 ▶ REVIEW QUESTIONS

1. List five of the major drivers of EC.
2. List the components of the business environment impact model and explain the model.
3. List the major factors in today's business environment.
4. List some of the major response activities taken by organizations (consult Exhibit 1.8).

EXHIBIT 1.7 Major Business Pressures		
Market and Economic Pressures	**Societal Pressures**	**Technological Pressures**
Strong competition	Changing nature of workforce	Increasing innovations and new technologies
Global economy	Government deregulation, leading to more competition	Rapid technological obsolescence
Regional trade agreements (e.g., NAFTA)	Compliance (e.g., Sarbanes-Oxley Act)	Increases in information overload
Extremely low labor costs in some countries	Shrinking government subsidies	Rapid decline in technology cost versus labor cost (technology becomes more and more attractive)
Frequent and significant changes in markets	Increased importance of ethical and legal issues	
Increased power of consumer	Increased societal responsibility of organizations	
Political and government	Rapid political changes	
	Terrorism	

EXHIBIT 1.8   Innovative Organizational Responses

Response Strategy	Descriptions
Strategic systems	Improve strategic advantage in industry.
Agile systems	Increase ability to adapt to changes and flexibility.
Continuous improvements and business process management	Using enterprise systems to improve business processes. Introduce e-procurement.
Customer relationship management	Introduce programs to improve customer relationships using the Internet and EC models.
Business alliances and partner relationship management (PRM)	Create joint ventures, partnerships, e-collaboration, virtual corporations, and others for win-win situations—even with competitors.
Electronic markets	Use both private and public electronic markets to increase efficiency and effectiveness.
Cycle time reduction	Increase speed of operation and reduce time to market.
Empowering employees, especially on the frontline (interacting with customers, partners)	Provide employees with computerized decision aids so they can make quick decisions on their own.
Mass customization in a build-to-order system	Produce customized products (services) rapidly at reasonable cost to many, many customers (mass) as Dell does.
Intrabusiness use of automation	Many intrabusiness activities, from sales force automation to inventory management can be improved with e-commerce and m-commerce.
Knowledge management	Appropriate creation, storage, and dissemination of knowledge using electronic systems, increases productivity, agility, and competitiveness.
Customer selection, loyalty, and service	Identify customers with the greatest profit potential; increase likelihood that they will want the product or service offering; retain their loyalty.
Human capital	Select the best employees for particular tasks or jobs, at particular compensation levels.
Product and service quality	Detect quality problems early and minimize them.
Financial performance	Better understand the drivers of financial performance and the effects of nonfinancial factors.
Research and development	Improve quality, efficacy, and where applicable, safety of products and services.
Social networking	Innovative marketing, advertising, collaboration, and innovation using the power of the crowd.

1.6 ELECTRONIC COMMERCE BUSINESS MODELS

One of the major characteristics of EC is that it enables the creation of new business models (Prahalad and Krishnan 2008). A **business model** is a method of doing business by which a company can generate revenue to sustain itself. The model also spells out where the company is positioned in the value chain; that is, by what activities the company adds value to the product or service it supplies. (The *value chain* is the series of value-adding activities that an organization performs to achieve its goals, such as making profit, at various stages of the production process.) One company may have several business models.

business model
A method of doing business by which a company can generate revenue to sustain itself.

Business models are a subset of a business plan or a business case (see the Online Tutorial at the book's Web site).

THE STRUCTURE AND PROPERTIES OF BUSINESS MODELS

Several different EC business models are possible, depending on the company, the industry, and so on.

A comprehensive business model is composed of the following elements:

- A description of the *customers* to be served and the company's relationships with these customers, including what constitutes value from the customers' perspective (*customers' value proposition*).
- A description of all *products* and *services* the business will offer and the markets in which they will be sold.
- A description of the *business process* required to make and deliver the products and services including distribution and marketing strategies.
- A list of the *resources* required and the identification of which ones are available, which will be developed in-house, and which will need to be acquired (including human resources).
- A description of the organization's *supply chain*, including *suppliers* and other *business partners*.
- A list of the major competitors, their market share, and strengths/weaknesses.
- The competitive advantage offered by the business model.
- The anticipated organizational changes and any resistance to change.
- A description of the revenues expected (*revenue model*), anticipated costs, sources of financing, and estimated profitability (*financial viability*).

Models also include a *value proposition*, which is an analysis of the benefits of using the specific model (tangible and intangible), including the customers' value proposition cited earlier. A detailed discussion of and examples of business models and their relationship to business plans is presented in the Online Tutorial.

This chapter presents two of the models' elements: revenue models and value propositions.

Revenue Models

A revenue model outlines how the organization, or the EC project, will generate revenue. For example, the revenue model for Godiva's online EC initiative shows revenue from online sales. The major revenue models are:

Sales. Companies generate revenue from selling merchandise or services over their Web sites. An example is when Zappos.com, Amazon.com, or Godiva sells a product online.

Transaction Fees. A company receives a commission based on the volume of transactions made. For example, when a home owner sells a house, he or she typically pays a transaction fee to the broker. The higher the value of the sale, the higher the total transaction fee. Alternatively, transaction fees can be levied *per transaction*. With online stock trades, for example, there is usually a fixed fee per trade, regardless of the volume.

Subscription Fees. Customers pay a fixed amount, usually monthly, to get some type of service. An example would be the access fee for AOL. Thus, AOL's primary revenue model is subscription (fixed monthly payments).

Advertising Fees. Companies charge others for allowing them to place a banner on their sites (see Chapter 4).

Affiliate Fees. Companies receive commissions for referring customers to others' Web sites.

Other Revenue Sources. Some companies allow people to play games for a fee or to watch a sports competition in real time for a fee (e.g., see espn.go.com). Another revenue source is licensing fees (e.g., see datadirect-technologies.com). Licensing fees can be assessed as an annual fee or a per usage fee. Microsoft takes fees from each workstation that uses Windows NT, for example.

A company uses its *revenue model* to describe how it will generate revenue and its *business model* to describe the *process* it will use to do so. Exhibit 1.9 summarizes five common revenue models.

The revenue model can be part of the value proposition or it may complement it.

Innovative Revenue Models for Individuals. The Internet allows for innovative revenue models, some of which can be utilized even by individuals, as demonstrated by the following two examples.

Example 1: Buy Low–Sell High. This strategy has been known for generations, but now you have a real chance. How about buying stuff cheap on Craigslist (or other online classified sites) and resell it for a 50 to 200 percent profit in an auction on

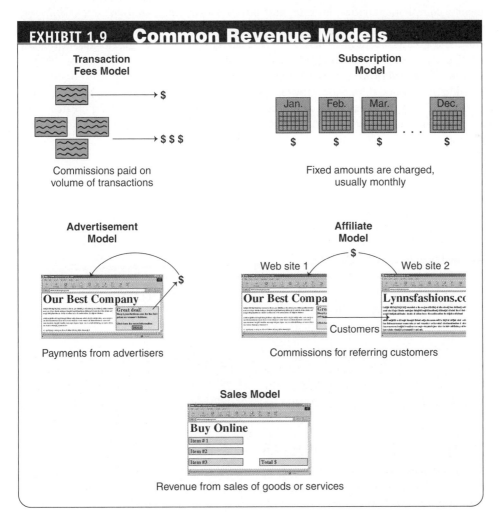

EXHIBIT 1.9   Common Revenue Models

Transaction Fees Model

Commissions paid on volume of transactions

Subscription Model

Jan.   Feb.   Mar.   Dec.

Fixed amounts are charged, usually monthly

Advertisement Model

Our Best Company

Payments from advertisers

Affiliate Model

Web site 1   Web site 2

Our Best Compa   Lynnsfashions.cc

Customers

Commissions for referring customers

Sales Model

Buy Online

Item #1
Item #2
Item #3   Total $

Revenue from sales of goods or services

eBay! Try it, you might make money. Some people make it even bigger. The person who bought the domain name *pizza.com* for $20 in 1994 sold it for $2.6 million in April 2008.

Example 2: Traffic Arbitrage.   This is a more complex implementation of buy low–sell high. Basically, you buy ad space on less expensive search engines (such as Microsoft's Ad Center). The search engine then directs traffic to your Web site via key words. Then you fill your personal Web site with Google's ads (see Chapter 4 for AdSense). When users come to your Web site and click on Google's ads, they are then directed to advertisers' Web sites. The advertisers pay Google for the referrals, and Google shares the fees with you.

Value Proposition

value proposition
The benefits a company can derive from using EC.

Business models also include a value-proposition statement. A **value proposition** refers to the benefits, including the intangible, nonquantitative ones, that a company can derive from using the model. In B2C EC, for example, a value proposition defines how a company's product or service fulfills the needs of customers. The *value proposition* is an important part of the marketing plan of any product or service.

Specifically, how do e-marketplaces create value? Amit and Zott (2001) identify four sets of values that are created by e-business: search and transaction cost efficiency, complementarities, lock-in, and novelty. *Search and transaction cost efficiency* enables faster and more informed decision making, wider product and service selection, and greater economies of scale—cost savings per unit as greater quantities are produced and sold (e.g., through demand and supply aggregation for small buyers and sellers). *Complementarities* involve bundling some goods and services together to provide more value than from offering them separately. Lock-in is attributable to the high switching cost that ties customers to particular suppliers. *Novelty* creates value through innovative ways for structuring transactions, connecting partners, and fostering new markets.

Functions of a Business Model

Business models have the following functions or objectives:

- Describe the major business processes of a company.
- Describe the business models' (the venture's) positioning within the value network linking suppliers and customers (includes identification of potential complementors and competitors). Also, describe the supply and value chains.
- Formulate the venture's competitive strategy and its long-range plans.
- Articulate a customer value proposition.
- Identify a market segment (who will use the technology for what purpose; specify the revenue-generation process; where the company will operate).
- Define the venture's specific value chain structure.
- Estimate the cost structure and profit potential.

TYPICAL EC BUSINESS MODELS

There are many types of EC business models. Examples and details of EC business models can be found throughout this text, and in Rappa (2008). The following are five common models. Additional models are listed in Online File W1.11.

1. **Online direct marketing.** The most obvious model is that of selling products or services online. Sales may be from a *manufacturer* to a customer, eliminating intermediaries or physical stores (e.g., Zappos), or from *retailers* to consumers, making distribution more efficient (e.g., Walmart). This model is especially efficient for digitizable products and services (those that can be delivered electronically). This model has several variations (see Chapters 3 and 5) and it uses different mechanisms (e.g., auctions). It is practiced in B2C (where it is called *e-tailing*) and in some B2B types of EC.

2. **Electronic tendering systems.** Large organizational buyers, private or public, usually make large-volume or large-value purchases through a **tendering (bidding) system**, also known as a *reverse auction*. Such tendering can be done online, saving time and money. Pioneered by General Electric Corp., e-tendering systems are gaining popularity. Indeed, several government agencies mandate that most of their procurement must be done through e-tendering.

   tendering (bidding) system
   Model in which a buyer requests would-be sellers to submit bids; the lowest bidder wins.

3. **Electronic marketplaces and exchanges.** Electronic marketplaces existed in isolated applications for decades (e.g., stock and commodities exchanges). But as of 1996, hundreds of e-marketplaces (old and new) have introduced new efficiencies to the trading process. If they are well organized and managed, e-marketplaces can provide significant benefits to both buyers and sellers. Of special interest are vertical marketplaces that concentrate on one industry (e.g., chemconnect.com for the chemical industry).

4. **Viral marketing.** According to the viral marketing model (see Chapter 4), an organization can increase brand awareness or even generate sales by inducing people to send influencing messages to other people or to recruit friends to join certain programs. It is basically Web-based *word-of-mouth* advertising, and it is popular in social networks.

5. **Social networking and Web 2.0 tools.** Many companies are deriving commercial benefits from social networking (Chapter 7) and Web 2.0 tools (see Chapter 2).

Section 1.6 ▶ REVIEW QUESTIONS

1. What is a business model? Describe its functions and properties.
2. Describe a revenue model and a value proposition.
3. Describe the following business models: direct marketing, tendering system, electronic exchanges, viral marketing, and social networking.
4. Identify business models related to buying and those related to selling.

1.7 BENEFITS, LIMITATIONS, AND IMPACTS OF ELECTRONIC COMMERCE

Few innovations in human history encompass as many benefits as EC does. The global nature of the technology, the opportunity to reach hundreds of millions of people, its interactive nature, the variety of possibilities for its use, and the resourcefulness and rapid growth of its supporting infrastructures, especially the Web, result in many potential benefits to organizations, individuals, and society. These benefits are just starting to materialize, but they will increase significantly as EC expands. It is not surprising that some maintain that the EC revolution is as profound as the change that accompanied the Industrial Revolution.

THE BENEFITS AND IMPACTS OF EC

EC provides benefits to *organizations*, *individual customers*, and *society*. These benefits are summarized in Exhibit 1.10. Many benefits can be found in the list of EC resources in Online File W1.12.

EXHIBIT 1.10   Benefits of E-Commerce

Benefit	Description
Benefits to Organizations	
Global reach	Locating customers and/or suppliers worldwide, at reasonable cost and fast.
Cost reduction	Lower cost of information processing, storage, distribution.
Facilitate problem solving	Solve complex problems that have remained unsolved.
Supply chain improvements	Reduce delays, inventories, and cost.
Business always open	Open 24/7/365; no overtime or other costs.
Customization/personalization	Make it to consumers' wish, fast and at reasonable cost (see Online File W1.15).
Seller's specialization (niche market)	Seller can specialize in a narrow field (e.g., dog toys), yet make money.
Ability to innovate, use new business models	Facilitate innovation and enable unique business models.
Rapid time to market and increased speed	Expedite processes; higher speed and productivity.
Lower communication costs	The Internet is cheaper then VAN private lines.
Efficient procurement	Saves time and reduces costs by enabling e-procurement.
Improved customer service and relationship	Direct interaction with customers, better CRM.
Fewer permits and less tax	May need fewer permits and be able to avoid sales tax.
Up-to-date company material	All distributed material is up-to-date.
Help SME to compete	EC may help small companies to compete against large ones by using special business models.
Lower inventories	Using customization inventories can be minimized.
Lower cost of distributing digitizable product	Delivery online can be 90 percent cheaper.
Provide competitive advantage	Innovative business models.
Benefits to Consumers	
Ubiquity	Can shop any time from any place.
More products/services	Large selection to choose from (vendor, products, styles).
Customized products/services	Can customize many products and/or services (see Online File W1.15).
Cheaper products/services	Can compare and shop for lowest prices.
Instant delivery	Digitized products can be downloaded immediately upon payment.
Information availability	Easy finding what you need, with details, demos, etc.
Convenient auction participation	Do auctions any time and from any place.
No sales tax	Sometimes.
Enable telecommuting	Can work or study at home.
Electronic socialization	Can socialize online in communities yet bet at home.
Find unique items	Using online auctions, collectible items can be found.
Benefits to Society	
Enable telecommuting	Facilitate work at home; less traffic, pollution.
More public services	Make education, health, etc., available for more people. Rural area can share benefits; more services for the poor.
Improved homeland security	Facilitate domestic security.
Increased standard of living	Can buy more and cheaper goods/services.
Close the digital divide	Allow people in developing countries and rural areas to accept more services and purchase what they really like.

EC as a Provider of Competitive Advantage

The business model created by EC and the benefits of the technology may result in significant changes in the way business is conducted. These changes may positively impact corporate operations resulting in a competitive advantage for the firms using EC. For a description and discussion see Online File W1.13.

THE LIMITATIONS AND BARRIERS OF EC

Barriers to EC can be classified as either technological or nontechnological. Representative major barriers are listed in Exhibit 1.11.

According to a 2006 study (*Harmony Hollow Software* 2006), the major barriers to EC are (1) resistance to new technology, (2) implementation difficulties, (3) security concerns, (4) lack of technology skills, (5) lack of potential customers, and (6) cost. Van Toorn et al. (2006) believe that the barriers are sectoral barriers (e.g., government, private sector, international organizations), internal barriers (e.g., security, lack of technical knowledge, and lack of time and resources), and external barriers (e.g., lack of government support). Van Toorn et al. (2006) also list the top barriers with regards to global EC: cultural differences, organizational differences, incompatible B2B interfaces, international trade barriers, and lack of standards. These limitations need to be addressed when implementing EC. One important area is that of ethics.

EXHIBIT 1.11 Limitations of Electronic Commerce

Technological Limitations	Nontechnological Limitations
Lack of universal standards for quality, security, and reliability.	Security and privacy concerns deter customers from buying.
The telecommunications bandwidth is insufficient, especially for m-commerce, videos, and graphics.	Lack of trust in EC and in unknown sellers hinders buying.
Software development tools are still evolving.	People do not yet sufficiently trust paperless, faceless transactions.
It is difficult to integrate Internet and EC software with some existing (especially legacy) applications and databases.	Many legal and public policy issues, including taxation, have not yet been resolved or are not clear.
Special Web servers are needed in addition to the network servers, which add to the cost of EC.	National and international government regulations sometimes get in the way.
Internet accessibility is still expensive and/or inconvenient.	It is difficult to measure some of the benefits of EC, such as online advertising. Mature measurement methodologies are not yet available.
Order fulfillment of large-scale B2C requires special automated warehouses.	Some customers like to feel and touch products. Also, customers are resistant to the change from shopping at a brick-and-mortar store to a virtual store.
	People do not yet sufficiently trust paperless, faceless transactions.
	In many cases, the number of sellers and buyers that are needed for profitable EC operations is insufficient.
	Online fraud is increasing.
	It is difficult to obtain venture capital due to the failure of many dot-coms.

Ethical Issues

ethics
The branch of philosophy that deals with what is considered to be right and wrong.

Ethical issues can create pressures or constraints on EC business operations. **Ethics** relates to standards of right and wrong, and *information ethics* relates to standards of right and wrong in information technology and EC practices. Ethical issues have the power to damage the image of an organization and morale of employees. Ethics is a difficult area, because ethical issues are not cut-and-dried. What is considered ethical by one person may seem unethical to another. Likewise, what is considered ethical in one country may be unethical in another.

Implementing EC use may raise ethical issues ranging from employee e-mail monitoring to invasion of privacy of millions of customers whose data are stored in private and public databases. In implementing EC, it is necessary to pay attention to these issues and recognize that some of them may limit, or even prohibit, the use of EC. An example of this can be seen in the attempted implementation of RFID tags in retail stores due to the potential invasion of buyers' privacy.

Despite these barriers, EC is expanding rapidly. As experience accumulates and technology improves, the cost-benefit ratio of EC will increase, resulting in even greater rates of EC adoption.

WHY STUDY E-COMMERCE?

The academic area of e-commerce started around 1995 with only a few courses and textbooks. Today, many universities offer complete programs in e-commerce or e-business (e.g., majors in e-commerce, minors in e-commerce and certificate programs; see University of Virginia, University of Maine). Recently, e-commerce topics have been integrated into all functional fields (e.g., Internet marketing, electronic financial markets). The reason for this proliferation is that e-commerce is penetrating more and more into business areas, services, and governments.

However, there are also some very tangible benefits to increased knowledge of EC. First, your chances of getting a good (or better) job are higher. The demand for both technical and managerial EC skills is growing rapidly, and so are the salaries (e.g., see salary comparison sites such as salary.com, cbsalary.com, and monster.com). Second, your chances for promotion could be higher if you understand EC and know how to seize its opportunities. Finally, it gives you a chance to become a billionaire, like the founders of Google, Facebook, and Yahoo!, or to make lots of money on eBay (see Joyner 2007). Even if you are not so lucky you can still make good money in Second Life (see Alter 2008 and Rymaszewski et al. 2008) or simply by selling on eBay, Yahoo!, or your own Web site. And you can do it while you are a student, as Lily, Shu, and Adrian did (see Case 1.3).

Section 1.7 ❯ REVIEW QUESTIONS

1. Describe some EC benefits to organizations, individuals, and society.
2. List the major technological and nontechnological barriers and limitations to EC.
3. Describe some of the benefits of studying EC.

1.8   OVERVIEW OF THIS BOOK

This book is composed of 11 chapters and an online chapter, grouped into seven parts, as shown in Exhibit 1.12. The seventh part, which comprises two chapters, is available at the text's Web site. Additional content, including a tutorial, a technical appendix, and online supplemental material for each chapter, is also available online at the book's Web site.

The specific parts and chapters of this textbook are as follows.

CASE 1.3
EC Application
HOW COLLEGE STUDENTS BECOME ENTREPRENEURS

Stanford University students Lily Kim, Shu Lindsey, and Adrian Mak use computers and the Internet extensively. They also do extensive writing (on paper) and especially like using ultra thin pens with a tip half the width of the average ballpoint. They learned about these pens when they visited Japan. Because these pens were not available in U.S. stores, they purchased them online directly from Japan. When they showed the pens to their friends (an example of the power of social marketing), they found that there was great interest in such pens in the United States.

Sensing the opportunity, in 2004 they decided to use their $9,000 savings to open a business, called JetPens (*jetpens.com*), selling pens they imported from Japan to their classmates. To keep costs low, they used open source free software (from osCommerce) to build and run the store. Soon after they opened an online storefront, they began advertising their products via e-mail to other students. By June 2009, they had over 5,000 registered users. To meet the demand, they initially kept an inventory of pens in their bedrooms, but now they rent storage space.

They also have a small advertising budget for Google ads. By using smart key words, their store ranks at the top of search engine discoveries when a user searches for "Japanese pens" (try a Google search to verify). This strategy is called *search engine* or *site optimization* (see search engine optimization in Chapter 4 and *en.wikipedia.org/wiki/Search_engine_optimization*).

In 2007, the owners expanded the product line by adding interesting office supplies, including a best-selling

eraser with 28 corners, which increased their sales volume to over 10,000 items per month. Other best sellers include a pen with a tip fine enough to write on a grain of rice, the Uni-ball Alpha Gel ballpoint pen with a squishy silicone-gel grip (this silicone gel is famous for keeping an egg from breaking when dropped from 5 feet), colorful and erasable gel pens that work just as well as pencils, and BeGreen environmentally friendly pens. To find friends and customers, they use Facebook, Flickr, and YouTube and they have a forum on the JetPens Web site.

By keeping a tight cap on operating expenses and using Internet advertising successfully, the young entrepreneurs have been able to do what many others have failed to do—generate a profit within two years, and grow by hundreds of percentage points every year.

Sources: Compiled from Blakely (2007) and *jetpens.com* (accessed June 2009).

Questions

1. Go to jetpens.com and examine the catalog. What impresses you the most?
2. Evaluate the site's ease of use.
3. Do you think that a business like this can succeed as an independent online-only store? Why or why not?
4. What is the purpose of the site's JetPress RSS Feed?

Source: Used with permission of *jetpens.com*.

EXHIBIT 1.12 Plan of the Book

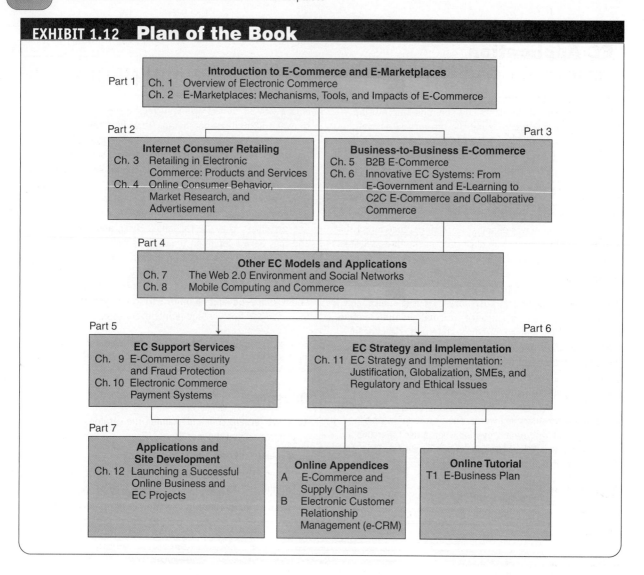

PART 1: INTRODUCTION TO E-COMMERCE AND E-MARKETPLACES

This section of the book includes an overview of EC and its content, benefits, limitations, and drivers, which are presented in Chapter 1. Chapter 2 presents electronic markets and their mechanisms, such as electronic catalogs and auctions. Chapter 2 also includes a presentation of Web 2.0 tools and mechanisms.

PART 2: INTERNET CONSUMER RETAILING

This section includes two chapters. Chapter 3 describes e-tailing (B2C), including some of its most innovative applications for selling products online. It also describes the delivery of services, such as online banking, travel, and insurance. Chapter 4 explains consumer behavior in cyberspace, online market research, and Internet advertising.

PART 3: BUSINESS-TO-BUSINESS E-COMMERCE

Part 3 is composed of two chapters. In Chapter 5, we introduce B2B EC and describe company-centric models (one buyer–many sellers, one seller–many buyers) as well as electronic exchanges (many buyers and many sellers). E-government, e-learning, C2C, and knowledge management are the major subjects of Chapter 6.

PART 4: OTHER EC MODELS AND APPLICATIONS

Several other EC models and applications are presented in Part 4. Chapter 7 examines social networking in the Web 2.0 environment. Finally, Chapter 8 introduces the topics of mobile commerce.

PART 5: EC SUPPORT SERVICES

Part 5 examines issues involving the support services needed for EC applications. Chapter 9 delves into EC security and fraud protection. Chapter 10 discusses electronic payments, order fulfillment, and other services.

PART 6: EC STRATEGY AND IMPLEMENTATION

Part 6 includes one chapter on EC strategy and implementation. Chapter 11 examines e-strategy and planning, including going global and the impact of EC on small businesses.

ONLINE PART 7: APPLICATION AND SITE DEVELOPMENT

An additional complete chapter is available online at the book's Web site (pearsonhighered. com/turban). Chapter 12 deals with creating, operating, and maintaining an Internet company. It also discusses initiating EC initiatives and creating EC content. Chapter 12 also addresses EC application development processes and methods, including software as a service (SaaS), Web Services, and service-oriented architecture (SOA).

ONLINE TUTORIAL

Online Tutorial T1 on *business plans* is available at the book's Web site (pearsonhighered. com/turban).

ONLINE APPENDICES

Online Appendix A on supply chain management (SCM) and Online Appendix B on e-CRM are available at the book's Web site (pearsonhighered.com/turban).

ONLINE SUPPLEMENTS

A large number of online files organized by chapter number support the content of each chapter.

MANAGERIAL ISSUES

Many managerial issues are related to EC. These issues are discussed throughout the book and also are summarized in a separate section (like this one) near the end of each chapter. Some managerial issues related to this introductory chapter are as follows.

1. **Is EC real?** For those not involved in EC, the first question that comes to mind is, "Is it real?" We believe that the answer is an emphatic "yes." The Internet is already an integral part of our lives. Banking from home, trading stocks online, and buying books from Amazon.com are now common practices for many people. The concern is not whether to start EC, but to what extent should it be developed and how to ensure the success of the e-business. Jack Welch, former CEO of General Electric, has commented, "Any company, old or new, that doesn't see this technology literally as important as breathing could be on its last breath" (McGee 2000).

2. **Why is B2B e-commerce so essential and successful?** B2B EC is essential for several reasons. First,

some B2B models are easier to implement than B2C models. The value of transactions is larger in B2B than in B2C, and the potential savings are larger and easier to justify in contrast to B2C, which has several major problems, ranging from channel conflict with existing distributors to a lack of a critical mass of buyers. Many companies can start B2B by simply buying from existing online stores and B2B exchanges or selling electronically by joining existing marketplaces or an auction house. The problem is determining *where* to buy or sell.

3. **What should be my business model?** Beginning in early 2000, the news was awash with stories about the failure of many dot-coms. Industry consolidation often occurs after a "gold rush." About 100 years ago, hundreds of companies tried to manufacture cars, following Ford's success in the United States; only three survived. The important thing is to learn from the successes and failures of others, and discover the right business model for each endeavor. For lessons that can be learned from EC successes and failures, see Chapters 3 and 5.

4. **How can we exploit social/business networking?** There are major possibilities here. Some companies even open their own social networks. Advertising is probably the first thing to consider. Recruiting can be a promising avenue as well. Offering discounted products and services should also be considered. Finally, the ultimate goal is associating the social network with commerce so that revenue is created.

5. **What are the top challenges of EC?** The top 10 technical issues for EC (in order of their importance) are security, adequate infrastructure, data access, back-end systems integration, sufficient bandwidth, network connectivity, up time, data warehousing and mining, scalability, and content distribution. The top 10 managerial issues for EC are budgets, project deadlines, keeping up with technology, privacy issues, the high cost of capital expenditures, unrealistic management expectations, training, reaching new customers, improving customer ordering services, and finding qualified EC employees. Most of these issues are discussed throughout this book.

SUMMARY

In this chapter, you learned about the following EC issues as they relate to the chapter's learning objectives.

1. **Definition of EC and description of its various categories.** EC involves conducting transactions electronically. Its major categories are pure versus partial EC, Internet versus non-Internet, and electronic markets versus interorganizational systems.

2. **The content and framework of EC.** The applications of EC, and there are many, are based on infrastructures and are supported by people; public policy and technical standards; marketing and advertising; support services, such as logistics, security, and payment services; and business partners—all tied together by management.

3. **The major types of EC transactions.** The major types of EC transactions are B2B, B2C, C2C, m-commerce, intrabusiness commerce, B2E, c-commerce, e-government, and e-learning.

4. **E-commerce 2.0.** This is the use of social computing in business, often through the use of Web 2.0 tools (such as blogs, wikis), as well as the emergence of enterprise social networking and commercial activities in virtual worlds. Social and business networks attract huge numbers of visitors. Many of the visitors are young (future EC customers). Therefore, advertisers are willing to spend money on advertising, either to an entire group or to individuals (e.g., using Google's technology).

5. **The elements of the digital world.** The major elements of the digital world are the digital economy, digital enterprises, and digital society. They are diversified and expanding rapidly.

6. **Drivers of EC.** EC is a major product of the digital and technological revolution, which enables companies to simultaneously increase both growth and profits. This revolution enables digitization of products, services, and information. The business environment is changing rapidly due to technological breakthroughs, globalization, societal changes, deregulation, and more. The changing business environment forces organizations to respond. Many traditional responses may not be sufficient because of the magnitude of the pressures and the pace of the changes involved. Therefore, organizations must

frequently innovate and reengineer their operations. In many cases, EC is driven by the needs of organizations to perform and even survive.

EC provides strategic advantage so organizations can compete better. Also, organizations can go into remote and global markets for both selling and buying at better prices. Organizations can speed time-to-market to gain competitive advantage. They can improve the internal and external supply chain as well as increase collaboration. Finally, they can better comply with government regulations.

7. **The major EC business models.** The major EC business models include online direct marketing, electronic tendering systems, name-your-own-price, affiliate marketing, viral marketing, group purchasing, online auctions, mass customization (make-to-order), electronic exchanges, supply chain improvers, finding the best price, value-chain integration, value-chain providers, information brokers, bartering, deep discounting, and membership.

8. **Benefits of EC to organizations, consumers, and society.** EC offers numerous benefits to all participants. Because these benefits are substantial, it looks as though EC is here to stay and cannot be ignored.

KEY TERMS

Brick-and-mortar (old economy) organizations	6	Consumer-to-business (C2B)	9	Extranet	6
Business model	29	Consumer-to-consumer (C2C)	9	Intrabusiness EC	9
Business-oriented networks	16	Corporate portal	22	Intranet	6
Business-to-business (B2B)	8	Digital economy	20	Social computing	13
Business-to-business-to-consumer (B2B2C)	8	Digital enterprise	22	Social network	14
		E-business	4	Social networking	15
Business-to-consumer (B2C)	8	E-government	9	Social network services (SNSs)	14
Business-to-employees (B2E)	9	E-learning	9	Tendering (bidding) system	33
Click-and-mortar (click-and-brick) organizations	6	Electronic commerce (EC)	4	Value proposition	32
		Electronic market (e-marketplace)	6	Virtual (pure-play) organizations	6
Collaborative commerce (c-commerce)	9	E-tailing	8	Virtual world	18
		Ethics	36	Web 2.0	13

QUESTIONS FOR DISCUSSION BY INDIVIDUAL STUDENTS

1. Compare brick-and-mortar and click-and-mortar organizations.

2. Why is buying with a smart card from a vending machine considered EC?

3. Why is e-learning considered EC?

4. How does EC facilitate customization of products and services? (Hint: See Online File W1.11.)

5. Explain how EC can reduce cycle time, improve employees' empowerment, and facilitate customer support.

6. Compare and contrast viral marketing with affiliate marketing. (Hint: See Online File W1.11.)

7. Identify the contribution of Web 2.0. What does it add to EC?

8. Distinguish an enterprise social network from a public one such as Facebook.

9. Carefully examine the nontechnological limitations of EC. Which are company-dependent and which are generic?

10. Why are virtual worlds such as Second Life related to EC?

11. Register at **ibm.com/enterpriseofthefuture** and download IBM's study "The Enterprise of the Future" (IBM 2008). In one page, summarize how the enterprise of the future differs from today's enterprise.

TOPICS FOR CLASS DISCUSSION

1. How can EC be a business pressure and an organizational response?

2. Some claim that digital businesses eliminate the "human touch." Discuss.

3. Why do companies frequently change their business models? What are the advantages? The disadvantages?

4. Discuss the seven lessons learned from the Zappos case. How has EC technology made this company so successful?

INTERNET EXERCISES

1. Visit bigboxx.com and identify the services the company provides to its customers. What type of EC is this? What business model(s) does Bigboxx use?

2. Visit amazon.com and locate recent information in the following areas:

   a. Find the five top-selling books on EC.

   b. Find a review of one of these books.

   c. Review the customer services you can get from Amazon.com and describe the benefits you receive from shopping there.

   d. Review the products directory.

3. Visit priceline.com and zappos.com and identify the various business models used by both.

4. Go to nike.com and design your own shoes. Next, visit office.microsoft.com and create your own business card. Finally, enter jaguar.com and configure the car of your dreams. What are the advantages of each activity? The disadvantages?

5. Try to save on your next purchase. Visit letsbuyit. com, kaboodle.com, yub.com, and buyerzone. com. Which site do you prefer? Why?

6. Enter espn.go.com and identify and list all of the revenue sources on the site.

7. Enter lala.com and listen to some of the commercial-free digital songs offered (cost 10¢). What other digital products and services do they offer? Write a summary.

8. Enter philatino.com, stampauctioncentral.com, and statusint.com. Identify the business model(s)

and revenue models they use. What are the benefits to sellers? To buyers?

9. Enter lowes.com. View the "design it" online feature and the animated "How Tos." Examine the Project Calculators and Gift Advisor features. Relate these to the business models and other EC features of this chapter.

10. Go to zipcar.com. What can this site help you do?

11. Enter digitalenterprise.org. Prepare a report regarding the latest EC models and developments.

12. Visit some Web sites that offer employment opportunities in EC (such as execunet.com and monster.com). Compare the EC salaries to salaries offered to accountants. For other information on EC salaries, check *Computerworld*'s annual salary survey, unixl.com, and salary.com.

13. Visit bluenile.com, diamond.com, and jewelry exchange.com. Compare the sites. Comment on the similarities and the differences.

14. Visit ticketmaster.com, ticketonline.com, and other sites that sell event tickets online. Assess the competition in online ticket sales. What services do the different sites provide?

15. Enter The Timberland Company (timberland. com) and design a pair of boots. Compare it to building your own sneakers at nike.com. Compare these sites to zappos.com/shoes.

TEAM ASSIGNMENTS AND PROJECTS

1. Reread the Blue Nile case (Online File W1.14) and discuss the following:

   a. What are the key success factors for Blue Nile?

   b. Amazon.com makes only a 15 percent margin on the jewelry products it sells. This enables Amazon.com to sell diamond earrings for $1,000 (traditional jewelers charge $1,700 for the same). Do you think that Amazon.com will succeed in selling this type of jewelry as Blue Nile did in selling expensive engagement rings?

   c. Competition between Blue Nile and Amazon.com will continue to increase. In your opinion, which one will win (visit their Web sites and see how they sell jewelry)?

   d. Why is "commoditization" so important in the diamond business?

   e. Compare the following three sites: diamond.com, ice.com, and bluenile.com.

   f. Follow the performance of Blue Nile's stock since 2003 (symbol: NILE, go to money.cnn.com). Compare it to the performance of the market average. What is your conclusion?

2. Create an online group for studying EC or a particular aspect of EC that interests you. You can do this via Google Groups, a social network of your choice, or Yahoo! Groups. Each member of the group must have an e-mail account. Go to Yahoo! Groups groups.yahoo.com and log in. At the bottom of the page, there is a section titled "Create your own Group."

   Step 1: Click on "Start a Group."

   Step 2: Select a category that best describes your group (use the Search Group Categories, or use Browse Group Categories tool). You must find a category.

   Step 3: Describe the purpose of the group and give it a name.

   Step 4: Set up an e-mail address for sending messages to all group members.

   Step 5: Each member must join the group (select "profile"); click on "Join this Group."

   Step 6: Go to Word Verification Section; follow instructions.

   Step 7: Finish by clicking "Continue."

   Step 8: Select a group moderator. Conduct a discussion online of at least two topics of the group's interest.

   Step 9: Arrange for messages from the members to reach the moderator at least once a week.

   Step 10: Find a similar group (use Yahoo!'s "find a group" and make a connection). Write a report for your instructor.

3. Each team will research two EC success stories. Members of the group should examine companies that operate solely online and some that extensively utilize a click-and-mortar strategy. Each team should identify the critical success factors for their companies and present a report to the other teams (see Online File W1.12 for some resources).

4. Each team selects a business-oriented social network such as LinkedIn, Xing, or Viadeo. Each team presents the essentials of the site, the attributes, etc. Each team will try to convince other students why their site is superior.

5. All class members that are not registered in Second Life need to register and create their avatars. Let each team address one of the following areas:

   ▶ Trading virtual properties
   ▶ Creating buildings, projects, stores
   ▶ Shopping and retail outlets
   ▶ Virtual jobs
   ▶ Learning and training
   ▶ Other topics

   a. Prepare a description of what is going on in that area.

   b. Have members' avatars interact with other avatars. Write a report about your experience.

   c. What can you learn from this project?

Closing Case

BEIJING 2008: A DIGITAL OLYMPICS

Known in China as "Superfish," Michael Phelps was on his way to achieving his goal of eight gold medals. His most difficult competition was the 100-meter butterfly. On PCs, cell phones, electronic billboards, and televisions, millions of viewers worldwide watched him win the event by .01 seconds. The results appeared on the screens almost in real time. If you did not see this exciting race, you can access it on YouTube. This was only one component in the "most wired," or digital, Olympics.

The Problem

It was not an easy task to manage 42 events in seven different cities in China. Competition results had to be displayed worldwide not only on PCs and televisions, but also on jumbo public display screens in stadiums and streets in hundreds of cities, and on millions of tiny mobile device screens.

But, this was only one problem. The Olympic organizers also had to manage the logistics of the participants and address the requirements of the media, while also accommodating over 100 million tourists. The following are some of the specific requirements that the Beijing Olympic organizers had to meet:

▶ Record the performance of all athletes and determine the winners instantly, sometimes based on millisecond differences. These results then had to be disseminated around the globe in real time.

▶ China hosted about 300,000 athletes, referees, trainers, journalists, and other workers from more than 200 countries, speaking dozens of languages. All needed to have accommodations, transportation, and food.

▶ Nearly 8 million visitors from abroad and close to 120 million domestic travelers attended the Olympics. They needed accommodation, transportation, and so forth.

▶ Tickets to all events had to be issued, many in advance, and to people in other countries. Protection against counterfeiting was necessary.

▶ Approximately 1,000 percent more Web-delivered videos were needed in 2008 than were needed by the 2004 Olympics.

▶ The organizers anticipated a greater than 1,000 percent increase in page views, and even more in video watching. Sufficient infrastructure had to be in place.

▶ In real time, the system had to collect and filter more than 12 million monitored events and identify potential security threats.

▶ Real-time, transoceanic coverage, including digital videos, required sophisticated hardware, software, and networks.

▶ Many visitors preferred to shop online and have Olympic souvenirs shipped to their homes.

▶ Overall, it was necessary to securely process more than 80 percent more information compared with the 2004 Olympics in Athens, Greece.

▶ Traffic in Beijing can be a major problem and is a major air pollutant, so monitoring and controls were needed to minimize it.

These problems and requirements can be classified into seven categories:

1. Information collection and monitoring
2. Information dissemination to the world
3. Tickets and souvenirs management
4. Food and supplies along the supply chain
5. Security and privacy monitoring and protection
6. Transportation and pollution control
7. Social networking for the public

The $4 Billion IT and EC Solutions

To address the administrative problems just discussed, as well as many others, the organizers employed the latest information technology tools, including electronic commerce. To explain how this was done, the seven requirements have been divided into five basic categories, as shown in the following exhibit (left side), which also shows the e-commerce solutions used (right side).

The following major e-commerce solutions were implemented:

▶ The instant display of the results was possible due to the use of sophisticated photo-finish cameras and computers. The system was capable of identifying winners accurately even when the difference was only milliseconds.

▶ The International Olympic Committee (IOC) launched a YouTube channel to broadcast clips that were accessible in 77 developing countries (but not in the United States). Viewers were able to watch free clips on demand from PCs, as well as news and commentaries. These clips were broadcast on television and display boards as well. Videos were downloaded with Microsoft's Silverlight and Adobe's Flash.

▶ Over 12 million tickets were available for the events. Many of these tickets were purchased online, using Beijing Gehua Ticketmaster, in what we call B2C electronic commerce.

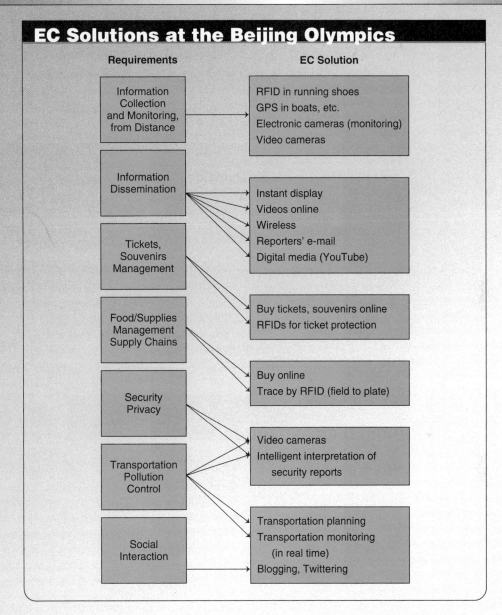

EC Solutions at the Beijing Olympics

Requirements	EC Solution
Information Collection and Monitoring, from Distance	RFID in running shoes GPS in boats, etc. Electronic cameras (monitoring) Video cameras
Information Dissemination	Instant display Videos online Wireless Reporters' e-mail Digital media (YouTube)
Tickets, Souvenirs Management	Buy tickets, souvenirs online RFIDs for ticket protection
Food/Supplies Management Supply Chains	Buy online Trace by RFID (field to plate)
Security Privacy	Video cameras Intelligent interpretation of security reports
Transportation Pollution Control	Transportation planning Transportation monitoring (in real time)
Social Interaction	Blogging, Twittering

- All the tickets were equipped with radio frequency identification (RFID) tags that were loaded with information designed to prevent counterfeit tickets. (See Online File W1.7 for an introduction to RFID.)

- Millions watched the Olympics through online videos and Internet-enabled cell phones and other mobile devices.

- Using RFID tags, the Olympic coordinators ensured the safety of athletes' food by tracking the ingredients from farms to plates.

- Global Positioning Systems (GPS) were used to track the position of sailing and rowing boats five times per second for comparison purposes.

- RFID tags were attached to one shoe of each marathon runner. When the runners passed RFID readers at certain locations along the running route, their whereabouts were known as well as their exact time of arrival there.

- More than 50 software applications supported the games' management. For example, a workforce management tool was used to manage the work of hundreds of telecommunication technicians and others during the games.

- Bloggers were encouraged to blog. For example, the Bank of America sponsored a site called "America's Cheer" where athletes were blogging. Others blogged on rotorblog.com, as well as thousands of other sites. Twitter (see Chapter 2) was also a great source of coverage and result dissemination. Social networking capabilities were provided by the "Olympic Network TV Station."

▶ Electronic collaboration among over a dozen IT companies and especially Cisco Systems, Microsoft, and Limelight Networks ensured the successful execution of the supporting IT and EC systems.

The Results

The organizing committee clearly deserved a gold medal. Everything was perfect, even the computer-generated fireworks that were displayed in the video of the opening and closing ceremonies! The EC solutions were able to handle over 20 times more video screens than the 2004 Olympics, satisfying approximately 60 million unique users (versus 11 million in 2004) who viewed more than 1 trillion pages (versus 230 million in Athens). All of this was accomplished without any major problems. The Olympics helped create many new online communities that provided instant feedback to NBC and Microsoft, which improved the coverage. Finally, a social network that covers all the Olympic

games was developed at *olympic-network.net*. No other Olympics had such sophisticated information processing capabilities and superb EC applications. Even the illegal e-commerce market that was selling pirated Olympic merchandise was minimized.

Sources: Compiled from Taft (2008), *IT Strategy* (2008), rotorblog.com (miscellaneous dates), *InformationWeek* (2008a and 2008b), Burger (2008), and Magnier (2008).

Questions

1. For each business requirement explain how the EC tools helped.
2. Identify the B2C and B2B activities described in this case.
3. Identify the major business models described in this case.
4. Relate the case to the concept of the digital enterprise.
5. Relate the case to social networks and communities.

ONLINE RESOURCES
available at pearsonhighered.com/turban

Online Files

Other Resources
Online Chapter

Online Tutorial
Online tutorial T1 on business plans is available at the book's Web site (pearsonhighered.com/turban).

Online Appendices
Online Appendix A on supply chain management (SCM) and Online Appendix B on electronic customer relationship management (e-CRM) are available at the book's Web site (pearsonhighered.com/turban).

Comprehensive Educational Web Sites
Electronic Resource Guide: Electronic Commerce (libraries.rutgers.edu/rul/rr_gateway/research_guides/busi/ecomm.shtml):
Offers resources and links to Internet statistics—see clickZstats, Nielsen/NetRatings, U.S. Census Bureau, ComScore.
Social Computing Journal (web2.socialcomputingjournal.com)

CHAPTER 2

E-MARKETPLACES: MECHANISMS, TOOLS, AND IMPACTS OF E-COMMERCE

Content

Learning Objectives

Upon completion of this chapter, you will be able to:

1. Describe the major electronic commerce (EC) activities and processes and the mechanisms that support them.

2. Define e-marketplaces and list their components.

3. List the major types of e-marketplaces and describe their features.

4. Describe electronic catalogs, search engines, and shopping carts.

5. Describe the major types of auctions and list their characteristics.

6. Discuss the benefits, limitations, and impacts of auctions.

7. Describe bartering and negotiating online.

8. List the major Web 2.0 tools and their use in EC.

9. Understand virtual worlds and their use in EC.

WEB 2.0 TOOLS AT EASTERN MOUNTAIN SPORTS

Eastern Mountain Sports (EMS) (*ems.com*) is a medium-sized specialty retailer (annual sales $29.3 million) that sells goods in more than 64 physical stores in 12 states, through mail-order catalogs and online. Operating in a very competitive environment, the company uses leading-edge information technologies. EMS is now using a complementary set of Web 2.0 tools in order to increase collaboration, information sharing, and communication among stores and their employees, suppliers, and customers. Let's see how this works.

The Business Intelligence Strategy and System

During the past few years, the company has implemented a business intelligence (BI) system (see Online File W4.7) that includes business performance management and dashboards. (A *dashboard* is a graphical presentation of results of reports about performance.) A BI system collects raw data from multiple sources, processes them into a data warehouse (or data mart), and conducts analyses that include comparing performance to operational

metrics in order to assess the health of the business (see details in Turban et al. 2011).

The illustration shows how the system works. Point-of-sale (POS) information and other relevant data, which are available on an IBM mainframe computer, are loaded into Microsoft's SQL server and into a data mart (see Online File W4.7). The data are then analyzed with Information Builders' WebFOCUS platform. The results are presented via a series of dashboards that users can view by using Web browsers.

The Web 2.0 Collaboration, Sharing, and Communication System

The company created a multifunctional employee workbench called *E-Basecamp*. E-Basecamp contains all information relevant to corporate goals integrated with productivity tools (e.g., Excel) and role-based content customized to each individual user. Then, EMS added a set of Web 2.0 tools. The system facilitates collaboration among internal and external stakeholders. EMS is using 20 operation metrics (e.g., inventory levels and turns). These metrics also cover e-tailing, where e-commerce managers monitor Web traffic and conversion rates on an hourly basis. The dashboard shows deviations from targets by means of a color code. The system uses the following Web 2.0 tools (see the following exhibit):

- **Wikis.** Wikis are used to encourage collaborative interaction throughout the company. Dashboard users are encouraged to post a hypothesis or request for help and then invite commentary and suggestions, almost like a notepad alongside the dashboard.

- **Blogs.** Blogs were created around specific data or a key metric. The blogs are used to post information and invite comment. Tools are then used to archive, search, and categorize blogs for easy reference. For example, store managers post an inquiry or explanation regarding sale deviations (anomalies). Keeping comments on blogs lets readers observe patterns they might have overlooked using data analysis alone.

- **RSS feeds.** RSS feeds (Chapter 7) are embedded into the dashboards to drive more focused inquiries. These feeds are the base for information sharing and online conversations. For example, by showing which items are selling better than others, users can collectively analyze the transaction characteristics and selling behaviors that produce the high sales. The knowledge acquired then cascades throughout the organization.

Eastern Mountain Sports Web 2.0 Collaboration, Sharing, and Communication System

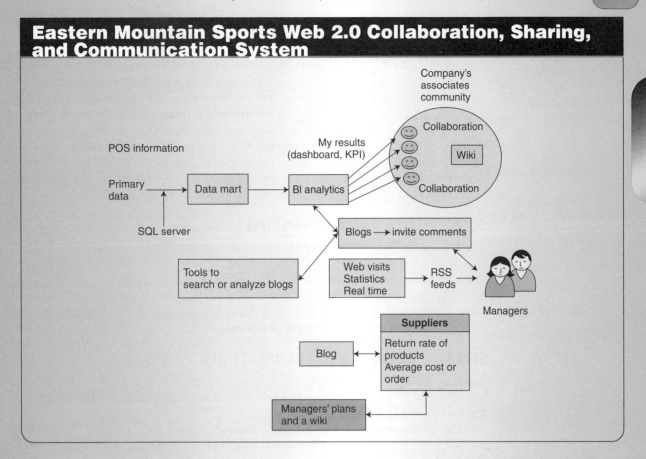

Going to Business Partners Externally

Suppliers can monitor the return rate of a product on the dashboard and invite store managers to provide explanations and suggestions using wikis or blogs. The objective is to build a tighter bond with business partners. For instance, by attaching a blog to suppliers' dashboards, the suppliers can view current sales information and post comments to the blogs. Product managers use a wiki to post challenges for the next season (such as a proposed percentage increase in sales) and then ask vendors to suggest innovative ways to achieve these goals. Several of the customers and other business partners subscribe to RSS feeds.

Called *Extreme Deals*, blogs are also embedded into the EMS product life-cycle management (PLM) tool. This allows vendors to have virtual conversations with the product development managers.

The major impact of the Web 2.0 collaboration tools is that instead of having conversations occur in the hallway (where you need to be in the right place at the right time), conversations take place on blogs and wikis where all interested parties can participate.

Sources: Compiled from Nerille (2007) and from *ems.com* (accessed November 2009).

WHAT WE CAN LEARN . . .

Eastern Mountain Sports was successful in bolstering communication and collaboration both among its own managers and with its suppliers. They did so with Web 2.0 tools: blogs, wikis, and RSS feeds. These tools facilitated the company's business processes and their existing information systems. The Web 2.0 tools enhance the activities of e-commerce, business-to-employee (B2E) information sharing, and e-tailing (business-to-consumer). The Web 2.0 tools are the newest mechanisms of EC and are introduced in this chapter together with the more traditional mechanisms that support selling and buying online.

2.1 ELECTRONIC COMMERCE MECHANISMS: AN OVERVIEW

The many EC models and types of transactions presented in Chapter 1 are enabled by different mechanisms. To begin, the generic enablers of any information system include databases, networks, security, operating systems, and hosting services need to be established. Then come the special EC enablers that are presented in this chapter such as electronic markets, e-stores, and e-catalogs. Also, there are different methods for executing EC, such as buying at a fixed price or at an auction, and each method has a different mechanism. In this chapter, the major EC mechanisms are described so that you will understand what they are when you read about them in other chapters.

EC ACTIVITIES AND MECHANISMS

The EC trading activities are divided into six categories, which are listed on the left side of Exhibit 2.1. Each activity is supported by one or more EC mechanisms, which are shown on the right side of Exhibit 2.1, along with the section numbers in this chapter, where they are presented. Additional mechanisms exist for special activities, such as payment (Chapter 10), security (Chapter 9), and order fulfillment (Online Appendix A).

Next, we present one of the major processes in EC.

SELLERS, BUYERS, AND TRANSACTIONS

Typically, a seller (retailer, wholesaler, or manufacturer) sells to customers. The seller buys either raw material (as a manufacturer) or finished goods (as a retailer) from suppliers. This process is illustrated in Exhibit 2.2.

The selling company, shown as "Our Company," appears in the center of the exhibit. Internally, processes and transactions are conducted in different functional areas and are supported by EC applications. The customers place orders (in B2C or B2B), and Our Company fulfills them. Our Company buys materials, products, and so on from suppliers, distributors (B2B), or from the government (G2B) in a process called *e-procurement*. Sometimes intermediaries are involved in this process. Let's zero in on what happens during a typical purchasing process.

The Purchasing Process

Customers buy goods online in different ways. The most common way is purchasing from catalogs at fixed prices. Sometimes prices may be negotiated or discounted. Another way is dynamic pricing, which refers to nonfixed prices such as those in auctions or stock (commodity) markets. The buyers use the process illustrated in Exhibit 2.3.

The process starts with logging into a seller's Web site, registering (if needed), and entering into an online catalog or the buyer's "my account." E-catalogs can be very large, so a search mechanism may be needed. Also, the buyer should compare prices. Some sellers (e.g., American Airlines) provide comparisons with competing vendors. Otherwise, the buyer may need to leave the site or do price comparisons *before* entering into the specific seller's store. If not satisfied, the buyer will abandon the site. If satisfied, the buyer will select an item and place it in a *shopping cart*. The buyer may return to the catalog to choose more items. Each selected item is placed in the shopping cart. When shopping is complete, the buyer goes to a checkout page, where a shipment option is selected from a menu. Also, a payment option may be available. For example,

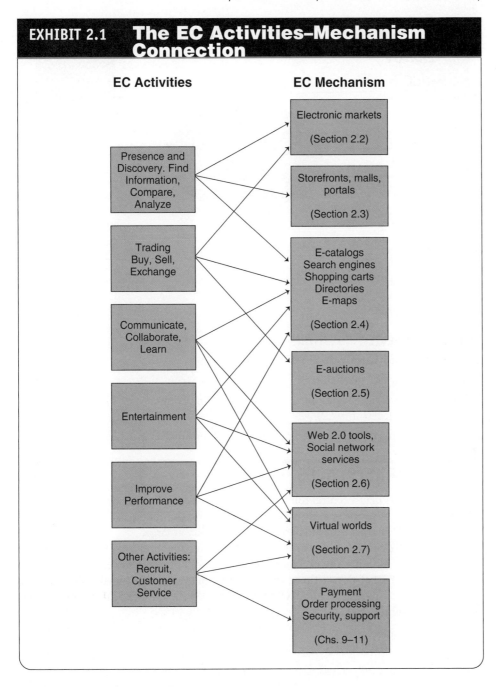

EXHIBIT 2.1   The EC Activities–Mechanism Connection

newegg.com lets you pay by credit card, with PayPal, by check after billing, in installments, and so on. After checking all details for accuracy, the buyer *submits* the order.

The major mechanisms that support this process are described in the remainder of this chapter. The place where these processes occur is an e-marketplace that we introduce next.

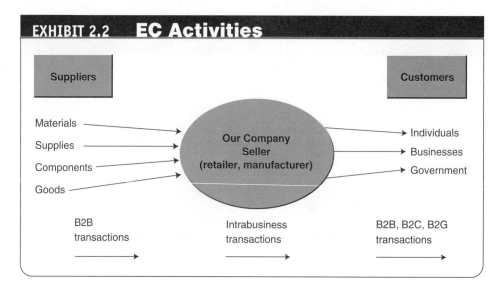

EXHIBIT 2.2   EC Activities

Section 2.1 ❯ **REVIEW QUESTIONS**

1. List the major EC activities.
2. List the major EC mechanisms.
3. Describe the selling–buying process among a selling company, its suppliers, and customers (consult Exhibit 2.2).
4. Describe the major steps in the buying process (consult Exhibit 2.3).

2.2 E-MARKETPLACES

Electronic markets play a central role in the digital economy, facilitating the exchange of information, goods, services, and payments. In the process, they create economic value for buyers, sellers, market intermediaries, and for society at large.

Markets (electronic or otherwise) have three main functions: (1) matching buyers and sellers; (2) facilitating the exchange of information, goods, services, and payments associated with market transactions; and (3) providing an institutional infrastructure, such as a legal and regulatory framework, that enables the efficient functioning of the market (see Exhibit 2.4).

ELECTRONIC MARKETS

e-marketplace
An online market, usually B2B, in which buyers and sellers exchange goods or services; the three types of e-marketplaces are private, public, and consortia.

The major place for conducting EC transactions is the electronic market. An **e-marketplace** is a virtual marketplace in which sellers and buyers meet and conduct different types of transactions. Customers exchange goods and services for money (or other goods and services if bartering is used). The functions of an e-market are the same as those of a physical marketplace; however, computerized systems tend to make electronic markets much more efficient by providing more updated information and diverse support services to buyers and sellers.

EC has increased market efficiencies by expediting or improving the functions listed in Exhibit 2.4. Furthermore, EC has been able to significantly decrease the cost of executing these functions.

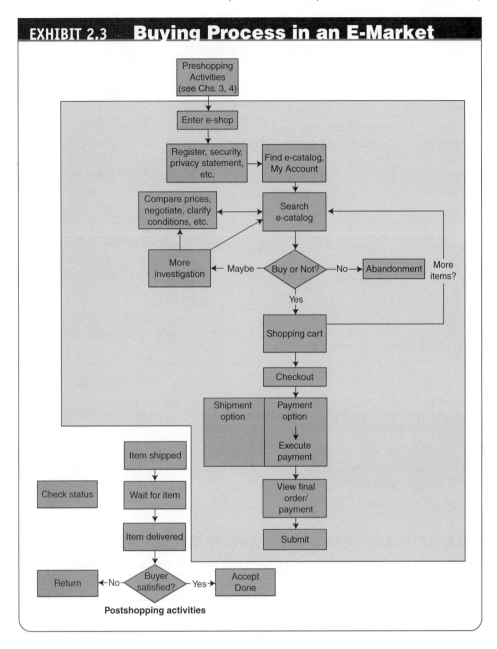

EXHIBIT 2.3 · Buying Process in an E-Market

The emergence of *electronic marketplaces* (also called *e-marketplaces, virtual markets,* or *marketspaces*), especially Internet-enabled ones, changed several of the processes used in trading and supply chains. These changes, driven by technology, resulted in:

▶ Greater information richness of the transactional and relational environment
▶ Lower information search time and cost for buyers
▶ Diminished information asymmetry between sellers and buyers
▶ Less time between purchase and possession of physical products purchased in the e-marketplace

EXHIBIT 2.4   Functions of a Market

Matching of Buyers and Sellers	Facilitation of Transactions	Institutional Infrastructure

• Determination of product offerings
    Product features offered by sellers
    Aggregation of different products
 	
• Search (of buyers for sellers and of sellers for buyers)
    Price and product information
    Organizing bids and bartering
    Matching seller offerings with buyer preferences
 	
• Price discovery
    Process and outcome in
        determination of prices
    Enabling price comparisons
 	
• Others
    Providing sales leads
	• Logistics
	    Delivery of information, goods,
	      or services to buyers
	
	• Settlement
	    Transfer of payments to sellers
	
	• Trust
	    Credit system, reputations,
	      rating agencies such as
	      Consumer Reports and the
	      BBB, special escrow and
	      online trust agencies
	
	• Communication
	    Posting buyers' requests
		• Legal
		    Commercial code, contract
		      law, dispute resolution,
		      intellectual property
		      protection
		
		• Regulatory
		    Rules and regulations,
		      compliance, monitoring,
		      enforcement
		
		• Discovery
		    Provides market information
		      (e.g., about competition,
		      government regulations)

Sources: Compiled from Bakos (1998) and from *E-Market Services* (2006).

> ▶ Greater temporal proximity between time of purchase and time of possession of digital products purchased in the e-marketplace
> ▶ The ability of buyers, sellers, and the virtual market to be in different locations
> ▶ The ability for EC to leverage capabilities with increased effectiveness and lower transaction and distribution costs, leading to more efficient "friction-free" markets. For more on e-marketplaces, see Li and Du (2005).

E-MARKETPLACE COMPONENTS AND PARTICIPANTS

marketspace
A marketplace in which sellers and buyers exchange goods and services for money (or for other goods and services), but do so electronically.

A **marketspace** includes electronic transactions that bring about a new distribution of goods and services. The major components and players in a marketspace are customers, sellers, products and services (physical or digital), infrastructure, a front end, a back end, intermediaries and other business partners, and support services. A brief description of each follows:

> ▶ **Customers.** More than 2 billion people worldwide who surf the Web are potential buyers of the goods and services offered or advertised on the Internet. These consumers are looking for bargains, customized items, collectors' items, entertainment, socialization, and more. They are in the driver's seat. They can search for detailed information, compare, bid, and sometimes negotiate. Organizations are the largest consumers, accounting for more than 85 percent of EC volume activities.
> ▶ **Sellers.** Millions of storefronts are on the Web, advertising and offering a huge variety of items. These stores are owned by companies, government agencies, or individuals. Every day it is possible to find new offerings of products and services. Sellers can sell direct from their Web sites or from e-marketplaces.

▶ **Products and services.** One of the major differences between the marketplace and the marketspace is the possible digitization of products and services in a marketspace. Although both types of markets can sell physical products, the marketspace also can sell **digital products**, which are goods that can be transformed to digital format and instantly delivered over the Internet. In addition to digitization of software and music, it is possible to digitize dozens of other products and services, as shown in Online File W2.1. Digital products have different cost curves than those of regular products. In digitization, most of the costs are fixed, and variable costs are very low. Thus, profits will increase very rapidly as volume increases, once the fixed costs are paid.

▶ **Infrastructure.** The marketspace infrastructure includes electronic networks, hardware, software, and more. (EC infrastructure is presented in Online Chapter 12.)

▶ **Front end.** Customers interact with a marketspace via a **front end**. The components of the front end can include the seller's portal, electronic catalogs, a shopping cart, a search engine, an auction engine, and a payment gateway.

▶ **Back end.** All the activities that are related to order aggregation and fulfillment, inventory management, purchasing from suppliers, accounting and finance, insurance, payment processing, packaging, and delivery are done in what is termed the **back end** of the business.

▶ **Intermediaries.** In marketing, an **intermediary** is typically a third party that operates between sellers and buyers. Intermediaries of all kinds offer their services on the Web. Some are manual, many are electronic. The role of these electronic intermediaries is frequently different from that of regular intermediaries (such as wholesalers), as will be seen throughout the text, especially in Chapters 3 and 5. For example, online intermediaries create and manage the online markets. They help match buyers and sellers, provide escrow services, and help customers and/or sellers institute and complete transactions. Intermediaries may be eliminated or done by computers as shown next.

digital products
Goods that can be transformed to digital format and delivered over the Internet.

front end
The portion of an e-seller's business processes through which customers interact, including the seller's portal, electronic catalogs, a shopping cart, a search engine, and a payment gateway.

back end
The activities that support online order fulfillment, inventory management, purchasing from suppliers, payment processing, packaging, and delivery.

intermediary
A third party that operates between sellers and buyers.

Intermediation may be eliminated, modified, or completely done by computers as shown next.

DISINTERMEDIATION AND REINTERMEDIATION

Intermediaries are agents that mediate between sellers and buyers. Usually, they provide two types of services: (1) They provide relevant information about demand, supply, prices, and requirements and, in doing so, help match sellers and buyers; (2) They offer value-added services such as transfer of products, escrow, payment arrangements, consulting, or assistance in finding a business partner. In general, the first type of service can be fully automated and thus is likely to be assumed by e-marketplaces, infomediaries, and portals that provide free or low-commission services. The second type requires expertise, such as knowledge of the industry, the products, and technological trends, and it can only be partially automated.

Intermediaries that provide only (or mainly) the first type of service may be eliminated; this phenomenon is called **disintermediation**. An example is the airline industry and its push for buying electronic tickets directly from the airlines. As of 2004, most airlines require customers to pay $5 or more per ticket if they buy a ticket from an agent or by phone, which is equivalent to the agent's commission. This is resulting in the *disintermediation* of travel agents from the purchasing process. In another example, discount stockbrokers that only

disintermediation
Elimination of intermediaries between sellers and buyers.

execute trades manually are disappearing. However, brokers who manage electronic inter-mediation are not only surviving but may also be prospering (e.g., Ameritrade Corp.). This phenomenon, in which disintermediated entities or newcomers take on new intermediary roles, is called *reintermediation* (see Chapter 3).

Disintermediation is more likely to occur in supply chains involving several intermediaries, as illustrated in the Blue Nile case (see Online File W1.14, Chapter 1).

TYPES OF E-MARKETPLACES

On the Web, the term *marketplace* differs from the physical one. We distinguish two types of e-marketplaces: private and public.

Private E-Marketplaces

Private e-marketplaces are those owned and operated by a single company. As seen in the Raffles Hotel case (Online File W2.2), private markets are either sell-side or buy-side. In a **sell-side e-marketplace**, a company, Cisco for example, will sell either standard or customized products to individuals (B2C) or to business (B2B); this type of selling is considered to be one-to-many. In a **buy-side e-marketplace,** a company purchases from many suppliers; this type of purchasing is considered to be *many-to-one*, and it is B2B activity. For example, Raffles Hotel buys its supplies from approved vendors that come to its e-market. Private marketplaces may be open only to selected members and are not publicly regulated. We will return to the topic of private e-marketplaces in Chapters 3 (B2C) and 5 (B2B).

**sell-side
e-marketplace**

A private e-marketplace in which one company sells either standard and/or customized products to qualified companies.

**buy-side
e-marketplace**

A private e-marketplace in which one company makes purchases from invited suppliers.

Public E-Marketplaces

Public e-marketplaces are usually B2B markets. They often are owned by a third party (not a seller or a buyer) or by a group of buying or selling companies (referred to as a consortium), and they serve many sellers and many buyers. These markets also are known as *exchanges* (e.g., a stock exchange). They are open to the public and usually are regulated by the government or the exchange's owners. Public e-marketplaces are presented in detail in Chapter 5.

Section 2.2 ▶ REVIEW QUESTIONS

1. Define e-marketplace and describe its attributes.
2. What is the difference between a physical marketplace and an e-marketplace (marketspace)?
3. List the components of a marketspace.
4. Define a digital product and provide five examples.
5. Describe private versus public e-markets.

2.3 CUSTOMER INTERACTION MECHANISMS: STOREFRONTS, MALLS, AND PORTALS

Several kinds of interactions exist among sellers, buyers, and e-marketplaces. The major B2C e-marketplaces are *storefronts* and *Internet malls*. Let's elaborate on these, as well as on the gateways to e-marketplaces—portals.

ELECTRONIC STOREFRONTS

A **Webstore** or an electronic or Web **storefront** refers to a single company's Web site where products and services are sold. It is an electronic store that usually has an online shopping cart associated with it. Many Webstores target a specific industry and find their own unique corner of the market. The storefront may belong to a manufacturer (e.g., geappliances.com and dell.com), to a retailer (e.g., zappos.com and wishlist.com.au), to individuals selling from home, or to another type of business. Note that companies that sell services (such as insurance) may refer to their storefronts as *portals*. An example of a service-related portal is a hotel reservation system, as shown in Online File W2.2.

A storefront includes several mechanisms that are necessary for conducting online sales. The most common mechanisms are an *electronic catalog*; a *search engine* that helps the consumer find products in the catalog; an *electronic cart* for holding items until checkout; *e-auction facilities* where auctions take place; a *payment gateway* where payment arrangements can be made; a *shipment court* where shipping arrangements are made; and *customer services*, which include product and warranty information.

Webstore (storefront)
A single company's Web site where products or services are sold and usually has an online shopping cart associated with it. Many Webstores target a specific industry and find their own unique corner of the market.

ELECTRONIC MALLS AND LARGE RETAILERS

In addition to shopping at individual storefronts, consumers can shop in electronic malls (e-malls). Similar to malls in the physical world, an **e-mall (online mall)** is an online shopping location where many stores are located. For example, Mall of Maine (emallofmaine.com) is an e-mall that aggregates products, services, and providers in the state of Maine. It contains a directory of vacation services and product categories and the vendors in each category. When a consumer indicates the category he or she is interested in, the consumer is transferred to the appropriate independent *storefront*. This kind of mall does not provide any shared services; it is merely a directory. Other malls, such as Choice Mall (choicemall.com), do provide shared services.

e-mall (online mall)
An online shopping center where many online stores are located.

Source: Reprinted by permission from Seeds of Change.

TYPES OF STORES AND MALLS

There are several different types of stores and malls:

▶ **General stores/malls.** These are large marketspaces that sell all kinds of products. Examples are amazon.com, choicemall.com, walmart.com, spree.com, and the major public portals (yahoo.com and msn.com). All major department and discount stores also fall into this category.

▶ **Specialized stores/malls.** These sell only one or a few kinds of products, such as shoes, books, flowers, wine, cars, or pet toys. 1800flowers.com sells flowers and related gifts; cars.com sells cars; fashionmall.com/beauty.html specializes in beauty products; and cattoys.com sells cat toys. Visit newegg.com for computer electronics and endless.com zappos.com for shoes and apparel.

▶ **Regional versus global stores.** Some stores, such as e-grocers or sellers of heavy furniture, serve customers that live nearby. For example, parknshop.com serves the Hong Kong community only; it will not deliver outside of Hong Kong. However, some local stores will sell to customers in other countries if the customer is willing to pay shipping, insurance, and other costs (e.g., see hothothot.com).

▶ **Pure-play versus click-and-mortar stores.** Stores may be pure online (i.e., virtual or pure-play) organizations, such as Blue Nile, Amazon.com, Buy.com, Newegg.com or Cattoys.com. They do not have physical stores. Others are physical stores that also sell online (e.g., Walmart with walmart.com, 1-800-Flowers.com with 1800flowers.com, and Woolworths with woolworths.com.au). This second category is called *click-and-mortar*. Both categories will be described further in Chapter 3.

WEB (INFORMATION) PORTALS

Web portal

A single point of access, through a Web browser, to critical business information located inside and outside (via Internet) an organization.

A *portal* is an information gateway that is used in e-marketplaces, e-stores, and other types of EC (e.g., in intrabusiness and e-learning). A **Web portal** is a single point of access, through a Web browser, to critical business information located inside and outside (via Internet) of an organization. Many Web portals can be personalized for the users. Note that wireless devices are becoming portals for enterprise and Internet access. A schematic view of a portal is shown in Exhibit 2.5. Information sources (external and internal) are shown on the left side, and integrated and process data are shown as output on the monitor's screen. For more on portals, see en.wikipedia.org/wiki/Web_portal.

Types of Portals

Portals can be described in many ways and assume many shapes. One way to distinguish among them is to look at their content, which can vary from narrow to broad, and their community or audience, which also can vary. The major types of portals are as follows:

▶ **Commercial (public) portals.** These portals offer content for diverse communities and are the most popular portals on the Internet. Although they can be customized by the user, they are still intended for broad audiences and offer fairly routine content, some in real time (e.g., a stock ticker and news about a few preselected items). Examples of such sites are yahoo.com, aol.com, and msn.com.

EXHIBIT 2.5   How a Portal Works

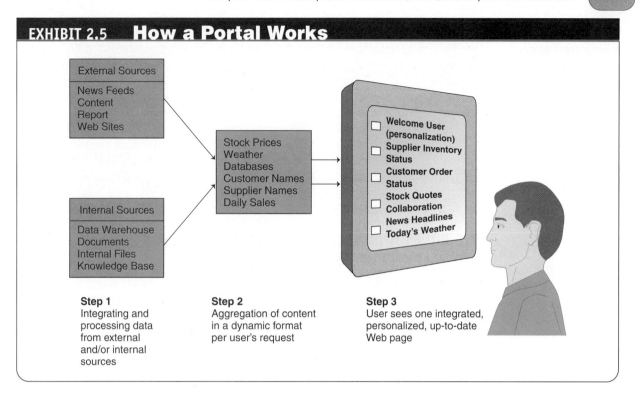

External Sources

News Feeds
Content
Report
Web Sites

Internal Sources

Data Warehouse
Documents
Internal Files
Knowledge Base

Stock Prices
Weather
Databases
Customer Names
Supplier Names
Daily Sales

☐ Welcome User (personalization)
☐ Supplier Inventory Status
☐ Customer Order Status
☐ Stock Quotes
☐ Collaboration News Headlines
☐ Today's Weather

Step 1
Integrating and
processing data
from external
and/or internal
sources

Step 2
Aggregation of content
in a dynamic format
per user's request

Step 3
User sees one integrated,
personalized, up-to-date
Web page

▶ **Corporate portals.** Corporate portals provide organized access to rich content within relatively narrow corporate and partners' communities. They also are known as *enterprise portals* or *enterprise information portals.* Corporate portals appear in different forms and are described in detail in Online File W2.3.

▶ **Publishing portals.** These portals are intended for communities with specific interests. These portals involve relatively little customization of content, but provide extensive online search features and some interactive capabilities. Examples of such sites are techweb.com and zdnet.com.

▶ **Personal portals.** These target specific filtered information for individuals. They offer relatively narrow content and are typically very personalized, effectively having an audience of one. Personalized portals, or homepages, pioneered by Netvibes (netvibes.com) are an alternative to a regular Web portal. They are offered by Yahoo!, Google, and many more. Netvibes lets individuals assemble their favorite widgets, Web sites, blogs, e-mail accounts, social networks, search engines, instant messenger, photos, videos, podcasts, and everything else they enjoy on the Web—all in one place. Today, Netvibes is a multilingual global community of users who are taking control of their digital lives by personalizing their Web experience. Netvibes is also a widget platform that is used by thousands of publishers around the world.

▶ **Mobile portals.** Mobile portals are portals that are accessible from mobile devices (see Chapter 8 for details). An increasing number of portals are accessible via mobile devices. One example of such a mobile portal is i-Mode.

mobile portal
A portal accessible via a
mobile device.

voice portal
A portal accessed by telephone or cell phone.

> **Voice portals.** Voice portals are Web sites, usually portals, with audio interfaces. This means that they can be accessed by a standard telephone or a cell phone. AOLbyPhone is an example of a service that allows users to retrieve e-mail, news, and other content from AOL via telephone. It uses both speech recognition and text-to-speech technologies. Companies such as Tellme (tellme.com) and BeVocal (bevocal.com) offer access to the Internet from telephones, and also tools to build voice portals. Voice portals are especially popular for 1-800 numbers (enterprise 800 numbers) that provide self-service to customers with information available in Internet databases (e.g., find flight status at delta.com).
>
> **Knowledge portals.** Knowledge portals enable access to knowledge by knowledge workers and facilitate collaboration.

THE ROLES AND VALUE OF INTERMEDIARIES IN E-MARKETPLACES

Intermediaries (brokers) play an important role in commerce by providing value-added activities and services to buyers and sellers. There are many types of intermediaries. The most well-known intermediaries in the physical world are wholesalers and retailers.

The two types of *online intermediaries* are brokers and infomediaries.

Brokers

A *broker* in EC is a company that facilitates transactions between buyers and sellers. The following are different types of brokers:

> **Buy/sell fulfillment.** A corporation that helps consumers place buy and sell orders (e.g., E*TRADE).

> **Virtual mall.** A company that helps consumers buy from a variety of stores (e.g., Yahoo! Stores).

> **Metamediary.** A firm that offers customers access to a variety of stores and provides them with transaction services, such as financial services (e.g., Amazon zShops).

> **Comparison agent.** A company that helps consumers compare different stores (e.g., bizrate.com).

> **Shopping facilitator.** A company that helps consumers use online shops by providing currency conversion, language translation, payment features, delivery solutions, and potentially a user-customized interface (e.g., puntomio.com).

> **Matching services.** These match jobs to openings, buyers to products, dating candidates, and so forth.

Infomediaries

infomediaries
Electronic intermediaries that provide and/or control information flow in cyberspace, often aggregating information and selling it to others.

In cyberspace, some intermediaries provide and/or control information flow. These electronic intermediaries are known as **infomediaries.** The information flows to and from buyers and sellers via infomediaries. Infomediaries are Web sites that gather and organize large amounts of data and act as intermediaries between those who want the information and those who supply the information (see webopedia.com/term/infomediary. html). There are two types of infomediaries:

> The first offers consumers a place to gather information about specific products and companies before making purchasing decisions (e.g., autobytel.com, cars.com, and bizrate.com).

▶ The second is not necessarily Web-based. It provides vendors with consumer information that will help the vendor develop and market products. The infomediary collects personal information from the buyers and sells that data to businesses.

WebMD and its parent company, Emdeon Inc., perform in both categories, as illustrated in Case 2.1.

CASE 2.1
EC Application
WEBMD

WebMD is the largest medical information services company in the United States. Although the company is known mainly for its consumer portal, *webmd.com*, the most visited medical-related Web site, its core business is being an e-intermediary.

A major instrument for medical cost control is the Health Insurance Portability and Accountability Act of 1996 (HIPAA), which requires digital medical records and standardized documents for the health care industry. WebMD is attempting to capitalize on this legislation by providing computer-related services to both the providers and purchasers of services (government, insurance companies, HMOs), mainly in terms of standardized electronic transactions. The company provides services to health care providers, vendors, customers, and government entities.

WebMD's major objective is to reduce costs for the participants by facilitating electronic communication and collaboration because paper-based transactions can be 20 to 30 times more expensive than electronic ones. It also seeks to speed health delivery times.

WebMD operates via several separate, but electronically linked, divisions:

▶ **WebMD Envoy.** This division (now a subsidiary of Emdeon) is the leading clearinghouse for real-time transactions (more than $2.5 billion a year) among more than 340,000 medical providers, 81,000 dental providers, 5,000 hospitals, 600 vendors partners, 55,000 pharmacies and laboratories, and 1,200 government and commercial health agencies.

▶ **WebMD Practice Services.** This division provides software and programs that help physicians and other providers manage their businesses. Hundreds of different applications are available (this service is referred to as *Intergy EHR*). Some provide access to patient information, whereas others retrieve medical knowledge. Practice Services is a leading provider of payment and transaction services at the vanguard of bringing innovative practice

management solutions to the rapidly changing health care industry.

▶ **WebMD Health.** This information gateway has portals for both consumers and professionals. For consumers, information is provided about wellness, diseases, and treatments. For professionals (physicians, nurses, medical technicians, and so forth), the Medscape portal provides medical news, medical education, research-related information, and more. HLTH Corp., WebMD Health, and Porex announced the intent to merge in June 2009.

▶ **Porex.** The medical product unit manufactures and sells specialty medical products. Of the many services available on the portal, notable are: News Center, A-Z Guides, Health Search, WebMD, Family and Pregnancy, Blogs for Experts, and Blogs for Readers.

According to O'Buyonge and Chen (2006), the success of WebMD is a result of the proper value proposition in its business model. Most important are the value-added services provided to health care providers, insurers, and other B2B participants.

Sources: Compiled from O'Buyonge and Chen (2006) and *webmd.com* (accessed November 2009).

Questions

1. Visit *webmd.com* to learn more about the types of intermediation that are available. Write a report based on your findings.

2. How do the types in Question 1 differ from traditional intermediation services?

3. WebMD Health does not bring in much revenue despite the hefty increase in ad revenue. Should the company be closed? Why or why not? (Check the financial reports at *money.cnn.com* or *business.yahoo.com*.)

The advantage of this approach is that consumer privacy is protected and some info-mediaries offer consumers a percentage of the brokerage deals.

Distributors in B2B

A special type of intermediary in e-commerce is the B2B *e-distributor*. These intermediaries connect manufacturers with business buyers (customers), such as retailers (or resellers in the computer industry). **E-distributors** basically aggregate the catalogs or product information from many manufacturers, sometimes thousands of them, in one place—the intermediary's Web site. An example is W.W. Grainger (see Chapter 5).

e-distributor

An e-commerce intermediary that connects manufacturers with business buyers (customers) by aggregating the catalogs of many manufacturers in one place—the intermediary's Web site.

Section 2.3 ▶ REVIEW QUESTIONS

1. Describe electronic storefronts and e-malls.
2. List the various types of stores and e-malls.
3. What are information portals? List the major types.
4. List the roles of intermediaries in e-markets.
5. Describe e-distributors.

2.4 ELECTRONIC CATALOGS, SEARCH ENGINES, AND SHOPPING CARTS

To enable selling online, a Web site usually needs *EC merchant server software*. Merchant software includes many functionalities. One example is OsCommerce.com, which is open-system software (see oscommerce.com and en.wikipedia.org/wiki/OsCommerce). The basic functionality offered by such software includes electronic catalogs, search engines, and shopping carts.

ELECTRONIC CATALOGS

electronic catalogs (e-catalogs)

The presentation of product information in an electronic form; the backbone of most e-selling sites.

Catalogs have been printed on paper for generations. Recently, electronic catalogs on CD-ROM and the Internet have gained popularity. **Electronic catalogs (e-catalogs)** consist of a product database, directory, and a presentation function. They are the backbone of most e-commerce sales sites. For merchants, the objective of electronic catalogs is to advertise and promote products and services. For the customer, the purpose of such catalogs is to locate information on products and services. Electronic catalogs can be searched quickly with the help of search engines, and they can be interactive. For example, *Change My Image* from Infinisys (en.infinisys.co.jp/product/cmimage/index.shtml) allows you to insert your photo and then change the hairstyle and color. Electronic catalogs can be very large; for example, the Library of Congress Web catalog (catalog.loc.gov) contains millions of records.

Most early online catalogs were replications of text and pictures from printed catalogs. However, online catalogs have evolved to become more dynamic, customized, and integrated with selling and buying procedures, shopping carts, order taking, and payment. They may even include video clips. The tools for building them are being integrated with merchant suites and Web hosting (e.g., see smallbusiness.yahoo.com/ecommerce). Examples of a product catalog can be seen at jetpens.com—see Case 1.3—in Chapter 1), and in the OfficeMax Application Case in Online File W2.4.

Although used only occasionally in B2C commerce, customized catalogs are used frequently in B2B e-commerce. For a comprehensive discussion of online catalogs, see jcmax.com/advantages.html.

Online Catalogs Versus Paper Catalogs

The advantages and disadvantages of online catalogs are contrasted with those of paper catalogs in Exhibit 2.6. Although online catalogs have significant advantages, such as ease of updating, the ability to be integrated with the purchasing process, coverage of a wide spectrum of products, interactivity, customization, and strong search capabilities, they also have disadvantages and limitations. To begin, customers need computers and Internet access to view online catalogs. However, as computer availability and Internet access continue to grow, many paper catalogs will be supplemented by, if not actually replaced by, electronic ones. The number of print newspapers and magazines may have diminished due to online ones, but the future of print will not disappear entirely. Paper catalogs probably will not disappear altogether either. There seems to be room for both media, at least in the near future. However, in B2B, paper catalogs may disappear more quickly.

Example. RadioShack (radioshack.com) builds and maintains electronic catalogs based on its customers' paper catalogs. The catalogs include search capabilities, the ability to feature large numbers of products, enhanced viewing capabilities, updating, and support.

EC SEARCH ACTIVITIES, TYPES, AND ENGINES

Search activities are popular in EC, and many tools for conducting searches are available. Here we describe only the essentials. First, though, we look at three major types of searches.

EXHIBIT 2.6 Comparison of Online Catalogs with Paper Catalogs

Type	Advantages	Disadvantages
Paper catalogs	• Easy to create without high technology • Reader is able to look at the catalog without computer system • More portable than electronic	• Difficult to update changed product information promptly • Only a limited number of products can be displayed • Limited information through photographs and textual description is available • No possibility for advanced multimedia such as animation and voice
Online catalogs	• Easy to update product information • Able to integrate with the purchasing process • Good search and comparison capabilities • Able to provide timely, up-to-date product information • Provision for globally broad range of product information • Possibility of adding on voice and animated pictures • Long-term cost savings • Easy to customize • More comparative shopping • Ease of connecting order processing, inventory processing, and payment processing to the system	• Difficult to develop catalogs, large fixed cost • Need for customer skill to deal with computers and browsers

Types of EC Searches

The three major types of EC searches are *Internet/Web search, enterprise search,* and *desktop search.*

Internet/Web Search. This is the standard search that involves any documents on the Web. According to Pew Internet and other statistical sites, finding information is one of the most important activities on the Web.

Enterprise Search. An **enterprise search** is the practice of identifying and enabling specific content across the enterprise to be indexed, searched, and displayed to authorized users. It describes the application of search technology to information *within* an organization. This is in contrast to the other two main types of horizontal search environment: Web search and desktop search.

Desktop Search. A **desktop search** is conducted by tools that search only the contents of a user's own computer files. The emphasis is on finding all the information that is available on the user's PC, including Web browser histories, e-mail archives, music, chats, photos, and word-processed documents.

One main advantage of desktop search programs is that search results come up in a few seconds. A variety of desktop search programs are available, such as Spotlight from Apple Computer, XI Enterprise, and Google's Desktop (see desktop.google.com). Desktop search is very useful: It is an efficient productivity tool that helps to increase information security.

Each search discussed here is accomplished with search engines and intelligent agents.

Search Engines

A **search engine** is a computer program that can access databases of Internet or intranet resources, search for specific information or key words, and report the results. For example, customers tend to ask for information (e.g., requests for product information or pricing) in the same general manner. This type of request is repetitive, and answering such requests is costly when done by a human. Search engines deliver answers economically and efficiently by matching questions with frequently asked question (FAQ) templates, which respond with "canned" answers.

Google, AltaVista, Lycos, and Bing (from Microsoft) are popular search engines. Portals such as AOL, Yahoo!, and MSN have their own search engines. Special search engines organized to answer certain questions or search in specified areas include Ask.com, Northern Light, Mama, and Looksmart. Thousands of different public search engines are available (see searchengineguide.com). These can be very specialized with different capabilities (see Martin 2008). In addition, hundreds of companies have search engines on their portals or storefronts. Endeca InFront (from endeca.com) is a special search engine for online catalogs.

Software (Intelligent) Agents

Unlike a search engine, a software (intelligent) agent can do more than just "search and match." It has capabilities that can be used to perform routine tasks that require intelligence. For example, it can monitor movements on a Web site to check whether a customer seems lost or ventures into areas that may not fit the customer's profile. If it detects such confusion, the agent can notify the customer and provide assistance. Software agents can be used in e-commerce to support tasks such as conducting complex searches, comparing prices, interpreting information, monitoring activities, and working as an assistant. Users can even chat or collaborate with intelligent agents as is done in

enterprise search
The practice of identifying and enabling specific content across the enterprise to be indexed, searched, and displayed to authorized users.

desktop search
Search tools that search the contents of a user's or organization's computer files, rather than searching the Internet. The emphasis is on finding all the information that is available on the user's PC, including Web browser histories, e-mail archives, and word-processed documents, as well as in all internal files and databases.

search engine
A computer program that can access databases of Internet resources, search for specific information or key words, and report the results.

Second Life, where the agents are avatars and some even "understand" a natural language interface.

Voice-Powered Search

To ease searching, especially when using a cell phone, Google introduced a voice-powered tool that allows you to skip the keyboard altogether. The first product was included as part of the iPhone's mobile search application. It allows you to talk into your phone, ask any question, and the results of your query are offered on your iPhone.

SHOPPING CARTS

An **electronic shopping cart** is an order-processing technology that allows customers to accumulate items they wish to buy while they continue to shop. In this respect, it is similar to a shopping cart in the physical world. The software program of an electronic shopping cart allows customers to select items, review what has been selected, make changes, and then finalize the list. Clicking on "buy" will trigger the actual purchase.

> **electronic shopping cart**
> An order-processing technology that allows customers to accumulate items they wish to buy while they continue to shop.

Shopping carts for B2C are fairly simple (visit amazon.com to see an example), but for B2B a shopping cart may be more complex. Shopping-cart software is sold or provided for free as an independent component (e.g., networksolutions.com/e-commerce/index.jsp and easycart.com). It also is embedded in merchants' servers, such as smallbusiness.yahoo.com/ecommerce. Free online shopping carts (trials and demos) are available at volusion.com and 1freecart.com. For more on shopping carts, see en.wikipedia.org/wiki/Shopping_cart_software.

Product Configuration

A key characteristic of EC is the ability to self-customize products and services, as done by Dell. Manufacturers need to produce customized products in economic and rapid ways so that the price of the products will be competitive. *Product configuration* systems support the acquisition of customer requirements while automating the order-taking process, and they allow customers to configure their products by specifying their technical requirements.

Section 2.4 ▶ REVIEW QUESTIONS

1. List and briefly describe the dimensions by which electronic catalogs can be classified.
2. List the benefits of electronic catalogs.
3. Explain how customized catalogs are created and used.
4. Compare search engines with software intelligent agents.
5. Describe an electronic shopping cart.

2.5 AUCTIONS, BARTERING, AND NEGOTIATING ONLINE

One of the most interesting market mechanisms in e-commerce is electronic auctions (Nissanoff 2006). They are used in B2C, B2B, C2C, G2B, G2C, and more.

DEFINITION AND CHARACTERISTICS

An **auction** is a market mechanism that uses a competitive process by which a seller solicits consecutive bids from buyers (forward auctions) or a buyer solicits bids from sellers (reverse auctions). Prices are determined dynamically by the bids. A wide variety

> **auction**
> A competitive process in which a seller solicits consecutive bids from buyers (forward auctions) or a buyer solicits bids from sellers (backward auctions). Prices are determined dynamically by the bids.

of online markets qualify as auctions using this definition. Auctions, an established method of commerce for generations, deal with products and services for which conventional marketing channels are ineffective or inefficient, and they ensure prudent execution of sales. For example, auctions can expedite the disposal of items that need to be liquidated or sold quickly. Rare coins, stamps, and other collectibles are frequently sold at auction.

There are several types of auctions, each with its own motives and procedures. (For details, see en.wikipedia.org/wiki/Online_auction_business_model.) They can be conducted in *public* auction sites, such as at eBay, or conducted in *private* auctions, which are by invitation only.

TRADITIONAL AUCTIONS VERSUS E-AUCTIONS

Traditional, physical auctions are still very popular. However, the volume traded on e-auctions is significantly larger and continues to increase.

Limitations of Traditional Offline Auctions

Traditional offline auctions, regardless of their type, have several limitations. They usually last only a few minutes, or even seconds, for each item sold. This rapid process may give potential buyers little time to make a decision, so they may decide not to bid. Therefore, sellers may not get the highest possible price; bidders may not get what they really want, or they may pay too much for the item. Also, in many cases the bidders do not have much time to examine the goods. Bidders have difficulty learning about auctions and cannot compare what is offered at each location. Bidders must usually be physically present at auctions; thus, many potential bidders are excluded.

Similarly, it may be difficult for sellers to move goods to an auction site. Commissions are fairly high because a physical location must be rented, the auction needs to be advertised, and an auctioneer and other employees need to be paid. Electronic auctioning removes these deficiencies.

Electronic Auctions

The Internet provides an infrastructure for executing auctions electronically at lower cost, with a wide array of support services, and with many more sellers and buyers. Individual consumers and corporations both can participate in this rapidly growing and very convenient form of e-commerce. Forrester Research projects that the Internet auction industry will reach $65.2 billion in sales by 2010 (*Edgar Online* 2006).

electronic auctions (e-auctions)
Auctions conducted online.

Electronic auctions (e-auctions) are similar to offline auctions except that they are conducted online. E-auctions have been in existence since the 1980s over LANs (e.g., flowers; see Saarinen et al. 2006). Host sites on the Internet, which were started in 1995, serve as brokers, offering services for sellers to post their goods for sale and allowing buyers to bid on those items.

Major online auctions, such as eBay (see Online File W2.5), offer consumer products, electronic parts, artwork, vacation packages, airline tickets, and collectibles, as well as excess supplies and inventories being auctioned off by B2B marketers. Another type of B2B online auction is increasingly used to trade special types of commodities, such as electricity transmission capacities and gas and energy options. Furthermore, conventional business practices that traditionally have relied on contracts and fixed prices are increasingly being converted into auctions with bidding for online procurements (e.g., Raffles Hotel, Online File W2.2). Some examples of innovative auctions are provided next.

INNOVATIVE AUCTIONS

Examples of innovative implementations of e-auctions are as follows:

▶ Every year, Warren Buffett, the famous U.S. stock investor and investment guru, invites a group of eight people to lunch with him. The eight pay big money for the pleasure. The money is donated to the needy in San Francisco. In the past, Buffett charged $30,000 per group. Since July 2003, Buffett has placed the invitation on an online auction (eBay). In 2003, bidders pushed the bid from $30,000 to $250,100. The winning bid in 2008 was $2,110,000. One of the winners commented that he was willing to pay whatever was needed so that he could express to Buffett his appreciation for investment guidance. Before the auction, he had no chance to be invited.

▶ A Harley-Davidson motorcycle autographed by celebrities and offered by talk-show host Jay Leno fetched $800,100 on eBay to benefit tsunami victims.

▶ JetBlue airlines started to auction flights in September 2008 on eBay. The initial offer was 300 flights and six vacation packages, with opening bids set between 5¢ and 10¢ (yes, cents). The flights are to more than 20 destinations, including four "mystery" JetBlue Getaways—vacation packages to undisclosed locations.

The three-, five-, and seven-day auctions included one- and two-person round-trip, weekend flights in September from Boston, Chicago, New York, Orlando, Salt Lake City, Fort Lauderdale, or Southern California.

Although no one was lucky enough to get a flight for 5¢ or 10¢, many auctions gave the winners a flight that was 10 to 20 percent cheaper than regular prices.

DYNAMIC PRICING AND TYPES OF AUCTIONS

One major characteristic of auctions is that they are based on dynamic pricing. **Dynamic pricing** refers to prices that are not fixed but that are allowed to fluctuate as supply and demand in a market change. In contrast, catalog prices are fixed, as are prices in department stores, supermarkets, and most electronic storefronts.

Dynamic pricing appears in several forms. Perhaps the oldest forms are negotiation and bargaining, which have been practiced for many generations in open-air markets. It is customary to classify dynamic pricing into the following four major categories based on how many buyers and sellers are involved.

dynamic pricing
Prices that change based on supply and demand relationships at any given time.

One Buyer, One Seller

In this configuration, one can use negotiation, bargaining, or bartering. The resulting price will be determined by each party's bargaining power, supply and demand in the item's market, and (possibly) business environment factors.

One Seller, Many Potential Buyers

In this configuration, the seller uses a **forward auction**, an auction in which a seller entertains bids from multiple buyers. (Because forward auctions are the most common and traditional form, they often are simply called *auctions*.) The four major types of forward auctions are *English* and *Yankee* auctions, in which bidding prices increase as the auction progresses, and *Dutch* and *free-fall* auctions, in which bidding prices decline as the auction progresses. Each of these can be used for either liquidation or for market efficiency.

forward auction
An auction in which a seller entertains bids from buyers. Bidders increase price sequentially.

reverse auction (bidding or tendering system)

Auction in which the buyer places an item for bid (tender) on a request for quote (RFQ) system, potential suppliers bid on the job, with the price reducing sequentially, and the lowest bid wins; primarily a B2B or G2B mechanism.

name-your-own-price model

Auction model in which a would-be buyer specifies the price (and other terms) he or she is willing to pay to any willing and able seller. It is a C2B model that was pioneered by Priceline.com.

double auction

An auction in which multiple buyers and their bidding prices are matched with multiple sellers and their asking prices, considering the quantities on both sides.

One Buyer, Many Potential Sellers

Two popular types of auctions in which there is one buyer and many potential sellers are reverse auctions (tendering) and name-your-own-price auctions.

Reverse Auctions. When there is one buyer and many potential sellers, a **reverse auction** (also called a **bidding** or **tendering system**) is in place. In a reverse auction, the buyer places an item he or she wants to buy for bid (or *tender*) on a *request for quote* (RFQ) system. Potential suppliers bid on the item, reducing the price sequentially (see Exhibit 2.7). In electronic bidding in a reverse auction, several rounds of bidding may take place until the bidders do not reduce the price further. The winner is the one with the lowest bid (assuming that only price is considered). Reverse auctions are primarily a B2B or G2B mechanism. (For further discussion and examples, see Chapter 5.)

The Name-Your-Own-Price Model. Priceline.com pioneered the **name-your-own-price model**. In this model, a would-be buyer specifies the price (and other terms) that he or she is willing to pay to any willing and able seller. For example, Priceline.com presents consumers' requests to sellers, who fill as much of the guaranteed demand as they wish at prices and terms requested by buyers. Alternately, Priceline.com searches its own database that contains vendors' lowest prices and tries to match supply against requests. Priceline.com asks customers to guarantee acceptance of the offer if it is at or below the requested price by giving a credit card number. This is basically a C2B model, although some businesses use it, too (see en.wikipedia.org/wiki/Name_Your_Own_Price).

Many Sellers, Many Buyers

When there are many sellers and many buyers, buyers and their bidding prices are matched with sellers and their asking prices based on the quantities on both sides. Stocks and commodities markets are typical examples of this configuration. Buyers and sellers may be individuals or businesses. Such an auction is called a **double auction** (see en.wikipedia.org/wiki/Double_Auction).

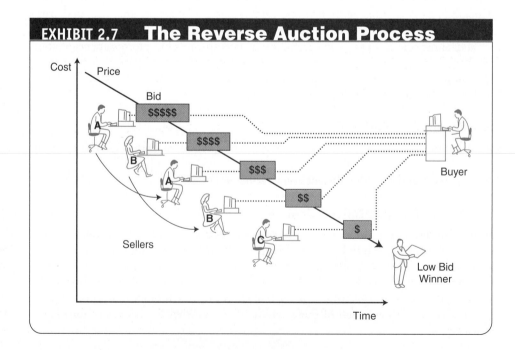

EXHIBIT 2.7   The Reverse Auction Process

BENEFITS, LIMITATIONS, AND IMPACTS OF E-AUCTIONS

E-auctions are becoming important selling and buying channels for many companies and individuals. E-auctions enable buyers to access goods and services anywhere auctions are conducted. Moreover, almost perfect market information is available about prices, products, current supply and demand, and so on. These characteristics provide benefits to all.

Benefits of E-Auctions

According to Nissanoff (2006), the auction culture will revolutionize the way customers buy, sell, and obtain what they want. A listing of the benefits of e-auctions to sellers, buyers, and e-auctioneers is provided in Exhibit 2.8.

Limitations of E-Auctions

E-auctions have several limitations. The most significant limitations are minimal security, the possibility of fraud, and limited participation.

Minimal Security. Some of the C2C auctions conducted on the Internet are not secure because they are done in an unencrypted environment. This means that credit card numbers could be stolen during the payment process. Payment methods such as PayPal (paypal.com) can be used to solve the problem (see Chapter 10). In addition, some B2B auctions are conducted over highly secure private lines.

EXHIBIT 2.8 **Benefits of E-Auctions**		
Benefits to Sellers	**Benefits to Buyers**	**Benefits to E-Auctioneers**
• Increased revenues from broadening bidder base and shortening cycle time. Can sell anywhere globally. • Opportunity to bargain instead of selling at a fixed price. Can sell any time and conduct frequent auctions. • Optimal price setting determined by the market (more buyers, more information). • Sellers can gain more customer dollars by offering items directly (saves on the commission to intermediaries; also, physical auctions are very expensive compared with e-auctions). • Can liquidate large quantities quickly. • Improved customer relationship and loyalty (in the case of specialized B2B auction sites and electronic exchanges).	• Opportunities to find unique items and collectibles. • Entertainment. Participation in e-auctions can be entertaining and exciting. • Convenience. Buyers can bid from anywhere, even with a cell phone; they do not have to travel to an auction place. • Anonymity. With the help of a third party, buyers can remain anonymous. • Possibility of finding bargains, for both individuals and organizations.	• Higher repeat purchases. Jupiter Research (*jupiterresearch.com*) found that auction sites, such as eBay, tend to garner higher repeat-purchase rates than the top B2C sites, such as Amazon.com. • High "stickiness" to the Web site (the tendency of customers to stay at sites longer and come back more often). Auction sites are frequently "stickier" than fixed-priced sites. Stickier sites generate more ad revenue for the e-auctioneer. • Easy expansion of the auction business.

Possibility of Fraud. Auction items are in many cases unique, used, or antique. Because the buyer cannot see the items, the buyer may get defective products. Also, buyers can commit fraud by receiving goods or services without paying for them. Thus, the fraud rate on e-auctions is relatively high. For a discussion of e-auction fraud and fraud prevention, see fraud.org/tips/internet/onlineauctions.htm.

Limited Participation. Some auctions are by invitation only; others are open to dealers only. Limited participation may be a disadvantage to sellers, who usually benefit from as large a pool of buyers as possible.

Impacts of Auctions

Because the trade objects and contexts for auctions are very diverse, the rationale behind auctions and the motives of the different participants for setting up auctions are quite different. The following are some representative impacts of e-auctions.

Auctions as a Social Mechanism to Determine a Price. For objects that are not traded in traditional markets, such as unique or rare items, or for items that may be offered randomly or at long intervals, an auction creates a marketplace that attracts potential buyers, and often experts. By offering many of these special items at a single place and time and by attracting considerable attention, auctions provide the requisite exposure of purchase and sale orders, and hence liquidity of the market in which an optimal price can be determined. Typical examples are auctions of fine arts or rare stamps, as well as auctions of communications frequencies, Web banners, and advertising space. For example, wine collectors can find a global wine auction at winebid.com.

Auctions as a Highly Visible Distribution Mechanism. Some auctions deal with special offers. In this case, a supplier typically auctions off a limited number of items, using the auction primarily as a mechanism to gain attention and to attract those customers who are bargain hunters or who have a preference for the gambling dimension of the auction process. The airline seat auctions by Cathay Pacific, American Airlines, and Lufthansa fall into this category (see Saarinen et al. 2006).

Auctions as an EC Component in a Business Model. Auctions can stand alone, or they may be combined with other e-commerce activities. An example of the latter is the combination of group purchasing with reverse auctions, as described in Online File W2.6.

Auctions for Profit for Individuals. As illustrated in Chapter 1, individuals can make money by selling things that they buy at bargain prices on eBay. If you are interested in learning how to do this, read Joyner (2007) and Weber (2008).

ONLINE BARTERING

bartering
The *exchange* of goods and services.

Bartering, the exchange of goods and services, is the oldest method of trade. Today, it is done primarily between organizations. The problem with bartering is that it is difficult to match trading partners. Businesses and individuals may use classified ads to advertise what they need and what they offer, but they still may not be able to find what they want. Intermediaries may be helpful, but they are expensive (20 percent to 30 percent commission) and very slow.

e-bartering (electronic bartering)
Bartering conducted online, usually in a bartering exchange.

E-bartering (electronic bartering)—bartering conducted online—can improve the matching process by attracting more partners to the barter. In addition, matching can be done faster, and as a result, better matches can be found. Items that are frequently bartered online include office space, storage, and factory space; idle facilities; and labor, products, and banner ads. (Note that e-bartering may have tax implications that need to be considered.)

bartering exchange
A marketplace in which an intermediary arranges barter transactions.

E-bartering is usually done in a **bartering exchange,** a marketplace in which an intermediary arranges the transactions. These exchanges can be very effective. Representative bartering Web sites include u-exchange.com, swapace.com, and barterdepot.com. The process works like this: First, the company tells the bartering exchange what it wants to offer. The exchange then assesses the value of the company's products or services and offers it certain "points" or "bartering dollars." The company can use the "points" to buy the things it needs from a participating member in the exchange.

Bartering sites must be financially secure. Otherwise, users may not have a chance to use the points they accumulate. (For further details see virtualbarter.8net and barternews.com.)

ONLINE NEGOTIATING

Dynamic prices also can be determined by *negotiation*. Negotiated pricing commonly is used for expensive or specialized products. Negotiated prices also are popular when large quantities are purchased. Much like auctions, negotiated prices result from interactions and bargaining among sellers and buyers. Negotiation also deals with nonpricing terms, such as the payment method and credit. Negotiation is a well-known process in the offline world (e.g., in real estate, automobile purchases, and contract work). In addition, in cases where there is no standard service or product to speak of, some digital products and services can be personalized and "bundled" at a standard price. Preferences for these bundled services differ among consumers, and thus they are frequently negotiated. A simple peer-to-peer (P2P) negotiation can be seen at ioffer.com. For more on negotiation in P2P money lending, see the ZOPA and Prosper cases in Online File W7.2. *Online (electronic) negotiation* may be more effective and efficient than offline negotiation.

Section 2.5 ▶ REVIEW QUESTIONS

1. Define auctions and describe how they work.
2. Describe the benefits of electronic auctions over traditional (offline) auctions.
3. List the four types of auctions.
4. Distinguish between forward and reverse auctions.
5. Describe the name-your-own-price auction model.
6. List the major benefits of auctions to buyers, sellers, and auctioneers.
7. What are the major limitations of auctions?
8. List the major impacts of auctions on markets.
9. Define bartering and describe the advantages of e-bartering.
10. Explain the role of online negotiation in EC.

2.6 WEB 2.0 TOOLS AND SERVICES: FROM BLOGS TO WIKIS TO TWITTER

The Web 2.0 environment is usually associated with its tools. The major tools and services are listed in Exhibit 2.9. For a comprehensive list, see Kathy Schrock's Guide for Educators at school.discoveryeducation.com/schrockguide/edtools.html and kathyschrock. net/web20.

The increased importance of social networking and social computing resulted in many innovative tools and services. Social networking, for example, is penetrating into enterprises and even becoming a B2B phenomenon. According to a Forrester survey, companies are spending money mostly on wikis, blogs, RSS, tagging, podcasting, and social networking (Farber 2008).

EXHIBIT 2.9   Social-Networking Software Tools

Tools for Online Communication
- Instant messaging
- VoIP and Skype
- Text chat
- Internet forums
- Blogs or weblogs
- Wikis
- Collaborative real-time editor
- Prediction markets

Types of Services
- Social network services
- Social network search engines
- Social guides
- Social bookmarking
- Social citations
- Social libraries
- Virtual worlds and massively multiplayer online games (MMOGs)
- Other specialized social applications
- Politics and journalism
- Content management tools

Emerging Technologies
- Peer-to-peer social networks
- Virtual presence
- Mobile tools for Web 2.0

Tools for Individuals
- Personalization
- Customization
- Search
- RSS
- File-sharing tools

Web 2.0 Development Tools
- Mushups
- Web services (Online Chapter 12)

Sources: Compiled from *en.wikipedia.org/wiki/Social_software* (accessed July 2009), Hinchcliffe (2006), Weblogs, Inc. (2007), and authors' experience.

In this chapter, we will cover blogs, wikis, micro-blogging, and Twitter (in this section) and virtual worlds in Section 2.7.

BLOGGING (WEBLOGGING)

blog
A personal Web site that is open to the public to read and to interact with; dedicated to specific topics or issues.

The Internet offers the opportunity for individuals to publish on the Web using a technology known as *Weblogging*, or *blogging*. A **blog** is a personal Web site, open to the public, in which the owner expresses his or her feelings or opinions. Blogs can result in two-way communication and collaboration, group discussion, and so on. As seen in the EMS opening case, blogs can be used in the company. The totality of blogs is known as the *blogosphere*. For coverage of blogs see en.wikipedia.org/wiki/Blog.

Many blogs provide commentary or news on a particular subject; others function as more personal online diaries. A typical blog combines text, images, and links to other blogs, Web pages, and other media related to its topic. A **vlog (or video blog)** is a blog with video content. Notice that almost 10,000 fake or spam blogs are created daily (out of 150,000 to 200,000) in total. The number of blogs is estimated to double every year. Most blogs are written in English and Japanese.

vlog (or video blog)
A blog with video content.

Building Effective Blogs

It is becoming easier and easier to build blogs. Programs from blogger.com, pitas.com, and others are very user-friendly. Blog space is free; the goal is to make it easy for users to create their own blogs. *Bloggers* (the people who create and maintain blogs) are handed a fresh space on their Web site to write in each day. They can easily edit, add entries, and broadcast whatever they want by simply clicking "send." Blogging software such as WordPress or Movable Type helps bloggers update their blogs easily. Bloggers also use a special terminology. See samizdata.net/blog/glossary.html for a dictionary of blog terms.

Microblogging and Twitter

Microblogging is a form of blogging that allows users to write short messages and publish them, either to be viewed by anyone or by a restricted group that can be chosen by the user. These messages can be submitted by a variety of means, including text messaging from cell phones, instant messaging, e-mail, MP3, or just on the Web.

The content of a microblog differs from that of a regular blog due to the limited space per message (usually up to 140 characters). Many microblogs provide short messages about personal matters.

The most popular service is Twitter. There are more than 100 competitors of Twitter worldwide (as of February 2009).

microblogging
A form of blogging that allows users to write messages (usually up to 140 characters) and publish them, either to be viewed by anyone or by a restricted group that can be chosen by the user. These messages can be submitted by a variety of means, including text messaging, instant messaging, e-mail, MP3, or just on the Web.

Twitter

Twitter is a free microblogging service that allows its users to send and read other users' updates, otherwise known as **tweets**, which are text-based posts (including updates), which are displayed on the user's profile page and delivered to other users who have signed up to receive them. The sender can restrict delivery to those in his or her circle of friends (delivery to everyone being the default). For capabilities and details, see en.wikipedia.org/wiki/Twitter. Twitter is described in detail in Chapter 7.

As of December 2008, Twitter claims to have more than 6 million registered accounts. Socialtext (socialtext.com) offers a Twitter for the enterprise. Twitter is becoming a useful enterprise tool.

Examples of Twitter as Enterprise Tools (based on business.twitter.com/twitter101).

Twitter
A free microblogging service that allows its users to send and read other users' updates.

tweets
Text-based posts up to 140 characters in length posted to Twitter.

▸ Dell Computers uses Twitter to disseminate information and interact with customers. With over 80 Dell-branded Twitter accounts, the company found Twitter useful in expanding awareness of its products and increased sales.

▸ JetBlue has about 1 million followers on Twitter. The company uses Twitter for customer service and market research. The company found customers wanted JetBlue to see them as a resource for helping JetBlue deliver a better product. The company posts questions and information to which people respond. Twitter helped tear down the artificial walls between customers and the company's employees.

▶ Tasti D-Lite offers guilt-free frozen treats in over 50 stores in New York. Twitter is being used to find out what customers are saying about the products and the competition. The company also mingles with customers on the customer's terms. Customers also help in problem solving (e.g., in delivery), and the company distributes paperless mobile coupons. Each store has its own Twitter account.

▶ Etsy is an online marketplace for buying and selling all things handmade. Over 250,000 sellers open up shops to sell handmade goods. The sellers are using Twitter to promote their shops and products. The company monitors the tweets of the followers to harness the collective brains of the participating community. They use RSS feeds of the relevant blogs, alert followers to particularly creative products from specific sellers, share valuable tips, and alert people about upcoming events and promotion on the site. Monitoring community concerns is another activity and is garnering feedback and ideas instantaneously, effectively creating focus groups from Etsy followers.

▶ Pepsi is using Twitter to supplement a toll-free telephone number to share product feedback faster and in a more personal way. The company monitors and talks with customers. The company reached a new audience that never bothered to call. And many of the new audience are very creative. The company also uses Twitter to handle complaints as well.

Commercial Uses of Blogs

The blog concept has transferred quickly to the corporate world. See Sloan and Kaihla (2006) for a survey of commercial uses of blogs. The examples in Online File W2.7 illustrate how companies use blogs for different purposes.

Potential Risks of Corporate Blogs

Some people see risks in corporate blogging. Two obvious examples are the risk of revealing trade secrets and of making statements that are or could be construed as libel or defamation. Many companies have corporate policies on blogging.

According to Flynn (2006), blog-related risks can be minimized by establishing a strategic *blog management* program that incorporates the three *E*'s of electronic risk management:

1. Establish comprehensive, written rules and policies. Make sure employees understand that all company policies apply to the blogosphere, regardless of whether employees are blogging at the office or from home.

2. Educate employees about blog-related risks, rules, and regulations. Be sure to address rights and privacy expectations, as well as the organization's blog-related risks and responsibilities.

3. Enforce blog policy with disciplinary action and technology. Take advantage of blog search engines to monitor the blogosphere and to keep track of what is being written about your company.

For a comprehensive discussion of corporate blogs, their risk, and how to mitigate this risk, see Cox et al. (2008).

MECHANISM AIDS FOR WEB 2.0 TOOLS: TAGS, FOLKSONOMY, AND SOCIAL BOOKMARKS

When you blog, you may see a notice that reads "Browse This Blog's Tags," followed by a list of key words. Tags are one of the most useful aids to Web 2.0 tools. (See en.wikipedia.org/wiki/Tag_(metadata) for details.)

Tags

A **tag** is a nonhierarchical key word or term assigned to a piece of information (such as an Internet bookmark, digital image, video clip, or any computer document). This kind of metadata (data about data) helps describe an item as a key word and allows it to be found by browsers when searching. Tags are chosen informally and personally by the item's creator or by its viewer, depending on the system. On a Web site in which many users tag many items, this collection of tags becomes a *folksonomy*.

Folksonomy

Folksonomy (also known as **collaborative tagging**, **social classification**, **social indexing**, or **social tagging**) is the practice and method of collaboratively creating, classifying, and managing tags to annotate and categorize content. In contrast to traditional subject indexing, key words (metadata) are generated not only by experts but also by creators and consumers of the content. Usually, freely chosen key words are used instead of a controlled vocabulary. *Folksonomy* (from *folk* and *taxonomy*) is a user-generated taxonomy. For additional information see en.wikipedia.org/wiki/Folksonomy.

Social Bookmarking

Social bookmarking is a method for Internet users to store, organize, search, and manage bookmarks of Web pages on the Internet with the help of metadata.

In a social-bookmarking system, users save links to Web pages that they want to remember and/or share. These bookmarks are usually public and can be saved privately, shared only with specified people, groups, or networks, and so forth. People can usually view these bookmarks chronologically, by category or tags, or via a search engine. For details, see en.wikipedia.org/wiki/Social_bookmarking.

WIKIS

A **wiki (wikilog)** can be viewed as an extension of a blog. Whereas a blog usually is created by an individual (or maybe a small group) and may have an attached discussion board, a *wikilog*, *wikiblog*, or *wiki* is essentially a blog that enables everyone to participate as a peer. Anyone may add, delete, edit, or change content. It is like a loose-leaf notebook with a pencil and eraser left in a public place. Anyone can read it, scrawl notes, tear out a page, and so on. Creating a wikilog is a *collaborative process*. For description and details, see the Meatball wiki at usemod.com/cgi-bin/mb.pl?WikiLog. Wikis can be implemented in many ways. One way is through a contribution by many, as in the case of Wikipedia. A similar concept is employed by the CIA in their "Intellipedia." For further discussion, see en.wikipedia.org/wiki/Wiki. A commercial use of a wiki was presented in the opening case. For a comprehensive list of wikis, see webtrends.about.com/od/wiki/a/guide_to_wikis.htm.

SOCIAL NETWORK SERVICES

Social network services, which were introduced in Chapter 1 and will be describe in detail in Chapter 7, use blogs, wikis, and other mechanisms and are considered Web 2.0 services. Social networks appear in a variety of forms; the most well-known, mostly social-oriented networks are MySpace and Facebook. LinkedIn is a business-oriented network. Covering both aspects via classified services is Craigslist, which is described in Case 2.2.

tag
A nonhierarchical keyword or term assigned to a piece of information (such as an Internet bookmark, digital image, video clip, or any computer document).

folksonomy (collaborative tagging, social classification, social indexing, social tagging)
The practice and method of collaboratively creating, classifying, and managing tags to annotate and categorize content.

social bookmarking
Web service for sharing Internet bookmarks. The sites are a popular way to store, classify, share, and search links through the practice of folksonomy techniques on the Internet and intranets.

wiki (wikilog)
A blog that allows everyone to participate as a peer; anyone may add, delete, or change content.

EC Application
CRAIGSLIST: THE ULTIMATE ONLINE CLASSIFIED SITE

If you want to find (or offer) a job, housing, goods and services, social activities, and much more in more than 500 cities in five languages and in more than 50 countries worldwide, go to Craigslist (*craigslist.org*). The site has much more information than you will find in all the newspapers in the individual cities. For example, more than 500,000 new jobs are listed from the more than 10 million new classified ads received by Craigslist every month. Each month there are more than 50 million visitors to the site. Craig Newmark, the founder of Craigslist, has said that everything is for sale on the site except the site itself. Although many other sites offer free classifieds, no other site even comes close to Craigslist.

In addition, Craigslist features 100 topical discussion forums with more than 120 million user postings. Every day, people in 450 cities worldwide check classified ads and interact on forums. No wonder that Craigslist has more than 9 billion page views per month, making it the seventh most visited site in the English language. Craigslist is considered by many as one of the few Web sites that could change the world because it is simply a free notice board with more than 4 billion readers (Naughton 2006). For more information, see *craigslist.org/about/factsheet*.

Users cite the following reasons for the popularity of Craigslist:

▶ It gives people a voice.
▶ It promotes a sense of trust, even intimacy.
▶ It is consistent and champions down-to-earth values.
▶ It illustrates simplicity.
▶ It has social-networking capabilities.
▶ It can be used for free in most cases (you can post free ads except for business, for rent, or for sale ads in a few large cities).
▶ It is effective and well visited. The site serves more than 9 billion page views per month.

As an example of the site's effectiveness, we provide the personal experience of one of the authors, who needed to rent his condo in Los Angeles. The usual process would take two to four weeks and $400 to $700 in newspaper ads, plus ads in the local online site for rent services, to get the condo rented. With Craigslist, it took less than a week at no cost. As more people discover Craigslist, the traditional newspaper-based classified ad industry will probably be the loser; ad rates may become lower, and fewer ads will be printed.

EBay owns 25 percent of Craigslist. Craigslist charges for "help wanted" ads and apartment broker listings in some larger cities. In addition, Craigslist may charge ad placers, especially when an ad has rich media features. Classified advertising is Craigslist's real money-making opportunity. According to Liedtke (2009), employment advertising is expected to account for $85 million of Craigslist's revenue this year. Other paid categories include housing ads (nearly $9 million) and adult-only ads (nearly $4 million). Further questions regarding the future of Craigslist have to do with the very hands-off mentality that made this site famous. Specifically, critics charge that users post illegitimate and possibly illegal ads on the site, and the Craigslist staff are unable to effectively police this practice. Some users have complained about questionable ads being posted, especially in the "jobs" section. This would include pyramid schemes and under-the-counter work. Craigslist also attracts criminals seeking to commit fraud by misleading the gullible into accepting false checks. The anonymity of Craigslist's users and the lack of ratings systems create an environment where deceitful users cannot be held accountable for their actions.

Another concern is that erotic services make up a significant portion of the total traffic on the site. There is a fear that many of the sexual encounters facilitated using Craigslist have been with underage girls. With the sheer volume of users and ads posted per day, such policing is not possible given the modest workforce of only 24 that the site employs.

In addition, many supporters contend that attempts to control Craigslist may simply cause users to relocate to a different, less-regulated site. Surely the design of Craigslist shouldn't be too difficult to duplicate. However, its brand is extremely strong.

Sources: Compiled from *craigslist.org* (accessed November 2009), Naughton (2006), Clark (2009), Copeland (2006), Liedtke (2009), and *en.wikipedia.org/wiki/Craigslist* (accessed November 2009).

Questions

1. Identify the business model used by Craigslist.
2. Visit *craigslist.org* and identify the social network and business network elements.
3. What do you like about the site? What do you dislike about it?
4. Why is Craigslist considered a site that "changes the world"?
5. What are some of the risks and limitations of using this site?

Section 2.6 ▶ REVIEW QUESTIONS

1. Define blogs and bloggers.
2. Discuss the critical features that distinguish a blog from a user-produced regular Web page.
3. Describe the potential advantages and risks of blogs.
4. Discuss the commercial uses of blogs and wikis.
5. Define tags, folksonomy, and social bookmarking.
6. Define wikis.

2.7 VIRTUAL WORLDS AS AN ELECTRONIC COMMERCE MECHANISM

According to en.wikipedia.org/wiki/Virtual_world, in virtual worlds the *computer-simulated* world offers the use of visual stimuli that in turn can manipulate elements of the modeled world and thus create *telepresence,* to a certain degree. The modeled world may motivate situations and rules based on the real world or some fantasy world. With the use of avatars, communication among users can include text, graphical icons, visual gesture, video clips, sound, and so forth.

AVATARS

Virtual worlds are populated with animated characters—software agents with personalities known as *avatars.* **Avatars** are animated representations of humanlike movements and behaviors in a computer-generated 3D world. Advanced avatars can "speak" and display behaviors such as gestures and facial expressions. They can be fully automated to act like robots. The purpose of avatars is to introduce believable emotions so that the computerized agents gain credibility with users. For example, the real estate giant RE/MAX uses hundreds of virtual sales agents as avatars. For a demonstration of avatars in business, see pulse3d.com.

Avatars are aimed at making the human–computer interface more natural. Avatars can improve customer satisfaction and retention by offering personalized, one-to-one service. They also can help companies get to know their customers and support advertising. For more on avatars, see en.wikipedia.org/wiki/Avatar_(computing).

avatars
Animated computer characters that exhibit humanlike movements and behaviors.

BUSINESS ACTIVITIES AND VALUE IN VIRTUAL WORLDS

As businesses compete in the real world, they also compete in virtual worlds. Many companies and organizations now incorporate virtual worlds as a new form of advertising and sales (see the Scion closing case in Chapter 4). An example of this would be Apple Computer creating a virtual store within Second Life. This allows users to browse Apple's latest innovative products. You cannot actually purchase a product (yet), but having these "virtual stores" is a way for vendors to access a different customer demographic as customers examine products in 3D and exchange opinions and recommendations.

There are several types of business activities in virtual worlds:

▶ Creating and managing a virtual business (see Terdiman 2008 for guidelines on how to do this)
▶ Conducting regular business activities (e.g., advertising, marketing, collaboration) within the framework of the virtual world
▶ Providing services for those who build, manage, or make money with virtual properties

For example, in a cover story in *BusinessWeek*, Hof (2008) discusses the various opportunities for conducting business in Second Life. Specifically, he introduces seven residents who are making substantial amounts of money. These include the Anshe Chung avatar, known as the "Rockefeller of Second Life," who buys virtual land from Second Life, "develops" it, and sells or rents it globally. Her business has grown so rapidly that she employs 20 people to design and program the development projects.

Following are two examples of how companies are using virtual worlds to bolster their physical businesses:

Example 1: Collaboration. More than 2,000 IBM employees signed up as members of Second Life, using the site to share ideas and work on projects. IBM holds an "alumni block party" in Second Life, allowing current and former employees from around the globe to get together in virtual meetings. IBM purchases islands for use as meeting places and technology showcases, and for experiments in virtual reality business. For example, IBM has set up a Sears appliance store as virtual commerce demonstration projects. IBM allows greater interactivity with products than a conventional store will allow. Users can, for example, customize appliances.

Example 2: Research and Marketing. Starwood Hotels constructed a prototype of the new Aloft brand hotels before they appeared in the real world in 2008. The company purchased two islands: Aloft, for the hotel prototype, and Argali, where visitors viewed the development project. Working from a preliminary architectural sketch, the designers began roughing out the layout, furnishings, and textures of the hotel, which were then refined in response to feedback from the *brick-and-mortar* architects and from Second Life residents who were invited to critique the design and layout. Then, the developers began remodeling the hotel in response to feedback from Second Life residents.

Using virtual worlds gives companies the opportunity to gauge customer reaction and receive feedback about new products or services. This can be crucial because it will give the companies insight into what the market and customers want from new products, which can give them a competitive edge. For more, see this chapter's closing case.

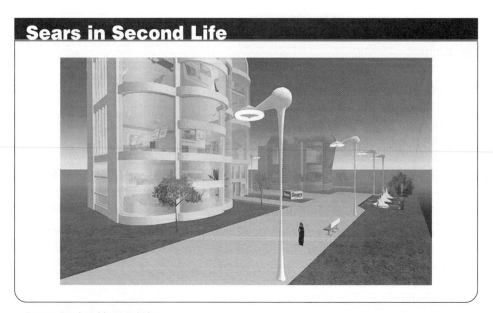

Source: Reprinted by permission.

Section 2.7 ▶ REVIEW QUESTIONS

1. Define virtual worlds.
2. Describe avatars. Why do we use them?
3. List some business activities in virtual worlds. Categorize them by type.

MANAGERIAL ISSUES

Some managerial issues related to this chapter are as follows.

1. **Should we auction?** A major strategic issue is whether to use auctions as a sales channel. Auctions do have some limitations, and forward auctions may create conflicts with other distribution channels. If a company decides to use auctions, it needs to select auction mechanisms and determine a pricing strategy. These days, auctions often allow an immediate purchase with a fixed price. These decisions determine the success of the auction and the ability to attract and retain visitors on the site. Auctions also require support services. Decisions about how to provide these services and to what extent to use business partners are critical to the success of high-volume auctions.

2. **Should we barter?** Bartering can be an interesting strategy, especially for companies that lack cash, need special material or machinery, and have surplus resources. However, the valuation of what is bought or sold may be hard to determine, and the tax implications in some countries are not clear.

3. **How do we select merchant software?** There are many products and vendors. Small businesses should consider offers from Yahoo! or eBay since the software is combined with hosting and offers exposure to the vendor-managed e-market. The functionalities of the software must be examined as well as the ease of building Webstores.

4. **How can we use Web 2.0 tools?** There are many possibilities that are presented throughout the book and especially in Chapter 7. The tools may be free or inexpensive, so at least try to experiment with them.

5. **Shall we take part in virtual worlds?** For many companies and applications the technology is still immature and cumbersome. A good strategy is to observe what other companies, especially in the same industry, are doing in Second Life.

SUMMARY

In this chapter, you learned about the following EC issues as they relate to the chapter's learning objectives.

1. **Activities and mechanisms.** The major activities are information dissemination and presence, trading, collaboration, entertainment, and search. The major mechanisms are marketplaces, storefronts, shopping carts, catalogs, Web 2.0 tools, and virtual worlds. The role of intermediaries will change as e-markets develop: Some will be eliminated (disintermediation); others will change their roles and prosper (reintermediation). In the B2B area, for example, e-distributors connect manufacturers with buyers by aggregating electronic catalogs of many suppliers. New value-added services that range from content creation to syndication are mushrooming.

2. **E-marketplaces and their components.** A marketspace, or e-marketplace, is a virtual market that does not suffer from limitations of space, time, or borders. As such, it can be very effective. Its major components include customers, sellers, products (some digital), infrastructure, front-end processes, back-end activities, electronic intermediaries, other business partners, and support services.

3. **The major types of e-marketplaces.** In the B2C area, there are storefronts and e-malls. In the B2B area, there are private and public e-marketplaces, which may be vertical (within one industry) or horizontal (across different industries). Different types of portals provide access to e-marketplaces.

4. **Electronic catalogs, search engines, and shopping carts.** The major mechanisms in e-markets

are electronic catalogs, search engines, software (intelligent) agents, and electronic shopping carts. These mechanisms facilitate EC by providing a user-friendly shopping environment.

5. **Types of auctions and their characteristics.** In forward auctions, bids from buyers are placed sequentially, either in increasing mode or in decreasing mode. In reverse auctions, buyers place an RFQ and suppliers submit offers in one or several rounds. In name-your-own-price auctions, buyers specify how much they are willing to pay for a product or service, and an intermediary tries to find a supplier to fulfill the request.

6. **The benefits and limitations of auctions.** The major benefits for sellers are the ability to reach many buyers, to sell quickly, and to save on commissions to intermediaries. Buyers have a chance to obtain bargains and collectibles while shopping from their homes. The major limitation is the possibility of fraud.

7. **Bartering and negotiating.** Electronic bartering can greatly facilitate the swapping of goods and services among organizations, thanks to improved search and matching capabilities, which is done in bartering exchanges. Software agents can facilitate online negotiation.

8. **Web 2.0 tools.** The major tools discussed in this chapter are blogs, wikis, and Twitter. Web 2.0 tools are used for several purposes, most commonly to improve communication and collaboration, to initiate viral marketing (word of mouth), to create branding awareness, and to foster interpersonal relationships.

9. **Virtual worlds.** These environments provide entertainment, trading virtual property, discussion groups, learning, training and much more. Everything is simulated, animated, and supported by avatars. Thousands of companies have established presences in virtual worlds, especially in Second Life, offering mainly dissemination of information and advertising.

KEY TERMS

QUESTIONS FOR DISCUSSION BY INDIVIDUAL STUDENTS

1. Compare marketplaces with marketspaces. What are the advantages and limitations of each?

2. Compare wikis and blogs.

3. Discuss the competitive advantage of Craigslist in classifieds.

4. Discuss the value of a virtual world as an EC environment. Why does it attract users? Why does it attract companies? How can it provide a competitive advantage to a company that has a presence there? What are its limitations?

5. Discuss how wikis, blogs, and virtual worlds can be used for collaboration.

6. Discuss the reasons why Twitter is becoming so popular.

7. Discuss the potential risks of using Web 2.0 tools.

8. Discuss the need for portals in EC.

TOPICS FOR CLASS DISCUSSION

1. Compare and contrast competition in traditional markets with that in digital markets.

2. Explain why sell-side and buy-side marketplaces in the same company are usually separated, whereas in an exchange they are combined.

3. Discuss the advantages of dynamic pricing over fixed pricing. What are the potential disadvantages of dynamic pricing?

4. Some say that blogs and wikis are going to eliminate e-mail. Discuss.

5. Should the content of Craigslist be monitored and controlled by the company? By users? By the government?

6. What is the advantage of a business using eBay instead of conducting auctions from its own site? Distinguish between C2C and B2B.

INTERNET EXERCISES

1. Go to cisco.com, google.com, and cio.com and locate information about the status of the "virtual close." Write a report based on your findings.

2. Examine how bartering is conducted online at tradeaway.com, buyersbag.com, and u-exchange.com. Compare and contrast the functionalities and ease of use of these sites.

3. Enter blogger.com and find its capabilities. Then enter blogsearch.google.com and find what this site helps you to do. Write a report.

4. Enter mfgquote.com and review the process by which buyers can send RFQs to merchants of their choice. Evaluate all the online services provided by the company. Write a report based on your findings.

5. Enter bloomsburgcarpet.com. Explain how the site solves the problem of sending carpet sample books to representatives all over the country.

6. Enter respond.com and send a request for a product or a service. Once you receive replies, select the best deal. You have no obligation to buy. Write a short report based on your experience.

7. Enter *Web 2.0 Journal* at web2.sys-con.com and find recent material on wikis, blogs, and Twitter. Write a report.

8. Enter yahoo.com and find what personalization methods it offers.

9. Enter cars.com. List all services available to sellers and to buyers of cars. Compare it to carsdirect.com. Also, identify the revenue sources of the sites.

10. Enter craigslist.org. From what you know about the design of Web sites and from comparisons with monster.com, what suggestions would you make to improve the site?

11. Enter ups.com.

   a. Find out what information is available to customers before they send a package.

   b. Find out about the "package tracking" system; be specific.

   c. Compute the cost of delivering a 10" × 20" × 15" box, weighing 40 pounds, from your hometown to Long Beach, California. Compare the fastest delivery against the lowest cost.

   d. Prepare a spreadsheet for two different types of calculations available on the site. Enter data to solve for two different calculators. Use Excel.

12. Register at Second Life, and enter the site.

   a. Find what IBM and Coca-Cola are doing on the site.

b. Find out what three universities that you are familiar with are doing on the site.

c. Write a report.

13. Create an avatar in Second Life. Let your avatar interact with avatars of some companies. Why do we consider an avatar as a mechanism for EC? Write a report.

14. Enter **ca.com/products** and register. Take the Clever Path Portal Test Drive. (Flash Player from Macromedia is required.) Then enter **ibm.com** and **oracle.com/bea**. Prepare a list of the major products available for building corporate portals.

15. Enter **findwhitepapers.com/knowledgemanagement/corporate-portals**. Find the white papers about corporate portals and their justification. Prepare a report based on your findings.

16. Enter **sap.com** and find the key capabilities of their enterprise portals. List the benefits of using five of the capabilities of portals.

17. Enter **networksolutions.com**. View the shopping cart demo. What features impress you the most and why? What related services does it provide? Compare it to **storefront.net** and **nexternal.com**.

18. Compare the shopping malls of Yahoo!, **amazon.com**, and **internetmall.net**.

TEAM ASSIGNMENTS AND PROJECTS

1. Read the opening case about EMS and answer the following questions.

a. Why not just have meetings and send e-mails rather than use blogs, wikis, and RSS feeds?

b. What are the benefits to EMS of combining its BI system with the Web 2.0 tools?

c. In what ways is corporate performance bolstered?

d. How can customers of the retail stores utilize the Web 2.0 tools?

e. Can the company use any other Web 2.0 technologies? What and how?

2. Assign each group to a large e-tailer (e.g., Amazon.com, Zappos.com, Walmart.com, Target.com, Dell.com, Apple.com, and HP.com). Trace the purchasing process. Look at the catalogs, search engines, shopping carts, Web 2.0 features, and any other mechanism that improves e-shopping. Make a presentation that will include recommendations for improving the existing process.

3. Enter **en.wikipedia.org/wiki/Businesses_and_organizations_in_Second_Life** and view the list of businesses. Identify some virtual companies and explore several in depth. Find what products (services) they offer and how much they charge if they sell their products (services). Then, identify several companies that are related to real-world businesses. (e.g., SL Bay auctions allow you to purchase real-world items with Linden dollars).

4. Build your own business in Second Life (SL). This can be each member or each group. Using the company cited in Question 3, determine what business you want to build. Then obtain a copy of Terdiman's book (2008) or a similar guide. Register at SL and go to work. In your project, do the following:

a. Select a business category and develop a business strategy.

b. Develop a business plan and model (see Online Tutorial T1) for your virtual enterprise.

c. Choose where to set up your business.

d. Conduct a budget and cash flow analysis (see Appendix B in Terdiman 2008).

e. Buy virtual land and other virtual properties.

f. Develop marketing and advertising plans (examine the competition).

g. Look for any possible revenues; make a pricing decision.

h. Examine the possibility of running your business in "Teen SL."

i. Plan all support business using the SL tools.

j. Watch for legal issues and other risks.

k. Build the business (using the SL tools).

l. Build a supporting blog. How would you use it for viral marketing?

5. GM and eBay are experimenting with selling new cars on eBay. In California, 250 GM dealers are using eBay as a channel to sell new cars. Customers can haggle with the dealers over the Internet. This is negotiation, not auctions. Find information on who is selling new and used cars online and how they do it. Write a report. Do you think the experiment will succeed? Why or Why not?

Closing Case

SECOND LIFE

In 2003, a 3D virtual world called Second Life (SL) was opened to the public. The world is entirely built and owned by its residents. In 2003, the virtual world consisted of 64 acres. By 2009 it had grown to about 100,000 acres and was inhabited by millions of residents from around the planet (see *secondlife.com*). The virtual world consists of a huge digital continent, people, entertainment, experiences, and opportunities.

Thousands of new residents join each day and *create their own avatars* through which they travel around the SL world meeting people, communicating, having fun, and buying virtual land and other virtual properties where they can open a business or build a personal space limited only by their imaginations and their ability to use the virtual 3D applications. Avatars have unique names and move around in imaginative vehicles including helicopters, submarines, and hot-air balloons.

SL is dedicated to creativity, and everything in SL is resident-created. Residents retain the rights to their digital creations and can buy, sell, and trade with other residents in SL marketplaces. Residents can also socialize and participate in group activities. Virtual businesses succeed due to the owners' ingenuity, artistic ability, entrepreneurial expertise, and reputation.

Residents get some free virtual land (and they can buy more) where they build a house, a city, or a business. They can then sell the virtual properties or the virtual products or services they create. Residents can also sell real-world products or services. For example, Copeland and Kelleher (2007) report that more than 25,000 aspiring entrepreneurs trade virtual products or services at SL. Virtual goods entrepreneurs, landowners, in-world builders, and service providers generated user-to-user transactions totaling US$350 million in 2008 (Linden 2009). Stevan Lieberman, an attorney, is one of these. He uses his expertise in intellectual property and the site to solicit work—mainly from programmers who are looking to patent their code. SL is managed by Linden Labs, which provides Linden dollars that can be converted to U.S. dollars. SL uses several Web 2.0 tools such as blogs, wikis, RSS, and tags (from *delicious.com*).

Many organizations use SL for 3D presentations of their products. Even governments open virtual embassies on "Diplomacy Island," located on the site. Many universities offer educational courses and seminars in virtual classrooms (see "EduIslands" on the SL site and Appendix A in Rymaszewski et al. [2008]).

Roush (2007) describes how to combine SL with Google Earth. Such combinations enable investigation of phenomena that would otherwise be difficult to visualize or understand. Shopping for virtual goods is popular in SL. You can start at the GNUbie Store (bargain prices), New Citizens Incorporates (NCI), and Free Dove. SL friends will help you choose! You can shop outside SL (for real goods) yet pay Linden dollars, the currency of SL (see *xstreetsl.com*). For SL fashion selection, try *blog.secondstyle.com*. Also *sluniverse.com/php/shop* lets you quickly and easily search and shop for many items. You can even use a shopping cart on this site.

Note: We suggest you build your own virtual business in SL in order to experience real-life thrills. For suggestions on how to profit in SL see Chapter 1 in Rymaszewski et al. (2008). You can work as a musician, hunter, financial speculator, or a writer. You can also work in many other virtual jobs—you are only limited by your imagination.

Example. For awhile now, real-world organizations have been taking a growing interest in SL. Educational institutions were the first to recognize the potential of the virtual world to act as a new communications, advertising, and learning platform, and they were quickly followed by corporations doing what most corporations do: Look for profit. Appendix C of Rymaszewski et al. (2008) provides information about real-life brand presence and retail outlets in SL.

At the time of this writing, corporate activity in SL is still in its infancy. Although an impressive number of companies have made or are in the process of making a foray into the virtual world, many treat it as an experiment whose only sure payoff is the media publicity it generates in the real world. However, to others—perhaps more visionary—SL offers very tangible advantages: A visit to *work.secondlife.com* will educate you in-depth on how organizations utilize SL's virtual environment. For readers interested in the corporate take on the virtual world, Rymaszweski et al. (2008) present three voices from three countries, representing companies in different fields of business.

The most common commercial activities in SL are:

- Advertising
- Joint designing and prototyping
- Market research
- Marketing and sales
- Corporate communication
- Broadcasting and entertainment
- Travel and tourism
- Training and e-learning

For details, see Chapter 1 and Robbins and Bell (2008).

An increasing number of businesses are using the virtual world. For example, IBM uses it as a location for meetings, training, and recruitment. American Apparel was the first major retailer to set up shop in SL. The Mexican Tourism Board and Morocco Tourism are examples of 3D presentations of major tourist attractions. Many companies use SL as a hot place to go to try new business ideas (see Rosedale 2007). For example, you can test-drive a Toyota Scion, toymakers prototype toys, and anyone can become a virtual architect.

Sources: Compiled from Copeland and Kelleher (2007), Linden (2009), Robbins and Bell (2008), Rosedale (2007), Rymaszewski et al. (2008), Roush (2007), and *secondlife.com* (accessed November 2009).

Questions

1. Enter the SL site (*secondlife.com*) and identify EC activities there. (You need to register for free and create an avatar.)
2. Which types of transactions are observable at the site?
3. Which business models are observable at the site?
4. If you were a travel agent, how would you utilize the site?
5. Have your avatar communicate with five others. Write a report on your experience.

ONLINE RESOURCES
available at pearsonhighered.com/turban

Online Files

W2.1   Examples of Digital Products
W2.2   Application Case: How Raffles Hotel Is Conducting E-Commerce
W2.3   Types of Corporate Portals
W2.4   Application Case: Electronic Catalogs at OfficeMax
W2.5   Application Case: EBay: The World's Largest Auction Site
W2.6   Application Case: Reverse Mortgage Auctions in Singapore

W2.7   How Companies Are Using Blogs

Comprehensive Educational Web Sites

wiki.secondlife.com/wiki/Video_Tutorials: Learn SL in a fun, easy way.

vectec.org/old_web/research_center: The Virginia Electronic Commerce Technology Center offers special reports, e-business news, and statistics.

allthingsweb2.com: An open directory for the interactive Web.

CHAPTER 3

RETAILING IN ELECTRONIC COMMERCE: PRODUCTS AND SERVICES

Content

Learning Objectives

Upon completion of this chapter, you will be able to:

1. Describe electronic retailing (e-tailing) and its characteristics.

2. Define and describe the primary e-tailing business models.

3. Describe how online travel and tourism services operate and their impact on the industry.

4. Discuss the online employment market, including its participants, benefits, and limitations.

5. Describe online real estate services.

6. Discuss online stock-trading services.

7. Discuss cyberbanking and online personal finance.

8. Describe on-demand delivery of groceries and similar products/services.

9. Describe the delivery of digital products and online entertainment.

10. Discuss various online consumer aids, including comparison-shopping aids.

11. Describe disintermediation and other B2C strategic issues.

AMAZON.COM: E-TAILING GROWS DESPITE THE SLUMPING ECONOMY

The Opportunity

Amazon.com (*amazon.com*) reported that its annual profit for 2008 had doubled, with a 41 percent revenue increase, despite adverse U.S. and global economic conditions.

Entrepreneur Jeff Bezos faced an opportunity rather than a business problem. In the early 1990s, Bezos saw the huge potential for retail sales over the Internet and identified books as the most logical product for e-tailing. In July 1995, Bezos started Amazon.com, an e-tailing pioneer, offering books via an electronic catalog from its Web site. Over the years, the company has recognized that it must continually enhance its business models and online storefront by expanding its product selection, improving the customer experience, and adding services and alliances. In addition, the company recognized early on the importance of order fulfillment and warehousing. It has invested hundreds of millions of dollars in building physical warehouses designed for shipping small packages to hundreds of thousands of customers. Amazon.com's challenge was, and remains, how to succeed where many have failed—namely, how to sell consumer products online, at a profit, and show a reasonable rate of return on investment.

The Solution: Reaching Out to Customers

In addition to its initial electronic bookstore, Amazon has expanded its offerings to a vast array of products and services segmented into three broad categories: media (books, music, DVDs, etc.); electronics and other merchandise (including its new wireless reading device, Kindle; office supplies; cameras; toys; etc.); and other (nonretail activities, such as Web services, Amazon Enterprise Solutions, etc.). Key features of the Amazon.com superstore are easy browsing, searching, and ordering; useful product information, reviews, recommendations, and personalization; broad selection; low prices; secure payment systems; and efficient order fulfillment.

The Amazon.com Web site has a number of features that make the online shopping experience more enjoyable. Its "Gift Ideas" section features seasonally appropriate gift ideas and services. AmazonConnect allows customers to select their favorite authors, read about them, and then receive e-mails from those authors.

Amazon.com also offers various marketplace services. Amazon Auctions hosts and operates auctions on behalf of individuals and small businesses throughout the world. The Shops service hosts electronic storefronts for a monthly fee, offering small businesses the opportunity to have customized storefronts supported by the richness of Amazon.com's order-fulfillment processing. Customers can use Web-enabled cell phones, PDAs, or pocket PCs to access Amazon.com and shop anywhere, anytime. Amazon.com also can be accessed via AT&T's #121 voice service.

Amazon.com is recognized as an online leader in creating sales through customer intimacy and customer relationship management (CRM), which are cultivated by informative marketing front ends and one-to-one advertisements. In addition, sales are supported by highly automated, efficient back-end systems. When a customer makes a return visit to Amazon.com, a cookie file (see Chapter 4) identifies the user and says, for example, "Welcome back, Sarah Shopper," and then proceeds to recommend new books from the same genre of the customer's previous purchases and a range of other items. It also provides detailed product descriptions and ratings to help consumers make informed purchase decisions. The site has an efficient search engine and other shopping aids. Amazon.com has a superb warehousing system that gives the company an advantage over the competition.

Customers can personalize their accounts and manage orders online with the patented "1-Click" order feature. 1-Click includes an electronic wallet (see Chapter 10), which enables shoppers to place an order in a secure manner without the need to enter their address, credit card number, and other information each time they shop and allows customers to view their order status, cancel or combine orders that have not yet entered the shipping process, edit the shipping options and addresses on unshipped orders, modify the payment method for unshipped orders, and more.

In 1997, Amazon.com started an extensive associates program. By 2009, the company had more than 2 million partners worldwide that refer customers to Amazon.com. Amazon.com pays a 4 to 10 percent commission on any resulting sale. Starting in 2000, Amazon.com has undertaken alliances with major "trusted partners" that provide knowledgeable entry into new markets. For example, clicking "Office Supplies" allows customers either to select from Amazon.com's office supplies or to browse those of Office Depot; clicking "Health and Personal Care" allows customers to benefit from great deals offered by Weight Watchers. In yet another extension of its services, in September 2001 Amazon.com signed an agreement with Borders Group Inc., providing Amazon.com's users with the option of picking up their merchandise at

The Vast Range of Products and Services at Amazon.com

Source: Courtesy of Amazon.com. Used with permission.

Borders' physical bookstores (in-store pickup). Amazon.com also is becoming a Web fulfillment contractor for national chains such as Target. AmazonFresh is a grocery delivery service. Amazon MP3 allows downloads, some free, others for 69¢ per song. AmazonConnect allows authors to post remarks on their book pages to customers who have bought their books. Amazon.com also has its own search engine, called A9 (*a9.com*), and offers a range of Web services to developers (Amazon WebStore).

In 1999, *Time* magazine named Bezos "Person of the Year," recognizing the company's success in popularizing online shopping. In January 2002, Amazon declared its first profit—for the 2001 fourth quarter. Since then, the company has remained profitable. Annual sales for Amazon.com have trended upward, driven largely by product diversification and its international presence.

This pioneer e-tailer now offers over 17 million book, music, and DVD/video titles to some 20 million customers.

Amazon.com also offers several features for international customers, including over 1 million Japanese-language titles. Amazon.com maintained its position as the number one e-tailer in 2008, generating revenues of $19.2 billion, with a net income of $645 million. In 2009, the Amazon.com Web site attracted at least 615 million visitors. Amazon.com, the king of e-tailers, which has shown all others the potential of B2C EC, is increasing its profitability, even in economic crises.

Sources: Compiled from Reuters (2008), Dignan (2008), and *amazon.com* (accessed November 2009).

WHAT WE CAN LEARN . . .

The case of Amazon.com, the most recognized and largest e-tailer in the world, demonstrates the evolution of e-tailing, some of the problems encountered by e-tailers, and the solutions employed by Amazon.com to expand its business. It also is indicative of a key trend in Internet retailing: The biggest online retailers are still growing and becoming more dominant, with the top 500 e-retailers accounting for 65 percent ($178.2 billion) of all online sales in 2009 (*Internet Retailer* 2009b). E-tailing, as demonstrated by the Amazon.com case, continues its double-digit, year-over-year growth rate despite the global economic downturn. This is, in part, because sales are shifting away from stores and also because online shoppers are, in general, more affluent. However, some experts argue that online retailers will need to better understand customer behavior and preferences if they are to achieve a better convergence between technological capability and customer desires (see Chapter 4). In this chapter, we will look at the delivery of both products and services online to individual customers. We also discuss e-tailing successes and failures.

3.1   INTERNET MARKETING AND ELECTRONIC RETAILING

The Amazon.com case illustrates how commerce can be conducted on the Internet. Indeed, the amount and percentage of goods and services sold on the Internet is increasing rapidly, despite the failure of many dot-com companies. According to *Internet Retailer* (2009a), approximately 60 percent of adult U.S. Internet users shop online and/or research offline sales online. With estimates of 228 million Internet users in the United States, this suggests that in 2009 there were approximately 139 million online shoppers. However, as the number of Internet users reaches saturation, the rate of increase of online shoppers may slow. On the other hand, the economic downturn may increase online shopping as a means of saving money. Still, one of the challenges for electronic retailers, therefore, is to increase the amount spent online. As discussed in Chapter 1, companies have many reasons to market and sell their goods and services online. Innovative marketing strategies and a deep understanding of online consumer behavior and preferences will be required for sustained success in a competitive online environment.

This chapter presents an overview of Internet retailing, its diversity, prospects, and limitations. Retailing, especially when conducted in a new medium, must be supported by an understanding of consumer buying behavior, market research, and advertising, topics that will be presented in Chapter 4. Let's begin our discussion of EC products and services with an overview of electronic retailing.

OVERVIEW OF ELECTRONIC RETAILING

A retailer is a sales *intermediary*, a seller that operates between manufacturers and customers. Even though many manufacturers sell directly to consumers, they usually supplement their sales through wholesalers and retailers (a *multichannel approach*). In the physical world, retailing is done in stores (or factory outlets) that customers must visit in order to make a purchase. Companies that produce a large number of products, such as Procter & Gamble, must use retailers for efficient distribution. However, even if a company sells only a relatively few products (e.g., Kodak), it still might need retailers to reach a large number of customers.

Catalog (mail order) sales offer companies and customers a relief from the constraints of space and time: Catalogs free a retailer from the need for a physical store from which to distribute products, and customers can browse catalogs on their own time. With the ubiquity of the Internet, the next logical step was for retailing to move online. Retailing conducted over the Internet is called **electronic retailing**, or **e-tailing**, and those who conduct retail business online are called **e-tailers**. E-tailing can be conducted through catalogs with fixed prices as well as via auctions. E-tailing makes it easier for a manufacturer to sell directly to the customer, cutting out the intermediary (e.g., Zappos.com in Chapter 1, now an Amazon.com company). This chapter examines the various types of e-tailing and related issues.

The concept of retailing and e-tailing implies sales of goods and/or services to individual customers—that is, B2C EC. However, the distinction between B2C and B2B EC is not always clear. For example, Amazon.com sells books mostly to individuals (B2C), but it also sells to corporations (B2B). Amazon.com's chief rival in selling books online, Barnes & Noble (barnesandnoble.com), has a special division that caters only to business customers. Walmart (walmart.com) sells to both individuals and businesses (via Sam's Club). Dell sells its computers to both consumers and businesses from

electronic retailing (e-tailing)
Retailing conducted online, over the Internet.

e-tailers
Retailers who sell over the Internet.

dell.com, Staples sells to both markets at staples.com, and insurance sites sell to both individuals and corporations.

SIZE AND GROWTH OF THE B2C MARKET

The statistics for the volume of B2C EC sales, including forecasts for future sales, come from many sources. Reported amounts of online sales *deviate substantially* based on how the numbers are derived, and thus it is often difficult to obtain a consistent and coherent picture of the growth of EC. Some of the variation stems from the use of different definitions and classifications of EC. For example, when tallying financial data, some analysts include the investment costs in Internet infrastructure, whereas others include only the value of the actual transactions conducted via the Internet. Another issue is how the items for sale are categorized. Some sources combine certain products and services; others do not. Some sources include online travel sales in the data for EC retail; others do not. Sometimes different time periods are used in the measurement. When reading data about B2C EC sales, therefore, it is very important that care is taken in interpreting the figures.

The sites listed in Exhibit 3.1 provide statistics on e-tailing as well as on other Internet and EC activities. Typical statistics used in describing e-tailing and consumer behavior include Internet usage by demographic (online sales by age, gender, country, etc.); online sales by item; online sales by vendor; and buying patterns online.

WHAT SELLS WELL ON THE INTERNET

With approximately 139 million shoppers online in the United States in 2009, e-tailers appreciate the need to provide excellent choice and service to an ever-increasing cohort of potential customers. Hundreds of thousands of items are available on the Web from numerous vendors. Exhibit 3.2 shows the major categories that are all selling well online. For some current trends in B2C, see Online File W3.1.

EXHIBIT 3.1	**Representative Sources of EC Statistics**

BizRate (*bizrate.com*)
Business 2.0 (*money.cnn.com/magazines/business2*)
comScore (*comscore.com*)
ClickZ Network (*clickz.com*)
Ecommerce Info Center (*ecominfocenter.com*)
eMarket (*emarket.com*)
Forrester Research (*forrester.com*)
Gartner (*gartner.com*)
Gomez (*gomez.com*)
InternetRetailer (*internetretailer.com*)
Nielsen Online (*nielsen-online.com*)
Shop.org (*shop.org*)
Ominture SiteCatalyst (*omniture.com*)
Pew Internet (*pewinternet.org*)
Yankee Group (*yankeegroup.com*)
U.S. Census Bureau (*census.gov/econ/estats*)

EXHIBIT 3.2   What Sells Well on the Internet?

Category	Description
Travel	Expedia and Travelocity are major players in this category. Online travel agents offer a range of services, including travel booking, hotel reservations, car rentals, and vacation packages.
Computer hardware and software	Dell and Gateway are the major online vendors of computer hardware and software. Computer hardware and software is the largest category of products sold online.
Consumer electronics	Consumer electronics include digital cameras, printers, scanners, and wireless devices. Consumer electronics is the second largest category of products sold online.
Office supplies	B2C and B2B sales of office supplies are increasing rapidly, all over the world, as companies increasingly use the Internet to place orders for stationery and the like.
Sport and fitness goods	Sporting goods sell very well on the Internet. However, it is difficult to measure the exact amount of sales because only a few e-tailers sell sporting goods exclusively online (e.g., *fogdog.com*).
Books and music (CDs, DVDs)	Amazon.com and Barnesandnoble.com are the major sellers of books. However, hundreds of other e-tailers sell books on the Internet, especially specialized books (e.g., technical books, children's books).
Toys and hobbies	In 2007, online sales of toys dropped again due to toy recalls, specifically those toys made in China (*Biz Report* 2007).
Health and beauty	A large variety of health and beauty products—from vitamins to cosmetics and fragrances—are sold online by most large retailers and by specialty stores.
Entertainment	This is another area where dozens of products, ranging from tickets to events (e.g., *ticketmaster.com*) to paid fantasy games (see Section 3.7), are embraced by millions of shoppers worldwide.
Apparel and clothing	With the possibility of buying customized shirts, pants, and even shoes, the online sale of apparel also is growing. Guaranteed returns policies and improving features on fitting clothing without first trying it on have increased customers' comfort zone for buying apparel online.
Jewelry	Online sales of jewelry are booming. With claims of prices about 40 percent less than would be paid in traditional stores, the trend toward online jewelry sales is likely to continue.
Cars	The sale of cars over the Internet is just beginning (people still like to "kick the tires"), but could be one of the top sellers on the Internet in the near future. Customers like the build-to-order capabilities, but even selling used cars online has advantages and is increasing rapidly. Support services such as financing, warranties, and insurance also are selling well online.
Services	Sales in service industries, especially travel, stock trading, electronic banking, real estate, and insurance, are increasing—more than doubling every year in some cases.
Food and drugs	Innovative delivery solutions help with food sales. Ordering prescription drugs online may save time and money. Many online pharmacies provide information about drug interactions. Some even e-mail alerts when a drug is recalled or a generic equivalent becomes available.
Pet supplies	Pet supplies are a new category in the top-seller list. As family pets become more and more integrated as members of the family, online spending on toys, edible treats, food, pet accessories, and veterinary products and services is soaring.
Others	Many other products, ranging from prescription drugs to custom-made shoes, are offered on the Internet. Many items are specialized or niche products.

Sources: *Biz Report* (2007) and Mulpuru et al. (2008).

CONSIDERED COMMERCE

The first-generation e-commerce sold books, software, and music—simple to understand items easy to ship to consumers. The second wave of online growth—that started in 2000 as consumers moved beyond simple transactions to research and purchase more complex products online. Consumers are researching and purchasing now online from categories like furniture, jewelry, appliances, cars, flooring, big-screen TVs, and building supplies. Consumers are buying many services as well. Now, we are starting to see what is known as considered commerce.

Conducting **considered commerce** means conducting e-commerce by new rules. The "island" concept used for simple items, where the online channel of a business is basically separate from the physical retail business, may not work for considered commerce. The following are five rules for setting up a successful considered commerce.

1. **Embedded e-commerce.** An e-commerce operation should be a coordinated, multichannel selling effort, with the head of e-commerce seated at the management table.

2. **Integration.** Use the same data and procedures as the rest of the business, simplifying coordination. Use existing people and their retail expertise wherever possible.

3. **Chainwide impact.** Instead of using the sole metric of online sales, take a holistic view of this channel. Set chainwide key performance indicators (KPIs) and track interactions across all channels.

4. **Localize.** E-commerce supports the overall retail strategy, and the Web sites should be as localized as your stores.

5. **Content, Content, Content.** Focus on your offering first, then optimize your online store around your offering. Do you have the right products? Richly and accurately described and displayed? At the right price? Are you solving a customer's problem (an installed floor in a week, a sofa in two days, removal of an old refrigerator)?

Despite the miserable retail outlook that resulted from the 2008–2009 recession, considered commerce experienced a 52 percent growth in the latter part of 2008 (Prindle 2009).

considered commerce
Conducting e-commerce where the online channel of a business is integrated with the physical retail business as opposed to being a separate channel.

CHARACTERISTICS AND ADVANTAGES OF SUCCESSFUL E-TAILING

Many of the same basic principles that apply to physical retail success also apply to e-tail success. Sound business thinking, visionary leadership, thorough competitive analysis and financial analysis, and the articulation of a well-thought-out EC strategy are essential. So, too, is ensuring appropriate infrastructure, particularly a stable and scalable technology infrastructure to support the online and physical aspects of EC business operations. Newly required capabilities (e.g., capabilities in logistics and distribution) might need to be obtained through external strategic alliances. Offering quality merchandise at good prices, coupled with excellent service, and cross-channel coordination and integration in which customers can almost seamlessly operate between the online and physical environments of a business are also important elements in successful e-tailing. In a sense, the online and traditional channels are not very different. However, e-tailers can offer expanded consumer services not offered by traditional retailers. For a comparison of e-tailing and retailing, including advantages, see Exhibit 3.3.

EXHIBIT 3.3   Retailing Versus E-Tailing

Factor	Retailers	E-Tailers
Physical expansion (when revenue increases as the number of visitors grows)	• Expansion of retailing platform to include more locations and space	• Expansion of e-commerce platform to include increased server capacity and distribution facilities
Physical expansion (when revenue does not increase as the number of visitors grows)	• May not need physical expansion • Expand marketing effort to turn "window shoppers" into effective shoppers	• May still need physical expansion to provide sustainable services • Expand marketing to turn "pane shoppers" into effective shoppers
Technology	• Sales automation technologies such as POS systems	• Front-end technologies • Benefit from browsing • Back-end technologies • "Information" technologies
Customer relations	• More stable due to nonanonymous contacts • More tolerable of disputes due to visibility • "Physical" relationships	• Less stable due to anonymous contacts • More intolerant of disputes due to invisibility • "Logical" relationships
Cognitive shopping overhead	• Lower cognitive shopping overhead due to easy-to-establish mutual trust	• Higher cognitive shopping overhead due to hard-to-establish mutual trust
Competition	• Local competition • Fewer competitors	• Global competition • More competitors
Customer base	• Local area customers • No anonymity • Fewer resources needed to increase customer loyalty • Customers remain loyal for future purchases	• Wide area customers • Anonymity • More resources needed to increase customer loyalty • Customers shift loyalty
Supply chain cost	• High, interruption	• Lower
Customization and personalization	• Expensive and slow	• Fast, efficient
Price changing and price discrimination	• Expensive to do, done not so often	• Inexpensive, anytime
Adaptability to market trends	• Slow	• Rapid

Sources: Compiled from Kwon and Lennon (2009) and Ha and Stoel (2009).

With all else being equal in the online environment, goods with the following characteristics are expected to facilitate higher sales volumes:

▶ High brand recognition (e.g., Lands' End, Dell, Sony)
▶ A guarantee provided by highly reliable or well-known vendors (e.g., Dell, Amazon.com, BlueNile.com)

- Digitized format (e.g., software, music, or videos)
- Relatively inexpensive items (e.g., office supplies, vitamins)
- Frequently purchased items (e.g., groceries, prescription drugs)
- Commodities with standard specifications (e.g., books, CDs, airline tickets), making physical inspection unimportant
- Well-known packaged items that cannot be opened even in a traditional store (e.g., foods, chocolates, vitamins)

The next section examines business models that have proven successful in e-tailing.

Section 3.1 ❯ REVIEW QUESTIONS

1. Describe the nature of B2C EC.
2. What sells well in B2C?
3. What are the characteristics of high-volume products and services?
4. Describe the major trends in B2C.
5. Describe considered commerce.

3.2 E-TAILING BUSINESS MODELS

In order to better understand e-tailing, let's look at it from the point of view of a retailer or a manufacturer that sells to individual consumers. The seller has its own organization and must also buy goods and services from others, usually businesses (B2B in Exhibit 3.4). As also shown in Exhibit 3.4, e-tailing, which is basically B2C (right side of the exhibit), is done between the seller (a retailer or a manufacturer) and the buyer. The exhibit shows other EC transactions and related activities that may impact e-tailing. In this section, we will look at the various B2C models and their classifications.

CLASSIFICATION OF MODELS BY DISTRIBUTION CHANNEL

A *business model* is a description of how an organization intends to generate revenue through its business operations. More specifically, it is an analysis of the organization's customers and, from that, a discussion of how that organization will achieve profitability and sustainability by delivering goods and services (value) to those customers. E-tailing business models can be classified in several ways. For example, some classify e-tailers by the scope of items handled (general purpose versus specialty e-tailing) or by the scope of the sales region covered (global versus regional), whereas others use classification by revenue models (see Chapter 1). Here we will classify the models by the distribution channel used, distinguishing five categories:

1. **Direct marketing by mail-order retailers that go online.** Most traditional mail-order retailers, such as QVC, Sharper Image, and Lands' End, simply added another distribution channel—the Internet. Several of these retailers also operate physical stores, but their main distribution channel is direct marketing.
2. **Direct marketing by manufacturers.** Manufacturers, such as Dell, Nike, LEGO, Godiva (Chapter 1), and Sony, market directly online from company sites to individual customers. Most of these manufacturers are click-and-mortar, also selling in their own physical stores or via retailers.

EXHIBIT 3.4   E-Tailing as an Enterprise EC System

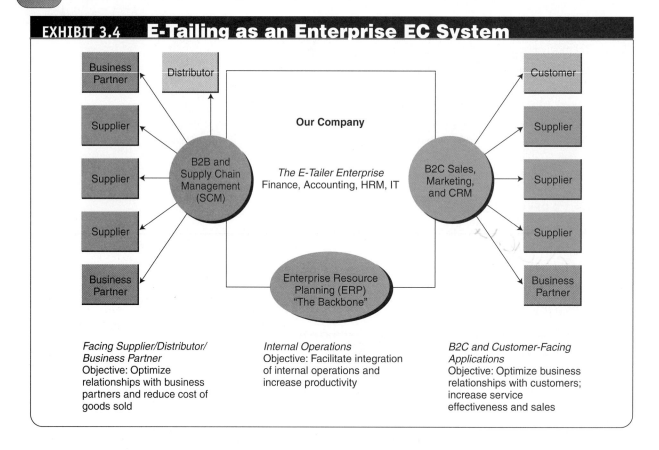

Facing Supplier/Distributor/Business Partner
Objective: Optimize relationships with business partners and reduce cost of goods sold

Internal Operations
Objective: Facilitate integration of internal operations and increase productivity

B2C and Customer-Facing Applications
Objective: Optimize business relationships with customers; increase service effectiveness and sales

3. **Pure-play e-tailers.** These e-tailers do not have physical stores, only an online sales presence. Amazon.com is an example of a pure-play e-tailer.

4. **Click-and-mortar retailers.** These are of two sorts, depending on how the businesses were originally founded. Originally, click-and-mortar referred to traditional businesses that developed Web sites to support their business activities in some way (e.g., walmart.com and homedepot.com). For details, see en.wikipedia.org/wiki/Bricks_and_clicks. However, we are now seeing the reverse trend. A small number of successful e-tailers are now creating physical storefronts, leveraging the brand power of the online environment to support more traditional trading activities via stores. For example, Dell, a pioneer of e-tailing and one of the largest sellers of computers online, has also opened physical stores. Expedia.com opened physical kiosks for tourists and Zappos.com has opened three physical outlets.

5. **Internet (online) malls.** As described in Chapter 2, these malls include large numbers of independent storefronts.

We will examine each of these distribution channel categories in the pages that follow.

Direct Marketing by Mail-Order Companies

direct marketing
Broadly, marketing that takes place without intermediaries between manufacturers and buyers; in the context of this book, marketing done online between any seller and buyer.

In a broad sense, **direct marketing** describes marketing that takes place without intermediaries. Direct marketers take orders directly from consumers, bypassing traditional wholesale or retail distribution.

Firms with established, mature mail-order businesses have a distinct advantage in online sales, given their existing payment processing, inventory management, and order-fulfillment operations.

Direct Sales by Manufacturers

The parties in direct marketing have a great opportunity to influence each other. Sellers can understand their markets better because of the direct connection to consumers, and consumers gain greater information about the products through their direct connection to the manufacturers. Dell is primarily using direct marketing combined with a build-to-order approach, customizing its products (see Online File W1.15 for more on build-to-order). Insights and Additions 3.1 describes the process by which customers can configure and order cars online.

WWW

Insights and Additions 3.1 Selling Cars Online: Build-to-Order

The world's automobile manufacturers operate in complex enterprises with thousands of suppliers and millions of customers. Their traditional channel for distributing cars has been the automobile dealer, who orders cars and then sells them from the lot. When a customer wants a particular feature or color ("options"), the customer might have to wait weeks or months until the "pipeline" of vehicles has that particular car on the production line.

In the traditional system, the manufacturers conduct market research in order to estimate which features and options will sell well, and then they make the cars they wish to sell. In some cases, certain cars are ultimately sold from stock at a loss when the market exhibits insufficient demand for a particular vehicle. The automakers have long operated under this "build-to-stock" environment, building cars that are carried as inventory during the outbound logistics process (ships, trucks, trains, and dealers' lots). General Motors (GM) estimates that it holds as much as $40 billion of unsold vehicles in its distribution channels. Other automakers hold large amounts as well.

Ford, GM, and Toyota, along with other automakers around the world, have announced plans to implement a build-to-order program, much like the Dell approach to building computers. These auto giants intend to transform themselves from build-to-stock companies to build-to-order companies, thereby cutting inventory requirements in half, while at the same time giving customers the vehicles they want in a short period (e.g., one to two weeks).

As an example of this trend toward build-to-order mass customization in the new car market, Jaguar car buyers can build a dream car online. On Jaguar's Web site (*jaguar.com*), consumers are able to custom configure their car's features and components, see it online, price it, and have it delivered to a nearby dealer. Using a virtual car on the Web site, customers can view in real time more

than 1,250 possible exterior combinations out of several million, rotate the image 360 degrees, and see the price updated automatically with each selection of trim or accessories. After storing the car in a virtual garage, the customer can decide on the purchase and select a dealer at which to pick up the completed car. (Thus, conflicts with the established dealer network channel are avoided.) The Web site helps primarily with the research process—it is not a fully transactional site. The configuration, however, can be transmitted to the production floor, thereby reducing delivery time and contributing to increased customer satisfaction. Similar configuration systems are available from all the major car manufacturers. Customers can electronically track the progress of the car, including visualization of the production process in the factory.

In the current economic times, (e.g., an economy without functioning credit markets), Detroit's build-to-forecast "push" distribution model has become unsustainable. A build-to-order "pull" distribution model is now a possible alternative to the build-to-forecast "push" system. The idea is to not ship a vehicle from its assembly plant until a retail customer asks for it. The proof-of-concept build-to-order model centralizes the completed vehicle inventory at the assembly plant and segments the market into "stock" vehicles and "special order" vehicles.

The competitive advantages of a "pull" vehicle distribution process are:

1. Improved customer satisfaction and better pricing
2. Large cost savings in finished vehicle inventory carrying costs
3. Virtually real-time market feedback
4. A barrier to entry against Indian and Chinese imports

Sources: Compiled from *jaguar.com* (accessed November 2009), McElroy (2009), and Weiner (2006).

Pure-Play E-Tailers

virtual (pure-play)
e-tailers
Firms that sell directly
to consumers over the
Internet without
maintaining a physical
sales channel.

Virtual (pure-play) e-tailers are firms that sell directly to consumers over the Internet without maintaining a physical sales channel. Amazon.com is a prime example of this type of e-tailer. Virtual e-tailers have the advantage of low overhead costs and streamlined processes. However, one drawback can be a lack of established infrastructure (including logistics) to support the online front-office activities. Virtual e-tailers are *general purpose* or *specialized* e-tailers.

General e-tailers, such as Amazon.com, selling a vast range of goods and services online, capitalize on the Internet to offer such variety to a diverse group of customers geographically without the need to maintain a large physical retail (storefront) network.

Specialty e-tailers can operate in a very narrow market, as does CatToys.com (cattoys.com), described in Online File W3.2, or Rugman.com (rugman.com), which offers more than 12,000 Oriental and Persian rugs online. Such specialized businesses would find it difficult to survive in the physical world because they would not have enough customers and could not hold the variety of stock.

Click-and-Mortar Retailers

**click-and-mortar
retailers**
Brick-and-mortar
retailers that offer a
transactional Web site
from which to conduct
business.

A **click-and-mortar retailer** is a combination of both the brick-and-mortar retailer and an online transactional Web site. Many click-and-mortar retailers started life as a traditional storefront with a physical retail presence only and over time adopted an online transactional capability as well (mortar-only to click-and-mortar; e.g., walmart.com). Another type of click-and-mortar business is a business that started online and then expanded to a physical storefront as well (click-only to click-and-brick; e.g., expedia.com).

**brick-and-mortar
retailers**
Retailers who do
business in the
non-Internet, physical
world in traditional
brick-and-mortar stores.

Brick-and-mortar retailers conduct business in the physical world, in traditional brick-and-mortar stores. Traditional retailing frequently involves a single distribution channel, the physical store. In some cases, traditional sellers also might operate a mail-order business.

**multichannel business
model**
A business model where
a company sells in
multiple marketing
channels simultaneously
(e.g., both physical and
online stores).

In today's digital economy, click-and-mortar retailers sell via stores, through voice phone calls to human operators, over the Internet through interactive Web sites, and via mobile devices. A firm that operates both physical stores and an online e-tail site is said to be a click-and-mortar business selling in a **multichannel business model**. Examples of retailers going from brick-only to brick-and-click are department stores, such as Macy's (macys.com) and Sears (sears.com), as well as discount stores, such as Walmart (walmart.com) and Target (target.com). It also includes supermarkets and all other types of retailing.

Expedia in the travel industry and Dell in the computer industry are examples of companies moving from click-only to click-and-brick.

Retailing in Online Malls

There are two types of online malls, as described in Chapter 2: referring directories and malls with shared shopping services.

Referring Directories. This type of mall is basically a directory organized by product type. Catalog listings or banner ads at the mall site advertise the products or stores. When users click on the product and/or a specific store, they are transferred to the storefront of the seller, where they then complete the transaction. Examples of referring directories can be found at bedandbreakfast.com. The stores listed in a directory either own the site collectively or they pay a subscription fee or a commission to the third party (e.g., a portal) that advertises their logos. This type of e-tailing is basically a kind of affiliate marketing.

Malls with Shared Services. In online malls with shared services, a consumer can find a product, order and pay for it, and arrange for shipment. The hosting mall provides these services.

Ideally, the customer would like to go to different stores in the same mall, use one shopping cart, and pay only once. This arrangement is possible in Yahoo! stores (smallbusiness.yahoo.com/ecommerce). Other examples of malls with shared services are firststopshops.com and bing.com/shopping.

OTHER B2C MODELS AND SPECIAL RETAILING

Several other business models are used in B2C. They are discussed in various places throughout the book. Some of these models also are used in B2B, B2B2C, G2B, and other types of EC. A summary of these other models is provided in Exhibit 3.5.

EXHIBIT 3.5   Other B2C Business Models

Model Name	Description	Revenue Model	Location in Book
Transaction brokers	Electronically mediate between buyers and sellers. Popular in services, the travel industry, the job market, stock trading, and insurance (e.g., Hotels.com).	Transaction fees	Chapter 3
Information portals	Besides information, most portals provide links to merchants, for which they are paid a commission (affiliate marketing). Some provide hosting and software (e.g., *store.yahoo.com*), and some also sell.	Advertising, subscription fees, transaction fees	Chapters 3, 4
Community portal and social networks	Combines community services with selling or affiliate marketing (e.g., *virtualcommunities.start4all.com*). Also see *facebook.com* and *myspace.com*.	Advertising, subscription, affiliate referral fees	Chapters 4, 7
Content creators or disseminators	Provide content to the masses (news, stock data). Also participate in the syndication chain (e.g., *espn.com*, *reuters.com*, and *cnn.com*).	Advertising, subscription fees, affiliate referral fees	Chapters 4, 7
Viral marketing	Use e-mail or SMS to advertise. Also can sell direct or via affiliates (e.g., *blueskyfrog.com*).	Sales of goods and services	Chapters 4, 7
Market makers	Create and manage many-to-many markets (e.g., *chemconnect.com*); also auction sites (e.g., *ebay.com* and *dellauction.com*). Aggregate buyers and/or sellers (e.g., *ingrammicro.com*).	Transaction fees	Chapter 5
Make (build)-to-order	Manufacturers that customize their products and services via online orders (e.g., *dell.com*, *nike.com*, and *jaguar.com*).	Sales of goods	Chapters 1–3, 5
B2B2C	Manufacturer sells to a business, but delivers to individual customers (*godiva.com*).	Sales of goods and services	Chapters 2, 3
Service providers	Offer online payments, order fulfillment (delivery), and security (e.g., *paypal.com* and *escrow.com*).	Sales of services	Chapter 10

Online Group Buying

In these depressed economic times, more people are using the Internet as a smart way to save money. Using online group buying, it is easy to quickly find people to share freight costs and buy in bulk so as to lower prices. It is also easier to get larger discounts when more people take part in a group purchase (see *Taipei Times* 2009 for details).

B2C IN SOCIAL NETWORKS

B2C sites such as Amazon.com (amazon.com) and Netflix (netflix.com) provide consumers with rich social context and relevancy to the purchases that they are making. The companies have promoted three activities that shoppers can do collectively via wikis, blogs, and other online tools: find, collect, and share/recommend. These three acts comprise the phenomenon of online group shopping. Such sites have a mechanism for intergroup feedback in that they allow users to leave a short review of the product they bought as well as the services obtained from the sellers. Meanwhile, other participants rely on group members who have previously rated the product/service and/or seller. B2C e-commerce relies on word of mouth among social network participants.

B2C in virtual worlds is also becoming popular. An example of this is the Dell Island in Second Life. Dell created a store on an island inside Second Life. Through the store it sells virtual computers for use in Second Life and real computers for use in real life, engaging users and fostering user interaction with each other and the products in the virtual world, which leads to purchases in the real world (Brown 2009).

Virtual Shopping

For the first few years e-commerce was taking hold, it was challenging for sites to get close to delivering the in-store experience online. But the much more intangible brick-and-mortar quality has been the fact that 85 percent of all purchases are made at the shelf, making impulse buys found money for retailers. Many consumers embrace impulse buying because they get interesting products they'd never have bought if they hadn't seen them. Theoretically, shoppers in a fully virtual 3D Second Life–like environment could get the same benefits.

One aspect of 3D is its ability to put dimensions and shape into a more physical context. A fully digitized depiction of a house interior could take the guesswork out of determining whether a large-screen television would fit in the intended space. Consider a consumer shopping for a home entertainment system drags a 3D CAD/CAM representation of his home to a consumer electronics e-commerce site. This large digital file includes window placements, the style and thickness of the rug and wall coverings, and a database that associates those items with their likely sound-dampening characteristics. Moving furniture around the room becomes a simple point and click. 3D applications could take the guesswork out of buying and installing home entertainment systems, as well as home furnishings, decorating, renovations, and so forth. See *Baseline* (2007) for details.

Section 3.2 ▶ REVIEW QUESTIONS

1. List the B2C distribution channel models.
2. Describe how mail-order firms are going online.
3. Describe the direct marketing model used by manufacturers.
4. Describe virtual e-tailing.
5. Describe the click-and-mortar approach.
6. Describe e-malls.
7. Describe B2C activities in social networks.

3.3 TRAVEL AND TOURISM (HOSPITALITY) SERVICES ONLINE

Some major travel-related Web sites are expedia.com, travelocity.com, and priceline.com. Online travel services also are provided by all major airlines (e.g., britishairways.com); vacation services (e.g., blue-hawaii.com); trains (e.g., amtrak.com); car rental agencies (e.g., autoeurope.com); hotels (e.g., marriott.com); commercial portals (e.g., cnn.com/travel); and tour companies (e.g., atlastravelweb.com). Publishers of travel guides such as Lonely Planet (lonelyplanet.com) provide considerable amounts of travel-related information on their Web sites, as well as selling travel services there.

The revenue models of online travel services include direct revenues (commissions), revenue from advertising, lead-generation payments, consultancy fees, subscription or membership fees, revenue-sharing fees, and more. With such rapid growth and success, the travel industry seems to have matured beyond initial concerns such as trust, loyalty, and brand image. However, competition among online travel e-tailers is fierce, with low margins, little customer loyalty, and increasing commoditization of products and services. Thus, guaranteed best rates and various loyalty programs are likely to be popular ways of affecting customer behavior.

Three important trends will drive further changes in the online travel industry. First, online travel agents may try to differentiate themselves through customer-service messaging and other related services, presenting themselves as adding value to the customer. Second, the number of travel meta search facilities, or "travel bots"— online sites or services that search through a range of related sites to find the best price or compare the value of travel products for a consumer—is likely to increase. Third, online travel companies are likely to increasingly use the growing phenomenon of social networking sites (such as myspace.com) to provide content to would-be travelers and also use these sites to study the behavior of potential customers (see discussion later in this section).

SERVICES PROVIDED

Virtual travel agencies offer almost all the services delivered by conventional travel agencies, from providing general information to reserving and purchasing tickets, accommodations, and entertainment. In addition, they often provide services that most conventional travel agencies do not offer, such as travel tips, fare tracking (free e-mail alerts on low fares to and from a city and favorite destinations), experts' opinions, detailed driving maps and directions within the United States and several other countries (see infohub.com), and chat rooms and bulletin boards. In addition, some offer several other innovative services, such as online travel auctions.

SPECIAL SERVICES ONLINE

Many online travel services offer travel bargains. Consumers can go to special sites, such as those offering standby tickets, to find bargain fares. Lastminute.com (lastminute.com) offers very low airfares and discounted accommodation prices to fill otherwise-empty seats and hotel rooms. Last-minute trips also can be booked on americanexpress.com, sometimes at a steep discount. Special vacation destinations can be found at priceline.com, stayfinder.com, and greatrentals.com. Flights.com (flights.com) offers cheap tickets and also Eurail passes. Travelers can access cybercaptive.com for a list of thousands of Internet cafés around the world. Similar information is available via many portals, such as Yahoo! and MSN.

Also of interest are sites that offer medical advice and services for travelers. This type of information is available from the World Health Organization (who.int), governments (e.g., cdc.gov/travel), and private organizations (e.g., tripprep.com, medicalert.org, and webmd.com).

Other special services include:

▶ **Wireless services.** Several airlines (e.g., Cathay Pacific, Delta, and Qantas) allow customers with cell phones with Internet access to check their flight status, update frequent flyer miles, and book flights.

▶ **Direct marketing.** Airlines sell electronic tickets over the Internet. When customers purchase electronic tickets online (or by phone), all they have to do is print the boarding pass from their computer's printer or upon arrival at the airport enter their credit card at an *electronic kiosk* to get a boarding pass.

▶ **Alliances and consortia.** Airlines and other travel companies are creating alliances to increase sales or reduce purchasing costs. For example, some consortia aggregate only fares purchased over the Internet.

Travel-Oriented Social Networks

Since 2005, online leisure travelers' use of social computing technologies, such as blogs, RSS, wikis, and user reviews, for researching travel has skyrocketed. Travel e-businesses, marketing executives, and managers realized that social computing was increasingly playing a larger role in corporate online strategy, even if all a company did was monitor what travelers were saying about a certain company in third-party forums.

As travelers forge connections and share information with like-minded travelers online, their needs and expectations change. They want more relevance and more correct information. Social computing has shifted online travel from passive selling to active customer engagement, which affects how travel companies and agents distribute and market their products. Several social networks have travel channels that cater to travelers. Examples of such networks are wikitravel.org and world66.com, which features a travel channel. Wikitravel was built in order to make it easy to share travel knowledge and let others share it. The site uses a wiki that allows any Internet reader to create, update, edit, and illustrate *any* article on the Web site. World66 believes that travelers are the best source of travel information. It is an open content travel guide, where people from all over the world can write about the places they love, hotels they stayed in, or restaurants where they have eaten. Every part of the travel guide can be directly edited. Case 3.1 shows an example of a social network for travelers.

BENEFITS AND LIMITATIONS OF ONLINE TRAVEL SERVICES

The benefits of online travel services to travelers are enormous. The amount of free information is tremendous, and it is accessible at any time from any place. Substantial discounts can be found, especially for those who have time and patience to search for them. Providers of travel services also benefit: Airlines, hotels, and cruise lines are selling otherwise-empty spaces. Also, direct selling saves the provider's commission and its processing.

Online travel services do have some limitations. First, many people do not use the Internet. Second, the amount of time and the difficulty of using virtual travel agencies can be significant, especially for complex trips and for inexperienced Internet surfers. Finally, complex trips or those that require stopovers might not be available online

EC Application
WAYN: A SOCIAL NETWORK FOR TRAVELERS

WAYN (which stands for "Where Are You Now?") is a social networking Web site (*wayn.com*) with a goal of uniting travelers from around the world. WAYN was launched in London in May 2003. It has grown from 45,000 to about 15 million members as of 2009, adding 20,000 new members each day. Approximately 2 million members are based in the United Kingdom. It also is strong in the United States, Canada, Australia, New Zealand, and countries in Western Europe.

As with many other social networking services, WAYN enables its users to create a personal profile and upload and store photos. Users can then search for others with similar profiles and link them to their profiles as friends. It also is possible to send and receive messages using discussion forums. Because it is designed for travelers, members are able to search for contacts based on a particular location. Using a world map, users can visually locate where each of their contacts is situated around the world. The goal of the service is for members to keep friends informed of where they are while traveling and, in turn, to be able to locate their friends.

In addition, users can send SMSs to any of their contacts worldwide, chat online using WAYN's Instant Messenger, and plan trips and notify their friends about them. Using WAYN, users can create discussion groups, ask for recommendations, and send smiley icons to all. Finally, chat bots (avatars) are dynamic and fully active,

representing one of the best ways of meeting people in the WAYN community.

WAYN is one of the very few sites that did not lose new subscriptions after introducing fees for its premier membership service, making it one of the few social networking communities that managed to quickly become profitable.

WAYN is now popular in 220 countries, becoming a global brand. It is not aimed at any particular age group, but it seems to be most popular with the 18-to-25 age group. It also has a strong position among the 35-to-45-plus age group. Members can find out who will be traveling to their next intended destination, at the same time as they are. The WAYN VIP Club, which offers 100 free international SMSs per month, has the ability to create private forums and other benefits.

Sources: Butcher (2008), *wayn.com* (accessed November 2009), and *en.wikipedia.org/wiki/WAYN* (accessed November 2009).

Questions

1. Visit *wayn.com*. What options do you find most exciting on the site?

2. Why has WAYN been so successful even though the site requires subscription fees?

because they require specialized knowledge and arrangements, which may be better done by a knowledgeable, human travel agent. Therefore, the need for travel agents as intermediaries remains, at least for the immediate future.

CORPORATE TRAVEL

The corporate travel market is huge and has been growing rapidly in recent years. Corporations can use all the travel services mentioned earlier. However, many large corporations receive additional services from large travel agencies. To reduce corporate travel costs, companies can make arrangements that enable employees to plan and book their own trips. Using online optimization tools provided by travel companies, such as those offered by American Express (americanexpress.com), companies can try to reduce travel costs even further. Travel authorization software that checks availability of funds and compliance with corporate guidelines is usually provided by travel companies such as American Express. Expedia (expedia.com), Travelocity (travelocity.com), and Orbitz (orbitz.com) also offer software tools for corporate planning and booking.

An example of how a major corporation uses online corporate travel services is described in Online File W3.3. For further discussion, see B2B travel in Chapter 5.

Note: A major issue emerged in 2009 when about 50 municipalities filed a class action suit against the online travel companies demanding the imposition of a fuel tax on the discounted fares (the travel companies pay a discount price). For details, see Bowling (2009).

Section 3.3 ▶ REVIEW QUESTIONS

1. What travel services are available online that are not available offline?
2. List the benefits of online travel services to travelers and to service providers.
3. How do social networks facilitate travel?
4. Describe corporate online travel services.

3.4 EMPLOYMENT PLACEMENT AND THE JOB MARKET ONLINE

The online job market connects individuals who are looking for a job with employers who are looking for employees with specific skills. It is a very popular approach, and, increasingly, both job seekers and prospective employers are turning away from traditional print-based advertising and recruitment methods in preference of online advertisements and recruitment activities. In addition to online job ads and placement services available through specialized Web sites (such as careerbuilder.com), larger companies are increasingly building career portals on their corporate Web sites as a way of trimming recruitment costs and reducing the time to fill vacancies. Advantages of the online job market over the traditional one are listed in Exhibit 3.6.

THE INTERNET JOB MARKET

The Internet offers a rich environment for job seekers and for companies searching for hard-to-find employees. Nearly all *Fortune* 500 companies now use the Internet for some of their recruitment activities, and studies reveal that online resources are now the most popular way to find suitably qualified applicants for job vacancies. Online job recruitment revenues and volume overtook print ad classifieds and in 2008 were estimated to reach $6 billion (Fisher 2008). More than 40,000 online job boards are now operating in the United States.

EXHIBIT 3.6 Traditional Versus Online Job Markets

Characteristic	Traditional Job Market	Online Job Market
Cost	Expensive, especially in prime space	Can be very inexpensive
Life cycle	Short	Long
Place	Usually local and limited if global	Global
Context updating	Can be complex, expensive	Fast, simple, inexpensive
Space for details	Limited	Large
Ease of search by applicant	Difficult, especially for out-of-town applicants	Quick and easy
Ability of employers to find applicants	May be very difficult, especially for out-of-town applicants	Easy
Matching of supply and demand	Difficult	Easy
Reliability	Material can be lost in mail	High
Communication speed between employees and employers	Can be slow	Fast
Ability of employees to compare jobs	Limited	Easy, fast

The U.S. market is dominated by three major players: Monster, Careerbuilder, and Yahoo! HotJobs, which together comprise about 55 percent of the market.

The following parties use the Internet job market:

> **Job seekers.** Job seekers can reply to employment ads. Or, they can take the initiative and place their résumés on their own homepages or on others' Web sites, send messages to members of newsgroups asking for referrals, and use the sites of recruiting firms, such as careerbuilder.com, hotjobs.yahoo.com, and monster.com. For entry-level jobs and internships for newly minted graduates, job seekers can go to collegerecruiter.com. Job seekers can also assess their market value in different U.S. cities at wageweb.com and use the Web to compare salaries and conditions, obtain information about employers, and get career advice. Passive job seekers, those just keeping an eye on opportunities, are using this medium, as well as those actively seeking new employment.

> **Employers seeking employees.** Many organizations, including public institutions, advertise openings on their Web sites. Others advertise job openings on popular public portals, online newspapers, bulletin boards, and with recruiting firms. Employers can conduct interviews and administer interactive intelligence, skills, and psychological tests on the Web. Forty percent of large U.S. firms are using computerized assessments to screen new hires or to identify up-and-comers for training and development (AlexFrankel.com 2008). The tests are designed to predict success by measuring behavioral or personality traits and comparing a candidate's profile with those of people who have succeeded in similar jobs. LinkedIn offers several tools that help recruiters to find employees registered at the site. Also see Yahoo!'s Resumix (at viviente.com/resumix/website).

> **Classified ads.** Classified ads for job openings and job seekers are available at craigslist.org, kijiji.com, webclassifieds.us, and in the online classified sections of many newspapers. Also, several social networks, including Facebook, allow posting of job openings.

> **Job agencies.** Hundreds of job agencies are active on the Web. They use their own Web pages to post available job descriptions and advertise their services in e-mails and at other Web sites. Job agencies and/or employers use newsgroups, online forums, bulletin boards, Internet commercial résumé services, and portals such as Yahoo! HotJobs and AOL. Most portals are free; others, such as MktgLadder (marketing-jobs.theladders.com), charge membership fees but offer many services.

> **Government agencies and institutions.** Many government agencies advertise openings for positions on their Web sites and on other sites; some are required by law to do so. In addition, some government agencies use the Internet to help job seekers find jobs elsewhere, as is done in Hong Kong and the Philippines. An initiative by the Australian Government, Jobsearch (jobsearch.gov.au), the largest free job board in Australia, offers free advertising to employers. It claims the largest candidate database in Australia and has over 1 million visitors per month, with an average of 80,000 jobs on offer at any one time. It links this online presence to an Australia-wide network of touch-screen kiosks. Employers are notified when a candidate's résumé matches an advertised job (*Workplace.gov.au* 2009).

Online Job Markets on Social Networking

In today's age of Web 2.0, the wide reach of social networking sites such as MySpace and LinkedIn can get people hired faster. As demonstrated in Exhibit 3.7, job referral social networking sites (e.g., jobster.com and bluechipexpert.com) solve the problem of finding the right people for the job in hours. The sites provide job seekers opportunities to promote their areas of expertise as well as help them get "found" by employers. The added incentive of getting paid for every successful referral makes it even more worthwhile to join these networks. The site's algorithms enable headhunters to sort qualified applicants by different criteria. When an offer is made, the job referral site receives payment on behalf of the employees, including a referral fee. Social networking commerce has certainly found its niche in the online job recruitment industry. While recruits text message thank-yous to hiring managers, mostly not well received, some recruiters are offering Facebook "friend" invitations to candidates they have interviewed (Bowers 2008).

Global Online Portals

The Internet is very helpful for anyone looking for a job in another country. An interesting global portal for Europe is described in Online File W3.4. An interesting global site for placing/finding jobs in different countries is xing.com (see Internet Exercise 8).

EXHIBIT 3.7   The Referral Power of Social Networks in Job Matching

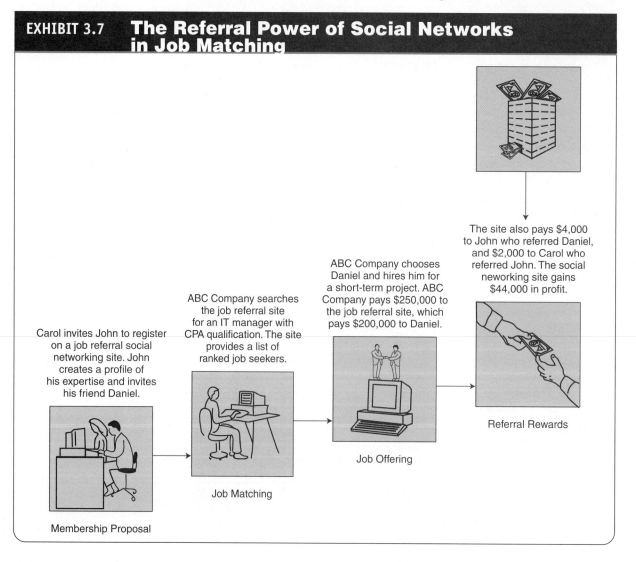

The site also pays $4,000 to John who referred Daniel, and $2,000 to Carol who referred John. The social neworking site gains $44,000 in profit.

ABC Company chooses Daniel and hires him for a short-term project. ABC Company pays $250,000 to the job referral site, which pays $200,000 to Daniel.

ABC Company searches the job referral site for an IT manager with CPA qualification. The site provides a list of ranked job seekers.

Carol invites John to register on a job referral social networking site. John creates a profile of his expertise and invites his friend Daniel.

Referral Rewards

Job Offering

Job Matching

Membership Proposal

Insights and Additions 3.2 Social Networking Sites for Business Professionals

Many business professionals use sites like LinkedIn, Twitter, and Facebook to promote their businesses. With the growing use of social networking by business professionals, there is a growing number of social networking sites focused on business users and meeting their needs. Some representative sites are:

▶ **Biznik** (*biznik.com*). Biznik is community of entrepreneurs and small businesses dedicated to helping each other succeed through the premise that collaboration beats competition. The site embraces people who are building real businesses, not looking for their next job. It's for sharing your ideas, not posting your résumé. All Biznik members use their real names, and provide real data. Biznik editors review profiles for compliance with this policy. It's the place where real conversations about small business and entrepreneurship are taking place. Biznik is not just online; it includes face-to-face meetings in order to build real, lasting business relationships.

▶ **E.Factor** (*efactor.com*). Over 750,000 members in 153 countries and 99 industries use this global network made by and for entrepreneurs. Members connect with like-minded people and investors.

▶ **Ecademy** (*ecademy.com*). Ecademy is a business network for creating contacts and sharing knowledge. Free membership allows you to introduce yourself by creating your profile, finding friends and colleagues, searching for new contacts, making new contacts by building your network, joining and/or running groups, commenting on blogs, and attending networking events. Higher levels of membership allow you to build trust by displaying a SafeNetworking badge on your profile when your identity has been verified; get found on Google when your profile and content is indexed by all major search engines; build your brand by hosting your own blog, posting Marketplace Adverts, and using advanced social media tools; and much more.

▶ **LinkedIn** (*linkedin.com*). More than 45 million professionals use LinkedIn to exchange information, ideas, and opportunities. Members can reconnect with past colleagues and classmates quickly, connect with current colleagues, and power their careers by finding connections when looking for a job or new business opportunity. They complete and update profiles that help recruiters find jobs or businesses related to individual careers, get recommendations on their personal profile to help make the best impression possible, and add connections to people within organizations they are interested in joining. LinkedIn Answers is a network of industry experts willing to share advice—just ask the question.

▶ **Xing.com** (*xing.com*). More than 8 million members from over 200 countries using 16 languages find XING a powerful tool for doing business and promoting their careers. XING makes networking and professional contact management simple, with made-to-measure networking functions and services. The site shows you how people are connected, which is an excellent tool in generating new contacts of your own.

A similar service is provided by linkedin.com. The electronic job market can also create high turnover costs for employers by accelerating employees' movement to better jobs. Finally, finding candidates online is more complicated than most people think, mostly due to the large number of résumés available online. The LinkedIn search engine can help employers quickly find the appropriate candidate. For more on social network sites for business professionals see Insights and Additions 3.2.

BENEFITS AND LIMITATIONS OF THE ELECTRONIC JOB MARKET

As indicated earlier, the electronic job market offers a variety of benefits for both job seekers and employers. These major advantages are shown in Exhibit 3.8.

Probably the biggest limitation of the online job market is the fact that some people do not use and do not have access to the Internet, although this problem has declined substantially. Nonetheless, the potential for an ever-increasing gap between those with skills and access to the Internet and those without is of concern. To overcome this problem, companies might use both traditional advertising approaches and the Internet. However, the trend is clear: Over time, more and more of the job market will be on the

| EXHIBIT 3.8 | **Advantages of the Electronic Job Market for Job Seekers and Employers** |

Advantages for Job Seekers	Advantages for Employers
Can find information on a large number of jobs worldwide	Can learn how to use their voice effectively in an interview (*greatvoice.com*)
Can communicate quickly with potential employers	Can access newsgroups that are dedicated to finding jobs (and keeping them)
Can market themselves directly to potential employers (e.g., *quintcareers.com*)	Can advertise to a large number of job seekers
Can write and post résumés for large-volume distribution (e.g., Personal Search Agent at *careerbuilder.com*, *brassring.com*)	Can save on advertisement costs
	Can reduce application-processing costs by using electronic application forms
Can search for jobs quickly from any location	Can provide greater equal opportunity for job seekers
Can obtain several support services at no cost (e.g., *hotjobs.yahoo.com* and *monster.com* provide free career-planning services)	Increased chance of finding highly skilled employees
	Can describe positions in great detail
	Can conduct interviews online (using video teleconferencing)
Can assess their market value (e.g., *wageweb.com* and *rileyguide.org* look for salary surveys)	Can arrange for testing online
	Can view salary surveys for recruiting strategies

Internet. One solution to the problem of limited access is the use of in-store Internet kiosks, as used by companies such as Home Depot or Macy's.

Security and privacy are another limitation. Résumés and other online communications are usually not encrypted, so one's job-seeking activities might not be secure, and thus confidentiality and data protection cannot be guaranteed. It also is possible that someone at a job seeker's current place of employment (possibly even his or her boss) might find out that that person is job hunting. LinkedIn, for example, provides protection of privacy, enabling job seekers to determine who can see their résumé online.

Section 3.4 ▶ REVIEW QUESTIONS

1. What are the driving forces of the electronic job market?
2. What are the major advantages of the electronic job market to the candidate? To employers?
3. Why is LinkedIn so useful for job seekers and for employees?

3.5 REAL ESTATE, INSURANCE, AND STOCK TRADING ONLINE

Online service industries are exploding on the Internet and are being embraced by customers. Internet and related technologies are more than just new distribution channels. They are a different way of providing these services. The major services are presented in this and the following section.

REAL ESTATE ONLINE

Changes in real estate transactions are reaching a tipping point, beyond which the nature of the business will be altered.

To get some idea of the changes, consider the following statistics. Borrell Associates forecasts that by 2013, 33.1 percent of a projected $35.3 billion in real estate–related advertising will be spent online, compared with online's 19.6 percent market share in 2005. Online advertising by real estate–related companies and mortgage lenders grew by nearly 20 percent in 2007 but will see slower growth during the current economic downturn (Ahorre.com 2009). The increase in Internet real estate advertising is understandably influencing buying behavior. Studies by the National Association of Realtors (NAR) have shown that over 80 percent of real estate buyers begin their searches for properties on the Internet (*Realtors Magazine* 2009).

In the face of such increases in consumer knowledge and control of the early parts of the identification and purchase of properties, some U.S. realtors have tried to restrict public access to some of the databases of properties, such as the local Multiple Listing Services. In many localities, local brokers have tried to restrict access to such databases to members of a professional association, such as the NAR.

In summary, e-commerce and the Internet are slowly but surely having an ever-increasing impact on the real estate industry. For example, despite the changes that are beginning to emerge, real estate agents have not been disintermediated. Home buyers today tend to use both real estate agents and the Internet. Thus, despite the fact that the Internet is shaking up the real estate industry, the emerging pattern is more complex than the simple disintermediation of agents, but their commission percentage starts to decline as more buyers find sales on the Internet.

Zillow, Craigslist, and Other Web 2.0 Real Estate Services

Craigslist and Zillow are examples of Web 2.0 free real estate services that have been intended to disintermediate unnecessary middlemen, such as newspaper and classified advertising.

Zillow (zillow.com) operates the "Make Me Move" function that allows users to shop for homes that are not necessarily for sale. Home owners who may have no intention of moving, but who certainly would for the right price, can list information about their homes on "Make Me Move" so that gutsy buyers can try to make a deal. A home owner can post a "Make Me Move" price without exposing any personal information. Zillow then enables interested buyers to contact the owner through an e-mail "anonymizer." The service is free. The company also provides free listings for all home owners and realtors. Listings can include photos, and realtors can also create Web sites for each listing. Another Web 2.0 function of Zillow is the Real Estate wiki, which has hundreds of articles on buying, selling, financing, or any topic an owner/buyer might need. Wiki visitors can edit or comment on articles or create new articles.

Craigslist (craigslist.org) has become a powerhouse site for advertising real estate listings, with more and more agents turning to the site for added exposure to buyers looking online. Property listings are free to list on Craigslist in all markets except New York, where brokers must pay $10 per listing. For more about real estate applications and services offered online, see Online File W3.5.

INSURANCE ONLINE

An increasing number of companies use the Internet to offer standard insurance policies, such as auto, home, life, or health, at a substantial discount, mostly to individuals. Furthermore, third-party aggregators offer free comparisons of available policies. Several large insurance and risk-management companies offer comprehensive insurance contracts online. Although many people do not trust the faceless insurance agent, others are eager to take advantage of the reduced premiums. For example, a visit to insurance.com will show a variety of different policies. At answerfinancial.com customers and businesses can compare car insurance offerings and then make a purchase online. At globaltravelinsurance.com, customers can book travel insurance. Another popular insurance site is insweb.com. Many insurance companies use a dual strategy, keeping human agents but also selling online. Like the real estate brokers, insurance brokers send unsolicited e-mails to millions of people. It is estimated that Web insurance transactions cost about 50¢ each to process, compared with up to $8 for those that are paper-based (McDougall 2007). The stiff competition will reduce the commission for the remaining agents.

ONLINE STOCK TRADING

The commission for an online trade is between $1 and $19, compared with an average fee of $100 from a full-service broker and $25 from a non-Internet discount broker. With online trading, there are no busy telephone lines, and the chance for error is small, because there is no oral communication in a frequently noisy environment. Orders can be placed from anywhere, at any time, day or night, and there is no biased broker to push a sale. Furthermore, investors can find a considerable amount of free research information about specific companies or mutual funds. Many services are provided to online traders, including online statements, tax-related calculations, extensive research on industries, real-time news, and even tutoring on how to trade.

Several discount brokerage houses initiated extensive online stock trading, notably Charles Schwab in 1995. Full-service brokerage companies, such as Merrill Lynch, followed in 1998–1999. By 2009, 97 percent of stock trades are executed automatically via the electronic communications networks including the Internet (Stokes 2009).

How does online trading work? Let's say an investor has an account with Schwab. The investor accesses Schwab's Web site (schwab.com), enters an account number and password, and clicks stock trading. Using a menu, the investor enters the details of the order (buy, sell, margin or cash, price limit, or market order). The computer tells the investor the current (real-time) "ask" and "bid" prices, much as a broker would do over the telephone, and the investor can approve or reject the transaction. The flow chart of this process is shown in Exhibit 3.9.

Some companies, including Schwab, are now also licensed as exchanges. This allows them to match the selling and buying orders of their own customers for many securities in one to two seconds. Some well-known companies that offer online trading are E*TRADE and Ameritrade.

E*TRADE is expanding rapidly into several countries, enabling global stock trading. In 2009, E*TRADE started allowing customers to trade online in seven different countries, taking care of the currency exchange rate.

With the rapid pace of adoption of mobile handsets, mobile banking will become more and more popular. Mobile banking services enable users to receive information on their account balances via SMS and to settle payments for bills and purchase stocks. See Online File W3.6 for more on investment information available online.

The Risk of Trading in an Online Stock Account

The major risk of online trading is security. Although all trading sites require users to have an ID and password, problems may still occur. For example, in 2004 it was discovered that hackers could steal users' ID numbers and passwords when they used the Windows operating system. The problem has been corrected. Problems of this nature also can occur when conducting online trading or online banking, our next topic.

EXHIBIT 3.9   Online Electronic Stock Trading

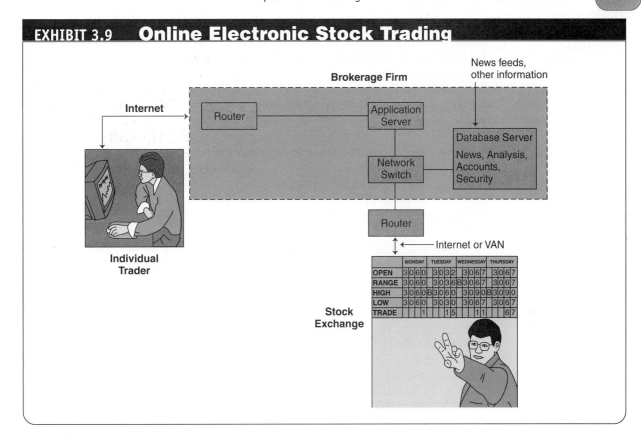

Section 3.5 ▶ REVIEW QUESTIONS

1. List the major online real estate applications.
2. What are the advantages of selling insurance online?
3. What are the advantages of online stock tracking?
4. What are some of the risks of trading stocks online?

3.6 BANKING AND PERSONAL FINANCE ONLINE

Electronic (online) banking, or **e-banking,** also known as cyberbanking, virtual banking, or home banking, includes various banking activities conducted via the Internet from home, business, or on the road rather than at a physical bank location. Consumers can use e-banking to check their accounts, pay bills online, secure a loan electronically, and much more. The credit crisis of 2007, banking collapses of 2008, and the resulting recession caused consumers to watch their spending more closely, fueling a desire for efficient but elegant online banking, bill pay, and personal finance management tools. Eight out of 10 online households now bank online. Paying bills online is now a routine practice for Americans. Javelin's 2009 survey data indicates that 70 percent of households paid a bill online in the previous month either through a financial institution, a biller, or both (Javelin Strategy and Research 2009).

electronic (online) banking or e-banking Various banking activities conducted from home or the road using an Internet connection; also known as cyberbanking, virtual banking, online banking, and home banking.

E-banking saves users time and money. For banks, it offers an inexpensive alternative to branch banking and a chance to enlist remote customers. Many physical banks now offer home banking services, and some use EC as a major competitive strategy. One such U.S. bank is Wells Fargo (wellsfargo.com). In Hong Kong, a leading bank is the Bank of East Asia (hkbea-cyberbanking.com). HSBC offers savings CDs online as well as checking accounts in the United States. Many banks offer wireless services.

An emerging innovation in online banking is peer-to-peer (P2P) online lending. Two examples are Zopa in the United Kingdom and Prosper in the United States, which offer P2P online lending (see Chapter 7). Note that despite the global credit crunch of 2008–2009 and the fact that neither has a government-backed guarantee, Zopa and Prosper are enjoying a boom. For example, in the third quarter of 2008 new borrowers of Zopa increased by nearly 50 percent, to 3,700, compared with the previous quarter (Keegan 2008). The default rate of these P2P lenders is very low, because the borrowers and the lenders know each other through social networking. Disintermediation of the banks also allows the lenders to get much more and the borrowers to pay much less.

Online banking has not only been embraced in the developed world; it is becoming an enabling feature of business growth in the developing world. For example, online banking in China is increasing rapidly in popularity, especially among China's new educated middle class in the developed cities. Consequently, the overall turnover of online banking activities is also growing rapidly. Many large and global corporations expect their businesses to become click-and-mortar banks.

The Bank of China and the China Merchants Bank started their online banking service in 1998. These online service offerings were followed by online offerings by China's other major banks and a number of smaller banks. These services have been enthusiastically embraced by China's new business classes.

HOME BANKING CAPABILITIES

Banking applications can be divided into the following categories: informational, administrative, transactional, portal, and others (see Exhibit 3.10). They also found that the larger the bank, the more services that were offered online.

Electronic banking offers several of the EC benefits listed in Chapter 1, both to the banks and to their customers, such as expanding the bank's customer base and saving on the cost of paper transactions.

VIRTUAL BANKS

In addition to regular banks adding online services, *virtual banks* have emerged; these have no physical location but only conduct online transactions. Security First Network Bank (SFNB) was the first such bank to offer secure banking transactions on the Web. Amid the consolidation that has taken place in the banking industry, SFNB has since been purchased and now is a part of RBC Centura (rbccentura.com). Another representative virtual bank in the United States is First Internet Bank (firstib.com). Virtual banks exist in many other countries (e.g., bankdirect.co.nz). In some countries, virtual banks are involved in stock trading, and some stockbrokers are doing online banking (e.g., see etrade.com). More than 97 percent of the hundreds of pure-play virtual banks failed by 2003 due to a lack of financial viability. Many more failed during 2007–2008. The most successful banks seem to be of the click-and-mortar type.

EXHIBIT 3.10 Online Banking Applications

Application Type	Information/Services Provided
Informational	General bank information and history
	Financial education information
	Employment information
	Interest rate quotes
	Financial calculators
	Current bank and local news
Administrative	Account information access
	Opening of new account online
	Applications for services
	Moving all banking online
	Personal finance software applications
Transactional	Account transfer capabilities
	Transfer funds housed at different financial institutions
	Bill-pay services
	Corporate services (e.g., cash management, treasury)
	Online insurance services
	Online brokerage services
	Real-time funds transfer
	Online trust services
Portal	Links to financial information
	Links to community information
	Links to local business
	Links to nonlocal businesses (and/or advertisers)
Others	Wireless capabilities
	Search function

Sources: Compiled from Acharya et al. (2008) and Cash Edge (2006).

A word of caution about virtual banking: Before sending money to any cyberbank, especially those that promise high interest rates for your deposits, make sure that the bank is a legitimate one. Several cases of fraud already have occurred.

INTERNATIONAL AND MULTIPLE-CURRENCY BANKING

International banking and the ability to handle trades in multiple currencies are critical for international trading. Although some international retail purchasing can be done by providing a credit card number, other transactions may require international banking support. Examples of such cross-border support include the following:

▶ TradeCard and MasterCard have developed a multiple-currency system for global transactions (see tradecard.com).
▶ Bank of America (bankofamerica.com) and most other major banks offer international capital funds, cash management, trades and services, foreign exchange, risk management investments, merchant services, and special services for international traders.
▶ Fxall.com is a multidealer foreign exchange service that enables faster and cheaper foreign exchange transactions. Special services are being established for stock market traders who need to pay for foreign stocks (e.g., at Charles Schwab or E*TRADE).

ONLINE FINANCIAL TRANSACTION IMPLEMENTATION ISSUES

As one would expect, the implementation of online banking and online stock trading can be interrelated. In many instances, one financial institution offers both services. The following are some other implementation issues for online financial transactions.

Securing Financial Transactions

Financial transactions for home banking and online trading must be very secure. In Chapter 10, we discuss the details of secure EC payment systems. In Case 3.2, we give an example of how a bank provides security and privacy to its customers.

CASE 3.2
EC Application

SECURITY FOR ONLINE BANK TRANSACTIONS

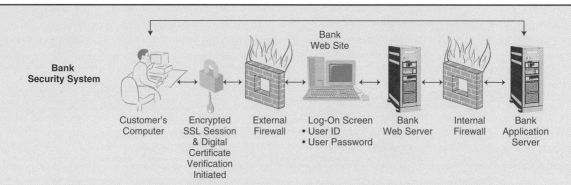

Banks provide extensive security to their customers. The following describes some of the safeguards provided.

Customers accessing a bank system from the outside must go through encryption provided by SSL (Secure Socket Layer) and digital certificate verification (see Chapter 9). The verification process assures users each time they sign on that they are indeed connected to their specific bank. The customer inquiry message then goes through an external firewall. Once the log-on screen is reached, a user ID and a password are required. This information flows through a direct Web server and then goes through an internal firewall to the bank's application server.

Information is shared among a bank's family of partners only for legitimate business purposes. Sharing information with outside companies is done with extreme care.

Banks do not capture information provided by customers when conducting "what-if" scenarios using planning tools (to ensure privacy). Most banks use cookies to learn about their customers; however, customers can control both the collection and use of the information. In addition, most banks provide suggestions on how users can increase security (e.g., "Use a browser with 128-bit encryption").

With the increased use of mobile devices (Chapter 8), the threat of security risks has increased. Banks are coming up with innovative solutions. For example, in January 2009 Bank of America introduced its "Safe Pass Card," a device that can generate a six-digit, one-time pass code that is necessary to complete an online transaction. The pass code is delivered via a text message to your mobile device.

Sources: Compiled from various security statements of online bank Web sites, including *co-operativebank.co.uk* (accessed November 2009) and *anz.com* (accessed November 2009).

Questions

1. Why is security so important for a bank?
2. Why is there a need for two firewalls?
3. Who is protected by the bank's security system—the customer, the bank, or both? Elaborate.
4. What might be the limitations of such a system?

Imaging Systems

Several financial institutions (e.g., Bank of America and Citibank) allow customers to view images of all of their incoming checks, invoices, and other related online correspondence. Image access can be simplified with the help of a search engine.

Fees Online Versus Fees for Offline Services

Computer-based banking services are offered free by some banks, whereas others charge $5 to $10 a month. Also, some banks charge fees for individual transactions (e.g., fee per check, per transfer, and so on). Financial institutions must carefully think through the pricing of online and offline services. Fee issues must take into account the costs of providing the different types of services, the organization's desire to attract new customers, and the prices offered by competitors.

Risks

Online banks, as well as click-and-mortar banks, might carry some risks and problems, especially in international banking. The first risk that most people think of is the risk of hackers getting into their account. In addition, some believe that virtual banks carry *liquidity* risk (the risk of not having sufficient funds to pay obligations as they come due) and could be more susceptible to panic withdrawals. Regulators are grappling with the safeguards that need to be imposed on e-banking.

ONLINE BILLING AND BILL PAYING

The era of e-payment is around the corner. The number of checks the U.S. Federal Reserve System processes has been decreasing while the volume of commercial automated clearinghouse (ACH) transactions has been increasing. Many people prefer to pay monthly bills, such as telephone, utilities, rent, credit cards, cable, and so on, online. The recipients of such payments are equally eager to receive money online because online payments are received much more regularly and quickly and have lower processing costs.

Another method to pay bills over the Internet is electronic bill presentment and payments (EBPP). With this method, the consumer makes payments at each biller's Web site either with a credit card or by giving the biller enough information to complete an electronic withdrawal directly from the consumer's bank account. The biller makes the billing information available to the customer (presentment) on its Web site or the site of a billing hosting service. Once the customer views the bill, he or she authorizes and initiates payment at the site. The payment can be made with a credit/debit card or an ACH debit. The biller then initiates a payment transaction that moves funds through the payment system, crediting the biller and debiting the customer. See Chapter 10 for more about EBPP.

Online billing and bill paying can be classified as B2C, B2B, or C2C. This section has focused largely on B2C services, which help consumers save time and payees save on processing costs. However, large opportunities also exist in B2B services, which can save businesses about 50 percent of billing costs. In Hong Kong, for example, Citicorp enables automatic payments by linking suppliers, buyers, and banks on one platform.

Taxes

One important area in personal finance is advice about and computation of taxes. Dozens of sites are available to help people in their federal tax preparations. Many sites will help people legally cut their taxes. The following list offers some sites worth checking:

- ❱ irs.gov: The official Web site of the Internal Revenue Service.
- ❱ webtax.com: A massive directory of tax-related information, research, and services.
- ❱ fairmark.com: A tax guide for investors.
- ❱ taxaudit.com: Offers advice on minimizing taxes.

Section 3.6 ❱ REVIEW QUESTIONS

1. List the capabilities of online banking. Which of these capabilities would be most beneficial to you?
2. How are banks protecting customer data and transactions?
3. List the major personal finance services available online.

3.7 ON-DEMAND DELIVERY OF PRODUCTS, DIGITAL ITEMS, ENTERTAINMENT, AND GAMING

This section examines B2C delivery issues related to on-demand items, including perishable products, as well as the delivery of digitizable items, entertainment, and games.

ON-DEMAND DELIVERY OF PRODUCTS

Most e-tailers use common logistics carriers to deliver products to customers. They might use the postal system within their country or they might use private shippers such as UPS, FedEx, or DHL. Delivery can be made within days or overnight if the customer is willing to pay for the expedited shipment.

Some e-tailers and direct marketing manufacturers own a fleet of delivery vehicles and incorporate the delivery function into their business plans in order to provide greater value to the consumer. These firms will either provide regular deliveries on a daily or other regular schedule or they will deliver items within very short periods of time, usually one hour. They might also provide additional services to increase the value proposition for the buyers. An example is Bigboxx.com (bigboxx.com), presented in Online File W5.2. An online grocer, or **e-grocer**, is a typical example of businesses in this category. Home delivery of food from restaurants is another example. In addition, another class of firms (groceries, office supplies, repair parts, and pharmaceutical products) promises virtually instantaneous or at least same-day delivery of goods to consumers.

Whether the delivery is made by company-owned vehicles or is outsourced to a carrier, an express delivery model is referred to as an **on-demand delivery service**. In such a model, the delivery must be done fairly quickly after an order is received. A variation of this model is same-day delivery. According to this model, delivery is done faster than "overnight" but slower than the 30 to 60 minutes expected with on-demand delivery of pizzas, fresh flowers, or blood. E-grocers often deliver using the same-day delivery model.

The Case of E-Grocers

In the United States, online grocery sales amounted to $7.3 billion in 2008 and are expected to reach $13.7 billion, 2 percent of total grocery sales, in 2012 (Mulpuru et al. 2008). It is a very competitive market, and margins are very thin. Many e-grocers are click-and-mortar retailers that operate in the countries where they have physical stores,

e-grocer
A grocer that takes orders online and provides deliveries on a daily or other regular schedule or within a very short period of time.

on-demand delivery service
Express delivery made fairly quickly after an online order is received.

such as Woolworths in Australia (woolworths.com.au) and Albertsons (albertsons.com) in the United States. (For statistics on the grocery industry, see retailindustry.about.com.)

Today, it is possible to shop for groceries from cell phones, BlackBerries, and PDAs. For e-grocery implementation issues, see Online File W3.7.

FreshDirect. FreshDirect is an online grocer that delivers to residences and offices in the New York City metropolitan area. The company uses SAP AG software to process thousands of orders placed on its Web site every night. Orders are dispatched to the kitchen, bakery, and deli as well as to fresh storage rooms, produce ripening rooms, and production areas within the company's refrigerated facility. All order components are custom-cut, packaged, weighed, and priced. In the case of dry goods or frozen foods, items are picked from storage before being placed inside bins that travel along conveyors to the sorting area. There, products in a customer's order are scanned and gathered in corrugated fiberboard boxes. The boxes are labeled, recorded, and loaded into refrigerated delivery trucks. FreshDirect adopts a *just-in-time* manufacturing practice that reduces waste and improves quality and freshness.

ONLINE DELIVERY OF DIGITAL PRODUCTS, ENTERTAINMENT, AND MEDIA

Certain goods, such as software, music, or news stories, can be distributed in a physical form (such as hard copy, CD-ROM, DVD, and newsprint), or they can be digitized and delivered over the Internet. For example, consumers can purchase shrink-wrapped CD-ROMs containing software (along with the owner's manual and a warranty card) or pay for the software at a Web site and immediately download it onto their computers (usually through File Transfer Protocol [FTP], a fast way to download large files).

Exhibit 3.11 provides examples of digital products that can be distributed either physically or digitally. Each delivery method has advantages and disadvantages for both sellers and buyers. Customers, for example, may prefer the formats available through physical distribution. They perceive value in holding a physical CD-ROM or music CD as opposed to a downloaded file. In addition, the related packaging of a physical product can be significant. In some cases, customers enjoy the "liner notes" that accompany a music CD. Paper-based software user manuals and other materials also have value and may be preferred over online help features. However, customers might have to wait days for physical products to be delivered.

For sellers, the costs associated with the manufacture, storage, and distribution of physical products (DVDs, CD-ROMs, paper magazines, etc.) can be enormous. Inventory management also becomes a critical cost issue, and so does delivery and

EXHIBIT 3.11	Distribution of Digital Versus Physical Products	
Type of Product	**Physical Distribution**	**Digital Distribution**
Software	Boxed, shrink-wrapped	FTP, direct download, e-mail
Newspapers, magazines	Home delivery, postal mail	Display on Web, "e-zines"
Greeting cards	Retail stores	E-mail, URL link to recipient
Images (e.g., clip art, graphics)	CD-ROM, magazines	Web site display, downloadable
Movies	DVD, VHS, NTSB, PAL	MPEG3, streaming video, RealNetworks, AVI, QuickTime, etc.
Music	CD, cassette tape	MP3, WAV, RealAudio downloads, wireless devices, iTunes

distribution. The need for retail intermediaries requires the establishment of relationships with channel partners and revenue-sharing plans. Direct sales of digital content through digital download, however, allow a producer of digital content to bypass the traditional retail channel, thereby reducing overall costs and capturing greater profits. However, retailers often are crucial in creating demand for a product through in-store displays, advertising, and human sales efforts, all of which are lost when the producer disintermediates the traditional channel.

A major revolution in the online entertainment industry occurred when Napster introduced the P2P file-sharing of music (see Online File W3.8). Another major phenomenon in the online delivery of entertainment is YouTube (see Chapter 7).

ONLINE ENTERTAINMENT

Online entertainment is growing rapidly. Online entertainment is now the most popular medium in the United States among young people between the ages of 8 and 17. There are many kinds of Internet entertainment. It is difficult to precisely categorize them because there tends to be a mixture of entertainment types, delivery modes, and personal taste and choice in deciding whether something is entertainment or not. Some online entertainment can be regarded as interactive, in that the user can interact, often in a somewhat conversational way, with the software and thus change the outcome or shape the direction of the entertainment activity. PriceWaterhouseCoopers (2008) forecasts that the global entertainment and media industry as a whole will reach $2.2 trillion in 2012. This includes online gaming, streaming video and audio, as well as mobile access to the entertainment field.

The major forms of traditional entertainment are television, film, radio, music, games, reading, and gambling. All of these are now available over the Internet. However, some have become much more popular in the new environment because the capabilities of modern technology mean that the experience can be enhanced for people who enjoy that activity. For example, online games offer multimedia experiences with colorful animations and sound and allow the player to affect the course and outcome of the game. Examples of online entertainment and services are described in Exhibit 3.12. For a more detailed summary of online entertainment, see Online File W3.9. For information on entertainment in the Web 2.0 environment, see Chapter 7.

EXHIBIT 3.12 Examples of Online Entertainment and Services

Online Entertainment	Entertainment-Related Services
Web browsing	Event ticketing
Internet gaming	Restaurant reservations
Fantasy sports games	Information retrieval
Single and multiplayer games	Retrieval of audio and video entertainment
Adult entertainment	
Card games	
Social networking sites	
Participatory Web sites	
Movies, TV online	
Live events	
Virtual worlds (trading, creating, etc.)	

Adult Entertainment

Online adult entertainment is probably the most profitable B2C model and accounts for a huge percentage of Internet usage. Adult content sites succeed because they offer three things unavailable in an offline store: anonymity, instant gratification, and choice. According to Nielsen Online, in October 2008 approximately a quarter of employees visited Internet porn sites during working hours, a 23 percent increase from October 2007 (Kuchment and Springen 2008). With little or no advertising effort to attract viewers, many of these sites are making good money. According to reports by market research firms that monitor the industry, such as Forrester, IDC, DataMonitor, Jupiter Media, and NetRating, viewers eagerly pay substantial subscription fees to view adult sites.

Internet Gaming

Internet gaming is comprised of all forms of gaming, including arcade gaming, lotteries, casino gaming, promotional incentives, and so on. In 2008, online gambling revenue continued to increase despite bad economic times. A 2008 study by Baranzelli indicated that although the offline market is anticipated to produce only a modest average development rate of 2.2 percent until 2012, the online market is going to accomplish average expansion rates of 10.3 percent per annum until 2012, hitting a total market volume of $24.4 billion, or 6.3 percent of the gaming market (Baranzelli 2008). The ease of access and use of broadband services throughout the world in recent years has been vital to the expansion of online gaming.

Online Dating Services

Online dating is a dating system that allows individuals, couples, and groups to make contact and communicate with each other over the Internet, usually with the objective of developing a personal romantic or sexual relationship. Online dating services usually provide unmoderated matchmaking over the Internet through the use of personal computers or cell phones. As a paid content category, online dating services are the third largest attractor of Internet users after music and games, earning 10 percent of the online audience in 2007. According to one study (*Jupiter Research* 2007), online dating sites are projected to increase revenue from $900 million in 2007 to $1.9 billion in 2012, an increase of 16 percent over five years.

Section 3.7 ❱ REVIEW QUESTIONS

1. Explain on-demand delivery service.
2. Describe e-grocers and how they operate.
3. What are the difficulties in shopping online for groceries?
4. Describe digital goods and their delivery.
5. What are the benefits and the limitations of digital delivery?
6. What are the major forms of online entertainment? (See Online File W3.9.)
7. Do you think people of different age groups and social classes might be attracted to different types of online entertainment?

3.8 ONLINE PURCHASE-DECISION AIDS

Many sites and tools are available to help consumers with online purchasing decisions. Some sites offer price comparisons as their primary tool (e.g., pricerunner.com and shopzilla.com); others evaluate services, trust, quality, and other factors. Shopping portals, shopping robots ("shopbots"), business ratings sites, trust verification sites, and other shopping aids also are available.

SHOPPING PORTALS

shopping portals
Gateways to e-storefronts and e-malls; may be comprehensive or niche oriented.

Shopping portals are gateways to storefronts and e-malls. Like any other portal, they can be comprehensive or niche-oriented. Comprehensive, or general-purpose, portals have links to many different sellers and present and evaluate a broad range of products. An example of a comprehensive portal is eCOST.com (ecost.com). Several public portals also offer shopping opportunities and comparison aids. Examples are shopping.com, shopping.yahoo.com, and bing.com/shopping. EBay is a shopping portal too because it offers shopping at fixed prices as well as auctions. All have clear shopping links from the main page of the portal, and they generate revenues by directing consumers to their affiliates' sites. Some of these portals even offer comparison tools to help identify the best price for a particular item. Several of these evaluation companies have purchased shopbots (see the following discussion) or other, smaller shopping aids and incorporated them into their portals.

Some shopping portals also offer specialized niche aids with information and links for purchasers of automobiles, toys, computers, travel, or some other narrow area. Such portals also help customers conduct research. Examples include review.zdnet.com and shopper.cnet.com for computer equipment. The advantage of niche shopping portals is their ability to specialize in a certain line of products and carefully track consumer tastes within a specific and relevant market segment.

SHOPBOTS SOFTWARE AGENTS

shopping robots (shopping agents or shopbots)
Tools that scout the Web on behalf of consumers who specify search criteria.

Savvy Internet shoppers may bookmark their favorite shopping sites, but what if they want to find other stores with good service and policies that sell similar items at lower prices? **Shopping robots** (also called **shopping agents** or **shopbots**) are tools that scout the Web for consumers who specify search criteria. Different shopbots use different search methods. For example, mySimon (mysimon.com) searches the Web to find the best prices and availability for thousands of popular items. This is not a simple task. The shopbot might have to evaluate different SKU (stock-keeping unit) numbers for the same item, because each e-tailer may have a different SKU rather than a standardized data-representation code. In addition to price, pricegrabber.com includes product details and features, product reviews from merchants and consumers, and additional information about the store selling the item.

"Spy" Services

In this context, "spy" services are not the CIA or MI5. Rather, they are services that visit Web sites for customers, at their direction, and notify them of their findings. Web surfers and shoppers constantly monitor sites for new information, special sales, ending time of auctions, stock updates, and so on, but visiting the sites to monitor them is time consuming. Several sites will track stock prices or airline special sales and send e-mails accordingly. For example, cnn.com, pcworld.com, and expedia.com will send people personalized alerts.

Of course, one of the most effective ways to spy on Internet users is to introduce cookies and spyware to their computers (see Chapter 4 for details.)

Wireless Shopping Comparisons

Users of mySimon (all regular services) and AT&T Digital PocketNet service have access to wireless shopping comparisons. Users who are equipped with an AT&T Internet-ready cell phone can find the service on the AT&T main menu; it enables shoppers to compare prices anytime from anywhere, including from any physical store.

BUSINESS RATINGS SITES

Many Web sites rate various e-tailers and online products based on multiple criteria. Bizrate.com (bizrate.com), Consumer Reports Online (consumerreports.org), Forrester Research (forrester.com), and Gomez Advisors (gomez.com) are such well-known sites. Bizrate.com organized a network of shoppers that reports on various sellers and uses the compiled results in its evaluations. Note that different raters provide different rankings. Alexa Internet, Inc. (alexa.com) is a California-based subsidiary company of Amazon.com that is best known for operating a Web site that provides information on Web traffic to other Web sites. Alexa ranks sites based on tracking information of users of its Alexa Toolbar for Internet Explorer and from integrated sidebars in Mozilla and Netscape. Online File W3.10 discusses ResellerRatings (resellerratings.com), an interesting example of a business ratings site.

TRUST VERIFICATION SITES

With so many sellers online, many consumers are not sure whom they should trust. A number of companies purport to evaluate and verify the trustworthiness of various e-tailers. One such company is TRUSTe (truste.com). The TRUSTe seal appears at the bottom of each TRUSTe-approved e-tailer's Web site. E-tailers pay TRUSTe for use of the seal (which they call a "trustmark"). TRUSTe's 1,300-plus members hope that consumers will use the seal as an assurance and as a proxy for actual research into their conduct of business, privacy policy, and personal information protection.

The most comprehensive trust verification sites are VeriSign and BBBOnline. VeriSign (verisign.com) tends to be the most widely used. Other sources of trust verification include Secure Assure (secureassure.com), which charges yearly license fees based on a company's annual revenue. In addition, Ernst and Young, the global public accounting firm, has created its own service for auditing e-tailers in order to offer some guarantee of the integrity of their business practices.

Recommendations from Other Shoppers and Friends

In marketing, a **referral economy** is the effect on sales of consumers receiving a referral or recommendation from other consumers. It occurs on the Internet via blogs, social networking sites, and review sites where users recommend items to other users. Because these recommendations take place over the Internet, potential customers perceive that the referring users are genuine and the recommendation is noncommercial. Therefore the recommendation has a higher perceived value. Many advertising agencies have launched word-of-mouth marketing departments designed to create viral campaigns via the Internet or "sneezing" campaigns. *Sneezing* describes the attention-grabbing behavior of agencies that go out to consumer environments and boast about how great a brand or item is in order to spread the word. Sites such as Kaboodle aim to tap into the referral economy and drive purchase through users' personal recommendation.

Kaboodle. Established in 2005, Kaboodle is a social shopping community where people find, recommend, and share products. Kaboodle's powerful shopping tools allow people to organize their shopping through lists, find new items from people with similar fashion approaches, get discounts on popular products, and find the best prices. Kaboodle is an entertaining community of people who love to shop. Community members create and join groups, share advice, feedback, and product suggestions, and personalize their profiles with polls and other widgets. The site has over 800,000 registered users who have added more than 8 million products to the site and boasts more than 12 million visitors per month.

referral economy
The effect upon sales of consumers receiving a referral or recommendation from other consumers.

OTHER SHOPPING TOOLS

Other digital intermediaries assist buyers or sellers, or both, with the research and purchase processes. For example, escrow services (e.g., escrow.com and fortis-escrow.com) assist buyers and sellers in the exchange of items and money. Because buyers and sellers do not see or know each other, a trusted third party frequently is needed to facilitate the proper exchange of money and goods. Escrow sites may also provide payment-processing support, as well as letters of credit (see Chapter 10).

Other decision aids include communities of consumers who offer advice and opinions on products and e-tailers. One such site is epinions.com, which has searchable recommendations on thousands of products. Pricescan.com is a price-comparison engine, pricegrabber.com is a comparison shopping tool that covers over 1 million products, and Onlineshoes.com specializes in all types of shoes. Other software agents and comparison sites are presented in Online File W3.11.

Another shopping tool is a *wallet*—in this case, an *electronic wallet*, which is a program that contains the shopper's information. To expedite online shopping, consumers can use electronic wallets so that they do not need to reenter the information each time they shop. Although sites such as Amazon.com offer their own specialized wallets, Microsoft has a universal wallet in its Passport program (see Chapter 10 for details).

Section 3.8 ❭ REVIEW QUESTIONS

1. Define shopping portals and provide two examples.
2. What are shopbots?
3. Explain the role of business and Web site rating and site verification tools in the purchase-decision process.
4. Why are escrow services and electronic wallets useful for online purchases?

3.9 ISSUES IN E-TAILING AND LESSONS LEARNED

The following are representative issues and problems that need to be addressed when conducting B2C.

DISINTERMEDIATION AND REINTERMEDIATION

disintermediation
The removal of organizations or business process layers responsible for certain intermediary steps in a given supply chain.

reintermediation
The process whereby intermediaries (either new ones or those that had been disintermediated) take on new intermediary roles.

Disintermediation refers to the removal of organizations or business process layers responsible for certain intermediary steps in a given supply chain. As shown in part B of Exhibit 3.13, the manufacturer can bypass wholesalers and retailers, selling directly to consumers. Also, e-tailers may drive regular retailers out of business. For a vivid case of such disintermediation, see the Blue Nile case in Online File W1.14.

However, consumers might have problems selecting an online vendor; vendors might have problems delivering to customers; and both might need an escrow service to ensure the transaction. Thus, new online assistance might be needed, and it might be provided by new or by traditional intermediaries. In such cases, the traditional intermediaries fill new roles, providing *added value* and assistance. This process is referred to as **reintermediation**. It is pictured in part C of Exhibit 3.13. Thus, for the intermediary, the Internet offers new ways to reach new customers, new ways to bring value to customers, and perhaps new ways to generate revenues.

The intermediary's role is shifting to one that emphasizes value-added services, such as assisting customers in comparison shopping from multiple sources, providing total

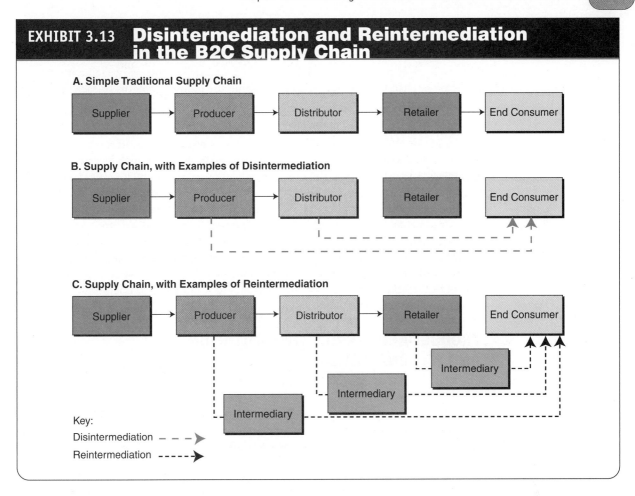

EXHIBIT 3.13 **Disintermediation and Reintermediation in the B2C Supply Chain**

A. Simple Traditional Supply Chain

Supplier → Producer → Distributor → Retailer → End Consumer

B. Supply Chain, with Examples of Disintermediation

Supplier → Producer → Distributor   Retailer   End Consumer

C. Supply Chain, with Examples of Reintermediation

Supplier → Producer → Distributor → Retailer   End Consumer

Intermediary   Intermediary   Intermediary

Key:
Disintermediation — — —▶
Reintermediation ------▶

solutions by combining services from several vendors, and providing certifications and trusted third-party control and evaluation systems. For instance, in the world of online new and used car sales, electronic intermediaries assist buyers and/or sellers. These are new *reintermediaries*, intermediaries that have restructured their role in the purchase process. An example of the new role of intermediaries is Edmunds (edmunds.com), which gives consumers a vast amount of information about cars, including price comparisons, ratings, the location of cars for sale, and the dealer's true costs.

CHANNEL CONFLICT

Many traditional retailers establish a new marketing channel when they start selling online. Similarly, some manufacturers have instituted direct marketing initiatives in parallel with their established channels of distribution, such as retailers or dealers. In such cases, channel conflict can occur. **Channel conflict** refers to any situation in which direct competition and/or damage caused by bypassing a former existing channel partner is perceived to have resulted from the introduction of a new, often online, channel. The extent of this conflict varies according to the nature of the industry and characteristics of particular firms, but sometimes, a move to sell online can damage old, valued relationships between trading partners. Channel conflict can also be said to occur when a move to online trading simply moves a company's customers from their traditional stores, for

channel conflict
Situation in which an online marketing channel upsets the traditional channels due to real or perceived damage from competition.

example, to an online environment, thus cannibalizing the sales from the former and potentially negatively impacting the traditional outlets by rendering them less profitable. However, careful management and the adoption of sound strategies can deliver a number of synergies for click-and-mortar e-tailers, especially those associated with encouraging cross-channel cooperation and exploiting the unique strengths of each channel to maximize the experience for the customer.

DETERMINING THE RIGHT PRICE

Pricing a product or service on the Internet, especially by a click-and-mortar company, is complicated. On the one hand, prices need to be competitive on the Internet. Today's comparison engines will show the consumer the prices at many stores, for almost all commodity products, at almost no cost to the consumer. However, balanced against this is the fact that for some items, transaction costs will decrease, the cost of distribution will decrease, and supply chains may become more efficient and shorter, meaning that e-tailers might be able to compete in the aggressive online marketspace. On the other hand, prices should be in line with the corporate policy on profitability and, in a click-and-mortar company, in line with the offline channel's pricing strategy. To avoid price conflict, some companies have created independent online subsidiaries.

PRODUCT AND SERVICE CUSTOMIZATION AND PERSONALIZATION

One significant characteristic of many online marketing business models is the ability of the seller to create an element of *personalization* for each individual consumer.

The Internet also allows for easy self-configuration ("design it your way"). This creates a large demand for customized products and services. Manufacturers can meet that demand by using a *mass customization* strategy. As indicated earlier, many companies offer customized products from their Web sites (e.g., see the Dell case in Online File W1.3).

Although pure-play e-tailing is risky and its future is unclear, e-tailing is growing rapidly as a complementary distribution channel to traditional stores and catalogs. In other words, the *click-and-mortar model is winning currently and all evidence suggests that this trend will continue.* (See the closing case at the end of the chapter.)

FRAUD AND OTHER ILLEGAL ACTIVITIES

A major problem in B2C is the increasing rate of online fraud. This can cause losses to both buyers and sellers. For a more detailed and thorough discussion of online fraud, see the discussion of online fraud in Chapter 9.

LESSONS LEARNED FROM FAILURES AND LACK OF SUCCESS

Online File W3.12 provides a sample of failed B2C companies. Some enduring principles can be distilled from the failures, and these "lessons learned" are discussed next.

Although thousands of companies have evolved their online strategies into mature Web sites with extensive interactive features that add value to the consumer purchase process, many other sites remain simple "brochureware" sites with limited interactivity. Many traditional companies are in a transitional stage. Mature transactional systems include features for payment processing, order fulfillment, logistics, inventory management, and a host of other services. In most cases, a company must replicate each of its physical business processes and design many more that can only be performed online. Today's environment includes sophisticated access to order information, shipping information, product information, and more through Web pages, touch-tone phones, Web-enabled cell phones, and PDAs over wireless networks. Faced with all of these variables, the challenges to implementing EC can be daunting.

A traditional brick-and-mortar store with a mature Web site that uses a click-and-mortar strategy is able to do the following:

> ▶ **Speak with one voice.** A firm can link all of its back-end systems to create an integrated customer experience. The online experience should be an extension of the experience encountered in traditional transactions.
>
> ▶ **Leverage the multichannels.** The innovative retailer will offer the advantages of each marketing channel to customers from all channels. Whether the purchase is made online or at the store, the customer should benefit from the presence of both channels.
>
> ▶ **Empower the customer.** The seller needs to create a powerful 24/7 channel for service and information. Through various information technologies, sellers can give customers the opportunity to perform various functions interactively, at any time. Such functions include the ability to find store locations, product information, and inventory availability online.

Section 3.9 ▶ REVIEW QUESTIONS

1. Define disintermediation.
2. Describe mediation issues, including disintermediation and reintermediation.
3. Describe channel conflict and other conflicts that may appear in e-tailing.
4. Describe price determination in e-tailing.
5. Explain personalization and mass customization opportunities in e-tailing.
6. What makes click-and-mortar companies successful?

MANAGERIAL ISSUES

Some managerial issues related to this chapter are as follows.

1. **What are the limitations of e-tailing?** In Korea, Internet retailing has become the second most important distribution channel, exceeding the national sales volume of all department stores. The question is what the limits of e-tailing will be. The large e-mall volume has grown faster than individual Webstores (see Chapter 2). The market concentration has already happened, making the entrance barrier to new e-tailers very high. However, small businesses can easily start their online channel as part of a stable e-mall service platform. The opportunity can be cultivated by redefining the merchant's business plan with the addition of click-and-mortar strategies or of alliances with both online or offline partners.

Because most easy sources of funding have dried up and revenue models are being scrutinized, vendor consolidation will continue until there is a greater stability within the e-tailing sector. Ultimately, there will likely be a smaller number of larger sellers with comprehensive general sites (e.g., Amazon.com) and many smaller, specialized niche sites.

2. **How should we introduce wireless shopping?** In some countries (e.g., Japan), shopping from cell phones is very popular (see Chapter 8). In other countries, mobile shopping is not popular, although the platform itself is available. Alternative channels and a culture of a variety of communication channels should be developed in different

countries in order to develop mobile strategies. Also, because the younger generation prefers the mobile platform, the age effect on the platform should be monitored closely. Offering mobile shopping might not be simple or appropriate to all businesses.

3. **Do we have ethics and privacy guidelines?** Ethical issues are extremely important in an agent-less system. In traditional systems, human agents play an important role in assuring the ethical behavior of buyers and sellers. Will online ethics and the rules of etiquette be sufficient to guide behavior on the Internet? Only time will tell. For example, as job-applicant information travels over the Internet, security and privacy become even more important. It is management's job to make sure that information from applicants is secure.

Also, e-tailers need to establish guidelines for protecting the privacy of customers who visit their Web sites. Security and privacy must be high priorities.

4. **How will intermediaries act in cyberspace?** The role of online intermediary has become more and more important. In the banking, stock trading, job market, travel industry, and book sales sectors, the Internet has become a most important service channel. These intermediary services create new business opportunities and convenience for users.

5. **Should we try to capitalize on social networks?** Many individuals began trading or selling products and services on Facebook and other social networks. Although large companies are concentrating on advertising at the moment, some are experimenting with B2C sales (see Chapter 7).

SUMMARY

In this chapter, you learned about the following EC issues as they relate to the chapter's learning objectives.

1. **The scope and characteristics of e-tailing.** E-tailing, the online selling of products and services, is growing rapidly. Computers, software, and electronics are the major items sold online. Books, CDs, toys, office supplies, and other standard commodities also sell well. More successful are services sold online, such as airline tickets and travel services, stocks, and insurance.

2. **E-tailing business models.** The major e-tailing business models can be classified by distribution channel—a manufacturer or mail-order company selling direct to consumers, pure-play (virtual) e-tailing, a click-and-mortar strategy with both online and traditional channels, and online malls that provide either referring directories or shared services.

3. **How online travel/tourism services operate.** Most services available through a physical travel agency also are available online. In addition, customers get much more information, much more quickly through online resources. Customers can even receive bids from travel providers. Finally, travelers can compare prices, participate in auctions and chat rooms, and view videos and maps.

4. **The online job market and its benefits.** The online job market is growing rapidly, with thousands and thousands of jobs matched with job seekers each year. The major benefits of online job markets are the ability to reach a large number of job seekers at low cost, to provide detailed information online, to take applications, and even to conduct tests. Also, using intelligent agents, résumés can be checked and matches made more quickly. Millions of job offers posted on the Internet help job seekers, who also can post their résumés for recruiters.

5. **The electronic real estate market.** The online real estate market is basically supporting rather than replacing existing agents. However, both buyers and sellers can save time and effort in the electronic market. Buyers can purchase distant properties much more easily and in some places have access to less expensive services. Eventually, commissions on regular transactions are expected to decline as a result of the electronic market for real estate, and more sales "by owner" will materialize.

6. **Online trading of stocks and bonds.** One of the fastest growing online businesses is the online trading of securities. It is inexpensive, convenient, and supported by a tremendous amount of financial

and advisory information. Trading is very fast and efficient, almost fully automated, and moving toward 24/7 global trading. However, security breaches are possible, so tight protection is a must.

7. **Cyberbanking and personal finance.** Branch banking is on the decline due to less expensive, more convenient online banking. The world is moving toward online banking; today, most routine banking services can be done from home. Banks can reach customers in remote places, and customers can bank with faraway institutions. This makes the financial markets more efficient. Online personal finance applications, such as bill paying, tracking of accounts, and tax preparation, also are very popular.

8. **On-demand delivery service.** On-demand delivery service is needed when items are perishable or when delivering medicine, express documents, or urgently needed supplies. One example of on-demand delivery is e-groceries; these may be ordered online and are shipped or ready for store pickup within 24 hours or less.

9. **Delivery of digital products.** Anything that can be digitized can be successfully delivered online. Delivery of digital products such as music, software, movies, and other entertainment online has been a success. Some print media, such as electronic versions of magazines or electronic books (see Chapter 6), also are having success when digitized and delivered electronically.

10. **Aiding consumer purchase decisions.** Purchase decision aids include shopping portals, shopbots and comparison agents, business rating sites, trust verification sites, and other tools.

11. **Disintermediation and other B2C strategic issues.** Direct electronic marketing by manufacturers results in disintermediation by removing wholesalers and retailers. However, online reintermediaries provide additional value, such as helping consumers make selections among multiple products and vendors. Traditional retailers may feel threatened or pressured when manufacturers decide to sell online; such direct selling can cause channel conflict. Pricing of online and offline products and services is one issue that always needs to be addressed.

KEY TERMS

Brick-and-mortar retailers	96	Electronic (online) banking or		Reintermediation	120
Channel conflict	121	e-banking	104	Shopping portals	118
Click-and-mortar retailers	96	Electronic retailing (e-tailing)	88	Shopping robots (shopbots,	
Considered commerce	91	E-tailers	88	shopping agents)	118
Direct marketing	94	Multichannel business model	96	Virtual (pure-play) e-tailers	96
Disintermediation	120	On-demand delivery service	114		
E-grocer	114	Referral economy	119		

QUESTIONS FOR DISCUSSION BY INDIVIDUAL STUDENTS

1. What are Amazon.com's critical success factors? Is its decision to offer a much broader selection of items a good marketing strategy? With the broader selection, do you think the company will dilute its brand or extend the value proposition to its customers?

2. Discuss the importance of comparison tools, product reviews, and customer ratings in online shopping.

3. Discuss the advantages of a specialized e-tailer, such as DogToys.com (dogtoys.com). Could such a store survive in the physical world? Why or why not?

4. Discuss the benefits of build-to-order to buyers and sellers. Are there any disadvantages?

5. Why are online travel services a popular Internet application? Why do so many Web sites provide free travel information?

6. Compare the advantages and disadvantages of online stock trading with offline trading.

7. It is said that the service Zuji.com (zuji.com) provides to travel agents will lead to their reintermediation. Discuss.

8. Compare the advantages and disadvantages of distributing digitizable products electronically versus physically.

TOPICS FOR CLASS DISCUSSION

1. Do you trust your personal data on social networks such as LinkedIn? How do you protect your privacy?

2. Discuss the advantages of established click-and-mortar companies such as Walmart over pure-play e-tailers such as Amazon.com. What are the disadvantages of click-and-brick retailers as compared with pure-play e-tailers?

3. Online employment services make it easy to change jobs; therefore, turnover rates may increase. This could result in total higher costs for employers because of increased costs for recruiting and training new employees and the need to pay higher salaries and wages to attract or keep them. What can companies do to ease this problem?

4. Discuss each of the following as limiting factors on the growth of B2C EC: (a) Too much competition, (b) expensive technology, (c) need a computer to shop, (d) people need the social interaction in face-to-face shopping, (e) many people cannot afford Internet access, (f) the EC market is already saturated.

5. How should a company handle channel conflict with its distributors?

6. Should online sales be an independent unit in a click-and-mortar firm?

7. Will P2P lending disrupt banking?

8. Would you use Monster.com or LinkedIn for recruiting?

INTERNET EXERCISES

1. Many consumer portals offer advice and ratings of products or e-tailers. Identify and examine two separate general-consumer portals that look at other sites and compare prices or other purchase criteria. Try to find and compare prices for a digital camera, a microwave oven, and an MP3 player. Visit clusty.com. How can this site help you in your shopping? Summarize your experience. Comment on the strong and weak points of such shopping tools.

2. Visit amazon.com and identify at least three specific elements of its personalization and customization features. Browse specific books on one particular subject, leave the site, and then go back and revisit the site. What do you see? Are these features likely to encourage you to purchase more books in the future from Amazon.com? Check the 1-Click feature and other shopping aids provided. List the features and discuss how they may lead to increased sales.

3. Visit landsend.com and prepare a customized order for a piece of clothing. Describe the process. Do you think this will result in better-fitting clothing? Do you think this personalization feature will lead to greater sales volume for Lands' End?

4. Make your résumé accessible to millions of people. Consult asktheheadhunter.com or careerbuilder.com for help rewriting your résumé. See monster.com for ideas about planning your career. Get prepared for a job interview. Also, use the Web to determine what salary you can get in the city of your choice in the United States.

5. Visit move.com, decisionaide.com, or a similar site and compute the monthly mortgage payment on a 30-year loan at 7.5 percent fixed interest. Also check current interest rates. Estimate your closing costs on a $200,000 loan. Compare the monthly payments of the fixed rate with that of an adjustable rate for the first year. Finally, compute your total payments if you take the loan for 15 years at the going rate. Compare it with a 30-year mortgage. Comment on the difference.

6. Access the Virtual Trader game at virtualtrader.co.uk and register for the Internet stock game. You will be bankrolled with £100,000 in a trading account every month. You also can play investment games at investorsleague.com and etrade.com.

7. Compare the price of a Sony digital camera at shopping.com, mysimon.com, bizrate.com, and pricescan.com. Which site locates the best deal? Where do you get the best information?

8. Enter xing.com and identify its job-related offerings. Prepare a list of support activities offered.

9. Enter Bazaarvoice (bazaarvoice.com) and find how consumers can engage in a dialog. Look at its Ask & Answer service. How is quality of content maintained. Write a report based on your findings.

10. Enter vivente.com/resumix/website, examine the capabilities of the tools, and write a report.

TEAM ASSIGNMENTS AND PROJECTS

1. Each team will investigate the services of two online car-selling sites from the following list (or other sites). When teams have finished, they should bring their research together and discuss their findings.

   a. Buying new cars through an intermediary (autobytel.com, carsdirect.com, autoweb.com, or amazon.com)

   b. Buying used cars (autotrader.com)

   c. Buying used cars by auto dealers (manheim.com)

   d. Automobile ratings sites (carsdirect.com and fueleconomy.gov)

   e. Car-buying portals (thecarportal.com and cars.com)

   f. Buying antique cars (classiccars.com and antiquecar.com)

2. Each team will represent a broker-based area (e.g., real estate, insurance, stocks, job finding). Each team will find a new development that has occurred in the assigned area over the most recent three months. Look for the site vendor's announcement and search for more information on the development with google.com or another search engine. Examine the business news at bloomberg.com. After completing your research, as a team, prepare a report on disintermediation in your assigned area.

3. Each team will examine fantasy games at various sites. Each team should examine the type of game, the rules, and the cost. Play at least one time. Each team should write a report based on its experiences. (Hint: See Online File W3.9.)

Closing Case

WALMART POWERS ONLINE

Walmart (walmart.com) is the largest retailer in the world, with $404 billion in sales for the fiscal year ending January 31, 2009. Walmart employs more than 2 million people, 1.4 million in the United States. The company has more than 8,100 stores in 55 countries. Each week, 200 million customers visit Walmart stores worldwide, including 2.1 million in the United States (see walmartfacts.com for current statistics).

Walmart maintains an intense strategic focus on the customer. Its standard company cheer ends with, "Who's number one? The customer." Walmart has also established itself as a master of the retail process by streamlining its supply chain and undercutting competitors with low prices.

Walmart has had an online presence since 1996. However, one problem with its strategy for growing online sales has been the demographics of its primary customer base. Walmart's target demographic is households with $25,000 in annual income, whereas the median income of online consumers is perhaps $60,000. Despite these demographics, online sales (primarily in music, travel, and electronics) through walmart.com already account for about 10 percent of Walmart's U.S. sales. Its long-time chief rival, Kmart, tried to attract its demographic audience to its Web site (kmart.com) by offering free Internet access. This appealed to its cost-conscious, lower-income constituency and provided the opportunity for those customers to access the site to conduct purchases. However, this move decreased company profits in the short run and was one of the major factors that led Kmart to file for bankruptcy in 2002.

Walmart also has concerns about cannibalizing its in-store sales. Its alliance with AOL is designed to provide cobranded low-cost Internet access to dwellers in both very rural and very urban areas, where there are no Walmart stores nearby. The intent is to lure new market segments and thus cancel the effect of cannibalization. Ultimately, a hybrid e-tailer that can offer a combination of huge selection with the click-and-mortar advantages of nearby stores (e.g., merchandise pickup or returns) might prove to be the 800-pound gorilla of online consumer sales.

In 2002, Walmart.com matured, offering order status and tracking, a help desk, a clear return policy and mechanisms, a store locator, and information on special sales and liquidations. Today, community services, such as photo sharing, are provided.

Walmart features 1 million products online plus easy-to-use music downloads and digital one-hour photo services, but the selection is increasing, including items not available in some or all stores (e.g., spas, mattresses). In 2004, Walmart started selling songs online for 88¢ each, competing with Apple's iTunes. Inexpensive items (e.g., those that sell for less than $5) are not available online. Also in 2004, during a four-day Thanksgiving special, Walmart began to court more affluent shoppers with new and more expensive items available only online. Products included cashmere sweaters and shiatsu massage chairs. The Web site averaged 8 million visitors each week prior to the promotion.

Walmart has added many new products to its online catalog. International customers can buy Walmart products directly from Walmart (if shipping is available) or from affiliate sites. For example, see ASDA (*asda.co.uk*), a Walmart-owned U.K. company.

In 2006, a fake "Walmarting Across America" blog—a very rough attempt at teen social networking—became a learning experience for the company. Also in 2006, the company revamped its site for the first time since 2000. The site now features a new four-click checkout process and rich media, including interactive functions in the toy section.

In 2007, Walmart rolled out its new order online/pickup in-store service. "Site to Store" enables customers to buy online and have products shipped for free to their store of choice. The new service also gives customers access to tens of thousands of products, many more than are available in stores. Delivery for such items is 7 to 10 days (*Internet Retailer* 2007). According to Competeinc, in July 2009 Walmart ranked second in the top 25 online retail sites behind Amazon.com (*Competeinc* 2009).

Walmart now adopts existing Web 2.0 social networks for its e-tailing activities. In late 2007, Walmart launched "Roommate Style Match" on Facebook, a site that allows students to design their dorm rooms with their roommates. Facebook users who join the Walmart group are able to take a quiz to determine their decorating style and get a list of "recommended products" they can buy at Walmart to mesh their style with their roommate's. Students can also download a shopping list of dorm room items sold at Walmart, link to Walmart's Web site promoting "earth-friendly" products, or click on Soundcheck, Walmart's Web site that shows musical performances by popular singers like Bon Jovi and Mandy Moore. It is believed that Walmart will soon make use of blogs and other Web 2.0 tools to support its online sales (e.g., customer product reviews). Walmart Watch (*myspace.com/walmartwatch*) is a page on MySpace where frustrated customers and employees get a chance to express their feelings.

In 2008, Walmart continued to gain market share and clout as cash-strapped shoppers sought out its low prices. It reported a stronger-than-expected 3.4 percent rise in sales at its U.S. stores during the 2008 holiday shopping season (Maestri 2008).

Sources: Compiled from Maestri (2008), Competeinc (2009), *Internet Retailer* (2007), and *walmart.com* (accessed February 2009).

Questions

1. Compare *walmart.com* with *amazon.com*. What features do the sites have in common? Which are unique to Walmart? To Amazon.com?

2. Will Walmart become the dominant e-tailer in the world, replacing Amazon.com, or will Amazon.com dominate Walmart online? What factors would contribute to Walmart's success in the online marketplace? What factors would detract from its ability to dominate online sales the way it has been able to dominate physical retail sales in many markets?

3. Check the shopping aids offered at *walmart.com*. Compare them with those at *amazon.com*.

4. What online services can be purchased on Walmart.com?

5. Compare buying a song from Walmart.com versus buying it from Apple's iTunes.

6. Walmart.com sells movies online for a monthly fee. How do similar sellers compare?

7. Visit *walmart.com*, *target.com*, *marksandspencer.com*, and *sears.com*. Identify the common features of their online marketing and at least one unique feature evident at each site. Do these sites have to distinguish themselves primarily in terms of price, product selection, or Web site features?

8. Investigate the options for international customers on the Walmart Web site.

ONLINE RESOURCES
available at pearsonhighered.com/turban

Online Files

W3.1   Some Current Trends in B2C EC
W3.2   Application Case: CatToys.com, a Specialty E-Tailer
W3.3   Application Case: Gateway's "Book-It-in-the-Box" E-Travel Solutions
W3.4   Application Case: The European Job Mobility Portal (EURES CV-Search) and Xing.com
W3.5   Real Estate Applications
W3.6   Investment Information
W3.7   Implementing E-Grocery
W3.8   Application Case: The Napster Experience: Its Rise, Collapse, and Revival
W3.9   Examples of Online Entertainment
W3.10   Application Case: Reseller Ratings: Making Online Retailers Accountable to Customers

W3.11   Representative Shopping Software Agents and Comparison Sites
W3.12   What Lessons Can Be Learned from These EC Failures?

Comprehensive Educational Web Sites

youtube.com/watch?v=DbwiRLbBg6U
youtube.com/watch?v=P18xwbZFCxM
dictionary.zdnet.com/definition/B2C.html
isos.com.my/ecommerce/b2c.htm
marketresearch.com/map/research/b2c/622.html
managementhelp.org/infomgnt/e_cmmrce/e_cmmrce.htm

ONLINE CONSUMER BEHAVIOR, MARKET RESEARCH, AND ADVERTISEMENT

Learning Objectives

Upon completion of this chapter, you will be able to:

1. Understand the decision-making process of consumer purchasing online.

2. Describe how companies are building one-to-one relationships with customers.

3. Explain how personalization is accomplished online.

4. Discuss the issues of e-loyalty and e-trust in EC.

5. Describe consumer market research in EC.

6. Describe the objectives of Web advertising and its characteristics.

7. Describe the major advertising methods used on the Web.

8. Understand how advertising is done in social networks and the Web 2.0 environment.

9. Describe various online advertising strategies and types of promotions.

10. Describe permission marketing, ad management, localization, and other advertising-related issues.

Content

Opening Case: Netflix Increases Sales Using DVD Recommendations and Advertisements

4.1 Learning About Consumer Purchasing Online

4.2 Personalization, Loyalty, Satisfaction, and Trust in EC

4.3 Market Research for EC

4.4 Web Advertising

4.5 Online Advertising Methods

4.6 Advertising in Social Networks and the Web 2.0 Environment

4.7 Advertising Strategies and Special Advertising Topics

4.8 Special Advertising Topics

Managerial Issues

Closing Case: Toyota Scion Goes Social for Advertising and Market Research

NETFLIX INCREASES SALES USING DVD RECOMMENDATIONS AND ADVERTISEMENTS

Netflix (*netflix.com*) is the world's largest online movie rental subscription company, offering 10 million members access to more than 100,000 DVD titles plus a growing library of more than 12,000 full-length movies and television episodes that are available for instant viewing on members' PCs in 2009. The company's appeal and success are built on providing the most comprehensive selection of DVDs, an easy way to choose movies, and fast, free delivery. Netflix distributes 2 million DVDs each day.

The Problem

Because of the large number of titles available on DVD, customers often had difficulty determining which ones they wanted to watch. In many cases, they chose the most recent and popular titles, which meant that Netflix had to maintain more and more copies of the same title. In addition, some unpopular titles were not renting well, even though they matched certain customers' preferences. For Netflix, matching titles with customers yet maintaining the right level of inventory is critical.

A second major problem facing Netflix is the competitive nature of the movie rental business. Netflix competes against Blockbuster and other rental companies, as well as against companies offering downloads of movies and videos. In 2008, Blockbuster started offering online movie rental subscription, including the most recent movies, increasing the direct competition with Netflix.

The Solution

Netflix reacted successfully to the first problem by offering a recommendation service called *CineMatch*. This software agent uses data mining tools to sift through a database of more than 2 billion film ratings, as well as through customers' rental histories. Using proprietary formulas, CineMatch recommends rentals to individuals. It is a personalized service, similar to the one offered by *amazon.com* that recommends books to customers. The recommendation is accomplished by comparing an individual's likes, dislikes, and preferences against people with similar tastes by using a variant of collaborative filtering (described later in this chapter). With the recommendation system, Netflix tells subscribers which DVDs they probably would like. CineMatch is like the geeky clerk at a small movie store who sets aside titles he knows you will like and tells you to return them whenever.

Netflix subscribers can also invite one another to become "friends" and make movie recommendations to each other, peek at one another's rental lists, and see how other subscribers have rated movies using a social network called *Friends*. All these personalized functions make the online rental store very customer friendly.

To improve CineMatch's accuracy, in October 2006 Netflix began a contest offering $1 million to the first person or team to write a program that would increase the prediction accuracy of CineMatch by 10 percent. The company understands that this will take quite some time; therefore, it is offering a $50,000 Progress Prize each year the contest runs. This prize goes to the team whose solution shows the most improvement over the previous year's accuracy bar (see *netflixprize.com*). On September 21, 2009, the *Wall Street Journal* reported that Netflix awarded $1 million to a team of researchers.

Netflix is advertising extensively on the Web using several advertising techniques, especially placing static banner ads on reputed sites, permission e-mail, blogs, social networks, classifieds, Really Simple Syndication (RSS), and more.

The Results

As a result of implementing its CineMatch system, Netflix has seen very fast growth in sales and membership. The benefits of CineMatch include the following:

- **Effective recommendations.** Approximately 60 percent of Netflix members select their movies based on movie recommendations tailored to their individual tastes.
- **Customer satisfaction.** More than 90 percent of Netflix members say they are so satisfied with the Netflix service that they recommend the service to family members and friends.
- **Inventory.** Netflix has more than 100,000 titles and more than 55 million DVDs. Every three months, Netflix members rent more than 95 percent of the 100,000 titles in the Netflix library. On any given day, more than 46,000 of the 100,000 titles available at Netflix are in distribution. (Netflix provides more than 10 million subscribers with access to more than 100,000 DVD titles plus a growing library of more than

12,000 choices that can be watched on their PCs. Netflix ships more than 2 million DVDs on a typical day, and subscribers rate an average of 2 million movies a day).

- **Ratings:** Netflix has more than 2 billion movie ratings from members. The average member has rated about 200 movies.
- **Rental habits:** Netflix members say they rent twice as many movies per month than they did prior to joining the service. Netflix members add 2 million movies to their queues (movies they want to get) every day.
- **Volume:** If you stacked every movie Netflix ships (on average, 2 million DVDs per day) in a single pile, the stack would be taller than Mt. Everest within a week.

- **Environment:** If Netflix members drove to and from a rental store, they would consume 800,000 gallons of gasoline and release more than 2.2 million tons of carbon dioxide emissions annually.

The domain Netflix.com attracted about 194 million visitors in 2008, according to a Compete.com survey. This is about five times the number of visitors to Blockbuster.com (*Compete.com* 2009).

CineMatch has become the company's core competence. Netflix's future relies heavily on CineMatch's making accurate recommendations and subscribers accepting them, which is why the company strives to increase its accuracy.

Sources: Compiled from Flynn (2006), *wikipedia.org/wiki/Netflix* (accessed October 2009), and *netflix.com* (accessed November 2009).

WHAT WE CAN LEARN . . .

This case illustrates that the use of online marketing is quite different from traditional marketing. In particular, Netflix uses intelligent agents in movie recommendation and gains a substantial advantage over its competitors. Netflix's CineMatch is designed to increase sales, customer satisfaction, and loyalty. The case also identifies some of the most popular advertising methods used in EC. All these previous topics are the main subjects of this chapter.

4.1 LEARNING ABOUT CONSUMER PURCHASING ONLINE

Companies are operating in an increasingly competitive environment. Therefore, they treat customers like royalty as they try to lure them to buy their goods and services. Finding and retaining customers is a major critical success factor for most businesses, both offline and online. One of the keys to building effective customer relationships is an understanding of consumer behavior online. A model of consumer behavior online is available in Online File W4.1.

A GENERIC PURCHASING-DECISION MODEL

From the consumer's perspective, a general purchasing-decision model consists of five major phases: (1) need identification, (2) information search, (3) evaluation of alternatives, (4) purchase and delivery, and (5) postpurchase behavior. Although these phases offer a general guide to the consumer decision-making process, one should not assume that every consumer's decision-making process will necessarily proceed in this order.

1. **Need identification.** The first phase occurs when a consumer is faced with an imbalance between the actual and the desired states of a need. A marketer's goal is to get the consumer to recognize such imbalance and then convince the consumer that the product or service the seller offers will fill this gap.

2. **Information search.** After identifying the need, the consumer searches for information on the various alternatives available to satisfy the need. Here, we differentiate between two decisions: what product to buy **(product brokering)** and from whom to buy it **(merchant brokering)**. During this phase, online product search and comparison engines, such as shopping.com, buyersindex. com, and mysimon.com, can be very helpful.

3. **Evaluation of alternatives.** The consumer's information search will eventually generate a smaller set of preferred alternatives. From this set, the would-be buyer will further evaluate the alternatives and, if possible, negotiate terms.

4. **Purchase decision and delivery.** After evaluating the alternatives, the consumer will make the purchasing decision, arrange payment and delivery, purchase warranties, and so on.

5. **Postpurchase behavior.** The final phase is a postpurchase phase, which consists of customer service and evaluation of the usefulness of the product (e.g., "This product is really great!" or "We really received good service when we had problems").

product brokering
Deciding what product to buy.

merchant brokering
Deciding from whom (from what merchant) to buy products.

CUSTOMER DECISION SUPPORT IN WEB PURCHASING

The preceding generic purchasing-decision model was widely used in research on consumer-based EC. In the Web-based environment, decision support is available in each phase. The framework shown in Exhibit 4.1 shows that each of the phases of the purchasing model can be supported by both consumer decision support system (CDSS) facilities and Internet and Web facilities. The CDSS facilities support the specific decisions in the process. Generic EC technologies provide the necessary mechanisms as well as enhance communication and collaboration. Specific implementation of this framework and explanations of some of the terms are provided throughout this chapter and the entire text.

The planner of B2C marketing needs to consider the Web purchasing models in order to better influence the customer's decision-making process (e.g., by effective one-to-one advertising and marketing).

PLAYERS IN THE CONSUMER DECISION PROCESS

Several different players may play roles in various phases of the consumer decision process. The following are five major roles:

- **Initiator.** The person who first suggests or thinks of the idea of buying a particular product or service.
- **Influencer.** A person whose advice or view carries some weight in making a final purchasing decision.
- **Decider.** The person who ultimately makes a buying decision or any part of it—whether to buy, what to buy, how to buy, or where to buy.
- **Buyer.** The person who makes an actual purchase.
- **User.** The person who consumes or uses a product or service.

A single person may play all five roles if the product or service is for personal use. In this case, the marketer needs to understand and target that individual. In many situations, however, different people may play different roles, For example, a newly graduated engineer proposed to buy a car for his mother, which was followed by suggestions from his father and friends. Finally, he followed his father's suggestion to buy the car. When

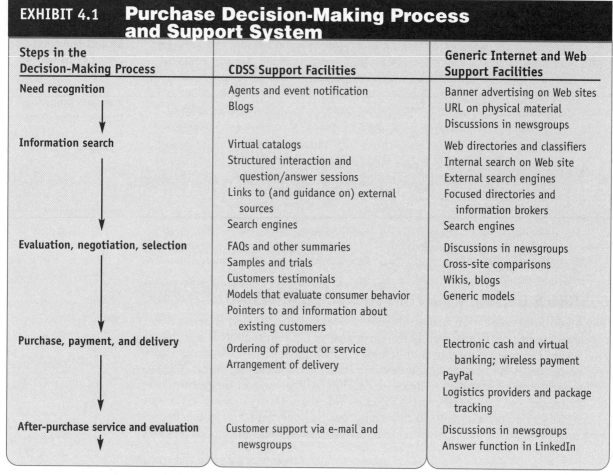

EXHIBIT 4.1   Purchase Decision-Making Process and Support System

Steps in the Decision-Making Process	CDSS Support Facilities	Generic Internet and Web Support Facilities
Need recognition	Agents and event notification Blogs	Banner advertising on Web sites URL on physical material Discussions in newsgroups
Information search	Virtual catalogs Structured interaction and question/answer sessions Links to (and guidance on) external sources Search engines	Web directories and classifiers Internal search on Web site External search engines Focused directories and information brokers Search engines
Evaluation, negotiation, selection	FAQs and other summaries Samples and trials Customers testimonials Models that evaluate consumer behavior Pointers to and information about existing customers	Discussions in newsgroups Cross-site comparisons Wikis, blogs Generic models
Purchase, payment, and delivery	Ordering of product or service Arrangement of delivery	Electronic cash and virtual banking; wireless payment PayPal Logistics providers and package tracking
After-purchase service and evaluation	Customer support via e-mail and newsgroups	Discussions in newsgroups Answer function in LinkedIn

Sources: O'Keefe and McEachern (1998) and authors' experience.

more than one individual comes into play, it becomes more difficult to properly target advertising and marketing. Different marketing efforts may be designed to target people playing different roles.

ONE-TO-ONE MARKETING

One of the greatest benefits of EC is its ability to match products (services) with individual consumers. Such a match is a part of *one-to-one marketing*, which treats each customer in a unique way to fit marketing and advertising with the customer's profile and needs. To learn about this approach and how it evolved from the traditional marketing approaches of mass marketing and market segmentation see Online File W4.2.

Section 4.1 ▶ REVIEW QUESTIONS

1. List the five phases of the generic purchasing-decision model.
2. Use an example to explain the five phases in the generic purchasing-decision model.
3. Describe the supporting functions available in Web-based purchasing.
4. Describe the major players in a buy decision.
5. Define the one-to-one marketing approach.

4.2 PERSONALIZATION, LOYALTY, SATISFACTION, AND TRUST IN EC

Internet marketing facilitates the use of market segmentation and one-to-one marketing (Online File W4.2). Here we will address several key issues related to one-to-one marketing: personalization, collaborative filtering, customer loyalty, permission marketing (Section 4.8), and trust. For details on these and other issues related to implementing EC-based one-to-one marketing, see Cant et al. (2009). For a discussion of how one-to-one marketing is related to CRM, see Online Appendix B.

PERSONALIZATION AND BEHAVIORAL TARGETING IN E-COMMERCE

Personalization refers to the matching of services, products, and advertising content to individuals and their preferences. The matching process is based on what a company knows about the individual user. This knowledge is usually referred to as a **user profile**. The user profile defines customer preferences, behaviors, and demographics. Profiles can be generated in several ways. The major strategies used to compile user profiles include the following:

personalization
The matching of services, products, and advertising content with individual consumers and their preferences.

▶ **Solicit information directly from the user.** This is usually done by asking the user to fill in a questionnaire or by conducting an interview with the user.

▶ **Observe what people are doing online.** A common way to observe what people are doing online is through the use of a **cookie**—a data file that is stored on the user's hard drive, frequently without disclosure or the user's consent. Sent by a remote Web server over the Internet, the information stored will surface when the user's browser accesses the specific Web server, and the cookie will collect information about the user's activities at the site (see cookiecentral.com). The use of cookies is one of the most controversial issues in EC, as discussed in Insights and Additions 4.1. Other tools, such as spyware and Web bugs, are described in Section 4.3. For an overview of personalization in EC, see Chan (2005) and Anke and Sundaram (2006).

user profile
The requirements, preferences, behaviors, and demographic traits of a particular customer.

cookie
A data file that is placed on a user's hard drive by a remote Web server, frequently without disclosure or the user's consent, that collects information about the user's activities at a site.

▶ **Build from previous purchase patterns.** For example, Amazon.com builds customer profiles to recommend books, CDs, and other products, based on what customers have purchased before, rather than asking customers, using cookies, or doing market research.

▶ **Perform marketing research.** Firms can research the market using tools described in Section 4.3 and in the Netflix case at the beginning of the chapter.

▶ **Make inferences.** Infer from information provided by customers on other issues or by analyzing similar customers. (See collaborative filtering in Section 4.3.) When the ad matching is based on information collected about the customers' behavior on the Internet, it is called **behavioral targeting**.

behavioral targeting
The use of information collected on an individual's Internet-browsing behavior to select which advertisements to display to that individual.

Once a customer profile is constructed, a company matches the profile with a database of products, services, or ads. Manual matching is time-consuming and expensive; therefore, the matching process is usually done by software agents. One-to-one matching can be applied through several different methods. One well-known method is *collaborative filtering* (Section 4.3).

Personalization can be done in different ways. For example, some stores send an instant alert to their customers' mobile devices and notify them when prices of particular items in their "watch list" drop to a predefined level or when an auction comes to a close. Some stores also allow users to personalize Web site attributes, such as the site's color or the greeting name. However, security, privacy, and trust concerns remain a limiting factor for personalization.

Insights and Additions 4.1 Cookies in E-Commerce

Are cookies bad or good? The answer is "both." When users revisit Amazon.com or other sites, they are greeted by their first name. How does Amazon.com know a user's identity? Through the use of cookies! Vendors can provide consumers with considerable personalized information if they use cookies that signal a consumer's return to a site. (A variation of cookies is known as e-sugging—*SUG-ing*, from "selling under the guise of research.") For example, consumers who visit travel sites may get more and more unsolicited travel related e-mails and pop-up ads.

Cookies can provide a wealth of information to marketers, which then can be used to target ads to consumers. Thus, marketers get higher rates of "click-throughs," and customers can view the most relevant information. Cookies can also prevent repetitive ads, because vendors can arrange for a consumer not to see the same ad twice.

Finally, advanced data mining companies, such as NCR and Sift, can analyze information in cookie files so companies can better meet the customers' needs.

However, some people object to cookies because they do not like the idea that "someone" is watching their activity on the Internet. Users who do not like cookies can disable them. However, some consumers might want to keep the friendly cookies. For example, many sites recognize a person as a subscriber so that they do not need to reregister. Internet Explorer (IE) 6.09 and higher also gives users control over third-party cookies. (Go to "Internet Options" under "Tools" and select "Private tab," click "Advanced," and put a check mark next to "Override automatic cookie handling." Then, direct IE to accept first-party cookies.) See *en.wikipedia.org/wiki/HTTP_cookie* and *webmaster. info.aol.com/aboutcookies.html* for more on cookies.

CUSTOMER LOYALTY

One of the major objectives of one-to-one marketing is to increase customer loyalty (recall the Netflix case). *Customer loyalty* refers to a deep commitment to rebuy or repatronize a preferred product/service consistently in the future, thereby causing repetitive same-brand purchasing.

Attracting and retaining loyal customers remains the most important issue for any selling company, including e-tailers. Increased customer loyalty can bring cost savings to a company in various ways: lower marketing and advertising costs; lower transaction costs; lower customer turnover expenses; lower failure costs, such as warranty claims; and so on. Customer loyalty also strengthens a company's market position because loyal customers are kept away from the competition. In addition, customer loyalty can lead to a decrease in price sensitivity, and an increase in favorable word-of-mouth advertising.

Loyalty programs were introduced over 100 years ago and are widely used among airlines, hotel chains, casinos, and credit card companies. Today, loyalty programs are computer-based and have been expanded to all kinds of businesses, as demonstrated by the following examples:

▶ Octopus Hong Kong (octopuscards.com) is a stored-value-card operator that launched a reward program for consumers aimed at increasing card usage across Hong Kong. Consumers earn reward points by purchasing at a number of leading merchants across the territory, including Watsons, UA Cinemas, and McDonald's. Each Octopus card can store up to 1,000 reward points, which can be redeemed on the next purchase.

▶ FANCL (fancl.com), a Japanese cosmetics and health care company, offers the "FANCL point program" where consumers earn FANCL points that are saved for gift redemption.

▶ Maxwell House Coffee has its own program where consumers earn "House Points" with each can of coffee they buy and redeem the points for gift rewards.

The introduction of EC decreases loyalty in general because customers' ability to shop, compare, and switch to different vendors becomes easier, faster, and less expensive given the aid of search and comparison engines. However, companies have found that loyal customers end up buying more when they have a Web site to shop from. For example, W.W. Grainger, a large industrial-supply company, found that loyal B2B customers increased their purchases substantially when they began using Grainger's Web site (grainger.com).

E-Loyalty

E-loyalty refers to a customer's loyalty to an e-tailer or a manufacturer that sells directly online or to loyalty programs delivered online or supported electronically. Customer acquisition and retention is a critical success factor in e-tailing. The expense of acquiring a new customer can be over $100; even for Amazon.com, which has a huge reach, it is more than $15. In contrast, the cost of maintaining an existing customer at Amazon.com is $2 to $4.

e-loyalty
Customer loyalty to an e-tailer or loyalty programs delivered online or supported electronically.

Companies can foster e-loyalty by learning about their customers' needs, interacting with customers, and providing superb customer service. A major source of information about e-loyalty is e-loyaltyresource.com. One of its major services is an online journal, the *e-Loyalty Resource Newsletter*, which offers numerous articles describing the relationships among e-loyalty, customer service, personalization, CRM, and Web-based tools. Another source of information is colloquy.com, which concentrates on loyalty marketing. Comprehensive reviews of the use of the Web and the Internet to foster e-loyalty are provided by Yeo and Chiam (2006).

Example. One of the most publicized computer-based loyalty programs is the one used by Harrah's, the largest casino chain in the world. The casino industry is extremely competitive, with more and more gambling channels and new physical casinos opening to the public. Standing out from the competition is becoming an increasingly enormous challenge. All casinos employ basic loyalty programs. They record the money spent in the machines, tables, restaurants, and so forth by each player and provide awards to frequent gamblers (e.g., a free night's stay in their hotels). Using data mining and business intelligence, Harrah's was able to learn more accurately about its customers and offer them the rewards on a one-to-one basis the players really like.

Lately, Harrah's moved one step further in order to increase its understanding of its customers and their loyalty by moving to a real-time rewards system. For example, if the casino knows who is playing on a specific slot machine and the birthdays of that player, it can arrange for a manager to come to the player with a birthday cake and a gift while playing the specific machine. And each player might receive its preferred gift. Using a Teradata data warehouse as well as SAS and Cognos software, an analysis of millions of customers becomes feasible and economical. This enables Harrah's to deliver the best in one-to-one marketing and to do it in real time. Customers feel that the company knows them and their needs, so they keep coming back.

According to Floh and Treiblmaier (2006), satisfaction and trust are the two most important factors in determining customer e-loyalty.

SATISFACTION IN EC

Satisfaction has received an enormous amount of attention in studies of consumer-based EC. ForeSee Results Inc., an online customer satisfaction measurement company, developed the American Customer Satisfaction Index (ACSI) (theasci.org) for measuring customer satisfaction with EC. For example, in the fourth quarter of 2005, the ACSI for e-commerce category had increased 1.3 percent over the previous quarter to an aggregate score of 79.6 on a 100-point scale (Tode 2006), below its all-time high of 80.8 in 2003. The Customer Respect Group (customerrespect.com) also provides an index to measure the customer's online experience. The Customer Respect Index (CRI) includes the following components: simplicity, responsiveness, transparency, principles, attitude, and privacy.

Researchers have proposed several models to explain the formation of satisfaction with online shopping. For example, Cheung and Lee (2005) proposed a framework for consumer satisfaction with Internet shopping by correlating the end-user satisfaction perspective with the service quality viewpoint. The framework has been updated and is shown in Online File W4.3. More discussion on EC satisfaction can be found in Collier and Bienstock (2006).

TRUST IN EC

trust

The psychological status of willingness to depend on another person or organization.

Trust is the psychological status of depending on another person or organization to achieve a planned goal. When people trust each other, they have confidence that as transaction partners they will keep their promises. However, both parties in a transaction assume some risk. In the electronic marketplace, sellers and buyers do not meet face to face. The buyer can see a picture of the product, but not the product itself. Promises of quality and delivery can be easily made—but will they be kept? To deal with these issues, EC vendors need to establish high levels of trust with current and potential customers. Trust is particularly important in global EC transactions due to the difficulty of taking legal action in cases of a dispute or fraud and the potential for conflicts caused by differences in culture and business environments.

In addition to sellers and buyers trusting each other, both must have trust in the EC computing environment and in the EC infrastructure. If people do not trust the security of the EC infrastructure, they will not feel comfortable about using credit cards to make EC purchases.

EC Trust Models

Several models have been put forth to explain the EC–trust relationship. For example, Lee and Turban (2001) examined the various aspects of EC trust and developed the model shown in Online File W4.4. According to this model, the level of trust is determined by numerous variables (factors) shown on the left side and in the middle of the figure. The exhibit illustrates the complexity of trust relationships, especially in B2C EC.

For a more comprehensive treatment of EC trust, see Jeanson and Ingham (2006) and Hoffman et al. (2006). For methods of increasing trust, see Online File W4.4.

Section 4.2 ▶ REVIEW QUESTIONS

1. Explain how personalization (matching people with goods/services) is done.
2. List the methods of customer profiling.
3. Define loyalty and describe e-loyalty.
4. Describe the issue of trust in EC and how to increase it.
5. What influences consumer satisfaction online? Why do companies need to monitor it?

4.3 MARKET RESEARCH FOR EC

The goal of market research is to find information and knowledge that describe the relationships among consumers, products, marketing methods, and marketers. Its aim is to discover marketing opportunities and issues, to establish marketing and advertising plans, to better understand the purchasing process, and to evaluate marketing performance. On the Web, the objective is to turn browsers into buyers. Market research includes gathering information about topics such as the economy, industry, firms, products, pricing, distribution, competition, promotion, and consumer purchasing behavior. Here we focus on the latter.

Businesses, educational institutions, and governments use various tools to conduct consumer market research both *offline* and *online*. The major ones that are used in e-commerce are described later in this section.

METHODS FOR CONDUCTING MARKET RESEARCH ONLINE

EC market research can be conducted through conventional methods, or it can be done with the assistance of the Internet. Although telephone or shopping mall surveys will continue, interest in Internet research methods is on the rise. Market research that uses the Internet frequently is faster and more efficient and allows the researcher to access a more geographically diverse audience than those found in many offline surveys (see FAQs at casro.org). Also, on the Web, market researchers can conduct a very large study much more cheaply than with other methods. The larger the sample size, the larger the accuracy and the predictive capabilities of the results. Telephone surveys can cost as much as $50 per respondent. This may be too expensive for a small company that needs several hundred respondents. An online survey will cost a fraction of a similarly sized telephone survey and can expedite research considerably, as shown in Case 4.1. As you may recall, marketers concentrate on market segmentation and one-to-one. Let's see how this is accomplished.

CASE 4.1
EC Application

INTERNET MARKET RESEARCH EXPEDITES TIME-TO-MARKET AT PROCTER & GAMBLE

For decades, Procter & Gamble (P&G), Johnson & Johnson, and Colgate-Palmolive have been competitors in the market for personal care products. Developing a major new product from concept to market launch used to take over five years. First, a concept test was conducted: The companies sent product photos and descriptions to potential customers, asking whether they might buy the product. If the feedback was negative, they tried to improve the product concept and then repeated previous tasks. Once positive response was achieved, sample products were mailed out, and the customers were asked to fill out detailed questionnaires. When customers' responses met the companies' internal hurdles, the companies would start with mass TV advertising.

However, thanks to the Internet, it took P&G only three and one-half years to get Whitestrips, the teeth-brightening product, onto the market and to a sales level of $200 million a year—considerably quicker than other oral care products. In September 2000, P&G threw out the old marketing test model and instead introduced Whitestrips on the Internet, offering the product for sale on P&G's Web site. The company spent several months studying who was coming to the site and buying the product and collecting responses to online questionnaires, which was much faster than the old mailers.

The online research, which was facilitated by data mining conducted on P&G's huge historical data (stored in a data warehouse) and the new Internet data, revealed the most enthusiastic groups. These included teenage girls, brides-to-be, and young Hispanic Americans. Immediately, the company started to target these segments with

appropriate advertising. The Internet created a product awareness of 35 percent, even before any shipments were made to stores. This buzz created a huge demand for the product by the time it hit the shelves.

In 2006, P&G began using on-demand solutions from RightNow Technologies (*rightnow.com*), including survey tools that execute opinion polls among selected segments of consumers who have opted into the company's market research programs. From these experiences, P&G learned important lessons about flexible and creative ways to approach product innovation and marketing. The whole process of studying the product concept, segmenting the market, and expediting product development has been revolutionized.

By 2009, all major competitors established groups in Facebook, purchased islands in Second Life, and used Twitter to engage customers in future product development. Not only did time to market decrease, but better accuracy has been achieved. For Johnson & Johnson's marketing activities in this area, see Ploof (2009).

Sources: Compiled from *RightNow.com* (2006), Buckley (2002), and *pg.com* (accessed November 2009).

Questions

1. How did P&G reduce time-to-market?
2. What was data mining used for?
3. What research methods were used?

WHAT ARE MARKETERS LOOKING FOR IN EC MARKET RESEARCH?

By looking at a personal profile that includes observed behaviors on the Web, it is possible for marketers to explain and predict online buying behavior. For example, companies want to know why some customers are online shoppers whereas others are not. Major factors that are used for prediction are (in descending order of importance): product information requested, number of related e-mails, number of orders made, products/services ordered, and gender.

Typical questions that online market research attempts to answer are: What are the purchase patterns for individuals and groups (market segmentation)? What factors encourage online purchasing? How can we identify those who are real buyers from those who are just browsing? How does an individual navigate—does the consumer check information first or do they go directly to ordering? What is the optimal Web page design? Knowing the answers to questions such as these helps a vendor to advertise properly, to price items, to design the Web site, and to provide appropriate customer service. Online market research can provide such data about individuals, about groups, and even about the entire Internet.

Internet-based market research is often done in an interactive manner, allowing personal contact with customers, and it provides marketing organizations with a greater ability to understand the customer, the market, and the competition. For example, it can identify early shifts in product and customer trends, enabling marketers to identify products and marketing opportunities and to develop those products that customers really want to buy. It also tells management when a product or a service is no longer popular. To learn more about market research on the Web, see the tutorials at webmonkey.com.

The following discussion describes some online market research methods.

MARKET SEGMENTATION RESEARCH

Because EC also has to identify an appropriate customer group for specific products and services, it is important first to understand how groups of consumers are classified. This classification is called *market segmentation* (see Online File W4.5).

MARKET RESEARCH FOR ONE-TO-ONE

The major one-to-one data collection approaches are:

- ▶ Direct solicitation of information from customers and experts (surveys, focus groups)
- ▶ Observing what customers are doing on the Web
- ▶ Collaborative filtering

Direct Solicitation of Information

Online direct solicitation methods range from one-to-one communication with specific customers, usually by e-mail, to moderated focus groups conducted in chat rooms, to questionnaires placed on Web sites, to tracking of customers' movements on the Web. Professional pollsters and marketing research companies frequently conduct online voting polls (e.g., see cnn.com and acnielsen.com). Polling consumer opinions is popular on social networks (e.g., Facebook Poll). A typical Internet-based market research process is shown in Exhibit 4.2. Representative methods of direct solicitation of information follow:

Implementing Web-Based Surveys. Web-based surveys are becoming popular with companies and researchers. For example, Mazda North America used a Web-based survey to help design its Miata line. Web surveys may be passive (a fill-in questionnaire) or

EXHIBIT 4.2 Online Market Research Process

Steps in Collecting Market Research Data
1. Define the research issue and the target market.
2. Identify newsgroups and Internet communities to study.
3. Identify specific topics for discussion.
4. Subscribe to the pertinent groups; register in communities.
5. Search discussion group topic and content lists to find the target market.
6. Search e-mail discussion group lists.
7. Subscribe to filtering services that monitor groups.
8. Read FAQs and other instructions.
9. Visit chat rooms.

Content of the Research Instrument
1. Post strategic queries to groups.
2. Post surveys on a Web site.
3. Offer rewards for participation.
4. Post strategic queries on a Web site.
5. Post relevant content to groups, with a pointer to a Web site survey.
6. Post a detailed survey in special e-mail questionnaires.
7. Create a chat room and try to build a community of consumers.

Target Audience of the Study
1. Compare audience with the target population.
2. Determine editorial focus.
3. Determine content.
4. Determine what Web services to create for each type of audience.

Sources: Compiled from Vassos (1996) and Moisander and Valtonen (2006).

interactive (respondents download the questionnaires, add comments, ask questions, and discuss issues). For more information and additional software tools, see supersurvey.com, surveymonkey.com, and clearlearning.com. For an introduction on how to conduct Web-based surveys, see Faught et al. (2004).

Online Focus Groups. Several research firms create panels of qualified Web regulars to participate in online focus groups. For example, Research Connections (researchconnections.com) recruits participants in advance by telephone and takes the time to help them connect to the Internet, if necessary. Use of preselected focus group participants helps to overcome some of the problems (e.g., small sample size and partial responses) that sometimes limit the effectiveness of Web-based surveys.

Hearing Directly from Customers. Instead of using focus groups, which are costly and possibly slow, customers can be asked directly what they think about a product or service. Toymaker LEGO used a market research vendor to establish a survey on an electronic bulletin board where millions of visitors read each other's comments and share opinions about LEGO toys. The research vendor analyzed the responses daily and submitted the information to LEGO. In addition, companies can use chat rooms, newsgroups, blogs, wikis, podcasts, and electronic consumer forums to interact with consumers.

Software tools that can be used to hear directly from customers include BetaSphere (voc-online.com), InsightExpress (insightexpress.com), and Survey.com (survey.com).

Data Collection in the Web 2.0 Environment

Collecting data in the Web 2.0 environment provides new and exciting opportunities. Here are some methods:

> **Discussion forums.** Subgroups in social networks operate discussion forums where members can exchange opinions on may topics.
>
> **Polling.** People like to vote (e.g., *American Idol*), expressing preferences (see the Netflix case). They provide opinions on products, services, and so forth. They do it in social networks (e.g., Facebook).
>
> **Blogging.** Bloggers can raise issues or induce others to express opinions.
>
> **Chatting.** Community members love to chat in public chat rooms. By following what goes on there, collection of current data is assured.
>
> **Live chat.** Here, interactive data from customers in real time is collected.
>
> **Chatterbots.** These can be partially interactive. Logs of communications can be analyzed. Sometimes, people are more honest when they chat with an avatar.
>
> **Collective wisdom for intelligence.** This is a kind of community brainstorming. Researchers can find out what arguments people are having and the degree of the disagreements.
>
> **Find expertise.** Expertise is frequently found in the Web 2.0 environment, many times for free. Finding experts can be easy with LinkedIn (e.g., use LinkedIn's "Answers" function.
>
> **Folksonomy.** This social tagging makes data easier to find and access.
>
> **Data in videos, photos, and other rich media.** Places where these media are shared contribute to valuable data collection.

Observing Customers' Movements Online

To avoid some of the problems of online surveys, especially the giving of false or biased information, some marketers choose to learn about customers by observing their behavior rather than by asking them questions. Many marketers keep track of consumers' Web movements by using methods such as transaction logs (log files) or cookie files.

transaction log
A record of user activities at a company's Web site.

Transaction Logs. A **transaction log** records user activities at a company's Web site. A transaction log is created from the computer log file of user actions that have occurred. With log file analysis tools, it is possible to get a good idea of where visitors are coming from, how often they return, and how they navigate through a site. The transaction-log approach is especially useful if the visitors' names are known (e.g., when they have registered with the site). In addition, data from the shopping cart database can be combined with information in the transaction log to reveal more insights.

clickstream behavior
Customer movements on the Internet.

Note that as customers move from site to site, they establish their **clickstream behavior,** a pattern of their movements on the Internet, which can be seen in their transaction logs. Both ISPs and individual Web sites are capable of tracking a user's clickstream.

Web bugs
Tiny graphics files embedded in e-mail messages and in Web sites that transmit information about users and their movements to a Web server.

Cookies, Web Bugs, and Spyware. Cookies and Web bugs can be used to supplement transaction-log methods. As discussed earlier, cookies allow a Web site to store data on the user's PC; when the customer returns to the site, the cookies can be used to find what the customer did in the past. Cookies are frequently combined with **Web bugs,** tiny graphics files embedded in e-mail messages and on Web sites. Web bugs transmit information about the user and his or her movements to a monitoring site.

Spyware is software that gathers user information through an Internet connection without the user's knowledge (see en.wikipedia.org/wiki/Spyware). Originally designed to allow freeware authors to make money on their products, spyware applications are typically bundled together with freeware for download onto users' machines. Many users do not realize that they are downloading spyware with the freeware. Sometimes the freeware provider may indicate that other programs will be loaded onto the user's computer in the licensing agreement (e.g., "may include software that occasionally notifies users of important news"). Spyware stays on the user's hard drive and continually tracks the user's actions, periodically sending information on the user's activities to the owner of the spyware. It typically is used to gather information for advertising purposes. Users cannot control what data are sent via the spyware, and unless they use special tools they often cannot uninstall the spyware, even if the software it was bundled with is removed from the system. Effective tools for fighting spyware include Ad-aware (lavasoftusa.com/software/adaware), Spykiller (spykiller.com), and Webwasher Spyware from Secure Computing (securecomputing.com, now part of McAfee). For more on spyware and banners, see Online File W4.6.

The use of cookies and Web bugs is controversial. Many believe that they invade the customer's privacy (see privacyfoundation.org). Tracking customers' activities *without their knowledge or permission* may be unethical or even illegal.

Analysis of B2C Clickstream Data. Large and ever-increasing amounts of B2C data can be collected on consumers, products, and so on. Such data come from several sources: internal data (e.g., sales data, payroll data, etc.), external data (e.g., government and industry reports), and clickstream data. **Clickstream data** are data generated in the Web environment; they provide a trail of a user's activities (the user's clickstream behavior) in a Web site. These data include a record of the user's browsing patterns: every Web site and every page of every Web site the user visits, how long the user remains on a page or site, in what order the pages were visited, and even the e-mail addresses of mail that the user sends and receives. By analyzing clickstream data, a firm can find out, for example, which promotions are effective and which population segments are interested in specific products.

Several companies offer tools that enable such an analysis. For example, WebTrends Marketing Lab 2 features several advanced tools for analyzing clickstream data (e.g., see webtrends.com).

Web mining refers to the use of data mining techniques for discovering and extracting information from Web documents. Web mining explores both *Web content* and *Web usage*. The usage analysis is derived from clickstream data. According to Gregg and Walczak (2006), Web mining has the potential to dramatically change the way we access and use the information available on the Web.

Collaborative Filtering

Once a company knows a consumer's preferences (e.g., music, movie, or book preferences), it would be useful if the company could predict, without asking the customer directly, what other products or services this consumer might enjoy. One way to do this is through **collaborative filtering,** which uses customer data to infer customer interest in other products or services. Similarly, if you know what certain customers like, you may want to infer what customers with similar profiles will prefer. These predictions are based on special formulas derived from behavioral sciences. Many personalization systems (recall the Netflix case) are based on collaborative filtering (e.g., backflip.com and choicestream.com). For details on collaborative filtering see en.wikipedia.org/wiki/Collaborative_filtering. For more about personalization and filtering, see knowledgestorm.com.

spyware
Software that gathers user information over an Internet connection without the user's knowledge.

clickstream data
Data that occur inside the Web environment; they provide a trail of the user's activities (the user's clickstream behavior) in the Web site.

Web mining
The use of data mining techniques for discovering and extracting information from Web documents and Web usage.

collaborative filtering
A market research and personalization method that uses customer data to predict, based on formulas derived from behavioral sciences, what other products or services a customer may enjoy; predictions can be extended to other customers with similar profiles.

Legal and Ethical Issues in Collaborative Filtering. Information often is collected from users without their knowledge or permission. This raises several ethical and legal questions, including invasion-of-privacy issues. Several vendors offer *permission-based* personalization tools. With these, companies request the customer's permission to receive questionnaires and ads (e.g., see knowledgestorm.com). See Section 4.8 for information on permission marketing.

LIMITATIONS OF ONLINE MARKET RESEARCH AND HOW TO OVERCOME THEM

One problem with online market research is that too much data may be available. To use data properly, one needs to organize, edit, condense, and summarize it. However, such a task may be expensive and time-consuming. One solution to this problem is to automate the process by using data warehousing and data mining. The essentials of this process, known as *business intelligence*, are provided in Online File W4.7 and Turban et al. (2011).

Some of the limitations of online research methods are accuracy of responses, loss of respondents because of equipment problems, and the ethics and legality of Web tracking. In addition, focus group responses can lose something in the translation from an in-person group to an online group. A researcher may get people online to talk to each other and play off of each other's comments, but eye contact and body language are two interactions of traditional focus group research that are lost in the online world. However, just as it hinders the two-way assessment of visual cues, Web research can actually offer some participants the anonymity necessary to elicit an unguarded response. Finally, a major limitation of online market research is the difficulty in obtaining truly representative samples.

Concerns have been expressed over the potential lack of representativeness in samples of online users. Online shoppers tend to be wealthy, employed, and well educated. Although this might be a desirable audience for some products and services, the research results might not be extendable to other markets. Although the Web-user demographic is rapidly diversifying, it is still skewed toward certain population groups, such as those with convenient Internet access (at home or work). Another important issue concerns the lack of clear understanding of the online communication process and how online respondents think and interact in cyberspace.

To overcome some of the limitations of online market research, companies can outsource their market research needs. Only large companies have specialized market research departments. Most other companies use third-party research companies, such as ACNielsen.

BIOMETRIC MARKETING

One problem with Web analytics, Web mining, clickstream data, and so on is that we observe and follow a *computer*, not knowing who is actually moving the mouse. Many households have several users; thus, the data collected may not represent any one person's preferences (unless of course, we are sure that there is one and only one user, as in the case of smart cell phones). A potential solution is suggested by Pons (2006) in the form of *biometric marketing*.

biometrics
An individual's unique physical or behavioral characteristics that can be used to identify an individual precisely (e.g., fingerprints).

A **biometric** is one of an individual's unique physical or behavioral characteristics that can be used to identify an individual precisely (e.g., fingerprints; see list at en.wikipedia.org/wiki/Biometrics and in Chapter 9). By applying the technology to computer users, we can improve both security and learn about the user's profile precisely. The question is how to do it? Indeed, there are programs by which users identify themselves to the computer by biometrics, and these are spreading rapidly. To utilize the technology for marketing involves social and legal acceptability. For these reasons, advertisers are using methods that target individuals without knowing their profiles. An example is search engine–based methods such as Google's AdWords (see Section 4.5).

Some researchers are wildly optimistic about the prospects for market research on the Internet; others are more cautious.

Section 4.3 ▶ REVIEW QUESTIONS

1. Describe the objectives of market research.
2. Define and describe market segmentation (see Online File W4.5).
3. Describe how market research is done online and the major market research methods.
4. List the major methods of data collection in the Web 2.0 environment.
5. Describe the role of Web logs and clickstream data.
6. Relate cookies, Web bugs, and spyware to market research.
7. Describe the limitations of online market research and how to overcome them.

4.4 WEB ADVERTISING

Advertising on the Web plays an extremely important role in e-commerce. Internet advertising is growing very rapidly, and companies are changing their advertising strategies to gain a competitive edge. According to a McKinsey global survey of marketers (*McKinsey Quarterly* 2007), online ads are also useful for brand building directly through response ads. Spending is expected to increase on all types of online advertising methods, including Web 2.0 tools over the next three years.

OVERVIEW OF WEB ADVERTISING

Advertising is an attempt to disseminate information in order to affect buyer–seller transactions. The traditional advertising was impersonal, one-way mass communication that was paid for by sponsors. Telemarketing and direct mail ads were attempts to personalize advertising to make it more effective. These direct marketing approaches worked fairly well but were expensive and slow and seldom truly one-to-one interactive. The cost–benefit was poor. For example, say a direct mail campaign costs about $1 per person and has a response rate of only 1 to 3 percent. This makes the cost per responding person in the range of $33 to $100. Such an expense can be justified only for high-ticket items (e.g., cars).

One of the problems with direct mail advertising was that the advertisers knew very little about the recipients. Market segmentation by various characteristics (e.g., age, income, gender) helped a bit but did not solve the problem. The concept of **interactive marketing** enables marketers and advertisers to interact directly with customers. But it was expensive and not very effective when done by phone. On the Internet, a consumer can click an ad to obtain more information or send an e-mail to ask a question. The consumer can live chat with the company or in a social network chat room. Besides the two-way communication and e-mail capabilities provided by the Internet, vendors also can target specific groups and individuals on whom they want to spend their advertising dollars. The Internet enables truly one-to-one advertising. A comparison of mass advertising, direct mail advertising, and interactive online advertising is shown in Online File W4.8.

The two major business models for advertising online are (1) using the Web as a channel to advertise a firm's own products and services and (2) making a firm's site a public portal site and using captive audiences to advertise products offered by other firms. For example, the audience might come to a P&G Web site to learn about Tide, but they might also get ads for products made by Coca-Cola there.

interactive marketing
Online marketing, facilitated by the Internet, by which marketers and advertisers can interact directly with customers, and consumers can interact with advertisers/vendors.

ad views

The number of times users call up a page that has a banner on it during a specific period; known as impressions or page views.

button

A small banner that is linked to a Web site. It can contain downloadable software.

click (click-through or ad click)

A count made each time a visitor clicks on an advertising banner to access the advertiser's Web site.

click-through rate

The percentage of visitors who are exposed to a banner ad and click on it.

click-through ratio

The ratio between the number of clicks on a banner ad and the number of times it is seen by viewers; measures the success of a banner in attracting visitors to click on the ad.

conversion rate

The percentage of clickers who actually make a purchase.

CPM (cost per thousand impressions)

The fee an advertiser pays for each 1,000 times a page with a banner ad is shown.

hit

A request for data from a Web page or file.

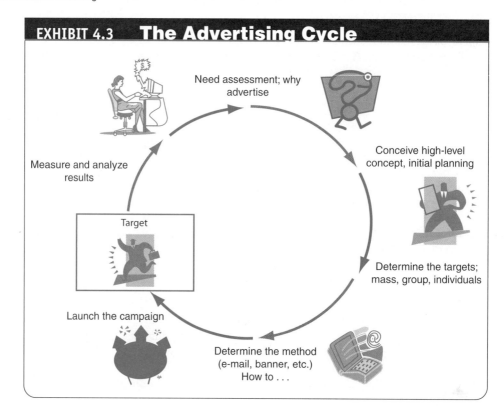

EXHIBIT 4.3   The Advertising Cycle

Need assessment; why advertise

Conceive high-level concept, initial planning

Determine the targets; mass, group, individuals

Determine the method (e-mail, banner, etc.) How to . . .

Launch the campaign

Target

Measure and analyze results

The Advertising Cycle

With closed-loop campaign management, companies are treating advertisement as a cyclical process, as shown in Exhibit 4.3. The cyclical process entails carefully planning a campaign to determine who the target audience is and how to reach that audience. Then, analyzing a campaign after its completion assists a company in understanding the campaign's success. This new knowledge is then used when planning future campaigns.

Before we describe the various steps of the cycle as it is implemented in Web advertising, let's learn some basic advertising terminology.

SOME BASIC INTERNET ADVERTISING TERMINOLOGY

The following list of terms and their definitions in the marginal glossary will be of use as you read about Web advertising.

- Ad views
- Button
- Click (click-through or ad click)
- Click-through rate
- Click-through ratio
- Conversion rate
- CPM (cost per thousand impressions)
- Hit

▶ Page
▶ Stickiness
▶ Unique visit
▶ Visit

WHY INTERNET ADVERTISING?

The major traditional advertising media are television, newspapers, magazines, and radio. However, the market is changing as many consumers are spending more time on the Internet and using mobile phones. Internet advertising is getting more attention. According to *eMarketer*, online ad spending is expected to reach $42.0 billion in 2011 from $21.4 billion in 2007 (reported in *New Media Trend Watch* 2009).

Companies advertise on the Internet for several reasons. To begin with, television viewers are migrating to the Internet. Internet users are spending time online that they previously spent viewing television. This trend will continue, especially as Internet-enabled cell phones become commonplace. In addition, many Internet users are well educated and have high incomes. These Internet surfers are a desired target for many advertisers.

Advertising Online and Its Advantages

The major advantages of using the Internet over mass advertising are precise targeting, interactivity, rich media (grabs attention), cost reduction, efficiency, and customer acquisition. In comparison to traditional media, the Internet is the fastest growing communication medium by far. Worldwide, the number of Internet users surpassed 1 billion in 2005; the 2 billion Internet user milestone is expected in 2011 (*Computer Industry Almanac* 2006). Of course, advertisers are interested in a medium with such potential reach, both locally and globally.

Other reasons why Web advertising is growing rapidly include:

> ▶ **Cost.** Online ads are sometimes cheaper than those in other media. In addition, ads can be updated at any time with minimal cost.
>
> ▶ **Richness of format.** Web ads can effectively use the convergence of text, audio, graphics, video, and animation. In addition, games, entertainment, and promotions can be easily combined in online advertisements. Also, services such as mysimon.com enable customers to compare prices and, using a PDA or cell phone, do it at any time from anywhere.
>
> ▶ **Personalization.** Web ads can be interactive and targeted to specific interest groups and/or individuals; the Web is a much more focused medium.
>
> ▶ **Timeliness.** Internet ads can be fresh and timely.
>
> ▶ **Location-basis.** Using wireless technology and GPS, Web advertising can be location based; Internet ads can be sent to consumers whenever they are in a specific location (e.g., near a restaurant or a theater) at a specific time.
>
> ▶ **Linking.** It is easy to link from an online ad to a storefront—one click does it.
>
> ▶ **Digital branding.** Even the most price-conscious online shoppers are willing to pay premiums for brands they trust. These brands may be click-and-mortar brands (e.g., P&G) or dot-coms such as Amazon.com. British Airways places many Internet banner ads; however, these ads are not for clicking on to buy: They are all about branding, that is, establishing British Airways as a brand.

page
An HTML (Hypertext Markup Language) document that may contain text, images, and other online elements, such as Java applets and multimedia files. It can be generated statically or dynamically.

stickiness
Characteristic that influences the average length of time a visitor stays in a site.

unique visits
A count of the number of visitors entering a site, regardless of how many pages are viewed per visit.

visit
A series of requests during one navigation of a Web site; a pause of a certain length of time ends a visit.

Each advertising medium, including the Internet, has its advantages and limitations. Online File W4.9 compares the advantages and limitations of Internet advertising against traditional advertising media. The combination of television–Web synergy can help attract more attention than either medium on its own.

Section 4.4 ▶ REVIEW QUESTIONS

1. Define Web advertising and the major terms associated with it.
2. Draw and explain the advertising cycle.
3. Describe the reasons for the growth in Web advertising.
4. Describe emerging Internet advertising approaches.
5. List the major benefits of Web advertising.

4.5 ONLINE ADVERTISING METHODS

A large number of online advertising methods exist. The following are a few major ones.

BANNERS

A **banner** is a graphic display that is used for advertising on a Web page. The size of the banner is usually 5 to 6.25 inches in length, 0.5 to 1 inch in width, and is measured in pixels. A banner ad is linked to an advertiser's Web page. When users "click" the banner, they are transferred to the advertiser's site. Advertisers go to great lengths to design a banner that catches consumers' attention. Banners often include video clips and sound. Banner advertising including pop-up banners is the most commonly used form of advertising on the Internet.

There are several types of banners. **Keyword banners** appear when a predetermined word is queried from a search engine. They are effective for companies that want to narrow their target audience. **Random banners** appear randomly, not as a result of some action by the viewer. Companies that want to introduce new products (e.g., a new movie or CD) or promote their brand use random banners. Static banners are always on the Web page. Finally, pop-up banners appear when least expected, as will be described later.

If an advertiser knows something about a visitor, such as the visitor's user profile or area of interest, it is possible to match a specific banner with that visitor. Obviously, such targeted, personalized banners are usually most effective.

In the near future, banner ads will greet people by name and offer travel deals to their favorite destinations. Such *personalized banners* are being developed, for example, by Dotomi (dotomi.com). Dotomi delivers ads to consumers who opt in to view its system. Initial results show a 14 percent click-through rate, which measures the success of a banner in attracting visitors to click, versus 3 to 5 percent with nonpersonalized ads.

Benefits and Limitations of Banner Ads

The major benefit of banner ads is that, by clicking on them, users are transferred to an advertiser's site, directly to the shopping page of that site. Another advantage of using banners is the ability to customize them for individual surfers or a market segment of surfers. Also, viewing of banners is common, because in many cases customers are forced to see banner ads while waiting for a page to load or before they can get the free information or entertainment that they want to see (a strategy called *forced advertising* and it is a banner spam). Finally, banners may include attention-grabbing multimedia.

banner

On a Web page, a graphic advertising display linked to the advertiser's Web page.

keyword banners

Banner ads that appear when a predetermined word is queried from a search engine.

random banners

Banner ads that appear at random, not as the result of the user's action.

The major disadvantage of banners is their cost. If a company demands a successful marketing campaign, it will need to allocate a large percentage of its advertising budget to place banners on high-volume Web sites. Another drawback is that a limited amount of information can be placed on the banner. Hence, advertisers need to think of a creative but short message to attract viewers.

However, it seems that viewers have become somewhat immune to banners and simply do not notice them as they once did. The click-through rate has been declining over time. Because of these drawbacks, it is important to decide where on the screen to place banners (e.g., the right side of the screen is better than the left; the top is better than the bottom). For more on the efficient use of banner ads, see Online File W4.10.

POP-UP AND SIMILAR ADS

One of the most annoying phenomena in Web surfing is the increased use of pop-up, pop-under, and similar ads. A **pop-up ad**, also known as *ad spawning*, appears due to the automatic launching of a new browser window when a visitor enters or exits a site, when a delay occurs, or when other triggers cause the display. A pop-up ad appears in front of the active window. A **pop-under ad** is an ad that appears underneath (in back of) the current browser window. When users close the active window, they see the ad. Pop-ups cover the user's current screen and may be difficult to close. Pop-up and pop-under ads are controversial: Many users strongly object to this advertising method, which they consider to be intrusive. Most browsers provide an option that allows the viewer to block pop-up windows. Legal attempts have also been made to control pop-ups because they are basically a form of spam.

Several other tactics, some of them very aggressive, are being used by advertisers, and their use is increasing (see Online File W4.11). These tactics may be accompanied by music, voice, and other rich multimedia.

E-MAIL ADVERTISING

Sending company or product information to people or companies that appear on mailing lists has become a popular way to advertise on the Internet. E-mail messages may be combined with brief audio or video clips to promote a product; some messages provide links that users can click on to make a purchase. E-mail continues to enjoy popularity among consumers and has become acknowledged as a legitimate and relied-upon marketing channel.

The advantages of e-mail advertising are its low cost and the ability to reach a wide variety of targeted audiences. E-mail is an interactive medium that can combine advertising and customer service. It can include a direct link to any URL, so it acts like a banner. A consumer may be more likely to respond to e-mail messages related to discounts or special sales. Most companies have a database of customers to whom they can send e-mail messages (e.g., Sears, most airlines, casinos, and financial institutions). However, using e-mail to send ads (sometimes floods of ads) without the receivers' permission is considered spamming.

A list of e-mail addresses can be a very powerful tool for a company, helping it to target a group of people that it knows something about. For information on how to create a mailing list, consult groups.yahoo.com (the service is free) or topica.com.

E-mail can also be sent to a PDA and to other mobile devices. Mobile phones, in particular, offer advertisers a real chance to advertise interactively and on a one-to-one basis with consumers—anytime, anyplace. In the future, e-mail ads will be targeted to individuals based not only on their user profiles but also on their physical location at any point in time. See Chapter 8 for a description of this concept, known as *l-commerce*.

pop-up ad
An ad that appears in a separate window before, after, or during Internet surfing or when reading e-mail.

pop-under ad
An ad that appears underneath the current browser window, so when the user closes the active window the ad is still on the screen.

E-Mail Hoaxes. E-mail hoaxes are very popular; some of them have been going on for years (e.g., Neiman Marcus's cookie recipe, the Nigerian treasure, the Koran and the Iraq invasion). Some of these are scams. For details, see ftc.gov and Chapter 9.

Fraud. Fraud also is a consideration. For example, a person may receive an e-mail stating that his or her credit card number is invalid or that his or her MSN service will be terminated unless another credit card number is sent in reply to the e-mail. For protection against such fraudulent practices, see scambusters.org and Chapter 9.

E-Mail Advertising Methods and Successes. E-mail advertising can be done in many different ways, as shown in Online File W4.12.

CLASSIFIED ADS

Classified ads can be found on special sites (e.g., craigslist.org and superpages.com), as well as on online newspapers, exchanges, and portals. In many cases, posting regular-size classified ads is free, but placing them in a larger size in color, or with some other noticeable features, is done for a fee. For examples, see traderonline.com and advertising.microsoft.com.

SEARCH ENGINE ADVERTISEMENT

Search engines are a good mechanism for most people to find information and, therefore, a good platform for online advertising. The two major forms of search engine advertising are listing URLs and keyword advertising.

URL Listing

Most search engines allow companies to submit their Internet addresses, called URLs (Universal Resource Locators), for free so that these URLs can be searched electronically. Search engine spiders crawl through each site, indexing its content and links. The site is then included as a candidate for future searches. Because there are quite a few search engines, advertisers who use this method should register URLs with as many proper search engines as possible. In some cases, URLs may be searched even if they are not submitted.

The major advantage of using search engines as an advertising tool is that it is free. Anyone can submit a URL to a search engine and be listed. Searchers for a company's products will most likely receive a list of sites that mention the products, including the company's own site. Search engine advertisement has become the most popular online advertising method, mainly thanks to Google.

However, the URL method has several drawbacks. The major one is location on the engine's list: The chance that a specific site will be placed at the top of a search engine's display list (say, in the first 10 items) is very slim. Furthermore, even if a company's URL makes it to the top, others can quickly displace it. Second, different search engines index their listings differently; therefore, making the top of several lists is difficult. The searcher may have the correct keywords, but if the search engine indexed the site listing using the "title" or "content description" in the meta tag, then the effort could be fruitless. A meta tag is a coding statement (in HTML) that describes the content of a Web page and is used by search engines in indexing.

Keyword Advertising

Google has created a new advertising technology by linking an advertisement with the user's keywords. Advertisers choose the keywords to which their advertisements will link. Advertisements appear on the screen along with the search results when the chosen keywords are searched. This can substantially increase the likelihood that the advertisement will be viewed because of its high relevance to user interests. In fact, more than 90 percent of Google's revenue is generated from this creative technology. Furthermore, Google allows the advertisers to bid for the order of appearance. Advertisers who pay more will appear higher on the list usually on the top or right side of the screen. It will appear as "sponsored advertisements."

Improving a Company's Search Engine Ranking (Optimization)

Because the URL appearing at the top of the search engine results usually receives more attention, each company wants its URL to be placed at the top. **Search engine optimization (SEO)** is the method of increasing site rank on search engines. To do so, the optimizer needs to know the ranking algorithm of the search engine (which may be different for different search engines) and best search phrases, and then tailor the ads accordingly.

In Google's ranking, for example, certain rules apply: Google ranks Web sites by their linkage popularity and tends to give weights to links from major companies, trade groups, government organizations, and sites built on the .edu domain. Wordtracker is a tool that helps find phrases that people tend to type when looking for a specific product. Wordtracker, however, has its own shortcomings: Popular phrases may not always be the best match for your target customers.

Another solution is to buy keyword ads on the page that contains Google's results of a search. Using Google Analytics or another system, users can track which phrases best convert into sales.

Finally, ads that appear on the side and top of the search results are attention grabbers, but they are expensive (see AdWords, later in this section). Several companies provide services that optimize Web content so that a site has a better chance of being discovered by a search engine—for example, Web Position from WebTrends (webtrends.com). More tips for improving a site's listing in various search engines can be found at searchenginewatch.com.

search engine optimization (SEO)
The craft of increasing site rank on search engines; the optimizer uses the ranking algorithm of the search engine (which may be different for different search engines) and best search phases, and tailors the ad accordingly.

Google: The Online Advertising King

No other EC company can match the success of Google and its meteoric rise. Google is considered by many to be not only changing the Internet but also the world. Google uses several varieties of search engine advertising methods that are generating billions of dollars in revenue and profits. In Insights and Additions 4.2, we describe two of these methods.

VIRAL MARKETING AND ADVERTISING

Viral marketing or advertising refers to word-of-mouth marketing in which customers promote a product or service by telling others about it. This can be done by e-mails, by text messaging, in conversations facilitated in chat rooms, via instant messaging, by posting messages in newsgroups, and in electronic consumer forums. Several of these are popular in social networks (Chapter 7). Having people forward messages to friends, asking them, for example, to "check out this product," is an example of viral marketing. This marketing approach has been used for generations, but now its speed and reach are multiplied by the Internet. This ad model can be used to build brand awareness at a minimal cost, because the people who pass on the messages are paid very little or nothing for their efforts.

viral marketing
Word-of-mouth method by which customers promote a product or service by telling others about it.

Insights and Additions 4.2   Google's Major Advertisement Methods

Google uses its Internet search technology to serve advertisements based on Web site content, the user's geographical location, and other factors. The major methods are AdWords and AdSense.

AdWords

AdWords is a self-service ad server that uses relevance-ranking algorithms similar to the ones that make the search engine so effective. Advertisers tell Google how much they want to spend and then "buy" pertinent keywords. When Web surfers type in a term that matches the advertiser's keyword, the advertiser is listed in a banner near the search results with the heading "Sponsored Links." Each time a user clicks the advertiser's banner ad, Google subtracts the cost-per-click for the advertiser's prepaid account; when the account's daily ad budget is depleted, Google stops displaying the ad.

The system is easy to use and remarkably effective. The click-through rate is about 15 percent, which is more than 10 times the rate of the average banner ad. According to industry experts, many Google advertisers have experienced a 20 to 25 percent increase in online sales.

Each time a visitor clicks on an ad (which takes the visitor to the advertiser's site), the site owner shares the commission paid by the advertiser with Google. The advertisers also participate in the AdWords program.

Despite its success, AdWords by itself does not provide the best one-to-one targeting. This may be achieved in many cases through a complementary program—AdSense.

AdSense

Google's AdSense is an affiliate program in which Google offers Web site owners a chance to earn a commission for their willingness to place ads of other advertisers on their sites. AdSense automatically delivers an advertiser's text and image ads that are precisely matched to each affiliate site. This is a major improvement over matching individuals based on their preferences, which is less accurate in many cases and much more expensive. The matching (called *contextual matching*) is based on a proprietary algorithm (Google filed for more than 60 patents on these and other innovations). The key is the quality and appearance of both the pages and the ads, as well as the popularity of the site. Hundreds of thousands participate in the affiliate program. Google provides the affiliates with analytics that help convert visitors to customers.

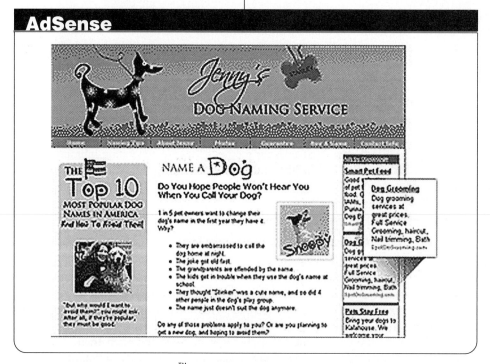

Source: Courtesy of Google AdSense™ advertising service (accessed January 2009).

Insights and Additions 4.2   (continued)

AdSense uses Google's relevance-scoring algorithms. Web site owners can enroll as affiliates in this program to enable ads of text, image, and more recently, video *advertisements* to be on their Web sites. These ads generate revenue for Google on either a *per-click* or *per-impression* basis. The revenue is shared with the Web site owners (affiliates).

AdSense has become a popular method of placing advertising on Web sites because the advertisements are less intrusive than most other banners, and the content of the advertisements is often more relevant to the Web site. For an example of a site using AdSense, see RTC (*rtcmagazine.com*). Google's success

is attributed to the quality of the matches, the large number of advertisers in its network, the ability to use ads in many languages, and the ability to understand the content of Web sites. Characteristics and demographics of the visitors that Google knows are considered in the match. This is also true of Google's competitors (e.g., MSN, with its AdCenter methodology). Similar programs are offered by eBay and Yahoo! (see eBay AdContex and Yahoo!'s Content Match). The closer the match, the less intrusive the ad is to the visitor, and the better the chance of the visitor's clicking on the ad.

Viral marketing has long been a favorite strategy of online advertisers pushing youth-oriented products. For example, advertisers might distribute, embedded within a sponsor's e-mail, a small game program that is easy to forward. By releasing a few thousand copies of the game to some consumers, vendors hope to reach hundreds of thousands of others. Viral marketing also was used by the founder of Hotmail, a free e-mail service that grew from zero to 12 million subscribers in its 18 initial months and to more than 50 million subscribers in about 4 years. Each e-mail sent via Hotmail carried an invitation for free Hotmail service. Also known as *advocacy marketing*, viral marketing, if properly used, can be effective, efficient, and relatively inexpensive. For further details, see en.wikipedia.org/wiki/Viral_marketing.

One of the downsides of this strategy is that several e-mail hoaxes have been spread this way. Another danger of viral advertising is that a destructive virus can be added to an innocent advertisement-related game or message.

Section 4.5 ▶ REVIEW QUESTIONS

1. Define banner ads and describe their benefits and limitations.
2. Describe banner swapping and banner exchanges.
3. Describe the issues surrounding pop-ups and similar ads.
4. Explain how e-mail is used for advertising.
5. Describe advertising via classified ads.
6. Describe the search engine optimization technique.
7. Describe Google's AdWords and AdSense.
8. Describe viral marketing (advertisement) on the Web.

4.6 ADVERTISING IN SOCIAL NETWORKS AND THE WEB 2.0 ENVIRONMENT

The emergence of social networks and the use of Web 2.0 tools provide new opportunities for advertisers.

SOCIAL NETWORK ADVERTISING

social network advertising
Online advertising that focuses on social networking sites.

Social network advertising describes online advertising that focuses on social networking sites. One of the major benefits of advertising in a social networking site is that advertisers can take advantage of the *users' demographic information* and target appropriate ads to the users. *eMarketer* estimated that $2 billion were spent in 2008 on social network advertising worldwide and that this market will continue to grow, reaching $3.8 billion in spending by 2011 (reported by *Marketing Charts* 2008).

Many claim that social network advertising will revolutionize the online advertising market. There is no doubt that social network advertising is a significantly new way of reaching customers; however, the market is far from being mature. The new forms of advertisement are more difficult to plan, measure, and quantify than regular Internet ads. Here we cover only some topics; others are covered in Online File W4.13.

Types of Social Network Advertising

According to en.wikipedia.org/wiki/Social_network_advertising, the three major classifications of social network advertising are as follows:

> ◗ **Direct advertising that is based on your network of friends.** This can be the most effective—but also the most controversial—format. An example is the Facebook Beacon Project. Based on an action your friend has taken, you might see a message in your news feed saying, "Bob has just bought a RadioHead CD from Music World." This can be an extremely effective mode of viral advertisement because people often make decisions to purchase something or do something based on their close group of friends. However, this form of advertising can be seen as exploiting the personal relationships you have with your friends; it also raises privacy concerns.
>
> ◗ **Direct advertising placed on your social network site.** This concept is similar to placing banner ads on any other site. An ad like this may be seen as a brick on a MySpace page or as a banner in a Facebook profile. However, there are two differences. One difference is that social network advertisers can take advantage of demographic data available on your profile and target ads directly to you. Second, these ads can be placed by developers on their application pages through ad networks such as AdParlor. Again, this raises the issue of privacy
>
> ◗ **Indirect advertising by creating "groups" or "pages."** With this innovative marketing technique, a company will create a "group" that users can join. The advertiser will target the "subscribers" or "fans" of this group to promote a contest, a new product, or simply just to increase brand awareness. These groups can grow quickly and become a very effective marketing tool. See the Scion case at the end of this chapter for an interesting example of innovative advertising to a market segment.

Sponsored Reviews by Bloggers

Companies are soliciting the help of paid bloggers to briefly mention their brands in regular blog entries or in video chips. For example, Apogee (apogee.com), instead of pouring money into search results as big companies do to get noticed, decided to explore the growing popularity of online communities (blogs and social networks) to get people talking about its Web site. For as little as $12.50 per post, Apogee's name and description of its business appear on blogs across the Web. For more on social network advertising, see Social Network Advertising (socialadblog.com).

ADVERTISING IN CHAT ROOMS AND FORUMS

Vendors also advertise to members of social networks. Sites such as Facebook offer targeted advertising opportunities, and vendors usually offer discounts to members on advertised products. Ads also link users to other sites that might be of interest to community members. Advertisers sometimes use online fantasy sports (e.g., available at Yahoo!) to send ads to specific sports fans (e.g., fans of the National Football League or Major League Baseball). According to *eMarketer* (2006), online fantasy sports attract millions of visitors every month.

Vendors frequently sponsor chat rooms. The sponsoring vendor places a chat link on its site, and the chat vendor does the rest (e.g., talkcity.com), including placing the advertising that pays for the session. The advertising in a chat room merges with the activity in the room, and the user is conscious of what is being presented.

The main difference between an advertisement that appears on a static Web page and one that comes through a chat room is that the latter allows advertisers to cycle through messages and target the chatters again and again. Also, advertising can become more thematic in a chat room. An advertiser can start with one message and build on it to a climax, just as an author does with a good story. For example, a toymaker may have a chat room dedicated to electronic toys. The advertiser can use the chat room to post a query such as, "Can anyone tell me about the new Electoy R3D3?" In addition, a company can go to competitors' chat rooms and observe the conversations there.

Chat rooms also are used as one-to-one connections between a company and its customers. For example, Mattel (mattel.com) sells about one-third of its Barbie dolls to collectors. These collectors use the chat room to make comments or ask questions that are then answered by Mattel's staff.

VIDEO ADS ON THE WEB AND IN SOCIAL NETWORKING

Videos ads are growing rapidly, mainly due to the popularity of YouTube and similar sites.

Video Ads

According to *Reuters* (2007), online video is expected to grow at nearly 40 percent annually through 2011 while TV viewing continues to fall. According to comScore, people watched 12 billion videos online in May 2008 alone. Video ads appear all over the Web, both as unsolicited pop-ups, or when you give permission to see a demo or information about a product. Video ads are very popular in the Web 2.0 environment and social networking.

Podcasting has begun to capture the public imagination. Content creators are now providing a growing stream of intriguing and diverse content for downloading on MP3 players or on personal computers, allowing consumers to control the time and place of their viewing or listening. And even advertising is emerging in podcasts. With the growth of online participation, consumers exert greater influence over the products and brands considered for purchase.

Two-minute YouTube clips were just the beginning as television comes to the Internet to become the network of tomorrow. For example, Diggnation (see digg.com) is a weekly tech/Web culture show based on the top social bookmarking news stories site. Diggnation drew about 250,000 viewers a week in 2008 and was among the most popular free video podcasts on Apple's iTunes service—alongside offerings from ABC, the BBC, and CNN. For example, KFC is among companies that are using consumer-generated videos and combining several of them to tell a story. Then, they show the story as an online ad or on television. For instance, homemade videos of the foam eruptions that come from dropping Mentos into a two-liter bottle of Diet Coke became a huge hit on video sites (see eepybird.com/dcm1.html).

YouTube has emerged as the largest advertising platform for video ads. By one estimate, YouTube currently had approximately 5 million videos and is growing at the rate of about 20 hours of new video content per minute in summer 2009 (Hodgin 2009). YouTube is already allowing marketers from brands like Wendy's (wendys.com) and Dove (dove.us) to upload videos to YouTube, just like anybody else. YouTube also began adding conventional ads to some of its videos and splitting the revenue with users who provide the content. Google AdSense's ad distribution network also offers ad-supported video clips.

Tracking the Success of an Online Video Campaign

Web video analytics
A way of measuring what viewers do when they watch an online video.

According to en.wikipedia.org/wiki/Online_video_analytics, online video analytics, also known as **Web video analytics,** is a way of measuring what viewers do when they watch an online video. A video is any length of video stream, such as a movie clip, video advertisement, movie trailer, television show, or full-length movie. Companies that provide Web video analytics are able to answer questions such as:

▶ How long did the viewer watch a particular video?

▶ Did the viewers pass it along to a friend? Embed it in their home page? Bounce out as soon as they clicked "play"?

▶ If there was an ad overlay with the video, did they watch it? If so, for how long? Did they click through to complete a sale proposed by the ad?

▶ Where do the viewers come from who watch videos on a particular site?

Using an analytics platform is an ideal way to track a campaign's success because it gives marketers real-time intelligence that allows them to continually optimize the campaign and ensure the highest ROI. Representative methods are as follows:

▶ *Analytics software* combines data from several sites. If advertisers are running a multi-platform campaign, they can assess the entire campaign via one analytics dashboard.

▶ *Search engine* rankings also are a quick way to gauge an online campaign's success. Search engines now crawl and rank sites based on blended content, including images, video, and audio.

▶ Another benchmark of success is the *traction* video content gets on sites such as youtube.com, metacafe.com, and blinkx.com, which allow viewers to tag, bookmark, rank, and comment on videos. Such feedback is a valuable way to gauge how video content is being perceived online.

▶ *Brand interaction* is another effective way to monitor the success of an online video campaign. Tracking how long viewers watch an advertisement, what percentage of the video clip viewers watch, and how often they see an advertisement can provide valuable information to online marketers.

VIRAL MARKETING IN SOCIAL NETWORKS

Social networks are a natural and ideal place for viral marketing. For example, Sears (sears.com) has been using social networking and e-commerce to drive prom-season sales. Sears kicked off a campaign that lets shoppers share their dress selections with friends on Facebook. There they have the option of sharing one of about 70 prom dresses with their Facebook friends. Choosing that option will either prompt users to select friends or place a photo of a model wearing the dress in their profile, along with a product description and a message requesting opinions. Prom dress selection is an important decision for high school girls who want to get feedback from a circle of trusted peers before buying.

Section 4.6 ▶ REVIEW QUESTIONS

1. Describe advertising on social networks.
2. Describe video ads and their advertising approach.
3. List success factors of video ads.
4. How do social networks provide viral marketing?

4.7   ADVERTISING STRATEGIES AND SPECIAL ADVERTISING TOPICS

Many advertising strategies are used on the Web. We present a representative sample of the major ones in this section.

AFFILIATE MARKETING AND ADVERTISING

Affiliate marketing is a revenue sharing model by which an organization refers consumers to the selling company's Web site. **Affiliate marketing** is used mainly as a revenue source for the referring organization and as a marketing tool for sellers. However, the fact that the selling company's logo is placed on many other Web sites is free advertising as well. Consider Amazon.com, whose logo can be seen on more than 1 million affiliate sites! Moreover CDNow (a subsidiary of Amazon.com) and Amazon.com are pioneers in the "get paid to view" or "listen to" commercials also used in affiliate marketing.

affiliate marketing
A marketing arrangement by which an organization refers consumers to the selling company's Web site.

ADS AS A COMMODITY (PAYING PEOPLE TO WATCH ADS)

With the ads-as-a-commodity approach, people are paid for time spent viewing an ad. This approach is used at mypoints.com and others. At MyPoints.com, interested consumers read ads in exchange for payment from the advertisers. Consumers fill out data on personal interests, and then they receive targeted banners based on their personal profiles. Each banner is labeled with the amount of payment that will be paid if the consumer reads the ad. If interested, the consumer clicks the banner to read it, and after passing some tests as to its content, is paid for the effort. Readers can sort and choose what they read, and the advertisers can vary the payments to reflect the frequency and desirability of the readers. Payments may be cash (e.g., $0.50 per banner) or product discounts. This method is used with smart phones too. For further details, see en.wikipedia.org/wiki/Online_advertising.

SELLING SPACE BY PIXELS

Million Dollar Homepage (milliondollarhomepage.com) was created by 21-year-old student Alex Tew in the United Kingdom. The Web site sold advertising space on a one-page grid, much as real estate is sold, displaying a total of 1 million pixels at $1 per pixel. The site was launched in August 2005 and sold out by January 13, 2006. Within a short time, people started to sell pixels in other countries (e.g., milliondollarhomepage.com.au, one of several Australian sites). Also, people who bought pixels at $1 each were selling them at higher prices through auctions. This is an innovative way of owning ad space because once you buy it, it's there forever. Incidentally, MillionDollarHomepage.com has been subjected to a distributed denial-of-service (DDoS) attack (Chapter 9) by malicious hackers, who have caused the site to be extremely slow to load or completely unavailable. Blackmailers at first asked for $5,000 to avert an attack on the site. The DDoS attack was launched after Alex Tew declined to pay, and the hackers then demanded $50,000 to stop attacking. A further refusal to pay prompted the attackers to deface the site, replacing the regular page with a message stating: "Don't come back, you sly dog!" The police solved the problem.

PERSONALIZED ADS AND OTHER PERSONALIZATION

The Internet has too much information for customers to view. Filtering irrelevant information by providing consumers with customized ads can reduce this information overload. BroadVision (broadvision.com) provides a customized ad service platform called *BroadVision eMarketing*. The heart of eMarketing is a customer database, which includes registration data and information gleaned from site visits. The companies that advertise via one-to-one use the database to send customized ads to consumers. Using this feature, a marketing manager can customize display ads based on user profiles. The product also provides market segmentation.

Webcasting

A free Internet news service that broadcasts personalized news and information, including seminars, in categories selected by the user.

Another model of personalization can be found in **Webcasting**, a free Internet news service that broadcasts personalized news and information as well as e-seminars. Users sign into the Webcasting system and select the information they would like to receive, such as sports, news, headlines, stock quotes, or desired product promotions. The users receive the requested information along with personalized ads based on their expressed interests and general ads based on their profile.

Adobe (adobe.com) with the help of Yahoo! launched an opt-in service that enables online commercial publishers to drive new revenue by including timely, contextual ads next to Adobe's Portable Document Format (PDF)–based content. The service has the potential to offer readers access to free content, enhanced with ads that match their interests. Every time the PDF content is viewed, contextual ads are dynamically matched to the content of the document.

ONLINE EVENTS, PROMOTIONS, AND ATTRACTIONS

Contests, quizzes, coupons (see coolsavings.com), and giveaways designed to attract visitors are as much a part of online marketing as they are of offline commerce. Some innovative ideas used to encourage people to pay attention to online advertising are provided in Online File W4.14.

Live Web Events

Live Web events (concerts, shows, interviews, debates, videos), if properly done, can generate tremendous public excitement and bring huge crowds to a Web site. Some of the best practices for successful live Web events are:

- Carefully planning content, audience, interactivity level, preproduction, and schedule
- Executing the production with rich media if possible
- Conducting appropriate promotion via e-mails, affinity sites, and streaming media directories, as well as conducting proper offline and online advertisement
- Preparing for quality delivery
- Capturing data and analyzing audience response so that improvements can be made

A global event can allow a product to debut in disparate locations. For example, Cisco Systems unveiled one of its products (ASR 1000 router) with the flair of an in-person event in 2008. It was covered by e-mail campaign and traditional media coverage but also by content distribution to bloggers and by ads in social networking sites such as Facebook. The company bought banner ads on prominent sites to drive traffic to marketing materials on their site. It also built a game around the new product and invited top prospects to take part in telepresence sessions that put them at a virtual table. The events and the marketing campaign created a strong response. For more details, see en.wikipedia.org/wiki/Telepresence.

Section 4.7 ▶ REVIEW QUESTIONS

1. Discuss the process and value of affiliate marketing.
2. How does the ads-as-a-commodity strategy work?
3. What are personalized ads?
4. What is a live event?
5. List some typical Internet promotions.

4.8 SPECIAL ADVERTISING TOPICS

The following are major representative topics related to Internet advertisement.

PERMISSION ADVERTISING

One of the major issues of one-to-one advertising is the flooding of users with unwanted (junk) e-mail, banners, pop-ups, and so on. The problem of flooding users with unsolicited ads is called spamming. **Spamming** typically upsets consumers and can keep useful advertising from reaching them.

    One solution used by advertisers is **permission advertising (permission marketing,** or the *opt-in approach*) in which users register with vendors and *agree* to accept advertising (see returnpath.net). For example, the authors of this book agreed to receive a large number of e-commerce newsletters knowing that some would include ads. This way we can keep abreast of what is happening in the field. We also agree to accept e-mail from research companies, newspapers, travel agencies, and more. These vendors push, for free, very valuable information to us. The accompanying ads pay for such services. One way to conduct permission advertisement is to provide incentives to the recipients. Note that Netflix asks permission to send users recommendations, but it does not ask whether it can use historical purchasing data to create them (see Team Assignment 4).

spamming
Using e-mail to send unwanted ads (sometimes floods of ads).

permission advertising (permission marketing)
Advertising (marketing) strategy in which customers agree to accept advertising and marketing materials (known as "opt-in").

ADVERTISEMENT AS A REVENUE MODEL

Many of the dot-com failures in 2000 to 2002 were caused by a revenue model that contained advertising income as the major, or only, revenue source. Many small portals failed, but several large ones are dominating the field: Google, AOL, Yahoo!, and MSN. However, even these heavy-traffic sites only started to show a significant profit in 2004. Too many Web sites are competing for advertising money. Therefore, almost all portals are adding other sources of revenue.

    However, if careful, a small site can survive by concentrating on a niche area. For example, playfootball.com is doing well. It pulls millions of dollars in advertising and sponsorship by concentrating on NFL fans. The site provides comprehensive and interactive content, attracting millions of visitors. For more on ad payments, see en.wikipedia.org/wiki/Online_advertising.

MEASURING ONLINE ADVERTISING'S EFFECTIVENESS

One managerial issue is how to measure the effectiveness of online advertisement. A related topic is how to charge for ads. These two topics are presented as a complete section in Online File W4.15. A related issue is the assessment of the number of visitors to sites where ads are placed. According to Sutel (2007), there are major disagreements among rating agencies regarding audience measurement.

MOBILE MARKETING AND ADVERTISING

The number of applications of *mobile commerce* (*m-commerce*) in marketing and advertising is growing rapidly, with advertising on cell phones and PDAs on the rise. One area is that of pervasive computing—the idea that computer chips can be embedded in almost any device (clothing, tools, appliances, homes, and so on), and then the device can be connected to a network of other devices. An interesting application of this is digital ads atop 12,000 taxis in various U.S. cities. The ads also include public service announcements. The technology comes from Vert (vert.net).

Vert displays live content and advertising messages very effectively by targeting specific zip codes, neighborhoods, and individual city blocks (see the accompanying photo). Ads can be scheduled for specific times during the day (e.g., promote coffee during the morning commute). Ads are beamed to Vert-equipped taxis like a cell phone signal. GPS satellites pinpoint where the cab is traveling, allowing ads to change from block to block.

Mobile Advertising

mobile advertising (m-advertising)
Ads sent to and presented on mobile devices.

Mobile advertising (m-advertising) refers to ads sent to and presented on mobile devices. M-advertising can be seen as a part of m-commerce. M-advertising enables the advertisers to send unique, personalized, and customized ads to mobile devices.

Examples. In September 2007, Blyk (blyk.co.uk), a then-new mobile operator, launched its service in Britain. It offered subscribers 217 free text messages and 43 free minutes of voice calls per month as long as they agreed to receive six advertisements by text message every day. To sign up for the service, customers must fill out a questionnaire about their hobbies and habits so advertisers can target their messages very precisely. In the United States, Virgin Mobile (virginmobileusa.com) tried something similar with its "Sugar Mama" program, which offers subscribers the choice between receiving an ad via text message or viewing a 45-second advertisement when browsing the Internet, in exchange for 1 free minute of talk time.

Vert Intelligent Displays: Advertising Used Atop Taxicabs

Source: Courtesy of VERT Incorporated.

Vodafone (vodafone.com), a large mobile operator in Europe, sees mobile advertising as a lucrative source of additional income. It gave an option of downloading footage from *Big Brother*, a popular television show, in exchange for viewing a promotional video clip.

Apple's iPhone now runs thousands of software programs, available at Apple's Application Store. Users downloaded more than 100 million applications in five months (July to December 2008). Those numbers have caught the attention of advertisers, who see social networking widgets, restaurant locators, mobile games, and other applications as prime targets.

Only 20 percent of the more than 3,000 software programs on Apple's Application Store are free, but they make up about 90 percent of the downloads. A growing number of the programs, such as the popular mobile game Tap Tap Revenge and Pandora Radio (a personalized music service), are already experimenting with ads. Play a round of Tap Tap, for instance, and you will likely see a banner ad for Jaguar cars on the bottom of your screen. Mobile ad networks like AdMob (admob.com), already have launched iPhone-specific ad services.

Some of the mobile phones that are equipped with GPS technology could be used to alert people to the availability and discounts of stores or restaurants that they are walking or driving by (see *l-commerce*, Chapter 8). Tying ads to online searches from mobile phones is another promising venture. A subscriber typing in "pizza," for instance, could receive ads for nearby pizza parlors with a discount coupon, along with his search results.

AD CONTENT

The content of ads is extremely important, and companies use ad agencies to help in content creation for the Web just as they do for other advertising media. A major player in this area is Akamai Technologies, Inc. (akamai.com). In several white papers (akamai.com/html/perspectives/whitepapers_content.html), the company points out how the right content can drive traffic to a site, how to evaluate third-party vendors and determine what content-related services are important, how to use user-generated content for successful social networking, and more.

Content is especially important to increase *stickiness*. Customers are expensive to acquire; therefore, it is important that they remain at a site, read its content carefully, and eventually make a purchase. The writing of the advertising content itself is, of course, important (see adcopywriting.com). Finding a good ad agency to write content and shape the advertising message is one of the key factors in any advertising campaign, online or offline. Some companies use input from consumers to create ads, including video clips.

SOFTWARE AGENTS IN MARKETING AND ADVERTISING APPLICATIONS

As the volume of customers, products, vendors, and information increases, it becomes uneconomical, or even impossible, for customers to consider all relevant information and to manually match their interests with available products and services. The practical solution to handling such information overload is to use software (intelligent) agents. In Chapter 3, we demonstrated how intelligent agents help online shoppers find and compare products, resulting in significant time savings.

In Online File W4.16, we concentrate on how software agents can assist customers in the online purchasing decision-making process as well as in advertisement. Depending on their level of intelligence, agents can do many things.

localization

The process of converting media products developed in one environment (e.g., country) to a form culturally and linguistically acceptable in countries outside the original target market.

LOCALIZATION

Localization is the process of converting media products and advertisement material developed in one environment (e.g., a country) to a form culturally and linguistically acceptable outside the original target market. It is usually done by a set of internationalization guidelines. Web page translation is just one aspect of internationalization. However, several other aspects also are important. For example, a U.S. jewelry manufacturer that displayed its products on a white background was astonished to find that this display might not appeal to customers in some countries where a blue background is preferred. For details see Online File W4.17.

Section 4.8 ▶ REVIEW QUESTIONS

1. Describe permission advertising.
2. What is localization? What are the major issues in localizing Web pages?
3. How is wireless advertising practiced?
4. What is the importance of ad content?
5. Describe the role of software agents in advertising.
6. Define localization in advertising.

MANAGERIAL ISSUES

Some managerial issues related to this chapter are as follows.

1. **Do we understand our customers?** Understanding customers, specifically what they need and how to respond to those needs, is the most critical part of consumer-centered marketing. To excel, companies need to satisfy and retain customers, and management must monitor the entire process of marketing, sales, maintenance, and follow-up service.

2. **Who will conduct the market research?** B2C requires extensive market research. This research is not easy to do, nor is it inexpensive. Deciding whether to outsource to a market research firm or maintain an in-house market research staff is a major management issue.

3. **Are customers satisfied with our Web site?** This is a key question, and it can be answered in several ways. Many vendors are available to assist you; some provide free software. For discussion on how to improve customer satisfaction, see astea. com/ben_increase_satisfaction.asp. For Web site improvements, see futurenowinc.com.

4. **How can we use social networks for advertising?** A company can capitalize on segmented audiences in a social network in a number of different ways. Companies can create their own social networks, pay to place banner ads on existing networks, do

affiliate marketing, and more. See Weber (2007) for guidelines and examples.

5. **How do we decide where to advertise?** Web advertising is a complex undertaking, and outsourcing its management should seriously be considered for large-scale ads. Some outsourcers specialize in certain industries (e.g., ebizautos.com for auto dealers). Companies should examine the adage.com site, which contains an index of Web sites, their advertising rates, and reported traffic counts, before selecting a site on which to advertise. Companies also should consult third-party audits.

6. **What is our commitment to Web advertising, and how will we coordinate Web and traditional advertising?** Once a company has committed to advertising on the Web, it must remember that a successful program is multifaceted. It requires input and vision from marketing, cooperation from the legal department, and strong technical leadership from the corporate information systems (IS) department. A successful Web advertising program also requires coordination with non-Internet advertising and top management support.

7. **Should we integrate our Internet and non-Internet marketing campaigns?** Many companies are

integrating their TV and Internet marketing campaigns. For example, a company's TV or newspaper ads direct the viewers/readers to the Web site, where short videos and sound ads, known as *rich media*, are used. With click-through ratios of banner ads down to less than 0.5 percent at many sites, innovations such as the integration of offline and online marketing are certainly needed to increase click-throughs.

8. **What ethical issues should we consider?** Several ethical issues relate to online advertising. One issue that receives a great deal of attention is spamming. Another issue is the selling of mailing lists and customer information. Some people believe not only that a company needs the consent of the customers before selling a list, but also that the company should share with customers the profits derived from the sale of such lists. Using cookies without an individual's consent is considered by many to be an ethical issue. The negative impacts of advertising need to be considered (see Gao et al. 2006).

9. **Are any metrics available to guide advertisers?** A large amount of information has been developed to guide advertisers as to where to advertise, how to design ads, and so on. Specific metrics may be used to assess the effectiveness of advertising and to calculate the ROI from an organization's online advertising campaign.

10. **Which Internet marketing/advertising channel should you use?** An increasing number of online methods are available from which to choose. These include banners, search engines, blogging, social networks, and more. Angel (2006) proposed a methodology to assess these alternatives with a matrix for selection and implementation.

SUMMARY

In this chapter, you learned about the following EC issues as they relate to the chapter's learning objectives.

1. **The online consumer decision-making process.** The goal of marketing research efforts is to *understand* consumers' online decision-making process and formulate an appropriate strategy to *influence* their behavior. For each step in the process, sellers can develop appropriate strategies.

2. **Building one-to-one relationships with customers.** EC offers companies the opportunity to build one-to-one relationships with customers that are not possible in other marketing systems. Product customization, personalized service, and getting the customer involved interactively (e.g., in feedback, order tracking, and so on) are all practical in cyberspace. In addition, advertising can be matched with customer profiles so that ads can be presented on a one-to-one basis.

3. **Online personalization.** Using personal Web pages, customers can interact with a company, learn about products or services in real time, or get customized products or services. Companies can allow customers to self-configure the products or services they want. Customization also can be done by matching products with customers' profiles.

4. **Increasing loyalty and trust.** Customers can switch loyalty online easily and quickly. Therefore, enhancing e-loyalty (e.g., through e-loyalty programs) is a must. Similarly, trust is a critical success factor that must be nourished.

5. **EC customer market research.** Several fast and economical methods of online market research are available. The two major approaches to data collection are: (1) soliciting voluntary information from the customers and (2) using cookies, transaction logs, or clickstream data to track customers' movements on the Internet and find what their interests are. Understanding market segmentation by grouping consumers into categories also is an effective EC market research method. However, online market research has several limitations, including data accuracy and representation of the statistical population by a sample.

6. **Objectives and characteristics of Web advertising.** Web advertising attempts to attract surfers to an advertiser's site. Once at the advertiser's site, consumers can receive information, interact with the seller, and in many cases, immediately place an order. With Web advertising, ads can be customized to fit groups of people with similar interests or even individuals. In addition, Web advertising can be interactive, is easily updated, can reach millions at a reasonable cost, and offers dynamic presentation by rich multimedia.

7. **Major online advertising methods.** Banners are the most popular online advertising method. Other frequently used methods are pop-ups and similar ads, e-mail (including e-mail to mobile devices),

classified ads, registration of URLs with search engines, and advertising in chat rooms. Some of these are related to search results obtained through search engines (especially Google).

8. **Advertising in social networks.** Social networks provide advertisers with the ability to target ads to market segments and individuals. This is also a source for viral marketing. Bloggers can be used to promote products (some are paid for their efforts).

9. **Various advertising strategies and types of promotions.** The major advertising strategies are ads associated with search results (text links), affiliate marketing, pay incentives for customers to view ads, viral marketing, ads customized on a one-to-one basis, and online events and promotions. Web promotions are similar to offline promotions. They include giveaways, contests, quizzes, entertainment, coupons, and so on. Customization and interactivity distinguish Internet promotions from conventional ones.

10. **Permission marketing, ad management, and localization.** In permission marketing, customers are willing to accept ads in exchange for special (personalized) information or monetary incentives. Ad management deals with planning, organizing, and controlling ad campaigns and ad use. Finally, in localization, attempts are made to fit ads to local environments.

KEY TERMS

Ad views	146	E-loyalty	137	Search engine optimization	
Affiliate marketing	157	Hit	146	(SEO)	151
Banner	148	Interactive marketing	145	Social network advertising	154
Behavioral targeting	135	Keyword banners	148	Spamming	159
Biometric	144	Localization	162	Spyware	143
Button	146	Merchant brokering	133	Stickiness	147
Click (click-through or ad click)	146	Mobile advertising		Transaction log	142
Clickstream behavior	142	(m-advertising)	160	Trust	138
Clickstream data	143	Page	147	Unique visit	147
Click-through rate	146	Permission advertising		User profile	135
Click-through ratio	146	(permission marketing)	159	Viral marketing (or advertising)	151
Collaborative filtering	143	Personalization	135	Visit	147
Conversion rate	146	Pop-under ads	149	Web bugs	142
Cookie	135	Pop-up ads	149	Webcasting	158
CPM (cost per thousand		Product brokering	133	Web mining	143
impressions)	146	Random banners	148	Web video analytics	156

QUESTIONS FOR DISCUSSION BY INDIVIDUAL STUDENTS

1. Discuss the similarities and differences between data mining and Web mining. (Hint: To answer this question, you will need to read Online File W4.7.)

2. Discuss the importance of videos as an advertising media.

3. Relate banner swapping to a banner exchange.

4. Discuss why banners are popular in Internet advertising.

5. Explain how Google generates targeted ads.

6. Discuss the relationship between market research and advertisement (see Atlas Solutions at **atlassolutions. com** for a start).

7. Discuss the advantages and limitations of listing a company's URL with many search engines.

8. How can a company use Facebook for advertising? (Hint: See Online File W4.13.)

9. Examine some Web avatars and try to interact with them (e.g., secondlife.com). Discuss the potential benefits and drawbacks of using avatars as an advertising medium.

10. When you buy a banner ad, you lease space for a specific time period. In **milliondollarhome-page.com**, you buy space forever. Compare and discuss.

11. Discuss the advantages and limitations of three methods of data collection about individual consumers.

12. Discuss the benefits of video ads in the social networking environment.

TOPICS FOR CLASS DISCUSSION

1. Is it ethical for a vendor to enter a chat room operated by a competitor and pose queries?

2. Some suggest that cookies should be made illegal. Discuss.

3. Netflix.com, amazon.com, and others view historical purchases as input available for use in their recommendation systems. Some believe that this is an invasion of privacy. Debate this issue.

4. Some say that you cannot provide one-to-one advertising without violating privacy. Discuss.

5. Some say that people come to social networks to socialize and they will not accept ads. Discuss.

6. What strategic implication do you see for companies that use videos, mobile devices, and social networks as platforms for advertising?

INTERNET EXERCISES

1. Enter netflix.com/affiliates. Describe the value of the program as a marketing channel.

2. Examine a market research Web site (e.g., nielsen.com or claritas.com). Discuss what might motivate a consumer to provide answers to market research questions.

3. Enter mysimon.com and share your experiences about how the information you provide might be used by the company for marketing in a specific industry (e.g., the clothing market).

4. Enter marketingterms.com and conduct a search by keywords as well as by category. Check the definitions of 10 key terms in this chapter.

5. Enter 2020research.com, infosurv.com, and marketingsherpa.com and identify areas for market research about consumers.

6. Enter en-us.nielsen.com/tab/industries/media and view the demos on e-market research. Then go to clickz.com and find its offerings. Summarize your findings.

7. Enter selfpromotion.com and find some interesting promotion ideas for the Web.

8. Enter hotwire.com and espn.com. Identify all the advertising methods used on each site. Can you find those that are targeted advertisements? What revenue sources can you find on the ESPN site? (Try to find at least seven.)

9. Visit adweek.com, wdfm.com, ad-tech.com, iab.com, and adage.com and find new developments in Internet advertisement. Write a report based on your findings.

10. Enter clairol.com to determine your best hair color. You can upload your own photo to the studio and see how different shades look on you. You can also try different hairstyles. It also is for men. How can these activities increase branding? How can they increase sales?

11. What resources do you find to be most useful at clickz.com, admedia.org, marketresearch.com, and wdfm.com?

12. Enter linkedin.com (you can sign in as a member for free) and find what marketing and advertising a company can conduct there.

13. Enter zoomerang.com and learn how it facilitates online surveys. Examine the various products, including those that supplement the surveys. Write a report.

14. Enter pewinternet.org and pewresearch.org. What research do they conduct that is relevant to B2C? To B2B? Write a report.

15. Enter omniture.com. How does it help with site optimization? What other services does it provide?

TEAM ASSIGNMENTS AND PROJECTS

1. Enter **harrisinteractive.com**, **infosurv.com**, and similar sites. Have each team member examine the free marketing tools and related tutorials and demos. Each team will try to find a similar site and compare the two. Write a report discussing the team's findings.

2. Each team will choose one advertising method and conduct an in-depth investigation of the major players in that part of the ad industry. For example, direct e-mail is relatively inexpensive. Visit **the-dma.org** to learn about direct mail. Then visit **ezinedirector.com**, **mailermailer.com**, and similar sites. Each team will prepare and present an argument as to why its method is superior.

3. In this exercise, each team member will enter **uproar.com** or similar sites to play games and win prizes. What could be better? This site is the destination of choice for game and sweepstakes junkies and for those who wish to reach a mass audience of fun-loving people. Relate the games to advertising and marketing.

4. Netflix, Amazon.com, and others view historical purchases as input available for use in their recommendation systems. Some believe that this is an invasion of privacy. Debate this issue.

5. Enter **autonlab.org** and download tools for conducting data mining analysis (these downloads are free). Get data on customer shopping and analyze it and write a report.

6. Create two teams. One will investigate advertising practices on **craigslist.org** and the other on **kijiji.com**. Each team will prepare a list of practices used by the sites. The differences should then be summarized.

Closing Case

TOYOTA SCION GOES SOCIAL FOR ADVERTISING AND MARKET RESEARCH

The Problem

The automotive industry is a global multibillion-dollar business where competition is very intense. At stake is not only how many cars can be sold, but also how much profit can be made and how to survive in economic downturns.

Toyota has been known for decades for its manufacturing innovations. Now it's taken an innovative lead on the Web. Here, we look at one of its newest brands, the Scion, geared toward Generation Y (Gen Y), which includes those born between 1980 and 1994. As of 2009, Gen Y and Gen X (the generation before Gen Y) combined are expected to account for at least 40 percent of vehicle sales. The problem faced by Scion has been how to reach Gen Y and Gen X.

Using Social Computing

Scion is using segmented advertising as its major media-based strategy in social networks. The company also uses search engine marketing, mass advertising, and one-to-one targeted marketing, all of which are aimed at increasing brand recognition.

Here are some representative activities:

▶ Scion uses display ads that reach urban audiences via sites such as *blastro.com* and *hiphopdx.com* (Rodgers 2007). Scion works with these sites to develop ad content in a way to make it attractive to the sites' membership. This ranges from photo galleries to social networking profile pages to offering interactive features.

▶ In August 2007, Scion launched *Club Scion*, a three-story virtual nightclub with dance floors, music, and hot tubs. Each level of the club reflects a different Scion model, which includes the xA hatchback, xB SUV, and tC sports coupe.

▶ Toyota targets children as a means to influence their parents. In April 2007, Toyota began placing its Scion on *whyville.net*, an online interactive community populated almost entirely by 8- to 15-year-olds. Toyota hopes *Whyvillians* will do two things: influence the users' parents' car purchases and grow up to buy Toyotas themselves. The power of younger consumers has grown stronger in recent years.

According to *MediaBuyerPlanner.com* (2006), a study by Packaged Facts showed that 39 percent of parents of 10- and 11-year-olds say their children have a significant impact on brand purchases.

▶ Scion maintains a presence in several large virtual worlds, including *secondlife.com, whyville.net, there.com*, and *gaia.com*. Each virtual world lends itself to a different marketing strategy. In *Whyville*, where users tend to fall between the ages 8 and 15,

the company launched a virtual driver's education program. Since *there.com* is populated by older teens, Scion made sure to create a more provocative social environment.

▶ Toyota made effective use of the Internet by using live chat to attract the 18- to 24-year-old audience. The campaign includes the use of *microapplication ads* that allow consumers to stencil designs over the picture of the Scion.

Source: Courtesy of Toyota Motor Sales. Used with permission.

▶ To capitalize on wireless technology, in 2004 Toyota launched a mobile *advergame* (game to advertise a product), called "Scion Road Trip." Players earn virtual miles when they send e-cards to friends and get back responses. The campaign lasted for several months.

▶ For the 2008 model xB SUV, Scion created a special Web site (*want2bsquare.com*). Visitors to the site can earn points by playing games, watching videos, and e-mailing others about the site. The site features eight *microsites,* including user community features; each has a unique theme and its own design. There are microsites that focus on music, resemble a Monty Python set, feature a haunted house, and include a town square and an urban zoo.

▶ Toyota also created its own social network site called *Scion Speak,* where Scion lovers can socialize, communicate, and play. Scion owners can choose from hundreds of symbols and create customized logos for their cars. They can then download the logo and make window decals, or have them painted on their cars (for a fee).

▶ Finally, like several other automakers, Scion is creating its own broadband channel. These channels are a way to move from push to pull marketing, where

the consumer decides what materials to view and when. A content-rich, broadband-friendly site is an always-on marketing channel to which people will return.

The Results

According to *MarketingVox.com* (2007a), Scion has 80 percent brand recognition, a very high value. As of April 2007, Scion was the number one brick-and-mortar e-tailer among consumers 35 years old and younger. Scion had not even made it into the top 25 sites in 2006; the amazing jump to the number one ranking was due to the interactive and community-oriented nature of the Scion online experiences.

The Scion Web site is highly personalized. Sophisticated customization tools allow people to build their own virtual cars on the site. This online information is then integrated offline—a local dealership locates the desired or similar vehicle for each virtual car builder and contacts them for a test drive. Other digital frills like a social network for Scion car buyers and a Web site that plays music and lists concert information create a superb brand experiences. Let's look at some of the specific advertising activities.

▶ The brand's Scion City in *Second Life* generated 10,000 blog posts between April and June 2007 and is the third most recognized brand behind Reuters in *Second Life* awareness.

▶ The on-site chat feature provides a forum for hundreds of conversations per week. Prior to the chat, users are asked a few questions, one of which is where they live. Interestingly, Toyota found that many of the chatters reside in areas where Scion is not even available, providing valuable information for dealer expansion plans.

▶ The *New York Times* reported that visitors to the site had used the word *Scion* in online chats more than 78,000 times; hundreds of virtual Scions were purchased using "clams," the currency of Whyville; and the community meeting place "Club Scion" was visited 33,741 times.

▶ SMS (*short messaging service* or *text message*) is being used to alert players of their accrued virtual miles and weekly contest events.

▶ Toyota Scion is now using Twitter to stay in contact with its customers (*twitter.com/scion*).

Sources: Compiled from *scion.com* (accessed March 2009), Bosman (2006), *MediaBuyerPlanner.com* (2006), *MarketingVox.com* (2007a, 2007b, and 2007c), and Rodgers (2007).

Questions

1. Identify all advertising actions and relate them to the methods described in this chapter.
2. Identify all activities that can be considered market research.
3. What can increase loyalty?
4. Identify personalization methods provided by Scion.
5. Find advertisement and market research activities conducted by Scion that are not cited in this case.
6. Identify viral marketing activities in this case.

ONLINE RESOURCES
Available at pearsonhighered.com/turban

Online Files

W4.1 A Model of Consumer Behavior Online
W4.2 From Mass Marketing to One-to-One Marketing
W4.3 Factors That Affect Customer Satisfaction with Internet Shopping
W4.4 How to Increase Trust in EC
W4.5 Online Market Segmentation Research
W4.6 Spyware
W4.7 Business Intelligence: From Data Collection to Data Mining and Analysis
W4.8 From Mass Advertising to Interactive Advertising
W4.9 Advantages and Limitations of Internet Advertising
W4.10 Click-Through and Conversion Ratios
W4.11 Pop-Up Advertising Methods
W4.12 E-Mail Advertising Methods
W4.13 Marketing and Advertising in the Web 2.0 Environment
W4.14 How to Attract Web Surfers
W4.15 Economics of Advertising
W4.16 Software Agents in Marketing and Advertising Applications
W4.17 Ad Management and Ad Localization

Comprehensive Educational Web Sites

▶ **marketresearch.com**: E-commerce market research reports (for free)
▶ **ecommerce-guide.com/news/research**: Comprehensive collection of resources
▶ **internet.com**: Many resources (for small business, in particular)
▶ **emarketer.com**: Statistics, news, products, laws
▶ **wilsonweb.com/research**: Case studies, articles, tutorials, videos, and more; the research room may require fees
▶ **lib.unc.edu/reference/busecon/ecommerce.html**: List of EC resources
▶ **ecommercetimes.com**: News and analysis
▶ **clickz.com/stat**: EC statistics
▶ **cio.com/white-papers**: White paper index for business technology and leadership

CHAPTER 5

B2B E-COMMERCE

Content

Opening Case: Auction for Supplies Helps Portsmouth Hospitals

Managerial Issues

Closing Case: iMarketKorea

Learning Objectives

Upon completion of this chapter, you will be able to:

1. Describe the B2B field.

2. Describe the major types of B2B models.

3. Discuss the characteristics and models of the sell-side marketplace, including auctions.

4. Describe the sell-side intermediaries.

5. Describe the characteristics of the buy-side marketplace and e-procurement.

6. Explain how reverse auctions work in B2B.

7. Describe B2B aggregation and group purchasing models.

8. Describe other procurement methods.

9. Define exchanges and describe their major types.

10. Describe B2B portals.

11. Describe third-party exchanges.

12. Describe how B2B can benefit from social networking and Web 2.0.

13. Describe Internet marketing in B2B, including organizational buyer behavior.

AUCTION FOR SUPPLIES HELPS PORTSMOUTH HOSPITALS

Portsmouth Hospitals NHS Trust is one of the largest trusts in the United Kingdom, providing health care services for over 500,000 people throughout Portsmouth and South East Hampshire.

The Problem

Like many other public health care facilities, Portsmouth Hospitals attempts to deliver quality health care within a "never enough" budget. Any cost-saving measure can help add more beds and services. The hospitals needed a new 20-bed ward. The problem was to cut costs without reducing the quality of care. An obvious place to begin was the administrative services, and one such area was the back-office purchasing processes.

The Solution

The target was pharmaceutical supplies, and the idea was to use e-auctions. The goals were:

- To purchase standard products at the lowest prices
- To release cash for frontline services
- To demonstrate benefits of auctions to suppliers
- To shorten the procurement cycle by streamlining sourcing
- To cut the cost of purchasing administration of traditional tendering processes

As a buyer, the NHS Trust used *reverse auctions* (Chapter 2), whereby suppliers are invited to place bids on what the buyer needs. Online auctions were seen by the Trust as an opportunity to negotiate savings on the cost of supplies it purchased in bulk, particularly when consolidating spending with other Trusts across the south of England (for more on group purchasing, see Section 5.7). Driving competition between suppliers by increasing price transparency through real-time bidding would ensure the lowest prices and most favorable trading conditions.

The first auction was conducted on a platform provided by an electronic auctioneer (UKprocure) that was powered by Oracle's Exchange and Sourcing products. The auctioneer provided both training and administrative support.

Being the first pharmaceutical auction in the United Kingdom, the process required extensive preparations. UKprocure worked with the Trust to put together a project plan and to familiarize suppliers with the processes and regulations surrounding online bidding.

Knowledge transfer was a key part of the preparation, with procurement and supply managers at the Trust being involved at every stage. On the day of the auction, 26 suppliers submitted a total of 185 tendered bids outlining their best deals for pharmaceutical supplies. Suppliers had to bid lower than the reserve price, with each having a 30-minute window to better the preceding offer. Supplier anonymity was assured, because the names of bidders were shown only to buyers at the Trust. At the end of the auction, Portsmouth and the successful suppliers agreed upon the lowest mutually acceptable purchase price.

The Results

The £640,000 (US$936) annual savings generated by combining the traditional procurement process with a reverse auction represented a 12 percent price reduction for the Trust. Online auctions also save the purchasing organizations substantial sums in administration by eliminating the need to evaluate tenders manually and help shorten the procurement cycle. The savings enabled the Trust to fund a 20-bed ward within 12 months of starting the auctions.

Suppliers also benefited from the reduced administrative and lower transaction costs afforded by online auctions. Seeing what prices are being offered for the same or similar products increases suppliers' market intelligence and can help improve their competitive advantage.

The trust expanded the auctions to clinical supplies and nonclinical items. It also experimented with auctioning from its own Web site.

Sources: Compiled from OCG (2004) and *portshosp.nhs.uk* (accessed January 2009).

WHAT WE CAN LEARN . . .

This case demonstrates one method of electronic procurement, a reverse auction, which is very popular with public organizations, where tendering is usually mandatory.

Electronic auctions increase performance by reducing costs and expediting processes. It is an example of a B2B buy-side application, a type of application discussed in this chapter. Other buy-side and sell-side methods, as well as relationships among B2B partners, are also examined in this chapter. The chapter also delves into implementation issues such as group purchasing and the use of intermediaries in conducting auctions. Finally, the new activities of B2B in social networking are discussed.

5.1 CONCEPTS, CHARACTERISTICS, AND MODELS OF B2B E-COMMERCE

B2B EC has some special characteristics as well as specific models, components, and concepts. The major ones are described next.

BASIC B2B CONCEPTS

Business-to-business e-commerce (B2B EC), also known as *eB2B* (*electronic B2B*), or just B2B, refers to transactions between businesses conducted electronically over the Internet, extranets, intranets, or private networks. Such transactions may take place between a business and its supply chain members, as well as between a business, a government, and any other business. In this context, a *business* refers to any organization, private or public, for profit or nonprofit. The major characteristic of B2B is that companies attempt to electronically automate trading or communication and collaboration processes in order to improve them. Note that B2B commerce is also done without the Internet.

Key business drivers for B2B are the need to gain competitive advantage; the availability of a secure broadband Internet platform and private and public B2B e-marketplaces; the need for collaboration between suppliers and buyers; the ability to save money, reduce delays, and improve collaboration; and the emergence of effective technologies for intra- and interorganizational integration (see en.wikipedia.org/Wiki/ Business-to-business).

business-to-business e-commerce (B2B EC) Transactions between businesses conducted electronically over the Internet, extranets, intranets, or private networks; also known as eB2B (electronic B2B) or just B2B.

MARKET SIZE AND CONTENT OF B2B

Market forecasters estimate that by 2012 the global B2B market (online and offline) could reach $15 trillion. Interactive Data Corporation (IDC) estimates B2B e-commerce sales will total $12.4 trillion worldwide in 2012 (*IDC* 2008). Chemicals, computer electronics, utilities, agriculture, shipping and warehousing, motor vehicles, petrochemicals, paper and office products, and food are the leading items in B2B. According to the authors' experience and several sources, the dollar value of B2B comprises at least 85 percent of the total transaction value of e-commerce, and in some countries it is 90 percent. (Note: This figure is considered current in 2009.)

The B2B market, which went through major consolidation in 2000–2002, is growing rapidly. Different B2B market forecasters use different definitions and methodologies. Because of this, predictions frequently change and statistical data often differ. Therefore, we will not provide any more estimates here. Data sources that can be checked for the latest information on the B2B market are provided in Chapter 3 (Exhibit 3.1).

B2B EC is now in its fifth generation, as shown in Online File W5.1. This generation includes collaboration with suppliers, buyers, government, and other business partners, internal and external supply chain improvements, and expert (intelligent) sales systems. Just starting is B2B social networking, which could usher in the sixth generation of B2B. Note that older generations coexist with new ones. Also, some companies are still using only EC from early generations. This chapter focuses on topics from the second and third generations. Topics from the fourth, fifth, and sixth generations are presented in Chapters 6 through 8.

THE BASIC TYPES OF B2B TRANSACTIONS AND ACTIVITIES

The number of sellers and buyers and the form of participation used in B2B determine the basic B2B transaction types:

- ▶ **Sell-side.** One seller to many buyers.
- ▶ **Buy-side.** One buyer from many sellers.
- ▶ **Exchanges.** Many sellers to many buyers.
- ▶ **Supply chain improvements and collaborative commerce.** This category includes activities other than buying or selling among business partners, for example, supply chain improvements, communicating, collaborating, and sharing of information for joint design, planning, and so on.

Exhibit 5.1 illustrates these four B2B types.

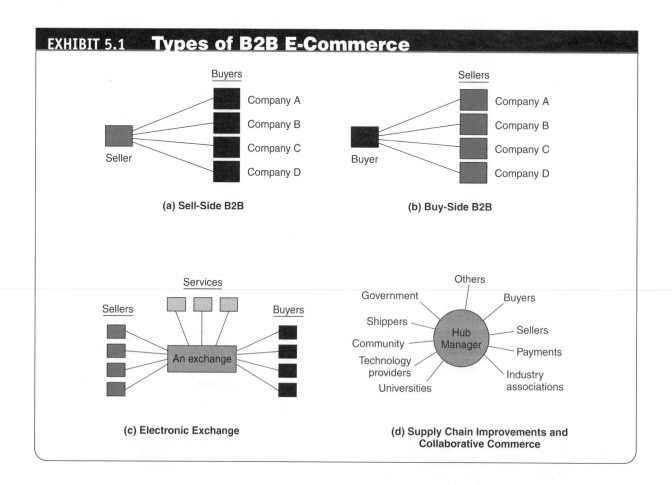

EXHIBIT 5.1   Types of B2B E-Commerce

(a) Sell-Side B2B

(b) Buy-Side B2B

(c) Electronic Exchange

(d) Supply Chain Improvements and Collaborative Commerce

THE BASIC TYPES OF B2B E-MARKETPLACES AND SERVICES

The following are the basic types of B2B e-marketplaces.

One-to-Many and Many-to-One: Private E-Marketplaces

In one-to-many and many-to-one markets, one company does either all the selling (*sell-side market*) or all the buying (*buy-side market*). Because EC is focused on a single company's buying or selling needs in these transactions, this type of EC is referred to as **company-centric EC**. Company-centric marketplaces—both sell-side and buy-side— are discussed in Sections 5.2 through 5.7.

In company-centric marketplaces, the individual sell-side or buy-side company has complete control over who participates in the selling or buying transaction and the supporting information systems. Thus, these marketplaces are essentially *private*. They may be at the sellers' Web sites or hosted by a third party (intermediary).

Many-to-Many: Exchanges

In many-to-many e-marketplaces, many buyers and many sellers meet electronically for the purpose of trading with one another. There are different types of such e-marketplaces, which are also known as **exchanges**, **trading communities**, or **trading exchanges**. We will use the term *exchanges* in this book. Exchanges are usually owned and run by a third party or by a consortium. They are described in more detail in Sections 5.8 and 5.9. Public exchanges are open to all interested parties (sellers and buyers), and thus are considered **public e-marketplaces**.

Supply Chain Improvers and Collaborative Commerce

B2B transactions are done along segments in the supply chain. Therefore, B2B initiatives need to be examined in light of other supply chain activities such as manufacturing, procurement of raw materials, shipments, and logistics.

Businesses deal with other businesses for purposes beyond just selling or buying. One example is that of *collaborative commerce*, which is communication, design, planning, and information sharing among business partners (see Chapter 6).

B2B CHARACTERISTICS

Here we examine various qualities by which B2B transactions can be characterized.

Parties to the Transaction: Sellers, Buyers, and Intermediaries

B2B commerce can be conducted *directly* between a *customer* and a *manufacturer* or it can be conducted via an **online intermediary**. The intermediary is a third party that brokers the transaction between the buyer and seller; it can be a virtual intermediary or a click-and-mortar intermediary. Some of the electronic intermediaries for consumers mentioned in Chapter 3 also can be referenced for B2B by replacing the individual consumers with business customers. Consolidators of buyers or sellers are typical B2B activities conducted by intermediaries (Section 5.3).

Types of Transactions

B2B transactions are of two basic types: *spot buying* and *strategic sourcing*. **Spot buying** refers to the purchasing of goods and services as they are needed, usually at prevailing market prices, which are determined dynamically by supply and demand. The buyers

company-centric EC
E-commerce that focuses on a single company's buying needs (many-to-one, or buy-side) or selling needs (one-to-many, or sell-side).

exchanges (trading communities or trading exchanges)
Many-to-many e-marketplaces, usually owned and run by a third party or a consortium, in which many buyers and many sellers meet electronically to trade with each other.

public e-marketplaces
Third-party exchanges open to all interested parties (sellers and buyers).

online intermediary
An online third party that brokers a transaction online between a buyer and a seller; may be virtual or click-and-mortar.

spot buying
The purchase of goods and services as they are needed, usually at prevailing market prices.

strategic (systematic) sourcing
Purchases involving long-term contracts that usually are based on private negotiations between sellers and buyers.

direct materials
Materials used in the production of a product (e.g., steel in a car or paper in a book).

indirect materials
Materials used to support production (e.g., office supplies or lightbulbs).

maintenance, repair, and operation (MRO)
Indirect materials used in activities that support production.

vertical marketplaces
Markets that deal with one industry or industry segment (e.g., steel, chemicals).

horizontal marketplaces
Markets that concentrate on a service, material, or a product that is used in all types of industries (e.g., office supplies, PCs).

and the sellers may not even know each other. Stock exchanges and commodity exchanges (oil, sugar, corn, etc.) are examples of spot buying. In contrast, **strategic (systematic) sourcing** involves purchases based on *long-term contracts*, and the parties know each other.

Spot buying can be conducted most economically on public exchanges (e.g., see this chapter's closing case). Strategic purchases can be supported more effectively and efficiently through direct buyer–seller offline or online negotiations, which can be done in private marketplaces or private trading rooms in public exchanges.

Types of Materials Traded

Two types of materials and supplies are traded in B2B: *direct* and *indirect*. **Direct materials** are materials used in making the products, such as steel in a car or paper in a book. The characteristics of direct materials are that their use is usually scheduled and planned for. They are frequently purchased in large quantities after extensive negotiation and contracting.

Indirect materials are items, such as office supplies or lightbulbs, that support production. They are usually used in **maintenance, repair, and operation (MRO)** activities. Collectively, they are known as *nonproduction materials*.

The Direction of the Trades

B2B marketplaces can be classified as *vertical* or *horizontal*. **Vertical marketplaces** are those that deal with one industry or industry segment. Examples include marketplaces specializing in electronics, cars, hospital supplies, steel, or chemicals. **Horizontal marketplaces** are those that concentrate on a service or a product that is used in all types of industries. Examples are office supplies, PCs, or travel services.

SUPPLY CHAIN RELATIONSHIPS IN B2B

In the various B2B transaction types, business activities are usually conducted along the supply chain of a company. The supply chain process consists of a number of interrelated subprocesses and roles. These extend from the acquisition of materials from suppliers, to the processing of a product or service, to packaging it and moving it to distributors and retailers. The process ends with the eventual purchase of a product by the end consumer. B2B e-commerce can make supply chains more efficient and effective or it can change the supply chain completely, eliminating one or more intermediaries.

SERVICE INDUSTRIES ONLINE IN B2B

In addition to trading products between businesses, services also can be provided electronically in B2B. Just as service industries such as banking, insurance, real estate, and stock trading can be conducted electronically for individuals, as described in Chapter 3, so they can be conducted electronically for businesses. The major B2B services are:

- **Travel and hospitality services.** Many large corporations arrange their travel electronically through corporate travel agents. To further reduce costs, companies can make special arrangements that enable employees to plan and book their own trips online. For instance, American Express Business Travel offers several tools to help corporate travel managers plan and control employee travel. Expedia, Travelocity, Orbitz, and other online travel services provide both B2C and B2B services.
- **Real estate.** Commercial real estate transactions can be large and complex. Therefore, the Web might not be able to completely replace existing human agents. Instead, the Web can help businesses find the right properties, compare properties,

and assist in negotiations. Some government-run foreclosed real estate auctions are open only to corporate real estate dealers and are conducted online.

▶ **Financial services.** Internet banking is an economical way of making business payments, transferring funds, or performing other financial transactions. For example, electronic funds transfer (EFT) is popular with businesses as are electronic letters of credit. Transaction fees over the Internet are less costly than any other alternative method. To see how payments work in B2B, see Chapter 10. Businesses can also purchase insurance online, both from pure online insurance companies and from click-and-mortar ones.

▶ **Online financing.** Business loans can be solicited online from lenders. Bank of America, for example, offers its commercial customers a matching service on IntraLoan (the bank's global loan syndication service), which uses an extranet to match business loan applicants with potential lending corporations. Several sites, such as garage.com, provide information about venture capital. Institutional investors use the Internet for certain trading activities.

▶ **Other online services.** Consulting services, law firms, health organizations, and others sell enterprise knowledge and special services online. Many other online services, such as the purchase of electronic stamps (similar to metered postage, but generated on a computer), are available online (see stamps.com). Also, recruiting and staffing services are done online.

THE BENEFITS AND LIMITATIONS OF B2B

The *benefits* of B2B are for buyers (B), sellers (S) or for both (J) and they depend on which model is used. In general, though, the major benefits of B2B (the beneficiaries are marked after each benefit) are that it:

> ▶ Creates new sales (purchase) opportunities (J)
> ▶ Eliminates paper and reduces administrative costs (J)
> ▶ Expedites processing and reduces cycle time (J)
> ▶ Lowers search costs and time for buyers to find products and vendors (B)
> ▶ Increases productivity of employees dealing with buying and/or selling (J)
> ▶ Reduces errors and improves quality of services (J)
> ▶ Makes product configuration easier (B)
> ▶ Reduces marketing and sales costs (S)
> ▶ Reduces inventory levels and costs (J)
> ▶ Enables customized online catalogs with different prices for different customers (J)
> ▶ Increases production flexibility, permitting JIT delivery (S)
> ▶ Reduces procurement costs (B)
> ▶ Facilitates customization via configuration (J)
> ▶ Provides for efficient customer service (B)
> ▶ Increases opportunities for collaboration (J)

B2B EC development has *limitations* as well, especially regarding channel conflict and the operation of public exchanges. Also, personal face-to-face interaction may be needed but unavailable. These will be discussed later in this chapter.

EXHIBIT 5.2   The Components of B2B

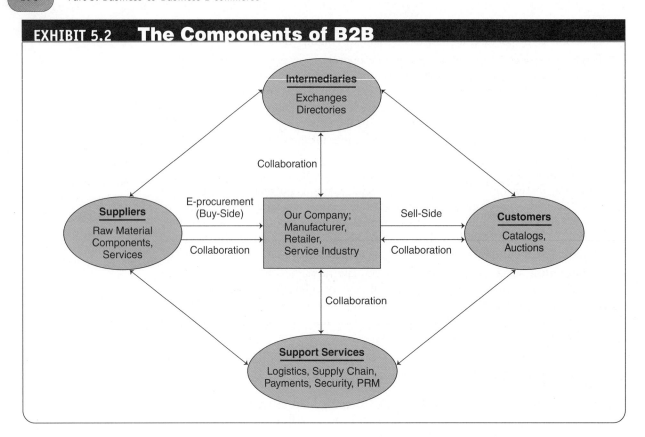

The development of B2B might eliminate the distributor or the retailer, which could be a benefit to the seller and the buyer (though not a benefit to the distributor or retailer). In previous chapters, such a phenomenon is referred to as *disintermediation*.

THE CONTENT OF THE B2B FIELD

The B2B field is very diverse depending on the industry, products and services transacted, volume, method used, and more. The diversity can be seen in Exhibit 5.2 where we distinguish five major components: (1) Our company, which may be a manufacturer, retailer, service provider, etc. (2) It has many types of suppliers (left) and, (3) customers (right). (4) Our company operations are supported by different services (bottom), and (5) we may work with several intermediaries (top of exhibit).

In the remainder of the chapter, we will look at the various components of this exhibit as well as the major types of B2B structural models (sell-side, buy-side, exchanges) as well as at transaction models (e.g., auctions) and other B2B topics.

Section 5.1 ▶ REVIEW QUESTIONS

1. Define B2B.
2. Discuss the following: spot buying versus strategic sourcing, direct materials versus indirect materials, and vertical markets versus horizontal markets.
3. What are company-centric marketplaces? Are they public or private?
4. Define B2B exchanges.
5. Relate the supply chain concept to B2B transactions.
6. List the B2B online services.
7. List the benefits of B2B.

5.2 ONE-TO-MANY: SELL-SIDE E-MARKETPLACES

Many B2B activities involve online selling.

SELL-SIDE MODELS

In the B2C model, a manufacturer or a retailer sells electronically directly to consumers from a *Webstore*. In a B2B **sell-side e-marketplace,** a business sells products and services to business customers electronically. The seller can be a manufacturer or an intermediary such as a distributor selling to wholesalers, to retailers, or to businesses (e.g., W.W. Grainger). In either case, sell-side e-marketplaces involve one seller and many potential buyers. In this model, both individual consumers and business buyers might use the same sell-side marketplace (e.g., dell.com), or they might use different marketplaces.

> **sell-side
> e-marketplace**
> A Web-based
> marketplace in which
> one company sells to
> many business buyers
> from e-catalogs or
> auctions, frequently
> over an extranet.

The architecture of this B2B model is similar to that of B2C EC. The major differences are in the process. For example, in B2B, large customers might be provided with customized catalogs and prices, another seller will arrange the delivery of the goods (by truck, ship, train). Usually, companies will separate B2C orders from B2B orders. One reason for this is that B2C and B2B orders have different *order-fulfillment processes* and different pricing models (i.e., wholesale versus retail pricing). Also, in B2B we use technologies such as RFID and XML, which are not usually used in B2C.

The one-to-many model has three major marketing methods: (1) selling from *electronic catalogs*, (2) selling via *forward auctions*, and (3) one-to-one selling, usually under a *negotiated* long-term contract. Such one-to-one negotiating is familiar: The buying company negotiates price, quantity, payments, delivery, and quality terms with the selling company.

B2B Sellers

Sellers in the sell-side marketplace may be click-and-mortar manufacturers or intermediaries (e.g., distributors or wholesalers). The intermediaries may even be pure online companies, as in the case of bigboXX.com, described in Online File W5.2.

Customer Service

Online sellers can provide sophisticated customer services. For example, General Electric receives over 20 million calls a year regarding appliances. Although most of these calls come from individuals, many come from businesses. By using the Internet and automatic-response software agents (autoresponders), GE has reduced the cost of handling calls from $5 per call when done by phone to $0.20 per electronically answered call. We now turn our attention to the most common sell-side method—selling online from electronic catalogs.

SELLING FROM CATALOGS

Companies can use the Internet to sell directly from their online catalogs. A company may offer one catalog for all customers or a *customized catalog* for each large customer (usually both).

Many sellers provide separate pages and catalogs to their major buyers. For example, Staples, an office-supply vendor, offers its business customers personalized software catalogs of about 100,000 products and pricing at stapleslink.com.

Another example of B2B direct sales from catalogs is Microsoft, which uses an extranet to sell over $60 billion of software annually to its distributors and larger customers. Using Microsoft's extranet-based order-entry tool (MOET), buyers can check inventory, make transactions, and look up the status of orders. The online orders are automatically fed into the customer's SAP applications. The extranet handles over 1 million transactions per year. The system significantly reduces the number of phone calls, e-mails, and incorrect product shipments.

In selling online to business buyers, manufacturers might encounter a similar problem to that of B2C, namely conflict with the regular distribution channels, including corporate dealers (channel conflict). An interesting solution is illustrated in Case 5.1, where Brady Corporation sells MRO and EOM identification products online across multiple channels.

Configuration and Customization

As with B2C EC, B2B direct sales offer an opportunity for efficient customization. As we will see in the case of Cisco, manufacturers can provide online tools for self-configuration, pricing, ordering, and so on. Business customers can self-configure customized products, get price quotes, and submit orders, all online.

Many click-and-mortar companies use a *multichannel distribution system*, in which the Internet is a supplemental channel that enables greater efficiency in the ordering process, as shown in the case of Whirlpool in Online File W5.3.

Benefits and Limitations of Online Sales from Catalogs

Successful examples of the B2B online direct sales model include manufacturers, such as Dell, Intel, IBM, and Cisco, and distributors, such as Ingram Micro (which sells to value-added retailers; the retailer adds some service along with the product). Sellers that use this model can be successful as long as they have a superb reputation in the market and a large enough group of loyal customers.

Although the benefits of direct online sales are similar to that of B2C, there also are limitations. One of the major issues facing direct sellers is how to find buyers. Many companies know how to advertise in traditional channels but are still learning how to contact would-be business buyers online. Also, B2B sellers may experience channel conflicts with their existing distribution systems. Another limitation is that if traditional electronic data interchange (EDI)—the computer-to-computer direct transfer of business documents—is used, the cost to the customers can be high, and they will be reluctant to go online. The solution to this problem is the transfer of documents over extranets (see Online File W5.4) and an Internet-based EDI (see Online File W5.5).

EXAMPLE: CISCO SYSTEMS

Cisco Systems (cisco.com) is the world's leading producer of routers, switches, and network interconnection services. Cisco's portal has evolved over several years, beginning with technical support for customers and developing into one of the world's largest direct B2B sales sites. Today, Cisco offers about a dozen Internet-based applications to both end-user businesses and reseller partners. For more on Cisco, see Online File W5.6.

Section 5.2 ▶ REVIEW QUESTIONS

1. List the types of sell-side B2B transaction models.
2. Distinguish between the use and nonuse of intermediaries in B2B sell-side transactions.
3. What are buy-side and sell-side transactions? How do they differ?
4. Describe customer service in B2B systems.
5. Describe the direct online B2B sales process from catalogs.
6. Discuss the benefits and limitations of direct online B2B sales from catalogs.

CASE 5.1
EC Application

BRADY CORPORATION REORGANIZES ITS E-CATALOG PRODUCTION

Brady Corporation (*bradycorp.com*), an ID product leader, is a company with over $1.3 billion in annual sales, selling identification solutions to more than 500,000 OEM and MRO customers worldwide through direct, catalog, and distributor channels. With 9,000 employees worldwide and more than 150,000 products, the company needed an e-catalog that could serve customers both efficiently and swiftly.

The Problem
The company was using Excel data to build the firm's online catalog. This method was labor-intensive as there was no way to make global data changes, forcing staff to manually update details on a given product in multiple locations in the company's e-catalog. Also, the system did not provide a means for storing product attributes, making it difficult to provide the Web site with information vital to customers' purchasing decisions. Exporting catalog data to any external system or providing custom catalog views was an undertaking of immense proportion and fraught with errors that had to be corrected manually, which was costly in terms of man-hours needed to maintain the e-catalog.

Another problem was the less than user friendly setup of the e-catalog. It was almost impossible for customers to find information for the products they needed, so they most often turned to Brady's direct sales team, call centers, or even distribution partners to find the best products for their needs. Therefore, customer satisfaction could only be improved through better search and navigation of the site and its product information.

The Solution
Brady chose FullTilt's Product Information Management Solution to store and organize its product data and attributes in a central repository for easy access and updating. By centralizing all product information in a single repository and creating a consistent set of product information that could be edited and exported for online use, the company was able to allow authorized users around the globe to edit product information yet maintain the accuracy and consistency of the product information.

If a product exists multiple times in the catalog, a change made in one place is automatically made in all the other locations. Users can also visually check the product descriptions against product images maintained

in the database, providing an extra layer of defense against data error. New product information is automatically imported from the marketing department, doing away with unnecessary manual steps. Updated information is uploaded to *bradyid.com*, Brady's e-commerce Web site, via an export file. Content managers can identify the types of products they want to upload, ranging from all new or active products to products only in certain categories. The system is so easy to use that Brady only needs two e-commerce content managers to maintain and update the system at the SKU level. FullTilt also allows the ability to create custom catalogs for different customers and users.

To meet the challenge of site navigation and search, Brady chose Endeca's Information Access Platform (IAP) to deliver the necessary product information from the FullTilt internal system. Using Endeca's Guided Summarization technique, the catalog could support featured products, make suggestions, and offer related information based on customer exploration of the site. In this way, customers could investigate options and select products best suited to their needs.

The Results
The FullTilt Information Access Platform resulted in reduced costs by decreasing the number of people needed to build and maintain the system, fast deployment of accurate and up-to-date custom catalogs, and more efficient catalog maintenance.

The Endeca Information Access Platform provided the single source of product information and resulted in an 84 percent increase in conversions (the number of customers who visited the site and went on to buy), more than 25 percent increase in leads for sales, and double-digit increase in online sales.

Sources: *FullTilt* (2004) and *Endeca* (2008).

Questions
1. Why did Brady need an e-catalog?
2. Why was the Excel-based catalog useless?
3. What are the benefits of the new e-catalog?
4. What did Endeca's product contribute?

5.3 SELLING VIA DISTRIBUTORS AND OTHER INTERMEDIARIES

Manufacturers can sell directly to businesses, and they do so if the customers are large buyers. However, frequently they use intermediaries to distribute their products to a large number of smaller buyers. The intermediaries buy products from many manufacturers and aggregate them into one catalog from which they sell to customers or to retailers. Now, many of these distributors also are selling online via Webstores.

Some well-known online distributors for businesses are Sam's Club (of Walmart), Avnet, and W.W. Grainger (Case 5.2). Most e-distributors sell in horizontal markets, meaning that they sell to businesses in a variety of industries. However, some specialize in one industry (vertical market), such as Boeing PART (see Online File W5.7). Most intermediaries sell at fixed prices; however, some offer quantity discounts, negotiated prices, or conduct auctions.

CASE 5.2

EC Application

W.W. GRAINGER AND GOODRICH CORPORATION

W.W. Grainger has a number of Web sites, but its flagship is *grainger.com*. In 2008, of Grainger's $6.9 billion in annual sales, more than $600 million was done over the Web, with the majority of those sales placed through *grainger.com*.

More than 870,000 products from more than 3,000 suppliers are offered at *grainger.com*, and a growing number of Grainger's 1.8 million customers from 150 countries are ordering online. The Web site continues the same kind of customer service and wide range of industrial products provided by Grainger's traditional offline business with the additional convenience of 24/7 ordering, use of search engines, and additional services.

This convenience is what first attracted BFGoodrich Aerospace (now called Goodrich Corporation) in Pueblo, Colorado. It found *grainger.com* to be one of the most convenient and easy purchasing sites to use. The purchasing agent of this relatively small Goodrich plant of approximately 250 employees used to call in an order to a supplier, give the salesperson a part number, and wait until the price could be pulled up. Goodrich's purchaser now can place orders online in a matter of minutes, and the purchaser's display has Goodrich's negotiated pricing built in.

Goodrich can get just about anything it needs from *grainger.com*. Grainger interfaces with other suppliers, so if Goodrich needs something specific that Grainger does not normally carry, Grainger will research and find the items through Grainger's Sourcing team. Consolidating their purchases through Grainger provided better prices.

Goodrich has achieved additional savings from the tremendous decrease in paperwork that has resulted from buying through *grainger.com*. Individuals in each department now have access to purchasing cards, which allow them to do some of their own ordering. Before, the central purchasing department had to issue purchase orders for every single item. Now, employees with purchasing cards and passwords can place orders according to the spending limits that have been set up based on their positions.

In 2002, the Goodrich Pueblo operation spent $200,000 for purchases from *grainger.com*, which reflected a 10 to 15 percent savings on its purchases. Goodrich has now signed a company-wide enterprise agreement that allows every Goodrich facility in the country to order through *grainger.com*, with an expected savings of at least 10 percent.

Sources: Compiled from *en/Wikipedia.org/wiki/w._w._Grainger* (accessed November 2009), *grainger.com* (accessed November 2009), *Fortune* (2000), and Lucas (2005).

Questions

1. Enter *grainger.com* and review all the services offered to online buyers. Prepare a list of these services.

2. Explain how Goodrich's buyers save time and money.

3. What other benefits does Goodrich enjoy by using *grainger.com*?

4. How was desktop purchasing (see details in Section 5.7) implemented at Goodrich Corporation?

Section 5.3 ▶ REVIEW QUESTIONS

1. What are the advantages of using intermediaries in B2B sales?
2. What types of intermediaries exist in B2B?
3. What special services are provided to buyers by Boeing Parts? (See Online File W5.7.)
4. Compare an e-distributor in B2B to Amazon.com. What are the similarities? What are the differences?

5.4 SELLING VIA E-AUCTIONS

Auctions are gaining popularity as a B2B sales channel. Some major B2B auction issues are discussed in this section.

USING AUCTIONS ON THE SELL SIDE

Many companies use *forward auctions* to liquidate their unneeded capital assets, obsolete or out of fashion products. In such a situation, items are displayed on an auction site (private or public) for quick disposal. Forward auctions offer the following benefits to B2B sellers:

> **Revenue generation.** Forward auctions support and expand online and overall sales. Forward auctions also offer businesses a new venue for quickly and easily disposing of excess, obsolete, and returned products (e.g., liquidation.com).

> **Cost savings.** In addition to generating new revenue, conducting auctions electronically reduces the costs of selling the auctioned items. These savings also help increase the seller's profits.

> **Increased "stickiness."** Forward auctions give Web sites increased "stickiness" (the number and length of visits by potential buyers). Stickiness is a characteristic that describes customer loyalty to a site, eventually resulting in higher revenue.

> **Member acquisition and retention.** All bidding transactions result in additional registered members, who are future business contacts. In addition, auction software aids enable sellers to search and report on virtually every relevant auction activity for future analysis and use.

Forward auctions can be conducted in two ways. A company can conduct its forward auctions from its own Web site or it can sell from an intermediary auction site, such as ebay.com. Let's examine these options.

AUCTIONING FROM THE COMPANY'S OWN SITE

For large and well-known companies that frequently conduct auctions, such as GM, it makes sense to build an auction mechanism on the company's own site. Why should a company pay a commission to an intermediary if the intermediary cannot provide the company with added value? Of course, if a company decides to auction from its own site, it will have to pay for infrastructure and operate and maintain the auction site. However, if the company already has an electronic marketplace for selling from e-catalogs, the additional cost for conducting auctions might not be too high. Note that a significant added value that could be provided by intermediaries is the attraction of many potential buyers to the auction site.

AUCTION RULES

The success of auctions depends also on complying with auction rules. These rules are intended to smooth the auction process and to prevent fraud. These rules can be divided into three major categories: bidding rules, clearing rules, and information-revelation rules. Examples of rules are provided by the U.S. government at ftc.gov/bcp/edu/pubs/consumer/tech/tec07.shtm. The rules provide definitions, restrictions, and timing constraints.

Auction rules may vary from country to country due to legal considerations. They may also vary within a country due to the nature of the items auctioned, the auctioneer's policies, and the nature of competition among the auction houses.

USING INTERMEDIARIES IN AUCTIONS

Several intermediaries offer B2B auction sites (e.g., see asset-auctions.com and liquidation.com). An intermediary might conduct private auctions for a seller, either from the intermediary's or the seller's site. Or a company might choose to conduct auctions in a public marketplace, using a third-party hosting company (e.g., eBay, which has a special "business exchange" for small companies).

Using a third-party hosting company for conducting auctions has many benefits. The first is that no additional resources (e.g., hardware, bandwidth, engineering resources, or IT personnel) are required. Nor are there any hiring costs or opportunity costs associated with the redeployment of corporate resources. B2B auction intermediary sites also offer fast time to market: They enable a company to have a robust, customized auction up and running immediately. Without the intermediary, it can take a company weeks to prepare an auction site in-house.

Another benefit of using intermediaries relates to billing and collection efforts, which are handled by the intermediary rather than the selling company. For example, intermediaries calculate merchant-specific shipping weights and charge customers for shipping of auctioned items. These services are not free, of course. They are provided as part of the merchant's commission to the intermediary; a cost often deemed worth paying in exchange for the ease of the service.

Example: Liquidation.com

Liquidation.com operates a market for production overruns, store returns, and goods from bankrupt firms. The company sells industrial goods and real estate in large lot sizes and operates four different marketplaces. Liquidity Service Inc. is the auction marketplace. Annual sales exceeded $200 million in 2008. The advantages of the company to its customers are:

- Offers a global marketplace with complete support.
- Includes presentation on Web site (graphics and text) and support for transactions (an auction and bidding engine).
- Offers at least twice as much value compared to an offline market.
- The firm is used by 750,000 professional buyers from 116 countries so there is wide exposure.
- For retail stores the return is 6 percent, compared to e-commerce at 12 percent of sales.

The Auction Process. The auction process consists of the following:

- Auctions close every two to three days.
- No sniping is allowed. Bidding is extended every three minutes until one bidder is left.
- Liquidation.com provides good descriptions of goods online, including extensive photos.
- Customer backing and support on goods sold is available.
- Batch sizes are adjusted for bids.

The company provides research and analysis services that benefit the sellers such as:

- Analyzing information to attract customers to the Web site.
- Building a tracking program to calculate conversion metrics such as average number of auctions viewed per name, average number of bids placed, average number of transactions, and the percent of visitors who registered.
- Focusing on search engine marketing.

For an example of using an intermediary to liquidate old equipment, see Online File W5.8.

EXAMPLES OF B2B FORWARD AUCTIONS

The following are examples of B2B auctions:

- Sam's Club (samsclub.com) auctions thousands of items (especially electronics) at auctions.samsclub.com. Featured auctions include the current bid, the number of bids, and the end date.
- ResortQuest, a large vacation rental company, uses auctionanything.com to auction rental space.
- At GovernmentAuctions.org (governmentauctions.org), businesses can bid on foreclosures, seized items, abandoned property, and more.
- Yahoo! conducts both B2C and B2B auctions of many items.

Section 5.4 ▶ REVIEW QUESTIONS

1. List the benefits of using B2B auctions for selling.
2. List the benefits of using auction intermediaries.
3. What are the major purposes of forward auctions, and how are they conducted?

5.5 ONE-FROM-MANY: BUY-SIDE E-MARKETPLACES AND E-PROCUREMENT

When a buyer goes to a sell-side marketplace, such as Cisco's, the buyer's purchasing department sometimes has to manually enter the order information into its own corporate information system. Furthermore, manually searching Webstores and e-malls to find and compare suppliers and products can be slow and costly. As a solution, large buyers can open their own marketplaces, as Portsmouth Hospitals (the opening case) did, called **buy-side e-marketplaces**, and invite sellers to browse and offer to fulfill orders. The term *procurement* is used to refer to the purchase of goods and services for organizations. It is usually done by *purchasing agents*, also known as *corporate buyers*.

buy-side e-marketplace
A corporate-based acquisition site that uses reverse auctions, negotiations, group purchasing, or any other e-procurement method.

PROCUREMENT METHODS

Companies use different methods to procure goods and services depending on what and where they buy, the quantities needed, how much money is involved, and more. The major procurement methods include the following:

▶ Conduct bidding in a system in which suppliers compete against each other. This method is used for large-ticket items or large quantities (Section 5.6).

▶ Buy directly from manufacturers, wholesalers, or retailers from their catalogs, and possibly by negotiation.

▶ Buy at private or public auction sites in which the organization participates as one of the buyers (Section 5.6).

▶ Buy from the catalog of an intermediary (e-distributor) that aggregates sellers' catalogs (Section 5.7).

▶ Buy from an internal buyer's catalog, in which company-approved vendors' catalogs, including agreed-upon prices, are aggregated. This approach is used for the implementation of *desktop purchasing*, which allows the requisitioners to order directly from vendors, bypassing the procurement department (Section 5.7).

▶ Join a group-purchasing system that aggregates participants' demand, creating a large volume. Then the group may negotiate prices or initiate a tendering process (Section 5.7).

▶ Buy at an exchange or industrial mall (Section 5.8).

▶ Collaborate with suppliers to share information about sales and inventory, so as to reduce inventory and stock-outs and enhance just-in-time delivery. (See Chapter 6 on collaborative commerce.)

Some of these activities are done in private marketplaces, others in public exchanges.

E-Procurement Organization and Types

E-procurement methods can be organized into four segments: (1) Buy at own Web site, (2) buy at seller's Webstore, (3) buy at exchanges, and (4) buy at other e-market sites. Each segment includes several activities, as illustrated in Exhibit 5.3. Some of these will be described in Sections 5.6 through 5.9.

According to Wikipedia (en.wikipedia.org/wiki/E-procurement), the seven main types of e-procurement are as follows:

▶ **E-Sourcing.** Identifying new suppliers for a specific category of purchasing requirements using Internet technology.

▶ **E-Tendering.** Sending requests for information and prices to known suppliers and receiving the suppliers' responses and bids using Internet technology.

▶ **E-Reverse auctioning.** Using Internet technology to buy goods and services from a number of known or unknown suppliers.

▶ **E-Informing.** Gathering and distributing purchasing information both from and to internal and external parties using Internet technology.

▶ **Web-based ERP (electronic resource planning).** Creating and approving purchasing requisitions, placing purchase orders, and receiving goods and services by using a software system based on Internet technology.

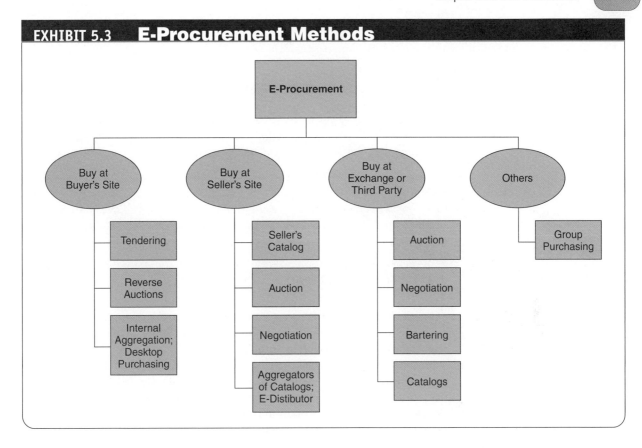

EXHIBIT 5.3   E-Procurement Methods

- **E-Marketsites.** Buying communities access favored suppliers' products and services, add products to shopping carts, create requisitions, seek approval, receive purchase orders, and process electronic invoices, integrating them into suppliers' supply chains and buyers' financial systems.
- **E-MRO (maintenance, repair, and operating).** The same as Web-based ERP except that the goods and services ordered are non-product-related MRO supplies.

INEFFICIENCIES IN TRADITIONAL PROCUREMENT MANAGEMENT

Procurement management refers to the planning, organizing, and coordinating of all the activities pertaining to the purchasing of the goods and services necessary to accomplish the mission of an enterprise. It involves the B2B purchase and sale of supplies and services, as well as the flow of required information and networking systems. Approximately 80 percent of an organization's purchased items, mostly MROs, constitute 20 to 25 percent of the total purchase value. Furthermore, a large portion of corporate buyers' time is spent on non-value-added activities, such as entering data, correcting errors in paperwork, expediting delivery, or solving quality problems.

procurement management
The planning, organizing, and coordinating of all the activities related to purchasing goods and services needed to accomplish the organization's mission.

The procurement process may be lengthy and complex due to the many activities performed. The following are the major activities that may be evidenced in a single purchase:

> *Search for items* using search engines, catalogs, showrooms, and sales presentations.
> *Learn details of items and terms* using comparison engines and quality reports, and research the items and vendors.
> *Negotiate or join group purchasing* using intelligent software agents (if available).
> *Sign agreement or contract* using contract management; arrange financing, escrow insurance, etc.
> *Create specific purchasing order(s)* using computerized system. Determine when and how much to order each time. Authorize corporate buyers.
> *Arrange packing, shipments, and deliveries* using electronic tracking, RFID, etc.
> *Arrange invoicing, payments, expense, management, and purchasing budgetary control* using software packages.

The traditional procurement process is often inefficient. For example, for high-value items, purchasing personnel spend a great deal of time and effort on procurement activities. These activities include qualifying suppliers, negotiating prices and terms, building rapport with strategic suppliers, and carrying out supplier evaluation and certification. If buyers are busy with the details of the smaller items (usually the MROs), they do not have enough time to properly deal with the purchase of the high-value items.

Other inefficiencies also may occur in conventional procurement. These range from delays to paying too much for rush orders. One procurement inefficiency is **maverick buying.** This is when a buyer makes unplanned purchases of items needed quickly, which results in buying at non-prenegotiated, usually higher, prices.

To correct the situation, companies reengineer their procurement systems, implement new purchasing models, and, in particular, introduce e-procurement.

maverick buying
Unplanned purchases of items needed quickly, often at non-prenegotiated higher prices.

THE GOALS AND BENEFITS OF E-PROCUREMENT

Improvements to procurement have been attempted for decades, usually by using information technologies. The real opportunity for improvement lies in the use of **e-procurement**, the electronic acquisition of goods and services for organizations. The general e-procurement process (with the exception of tendering) is shown in Online File W5.9.

By automating and streamlining the laborious routines of the purchasing function, purchasing professionals can focus on more strategic purchases, *achieving the following goals and benefits:*

e-procurement
The electronic acquisition of goods and services for organizations.

> Increasing the productivity of purchasing agents (providing them with more time and reducing job pressure)
> Lowering purchase prices through product standardization, reverse auctions, volume discounts, and consolidation of purchases
> Improving information flow and management (e.g., supplier's information and pricing information)
> Minimizing the purchases made from noncontract vendors (minimizing maverick buying)

- Improving the payment process and savings due to expedited payments (for sellers)
- Establishing efficient, collaborative supplier relations
- Ensuring delivery on time, every time
- Slashing order-fulfillment and processing times by leveraging automation
- Reducing the skill requirements and training needs of purchasing agents
- Reducing the number of suppliers
- Streamlining the purchasing process, making it simple and fast (may involve authorizing requisitioners to perform purchases from their desktops, bypassing the procurement department)
- Streamlining invoice reconciliation and dispute resolution
- Reducing the administrative processing cost per order by as much as 90 percent (e.g., GM achieved a reduction from $100 to $10)
- Finding new suppliers and vendors that can provide goods and services faster and/or cheaper (improved sourcing)
- Integrating budgetary controls into the procurement process
- Minimizing human errors in the buying or shipping processes
- Monitoring and regulating buying behavior

For an example of a successful implementation, see Case 5.2 (p. 180). For implementation process and strategy, see Online File W5.10.

Section 5.5 ▶ REVIEW QUESTIONS

1. Define procurement and list the major procurement methods.
2. Describe the inefficiencies of traditional procurement.
3. Define e-procurement and list its goals.
4. List the major e-procurement segments and some activities in each.
5. List the benefits of e-procurement.

5.6 BUY-SIDE E-MARKETPLACES: REVERSE AUCTIONS

Recall from our previous chapters that a *reverse auction* is a tendering system in which suppliers are invited to bid on the fulfillment of an order and the lowest bid wins. In B2B usage of a reverse auction, a buyer may open an electronic market on its own server and invite potential suppliers to bid on the items the buyer needs. The "invitation" to such reverse auctions is a form or document called a **request for quote (RFQ)**. Traditional tendering usually implied one-time sealed bidding, whereas an e-reverse auction opens the auction to competing sequential bidding. See en.wikipedia.org/wiki/Reverse_auction for a comprehensive overview of reverse auctions.

Governments and large corporations frequently mandate reverse auctions, which may provide considerable savings. The electronic process is faster and administratively much less expensive. It also can benefit buyers in locating the cheapest possible products or services.

request for quote (RFQ)
The "invitation" to participate in a tendering (bidding) system.

CONDUCTING REVERSE AUCTIONS

As the number of reverse auction sites increases, suppliers will not be able to manually monitor all relevant tendering sites. This problem has been addressed with the introduction of online directories that list open RFQs. Another way to solve this problem is through the use of monitoring software agents. Software agents also can aid in the bidding process itself. Examples of agents that support the bidding process are auctionsniper.com and auctionflex.com.

Alternatively, third-party intermediaries may run the electronic bidding, as they do for forward auctions. General Electric's GXS (now an independent company, described in detail in Online File W5.11) is open to any buyer. Auction sites such as govliquidation.com, liquidation.com, and asset-auctions.com also belong to this category. Conducting reverse auctions in B2B can be a fairly complex process. This is why an intermediary may be beneficial.

The reverse auction process is demonstrated in Exhibit 5.4. As shown in the exhibit, the first step is for the would-be buyer to post bid invitations. When bids

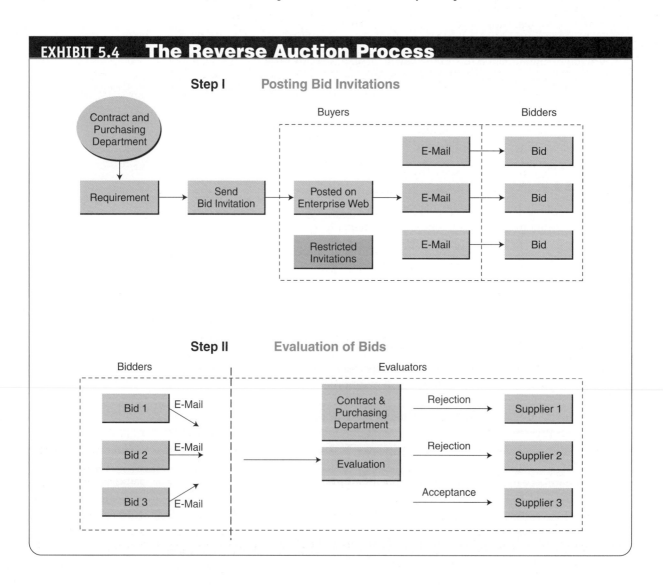

EXHIBIT 5.4   The Reverse Auction Process

arrive, contract and purchasing personnel for the buyer evaluate the bids and decide which one(s) to accept.

E-Tendering by Governments

Most governments must conduct tendering when they buy or sell goods and services. Doing this manually is slow and expensive. Therefore, many are moving to e-reverse auctions.

GROUP REVERSE AUCTIONS

B2B reverse auctions are done in a private exchange or at an aggregator's site for a group of buying companies. Such *group reverse auctions* are popular in South Korea and usually involve large conglomerates. For example, the LG Group operates the LG MRO Auction for its members, and the Samsung Group operates iMarketKorea, as described in this chapter's closing case.

Section 5.6 ▶ REVIEW QUESTIONS

1. Describe the manual tendering system.
2. How do online reverse auctions work?
3. List the benefits of Web-based reverse auctions.
4. Describe the business drivers of GE's TPN now (GXS) and its evolution over time. (See Online File W5.11.)

5.7 OTHER E-PROCUREMENT METHODS

Companies have implemented other innovative e-procurement methods. Some common ones are described in this section and the next.

AN INTERNAL PURCHASING MARKETPLACE: AGGREGATING SUPPLIERS' CATALOGS AND DESKTOP PURCHASING

Large organizations have many corporate buyers that are usually located in different departments and locations. These agents buy from a large number of suppliers. The problem is that even if all purchases are made from approved suppliers, it is difficult to plan and control procurement when many buyers purchase individually. In many cases, to save time, buyers engage in *maverick buying*. This situation is especially serious in government agencies and multinational entities where many buyers and large numbers of purchases are involved.

One effective solution to such a procurement problem is to aggregate the catalogs of all approved suppliers, combining them into a single internal electronic catalog. By aggregating the suppliers' catalogs on the buyer's server, it also is easier to centralize and control all procurement. Such an aggregation is called an **internal procurement marketplace**.

Benefits of Internal Aggregated Catalogs

Corporate buyers can use search engines to look through internal aggregated catalogs to quickly find what they want, check availability and delivery times, and complete electronic requisition forms. Another advantage of such aggregation is that a company can

internal procurement marketplace
The aggregated catalogs of all approved suppliers combined into a single internal electronic catalog.

reduce the number of suppliers it uses. Buying from fewer sellers typically increases the quantities bought from each, lowering the per unit price.

Example: MasterCard International. MasterCard International aggregates more than 10,000 items from the catalogs of approved suppliers into an internal electronic catalog. The goal of this project is to consolidate buying activities from multiple corporate sites, improve processing costs, and reduce the supplier base. Payments are made with MasterCard's corporate procurement card. The system is used by all corporate buyers (about 3,000). MasterCard is continually adding suppliers and catalog content to the system (see MasterCard 2009).

Finally, internal catalogs allow for easy financial controls. As buyers make purchases, their account balances are displayed. Once the balance is depleted, the system will not allow new purchase orders to go through. Therefore, this model is especially popular in public institutions and government entities. The implementation of internal purchasing marketplaces is frequently done via a process known as *desktop purchasing*.

Desktop Purchasing

desktop purchasing
Direct purchasing from internal marketplaces without the approval of supervisors and without the intervention of a procurement department.

Desktop purchasing implies purchasing directly from internal marketplaces without the approval of supervisors and without the intervention of a procurement department. This is usually done by using a *payment card* (see Chapter 10; also known as purchasing card [p-card]). Desktop purchasing reduces the administrative cost and cycle time involved in purchasing urgently needed or frequently purchased items of small dollar value. This approach is especially effective for MRO purchases.

Example: Microsoft. Microsoft built its internal marketplace, MS Market, for the procurement of small items. The aggregated catalog that is part of MS Market is used by Microsoft employees worldwide, whose purchasing totals over $3.5 billion annually. The system has drastically reduced the role and size of the procurement departments at Microsoft.

The desktop-purchasing approach also can be implemented by partnering with external private exchanges. For instance, Samsung Electronics of South Korea, a huge global manufacturer and its subsidiaries, has integrated its iMarketKorea exchange (see this chapter's closing case) with the e-procurement systems of its buying agents. This platform can be easily linked with *group purchasing*, which is described later in this section.

BUYING AT SELLERS' E-AUCTIONS

Another popular approach to procurement is e-auctions. As described earlier, sellers are increasingly motivated to sell surpluses and even regular products via auctions. In some cases, e-auctions provide an opportunity for buyers to find inexpensive or unique items fairly quickly. A prudent corporate buyer should certainly look at both those manufacturers and distributors that conduct auctions periodically (e.g., Dell) and at third-party auctioneers (e.g., eBay or dir.yahoo.com/Business_and_Economy/Shopping_and_ Services/Auctions). Auction aggregators can help purchasers find where and when auctions of needed items are being conducted. Auctions can be conducted at the seller's site, at an auctioneer's site, or at an exchange.

GROUP PURCHASING

group purchasing
The aggregation of orders from several buyers into volume purchases so that better prices can be negotiated.

Many companies, especially small ones, are moving to group purchasing. With **group purchasing**, orders from several buyers are aggregated into volume purchases so that better prices can be negotiated. Two models are in use: internal aggregation and external (third-party) aggregation.

Internal Aggregation of Purchasing Orders

Large companies, such as GE, spend billions of dollars on MROs every year. Company-wide orders, from GE companies and subsidiaries, for identical items are aggregated using the Web and are replenished automatically. Besides economies of scale (lower prices for large purchases) on many items, GE saves on the administrative cost of the transactions, reducing transaction costs.

External Aggregation for Group Purchasing

Many SMEs would like to enjoy quantity discounts but have difficulty finding others to join group purchasing to increase the procurement volume. Finding partners can be accomplished by an external third party such as BuyerZone (buyerzone.com), HIGPA (higpa.org), or the United Sourcing Alliance (usa-llc.com). The idea is to provide SMEs with better prices, selection, and services by aggregating demand online and then either negotiating with suppliers or conducting reverse auctions. The external aggregation group purchasing process is shown in Exhibit 5.5.

Several large companies, including large CPA firms, EDS, and Ariba, are providing similar aggregation services, mainly to their regular customers. Yahoo! and AOL also offer such services. A key to the success of these companies is a critical mass of buyers. An interesting strategy is for a company to outsource aggregation to a third party. For example, energysolutions.com provides group buying for community site partners in the energy industry.

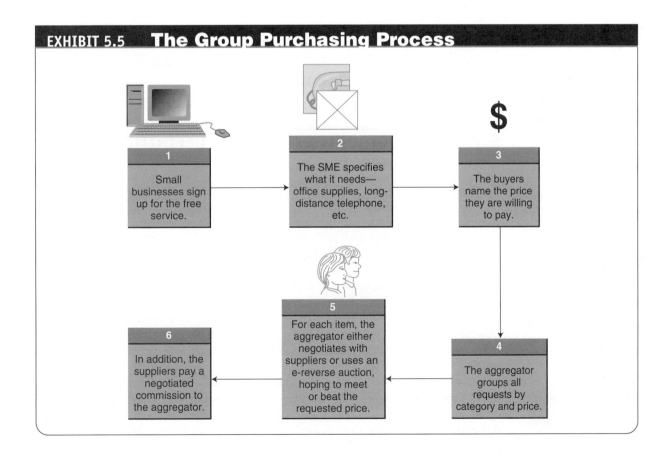

EXHIBIT 5.5 The Group Purchasing Process

BUYING AT SELLERS' SITES AND COLLABORATIVE COMMERCE

Section 5.3 described how companies use e-distributors as a sales channel (recall the case of W.W. Grainger). When buying small quantities, purchasers often buy from an e-distributor. If they buy online, it is considered e-procurement.

ACQUISITION VIA ELECTRONIC BARTERING

bartering exchange
An intermediary that links parties in a barter; a company submits its surplus to the exchange and receives points of credit, which can be used to buy the items that the company needs from other exchange participants.

Bartering is the exchange of goods or services without the use of money. The basic idea is for a company to exchange its surplus for something that it needs. Companies can advertise their surpluses in classified ads and may find a partner to make an exchange, but in many cases a company will have little success in finding an exact match on its own. Therefore, companies usually ask an intermediary to help.

A bartering intermediary can use a manual search-and-match approach or it can create an electronic bartering exchange. With a **bartering exchange,** a company submits its surplus to the exchange and receives points of credit, which the company can then use to buy items that it needs. Popular bartering items are office space, idle facilities and labor, products, and even banner ads. Examples of bartering companies are u-exchange.com and itex.com.

Section 5.7 ▶ REVIEW QUESTIONS

1. Describe a buyer-operated procurement marketplace and list its benefits.
2. Describe the benefits of desktop purchasing.
3. Discuss the relationship of desktop purchasing with internal procurement marketplaces and with group purchasing.
4. Explain the logic of group purchasing and how it is organized.
5. Describe how e-distributors operate and discuss their appeal to buyers.
6. How does B2B bartering work? What are its benefits?

5.8 B2B ELECTRONIC EXCHANGES: DEFINITIONS AND CONCEPTS

Companies can buy and/or sell in B2B exchanges. The term *exchange* implies many-to-many e-marketplaces. In addition to being trading venues, many exchanges support community activities, such as distributing industry news, sponsoring online discussion groups, blogging, and providing research. Some also provide support services such as payments and logistics (see Papazoglou and Ribbers 2006).

Exchanges are known by a variety of names: *e-marketplaces* and *trading exchanges* (*trading communities, exchange hubs, Internet exchanges, Net marketplaces,* and *B2B portals*).

Despite their variety, all exchanges share one major characteristic: Exchanges are electronic trading-community meeting places for many sellers and many buyers, and possibly for other business partners, as shown in Exhibit 5.6. At the center of every exchange is a market maker, the third party that operates the exchange and, in some cases, may also own it.

In an exchange, just as in a traditional open-air marketplace, buyers and sellers can interact and negotiate prices and quantities. Generally, free-market economics rules the exchange community, as demonstrated by ChemConnect (see Online File W5.12). A thriving example of a third-party exchange is Agentrics.com, which is described in Case 5.3.

EXHIBIT 5.6 **The Community of an Exchange: Flow and Access to Information**

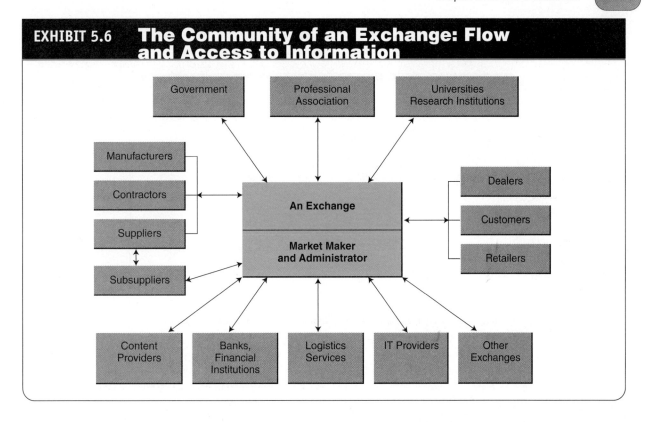

CASE 5.3
EC Application
AGENTRICS: A GIANT RETAIL EXCHANGE

Agentrics (*agentrics.com*) is the world's largest exchange for retail and packaged consumer goods. It was formed from the mergers of several exchanges, including the World Wide Retail Exchange (WWRE) and GNX. As of May 2009, its membership included 250 manufacturers among them Kraft, Pepsi, Coca-Cola, GlaxoSmithKline, as well as 50 of the world's largest retailers, including 15 of the top 25 retailers (e.g., Kroger, Tesco, and Walgreens). Its primary objective is to enable participating retailers and manufacturers to simplify, rationalize, and automate supply chain processes, thereby eliminating inefficiencies in the supply chain.

Today, Agentrics is the premier Internet-based B2B exchange in the retail e-marketplace. Utilizing the most sophisticated Internet technology available, the exchange enables retailers and manufacturers in the food, general merchandise, textile/home, and drugstore sectors to substantially reduce costs across product development, e-procurement, and

supply chain processes. The exchange is used by more than 100,000 suppliers, partners, and distributors worldwide.

The exchange operates as an open, independently managed company that generates benefits for its members and ultimately the consumer. Agentrics is run as a private company with no plans of going public. Rather, it concentrates on bringing value to its members and customers.

Founding Principles
The following six principles guide the exchange's development and growth:

1. Openness
2. Commitment to utilizing the best available technology
3. Focus on improving efficiency and lowering costs for the retail industry
4. Operation as a neutral company
5. Equivalent fee structures for all participants
6. Confidentiality of transaction information

(continued)

CASE 5.3   (continued)

Source: Courtesy of Agentrics.com. Used with permission.

Value Proposition

Members realize value in seven key ways:

1. Low-cost product offerings that are robust, scalable, integrated, and fully supported
2. Shared technology investments and outsourced assets
3. Ability to access a global membership community and network with other retailers/manufacturers
4. Value-added services from a trusted source, at competitive costs
5. Participation in collaborative activities
6. Complex transactions and interactions made easy through automation
7. Standard-setting benefits for all B2B activities

   The exchange offers about 20 different products and services. They are classified as those related to WWRE (e.g., global data synchronization, trading, sourcing,

supply chain solutions) and those related to GNX (e.g., collaboration, performance and life-cycle management, CPFR, and negotiation).

Sources: Compiled from *agentrics.com* (accessed August 2009), webMethods (2005), and *webmethods.com* (accessed August 2009).

Questions

1. Enter *agentrics.com* and find information about services offered, including auctions and negotiations. Write a report.
2. Enter *agentrics.com* and identify the services offered for retailers and for suppliers. Write a summary.
3. Does it make sense to have such a large exchange? Why?

FUNCTIONS OF EXCHANGES

Exchanges have three major sets of functions:

1. **Matching buyers and sellers.** The matching of buyers and sellers includes such activities as:
   ▶ Establishing product offerings
   ▶ Aggregating and posting different products for sale
   ▶ Providing price and product information
   ▶ Organizing bids, bartering, and auctions

- Matching supplier offerings with buyer preferences
- Enabling price and product comparisons
- Supporting negotiations and agreements between buyers and suppliers
- Providing directories of buyers and sellers

2. **Facilitating transactions.** Facilitating transactions includes the following activities:
   - Providing the trading platform and mechanisms such as arranging logistics of delivering information, goods, or services to buyers
   - Providing billing and payment information, including addresses
   - Defining terms and other transaction values
   - Inputting searchable information
   - Granting exchange access to users and identifying company users eligible to use the exchange
   - Settling transaction payments to suppliers, collecting transaction fees and providing other escrow services
   - Registering and qualifying buyers and suppliers
   - Maintaining appropriate security over information and transactions
   - Arranging for group (volume) purchasing

3. **Maintaining exchange policies and infrastructure.** Maintaining institutional infrastructure involves the following activities:
   - Ascertaining compliance with commercial code, contract law, export and import laws, and intellectual property law for transactions made within the exchange
   - Maintaining technological infrastructure to support volume and complexity of transactions
   - Providing interface capability to standard systems of buyers and suppliers
   - Obtaining appropriate site advertisers and collecting advertising and other fees

Services Provided by Exchanges

Exchanges provide many services to buyers and sellers. The types of services offered depend on the nature of the exchange. For example, the services provided by a stock exchange are completely different from those provided by a steel or food exchange or by an intellectual property or patent exchange. However, most exchanges provide the services shown in Exhibit 5.7.

DYNAMIC PRICING IN B2B EXCHANGES

Exchanges facilitate the relationships among business partners (see Online File W5.13). The market makers in both vertical and horizontal exchanges match supply and demand in their exchanges, and this matching determines prices, which are usually *dynamic* and are based on changes in supply and demand. **Dynamic pricing** refers to a rapid movement of prices over time and possibly across customers. Stock exchanges are the prime example of dynamic pricing. Another good example of dynamic pricing occurs in auctions, where prices vary all the time.

dynamic pricing
A rapid movement of prices over time and possibly across customers, as a result of supply and demand matching.

EXHIBIT 5.7 Services in Exchanges

The Exchange and Its Services

Sellers
A
B
C
D
•
•
•

- Buyer–seller registration, qualification, coordination
- Catalog management (conversion, integration, maintenance)
- Communication/protocol translation (EDI, XML, CORBA)
- Sourcing—RFQ, bid coordination (product configuration, negotiation)
- Security, anonymity
- Software: groupware, workflow
- Integration with members' back-office systems
- Auction management
- News, information, industry analysis
- Support services (financing, payment, insurance, logistics, tax, escrow, order tracking)
- Administration—profiles, statistics, etc.

Buyers
X
Y
Z
•
•
•

The typical process that results in dynamic pricing in most exchanges includes the following steps:

1. A company posts a bid to buy a product or an offer to sell one.
2. An auction (forward or reverse) is activated.
3. Buyers and sellers can see the bids and offers but might not always see who is making them. Anonymity often is a key ingredient of dynamic pricing.
4. Buyers and sellers interact with bids and offers in real time. Sometimes buyers join together to obtain a volume discount price (group purchasing).
5. A deal is struck when there is an exact match between a buyer and a seller on price, volume, and other variables, such as location or quality.
6. The deal is consummated, and payment and delivery are arranged.

ADVANTAGES, LIMITATIONS, AND THE REVENUE MODEL OF EXCHANGES

Exchanges have several benefits, including making markets more efficient, providing opportunities for sellers and buyers to find new business partners, cutting the administrative costs of ordering MROs, and expediting trading processes. They also facilitate global trade and create communities of informed buyers and sellers.

The potential gains and risks of B2B exchanges for buyers and for sellers are summarized in Exhibit 5.8. As the exhibit shows, the gains outnumber the risks. Quantitative benefits usually result from revenue models.

Revenue Models

Exchange owners, whoever they are, must decide how they will earn revenue. The revenue sources cited in Section 1.5 (Chapter 1) are applicable here too.

Section 5.8 ▶ REVIEW QUESTIONS

1. Define B2B exchanges and list the various types of public exchanges.
2. List the major functions of exchanges.
3. What is dynamic pricing? How does it work?
4. List the potential advantages, gains, limitations, and risks of exchanges.

EXHIBIT 5.8 Potential Gains and Risks in B2B Exchanges

	For Buyers	For Sellers
Potential gains	• One-stop shopping, huge variety • Search and comparison shopping • Volume discounts • 24/7 ordering from any location • Make one order from several suppliers • Huge, detailed information • Access to new suppliers • Status review and easy reordering • Community participation • Fast delivery • Less maverick buying • Better partner relationship management	• New sales channel • No physical store is needed • Reduced ordering errors • Sell 24/7 • Community participation • Reach new customers at little extra cost • Promote the business via the exchange • An outlet for surplus inventory • Can go global more easily • Efficient inventory management • Better partner relationship management
Potential risks	• Unknown vendors; may not be reliable • Loss of customer service quality (inability to compare all services)	• Loss of direct CRM and PRM • More price wars • Competition for value-added services • Must pay transaction fees (including on seller's existing customers) • Possible loss of customers to competitors

5.9 B2B PORTALS, DIRECTORIES, AND OWNERSHIP OF B2B MARKETPLACES

Two major varieties of B2B marketplaces exist: *portals* and *directories*.

B2B PORTALS

B2B portals are information portals for businesses. Some e-marketplaces act as pure information portals. They usually include *directories* of products offered by each seller, lists of buyers and what they want, and other industry or general information. Buyers then visit sellers' sites to conduct their transactions. The portal may get commissions for referrals or only derive revenue from advertisements. Thus, information portals sometimes have a difficult time generating sufficient revenues. Because of this, many information portals are beginning to offer, for a fee, additional services that support trading, such as escrow and shipments. An example of a B2B portal is MyBoeingFleet (myboeingfleet.com), which is a Web portal for airplane owners, operators, and MRO operators. Developed by Boeing Commercial Aviation Services, MyBoeingFleet provides customers (primarily businesses) direct and personalized access to information essential to the operation of Boeing aircraft.

Like exchanges, information portals may be horizontal (e.g., Alibaba.com, described in Case 5.4), offering a wide range of products to different industries. Or they may be vertical, focusing on a single industry or industry segment. Vertical portals often are referred to as **vortals**.

The two examples that follow are portals that illustrate some of the differences between *portals* and *exchanges*.

B2B portals
Information portals for businesses.

vortals
B2B portals that focus on a single industry or industry segment; "vertical portals."

CASE 5.4
EC Application
ALIBABA.COM

Alibaba.com Limited is the global leader in B2B EC and the flagship company of Alibaba Group. Founded in 1999, Alibaba.com makes it easy for millions of buyers and suppliers around the world to do business online through three marketplaces: a global trade marketplace (*alibaba.com*) for importers and exporters, a Chinese marketplace (*alibaba.com.cn*) for domestic trade in China, and, through an associated company, a Japanese marketplace (*alibaba.co.jp*) facilitating trade to and from Japan. Together, its marketplaces form a community of 40 million registered users from more than 240 countries and regions. Headquartered in Hangzhou, China, Alibaba.com has offices in more than 40 cities across Greater China as well as in Europe and the United States.

In 10 short years, Alibaba.com has grown into a premier e-commerce brand and a vibrant online marketplace for businesses from around the world. To date, Alibaba.com's international marketplace is serving more than 8.6 million members from over 240 countries and regions, offering products in more than 3,500 different categories, and its China marketplace is also facilitating domestic trade for 31.6 million registered users in China, offering products in more than 6,000 different categories. Alibaba.com offers trade information in both breadth and depth and matches buyers and sellers 24/7.

Trust and safety are fundamental to e-commerce. Paid suppliers on Alibaba.com must pass an authentication and verification process conducted by an independent third-party agency. Only those who have been successfully verified by the third party can obtain an Alibaba "TrustPass."

Alibaba International (*alibaba.com*) is an English-language global trade marketplace, serving small and medium-sized enterprises (SMEs) in the international trade community. Alibaba.com offers a broad range of products and services to both suppliers and buyers. Basic features such as standard supplier Webstores, product listings, and communication tools are available for free. It also offers paid membership packages to verified suppliers. The subscription fee of the membership includes authentication and verification of the member's identity, which is performed by a third-party credit reporting agency. Alibaba is prospering from a business model dedicated to serving a vital, but disadvantaged, segment of China's economy: SMEs. Fewer than 1 million of the nation's 42 million small and medium-sized enterprises have any Internet capability. Alibaba offers simple and efficient Internet solutions for fledgling ventures to such companies.

Alibaba China (*alibaba.com.cn*) is China's largest online marketplace in the Chinese language for domestic trade among businesspeople. With more than 30 million registered users, Alibaba China is a trusted community of members who regularly meet, chat, search for products, and do business online. Just as in the international marketplace, customers pay an annual subscription fee for membership, which entitles them to post trade offers and products online.

In addition, Alibaba Group owns and maintains the following:

▶ *Yahoo.china.cn* is a marketplace for suppliers and buyers trading domestically in China with more than 30 million registered users.
▶ *Taobao.com* is China's largest Internet retail site. Taobao has 100 million registered users, and more than 1.5 million sellers have opened up stores on the site.
▶ *Alimama.com* was China's leading online advertising exchange, helping to connect Web publishers to advertisers; an affiliate network for more than 400,000 publishers in China was merged into Taobao in 2008.
▶ *Alipay.com* is China's leading third-party online payment platform that enables individuals and businesses to execute payments online in a safe and secure manner. In August 2007, Alipay launched an online payment solution to help merchants worldwide sell directly to consumers in China, cooperating with more than 300 global retail brands and supports transactions in 12 major foreign currencies.
▶ *Alisoft.com* offers Internet-based business management solutions. It develops, markets, and delivers Internet-based business management software to SMEs in China. It commands more than 40 percent of the Software as a Service (SaaS) model offering enterprise management tools, such as e-mail, customer support software, and information management, and basic financial management tools, such as invoicing and bookkeeping.

To understand the capabilities of Alibaba.com, explore its marketplace by taking the multimedia tour!

The Database

The center of Alibaba.com is its huge database, which is basically a horizontal information portal with offerings in a wide variety of product categories. The portal is organized into 44 major industry categories (as of 2009), including agriculture, apparel and fashion, automobiles, and toys. Each industry category is further divided into subcategories (over 700 in total). For example, the toy category includes

CASE 5.4   *(continued)*

items such as dolls, electrical pets, and wooden toys. Each subcategory includes classified postings organized into four groups: sellers, buyers, agents, and cooperation.

Reverse Auctions

Alibaba.com also allows buyers to post RFQs. Would-be sellers can then send bids to the buyer, conduct negotiations, and accept a purchase order when one is agreed upon (all via the exchange). The RFQ process can be fully automated, partially automated, or done entirely manually. (To see how the process works, go to "My trade activity" and take the tour, initiate a negotiation, and issue a purchase order.)

Features and Services

Alibaba.com provides the following major features: free e-mail, instant messenger Trade Manager, Trust Service, FAQs, tutorials for traders, free e-mail alerts, news (basically related to importing and exporting), trade show information, legal information, arbitration, forums and discussion groups and trade trends, etc. In addition, a member can create a personalized company Web page as well as a "product showroom," and members also can post their own marketing leads (where to buy and sell).

Revenue Model

Sourcing on Alibaba.com is always free, attracting buyers to constantly source from Alibaba. While offering free Web site features, Alibaba.com offers paid membership service to suppliers. Income is generated through paid memberships, and value-added services. As of 2009, company profits were growing very rapidly. Gross profit for 2008 was US$3.8 million, a 39 percent increase over 2007.

Going Public with an IPO

Alibaba's founder Jack Ma took the company public in November 2007 (on the Hong Kong stock exchange; it is also traded on the OTC market in the United States) using $1.7 billion of outside capital to deploy its business model on a full scale in order to show that e-commerce in China can make money (see Chandler 2007). The influx of capital allows Alibaba to continue building its customer base by offering the bulk of its services at no charge. And that may prove to be a winning strategy.

Sources: Compiled from *alibaba.com* (accessed May 2009), Alibaba.com (2009a), Alibaba.com (2009b), Alibaba.com (2009c), Chandler (2007).

Questions

1. When the company's IPO started trading, hundreds of large corporations rushed to invest in it. Why?
2. Trace Alibaba's revenue sources.
3. List the major services provided by Alibaba.

Thomas Global

Thomas Global (thomasglobal.com) is a directory of over 700,000 manufacturers and distributors from 28 countries, encompassing over 11,000 products and service categories in 9 languages. It covers regional guides, such as Thomas Register of America (thomasnet.com), an information portal, which publishes a directory of millions of manufacturing companies. Thomas Register is basically an information portal for buyers using search engines, because it does not offer any opportunity for transactions on its site. For example, it does not offer a list of products with quantities needed (requests to buy) or offer what is available from sellers. A similar information-only service is provided by Manufacturing.net (manufacturing.net).

Alibaba.com Corporation

Another intermediary that started as a pure information portal but that is moving toward becoming a trading exchange is Alibaba.com (alibaba.com). Launched in 1999, Alibaba.com initially concentrated on China. Today it includes a large, robust community of international buyers and sellers who are interested in direct trade without an intermediary. Initially, the site was a huge posting place for classified ads. Alibaba.com is a portal in transition, showing some characteristics of an information portal plus some services of an exchange. Today, Alibaba.com has two complementary markets, as described in Case 5.4.

Directory Services and Search Engines

The B2B landscape is huge, with hundreds of thousands of companies online. Directory services can help buyers and sellers manage the task of finding specialized products, services, and potential partners. However, specialized search engines are becoming a necessity in many industries due to the information glut. The most useful search engines are those concentrating on vertical searches. Examples of vertical search engines and their services can be found at globalspec.com. In contrast to vertical searches, products such as Google Search provide search capabilities on many topics within one enterprise or on the Web in general.

OWNERSHIP OF B2B MARKETPLACES

Exchanges may be owned by a third-party operator. This arrangement is preferred by both sellers and buyers. Alternatively, an exchange may be owned by a few major sellers or buyers. This kind of arrangement is referred to as a *consortium*.

Third-Party Exchanges

Third-party exchanges are electronic intermediaries. In contrast with a portal such as Alibaba.com, the intermediary not only presents catalogs (which the portal does), but also tries to *match* buyers and sellers and encourages them to make transactions by providing electronic trading floors and rooms (which portals, in general, do not).

Third-party exchanges are characterized by two contradicting properties. On the one hand, they are *neutral* because they do not favor either sellers or buyers. On the other hand, because they do not have a built-in constituency of sellers or buyers, they sometimes have a problem attracting enough buyers and sellers to attain financial viability. Therefore, to increase their financial viability, these exchanges try to team up with partners, such as large sellers or buyers, financial institutions that provide payment schemes (as ChemConnect did with Citigroup), and logistics companies that fulfill orders.

Online File W5.12 introduced ChemConnect, a neutral, public, third-party-owned vertical market maker. ChemConnect's initial success was well publicized, and dozens of similar third-party exchanges, mostly in specific industries, have been developed since.

Consortium Exchanges

consortium trading exchange (CTE)
An exchange formed and operated by a group of major companies in an industry to provide industry-wide transaction services.

A subset of third-party exchanges is a **consortium trading exchange (CTE)**, an exchange formed and operated by a group of major companies in one industry. The major goal of CTEs (also called *consortia*) is to provide industry-wide transaction services that support buying and selling. These services include links to the participants' back-end processing systems as well as collaborative planning and design services.

Markets operate in three basic types of environments, which are shown in the following list. The type of environment indicates which type of exchange is most appropriate.

1. **Fragmented markets.** These markets have large numbers of both buyers and sellers. Examples include the life sciences and food industries. When a large percentage of the market is fragmented, third-party managed exchanges are the most appropriate.

2. **Seller-concentrated markets.** In this type of market, several large companies sell to a very large number of buyers. Examples are the plastics and transportation industries. In this type of market, consortia may be the most appropriate.

3. **Buyer-concentrated markets.** In this type of market, several large companies do most of the buying from a large number of suppliers. Examples are the automotive, airline, and electronics industries. Here, again, consortia may be the most appropriate.

EXHIBIT 5.9	Comparing the Major B2B Many-to-Many Models	
Name	**Major Characteristics**	**Types**
B2B portals and directories	• Community services, news, information • Communication tools • Classified ads • Employment markets • May support selling (buying) • Fixed prices • May do auctions	• Vertical (vortals), horizontal • Shopping directory, usually with hyperlinks
B2B trading exchanges	• Matches buyer/seller orders at dynamic prices, auctions • Provides trading-related information and services (payment, logistics) • Highly regulated • May provide general information, news, etc. • May provide for negotiations	• Vertical, horizontal • Forward auctions • Reverse auctions • Bid/ask exchanges

COMPARING THE MANY-TO-MANY B2B MODELS

Exhibit 5.9 summarizes the many-to-many models presented in this chapter.

Section 5.9 ▶ REVIEW QUESTIONS

1. Define B2B portals.
2. Distinguish a vortal from a horizontal portal.
3. Describe some directory services in B2B.
4. What is a third-party-owned exchange?
5. Define consortium trading exchanges.

5.10 B2B IN THE WEB 2.0 ENVIRONMENT AND SOCIAL NETWORKING

Although a large number of companies practice social networking that targets individual consumers (B2C), there is much less activity in the B2B arena. However, the potential is large, and new applications are added daily. The potential of B2B social networking depends on the companies' goals and the perceived benefits and risks involved.

THE OPPORTUNITIES

Companies that use B2B social networking may experience the following advantages:

▶ Discover new business partners.
▶ Enhance their ability to learn about new technologies, competitors, and the business environment.
▶ Find sales prospects.

▶ Improve participation in industry association activities (including lobbying).

▶ Create brand awareness (e.g., through the release of *widgets*, smart devices for customizing Web pages; see en.wikipedia.org/wiki/Social_networking for details).

▶ Advertise products and services and promote new ones.

▶ Create buzz about upcoming product releases.

▶ Drive traffic to their online Web properties in the hopes of enticing users to engage with their sites, products, or solutions.

▶ Create social communities to encourage discussions among business partners (e.g., suppliers) about their products and/or act as a feedback mechanism about their products/services (for business improvements).

▶ Improve recruitment (mostly B2C, but some B2B).

▶ Use social networks, such as Facebook and LinkedIn, to recruit new talent. Some HR departments are using social networks to obtain more insight into potential new hires.

More uses of B2B social networking are evidenced in what we call *enterprise social networking* that are private networks within enterprises (see Chapter 7).

THE USE OF WEB 2.0 TOOLS IN B2B

More companies are using blogs, wikis, RSS feeds, and other tools in B2B EC. For example, at Eastern Mountain Sports (opening case Chapter 2), the company uses blogs, RSS feeds, and wikis to communicate and collaborate with suppliers and distributors. Thousands of other companies are using (or experimenting with) these tools.

SOCIAL NETWORKS IN THE B2B MARKETPLACE

The importance of social networks has yet to be fully realized in the B2B marketplace. According to a 2008 study by KnowledgeStorm, 77 percent of respondents had little or no interaction with social networks (Spagnuolo 2008). Of the social networks frequented by business and EC professionals, LinkedIn (linkedin.com) was the most well known (see closing case in Chapter 7). Does this mean that B2B buyers and sellers are antisocial? Well, not really; it just means that because social networks are still fairly new they have not been used much for B2B applications. It may also indicate that there is a need for more B2B social networking sites. Also, it is difficult to demonstrate tangible benefits from the use of B2B social networks, so firms may be reluctant to invest in them.

Businesses can use B2B social networking to improve knowledge sharing, collaboration, and feedback. Furthermore, social networking sites may also prove beneficial in aiding troubleshooting and problem-solving efforts. Companies (especially small ones) are using LinkedIn Answers, for example, for problem solving. B2B participants need to look into social networking as part of their overall EC strategy, otherwise they may miss an opportunity to reach the B2B audience and differentiate themselves from the competition.

According to eMarketer (2008), B2B advertising on social networking sites will grow from $15 million in 2007 to $240 millions in 2012 (about a 13-fold increase). The same report attempted to answer the following key questions:

▶ How much will marketers spend on social network advertising aimed at a business audience?

▶ What types of B2B advertising can businesses do on social network sites?

▶ Why are companies creating social networks to market to business customers, vendors, distributors, and channel partners?

▶ What are the challenges of developing such networks?

EXAMPLES OF OTHER ACTIVITIES OF B2B SOCIAL NETWORKS

The following are examples of some social-network-oriented B2B activities:

▶ **American Express–sponsored Business Travel Social Network.** In October 2008, American Express launched an online social network, Business Travel Connexion (BTX, businesstravelconnexion.com), for the corporate travel industry. American Express hopes that BTX will be a dynamic network that will harness the collective intelligence of the business industry. It is designed for travel professionals who wish to become more informed and better equipped to optimize their travel and entertainment programs. The site offers an array of tools—blogs, photo albums, videos, galleries, community calendars, mobile alerts, a friends list, and the ability to form subgroups—to leverage the power of social networking.

▶ **Corporate profiles on social networks.** LinkedIn and Facebook include substantial information on companies and their individual employees. In fact, employees' profiles can be part of a company's brand. For example, IBM currently has approximately 116,000 employees registered on LinkedIn; Microsoft has around 78,000 as of November 2008. In addition, some sites feature company profiles, with comments by employees and customers.

THE FUTURE OF B2B SOCIAL NETWORKING

Products such as Google's OpenSocial may spark interest from the B2B community with regard to social networking. OpenSocial is a programming standard that lets developers create applications that can run on a wide range of social networking platforms. More important, OpenSocial promises users the choice of which social networks they want to use for their applications (see en.wikipedia.org/wiki/OpenSocial).

Businesses must embrace social networking in order to understand the needs and wants of their prospects and clients. Establishing trust with business partners and generating brand awareness will force B2B companies to become more involved in social networking.

Section 5.10 ▶ REVIEW QUESTIONS

1. List some of the reasons corporations are using social networking in B2B EC.
2. What are some of the benefits of social networking for B2B EC?
3. Describe some of the applications of B2B in social networks.
4. Discuss the future of B2B social networking.

5.11 INTERNET MARKETING IN B2B EC

B2B marketing is different from B2C marketing. Major differences also exist between B2B and B2C EC with respect to the nature of demand and supply and the trading process. Here we discuss the corporate purchaser's buying behavior and some marketing and advertising methods used in B2B EC.

ORGANIZATIONAL BUYER BEHAVIOR

Organizations buy large quantities of direct materials that they consume or use in the production of goods and services and in the company's operations. They also buy indirect materials, such as PCs, delivery trucks, and office supplies to support their production and operations processes.

Although the number of organizational buyers is much smaller than the number of individual consumers, their transaction volumes are far larger, and the terms of negotiations and purchasing are more complex. In addition, the purchasing process itself usually is more complex than the purchasing process of an individual customer. Also, the organization's buyer may be a group. In fact, decisions to purchase expensive items are usually made by a group. Therefore, factors that affect individual consumer behavior and organizational buying behavior are quite different.

A Behavioral Model of Organizational Buyers

The behavior of an organizational buyer is described by the model illustrated in Online File W5.14. A B2B model includes the organization's purchasing guidelines and constraints (e.g., contracts with certain suppliers) and the purchasing system used. Interpersonal influences, such as authority, and the possibility of group decision making must be considered.

THE MARKETING AND ADVERTISING PROCESSES IN B2B

The marketing and advertising processes for businesses differ considerably from those used for selling to individual consumers. For example, traditional (offline) B2B marketers use methods such as physical trade shows, advertisements in industry magazines, paper catalogs, and salespeople who call on existing customers and potential buyers.

In the digital world, these approaches may not be effective, feasible, or economical. Therefore, organizations use a variety of online methods to reach business customers. Popular methods include online directory services, matching services, the marketing and advertising services of exchanges, cobranding or alliances, affiliate programs, online trade shows, online marketing services (e.g., see digitalcement.com), or e-communities. Several of these methods are discussed next.

METHODS FOR B2B ONLINE MARKETING

When a B2C niche e-tailer seeks to attract its audience of skiers, musicians, or cosmetic customers, it may advertise in traditional media targeted to those audiences, such as magazines or television shows, or use Internet ads. The same is true in B2B when trade magazines and directories are used. But when a B2B vendor wants to grow by adding new customers or products, it may not have a reliable, known advertising channel. How can it reach new customers?

Targeting Customers

A B2B company, whether a provider of goods or services, an operator of a trading exchange, or a provider of digital real-time services, can contact all of its targeted customers individually when they are part of a well-defined group. For example, to attract companies to an exchange for auto supplies, one might use information from industry trade association records or industry magazines to identify potential customers.

Another method of bringing new customers to a B2B site is through an affiliation service, which operates just as a B2C affiliate program does. A company pays a small commission every time the affiliate company "drives traffic" to the payer's site.

An important part of any marketing effort is advertising. Several of the advertising methods that will be presented later in this chapter are applicable both to B2C and B2B. For example, an ad server network provider, such as DoubleClick (doubleclick.com, now a Google company), can be used to target customers in B2B2C EC.

Electronic Wholesalers

One of the interesting B2B ventures is the e-wholesaler. Like click-and-mortar e-tailer Sam's Club, this kind of intermediary sells directly to businesses but does so exclusively online. An example is bigboXX.com, described in Online File W5.2.

AFFILIATE PROGRAMS, INFOMEDIARIES, AND DATA MINING

Many more methods and approaches can be used in B2B marketing and advertising. Here we examine three popular methods: affiliate programs, infomediaries, and online data mining services.

Affiliate Programs

There are several types of affiliate programs. With the simplest type, which is used extensively in B2C EC, an affiliate puts a banner of another vendor, such as amazon.com, on its site. When a consumer clicks the vendor's banner, the consumer is taken to that vendor's Web site, and a commission is paid to the affiliate if the customer makes a purchase. Examples include the Netflix opening case in Chapter 4. The same method works for B2B.

With B2B, additional types of affiliate programs are possible. Schaeffer Research (schaeffersresearch.com), for example, offers financial institutions a content alliance program in which content is exchanged so that all obtain some free content. For more on B2B affiliate programs, see en.wikipedia.org/ wiki/Affiliate_marketing.

Infomediaries start by processing existing information until new, useful information is extracted from it. This new information is sold to B2B customers or exchanged for more information, which is manipulated yet again, until even more valuable information can be extracted. B2B vendors use the information from infomediaries to identify likely buyers with much greater precision than ever before—leading to increased sales and drastically reduced marketing expenses. Representative infomediary specialists are SAS Institute (sas.com), Unica NetTracker (unica.com), and WebTrends (webtrends.com).

Section 5.11 ▶ REVIEW QUESTIONS

1. Distinguish between organizational buyers and individual consumers.
2. Describe B2B EC marketing and advertising methods.
3. Explain how affiliate programs and data mining work in B2B EC.
4. What are infomediaries and what is their role in B2B?

MANAGERIAL ISSUES

Some managerial issues related to this chapter are as follows.

1. **Which B2B model(s) should we use for e-procurement?** Among the various upstream B2B models, we need to match the suitable e-procurement goals with solution strategies depending on whether the purchases are direct material or indirect material. Four typical goals that should be distinguished are interorganizational operational efficiency, minimum price, minimum inventory and stock-out, and purchase administrative cost. For each of these goals, the appropriate solution and system should be designed accordingly. Many third-party portal sites have provided mismatched solutions and failed their business. Handling many small and medium suppliers that do not have sophisticated systems is a challenging issue.

2. **Which exchange to join?** One of the major concerns of management is selecting exchanges in which to participate. At the moment, most exchanges are not tightly connected, so there may be a substantial start-up effort and cost for joining multiple exchanges. This is a multicriteria decision that should be analyzed carefully. A related issue is whether to join a third-party public exchange or a consortium or to create a private exchange. Companies must take very seriously the issues listed in Exhibit 5.8. The risks of joining an exchange must be carefully weighed against the expected benefits. Joining an exchange may require a restructuring of the internal supply chain, which may be expensive and time consuming. Therefore, this possibility must be taken into consideration when deciding whether to join an exchange.

3. **What is the organizational impact of B2B?** The B2B system will change the role of the procurement department by redefining the role and procedures of the department. The function of the procurement department may be completely outsourced. A procurement policy portfolio is necessary to balance strategic sourcing items and spot purchasing items and to design a supply relationship management system.

4. **What are some ethical issues in B2B?** Because B2B EC requires the sharing of proprietary information, business ethics are a must. Employees should not be able to access unauthorized areas in the trading system, and the privacy of trading partners should be protected both technically and legally. Control of partner relationship management is important in this regard.

5. **How shall we manage our suppliers?** Global suppliers can be evaluated periodically with regard to price, quality, and timely delivery. A supplier relationship management system can support the evaluation of suppliers. Management must decide whether to negotiate a quantity discount or to compel the suppliers to compete in reverse auctions.

6. **Which type of social network? Private (proprietary) or public?** There are successes and failures in both types. Some large companies have both types (e.g., Toyota, Coca-Cola, Disney). In most cases it is better to go with public networks such as LinkedIn and Facebook (see discussion in Chapter 7).

SUMMARY

In this chapter, you learned about the following EC issues as they relate to the chapter's learning objectives.

1. **The B2B field.** The B2B field comprises e-commerce activities between businesses. B2B activities account for 77 to 85 percent of all EC. B2B e-commerce can be done using different models.

2. **The major B2B models.** The B2B field is diversified. It can be divided into the following segments: sell-side marketplaces (one seller to many buyers), buy-side marketplaces (one buyer from many sellers), and trading exchanges (many sellers to many buyers).

Intermediaries play an important role in some B2B models.

3. **The characteristics and models of sell-side marketplaces.** Sell-side B2B EC is the online direct sale by one seller (a manufacturer or an intermediary) to many buyers. The major technology used is electronic catalogs, which also allow for efficient customization, configuration, and purchase by customers. In addition, forward auctions are becoming

popular, especially for liquidating surplus inventory. Sell-side auctions can be conducted from the seller's own site or from an intermediary's auction site. Sell-side activities can be accompanied by extensive customer service. E-commerce allows customization of products and personalized catalogs.

4. **Sell-side intermediaries.** The role of intermediaries in B2B primarily is to provide value-added services to manufacturers and business customers. They can also aggregate buyers and conduct auctions. Intermediaries can be distributors that aggregate catalogs of many sellers.

5. **The characteristics of buy-side marketplaces and e-procurement.** Today, companies are moving to e-procurement to expedite purchasing, save on item and administrative costs, and gain better control over the purchasing process. Major procurement methods are reverse auctions (bidding system); buying from Webstores and catalogs; negotiation; buying from an intermediary that aggregates sellers' catalogs; internal marketplaces and group purchasing; desktop purchasing; buying in exchanges or industrial malls; and e-bartering. E-procurement offers the opportunity to achieve significant cost and time savings.

6. **B2B reverse auctions.** A reverse auction is a tendering system used by buyers to get better prices from suppliers competing to fulfill the buyers' needs. Auctions can be done on a company's Web site or on a third-party auction site. Reverse auctions can dramatically lower buyers' costs, both product costs and the time and cost of the tendering process.

7. **B2B aggregation and group purchasing.** Increasing the exposure and the bargaining power of companies can be done by aggregating either the buyers or the sellers. Aggregating suppliers' catalogs into an internal marketplace gives buying companies better control of purchasing costs. In desktop purchasing, buyers are empowered to buy from their desktops up to a set limit without the need for additional approval. They accomplish this by viewing internal catalogs with pre-agreed-upon prices with the suppliers. Industrial malls specialize in one industry (e.g., computers) or in industrial MROs. They aggregate the catalogs of thousands of suppliers. A purchasing agent can place an order at an industrial mall, and shipping is arranged by the supplier or the mall owner. Buyer aggregation through group purchasing is very popular because it enables SMEs to get better prices on their purchases. In addition to direct purchasing, items can be acquired via bartering.

8. **Other procurement methods.** Common procurement methods include: internal marketplaces and desktop purchasing, buying at e-auctions, group purchasing, buying from distributors, bartering, and buying at exchanges.

9. **E-marketplaces and exchanges defined and the major types of exchanges.** Exchanges are e-marketplaces that provide a trading platform for conducting business among many buyers, many sellers, and other business partners. Types of public e-marketplaces include B2B portals, directories, third-party trading exchanges, and consortium trading exchanges. Exchanges may be vertical (industry oriented) or horizontal. They may target systematic buying (long-term relationships) or spot buying (for fulfilling an immediate need).

10. **B2B portals.** B2B portals are gateways to B2B community-related information. They are usually of a vertical structure, in which case they are referred to as *vortals*. Some B2B portals offer product and vendor information and even tools for conducting trades, sometimes making it difficult to distinguish between B2B portals and trading exchanges.

11. **Third-party exchanges.** Third-party exchanges are owned by an independent company and usually operate in highly fragmented markets. They are open to anyone and, therefore, are considered public exchanges. They try to maintain neutral relations with both buyers and sellers.

12. **B2B in Web 2.0 and social networks.** Although there are considerable B2C activities, B2B activities are just beginning. A major success has been seen in the use of blogs and wikis to collaborate with suppliers and customers. Large companies use social networking to create and foster business relationships. Smaller companies use social networking for soliciting experts' opinions. Other companies use it for finding business partners, business opportunities, employees, and sales leads as well as for generating sales leads.

13. **B2B Internet marketing methods and organizational buyers.** Marketing methods and marketing research in B2B differ from those of B2C. A major reason for this is that the buyers must observe organizational buying policies and frequently conduct buying activities as a committee. Organizations use modified B2C methods such as affiliate marketing. Buying decisions in B2B may be determined by a group, and purchasing is controlled by rules and constraints.

KEY TERMS

QUESTIONS FOR DISCUSSION BY INDIVIDUAL STUDENTS

1. Explain how a catalog-based sell-side e-marketplace works and describe its benefits.

2. Discuss the advantages of selling through online auctions over selling from catalogs. What are the disadvantages?

3. Discuss the role of intermediaries in B2B. Distinguish between buy-side and sell-side intermediaries.

4. Discuss and compare all the mechanisms that group-purchasing aggregators can use.

5. Should desktop purchasing only be implemented through an internal marketplace?

6. Suppose a manufacturer uses an outside shipping company. How can the manufacturer use an exchange?

7. Compare and contrast a privately owned exchange with a private e-marketplace.

8. How does ChemConnect change the market for commodity chemicals?

9. Compare external and internal aggregation of catalogs.

TOPICS FOR CLASS DISCUSSION

1. Discuss B2B opportunities in social networking.

2. Discuss risk in B2B social networking.

3. Discuss how globalization impacts B2B.

4. Relate B2B to the four P's of marketing (product, pricing, placement, promotion).

5. Discuss potential channel conflict in B2B, and how to deal with such conflicts.

6. What is the contribution of Alibaba.com to global trade? What are its potential limitations?

7. Some say that exchanges must be owned by a third-party intermediary and that consortiums should not be allowed to exist. Discuss.

INTERNET EXERCISES

1. Enter gxs.com and review GXS Express's bidding process. Describe the preparations a company would have to make in order to bid on a job.

2. Visit supplyworks.com and procuri.com. Examine how each company streamlines the purchase process.

3. Visit ebay.com and identify all the activities related to its small business auctions. What services are provided by eBay? Enter eBay's Business Industrial area (business.shop.ebay.com or ebay.com and select "wholesale"). What kind of e-marketplace is this? What are its major capabilities?

4. Enter ondemandsourcing.com and view the demo. Prepare a list of benefits to small and midtier organizations.

5. Visit iasta.com, purchasing.com, and cognizant.com. Examine the tools they sell for conducting various types of e-procurement. List and analyze each tool.

6. Enter bambooweb.com and find information about EDI. Prepare a report.

7. Enter thebuyinggroup.com, tidewatergpo.com, and other group purchasing sites. Report on B2B group buying activities.

8. Go to procurenet.com.au. Prepare a list of resources related to e-procurement.

9. Go to alibaba.com and sign up as a member (membership is free). Create a product and post it. Tell your instructor how to view this product.

10. Compare the services offered by globalsources.com with those offered by alibaba.com Assuming you are a toy seller, with which one would you register? Why? If you are a buyer of auto parts, which one would you join and why?

11. Enter chemconnect.com and view the demos for different trading alternatives. Examine the revenue model. Evaluate the services from both the buyer's and seller's points of view. Also, examine the site policies and legal guidelines. Are they fair?

12. Visit converge.com. What kind of exchange is this? What services does it provide? How do its auctions work? Summarize in a report.

13. Enter dir.yahoo.com/Business_and_Economy/Business_to_Business. Prepare a list of resources about exchanges and B2B directories.

14. Enter smallbusiness.yahoo.com/r-mainCat-m-1-getting_started-i and summarize the sell-side case.

TEAM ASSIGNMENTS AND PROJECTS

1. Predictions about the future magnitude of B2B and statistics on its actual volume in various countries keep changing. In this activity, each team will locate current B2B predictions and statistics for different world regions (e.g., Asia, Europe, North America). Using at least five sources, each team will find the predicted B2B volume (in dollars) for the next three to five years in its assigned region. Sources of statistics are listed in Exhibit 3.1 (page 89).

2. Each team should explore a different e-procurement method and prepare a summary paper for a class presentation. The paper should include the following about the e-procurement method:
   a. The mechanisms and technologies used
   b. The benefits to buyers, suppliers, and others (if appropriate)
   c. The limitations
   d. The situations for which each method is recommended

3. Form two teams (A and B) of five or more members. On each team, person 1 plays the role of an assembly company that produces television monitors. Persons 2 and 3 are domestic parts suppliers to the assembling company, and persons 4 and 5 play foreign parts suppliers. Assume that the TV monitor company wants to sell televisions directly to business customers. Each team is to design an environment composed of membership in exchanges they can use. Present a report. The design should include business processes and activities involved.

4. Enter gtnexus.com and examine its offerings. Prepare a report on how exchanges can benefit from its services. How does GT Nexus facilitate supply chains? Can it help e-marketplaces?

Closing Case

IMARKETKOREA

Established in 2000, iMarketKorea (IMK) is South Korea's largest e-marketplace (exchange) specializing in MRO items for various industries and direct materials for the electronics industries. IMK's e-catalog includes over 1 million items. In 2008, sales revenues were $722 million, with 180,000 monthly purchase orders. IMK was originally established as the online procurement sourcing company of Samsung Group in 2000; since then it has expanded its customer groups to various industries, including manufacturing, finance, retail, universities, and hospitals. Since its inception, the company has grown rapidly (an average annual growth rate of 23 percent).

From a market for Samsung's 45 affiliated companies, IMK has grown to serve approximately 350 companies in 2008. Currently, 70 percent of customers are Samsung related, whereas 30 percent are non-Samsung related. Many of the newly added customers are not Samsung affiliates, including some from outside South

Korea. The site offers Korean, English and Japanese options to registered users.

Initially, IMK concentrated on acting as a procurement agent to the Samsung companies. By 2007, however, the company shifted its mission to become a B2B procurement service provider, providing end-to-end procurement and logistics services for a variety of industries.

Among its most popular services for buyers are payments, deliveries, purchasing, budget management, internal approval processes, inventory management, storage, and more. In addition, IMK helps to smooth its customers' supply chains (e.g., process improvement and workflow management). IMK also supports connectivity to enterprise systems (e.g., ERP, legacy systems). The system architecture and the major participants are shown in the following exhibit.

IMK's business model is interesting because IMK does not charge fees for its services, but rather shares

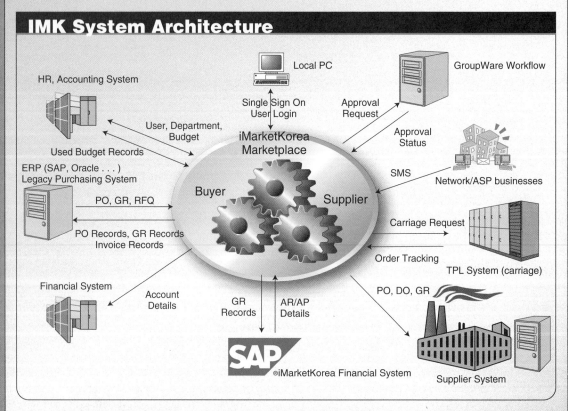

Source: iMarketKorea, "Purchasing Innovation: Value Proposition," 2009. *imartketkorea.co.kr/en_HD/DC9553ED_IMK_homepage_en_200408.pdf* (accessed April 2009).

the reduced costs with its buying customers. In this manner, IMK removes the risk from the customer side. IMK pursues a 3S leadership strategy: sourcing, service, and system leadership. The strategic sourcing suites that IMK provides include SRM, sourcing DSS, and e-catalog collaboration tools. They include features such as the following:

▶ Tools to calculate "total cost of ownership" (for purchasing)

▶ Strategic sourcing processes

▶ A scorecard grading system tool to perform a formal evaluation of suppliers (assessment, selection, monitoring)

▶ Knowledge sharing about best practices of procurement

▶ B2B auctions (forward and reverse, either as supporting the entire process or in helping customers take charge of the major activities, helping only with procedural matters during the auction)

▶ Spend management analysis and control tools

▶ Collaborative e-sourcing tools

▶ Decision support and optimization models for buyers

▶ Contract management features

▶ Integration of suppliers by selecting those who are reliable and sound and who are able to provide value (price matters, too, of course), leading to long-term strategic relationships (win-win situation)

▶ Risk assessment and management

▶ Item standardization for inventory and cost reduction at the suppliers' level, enabling better cataloging and faster and easier search (e.g., simultaneous search of many items)

▶ Analyzes replies to RFQs quickly, considering large amounts of computerized information and knowledge

▶ Joint process improvement, attempting to reduce supplier's TCO (providing suppliers with a comprehensive program of how to do it)

The following are some recent IMK initiatives:

▶ An alliance with the Japanese Sumitomo Corp. (a top online trading company), kicking off global business expansion. IMK is already exporting MROs to 12 countries.

▶ IMK exported over $87 million in MROs in 2008, plus $18 million in direct materials (a 37 percent increase over 2007).

▶ In collaboration with Woori Bank, IMK opened B2C and B2B2C channels for selling gifts over the Internet to the bank's employees.

The results speak for themselves. IMK's customers have experienced the following benefits:

▶ On-time delivery has increased from 72 to 94.5 percent.

▶ Average lead time has been reduced from 5.3 to 3.31 days.

▶ Catalog search speed has increased 40 percent.

▶ 12 to 18 percent savings in purchase prices.

▶ 30 to 50 percent savings in process costs.

▶ 5 to 15 percent savings in inventory management costs.

▶ 40 to 60 percent savings in reduced inventory.

All these savings have contributed to the success and growth of IMK.

Sources: Compiled from iMarketKorea (2006), Lee and Lee (2007), and *imarketkorea.com* (accessed November 2009).

Questions

1. How do the support services benefit the exchange?

2. Relate this case to desktop purchasing.

3. Write a summary of the benefits of the exchange to buyers.

4. Write a summary of the benefits of the exchange to sellers.

5. Compare IMK to Alibaba.com. What are the similarities and the differences?

6. Much of IMK's success is attributed to the understanding of the Korean culture and business environment. Given that IMK wants to expand internationally, what could be some of its stumbling blocks?

7. Check the recent news and press releases (last six months) at *imarketkorea.com*. Identify expansion patterns.

ONLINE RESOURCES
available at pearsonhighered.com/turban

Comprehensive Educational Web Sites

b2btoday.com: B2B resources
optimizeandprophesize.com: Optimize and Prophesize, Jonathan Mendez's blog
silicon.com: Case studies, publications
directoryb2b.com: B2B topics, news, software, etc.
netb2b.com: *B2B* magazine
www-01.ibm.com/software/success/cssdb.nsf/topstoriesFM?OpenForm&Site=corp: Case studies from IBM

INNOVATIVE EC SYSTEMS: FROM E-GOVERNMENT AND E-LEARNING TO C2C E-COMMERCE AND COLLABORATIVE COMMERCE

Content

Learning Objectives

Upon completion of this chapter, you will be able to:

1. Describe various e-government initiatives.
2. Understand e-government implementation issues including e-government 2.0 and m-government.
3. Describe e-learning, virtual universities, and e-training.
4. Describe e-books.
5. Describe knowledge management and dissemination as an e-business.
6. Describe C2C activities.
7. Describe collaborative commerce.

CATERPILLAR CHAMPIONS E-LEARNING

Caterpillar Inc. (CAT) is a large global manufacturer of heavy construction and mining equipment and a service provider to its products. It is also a major financial services provider. In 2008, CAT generated over $51 billion in revenue from the sale of its products and services.

The Problem

CAT has more than 100,000 employees and sells through more than 480 dealerships in 200 countries. The company has experienced explosive growth, more than doubling its size from 2003 to 2006. Reaching so many employees in so many locations and in different countries and time zones had become a major challenge for the company. In addition, with so many newcomers, as well as new and improved products and services, CAT needed to train new employees and retrain existing ones.

Another problem was knowledge drain. By early 2000, nearly half of CAT's senior leadership team and the general employee population were eligible to retire. Also, the industry is very competitive (e.g., competition from Japan is very strong), so employees and dealers need to have the skills and knowledge to succeed in the twenty-first-century workforce.

The Solution

The company spends more than $100 million a year on training and learning. It created a learning infrastructure that includes three major elements: governance, a learning technology infrastructure (mainly Web based), and an alignment strategy to create a lifelong culture of learning in accord with the firm's business goals. Caterpillar created Caterpillar University (CAT U) to meet its training and learning needs. CAT U uses a universal virtual collaboration tool, a synchronous online learning management system (LMS), and a knowledge network.

Caterpillar's LMS is a worldwide platform that supports both employees and dealers. A new release was implemented in 2007. The LMS has a learner-centric user interface that allows individual users to experience it in a customized fashion. It dynamically constructs each individual's learning plan on his or her desktop.

One of the biggest challenges facing any organization, let alone a large global one with a tightly integrated dealer network, is how to enable learning across an extended enterprise that includes employees, dealers, suppliers, and customers. CAT U enables e-learning through its knowledge management system, the Caterpillar Knowledge Network. Caterpillar employees, dealers, suppliers, and customers make use of more than 4,000 communities of practice organized around specific business-related topics to exchange information, share files, ask questions, and contact subject-matter experts around the world. The knowledge network provides a deep mine of searchable data, giving users access to information created everywhere, anytime, in every area of the organization.

The company also created the CAT Knowledge Network to help preserve the knowledge of retiring executives and experts. Approximately 10,000 experts have been identified and listed. These experts' searchable "expert descriptions" serve as expertise locators for users within Caterpillar and throughout the value chain. Users can search online for experts by area of expertise.

In addition, the knowledge network includes "lessons learned," which capture past experiences in a formal template and are searchable, too. The knowledge network also includes a discussion bulletin board.

The network is also a powerful tool for making personal connections. Users no longer have to rely on a personal network built through years of experience and various job assignments; instead, they rely on a keyword search in the knowledge network. This allows a wheel-loader engineer in China, for instance, to quickly locate a transmission software expert in Europe.

Synchronous online learning allows the virtual delivery of learning across the globe. In this setting, a live instructor interacts with dispersed learners who are attending virtually. Online learning saves time and money by allowing information to be distributed quickly and by reducing travel costs. Conducting meetings via virtual collaboration has reduced travel costs. Between January and October 2007, more than 2,100 classes were conducted using synchronous online learning, and more than 300,000 meetings were conducted using virtual collaboration.

The Results

Caterpillar's learning technology enables its employees to quickly build both competence and confidence. In addition, the technology infrastructure is an important contributor to business sustainability by dramatically reducing travel and other expenses and increasing employee productivity. By aligning learning needs and strategies at the division and enterprise levels, Caterpillar is able to improve enterprise performance by providing the right skills and knowledge through learning. This increases engagement and increases

discretionary effort, which leads to better performance. Engagement is the extent to which employees commit, rationally or emotionally, to the organization, how hard they work as a result of this commitment, and how long they intend to stay. This all leads to a bottom-line benefit, because better enterprise performance results in increased profitability. Finally, the knowledge-sharing platform was so successful that its software and procedures have been sold to many companies.

Sources: Compiled from Glynn (2008) and Boehle (2007).

WHAT WE CAN LEARN . . .

E-learning is an EC application that helps organizations teach and retrain a large number of learners to ensure that they can grow and handle their jobs effectively. E-learning at Caterpillar is based in part on the knowledge and best practices accumulated by employees over the years. This knowledge is managed in a knowledge management (KM) system and is accessible to learners and problem solvers electronically. E-learning and KM are two innovative systems introduced in this chapter that illustrate the benefits of EC. Other topics discussed in this chapter are e-government, online publishing and e-books, and consumer-to-consumer EC.

6.1 E-GOVERNMENT: AN OVERVIEW

Electronic government, or *e-government*, is a growing e-commerce application that encompasses many topics. This section presents the major e-government topics.

DEFINITION AND SCOPE

As e-commerce matures and its tools and applications improve, greater attention is being given to its use in improving the business of public institutions and governments (country, state, county, city, etc.). **E-government** is the use of information technology in general, and e-commerce in particular, to provide citizens and organizations with more convenient access to government information and services, and to provide delivery of public services to citizens, business partners, and those working in the public sector. It also is an efficient and effective way of conducting government business transactions with citizens and businesses and within governments themselves. See Shark and Toporkoff (2008) and Wikipedia (en.wikipedia.org/wiki/E-Government) for details.

e-government
E-commerce model in which a government entity buys or provides goods, services, or information to businesses or individual citizens.

In this book, the term *e-government* will be used in its broader context—the bringing together of governments, citizens, and businesses in a network of information, knowledge, and commerce. In this broader view, e-government offers an opportunity to improve the efficiency and effectiveness of the functions of government and to make governments more transparent to citizens and businesses by providing access to more of the information generated by government, as well as facilitating transactions with and within governments.

Several major categories fit within this broad definition of e-government: government-to-citizens (G2C), government-to-business (G2B), government-to-government (G2G), internal efficiency and effectiveness (IEE), and government-to-employees (G2E). The performance objectives of the first four categories are provided in Exhibit 6.1. For a description of the range of e-government activities in the United States, see whitehouse.gov/omb/egov.

EXHIBIT 6.1 Categories of E-Government Performance Objectives

G2C	G2B
• Create easy-to-find single points of access to government services for individuals. • Reduce the average time for citizens to find benefits and determine eligibility. • Increase the number of citizens who use the Internet to find information on recreational opportunities. • Meet the high public demand for information. • Improve the value of government to citizen. • Expand access to information for people with disabilities. • Make obtaining financial assistance from the government easier, cheaper, quicker, and more comprehensible.	• Increase the ability for citizens and businesses to find, view, and comment on rules and regulations. • Reduce the burden on businesses by enabling online tax filing. • Reduce the time to fill out export forms and locate information. • Reduce time for businesses to file and comply with regulations. • Make transactions with the government easier, cheaper, quicker, and more comprehensible.
G2G	**IEE**
• Decrease response times for jurisdictions and disciplines to respond to emergency incidents. • Reduce the time to verify birth and death entitlement information. • Increase the number of grant programs available for electronic application. • Share information more quickly and conveniently between the federal and state, local, and tribal governments. • Improve collaborations with foreign partners, including governments and institutions. • Automate internal processes to reduce costs within the federal government by disseminating best practices across agencies. • Plan IT investments more effectively. • Secure greater services at a lower cost. • Cut government operating costs.	• Increase availability of training programs for government employees. • Reduce the average time to process clearance forms. • Increase use of e-travel services within each agency. • Reduce the time for citizens to search for federal jobs. • Reduce time and overhead cost to purchase goods and services throughout the federal government.

Sources: U.S. Government (2003), Lee et al. (2005), and Hyperion (2007).

GOVERNMENT-TO-CITIZENS

government-to-citizens (G2C)
E-government category that includes all the interactions between a government and its citizens.

The **government-to-citizens (G2C)** category includes all the interactions between a government and its citizens that can take place electronically. As described in the closing case about the government of New Zealand and in Online File W6.1 about the government of Hong Kong, G2C can involve dozens of different initiatives. The basic idea is to enable citizens to interact with the government from anywhere. G2C applications enable citizens to ask questions of government agencies and receive answers, pay taxes, receive payments and documents, and so forth. For example, in many U.S. states, residents can renew driver's licenses, pay traffic tickets, and make appointments for vehicle emission inspections and driving tests. Governments also can disseminate information on the Web, conduct training, help citizens find employment, and more. In California, for example, drivers' education classes are offered online and can be taken anytime, anywhere.

EXHIBIT 6.2	Sample G2C Municipal Services in Denmark
Service	**Description**
Your real estate	Information on your real estate holdings in a particular municipality.
Government housing eligibility	Self-calculate eligibility for government housing; online application is available.
Child care option	Child care options in your municipality; child care guides.
Facts and statistics	Data on your municipality of choice.
Change of address	Do it yourself and get a receipt online.
Pay tax and for services	Pay municipalities tax and pay for services (e.g., child care).
Calculate social benefits	Calculate available benefits (e.g., for elderly, children, pensions, maternity/paternity leave, sickness benefits for employees).
Budget preparation	Calculators for individuals and small businesses.
Tax calculations and matters	Calculate taxes; forms and guides are available.
Real estate information	Statistics, facts, and availability of real estate in Denmark, by municipality.
Building guides	Building guides for different municipalities; forms and guides.
Utility guides	Reports on water and electricity consumption in different cities.
Education	Information on how to sign up for wait lists for educational institutions.
Scholarships for nursery school	Applications for scholarships for nursery schools (not provided to everyone).
Real estate appraisers/valuation	The official valuation of any real estate in Denmark.

Sources: Compiled from Henriksen (2006) and *dst.dk* (accessed September 2009).

Government services to citizens are provided via citizen portals. The services will vary depending on the country, on the level (city, county, country), and on the users' skills in using computers. An example of representative services in municipalities in Denmark is provided in Exhibit 6.2. For the diversity of services, see the Hong Kong case in Online File W6.1.

The major features of government Web sites are phone and address information, links to other sites, publications, and databases. The major areas of G2C activities are tourism and recreation, research and education, downloadable forms, discovery of government services, information about public policy, and advice about health and safety issues. G2C is available now in many countries on mobile/wireless devices.

An interesting recent application is the use of the Internet by politicians, especially during election periods. For example, the French political parties pursued millions of voters in the blogosphere for the 2007 presidential election. In the United States, during the 2008 presidential election both major-party candidates sent e-mail messages to potential voters and had comprehensive information portals. Barack Obama even created a social network site (my.barackobama.com) and had pages on MySpace, Facebook, and Second Life, much earlier than his competitors who followed with similar activities (see Mark 2007). In South Korea, politicians log on to the Internet to recruit voters, because many people who surf the Internet rarely read newspapers or watch TV. The target audience of these politicians is 20- to 30-year-olds, the vast majority of whom surf the Internet. Pasdaq, the Seoul-based over-the-counter stock exchange, offers an Internet game that simulates the stock market and measures the popularity of some 300 politicians by allowing players to buy "stocks" in a politician. In one year, over 500,000 members signed up. Some politicians make decisions based on citizens' opinions collected on the Internet.

Another area of G2C activity is in solving constituents' problems. The government (or a politician) can use CRM-type software to assign inquiries and problem cases to the appropriate staff member (as shown in the New Zealand case, at the end of the chapter) .Workflow CRM software can then be used to track the progress of the problem's resolution.

Note that over 20 countries block Web sites for political, social, or other reasons (e.g., China, Iran, Syria). For more on G2C, see nbc.gov/egov/g2c.html. Two popular examples of G2C are provided next.

Electronic Voting

Voting processes inherently are subject to error and also are historically subject to manipulation and fraud. In many countries, there are attempts to "rig" the votes; in others, the losers want to recount. Voting may result in major political crises, as happened in the Ukraine in November 2004. Problems with the U.S. 2000 and 2004 presidential elections have accelerated the trend toward electronic voting.

Voting encompasses a broad spectrum of technological and social problems that must be systematically addressed—from registration and voter authentication to the casting of ballots and subsequent tallying of results. Electronic voting automates some or all steps in the process.

Fully electronic voting systems have raised considerable controversy because of a variety of factors, such as the proprietary nature of the software, the weakness of the certification criteria, the inability of black-box testing to provide full assurances of correctness, the general secrecy of the evaluation process, vendor-commissioned evaluations, and the lack of any mechanism whereby independent recounting of the ballots and auditing of the vote totals can be performed.

The first country to use fully computerized balloting was Brazil. In the United States, electronic systems have been in use since 1980 (mainly for counting the results); large-scale implementation of touch-screen systems occurred only in 2008. It is interesting to note that several states (e.g., California, Nevada) require that touch-screen machines be able to produce a printed record. A good voting machine should show the voter what he or she has entered and ask for confirmation, much like when purchasing a book online from Amazon.com, transferring funds, or selling stocks.

From a technology point of view, election fraud could be carried out by changing a program to count votes for X twice or not to count votes for Y at all (see Gibson and Brown 2006). Therefore, security and auditing measures are key to the success of e-voting. However, considering the amount of fraud that occurs with traditional, non-e-voting systems and the fact that e-security is improving (see Epstein 2007), e-voting eventually could be the norm. For more information on e-voting, see fcw.com.

Aspiring politicians are using blogs to promote themselves. Many continue to use blogs after being elected. Social networks, especially MySpace, Facebook, and YouTube, are being used to reach the voters directly, especially young voters. For example, Keen (2006) reported that Facebook (facebook.com) had over 1,400 candidate profiles for the November 2006 U.S. elections. All the major-party presidential candidates had profiles for the 2008 election.

Electronic Benefits Transfer

One e-government application that is not new is electronic benefits transfer (EBT), which has been available since the early 1990s. The U.S. government, for example, transfers around $1,000 billion in benefits to its citizens annually. In 1993, the U.S. government launched an initiative to develop a nationwide EBT system to deliver government benefits electronically. Initially, the attempt was made to deliver benefits to recipients' bank accounts. However, more than 20 percent of these transfers go to citizens who do not have bank accounts. To solve this problem, the government initiated the use of smart cards (see Chapter 10). Benefit recipients can load electronic funds onto the cards and use the cards at automated teller machines (ATMs), point-of-sale locations, and grocery and other stores, just like other bank card users do. The advantage is not only the reduction in processing costs (from about 50 cents per paper check to 2 cents for electronic payment) but also the reduction of fraud. With biometrics (see Chapter 9) coming to smart cards and PCs, officials expect fraud to be reduced substantially. For more information on EBT in government, see fns.usda.gov/snap/ebt.

GOVERNMENT-TO-BUSINESS

Governments seek to automate their interactions with businesses. Although we call this category **government-to-business (G2B)**, the relationship works two ways: government-to-business and business-to-government. Thus, G2B refers to e-commerce in which government sells products to businesses or provides them with services as well as to businesses selling products and services to government. Two key G2B areas are e-procurement and the auctioning of government surpluses. For other U.S. G2B initiatives, see nbc.gov/egov/g2b.html.

government-to-business (G2B)
E-government category that includes interactions between governments and businesses (government selling to businesses and providing them with services and businesses selling products and services to the government).

Government E-Procurement

Governments buy large amounts of MROs and other materials directly from suppliers. In many cases, RFQ (or tendering) systems are mandated by law. For years, these RFQs were done manually; the systems are now moving online. These systems employ reverse (buy-side auction systems), such as those described in Chapter 5. An example of a reverse auction used for G2B procurement in Hong Kong is described in Online File W6.1 and at info.gov.hk. For additional information about such reverse auctions, see gsa.gov. In the United States, for example, the local housing agencies of HUD (Housing and Urban Development), which provides housing to low-income residents, are moving to e-procurement (see Kumar and Peng 2006 and U.S. Department of Housing and Urban Development 2008). Governments provide all the support for such tendering systems.

The Procurement Marketing and Access Network from the Small Business Administration has developed a service called PRO-Net (pro-net.sba.gov), a searchable database that contracting officers in various U.S. government units can use to find products and services sold by small, disadvantaged, or women-owned businesses.

Group Purchasing

The U.S. government also uses online group purchasing, which was described in Chapter 1. For example, the EFAST service conducts reverse auctions for aggregated orders (see gsa.gov). Suppliers post group-purchasing offers, and the prices fall as more orders are placed. Alternatively, government buyers may post product requests that other buyers may review and join.

Forward E-Auctions

Many governments auction equipment surpluses or other goods, ranging from vehicles to foreclosed real estate. These auctions are now moving to the Internet. Governments can auction from a government Web site or they can use third-party auction sites such as ebay.com, bid4assets.com, or governmentauctions.org for this purpose. The U.S. General Services Administration (GSA) operates a property auction site online (auctionrp.com) where real-time auctions for surpluses and seized goods are conducted. Some of these auctions are restricted to dealers; others are open to the public (see governmentauctions.org).

GOVERNMENT-TO-GOVERNMENT

government-to-government (G2G)
E-government category that includes activities within government units and those between governments.

The **government-to-government (G2G)** category consists of EC activities between units of government, including those within one governmental body. Many of these are aimed at improving the effectiveness or the efficiency of the government. Here are a few examples from the United States:

▶ **Intelink.** Intelink is an intranet that contains classified information that is shared by the numerous U.S. intelligence agencies.

▶ **Procurement at GSA.** The GSA's Web site (gsa.gov) uses technologies such as demand aggregation and reverse auctions to buy for various units of the federal government. (See also governmentauctions.org and liquidation.com.) The agency seeks to apply innovative Web-based procurement methods to government buying.

▶ **Federal Case Registry (Department of Health and Human Services).** This service helps state governments locate information about child support, including data on paternity and enforcement of child-support obligations. It is available at acf.hhs.gov/programs/cse/newhire/fcr/fcr.htm.

For more examples of G2G services, see govexec.com, nbc.gov/egov/g2g.html, and the closing case about e-government in New Zealand.

GOVERNMENT-TO-EMPLOYEES AND INTERNAL EFFICIENCY AND EFFECTIVENESS

Governments are introducing various EC models internally. Two areas are illustrated next.

Government-to-Employees (G2E)

government-to-employees (G2E)
E-government category that includes activities and services between government units and their employees.

Governments are just as interested as private-sector organizations are in providing services and information electronically to their employees. Indeed, because employees of federal and state governments often work in a variety of geographic locations, **government-to-employee (G2E)** applications may be especially useful in enabling efficient communication.

Example: G2E in the U.S. Navy. The U.S. Navy uses G2E to improve the flow of information to sailors and their families. Because long shipboard deployments cause strains on Navy families, in 1995 the Navy began seeking ways to ensure that quality-of-life information reaches Navy personnel and their loved ones all over the world. Examples of quality-of-life information include self-help, deployment support, stress management, parenting advice, and relocation assistance.

To help Navy families, the Navy developed Lifelines. Lifelines uses the Internet, simulcasting, teleconferencing, cable television, and satellite broadcasting to reach overseas personnel. The Navy has found that certain media channels are more appropriate for different types of information. Lifelines regularly features live broadcasts, giving forward-deployed sailors and their families welcome information and, in some cases, a taste of home. On the Web, several thousands of people access the Lifelines portal each day. In 2008, the portal covered dozens of topics ranging from jobs to recreation.

The government provides several other e-services to Navy personnel. Notable are online banking, personal finance services, and insurance. Education and training also are provided online. The Navy provides mobile computing devices to sailors while they are deployed at sea. The handheld devices offer both entertainment and information to Navy personnel on active duty. For details, see lifelines.navy.mil.

Internal Efficiency and Effectiveness (IEE)

These internal initiatives provide tools for improving the effectiveness and efficiency of government operations, and the processes are basically intrabusiness applications implemented in government units. For example, the U.S. Office of Management and Budget provides the following services:

- ▶ **E-payroll.** Consolidates systems at more than 14 processing centers across government.
- ▶ **E-records management.** Establishes uniform procedures and standards for agencies in converting paper-based records to electronic files.
- ▶ **E-training.** Provides a repository of government-owned courseware.
- ▶ **Enterprise case management.** Centralizes justice litigation case information.
- ▶ **Integrated acquisition.** Agencies share common data elements to enable other agencies to make better informed procurement, logistical, payment, and performance-assessment decisions.
- ▶ **Integrated human resources.** Integrates personnel records across government.
- ▶ **One-stop recruitment.** Automates federal government information on career opportunities, résumé submission and routing, and assessment. Streamlines the federal hiring process and provides up-to-the-minute application status for job seekers.

Improving homeland security can be considered an IEE activity. The government is using different EC-related systems to improve security. For more information on security in e-government, go to dhs.gov/index.shtm. For more on using EC to improve the efficiency and effectiveness of government, see nbc.gov/egov/iee.html.

IMPLEMENTING E-GOVERNMENT

Like most other organizations, government entities want to move into the digital era and become click-and-mortar organizations. Therefore, one can find a large number of EC applications in government organizations. This section examines some of the issues involved in implementing e-government. Huang et al. (2006) review many implementation issues and trends in e-government. These are summarized in Online File W6.2.

THE TRANSFORMATION TO E-GOVERNMENT

The transformation from traditional delivery of government services to full implementation of online government services may be a lengthy process. The business consulting firm Deloitte & Touche conducted a study that identified six stages in the transformation to e-government. These stages do not have to be sequential, but frequently they are, with a seventh stage added by the authors. Online File W6.2 also presents some implementation issues.

E-GOVERNMENT 2.0 AND SOCIAL NETWORKING

According to Baumgarten and Chui (2009), government agencies often fail to meet users' needs despite spending enormous amounts on Web-based initiatives. By employing Web 2.0 tools, new business models, and embracing social networks and user participation, government agencies can raise the effectiveness of their online presence. Thus, government agencies around the world are experimenting with social networking tools as well as with their own pages and presence on public social networking sites. Governments are using Web 2.0 tools mainly for collaboration, dissemination of information, e-learning, online forums, and citizen engagement. An interesting example is the initiatives going on in New Zealand, where social networking tools are being used extensively both for internal as well as external use (see this chapter's closing case about New Zealand's e-government).

Some people believe that social networking will replace the current portal-based e-government and that the trend is clearly away from the "one-stop shop" portal. Government initiatives are very diversified with the Web 2.0 approach. For example, many governments own islands on Second Life on which they present diplomatic issues and advertise tourist attractions. Gartner cites a number of adventurous e-government Web 2.0 initiatives. With such initiatives, it is important to have strict security, accountability, and compliance functionality in place, which has proven challenging when implementing wikis and blogs. Gartner encourages e-government efforts to "experiment with innovative means to better serve and engage constituents," but it warns that "such pilots have to remain very well-focused and somewhat isolated from mainstream processes for at least the next two years." However, products such as Atlassian, which integrates with Microsoft SharePoint, have more than enough "control" to satisfy most government security requirements (reported by *Government Technology* 2008).

Note that politicians are using social networking extensively. For example, during the 2008 U.S. presidential election, Democratic candidate Barack Obama created a page at LinkedIn, where he received thousands of connections and responses to his question, "What ideas do you have to keep America competitive in the years ahead?" Many of the responses were very interesting and insightful. Obama also added a LinkedIn interest group. One of the keys to Obama's success was that his LinkedIn profile was set up much like a "regular person" in tone and language, fitting with his strategy of not appearing to be an old-school Washington insider.

All the major-party candidates for the 2008 presidential election had official pages where videos were viewed by millions. They also created pages on Facebook and MySpace, and some used Twitter.

M-GOVERNMENT

mobile government (m-government)
The wireless implementation of e-government mostly to citizens but also to businesses.

Mobile government, or **m-government**, is the wireless implementation of e-government applications (see en.wikipedia.org/M-government) mostly to citizens (e.g., Government of Canada Wireless Portal), but also to business. M-government uses wireless Internet infrastructure and devices. It is a value-added service, because it enables government to reach a larger number of citizens and is more cost-effective than other IT applications; it is convenient to users as well (per Trimi and Sheng 2008). In addition, governments employ large numbers of mobile workers who can be supported by wireless devices.

Example

An example is the bus-location system in Honolulu, Hawaii. Using your cell phone you can find the estimated arrival time to any of the more than 4,000 bus stops. Buses are equipped with GPSs (Chapter 8) that transmit the bus location every two minutes. The system then calculates the estimated arrival time.

Proponents of m-government argue that it can help make public information and government services available "anytime, anywhere" and that the ubiquity of these devices mandates their employment in government functions. An example of such beneficial use of mobile technologies would be the sending of a mass alert to registered citizens via short message service (SMS) in the event of an emergency.

Some implementation issues are:

▶ Wireless and mobile networks and related infrastructure, as well as software, must be developed.

▶ To increase citizen participation and provide citizen-oriented services, governments need to offer easy access to m-government information in several forms.

▶ Mobile phone numbers and mobile devices are relatively easy to hack, and wireless networks are vulnerable because they use public airwaves to send signals.

▶ Many countries have not yet adopted legislation for data and information practices that spell out the rights of citizens and the responsibilities of the data holders (government).

Several wireless applications suitable for e-government are presented in Chapter 8. Notable are B2E applications, especially for field employees, and B2C information discovery, such as the U.S. Government 511 system. Another example is the city of Bergen, Norway, which provides extensive wireless portable tourism services.

For implementation issues, success stories, applications, benefits, and more, see Massey and Taylor (2007).

Section 6.1 ▶ REVIEW QUESTIONS

1. Define e-government.
2. What are the four major categories of e-government services?
3. Describe G2C.
4. Describe how EBT works.
5. Describe the two main areas of G2B activities.
6. How does government use EC internally and when dealing with other governments?
7. Describe e-government social networking activities.
8. Describe m-government and its implementation issues.

6.2 E-LEARNING

The topic of e-learning is gaining much attention, especially because world-class universities such as MIT, Harvard, and Stanford in the United States and Oxford in the United Kingdom are implementing it. Exhibit 6.3 shows the forces that are driving the transition from traditional education to online learning. Details are provided in Online File W6.3. E-learning also is growing as a method for training and information delivery in the business world and is becoming a major e-business activity. In this section, we will discuss several topics related to e-learning (see Wagner 2008).

THE BASICS OF E-LEARNING: DEFINITIONS AND CONCEPTS

E-learning is the online delivery of information for purposes of education, training, or knowledge management (see elearnmag.org). It is a Web-enabled system that makes knowledge accessible to those who need it, when they need it, anytime, anywhere. It appears in a variety of formats, ranging from virtual classrooms to mobile learning (see Wagner 2008).

According to Wikipedia (en.Wikipedia.org/wiki/E-learning), e-learning can refer to any method of computer-enhanced learning. This could be as simple as the extension of traditional mail-order distance learning where CD-ROMs are used for media-rich interaction

e-learning
The online delivery of information for purposes of education, training, or knowledge management.

EXHIBIT 6.3   The Drivers of E-Learning

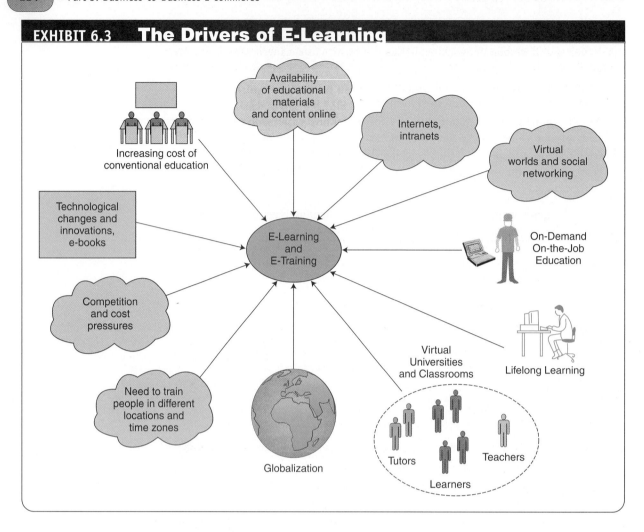

with the student. Alternatively, it can be extended all the way to fully interactive, institution-wide "managed learning environments" in which students communicate with professors and classmates, which is the same as with face-to-face delivered courses. E-learning may include the use of Web-based teaching materials and hypermedia in general, multimedia CD-ROMs, Web sites, discussion boards, collaborative software, e-mail, blogs, wikis, chat rooms, computer-aided assessment, educational animation, simulations, games, learning management software, electronic voting systems, and more (possibly a few of these combined).

E-learning is also broader than the term *online learning,* which generally refers to purely Web-based learning. The term *m-learning* has been proposed when the material is delivered wirelessly to cell phones or PDAs.

E-learning can be useful both as an environment for facilitating learning at schools and as an environment for efficient and effective corporate training, as shown in Online File W6.4.

Technological advances, such as simulations, virtual worlds, and open source software, have reshaped the e-learning landscape. Rapid development tools enable organizations to create e-learning environments quickly and easily. Comprehensive sites about e-learning, including videos and PowerPoint presentations, are available at e-learningcenter.com and e-learningcentre.co.uk.

BENEFITS AND DRAWBACKS OF E-LEARNING

E-learning has many benefits. These benefits are presented in the following discussion and in Wagner (2008). However, it also has several drawbacks, thus making it a controversial topic.

Benefits of E-Learning

E-learning can be a great equalizer: By eliminating barriers of time, distance, and socioeconomic status, it can enable individuals to take charge of their own lifelong learning. In the information age, skills and knowledge need to be *continually updated* and refreshed to keep up with today's fast-paced business environment. E-learning of new content will help organizations and countries adapt to the demands of the Internet economy by training their workers and educating their citizens. E-learning can save money, reduce travel time, increase access to experts, enable large numbers of students to take classes simultaneously, provide on-demand education, and enable self-paced learning. It also may make learning less frustrating by making it more interactive and engaging.

More specific benefits of e-learning are as follows:

> **Time reduction.** E-learning can reduce training time by 50 percent.
> **Large volume and diversity.** E-learning can provide training to a large number of people from diverse cultural backgrounds and educational levels even though they are at different locations in different time zones.
> **Cost reduction.** The cost of providing a learning experience can be reduced by 50 to 70 percent when classroom lectures are replaced by e-learning sessions.
> **Higher content retention.** E-learning students usually are self-initiated and self-paced. Their motive for acquiring more knowledge may be to widen their scope of view or to develop career skills. Such self-motivation may result in content retention that could be 25 to 60 percent higher than with traditional lecturer-led training.
> **Flexibility.** E-learners are able to adjust the time, location, content, and speed of learning according to their own personal schedules. For example, if necessary, they can refer back to previous lectures without affecting the learning pace of other students.
> **Updated and consistent material.** It is almost impossible to economically update the information in textbooks more frequently than every two or three years; e-learning can offer just-in-time access to timely information. E-learning may be more consistent than material presented in traditional classroom learning, because variations among teachers are eliminated.
> **Fear-free environment.** E-learning can facilitate learning for students who may not wish to join a face-to-face group discussion or participate in class. This kind of behavior usually is attributed to their reluctance to expose their lack of knowledge in public. E-learning can provide a fear-free and privacy-protected environment in which students can put forth any idea without fear of looking stupid.

Tutoring services that once required face time can now be profitably handled online and offshored to low-cost countries such as India. For more discussion of the benefits of e-learning, see e-learningguru.com and elearnmag.org. For current topics, see icl-conference.org and their International Conference.

E-Learning Management

One of the most effective tools for learning management is Blackboard (which was combined with WebCT). A brief description follows.

Example: Blackboard. Blackboard Inc. is the world's largest supplier of course management system software to educational institutions (5,000 institutions in 60 countries in 2008). There is a good chance that you will use the Blackboard framework when using this textbook. These products provide the Internet software needed for e-learning.

How do these products work? A publisher places a book's content, teaching notes, quizzes, and other materials on Blackboard in a standardized format. Instructors can access modules and transfer them into their own Blackboard sites, which can be accessed by their students.

Blackboard offers a complete suite of enterprise software products and services that power a total "e-education infrastructure" for schools, colleges, universities, and other education providers. Blackboard's two major lines of business are Course & Portal Solutions and Commerce & Access Solutions. The Blackboard Connect service provides millions nationwide with time-sensitive information—via voice, text, e-mail and more. It uses mass communication to alert its users' communities and enhance their safety by keeping them informed, involved, and prepared.

A professor can easily incorporate a book's content into the software that is used by thousands of universities worldwide. As of 2009, Blackboard also delivers corporate and government employee training programs in every major region of the world that increase productivity and reduce costs. For details, see blackboard.com and en.wikipedia.org/wiki/Blackboard_Inc.

Drawbacks and Challenges of E-Learning

Despite the numerous benefits, e-learning does have some drawbacks. The following issues have been cited as possible drawbacks of e-learning:

- **Need for instructor retraining.** Some instructors are not competent in teaching by electronic means and may require additional training. It costs money to provide such training.
- **Equipment needs and support services.** Additional funds are needed to purchase multimedia tools to provide support services for e-learning creation, use, and maintenance.
- **Lack of face-to-face interaction and campus life.** Many feel that the intellectual stimulation that takes place through instruction in a classroom with a "live" instructor cannot fully be replicated with e-learning.
- **Assessment.** In the environment of higher education, one criticism is that professors may not be able to adequately assess student work completed through e-learning. There is no guarantee, for example, of who actually completed the assignments or exams.
- **Maintenance and updating.** Although e-learning materials are easier to update than traditionally published materials, there are practical difficulties (e.g., cost, instructors' time) in keeping e-learning materials up-to-date. The content of e-learning material can be difficult to maintain due to the lack of ownership of and accountability for Web site material. In addition, no online course can deliver real-time information and knowledge in the way a "live" instructor can.

> ▶ **Protection of intellectual property.** It is difficult and expensive to control the transmission of copyrighted works downloaded from the e-learning platform.
> ▶ **Computer literacy.** E-learning cannot be extended to those students who are not computer literate or do not have access to the Internet.
> ▶ **Student retention.** Without some human feedback, it may be difficult to keep some students mentally engaged and enthusiastic about e-learning over a long period of time.

Some of these drawbacks can be reduced by advanced technologies. For example, some online products have features that help stimulate student thinking. Offsetting the assessment drawback, biometric controls can be used to verify the identity of students who are taking examinations from home. However, these features add to the costs of e-learning.

From the learner's perspective, the challenge is simply to change the mind-set of how learning typically takes place. Learners must be willing to give up the idea of traditional classroom training, and they must come to understand that continual, lifelong learning will be as much a part of normal work life, past the college years, as voice mail and e-mail. From the teaching perspective, all learning objects must be converted ("tagged") to a digital format. This task can be difficult. Finally, another challenge for e-learning systems is the updating of the knowledge in them—who will do it and how often? Also, who will pay the cost of the updating? For ways to prevent e-learning failures see Online File W6.5.

DISTANCE LEARNING AND ONLINE UNIVERSITIES

The term **distance learning** refers to formal education that takes place off campus, often from home. The concept is not new. Educational institutions have been offering correspondence courses and degrees for decades. What is new, however, is the application of IT in general, and the Web in particular, to expand the opportunities for distance learning to the online environment. Neal (2007) describes the role of the Web 2.0 tools in distance learning in higher education, surveying implementation issues in terms of technology, course content, and pedagogy.

distance learning
Formal education that takes place off campus, usually, but not always, through online resources.

The concept of **virtual universities**, online universities from which students take classes from home or an offsite location via the Internet, is expanding rapidly. Hundreds of thousands of students in dozens of countries, from the United Kingdom to Israel to Thailand, are studying in such institutions. A large number of existing universities, including Stanford University and other top-tier institutions, offer online education of some form; for example, MIT is offering its entire 1,800 course curriculum online. Over 1.5 million independent learners (students, professors, self-learners) log on to the MIT OpenCourseWare site each month. Some universities, such as University of Phoenix (phoenix.edu), California Virtual Campus (cvc.edu), and the University of Maryland (umuc.edu/online_ed.shtml), offer hundreds of courses and dozens of degrees to students worldwide, all online. See distancelearn.about.com for more resources of distance learning and online universities. For a list of the top online MBA programs in the world, see onlinedegrees.com/Online-MBA-Degrees.html.

virtual university
An online university from which students take classes from home or other offsite locations, usually via the Internet.

The virtual university concept allows universities to offer classes worldwide. Moreover, integrated degrees may soon appear by which students can customize a degree that will best fit their needs and take courses at different universities. Several other virtual schools include eschool.com.hk/hongkong, waldenu.edu, and trainingzone.co.uk.

ONLINE CORPORATE TRAINING

Like educational institutions, a large number of business organizations are using e-learning on a large scale (e.g., see Neal 2007). Many companies offer online training, as Cisco does. Some, such as Barclays Bank, COX Industries, and Qantas Airways, call such learning centers "universities." New employees at IBM Taiwan Corp. are given Web-based "electronic training," and KPMG Peat Marwick offers e-learning to its customers.

Corporate training is driven by multiple factors, as shown in Online File W6.6, and is often done via intranets and corporate portals. It has several variations, one of which is on-demand online training, which is offered by companies such as Citrix Systems (citrix.com). However, in large corporations with multiple sites and for studies from home, the Internet is used to access the online material. For a discussion of strategies for implementing corporate e-learning, see Chan and Ngai (2007). Vendors and success stories of online training and educational materials can be found at convergys.com and brightwave.co.uk.

Examples: Corporate Training. The following are two examples of successful e-training:

- Shoney's restaurant chain (over 400 restaurants) needs to provide training continuously to its thousands of employees, from busboys to managers. A multicasting solution (RemoteWare from XcelleNet) is used to offer computer-based training. With multicasting, files are sent by telephone line or satellite from a server to many remote computers at the same time. The system helps both in communication and information dissemination as well as in training. These capabilities have allowed Shoney's to use PCs located at the chain's sites for computer-based training (CBT). Each restaurant has one computer (with speakers) used exclusively for staff training. Training files containing video clips, animation, and spot quizzes are easily transferred to the restaurants' computers. The solution also offers management and evaluation tools (e.g., which employees have completed which courses and how they scored on tests). Course evaluation also is done online. Test results provide indications that aid in improving content. The cost is much lower than training offered via videotape or CD-ROM. Training material is kept up-to-date and is consistent across the corporation. High-quality training has helped the company reduce employee attrition, which means people stay longer at their jobs and provide better customer service.

- The University of Toyota (UOT), a division of Toyota Motor Sales, was established in 1999 to develop training for its 8,500 employees and 104,000 dealership associates. In addition to classroom training, UOT develops dozens of e-learning courses per year, all distributed via a commercially available learning management system (LMS). External vendors produce the majority of these courses. UOT uses a single set of development standards, benchmarks, purchasing specifications, and best practices to ensure standardization and quality of the work of the many vendors. This also helps in avoiding duplications and encourages the dissemination of new information among vendors. A major task was to coordinate all e-training efforts. Because each division (e.g., Lexus, Scion, etc.) is fairly independent in managing training, UOT arranges a corporate e-learning team from all divisions to work together with the vendors and the IT units. The best practices of each division are observed and shared among all. These efforts have been more than successful (Morrison 2008). The training is done via the UOT Web site (called E-source). Ease of use and clarity are achieved via standardization and detailed instructions are sent via a bimonthly e-mail bulletin. E-learning enables the elimination of delays in the deployment of new courses and increases learners' satisfaction.

IMPLEMENTING E-LEARNING AND E-TRAINING

Most schools and industries use e-learning as a supplementary channel to traditional classrooms. One facility that is used in industry is the learning center. A *learning center* is a focal point for all corporate training and learning activities, including online ones. Some companies have a learning center dedicated only to online training. However, most companies combine online and offline activities, as done by W. R. Grace and described in Online File W6.6. In industry, an increasing number of companies are using e-learning for teaching all skills, including managerial ones (see Roberts 2008). Large corporations refer to their learning centers as "universities." For additional information about e-learning, see training mag.com, elearn mag.org, and astd.org/lc.

SOCIAL NETWORKS AND E-LEARNING

Since its inception, social networking has been interrelated with learning. Social networks are virtual spaces where people of all ages can make contacts, share information and ideas, and build a sense of community. Like all technologies, they are built with tools that can serve many purposes.

Well-constructed social environments provide an excellent opportunity to model high-tech learning in a safe online environment, making it possible for employees to share their experiences with others. Several companies are using social networking for training and development (e.g., see advancinginsights.com).

Some students use MySpace, Facebook, and so forth, to connect with other learners. For example, learners can get together and study or hold a discussion online. Unfortunately the clutter and distractions found on these networks can make it difficult to focus on learning. Many MySpace users are seeking other virtual spaces geared to more specific needs, such as study or discussion.

Several social networks (or communities) are dedicated to learning and training (e.g., see e-learning.co.uk). For example, in 2008 Wi5Connect launched CommSocial, a Web 2.0 network platform, to fully leverage social networking's unique power to create "social communities" that can produce business value. The company also launched LearnSocial, which integrates social networking with LMS. Another example of a social network for learning is learnhub.com. Study Curve (studycurve.com) combines social networking and learning for middle schoolers through adults. Users can find experts to answer questions and rate the quality of their responses.

Many universities combine e-learning and social networks; also numerous professors have blogs and wikis for their classes.

LEARNING IN VIRTUAL WORLDS AND SECOND LIFE

A number of interesting learning initiatives have been implemented in virtual worlds, especially in Second Life (SL). Users can participate in simulations, role-plays, construction projects, and social events (see Robbins and Bell 2008 for details). Learners can use virtual worlds to explore ancient civilizations, gothic castles, or fantasy worlds. These places can be springboards to fiction writing, sociology studies, and historical reenactments.

Many people see SL and other virtual worlds as an opportunity to carry out learning projects that would be impossible in the real world because of constraints such as geography or cost. Others see it as a chance to engage a younger generation of learners, many of whom are impatient with traditional forms of education and training. Many see it as a way to advance the practice of learning itself, creating new pedagogies and extending and modifying old ones. Therefore, many refer to SL as the classroom of the future.

Learning in virtual worlds also offers the possibility of collaboration. With the growth in bandwidth, online games are not only multiplayer, but massively multiplayer when played on the Internet. It is no longer a matter of a learner interacting with a learning program. Now learners can interact with each other as well, across dispersed teams and communities of practice around the globe. This further extends the range of the types of learning that can, theoretically, take place in an online environment like SL. Learning a foreign language, team building, and leadership all benefit from group interaction. In addition, students report that they are learning more in SL than they would in the traditional classroom.

Learning in virtual worlds in general, and in SL in particular, is growing rapidly, with many activities and projects. According to Lagorio (2007), scores of universities have set up campuses on SL's islands, where classes meet and students interact in real time. They hold chat discussions and create multimedia presentations. Education-related SL applications are demonstrated in Online File W6.7.

VISUAL INTERACTIVE SIMULATION

An effective technology for e-training and e-learning is *visual interactive simulations* (VIS), which uses computer graphic displays to present the impact of decisions. It differs from regular graphics in that the user can adjust the decision-making process and see the results of the intervention. Some learners respond better to graphical displays, especially when it is done interactively. For example, VIS was used to examine the operations of a physician clinic environment within a physician network in an effort to provide high-quality, cost-effective health care in a family practice. The simulation system identified the most important input factors that significantly affected performance. These inputs, when properly managed, led to lower costs and higher service levels (Swisher et al. 2001).

VIS can represent a static or a dynamic system. Static models display a visual image of the result of one decision alternative at a time. Dynamic models display systems that evolve over time, and the evolution can be presented by animation. The learner can interact with the simulated model, watch the results develop over time, and try different activities or decision strategies.

Such systems provide the following major potential benefits:

- Shorten learning time
- Aid in teaching how to operate complex equipment
- Enable self-paced learning, any place, any time
- Aid in memorization
- Lower overall training costs
- Record an individual's learning progress and improve on it

Several companies provide the necessary software and learning procedures for VIS. One product is SimMAGIC from HamaStar Technology Co. (hamastar.com.tw). Exhibit 6.4 shows how the application is applied at a pharmaceutical company. Exhibit 6.5 provides a trainee progress chart.

E-LEARNING TOOLS AND MANAGEMENT

Many e-learning tools are available (e.g., see the directories of products and services at trainingmag.com). One of the facilitators of e-learning is Web 2.0 technologies, such as blogs and wikis .The following are several examples of the use of Web 2.0 in e-learning:

- IBM Workplace Collaborative Learning 2.0 software (ibm.com/software/workplace/collaborativelearning) is a Web-based tool that can be customized to fit a company's training needs. It uses customer-supplied job profile information to deliver role-based learning resources right to the users' desktops.

EXHIBIT 6.4   SimMAGIC Training Application

Source: Courtesy of HamaStar Technology Co., Ltd. Used with permission.

EXHIBIT 6.5   SimMAGIC Trainee Progress Chart

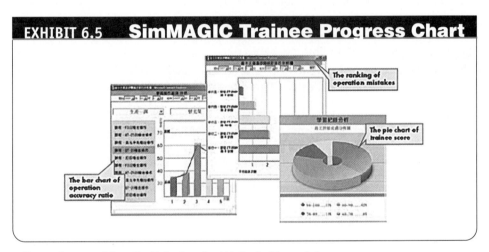

Source: Courtesy of HamaStar Technology Co., Ltd. Used with permission.

▶ ComputerPREP (computerprep.com) offers almost 400 e-learning products, including a comprehensive library of Web-based classroom, distance-learning, and self-study curricula. Students can even combine products from different categories to customize their learning environments.

▶ Macromedia offers tools for wireless devices at adobe.com/software.

▶ eCollege (ecollege.com) offers an e-learning platform that includes free collaboration tools.

▶ Camtasia studio offers many e-learning tools, some of which instructors and students can use to create video tutorials (see techsmith.com/camtasia).

For additional information about e-learning, see trainingmag.com, elearnmag.org, and learningcircuits.org.

E-learning content can be facilitated with the aid of e-books, and knowledge management (Section 6.3).

ELECTRONIC BOOKS

e-book

A book in digital form that can be read on a computer screen or on a special device.

An **electronic book**, or **e-book**, is a book in digital form that can be read on a computer screen, including handheld computers and a special reader. A major event in electronic publishing occurred on March 24, 2000, when Stephen King's book *Riding the Bullet* was published exclusively online. For $2.50, readers could purchase the e-book at amazon.com, ebooks.com, and other e-book providers. Several hundred thousand copies were sold in a few days. However, the publishing event did not go off without some problems. Hackers breached the security system and distributed free copies of the book. There are several distinct types of e-books, as described in Online File W6.8.

Publishers of e-books have since become more sophisticated, and the business of e-publishing has become more secure. E-books can be delivered and read in various ways:

- **Via Web access.** Readers can locate a book on the publisher's Web site and read it there. The book cannot be downloaded. It may be interactive, including links and rich multimedia.
- **Via Web download.** Readers can download the book to a PC.
- **Via a dedicated reader.** The book must be downloaded to a special device (an e-book reader).
- **Via a general-purpose reader.** The book can be downloaded to a general-purpose device, such as a Palm Pilot.
- **Via a Web server.** The contents of a book are stored on a Web server and downloaded for print-on-demand (which is discussed later in this book).

Most e-books require some type of payment. Readers either pay before they download a book from a Web site, or they pay when they order the special CD-ROM edition of a book. Amazon.com offers hundreds of thousands of e-books, newspapers (including international ones), and much more. All are cheaper than the hard-copy version (e.g., new releases of books cost only $10).

Devices for Reading E-Books

The major device used to read an e-book is an e-book reader. Most e-book readers are lightweight (about 10 ounces) and convenient to carry. The major readers are:

- Kindle 2 from Amazon.com (see the following photo). This popular reader cost $359 in 2008, and it can hold over 200 titles. For capabilities, photos, and a video demonstration, go to amazon.com and search for "Kindle 2.0." For more on Kindle, see Perenson (2009).
- The Sony PRS-200, which costs $400, can store 350 e-books in its internal memory. An older model, PRS-505, is available for $300. More content can be loaded onto special memory cards that (in 2007) can store up to 100 GB (see tigerdirect.com).
- Barnes and Noble's Nook with color touchscreen costs $259 and can store 1,500 books on its 2 GB internal storage (see barnesandnoble.com/nook/features/techspecs).

Kindle 2.0

Several other aids are available to help readers who want to read large amounts of material online. For example, ClearType from Microsoft and CoolType from Adobe can be used to improve screen display, colors, and font sizes.

Advantages and Limitations of E-Books

For e-books to make an impact, they must offer advantages to both readers and publishers. Otherwise, there would be little incentive to change from the traditional format. E-books, like other books, can be used for pleasure reading and as textbooks to support learning (see Chu and Lam 2006).

The major advantage of e-books to readers is lower cost and portability. Readers can carry as many as 200 books wherever they go (and more when portable memory drives are used). Other advantages are easy search capabilities and links; easy downloading; the ability to quickly and inexpensively copy material, including figures; easy integration of content with other text; easy updating; no wear and tear on a physical book; ability to find out-of-print books; and books can be published and updated quickly, so they can be kept current.

E-books also can reduce some of the physical burdens of traditional books. A number of studies have shown that 6 out of 10 students ages 9 to 20 report chronic back pain related to heavy backpacks filled with books. Some schools have eliminated lockers for safety reasons, causing students to carry heavy backpacks not only to and from school, but all day long. A number of schools are experimenting with eliminating textbooks altogether and using an Internet-based curriculum or school materials on CD-ROMs.

The primary advantage that e-books offer publishers is lower production, marketing, and delivery costs, which have a significant impact on the price of books (e-textbooks are about 50 percent cheaper than print versions). Other advantages for publishers are lower updating and reproduction costs; the ability to reach many readers; the ease of combining several books, so professors can customize textbooks by using materials from different books by the same publisher; and lower advertising costs (see Chu and Lam 2006).

Of course, e-books have some limitations: They require hardware and software that may be too expensive for some readers; some people have difficulty reading large amounts of material on a screen; batteries may run down; and there are multiple, competing standards.

Section 6.2 ▶ REVIEW QUESTIONS

1. Define e-learning and describe its drivers and benefits.
2. List some of the major drawbacks of e-learning and describe how they can be prevented.
3. Describe virtual universities and distance learning.
4. Define e-training and describe how it is done.
5. Describe the connection between learning and social networking.
6. Describe learning in virtual worlds.
7. List some e-learning tools, and describe Blackboard and visual interactive simulation.
8. Describe e-books and list their advantages and limitations.

6.3 KNOWLEDGE MANAGEMENT, LEARNING, AND ELECTRONIC COMMERCE

The term *knowledge management* frequently is mentioned in discussions of e-learning. Why is this? To answer this question, you first need to understand what knowledge management is.

AN OVERVIEW OF KNOWLEDGE MANAGEMENT

knowledge management (KM)
The process of capturing or creating knowledge, storing it, updating it constantly, disseminating it, and using it whenever necessary.

Knowledge management and e-learning both use the same "coin of the realm"—knowledge. Whereas e-learning uses that "coin" for the sake of individual learning, knowledge management uses it to improve the functioning of an organization. Knowledge is one of the most important assets in any organization, and thus it is important to capture, store, and apply it. These are the major purposes of knowledge management. Thus, **knowledge management (KM)** refers to the process of capturing or creating knowledge, storing and protecting it, updating it constantly, disseminating it, and using it whenever necessary. For a comprehensive discussion of KM, see Holsapple (2003), kmworld.com, and en.wikipedia.org/wiki/Knowledge_management.

Knowledge is collected from both external and internal sources. Then it is examined, interpreted, refined, and stored in what is called an *organizational knowledge base*, the repository for the enterprise's knowledge. A major purpose of an organizational knowledge base is to allow for *knowledge sharing*. Knowledge sharing among employees, with customers, and with business partners has a huge potential payoff in improved customer service, the ability to solve difficult organizational problems, shorter delivery cycle times, and increased collaboration within the company and with business partners. Furthermore, some knowledge can be sold to others or traded for other knowledge.

KM TYPES AND ACTIVITIES

Organizational knowledge is embedded in the following resources: (1) human capital, which includes employee knowledge, competencies, and creativity; (2) structured capital (organizational capital), which includes organizational structure and culture, processes, patents, and the capability to leverage knowledge through sharing and transferring; and (3) customer capital, which includes the relationship between organizations and their customers and other partners.

This organizational knowledge must be properly managed, and this is the purpose of KM. KM has the following major tasks:

- **Create knowledge.** Knowledge is created as people determine new ways of doing things or develop know-how. Sometimes external knowledge is brought in.
- **Capture knowledge.** New knowledge must be identified as valuable and be represented in a reasonable way.
- **Refine knowledge.** New knowledge must be placed in context so that it is actionable. This is where human insights (tacit qualities) must be captured along with explicit facts.
- **Store knowledge.** Useful knowledge must then be stored in a reasonable format in a knowledge repository so that others in the organizational can access it.
- **Manage knowledge.** Like a library, the knowledge must be kept current. It must be reviewed to verify that it is relevant and accurate.
- **Disseminate knowledge.** Knowledge must be made available in a useful format to anyone in the organization who needs it, anywhere and anytime.

These tasks can be viewed as a cyclical process, as shown in Exhibit 6.6.

For a comprehensive list of KM activities and tools, see en.wikipedia.org/wiki/Knowledge_management and kmworld.com.

Knowledge Sharing

Knowledge is of limited value if it is not updated and shared. The ability to share knowledge decreases its cost and increases its effectiveness for greater competitive advantage. Thus, a major purpose of KM is to increase knowledge sharing. Shared knowledge can also decrease risk and uncertainty. KM is about sharing a company's knowledge repository, but increasingly it is also about sharing the information stored in people's heads. An example of a knowledge-sharing system at Infosys Technologies is provided in Case 6.1.

EXHIBIT 6.6   The Knowledge Management System Cycle

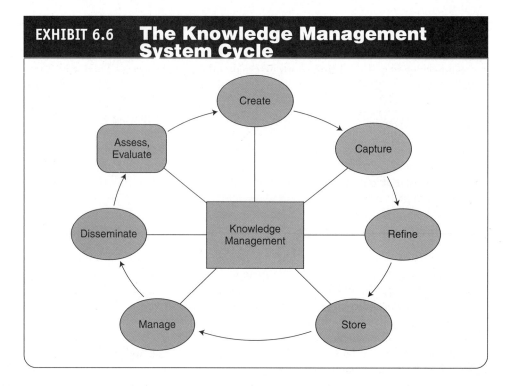

CASE 6.1
EC Application
KNOWLEDGE MANAGEMENT AT INFOSYS TECHNOLOGIES

The Problem

Infosys Technologies, a global software services company based in India, is a worldwide leader in outsourcing. With over 23,000 employees and globally distributed operations, Infosys develops IT solutions for some of the largest corporations in the world. During the past 10 years, Infosys has experienced annual growth of 30 percent. Infosys faced a challenge of keeping its large employee base up-to-date, staying ahead of both its competitors and clients, and ensuring that the lessons learned in one part of the organization were available to its consultants so they could reuse the knowledge accumulated in the company. The company's motto is "Learn once, use anywhere." The company's vision is that every instance of learning within Infosys should be available to every employee. But how does an organization turn such a vision into a reality?

The Solution

Infosys Technologies' effort to convert each employee's knowledge into an organizational asset started in the early 1990s and extended well into the first decade of the 2000s.

In the early 1990s, Infosys launched its *bodies of knowledge (BOK)* initiative, which involved encouraging employees to provide written accounts of their experiences across various topics, such as technologies, software development, and living abroad. These experiences were then shared in hard-copy form with all other employees. This early effort ballooned into a full-fledged KM effort supported by e-mail, bulletin boards, and various knowledge repositories. In 1996, a corporate intranet was developed to make BOKs, in HTML format, easily accessible to all. In 1999, Infosys began an organization-wide program to integrate the various knowledge initiatives. A central *knowledge portal* was created, called KShop, and although the KM group developed the technology infrastructure, local groups were encouraged to maintain their own content on KShop.

The content of KShop consisted of different content types—BOKs, case studies, reusable artifacts, and downloadable software—each with its own homepage. Content was carefully categorized by the KM group to ensure that as the amount of content increased, it would still be possible for people to quickly find what they needed.

(continued)

CASE 6.1   (continued)

In early 2000, Infosys appeared to have a very functional KM system, and yet patronage by employees remained low. The KM group therefore initiated a reward scheme to increase both use and contribution. The scheme gave employees who contributed to KShop knowledge currency units (KCUs) that could be accumulated and exchanged for monetary rewards or prizes.

As you can see, KM initiatives are much more than the implementation of technology tools to allow employees to create or document knowledge. Infosys's KM initiatives involved processes to organize knowledge, to categorize knowledge, and to rate knowledge usefulness, as well as strategies to encourage knowledge sharing and reuse.

The Results

Within a year of the introduction of the incentive KCU scheme, 2,400 new knowledge assets had been contributed to KShop by some 20 percent of Infosys's employees. However, as the volume of content increased, so, too, did problems relating to finding the needed information. Moreover, the heavy growth in contributions taxed the limited number of volunteer reviewers, who served an important quality-control function. The KM group therefore modified the KCU incentive scheme. It developed a new KCU scheme that rated the usefulness of knowledge from the perspective of the users of the knowledge, rather than the reviewers. And, to increase accountability, the KM group requested tangible proof to justify any high ratings. Finally, the KM group raised the bar for cashing in KCU points for monetary awards.

Sources: Compiled from *infosys.com* (accessed October 2009) and Garud and Kumaraswamy (2005).

Questions

1. Why are consulting organizations interested in KM?
2. Identify the KM cycle in this case.
3. Why is a reward system beneficial? Compare the old and new reward systems.
4. Why was using a single portal beneficial?

HOW IS KNOWLEDGE MANAGEMENT RELATED TO E-COMMERCE?

To better perform their EC tasks, organizations need knowledge, which is provided by KM. For example, strategic planning in traditional organizations needs considerable amounts of knowledge. To mitigate this problem, e-commerce can proactively incorporate KM processes to facilitate quick access to different types of knowledge.

By analyzing database marketing data in a timely manner, organizations can learn about their customers and generate useful knowledge for planning and decision making. For these activities to be successful in both B2B and B2C, appropriate knowledge is needed to interpret information and to execute activities.

Core knowledge management activities for companies doing EC should include the following electronically supported activities: identification, creation, capture and codification, classification, distribution, utilization, and evolution of the knowledge needed to develop products and partnerships. *Knowledge creation* involves using various computer-based tools and techniques to analyze transaction data and generate new ideas. *Knowledge capture and codification* includes gathering new knowledge and storing it in a machine-readable form. *Knowledge classification* organizes knowledge using appropriate dimensions relating it to its use. *Knowledge distribution* is sharing relevant information with suppliers, consumers, and other internal and external stakeholders through electronic networks—both public and private. *Knowledge utilization* involves appropriate application of knowledge to problem solving. *Knowledge evolution* entails updating knowledge as time progresses.

Some managers believe that a major role of KM is linking EC and business processes. Specifically, knowledge generated in EC contributes to the enhancement of three core processes: CRM, SCM, and product development management. For more on KM-enabling technologies and how they can be applied to business unit initiatives, see kmworld.com and knowledgestorm.com.

KM and Social Networks

A major area of KM is knowledge creation in communities, which is also known as the *wisdom of the crowd* and *communities of practice*. This area has several variations. One variety is limited within a single company (see the Knowledge Network in the Caterpillar opening case). Another is a public community whose members are interested in a common area of interest. Yet another type is a combination of the two. The major purposes of such communities are:

▶ **Knowledge creation.** The creation of knowledge for a specific problem or area. Individuals are asked to contribute to a solution or offer valuable advice. For example, IBM, GE, and other companies have communities of employees and business partners who contribute to knowledge creations.

▶ **Knowledge sharing.** Members share knowledge by telling other members where to find knowledge of interest to the community. For example, Microsoft Vine is a community that supports those interested in emergency services information exchange.

Web 2.0 applications help aggregate corporate knowledge and simplify the building of repositories of best practices, as demonstrated by the following example.

Example: IBM's Innovation Jam. IBM has long used communities for problem solving. One of its best-known communities is the Innovation Jam, an online brainstorming session. This community of over 150,000 employees and business partners tries to move the latest technologies to the market. IBM has been hosting online brainstorming sessions since 2001. For example, in July 2006, IBM invited employees, partners, and customers to contribute ideas about a certain new product. Within 72 hours, more than 50,000 ideas were posted. These ideas were then winnowed down by using sophisticated analytical software.

Virtual meetings where IBM employees can participate in Innovation Jam launches are conducted in SL. IBM's CEO has even created an avatar to represent him. Topics that have been explored by recent Innovation Jams have included new technologies for water filtration, 3D Internet, and branchless banking. For more on IBM's Innovation Jams and use of virtual worlds, see Bjelland and Wood (2008) and en.wikipedia.org/wiki/IBM_Virtual_Universe_Community.

ONLINE ADVICE AND CONSULTING

Another use of knowledge online is offering advice and consulting services. The online advice and consulting field is growing rapidly as tens of thousands of experts of all kinds sell (or provide for free) their expertise over the Internet. The following are some examples:

▶ **Medical advice.** Companies such as WebMD (webmd.com) (see Chapter 2) and others (see liveperson.com) provide health-advice consultations with top medical experts. Consumers can ask specific questions and get an answer from a specialist in a few days. Health sites also offer specialized advice and tips for travelers, for pet owners, and more.

▶ **Management consulting.** Many consultants are selling their accumulated expertise from organizational knowledge bases. A pioneer in this area was Andersen Consulting (now Accenture at accenture.com). Other management consultants that sell knowledge online are Aberdeen (aberdeen.com) and Forrester Research (forresterresearch.com). Because of their high consultation fees, such services mainly are used by corporations.

▶ **Legal advice.** Delivery of legal advice to individuals and businesses by consultation services has considerable prospects. For example, Atlanta-based law firm Alston & Bird coordinates legal counseling with 12 law firms for a large health care company and for many other clients.

▶ **Gurus.** Several sites provide diversified expert services, some for free. One example is guru.com, which provides businesses with the most efficient platform to connect and perform transactions with freelance professionals locally, nationally, and globally. As of 2009, it had more than 1 million registered members and 100,000 active freelancer profiles. Expertise is advertised at elance.com—companies find, hire, manage, and pay contractors online. On Elance, companies gain instant access to 100,000 rated and tested professionals who offer technical, marketing, and business expertise. Of special interest is scientificamerican.com/sciammag, which offers advice from science experts at *Scientific American.* Some of the most popular services that offer information from experts are answers.com (previously GuruNet), answers.yahoo.com, catholic.com, healthanswers.com, wineanswers.com, and many more. Some provide answers for free; others charge fees for premium services.

▶ **Financial advice.** Many companies offer extensive financial advice. For example, Merrill Lynch Online (totalmerrill.com) provides free access to some of the firm's research reports and analyses.

▶ **Social networks.** Several social networks allow users to post questions and get answers. For business-oriented questions, go to linkedln.com.

▶ **Other advisory services.** Many other advisory services are available online—some for free and others for a fee. For example, guestfinder.com makes it easy for people who work in the media to find guests and interview sources.

One word of caution about advice: It is not wise to risk your health, your money, or your legal status on free or even for-fee online advice. Always seek more than one opinion, and carefully check the credentials of any advice provider.

EMPLOYEE KNOWLEDGE NETWORKS AND EXPERT LOCATION SYSTEMS

Expert advice can be provided within an organization in a variety of ways. Human expertise is rare; therefore, companies attempt to preserve it electronically in corporate knowledge bases. Alternatively, electronic expert systems may be used.

Finding Experts Electronically

People who need help may post their problem on the corporate intranet (e.g., using blogs) or on public social networks such as LinkedIn (linkedin.com) and ask for help internally and/or externally. Similarly, companies may ask for advice on how to exploit an opportunity. IBM frequently uses this method. Sometimes it obtains hundreds of useful ideas within a few days. It is a kind of brainstorming. The problem with this approach is that it may take days to get an answer, if an answer is even provided, and the answer may not be from the top experts.

Expert Location Systems

Expert location systems (ELS) are interactive computerized systems that help employees find and connect with colleagues with expertise required for specific problems—whether they are across the country or across the room—in order to solve specific, critical business problems in seconds. Expertise location systems are designed to:

▶ Connect people to people.
▶ Link people to information about people.
▶ Identify people with expertise and link them to those with questions or problems.
▶ Identify potential staff for projects requiring specific expertise.
▶ Assist in career development.
▶ Provide support for teams and communities of practice.

expert location systems (ELS)
Interactive computerized systems that help employees find and connect with colleagues who have expertise required for specific problems— whether they are across the country or across the room—in order to solve specific, critical business problems in seconds.

Software for such systems is made by companies such as AskMe, RightNow Technologies, and Tacit Knowledge Systems, Inc. For example, AskMe Realcom, a software solution for deploying employee knowledge networks, enables organizations to fully leverage employee knowledge and expertise to drive innovations and improve bottom-line performance. The solution is the result of AskMe's collaboration, experience and success with real-world customer deployments and many companies. For benefits, features, and demonstrations, see realcom-inc.com. Most expert location systems work similarly, exploring knowledge bases for either an answer to the problem (if it exists there) or locating qualified experts. The generic process is shown in Exhibit 6.7. The four steps of the process are:

1. An employee submits a question to the ELS.

2. The software searches its database to see if an answer to the question already exists. If it does, the information (research reports, spreadsheets, etc.) is returned to the employee. If not, the software searches documents and archived communications for an "expert."

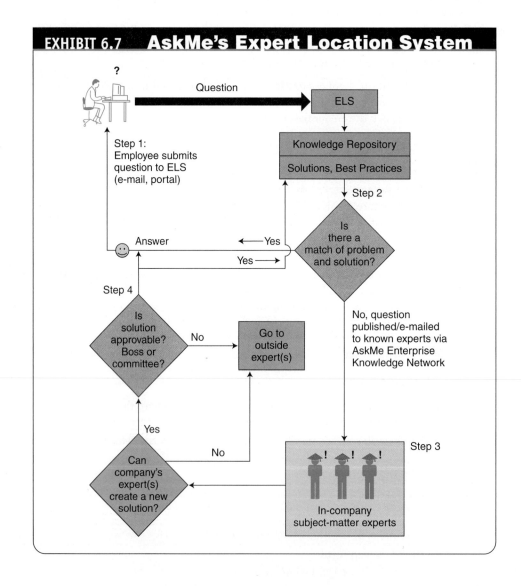

EXHIBIT 6.7   AskMe's Expert Location System

3. Once a qualified candidate is located, the system asks if he or she is able to answer a question from a colleague. If so, the expert submits a response. If the expert is unable to respond, he or she can elect to pass on the question. The question is then routed to the next appropriate candidate until one responds.

4. After the response is sent, it is reviewed for accuracy and sent back to the person who made the query. At the same time, the question and its response are added to the knowledge database. This way, if the question comes up again, it will not be necessary to seek real-time assistance.

Case 6.2 demonstrates how such a system works for the U.S. government.

Seeking Expertise in Social Networks

Seeking expertise (and experts) is becoming a very popular activity. People post their problems on bulletin boards, forums, and blogs and wait for responses. The New Zealand closing case describes several initiatives of this nature. One of the features of LinkedIn is the free "LinkedIn Answers," where users ask questions for the community to answer.

CASE 6.2
EC Application

HOW THE U.S. DEPARTMENT OF COMMERCE USES AN EXPERT LOCATION SYSTEM

The U.S. Commercial Service Division at the Department of Commerce (DOC) conducts approximately 200,000 counseling sessions a year involving close to $40 billion in trade. The division employs many specialists who frequently need to do research or call on experts to answer a question posed by a U.S. corporation.

For example, in May 2004 a U.S.–based software company called Brad Anderson, a DOC specialist, for advice. The software company wanted to close a deal with a customer in Poland, but the buyer wanted to charge the U.S. company a 20 percent withholding tax, a tax it attributed to Poland's recent admission into the European Union. Was the tax legitimate?

To find out, Anderson turned to the DOC Insider, an expertise location system (from AskMe). After typing in his question, Anderson first found some documents that were related to his query, but they did not explain the EU tax code completely. Anderson next asked the system to search the 1,700-strong Commercial Service for a real "live" expert, and within seconds, he was given a list of 80 people in the DOC who might be able to help him. Of those, he chose the six people he felt were most qualified and then forwarded to them his query.

Before the DOC Insider was in place, Anderson says, it would have taken him about three days to get an answer to the same question. "You have to make many phone calls and deal with time zones," he says. Thanks to the expertise location system, however, he had three responses within minutes, a complete answer within an hour, and the sale went through the following morning. Anderson estimates that he now uses the system for roughly 40 percent of the work he does.

The DOC Insider is an invaluable tool. Anderson thinks the tool is vital enough to provide it to other units at the agency. In the first nine months the system was in place, it saved more than 1,000 man hours.

Sources: Compiled from D'Agostino (2004) and *realcom-inc.com* (accessed November 2009).

Questions

1. What are the benefits of the expertise location system to the DOC? To U.S. companies?

2. Review Exhibit 6.7 and relate it to this case.

3. What, in your opinion, are the limitations of this system? Can they be overcome? How?

In many organizations, social networking and the location of expertise are converging. Some organizations use the same internal social networking site, intranet, or portal for internal expertise location as they do for communication and general networking. Many consider expertise location to be an extension of knowledge management, in that the goal is to capture and reuse the skills and experience of internal staff members in order to increase competitive advantage. For discussion and details of when to use social networking for expert location, see kmedge.org/wp/snel-whentouse.html.

Section 6.3 ▶ REVIEW QUESTIONS

1. Define knowledge management.
2. Discuss the relationship between KM and EC.
3. Describe online advisory services.
4. Describe expert location systems and their benefits.

6.4 CONSUMER-TO-CONSUMER ELECTRONIC COMMERCE

consumer-to-consumer (C2C)
E-commerce model in which consumers sell directly to other consumers.

Consumer-to-consumer (C2C) EC, which is sometimes referred to as *peer-to-peer (P2P) networks* or *exchanges,* involve all transactions between and among individual consumers. These transactions can also include third parties, usually in the form of those who facilitate the marketplace, such as eBay or a social network site. C2C networks can include classified ads, music and file sharing, career and job Web sites (linkedln.com and careerone.com.au), and also personal services, such as dating Web sites (match.com).

In C2C EC, consumers sell goods and services to other consumers. There are millions of sellers with different items to sell and an equally large number of buyers. Finding each other may take a long time and can even incur high costs to both buyers and sellers, and this is why intermediaries such as eBay or Craigslist are so important. They simply mediate between consumers who want to buy and sell. Some take small cuts of a seller's profit as a fee for bringing customers to the marketplace.

C2C EC has given online shopping and trading a new dimension. Although this sort of trading is prevalent in the offline world (classified newspaper ads, garage sales, etc.), it was not expected to take off online due to the anonymity of users. This problem was solved by using a third-party payment provider (e.g., PayPal) and insurance provided by eBay and others. One advantage of C2C EC is that it reduces the cost to buyers. It also gives many individuals and small business owners a low-cost way to sell their goods and services.

Social networks have become a popular place for C2C activities such as selling products and services via classified ads, sharing or selling music, bartering, selling virtual properties, and providing personal services.

E-COMMERCE: C2C APPLICATIONS

EC has redefined the traditional structure of business by giving small firms and individuals the same opportunities to conduct business as multinational corporations. As a result, many Web sites have been created that encourage and assist with commerce between consumers. We cover several representative applications next.

C2C Auctions

The most successful example of a C2C application is auctions. In dozens of countries, selling and buying on auction sites is exploding. Most auctions are conducted by intermediaries (the most well-known is eBay). Consumers can visit auctions at general sites such as ebay.com or auctionanything.com or they can use specialized sites, such as bidz.com that specializes in exclusive and brand name jewelry. In addition, many individuals are conducting their own auctions with the use of special software. For example, greatshop.com provides software to create C2C reverse auction communities online.

Classified Ads

People sell to other people every day through classified ads. Internet-based classified ads have several advantages over newspaper classified ads. They offer a national, rather than a local, audience. This greatly increases the supply of goods and services available and the number of potential buyers. One of the most successful sites of C2C classified ads is Craigslist (see Chapter 2). Other examples are iclassifieds2000.com, which contains a list of about 500,000 cars, compared with the much smaller number you might find locally. It also includes apartments for rent across the United States (powered by forrent.com) and personal ads (powered by match.com). Another example is freeclassified.com. Both Google and Yahoo! are expanding their online classifieds. Many newspapers also offer their classified ads online. In many cases, placing an ad on one Web site brings it automatically into the classified sections of numerous partners. This increases ad exposure at no additional cost. To help narrow the search for a particular item, on some sites shoppers can use search engines.

Classified ads appear in thousands of Web sites including popular social networks such as LinkedIn, Facebook, and SL.

Personal Services

Numerous personal services are available on the Internet (lawyers, handy helpers, tax preparers, investment clubs, dating services). Some are in the classified ads, but others are listed in specialized Web sites (e.g., hireahelper.com) and directories. Some are free, some charge a fee. Be very careful before purchasing any personal services. Fraud or crime could be involved (e.g., a lawyer online may not be an expert in the area professed or may not deliver the service at all). Online advising and consulting, described in Section 6.3, also are examples of personal services.

Napster and Others—File-Sharing Utilities

It all started in 2001. By logging onto services such as Napster, people could download files that others were willing to share. Such P2P networks enabled users to search other members' hard drives for a particular file, including data files created by users or copied from elsewhere. Digital music and games were the most popular files accessed. Then came the movies and videos. Napster had more than 60 million members in 2002 before it went out of business.

The Napster server functioned as a directory that listed the files being shared by other users. Once logged into the server, users could search the directory for specific songs and locate the file owner. They could then directly access the owner's computer and download the songs they had chosen. Napster also included chat rooms to connect its millions of users.

However, a U.S. federal court found Napster to be in violation of copyright laws because it enabled people to obtain music files without paying the creators of the music for access to their material. Following this ruling, in March 2002, Napster closed its free services. Napster continued to operate, with users paying a fee for file sharing and Napster passing along part of the fee to copyright owners.

A number of free file-sharing programs still exist. For example, an even purer version of P2P is Gnutella (downloadable software), a P2P program that dispenses with the central database altogether in connecting the peer computers. To access games over P2P networks, try trustyfiles.com. ICQ (the instant messenger-type chat room) can be considered a hybrid P2P technology because the chatters share the same screen.

Despite the temptation to get "something for nothing," remember that downloading copyrighted materials for free is against the law; violators are subject to penalties if caught.

C2C Activities in Social Networks and Trading Virtual Properties

C2C activities in social networks include the sharing of photos, videos, music, and other files, trading of virtual properties, and much more. Trading virtual properties is very popular in virtual worlds, especially in SL.

Section 6.4 ▶ REVIEW QUESTIONS

1. Define C2C e-commerce.
2. Describe the major e-commerce applications.
3. Define file sharing.
4. How is C2C practiced in social networking?

6.5   COLLABORATIVE COMMERCE

Collaborative commerce is an e-commerce technology that can be used to improve collaboration within and among organizations, including in supply chains and their management.

ESSENTIALS OF COLLABORATIVE COMMERCE

collaborative commerce (c-commerce) The use of digital technologies that enable companies to collaboratively plan, design, develop, manage, and research products, services, and innovative EC applications.	**Collaborative commerce (c-commerce)** refers to the use of digital technologies that enable companies to collaboratively plan, design, develop, manage, and research products, services, and innovative EC applications. An example would be a manufacturer that is collaborating electronically with a supplier that designs a product or a part for the manufacturer, as was shown in the Boeing case in Online Appendix A. C-commerce implies communication, information sharing, and collaborative planning done electronically through tools such as groupware, blogs, wikis, and specially designed EC collaboration tools. In the supply chain, major benefits are cost reduction, increased revenue, and better customer retention. These benefits are the results of fewer stock-outs, less exception and rush-order processing, reduced inventory throughout the supply chain, lower materials costs, increased sales volume, and increased competitive advantage.

The Elements and Processes of C-Commerce

The elements of processes of c-commerce vary according to situations. For example, in many cases collaboration involves a manufacturer (or assemblers) with its suppliers, designers, and other business partners as well as its customers and possibly government, along the supply chain. The major elements of the collaboration are illustrated in Exhibit 6.8. Notice that the collaboration is based on the analysis of internal and external data that are made visible via a portal. On the left side of the exhibit, we show the cyclical process of collaborative commerce. The people involved in this cycle use the information in the displays as well as the interactions among the major groups of participants. The elements of c-commerce can be arranged in different configurations, one of which is the hub.

COLLABORATION HUBS

collaboration hub The central point of control for an e-market. A single c-hub, representing one e-market owner, can host multiple collaboration spaces (c-spaces) in which trading partners use c-enablers to exchange data with the c-hub.

One of the most popular forms of c-commerce is the *collaboration hub*, which is often used by the members of a supply chain. A **collaboration hub** (c-hub) is the central point

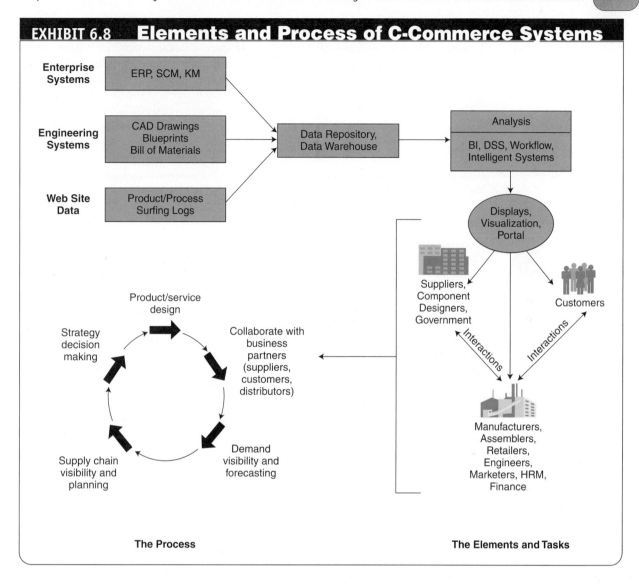

EXHIBIT 6.8   Elements and Process of C-Commerce Systems

of control for an e-market. A single c-hub, representing one e-market owner, can host multiple collaboration spaces (c-spaces) in which trading partners use c-enablers to exchange data with the c-hub.

C-commerce activities usually are conducted between and among supply chain partners. Leightons Opticians, as shown in Online File W6.9, uses a hub to communicate among all its business partners and is thus able to improve customer service. Finally, in Online File W6.10, the case of Webcor, a company using special software to better collaborate with its partners electronically, is described.

There are several varieties of c-commerce, ranging from joint design efforts to forecasting. Collaboration can be done both between and within organizations. For example, a collaborative platform can help in communication and collaboration between headquarters and subsidiaries or between franchisers and franchisees. The platform provides e-mail, message boards and chat rooms, and online corporate data access around the globe, no matter what the time zone. The following sections demonstrate some types and examples of c-commerce.

IMPLEMENTING C-COMMERCE

Leading companies such as Dell, Cisco, and HP use collaborative commerce strategically, enabling sophisticated business models while transforming their value chains. They also have implemented e-procurement and other mature collaboration techniques to streamline operations, reduce overhead, and maintain or enhance margins in the face of intense competition. For example, Dell implemented end-to-end integrated configuration and ordering, a single enterprise middleware backbone, and multitier collaborative planning. This has enabled Dell to support a make-to-order business model with best-in-class speed and efficiency. Cisco chose to support a virtual business model focusing on time to market and customer satisfaction. Cisco has integrated its order process with back-end processes, implemented purchase order automation, and enabled collaborative product development.

Example: Design with C-Commerce

Collaborative efforts are common in joint design, as illustrated in the Boeing case in Online Appendix A. This is one of the oldest areas of electronic collaboration, which is becoming even more popular due to EC Web 2.0 tools, as discussed in Online File W6.11.

BARRIERS TO C-COMMERCE

Despite the many potential benefits, c-commerce is moving ahead fairly slowly. Reasons cited in various studies include technical factors involving a lack of internal integration, standards, and networks; security and privacy concerns, and some distrust over who has access to and control of information stored in a partner's database; internal resistance to information sharing and to new approaches; and lack of internal skills to conduct c-commerce. Gaining agreement on how to share costs and benefits can also prove problematic.

A big stumbling block to the adoption of c-commerce has been the lack of defined and universally agreed-upon standards. New approaches, such as the use of XML and its variants and the use of Web Services, could significantly lessen the problem of standards. Also, the use of collaborative Web 2.0 tools that are based on open source could be helpful. Finally, global collaboration may be complicated by additional barriers ranging from language incompatibility to cultural misunderstandings.

Specialized c-commerce software tools will break down some of the barriers to c-commerce. In addition, as companies learn more about the major benefits of c-commerce—such as smoothing the supply chain, reducing inventories and operating costs, and increasing customer satisfaction and the competitive edge—it is expected that more will rush to jump on the c-commerce bandwagon.

C-commerce is a typical response to business pressures, as can be seen in the case of a global supply chain in the fashion retailing industry. The fashion retail supply chain poses some unique and very challenging decisions for managers, and the adoption of appropriate technologies to support such supply chains is obviously critical. Some fashion retailers are achieving extraordinary levels of success and are the envy of nearly all other players in this industry, even if they have not adopted all the prescriptions we have detailed here.

Section 6.5 ▶ REVIEW QUESTIONS

1. Define c-commerce.
2. List the major types and characteristics of c-commerce.
3. Describe some examples of c-commerce.
4. Describe the elements and process of c-commerce.
5. List some major barriers to c-commerce. How might these limitations be overcome?

MANAGERIAL ISSUES

Some managerial issues related to this chapter are as follows.

1. **What are the e-government opportunities?** If an organization is doing business with the government, eventually some or all of it may be moved online. Organizations may find new online business opportunities with the government because governments are getting serious about going online; some even mandate it as a major way to conduct B2G and G2B.

2. **How do we design the most cost-efficient government e-procurement system?** How much can the governmental e-procurement system save on procurement costs? How can it enhance the transparency of the procurement process and prevent illegal bribery? How should the online and offline procurement systems be designed? How should the portfolio of auctions and desktop purchasing be constructed? Can the government use commercial B2B sites for procurement? Can businesses use the government procurement system for their own procurement? Would the boundary between G2B and B2B blur as the channel of procurement?

3. **How do we design the portfolio of e-learning knowledge sources?** There are many sources of e-learning services. The e-learning management office needs to design the portfolio of the online and offline training, internal and external sources, paid and nonpaid sources, and know-how and know-who choices. The internal knowledge management system is an important source for large corporations, whereas external sources will be more cost-effective for small corporations. Obviously, justification is needed and goes hand-in-hand with the selection of supporting tools (see West 2007). For illustrative case studies, see brightwave.co.uk.

4. **How do we incorporate social networking–based learning and services in our organization?** With the proliferation of social networking initiatives in the enterprise comes the issue of how to integrate these with the enterprise system, including CRM, KM, training, and other business processes. An issue is how to balance the quality of knowledge with the scope of knowledge.

5. **Can we capitalize on C2C EC?** Businesses cannot capture much C2C activity unless they provide secure payment services such as paypal.com or an escrow service. Businesses may consider sponsoring C2C activities in order to increase viral marketing and advertising.

6. **How do we connect our expert location system and social networking initiatives?** Expert location systems and knowledge management systems can be developed to assist in finding experts both internally and externally. This service can be linked with the job match portal and professional social networks.

7. **What will be impact of the e-book platform?** If the e-book is widely adopted by readers, the distribution channel of online book sales may be disruptive. This new platform may cannibalize the online book retail business and impact the platform of e-learning as well. A threat is the protection of the intellectual property of digital contents.

8. **How difficult is it to introduce e-collaboration?** Dealing with the technology may be the easy part. Tackling the behavioral changes needed within an organization and its trading partners may be the greater challenge. Change management requires an understanding of the new interdependencies being constructed and the new roles and responsibilities that must be adapted in order for the enterprise and its business partners to collaborate. Finally, e-collaboration costs money and needs to be justified. This may not be an easy task due to the intangible risks and benefits involved.

SUMMARY

In this chapter, you learned about the following EC issues as they relate to the chapter's learning objectives.

1. **E-government activities.** Governments, like any other organization, can use EC applications for great savings. Notable applications are e-procurement using reverse auctions, e-payments to and from citizens and businesses, auctioning of surplus goods, and electronic travel and expense management

systems. Governments also conduct electronic business with other governments. Finally, governments can facilitate homeland security with EC tools.

2. **Implementing e-government to citizens, businesses, and its own operations.** Governments worldwide are providing a variety of services to citizens over the Internet. Such initiatives increase citizens' satisfaction and decrease government expenses in providing customer service applications including electronic voting. Governments also are active in electronically trading with businesses. Finally, EC is done within and between governments. E-government's growth is strengthening through the use of wireless systems in what is described as mobile or m-government. E-government 2.0 is becoming increasingly popular with tools such as wikis, blogs, and Twitter.

3. **E-learning and training.** E-learning is the delivery of educational content via electronic media, including the Internet and intranets. Degree programs, lifelong learning topics, and corporate training are delivered by thousands of organizations worldwide. A growing area is distance learning via online university offerings. Some are virtual; others are delivered both online and offline. Online corporate training also is increasing and is sometimes conducted at formal corporate learning centers. Implementation is done in steps starting with just presence and ending with activities on social networks. New e-book readers contain easy-to-read text, search capabilities, and many other functions. Add to this the low cost of books and the capability of storing many books on a small device and you can understand the increased popularity of the device.

4. **Knowledge management and dissemination as an e-business.** Knowledge has been recognized as an important organizational asset. It needs to be properly captured, stored, managed, and shared. Knowledge is critical for many e-commerce tasks. Knowledge can be shared in different ways; expert knowledge can be provided to nonexperts (for a fee or free) via a knowledge portal or as a personal service (e.g., via e-mail).

5. **C2C activities.** C2C consists of consumers conducting e-commerce with other consumers, mainly in auctions (such as at eBay), classified ads, matching services, and file sharing.

6. **C-commerce: Definitions and types.** Collaborative commerce (c-commerce) refers to a planned use of digital technology by business partners. It includes planning, designing, researching, managing, and servicing various partners and tasks, frequently along the supply chain. Collaborative commerce can be between different pairs of business partners or among many partners participating in a collaborative network.

7. **Collaboration 2.0.** Collaboration with Web 2.0 tools and in social networks adds a social dimension that could improve communication, participation, and trust. There are many new tools, some of which are being added to traditional collaboration tools. Better collaboration may improve supply chain operation, knowledge management, and performance.

KEY TERMS

QUESTIONS FOR DISCUSSION BY INDIVIDUAL STUDENTS

1. Discuss the advantages and disadvantages of e-government using social networking versus the traditional e-government portal.

2. Discuss the advantages and shortcomings of e-voting.

3. Discuss the advantages and disadvantages of e-books.

4. Discuss the advantages of e-learning in the corporate training environment.

5. In what ways does KM support e-commerce?

6. Why do you think people trade virtual properties online?

7. Some say that B2G is simply B2B. Explain.

8. Compare and contrast B2E with G2E.

9. Which e-government EC activities are intrabusiness activities? Explain why they are intrabusiness.

10. Identify the benefits of G2C to citizens and to governments.

11. Relate IBM's Innovation Jam to KM and social networks.

12. Relate KM to learning, to e-publishing, and to C2C.

TOPICS FOR CLASS DISCUSSION

1. Discuss the advantages of e-learning for an undergraduate student and for an MBA student.

2. Discuss the advantages of expert location systems over corporate databases that contain experts' information and knowledge. What are the disadvantages? Can they be combined? How?

3. Discuss the benefits of using virtual worlds to facilitate learning. What are the limitations? The disadvantages?

4. Will e-books replace traditional paper books?

5. Will e-universities replace universities?

6. Why aren't all firms embracing KM?

INTERNET EXERCISES

1. Enter tamago.us and nextag.com and learn how they operate. What do they offer? Write a report.

2. Enter e-learningcentre.co.uk, elearnmag.org, and elearningpost.com. Identify current issues and find articles related to the effectiveness of e-training. Write a report. Also prepare a list of the resources available on these sites.

3. Enter adobe.com and find the tools it offers for e-learning, knowledge management, and online publishing.

4. Identify a difficult business problem. Post the problem on elance.com, linkedln.com, and answers.com. Summarize the offers to solve the problem.

5. Enter blackboard.com and en.wikipedia.org/wiki/Blackboard and find the major services provided by the company, including its community system. Write a report.

6. Enter oecd.org and identify the studies conducted by the Organization for Economic Cooperation and Development (OECD) on the topic of e-government. What are the organization's major concerns?

7. Enter fcw.com and read the latest news on e-government. Identify initiatives not covered in this chapter. Check the B2G corner. Then enter gcn.com. Finally, enter estrategy.gov. Compare the information presented on the three Web sites.

8. Enter procurement.org and govexec.com. Identify recent e-procurement initiatives and summarize their unique aspects.

9. Enter insight24.com and opentext.com and find the most recent and most popular videos about knowledge management. Prepare a list of five and view one in each category. Prepare a report.

10. Enter learn.gotomeeting.com/forms/G2MC-WBRARC-100208 and find the Webinar titled "How to Build an On-Demand Training Program"

sponsored by Citrix Online. View it (45 minutes) and write a report on what it is and what the benefits are.

11. Enter amazon.com and sony.com and find the latest information about their e-book readers. Compare their capabilities and write a report.

12. Enter wi5connect.com and find what product it has for learning in social networking. Prepare a list of capabilities of each product.

13. Enter kolabora.com or mindjet.com. Find out how collaboration is done. Summarize the benefits of the site to the participants.

14. Enter vignette.com or share360.com and read the company vision for collaborative commerce. Then view the demo. Explain in a report how the company facilitates c-commerce.

TEAM ASSIGNMENTS AND PROJECTS

1. Assign each team to a different country. Each team will explore the e-government offerings of that country. Have each team make a presentation to convince the class that its country's offerings are the most comprehensive. (Exclude Hong Kong and New Zealand.)

2. Create four teams, each representing one of the following: G2C, G2B, G2E, and G2G. Each team will prepare a plan of its major activities in a small country, such as Holland, Denmark, Finland, or Singapore. A fifth team will deal with the coordination and collaboration of all e-government activities in each country. Prepare a report.

3. Have teams search for online universities (e.g., the University of Phoenix, phoenix.edu), Liverpool University in the United Kingdom, or ecollege.com). Write a summary of the schools' e-learning offerings.

4. Have each team represent one of the following sites: netlibrary.com, ebooks.com, and cyberread.com. Each team will examine the technology, legal issues, prices, and business alliances associated with its site. Each team will then prepare a report answering the question, "Will e-books succeed?"

5. Have teams explore KM videos and other resources at portal.brint.com and kmworld.com. Relate them to the topics of this chapter. Prepare a report.

Closing Case

SOCIAL NETWORKING INITIATIVES BY THE NEW ZEALAND GOVERNMENT

For such a small country, the New Zealand government is very active in implementing new technologies. As of 2008, it has created a number of e-government social networking initiatives.

Cross-Government Initiatives

A number of Web 2.0 initiatives have been implemented to help various government agencies and their employees to work together:

▶ **Shared Workspaces.** A suite of online tools that supports information sharing and interagency collaboration, enabling specialist groups and networks to share expertise, experience, and good practices. Over 250 shared workspaces are used in 50 agencies by over 5,000 employees. The major tools are blogs and wikis.

▶ **E-Initiatives Wiki.** An online library of IT projects across government that allows those working on similar projects to share information and experience.

▶ **TiWiki.** The Ministry of Education's collaborative Web site for people from various agencies in the tertiary education sector.

▶ **Principals Electronic Network.** An interactive online community of school principals and school leaders, established as a space for reflection and discussion and to facilitate learning from colleagues' knowledge and expertise.

▶ **Best Practices Forum.** A blog that seeks to provide leadership around best practices in significant work programs, including online authentication, strategy and policy, and Web standards.

▶ **Research e-Labs.** A blog that explores Web trends, open source software, and technology in government. It aims to publish practical technical research and case studies and generate conversations on related topics.

▶ **Sustainable living forums.** A forum provided by government for people to discuss sustainable living and eco-building experiences.

Public Engagement

Most of the government's social networking initiatives have been developed by agencies for the purpose of engaging with the public. The following are key examples:

▶ **Police Act Wiki.** An initiative by the New Zealand Police to encourage public contributions to inform the drafting of the new Policing Act. The wiki was one of a number of initiatives undertaken by the New Zealand Police to enable people to participate in the project. The experiment resulted in thousands of visits and a huge number of ideas and suggestions from the public during a brief time. All were posted publicly online, and this material was provided to the special committee considering submission on the bill.

▶ **National Library of New Zealand.** The National Library has created a number of initiatives. Create Readers is a blog about youth literature and literacy that is run by school services staff around the country. On the Library TechNZ blog, Web development staff share their thoughts about work progress on the National Library's technology. The 2007 New Zealand Poet Laureate has a blog where she shares her own poetry news and events. In addition, portions of the National Library's image collection are posted on Flickr with the aim of helping people discover new material.

▶ **Web Standards wiki.** A collaborative space in which to share knowledge and make suggestions on the New Zealand Government Web Standards. These standards exist to ensure that government Web sites are accessible regardless of a user's computer literacy level, Web browser, mobile device, or connection speed.

▶ **Participation Project wiki.** A vehicle for collaborative policy making developed by the State Services Commission. This wiki attracted comments from more than 1,200 people over eight days during the process of developing the Guide to Online Participation—far more input than had ever been received from a conventional public forum.

▶ **NZAID Field blog.** A forum for staff of New Zealand's international aid and development agency to write about their experiences as they travel on New Zealand–funded projects and to discuss issues relevant to development work.

▶ **Ministry for Culture and Heritage.** The Ministry for Culture and Heritage offers Lively, a blog for "everyone involved in New Zealand's cultural sector," with topics such as identity, social media, and cultural research. New Zealand History Online discussion forums offer community forums on specific topics. Selected images of New Zealand from Te Ara, the Encyclopedia of New Zealand, are posted on Flickr, where users can comment and post their own photos.

▶ **Ministry for the Environment.** The Ministry for the Environment offers a discussion forum where visitors can post comments on topics related to energy, water, rubbish, and reducing adverse impacts on the environment. It also offers a Web site for people to show (and share with others) their films about what sustainability means to them. The films are posted on the Ministry for the Environment's YouTube page. The Sustainability Challenge group in Facebook encourages people to post ideas about steps that can be taken to reduce adverse impacts on the environment.

▶ **Ministry of Youth Development.** The Ministry's ID360 short-film competition provides an opportunity for young people to tell their stories through films about what identity and diversity means to them. The films are posted on YouTube with links from the Ministry's Web site, and the public are invited to vote and comment on them. The Ministry also offers an online forum and blog for young people to discuss various topics and ideas about community participation.

▶ **Families Commission.** The Families Commission set up "The Couch" to hear the views of New Zealanders on issues relating to families. It is part of a wider community engagement program in which the commission seeks feedback from families, as well as community groups and organizations, through forums and meetings. The responses from polls and questionnaires help in advocacy work to improve services and support for families, and improve advice on proposed government policies

▶ **ePetitions.** A Wellington City Council initiative to allow anyone to make suggestions relevant to Council business via the Internet and for others to endorse them. Petitioners can provide links to background information to support their cases.

▶ **Audio Visual wiki.** An Archives of New Zealand initiative to enable the public to view films online, add information about the content or context of the films, and discuss them with other users.

Other Agency-Related Social Media Initiatives

Agencies are also using social networking tools in collaboration with nongovernment organizations. In some instances, intermediaries are using them on behalf of agencies; in others, an agency's relationship with the service being provided is not made explicit. The following are examples of such initiatives:

▶ **Wikipedia.** Nearly every New Zealand government agency has a listing on this site (many of which are quite extensive). However, these public profiles may not have been created, monitored, or managed by New Zealand government agencies.

▶ **Business online discussion groups.** Discussion groups accessed via *business.govt.nz* are in fact hosted by a private company, which in turn has relationships with the various subject experts who comment on postings.

▶ **LG Online Groups.** A Web forum and shared workspace for local government personnel to communicate about best practices and seek responses to general inquiries.

▶ **100% Pure New Zealand.** A layer on Google Earth provided by Tourism New Zealand. Google Earth provides geographic information by combining satellite imagery, maps, terrain information, and 3D building imagery. Anyone can write articles in Wikipedia or post photos in Panoramio, videos in YouTube, or comments in Google Earth Community and "geotag" them with coordinates so they appear in the Google Earth layer. This enables a user to browse other people's comments, photographs, and posts about a particular place.

Sources: Compiled from New Zealand E-Government (2008a and 2008b).

Questions

1. Given the richness of New Zealand's offerings, do you believe that the portal style of e-government will disappear?
2. What are the benefits of the internal initiatives?
3. Comment of the connections to YouTube, Flickr, and Facebook.
4. Why do wikis and blogs play an important role in many of these initiatives?
5. Which alternatives are related to e-learning? In what ways?

ONLINE RESOURCES
available at pearsonhighered.com/turban

Online Files

W6.1 Application Case: A Decade of E-Government Development in Hong Kong (1998 to 2009)
W6.2 Key Issues and Trends of E-Government Development and Implementation
W6.3 The Driving Forces of E-Learning
W6.4 Application Case: E-Learning at Cisco Systems
W6.5 Preventing E-Learning Failures
W6.6 Application Case: Online Global Learning Center at W. R. Grace
W6.7 Education-Related Activities in Second Life
W6.8 Types of E-Books
W6.9 Application Case: Leightons Opticians Sees the Value of Collaborative Hubs
W6.10 Application Case: Webcor Builders Goes Online with Its Partners
W6.11 Application Case: Cadence Design Systems: Deploying a Corporate Portal on Its Intranet

Comprehensive Educational Web Sites

e-learningcentre.co.uk: A vast collection of selected and reviewed links to e-learning resources.
wwwords.co.uk/elea: An e-learning journal and comprehensive portal.
metakm.com: A portal for KM.
tools.kmnetwork.com: A portal on KM tools and techniques.
portal.brint.com: A portal for KM.
kmworld.com: A collection of KM solutions.
egov.vic.gov.au: A major resource center on e-government.
updates.zdnet.com/tags/e-government.html: White papers, case studies, technical articles, and blog posts relating to e-government
forums.e-democracy.org: A portal focused on e-democracy.
egov.gov: Official e-government site of the U.S. government.

Part 4: Other EC Models and Applications

THE WEB 2.0 ENVIRONMENT AND SOCIAL NETWORKS

Content

Learning Objectives

Upon completion of this chapter, you will be able to:

1. Understand the Web 2.0 revolution, social and business networks, and industry and market disruptors.

2. Understand the concept, structure, types, and issues of virtual communities.

3. Understand social networking and social network services sites.

4. Describe some of the major social networks.

5. Describe business-oriented and enterprise social networks.

6. Understand the commercial aspects of social networking.

7. Describe Web 2.0 entertainment.

8. Describe the potential of Web 3.0 and Web 4.0.

WIKIPEDIA AND ITS PROBLEMS OF CONTENT, QUALITY, AND PRIVACY PROTECTION

The Problem

Wikipedia is a free online collaborative encyclopedia. In September 2009, it had over 12 million articles in over 262 languages and generated some 80 million hits per day. By comparison, Wikipedia is 100 times bigger than the *Encyclopedia Britannica*, which contains 120,000 articles.

Wikipedia's greatest strength is also its biggest weakness. Users create the content; therefore, sometimes people with no special expertise in their chosen topics or people with malicious agendas post so-called "facts." For instance, once a contributor to an article on Pope Benedict substituted the Pontiff's photo with that of Emperor Palpatine from the *Star Wars* films. According to Farrell (2007), Microsoft paid experts to write information about the company that was later found to be inaccurate.

In another, more serious, example, a contributor made the accusation that distinguished journalist and long-time civil rights advocate John Seigenthaler had been involved in the assassinations of President John Kennedy and his brother Bobby Kennedy. The contributor practically fabricated the entire article. Seigenthaler pursued legal action against the anonymous Wikipedia contributor, via the poster's IP address, and charged the unidentified accuser with defamation. For Seigenthaler, Wikipedia is "populated by volunteer vandals with poison-pen intellects" and should not be permitted to exist in its current form.

Another problem is invasion of privacy. Even if information about a certain individual or company is correct (i.e., it is not defamatory), the individual may not want the information to be made public. Because most contributors do not ask permission from those they are writing about, an invasion of privacy occurs. Yet, another problem is that the bulk of Wikipedia is written by only 1,400 of its more than 100,000 contributors (see Blodget 2009), introducing possible bias.

The Solution

In order to avoid false or misleading entries, the Wikimedia Foundation, which operates Wikipedia, along with several other wiki initiatives (such as Wikibooks), has promoted several alternatives to improve the quality of Wikipedia articles. The first step was the creation of a more formal advisory board. The second step was to empower system administrators to block access to the site to certain users who repeatedly vandalized entries. Next, the process of handling complaints was improved.

Ultimately, the owners plan to change the site to Wikipedia 2.0 and are considering the following three options:

1. The editing of mediocre Wikipedia articles by experts in the specific field; especially the use of quality art editors to improve Wikipedia's humanities coverage.

2. The creation of original articles from the ground up. According to Larry Sanger, one of Wikipedia's cofounders, this could provide a more distinctive culture that will provide more pride in the articles. In this case, the name of the site would change to *citizendium*.

3. Make the users' policy more interactive. Wikipedia is asking readers to notify the company whenever they read inaccurate or incomplete content.

The Results

While the Seigenthaler issue was debated in fall 2005, early quality measures were instituted, and the site's founder, Jimmy Wales, appeared on CNN with Seigenthaler in December 2005. During this time, traffic to Wikipedia nearly tripled, mostly due to the publicity of the CNN presentation and the subsequent publicity in newspapers and TV. Yet problems still exist, with continued complaints against both inaccurate content and privacy invasion. And, after years of enormous growth, the rate of editing articles, new account registration, user blocks, article protection and deletion, and uploads have all declined. In addition, in 2008 Google launched a potential Wikipedia competitor with its service called Knol.

Sources: Compiled from Blodget (2009) and Farrell (2007).

WHAT WE CAN LEARN . . .

The Wikipedia case illustrates a *wiki*, a collaborative online encyclopedia jointly written by volunteers. Murray-Buechner (2006) lists it as one of the 25 sites "we cannot live without" and labeled it as a "real Web wonder." It is a typical Web 2.0 application; it is done for people by people. Also, it illustrates the phenomenon of the "wisdom of the crowd"; namely, many people contributing their knowledge to create better resources and to solve problems. Finally, it is a wiki where people jointly create a knowledge document, editing, modifying, and adding to the contributions of others.

Many companies are now using a similar concept internally; for example, the pharmaceutical company Pfizer implemented an internal wiki, called Pfizerpedia, to accumulate knowledge about its pharmaceutical products and research. Many other companies use the wisdom of its employees to create corporate knowledge bases.

The Wikipedia case illustrates both the benefits to society and the problems of content created by volunteers. The Wikipedia case also illustrates the potential risk of invasion of privacy, potential of litigation against a site, and the need for financial viability, especially when money is needed to check the content people contribute.

This chapter examines several Web 2.0 applications, namely virtual communities and social networking, and their impact on the way we live and do business. Specific companies, such as LinkedIn, Facebook, YouTube, Twitter, and Flickr, which have already changed the work and/or lives of millions of people, also are discussed. Finally, the chapter describes the commercialization of social networking and its major implementation issues.

7.1   THE WEB 2.0 REVOLUTION, SOCIAL MEDIA, AND INDUSTRY DISRUPTORS

This chapter deals with the newest areas of EC—social networks and other Web 2.0 applications. Let's see what it is all about.

WHAT IS WEB 2.0?

Web 2.0 is the popular term for describing advanced Web technologies and applications, including blogs, microblogs, wikis, RSS, mashups, user-generated content, and social networks. A major objective of Web 2.0 is to enhance creativity, information sharing, and collaboration.

One of the most significant differences between Web 2.0 and the traditional Web is the greater collaboration among Internet users and other users, content providers, and enterprises. As an umbrella term for an emerging core of technologies, trends, and principles, Web 2.0 is not only changing what is on the Web, but also how it works. Web 2.0 concepts have led to the evolution of Web-based virtual communities and their hosting services, such as social networking sites, video-sharing sites, and more. Many believe that companies that understand these new applications and technologies—and apply the capabilities early on—stand to greatly improve internal business processes and marketing. Among the biggest advantages is better collaboration with customers, partners, and suppliers, as well as among internal users (see the opening case about Eastern Mountain Sports in Chapter 2, en.wikipedia.org/wiki/WEB_2.0, and web2.socialcomputingjournal.com).

Web 2.0
The popular term for advanced Internet technology and applications, including blogs, wikis, RSS, and social bookmarking. One of the most significant differences between Web 2.0 and the traditional World Wide Web is greater collaboration among Internet users and other users, content providers, and enterprises.

REPRESENTATIVE CHARACTERISTICS OF WEB 2.0

The following are representative characteristics of the Web 2.0 environment:

> ▶ The ability to tap into the collective intelligence of users. The more users contribute, the more popular and valuable a Web 2.0 site becomes.
> ▶ Data is made available in new or never-intended ways. Web 2.0 data can be remixed or "mashed up," often through Web service interfaces, much the way a dance-club DJ mixes music.
> ▶ Web 2.0 relies on user-generated and user-controlled content and data.
> ▶ Lightweight programming techniques and tools let nearly anyone act as a Web site developer.
> ▶ The virtual elimination of software-upgrade cycles makes everything a *perpetual beta* or work in progress and allows rapid prototyping, using the Web as an application development platform.
> ▶ Users can access applications entirely through a browser.
> ▶ An architecture of participation and *digital democracy* encourages users to add value to the application as they use it.
> ▶ A major emphasis on social networks and computing.
> ▶ Strong support of information sharing and collaboration.
> ▶ Rapid and continuous creation of new business models.

Other important features of Web 2.0 are its dynamic content, rich user experience, metadata, scalability, open source basis, and freedom (net neutrality).

Most Web 2.0 applications have a rich, interactive, user-friendly interface based on Ajax (Asynchronous JavaScript and XML) or a similar framework. Ajax is an effective and efficient Web development technique for creating interactive Web applications. The intent is to make Web pages feel more responsive by exchanging small amounts of data with the server behind the scenes so that the entire Web page does not have to be reloaded each time the user makes a change. This is meant to increase the Web page's interactivity, loading speed, and usability.

WEB 2.0 COMPANIES AND NEW BUSINESS MODELS

A major characteristic of Web 2.0 is the global spreading of innovative Web sites and start-up companies. As soon as a successful idea is deployed as a Web site in one country, other similar sites appear around the globe. This section presents some of these sites. Others appear in different chapters of this book. For example, approximately 120 companies specialize in providing Twitter-like services in dozens of countries. An excellent source for material on Web 2.0 is Search CIO's *Executive Guide: Web 2.0* (see searchcio.techtarget. com/general/0,295582,sid19_gci1244339,00.html#glossary).

A new business model that has emerged from Web 2.0 is the accumulation of the "power of the crowd," which was discussed in Chapters 2 and 6. The potential of such a business model is unlimited. For example, wikia.com is working on community-developed Web searches. If they can create a successful one, Google may be in trouble. A key feature of the new business model is participation, the architecture of which is shown in Online File W7.1.

Many companies provide the technology for Web 2.0 activities (see the list of activities in Chapter 2), and dozens of firms have emerged as providers of infrastructure and services for social networking. A large number of start-ups appeared in 2005–2009. For a guide to the 25 hottest Web 2.0 companies and the powerful trends that are driving them, see money.cnn.com/magazines/business2/business2_archive/2007/03/01/8401042/index.htm.

Several start-ups created new business models. For example, Joost.com invented a P2P service that sends broadcast-quality video over the Internet (disrupting television providers). One of the major phenomena of Web 2.0 is the rise of mass social media.

SOCIAL MEDIA

Social media refers to the online platforms and tools that people use to share opinions, experiences, insights, and perceptions with each other. Social media can take many different forms, including text, images, audio, or video. The key is that *users,* rather than organizations, control and use the media, often at little or no cost. It is a powerful force of democratization; the network structure enables communication and collaboration on a massive scale. For details on social media, see web2.socialcomputingjournal.com.

Exhibit 7.1 depicts the emergence and rise of mass social media, comparing traditional media with social media. It describes the new tools of social media (e.g., blogs, video blogs, etc.) as being under the consumer's control. With social media, content is produced and consumed by the users. This is in contrast to traditional media, whereby content is created by a company and pushed to or observed by the users.

Social media and Web 2.0 tools may act as market disruptors.

social media
The online platforms and tools that people use to share opinions, experiences, insights, perceptions, and various media, including photos, videos, and music, with each other.

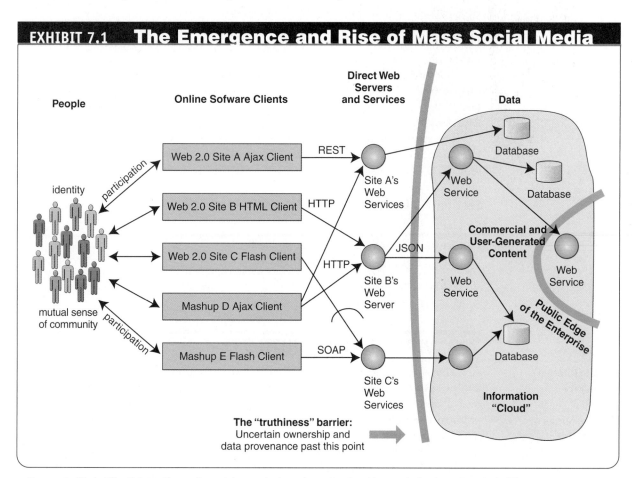

EXHIBIT 7.1   The Emergence and Rise of Mass Social Media

Source: D. Hinchcliffe, *Web 2.0 Blog*, web2.socialcomputingjournal.com. Reprinted by permission from Dion Hinchcliffe.

disruptors
Companies that introduce a significant change in their industries, thus causing a disruption in normal business operations.

INDUSTRY AND MARKET DISRUPTORS

Several companies have introduced Web 2.0 innovations that could disrupt and reorder markets, or even entire industries, introducing major changes in the way companies do business. Some refer to such companies as **disruptors**.

Example 1. Zopa (us.zopa.com), which facilitates person-to-person money lending, may disrupt the lending business (see Online File W7.2). Consumer-generated content is disrupting traditional media. Specifically, large numbers of blogs and videos are posted everyday and then viewed by millions around the globe. Content is created continuously by millions of people. The result is that individuals are becoming both publishers of Web-based content and consumers of that content.

Example 2: Real Estate Industry Disruptors. Companies such as Zillow (zillow.com) and HomeGain (homegain.com) are disrupting the real estate industry, providing more services and information than their Web 1.0 counterparts, such as realtor.com and realtytrac.com.

At zillow.com, users can get an estimate of their homes' market value. The market value estimate can be changed by adding extra features to the house's profile. In addition, Zillow provides neighborhood maps that show the estimated values of other homes in the neighborhood (see Team Assignments and Projects at the end of this chapter). Users can also list their homes for free. The service is good not only for sellers. Buyers can use Zillow to buy a house that is not even on the market, avoiding open houses and bidding wars, and get it cheaper by avoiding commissions.

Will real estate agents become extinct? Some will. More likely, the 6 percent realtor commission paid in the United States will move closer to the 1 percent commission commonly paid in other countries.

Many other disruptors exist. For the description of 15 disruptors that Schonfeld and Morrison (2007) believe will change the world, such as Blinkx, Zipcar, and Expensr, see money.cnn.com/magazines/business2/business2_archive/2007/09/01/100169862/index.htm.

The major applications of Web 2.0 are social networks such as MySpace and Facebook. These are based on the concept of *virtual communities*, the topic we present next.

Section 7.1 ▶ REVIEW QUESTIONS

1. Define Web 2.0.
2. List the major characteristics of Web 2.0.
3. Identify the major Web 2.0 technologies.
4. Define social media.
5. What is a disruptor? Provide an example.

7.2 VIRTUAL COMMUNITIES

virtual (Internet) community
A group of people with similar interests who interact with one another using the Internet.

A *community* is a group of people with common interests who interact with one another. A **virtual (Internet) community** is one in which the interaction takes place over a computer network, mainly the Internet. Virtual communities parallel typical physical communities, such as neighborhoods, clubs, or associations, but people do not meet face-to-face. Instead, they meet online. A virtual community is a social network organized around a common interest, idea, task, or goal; members interact across time, geographic location, and organizational boundaries to develop personal

EXHIBIT 7.2	Elements of Interaction in a Virtual Community
Category	**Element**
Communication	Bulletin boards (discussion groups)
	Chat rooms/threaded discussions (string Q&A)
	E-mail and instant messaging and wireless messages
	Private mailboxes
	Newsletters, "netzines" (electronic magazines)
	Blogging, wikis, and mashups
	Web postings
	Voting
Information	Directories and yellow pages
	Search engine
	Member-generated content
	Links to information sources
	Expert advice
EC element	Electronic catalogs and shopping carts
	Advertisements
	Auctions of all types
	Classified ads
	Bartering online

relationships. Virtual communities offer several ways for members to interact, collaborate, and trade (see Exhibit 7.2). Similar to the EC click-and-mortar model, many physical communities have Web sites to support Internet-related activities that supplement physical activities.

CHARACTERISTICS OF TRADITIONAL ONLINE COMMUNITIES AND THEIR CLASSIFICATION

Many thousands of communities exist on the Internet, and the number is growing rapidly. Pure-play Internet communities may have thousands, or even hundreds of millions, of members. MySpace (see Case 1.2 in Chapter 1) grew to 100 million members in just one year. This is one major difference from traditional purely physical communities, which usually are smaller. Another difference is that offline communities frequently are confined to one geographic location, whereas only a few online communities are geographically confined. For more information on virtual communities, see en.wikipedia.org/wiki/Virtual_community.

Types of Communities

The major types of online communities are provided in Online File W7.3. Some popular categories of communities with examples follow.

Public Versus Private Communities. Communities can be designated as *public*, meaning that their membership is open to anyone. The owner of the community may be a privately held corporation or a public one. Most of the social networks, including MySpace and Facebook, belong to the public category.

In contrast, *private* communities belong to a company, an association, or a group of companies, and their membership is limited to people who meet certain requirements (e.g., work for a particular employer or work in a particular profession). Private communities may be internal (e.g., only employees can be members) or external.

Example: IBM's Virtual Universe Community. This is a private, internal community of over 5,500 individuals (in January 2009) who are active in virtual worlds. It was launched in 2006 with the goal of moving IBM into a range of new and profitable industries, from the creation of IBM mainframes for virtual worlds to 24-hour virtual service desks staffed by avatars.

Internal and External Private Communities. *Internal communities* exist within organizations. Such communities include employees, retirees, suppliers, and customers who share a common interest. The focus of such communities is on knowledge sharing, collaboration, expert location, and knowledge creation. Companies such as Pfizer, FedEx, Caterpillar, Wells Fargo, and IBM have such communities.

External private communities include one organization and its business partners, government agencies, and prospects. The participants share information on a variety of issues. For example, customers may collaborate around product issues. External private communities have fewer restrictions with regard to participation and security than do internal communities. External communities are used for collaboration, market research, product innovation, or improved customer and supplier support.

Example: A Virtual World Community. In 2008, Sony launched a virtual community service for its PlayStation 3 (PS3) video game network, which attracted 8 million members in its first year. The 3D service called Home allows users to create avatars, decorate homes, and interact and socialize with other users in a virtual world. Sony considers this an important part of the game-playing experience. Avatars can interact with each other, and users can play games with friends at a virtual arcade. The community is regional due to language and cultural considerations. As an extension, the service allows downloading of content and movies to the PS3.

Other Classifications of Virtual Communities

Virtual communities can be classified in several other ways. One possibility is to classify the members as *traders, players, just friends, enthusiasts,* or *friends in need.* A more common classification recognizes six types of Internet communities: (1) transaction, (2) purpose or interest, (3) relations or practices, (4) fantasy, (5) social networks, and (6) virtual worlds. Exhibit 7.3 explains and provides examples of these communities. For issues of participation and design of communities, see en.wikipedia.org/wiki/Virtual_community.

Section 7.2 ▶ REVIEW QUESTIONS

1. Define virtual (Internet) communities and describe their characteristics.
2. List the major types of virtual communities. (Hint: Consult Online File W7.3.)
3. Distinguish between private and public communities.
4. Distinguish between internal and external communities.

EXHIBIT 7.3   Types of Virtual Communities

Community Type	Description
Transaction and other business activities	Facilitate buying and selling (e.g., *ausfish.com.au*). Combine an information portal with an infrastructure for trading. Members are buyers, sellers, intermediaries, etc., who are focused on a specific commercial area (e.g., fishing).
Purpose or interest	No trading, just exchange of information on a topic of mutual interest. Examples: Investors consult The Motley Fool (*fool.com*) for investment advice; rugby fans congregate at the Fans Room at *nrl.com*; music lovers go to *mp3.com*; *geocities.yahoo.com* is a collection of several areas of interest in one place.
Relations or practices	Members are organized around certain life experiences. Examples: *ivillage.com* caters to women, and *seniornet.com* is for senior citizens. Professional communities also belong to this category. Example: *isworld.org* is a space for information systems faculty, students, and professionals.
Fantasy	Members share imaginary environments. Examples: sport fantasy teams at *espn.com*; GeoCities members can pretend to be medieval barons at *dir.yahoo.com/Recreation/games/role_playing_games/titles*. See *games.yahoo.com* for many more fantasy communities.
Social networks	Members communicate, collaborate, create, share, form groups, entertain, and more. MySpace.com is the leader.
Virtual worlds	Members use avatars to represent them in a simulated 3D environment where they can play, conduct business, socialize, and fantasize. Second Life (*secondlife.com*) is currently the most well-known virtual world.

7.3 ONLINE SOCIAL NETWORKING: BASICS AND EXAMPLES

Social networking is built on the idea that there is determinable structure to how people know each other and interact. The basic premise is that social networking gives people the power to share, making the world more open and connected. Although social networking is usually practiced in social networks such as MySpace and Facebook, aspects of it also are found in Wikipedia and YouTube.

Let's first define social networks and then look at some of the services they provide and their capabilities.

A DEFINITION AND BASIC INFORMATION

A *social network* as a place where people create their own space, or homepage, on which they write blogs (Web logs); post pictures, videos, or music; share ideas; and link to other Web locations they find interesting. In addition, members of social networks can tag the content they create and post it with keywords they choose themselves, which makes the content searchable. The mass adoption of social networking Web sites points to an evolution in human social interaction.

Social networking includes social networks and activities conducted there. It also includes activities conducted using Web 2.0 (e.g., wikis, microblogs) not within social networks.

social networking
Social networks and activities conducted in social networks. It also includes activities conducted using Web 2.0 (e.g., wikis, microblogs) not within social networks.

A lengthy list of the characteristics and capabilities of social networks was provided in Section 1.3.

The Size of Social Network Sites

Social network sites are growing rapidly, with some having over 100 million members. The typical annual growth of a successful site is 40 to 50 percent in the first few years and 15 to 25 percent thereafter. For a list of the major sites, including user counts, see en.wikipedia.org/wiki/List_of_social_networking_websites. Exhibit 7.4 shows the size of some major social networks as of January 2009. Note that many changes take place in a short amount of time. For example, by June 2010 Facebook had more than 450,000,000 members and LinkedIn had grown to 70,000,000.

New Business Models

Social networking sites provide innovative business models, ranging from customer reviews of food and night life in India (mumbai.burrp.com) to users who dress up dolls that look like celebrities (stardoll.com). New revenue models are being created daily. Although some generate limited revenue, others succeed wildly.

Many communities attract advertisers. For example, Vivapets (vivapets.com) attracts pet lovers with Wikipedia-like contributions in its quest to catalog every pet breed. The site attracts about 300,000 unique visitors per month. Obviously, pet-food-related vendors are willing to place ads there.

Social Network Analysis Software

social network analysis (SNA)
The mapping and measuring of relationships and information flows among people, groups, organizations, computers, and other information- or knowledge-processing entities. The nodes in the network are the people and groups, whereas the links show relationships or flows between the nodes. SNAs provide both visual and a quantitative analysis of relationships.

Social network analysis (SNA) is software used to identify, represent, analyze, visualize, or simulate network nodes (e.g., agents, organizations, or knowledge) and edges (relationships) from various types of input data (relational and nonrelational),

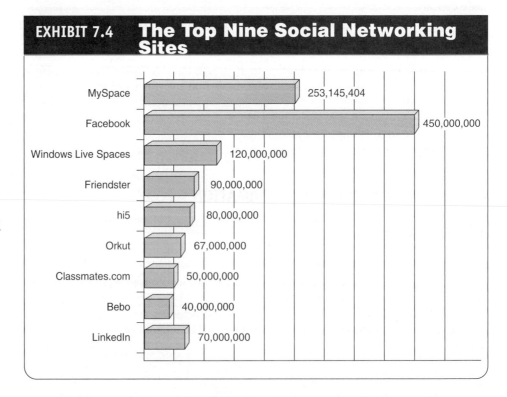

EXHIBIT 7.4   The Top Nine Social Networking Sites

Site	Members
MySpace	253,145,404
Facebook	450,000,000
Windows Live Spaces	120,000,000
Friendster	90,000,000
hi5	80,000,000
Orkut	67,000,000
Classmates.com	50,000,000
Bebo	40,000,000
LinkedIn	70,000,000

including mathematical models of social networks. Various input and output file formats exist.

Network analysis tools enable researchers to investigate representations of networks of different forms and different sizes, from small (e.g., families, project teams) to very large. Visual representations of social networks are popular and important to understand network data and to convey the results of the analysis.

Some of the representative tools that enable such presentations are:

▶ Business-oriented social network tools such as InFlow and NetMiner
▶ Social Networks Visualizer, or SocNetV, which is a Linux-based open source package

For details, see en.wikipedia.org/wiki/Social_network_analysis_software.

Now let's look at several social networks and sites that provide social networking services.

REPRESENTATIVE SOCIAL NETWORKS SITES AND SERVICES

Here, we provide a sampling of representative social networking sites. Additional information is available at pcworld.com/article/142700/the_right_social_network_for_you.html. Some social networking sites are discussed in more detail in Section 7.4. One of the most popular social networking services is YouTube, which is described in detail in Online File W7.4. It is having a major impact on the media and advertising industries. Some other specific sites include the following.

Classmates Online

Classmates Online (classmates.com) helps members find, connect, and keep in touch with friends and acquaintances they have made throughout their lives, from kindergarten through college to work and the U.S. military. Classmates Online has more than 40 million active members in the United States and Canada.

The site's basic membership is free and allows users to list themselves to be found and to search the Classmates Online database for friends. Basic members may also post photographs, announcements, and biographies; read community message boards; and learn about upcoming reunions. Gold members, who pay a fee, can also send an e-mail to any member, use Web site tools for planning reunions and events, form private groups, and use My Network to communicate with friends.

The site is owned by United Online, which also operates social networking sites in Germany and Sweden. The site is profitable, generating income from advertisements and membership fees.

Xanga

Xanga (xanga.com), which is operated by Xanga.com, Inc., hosts blogs, photoblogs, and social networking profiles. Users of Xanga are referred to as "Xangans." Xanga's origins can be traced back to 1999, when it was launched as a site for sharing book and music reviews. It has since evolved into one of the most popular blogging and networking services on the Web, with an estimated 40 million users worldwide.

A *blogring* connects a circle of Weblogs with a common focus or theme. All Xanga users are given the ability to create a new blogring or join an existing one. Blogrings are searchable by topic. A list of blogrings that the user is associated with appears in a module, typically on the left side of the Web site. Each user is allowed a maximum of eight blogrings.

Digg

Digg (digg.com) is a community-based popularity Web site with an emphasis on technology and science articles (see en.wikipedia.org/wiki/Digg). The site expanded in 2008 to provide a variety of other categories, including politics and videos. It combines social bookmarking, blogging, and syndication with a form of nonhierarchical, democratic editorial control. Users submit news stories and Web sites, and then a user-controlled ranking system promotes these stories and sites to the front page. This differs from the hierarchical editorial system that many other news sites employ. When users read news items, they have the option to "digg it" or "digg that."

Readers can view all the stories that fellow users have submitted in the "digg/All/ Upcoming" section of the site. Once a story has received enough "diggs," it appears on Digg's front page. Should the story not receive enough diggs, or if enough users report a problem with the submission, the story will remain in the "digg all" area, from which it may eventually be removed. For additional details, see en.wikipedia.org/ wiki/Digg.

Many social networking sites are strongly related to mobile devices and networks, which we'll discuss next.

MOBILE SOCIAL NETWORKING

mobile social networking

Members converse and connect with one another using cell phones or other mobile devices.

Mobile social networking refers to social networking where members converse and connect with one another using cell phones or other mobile devices. A current trend for social networking Web sites such as MySpace and Facebook is to offer mobile services. Some social networking sites offer mobile-only services (e.g., Brightkite [brightkite.com]).

There are two basic types of mobile social networks. The first type is companies that partner with wireless carriers to distribute their communities via the default start pages on cell phone browsers. For example, users can access MySpace via Cingular's wireless network (now AT&T wireless; [wireless.att.com]). The second type is companies that do not have such carrier relationships (also known as "off deck") and rely on other methods to attract users. Examples of this second type include MocoSpace (mocospace.com) and Peperonity (peperonity.com).

Windows Live Spaces Mobile can be viewed on mobile devices with limited screen size and slow data connections. It allows users to browse and add photos, blog entries, and comments directly from their mobile devices. However, it has also introduced several other features to improve the user experience with handheld devices. For more information on Windows Live Spaces Mobile, see mobile.spaces.live.com and en.wikipedia.org/ wiki/Windows_Live_Spaces_Mobiles.

Mobile social networking is much more popular in Japan, South Korea, and China than it is in the West, generally due to better mobile networks and data pricing (flat rates are widespread in Japan). Experts predict that mobile social networks will experience explosive growth, increasing from 50 million members in 2006 to 607.5 million in 2013 (Ankeny 2009). For more predictions, see emarketer.com/reports. The explosion of mobile Web 2.0 services and companies means that many social networks can be based from cell phones and other portable devices, extending the reach of such networks to the millions of people who lack regular or easy access to computers.

With the current software that is available, interactions within mobile social networks are not limited to exchanging simple text messages on a one-to-one basis. In many cases, they are evolving toward the sophisticated interactions of Internet virtual communities.

Mobile Enterprise Networks

Several companies have developed (or fully sponsor) mobile-based social networks. For example, in 2007 Coca-Cola created a social network that could only be accessed by cell phones in an attempt to lure young people to its sodas and other products.

Mobile Community Activities

In many mobile social networks, members can use their mobile devices to create their profiles, make friends, participate in chat rooms, create chat rooms, hold private conversations, and share photos, videos, and blogs. Some companies provide wireless services that allow their customers to build their own mobile community and brand it (e.g., Sonopia at sonopia.com).

Mobile video sharing, which is sometimes combined with photo sharing, is a new technological and social trend. Mobile video-sharing portals are becoming popular (e.g., see myubo.com and myzenplanet.com). Many social networking sites are offering mobile features. For example, MySpace has partnership agreements with a number of U.S. wireless providers to support its MySpace Mobile service. Similarly, Facebook is available in both the United States and Canada via a number of wireless carriers. Bebo has joined forces with O2 Wireless in the United Kingdom and Ireland. This phenomenon is just the next step in the race to establish access to social networking sites across multiple mediums. Some argue that these deals do more to sell mobile phones than to promote the social networking sites; however, the social networks are more than happy to collect the residual attention.

Section 7.3 ▶ REVIEW QUESTIONS

1. Define social network.
2. List some major social network sites.
3. Describe the global nature of social networks.
4. Discuss how social networking can drive new business models.
5. Describe mobile social networking.

7.4 MAJOR SOCIAL NETWORK COMPANIES: FROM FACEBOOK TO FLICKR

Now that you are familiar with social network services, let's take a closer look at some of the most popular ones.

FACEBOOK: THE NETWORK EFFECT

Facebook (facebook.com), which was launched in 2004 by former Harvard student Mark Zuckerberg, is probably largest social network service in the world, with more than 450 million active users worldwide as of June 2010. When Zuckerberg first created Facebook, he had very strong social ambitions and wanted to help people connect to others on the Web.

A primary reason why Facebook has expanded so rapidly is the network effect—more users mean more value. As more users become involved in the social space, more people are available to connect with. Initially, Facebook was an online social space for college and high school students that automatically connected students to other students at the same school. However, Facebook realized that it could only keep college and university users for four years. In 2006, Facebook opened its doors to anyone age 13 or older with a valid e-mail address. Expanding to a global audience has enabled Facebook to compete directly with MySpace.

The lack of privacy controls (e.g., tools that restrict who sees your profile) was the biggest reason why many people initially resisted joining Facebook. However, in 2008 Facebook introduced controls enabling users to set different levels of access to information about themselves for each of their groups (e.g., family, friends from school, friends from work). For example, only close friends might see your mobile phone number, music favorites, e-mail address, and so forth, whereas other friends might only see the basics of your résumé (Abram and Pearlman 2008).

Today, Facebook has a number of applications that support photos, groups, events, marketplaces, posted items, and notes. Facebook also has an application called "People You May Know," which helps users connect with people they might know. More applications are being added constantly. A special feature on Facebook is the News Feed, which enables users to track the activities of friends in their social circles. For example, when a user changes his or her profile, the updates are broadcast to others who subscribe to the feed. Users can also develop their own applications or use any of the millions of Facebook applications that have been developed by other users.

Facebook is expanding to the rest of the world. In fact, two-thirds of its members are from outside the United States. Even Chinese Premier Wen Jiabao created a profile, and within two weeks had more supporters than President Bush. Facebook has adopted a wiki-like approach to translate itself into other languages: Specialists first collect thousands of English words and phrases throughout the site and then members are invited to translate those bits of text into another language. Members then rate the translations, until a consensus is reached. For example, the Spanish version was completed by about 1,500 volunteers in less than a month. The German version was prepared by 2,000 volunteers in less than two weeks. In early March 2008, Facebook invited French members to help out. They finished the translations in a few days. The team is continuing to translate to other languages, even relatively rare ones.

To generate revenue, Facebook supports advertising for businesses and for developers who offer tools for building applications. In June 2009, Facebook finally had a positive cash flow.

In December 2008, Facebook introduced Facebook Connect, which enables users to log in to other sites (e.g., to CitySearch) using their Facebook IDs and to share their activities from these third-party sites with their Facebook friends. For the basics of Facebook and its enterprise efforts, see Abram and Pearlman (2008). For current information, see insidefacebook.com. For a case study, see startup-review.com/blog/facebook-case-study-offline-behavior-drives-online-usage.php.

BEBO

Bebo (bebo.com), an acronym for the phrase "blog early, blog often," was launched in January 2005 and quickly become one of the foremost social networking platforms. Michael and Xochi Birch met in a London bar and started four online businesses that either failed or were minor successes before developing Bebo. Michael, a physicist, was the CEO and in charge of programming, and Xochi handled finance and customer relations. Acknowledging that they had neither business qualifications nor any grasp of marketing, they relied on word of mouth for the Web site's popularity. Based in San Francisco, Bebo boasts more than 40 million users who generate billions of page views per month.

Bebo was acquired by AOL for $850 million in March 2008, placing the site alongside MySpace and YouTube, which also were acquired by media conglomerates for enormous sums of money despite possessing mostly intangible property. Similar to Facebook and MySpace, Bebo provides a canvas for users to display personal profiles using such media as photos, diaries, music, embedded video, commercial applications, quizzes, and so forth. It allows its users to add other users as friends who can then view their profiles and post messages. Bebo adopts a private setting whenever a new friend is added, limiting the friend's access to information on the user's profile unless the owner grants special authorization. This tactic ensures more privacy for its users, which has been an issue with social networking sites.

In November 2007, Bebo allowed dozens of business partners (e.g., CBS, BBC, MTV, ESPN) to link to its millions of registered members free of charge. Partners can use Bebo's "channel profiles" to determine how their content is delivered and to encourage communities to grow around it through comments, reviews, forums, blogs, photos, and cross-promotions. In return, users get free and open access to entertainment and news. They can store their favorite music and video content through features such as personal video profiles, which distribute content through "friend networks."

As of January 2009, Bebo faces the challenge of penetrating the North American market, where MySpace and Facebook are both deeply entrenched. Given that social networking sites are so new and that there are so many directions in which they can grow, the idea that this market is becoming mature seems odd. However, the torrid pace at which these sites grow could make it difficult for Bebo to jostle its way into other geographic markets in order to maintain its phenomenal growth rate. This would eventually mean direct competition with sites popular in North America or other foreign markets such as Europe, Asia, and Latin America. In 2008 and 2009, Bebo launched a Polish site.

TWITTER IS ALSO FOR BUSINESSES

Twitter is a microblogging-based communication platform that helps people stay connected with other people and businesses stay connected to their customers (see business.twitter.com/twitter101). As a business, you can use it to quickly share information with people interested in your company, gather real-time market intelligence and feedback, and build relationships with customers, partners, and other people who care about your company. As an individual user, you can use Twitter to tell a company (or anyone else) that you've had a great—or disappointing—experience with their business, offer product ideas, and learn about great offers. Twitter is also considered a social network since users and their friends (followers) have homepages, profiles, and other features of social networks.

How Does Twitter Work?

Twitter began as an instant communication network during shared events like earthquakes, conferences, Obama's announcement of his running mate for vice president in 2008, and festivals. Twitter lets you write and read messages of up to 140 characters. You can send and receive Twitter messages, or Tweets, from your desktop or your mobile phone. It is known as the SMS of the Internet.

The Key Business Benefits of Twitter

Twitter connects you to your customers in real time, in a way that was never before possible. For example, let's say you work for a custom bike company. If you run a search for your brand, you may find people posting messages about how happy they are riding your bikes in the French Alps—giving you a chance to share tips about cyclist-friendly cafés along their route.

Others may post minor equipment complaints or desired features that they would never bother to contact you about—providing you with invaluable customer feedback that you can respond to right away or use for future planning. Still others may twitter about serious problems with your bikes—letting you offer customer service that can positively handle complaints.

One of Twitter's key benefits is that it gives you the chance to communicate casually with customers on their terms, creating friendly relationships along the way, which is tough for corporations to do in most other mediums. The conversational nature of the medium lets you build relationships with customers, partners, and other people important to your business. Beyond transactions, Twitter gives your constituents direct access to employees and a way to contribute to your company; as marketers say, it shrinks the emotional distance between your company and your customers.

For example, let's say you run a big retail Web site. In addition to learning more about what your customers want, you can provide exclusive Twitter coupon codes, link to key posts on your blog, share tips for shopping online, and announce specials at store locations. And you can take things a step further by occasionally posting messages about fun, quirky events at your headquarters. For further information especially on Twitter "Best Practices" and "Case Studies" see en.wikipedia.org/wiki/Twitter, business.twitter.com/twitter101, and tweeternet.com.

FLICKR TICKS OFF SOME OF ITS USERS

Flickr (flickr.com) was created by a small Vancouver-based company called Ludicorp. The site, which allows for the storage and organization of photos, was launched in 2004 and drew fans who were seeking a place to manage and share their photos. One of the original Web 2.0 applications, Flickr had more than 2 billion images by May 2008, and it continues to grow rapidly.

Initially, users had to have an individual account (free) in order to add friends to their network and to share their photos. When Yahoo! acquired Flickr in 2005, users were not required to obtain a Yahoo! account in order to access their Flickr profile. However, two years later Yahoo! required Flickr's users to register with Yahoo! This stipulation ruffled the feathers of many of Flickr's users, who preferred to have their Flickr content separate from their Yahoo! account. Some users felt that having the accounts remain separate would create a safer and more comfortable environment. Some users were angry because the Yahoo! account requirement would mean that Flickr's users would be bound to Yahoo!'s terms and conditions and be accessible to Yahoo!'s advertisers. Yahoo! claimed the change was largely a strategy to limit the costs of maintaining an independent means of authentication; however, existing users suspect corporate interests are to be credited for the restriction.

Section 7.4 ▶ REVIEW QUESTIONS

1. Identify the major strategic issues of Facebook (e.g., look at the marketing efforts at insidefacebook.com and at facebook.com).

2. Much of Facebook's early success was due to the close affiliation of its members' networks. How does Facebook expand into new markets *without* losing what originally made the site popular and alienating existing users?

3. What strategies should Bebo pursue in order to compete directly with other social networking sites?

4. What makes Orkut (see Online File W7.5) different from other social networks? How should it respond to the demands of local governments that disapprove of some of the ideas and practices associated with social networking sites?

5. What makes Twitter so popular for business use?

6. Most social networking sites now offer services similar to those provided by Flickr. Will this cause the demise of Flickr?

7.5 BUSINESS AND ENTERPRISE SOCIAL NETWORKS

Chapter 1 introduced a business-oriented network called Xing (xing.com). This is only one way that enterprises can interact with social networking. Here, we describe other business- and enterprise-oriented networking activities.

DEFINITIONS, CONCEPTS, TYPES, AND EXAMPLES

A **business network** is a group of people who have some kind of commercial or business relationship—for example, the relationships between sellers and buyers, buyers among themselves, buyers and suppliers, and professionals and their colleagues. Such networks of people form **business social networks**, and they can exist offline or online. Business networking can take place outside the traditional corporate physical environments. For example, public places such as airports or golf courses provide opportunities to make new face-to-face business contacts if an individual has good social skills. Similarly, the Internet is also proving to be a good place to network. The most popular business-oriented social network service is LinkedIn (see closing case in this chapter).

Commercial activities related to social networks are on the rise. An increasing number of people and companies are engaged in *business-oriented social networking*, which refers to business activities, especially marketing and operations, by which business opportunities are created through social networks of businesspeople. For example, people might offer to help others find connections rather than "cold-calling" on prospects themselves (see en.wikipedia.org/wiki/Business_networking).

Recall from Chapter 1 that we distinguished the *business-oriented social networks* from *enterprise social networks*, which are social networks owned and operated within one enterprise, whose members are usually the employees of that enterprise. An example of an enterprise social network is IBM's Beehive (which we'll describe later).

business network
A group of people who have some kind of commercial relationship; for example, sellers and buyers, buyers among themselves, buyers and suppliers, and colleagues and other colleagues.

business social network
A social network whose primary objective is to facilitate business connections and activities.

BUSINESS SOCIAL NETWORKING: CONCEPTS AND BENEFITS

Many professionals contend that advertising in business social networking is a more cost-effective method of generating new business than traditional advertising or public relations efforts. This is because networking, especially when done online, is a low-cost activity that involves more personal commitment than just the company spending money on ads.

The major reasons to use or deploy a business social network are:

▶ To build better customer relationships
▶ To improve knowledge management
▶ To facilitate recruiting and retention
▶ To increase business opportunities
▶ To build a community
▶ To gain expert advice
▶ To improve trade show experiences
▶ To improve communication and collaboration

Many believe that the ability to communicate and collaborate with people both inside and outside the company via social networking is a key business differentiator that may enable a company to outperform the competition by allowing it to see opportunities that others miss.

BUSINESS-ORIENTED SOCIAL NETWORKING

Social networking activities can be conducted both in private and public social networking sites, as well as in internal and external communities. For example, Xing (see Chapter 1) is an example of a business-oriented public network, whereas Facebook is primarily a public social network for social-oriented activities. However, Facebook allows its members to conduct business-oriented activities.

The following are some examples of business-oriented social networks:

▶ **Ryze.** Similar to LinkedIn, with Ryze (ryze.com) users create profiles that can be viewed and invite friends and business associates into special-interest "tribes."

▶ **The Business Social Network.** A social network site (thebusinesssocialnetwork.com) that connects businesspeople who want to make connections and identify businesses with similar goals, products, or services. It is a clone of LinkedIn, operating mainly in the United Kingdom.

▶ **Viadeo.** Viadeo (viadeo.com) is a network of over 3 million professionals, mostly in Europe and China. Its primary use is for connecting with business contacts. It is a European clone of LinkedIn, with an emphasis on localization.

▶ **APSense.** APSense (apsense.com) is a business social network where people get paid to come together to share their business through networking, deciding, exploring, and creating quality business content. Users build their own social networks by inviting their friends to APSense. Friends of friends can also be placed in users' networks.

Several other networks similar to LinkedIn have been launched: Wealink (wealink.com) in China, Rediff Connexions (connexions.rediff.com) in India, International Jobs and Internships (ihipo.com) in Mexico, and Moikrug (moikrug.ru) in Russia.

ENTERPRISE SOCIAL NETWORKS

An increasing number of companies have created their own social networks for their employees, former employees, and/or customers. Such networks are considered to be "behind the firewall," and are often referred to as *corporate social networks.*

Such networks come in several formats, depending on their purpose, the industry, the country, and so forth. The following are guidelines regarding enterprise social networking activities (see searchcio.techtarget.com/originalContent/0,289142,sid182_gci1226050,00.htm):

▶ Allow employees to collaborate and communicate in an employee-driven system (e.g., see the closing case of this chapter).
▶ Promote the use of enterprise wikis via demonstrations.
▶ Set up internal blogs and incorporate them into internal directories so users can see who has a blog.
▶ Set up enterprise social bookmarking systems so users can see what sort of content their colleagues are tagging.
▶ CIOs should be involved from the beginning to make sure the right infrastructure and tools are in place.

For more on enterprise social networks see web2.socialcomputingjournal.com; for a demo on enterprise social networking, see news.zdnet.com/2422-19178_22-246969.html. For additional tips and sources see Kolakowski (2009).

Let's look at two examples of enterprise social networks.

Example 1: IBM'S Beehive. IBM's Beehive is an internal social networking site that gives IBM employees a rich connection to the people they work with on both a personal and a professional level. Beehive helps employees make new connections, track current friends and coworkers, and renew contacts with people they have worked with in the past. When employees join Beehive, they get a profile page. They can use the status message field and the free-form "About Me" section on their profile page to let other people at IBM know where they are, what they are doing, and even what they are thinking. Employees can use Beehive to find out what team members they spent late nights with a couple of years ago working toward a deadline are doing now by checking out their coworkers' profiles.

Employees can also use Beehive to post photos, create lists, and organize events. If users are hosting an event, they can create an event page in Beehive and invite people to attend. The page can be a place to spread the buzz about the event and get people talking about it through the comments feature.

Users can create top five lists, called "hive fives," to share their thoughts on any topic they are passionate about. For example, they can add a "hive five" list that outlines their ideas about their project, and then invite their team members to examine the list and voice their opinions.

Beehive can also come in handy when preparing for conference calls. If users do not know the other people on the call, they can check out the participants' Beehive profiles beforehand and find out if they have common interests, either work-related or recreational, or if they have colleagues in common.

In addition to the social goal, the Beehive team created the site to help IBM employees to meet the challenge of building relationships that are vital to working in large, distributed enterprises. Beehive can help IBM employees discover people with common interests or the right skills for a project. Learning more about someone— personally and professionally—facilitates making contact and might entice people to learn about ongoing projects and activities beyond their immediate project.

Beehive is related to the IBM's Innovation Jam project (see Chapter 6). For additional details, see domino.research.ibm.com/cambridge/research.nsf/99751d8eb5a20c1f852568 db004efc90/8b6d4cd68fc12b52852573d1005cc0fc? OpenDocument.

Example 2: Wells Fargo. Wells Fargo (wellsfargo.com) is a large financial holding company. Wells Fargo introduced its social networking service to about 150,000 employees in 2008. Like the popular Facebook service, the network allows users to upload photos of themselves—not just corporate ID mug shots either—and personal information. One of the goals of the project is community-building across the vast company.

The network is entirely business oriented. Think of it as a nervous system for the enterprise, one that gets more valuable the more it is used. Wells Fargo envisions a sophisticated knowledge-management platform integrated with multiple applications to let workers locate information—and the people who use it—simply and intuitively. Employees can look up coworkers and see their relationships to other employees and departments and determine their availability at any given moment. Employees can also search for the best practices by topic and review blogs and wikis written by informed employees. An in-house encyclopedia also is available.

Interfacing with Social Networks

Enterprises can interface with public and/or private social networks in several ways. One way is participating in business-oriented public networks, such as LinkedIn, or in enterprise social networks. Companies can interface with social networking in several other ways as well. The major interfaces are:

> Use existing public social networks, such as Facebook or MySpace, or virtual worlds, such as Second Life, to create pages and microcommunities; advertise products or services; and post requests for advice, job openings, and so forth. (For examples, see Weber 2007.)

> Create an in-house private social network and then use it for communication and collaboration among employees and retirees or with outsiders (e.g., customers, suppliers, designers). Employees can create virtual rooms in their company's social networks where they can deploy applications to share information (e.g., see wiki.oracle.com).

> Conduct business activities in a business-oriented social network (such as LinkedIn) or sponsor such a site.

> Create services for social networks, such as software development, security, consulting services, and more (e.g., Oracle, IBM, Microsoft).

> Use Web 2.0 tools, mostly blogs, wikis, workspaces, microblogging (Twitter), and team rooms, and create innovative applications for both internal and external users (see the opening case in Chapter 2).

> Create and/or participate in a social marketplace (such as fotolia.com).

Many large corporations, including Coca-Cola, Cisco, GE, and Deloitte & Touche, have developed innovative in-house social networks. Others create groups within MySpace or other social networks (see Weber 2007 for examples). For a more detailed description of one innovative application used for recruiting, see Online File W7.6.

Some corporate-based social networks do not fly. They simply do not attract enough members and/or visitors. An example is Walmart's failed attempt at a corporate social network (see Section 7.6).

OTHER SOCIAL NETWORKING STRUCTURES

Several other social networking structures exist. Here we present one of them.

Enterprise 2.0

Enterprise 2.0
Technologies and business practices that free the workforce from the constraints of legacy communication and productivity tools such as e-mail. Provides business managers with access to the right information at the right time through a Web of interconnected applications, services, and devices.

Enterprise 2.0 refers to collaboration within enterprises via Web 2.0 tools such as blogs and wikis. Thousands of companies use Web 2.0. For example, Motorola supports 3,900 blogs. Procter & Gamble uses Microsoft SharePoint and Office Communications for the company's 140,000 employees, many of whom use the blogs embedded in SharePoints.

According to an *InformationWeek* survey of business technology experts, the most useful Web 2.0 tools in Enterprise 2.0 are instant messaging (69 percent), collaborative tools (61 percent), integrated search tools (56 percent), unified communication (49 percent), wikis (47 percent), and mashups (43 percent). Also of importance were Ajax, RSSs, blogs, and presence awareness (30 to 40 percent each). The experts identified the following major concerns with Enterprise 2.0: security issues (64 percent), lack of expertise (56 percent), integration with existing IT systems (52 percent), and difficulty in proving ROI (51 percent) (Hoover 2007).

Social Marketplaces

The term **social marketplace** is derived from *social networking* and *marketplaces*. Thus, a social marketplace essentially acts like an online intermediary that harnesses the power of one's social networks for introducing, buying, and selling products and services and mobilizing resources for social networking. Ideally, a social marketplace should enable the marketing of members' own creations.

Examples of social marketplaces include:

- **Craigslist.** Craigslist can be considered a social network marketplace in that it provides online classifieds in addition to supporting social activities (meetings, dating, events) (see Chapter 2).
- **Fotolia.** Fotolia (fotolia.com) is a social marketplace for a huge community of creative people who enjoy sharing, learning, and expressing themselves through images, forums, and blogs. Members provide royalty-free stock images that other individuals and professionals can legally buy and share.
- **Flipsy.** Anyone can use Flipsy (flipsy.com) to list, buy, and sell books, music, movies, and games. It was created to fill the need for a free and trustworthy media marketplace. Flipsy does not charge commissions in order to foster increased trading. Payment processing is handled by a third party, such as PayPal.

social marketplace
The term is derived from the combination of *social networking* and *marketplace*. An online community that harnesses the power of one's social networks for the introduction, buying, and selling of products, services, and resources, including one's own creations. Also may refer to a structure that resembles a social network but is focused on individual members.

Section 7.5 ▶ REVIEW QUESTIONS

1. What is a business-oriented network?
2. What is an entrepreneurial network?
3. Define enterprise social network.
4. List six ways organizations can interface with Web 2.0 tools and social networks.
5. What is a social marketplace?

7.6 COMMERCIAL ASPECTS OF WEB 2.0 AND SOCIAL NETWORKING APPLICATIONS

Implementing Web 2.0 applications, especially social networks and similar communities, attracts a large number of visitors. Therefore, it provides an opportunity for vendors to advertise (see Chapter 4) and try to sell to community members.

WHY IS THERE AN INTEREST?

Web 2.0 applications are spreading rapidly, and many of them cater to a specific *segment* of the population (e.g., music lovers, travelers, game lovers, and car fans), enabling segmented advertising. Finally, many users of Web 2.0 tools are young, and they will grow older and have more money to spend. For these reasons, many believe that social networks, blogging, and other Web 2.0 activities will play a major role in the future of e-commerce. In this section, we describe a few areas where success has already been achieved.

Retailers stand to benefit from online communities in several important ways:

> ▶ Consumers can provide feedback on the design of proposed or existing products, on marketing and advertising campaigns, and on how well customer service and support are performing, which can lead to improvements and innovations for manufacturers and retailers.

> ▶ Word of mouth (i.e., *viral marketing*) is free advertising that can increase the visibility of niche retailers and products.
>
> ▶ Increased Web site traffic, a common effect of viral marketing, inevitably brings more ad dollars with it.
>
> ▶ Increased sales can come from harnessing techniques based on personal preferences such as collaborative filtering. At a more advanced level, retailers strive for a higher degree of relevance in matching the knowledge of one person to someone of similar interests who has a need to know (the "twinsumer" concept). The twinsumer trend involves consumers looking for the best of the best, the first of the first, the most relevant of the relevant. Using collaborative filtering in recommendation centers, these consumers connect with and listen to their *taste twins*; fellow consumers somewhere in the world who think and consume the way they do.

ADVERTISING USING SOCIAL NETWORKS, BLOGS, AND WIKIS

Many advertisers are placing ads on MySpace, Facebook, and YouTube or are using Google AdSense with user searches in social networking sites. Although a social media campaign may have a small impact on actual online retail sales, it may have huge benefits with regard to increasing brand awareness.

Facebook features hundreds of thousands of third-party software applications on its site. One popular application area is travel. For example, one application is "Where I've Been," a map that highlights places where users have visited or hope to visit. You can plan trips, group travel, and find and rate free in-home accommodations (at CouchSwap). This information can be sold to travel-oriented vendors, who in turn advertise their products to Facebook members.

Viral (Word-of-Mouth) Marketing

Young adults are especially good at viral marketing. If members like a certain product or service, word-of-mouth advertising works rapidly. What they like can spread very quickly—sometimes to millions of people at a minimal cost to companies (e.g., see Weber 2007). For example, YouTube conducted almost no advertising in its first few months, but millions joined because of word-of-mouth marketing. According to Megna (2007), many retailers are capitalizing on word-of-mouth marketing by bloggers. When viral marketing is done by bloggers, it is referred to as **viral blogging**. Viral marketing can be effective with the use of tools such as Twitter (e.g., see business.twitter.com/ twitter101/case_dell).

viral blogging
Viral (word-of-mouth) marketing done by bloggers.

Example 1. An example of viral marketing on social networks is the story of Stormhoek Vineyards (stormhoek.com). The company first offered a free bottle of wine to bloggers. About 100 of these bloggers posted voluntary comments about the winery on their own blogs within six months. Most had positive comments that were read by other bloggers.

The Stormhoek example raises an interesting question: Can bloggers be bought? The criticism is that bloggers are not required to disclose that they are being paid for their endorsements. Companies can pay bloggers to endorse products via an intermediary such as PayPerPost.

Example 2. PayPerPost (payperpost.com) runs a marketplace where advertisers can find bloggers, video bloggers, online photographers, and podcasters willing to endorse the advertisers' products.

A company with a product or a service to advertise registers with PayPerPost and describes what it wants. A sneaker company, for example, might post a request for people willing to write a 50-word blog entry about their sneakers or upload a video of themselves playing basketball wearing the sneakers. The company also says what it is willing to pay for the posting.

Bloggers create the blog post (or whatever content is requested) and inform PayPerPost, which checks to see that the content matches what the advertiser asked for, and PayPerPost arranges payment. Note that the PayPerPost bloggers *are* required to disclose that they are being paid for their posting.

Classified Ads, Job Listings, and Recruitment

MySpace has provided classifieds and job listings since fall 2005, competing with Craigslist and CareerBuilder. MySpace is already a large force in e-commerce, sending more traffic to shopping and classified sites than MSN, and it is fast closing in on Yahoo! Facebook, LinkedIn, and many other social networks that offer classifieds and job listings as well. Google partnered with eBay in 2006 to roll out "click-to-call" advertising across Google and eBay sites—a deal that is expanding to MySpace's giant network.

One interesting example is Salesforce.com (salesforce.com). The CRM software company has partnered with Facebook to allow Salesforce.com customers to build applications on its Force.com platform inside Facebook. For example, employees could embed a recruitment application within their Facebook page, and then use their social connections to recruit new employees for their company.

Special Advertising Campaigns

Some retailers have successfully used the fall back-to-school season as a social networking focus. For example, in fall 2008, JCPenney created an online game called Dork-Dodge for girls in Facebook. Players had to navigate their way past undesirable boyfriends to get to their dream date. The retailer also had an interactive video (a modern-day take on the movie *The Breakfast Club*) where users could choose clothes from JCPenney for the actors. Similarly, Sears had a fall 2008 marketing campaign that featured actress Vanessa Hudgens from *High School Musical* playing various characters to show the different styles that could be put together with clothing from Sears.

Shoppers at Sears.com have the option of sharing prom dresses with their Facebook friends using a feature called Prom Premier 2008. Sears supplemented the option with an ad campaign on Facebook. Sears is using the program to test the benefits of melding EC with social networking. The company is monitoring the clickstream at the site using Web analytics tools. Many of MySpace's most popular pages are from e-tailers who stock the site with low-cost cosmetics ads, other Web site ads, and the like. The advertisement value is $140 million or more per year and growing rapidly (Kafka 2007).

MySpace lets brand owners create profile pages for their property. For example, the Burger King mascot, "The King," has a MySpace page. This has been a tremendous success.

MySpace is starting its own *behavioral targeting*, which is similar to collaborative filtering (Chapter 4). Based on the members' voluntary information on what they like and what they do not, MySpace serves up its users to relevant advertisers with the users' permission. For example, DaimlerChrysler's Jeep already has its own MySpace page from which it can conduct sales campaigns to targeted individuals.

Mobile Advertising

Mobile advertising is a rapidly developing area. It refers to advertisement on cell phones and other mobile devices. The competition for mobile ad revenue is intensifying, especially with the increased use of cell phones with access to the Internet. Recently, watching video clips has become popular on cell phones. Advertisers are starting to attach ads to these video clips (see Chapter 4). Finally, advertisers use microblogging, especially Twitter, to reach large audiences.

SHOPPING IN SOCIAL NETWORKS

Shopping is a natural area for social networks to become involved in. Although shopping in social networks is only beginning to grow, it has enormous potential. Consider the following examples:

▶ MySpace's music-download service allows the site's independent musicians to sell their work directly from their profile pages. Snocap, a copyright-services company cofounded by Napster creator Shawn Fanning, supports the project. MySpace and Snocap get a cut of every piece of music sold. By allowing users to self-publish, MySpace has become a launching pad for about 3 million musicians, from garage bands to big names. MySpace is also doing it with its Japanese site, where 90,000 musicians and game writers are trying to fulfill the demand for their services. The users of this model actually create an EC storefront in their Facebook page in just a few minutes.

▶ In 2006, Google signed an agreement to pay more than $900 million in ad revenue over five years to MySpace for the right to provide searches inside MySpace. The deal includes the extension of Google's checkout payment service (enabling customers to pay once for several vendors) to MySpace.

▶ YouTube joined Amazon.com and Apple's iTunes in creating the eCommerce Platform. YouTube sells music and games from iTunes and Amazon.com's stores on its site (see the "click-to-buy" icon). YouTube adds more products and vendors continuously.

An overview of selling in social networks is provided by Jefferies (2008), who cites the following drivers (by decreasing level of importance) of selling in social networks:

▶ Pressure to increase top-line revenue growth

▶ Efforts to improve overall sales productivity

▶ Need to compete with increasing customer and prospect knowledge of products and competitive differentiators

For more on social shopping, see genuinevc.com/archives/2006/11/the_meaning_of_2.htm and blog.comtaste.com.

FEEDBACK FROM CUSTOMERS: CONVERSATIONAL MARKETING

Companies are starting to utilize Web 2.0 tools to get feedback from customers. This trend is referred to as *conversational marketing*. In Chapter 4, we described customer feedback via questionnaires, focus groups, and other methods. However, Web 2.0 enables customers to supply feedback via blogs (e.g., see bloombergmarketing.blogs.com/Bloomberg_marketing), wikis, online forums, chat rooms, and social networking sites.

Companies are finding that these tools not only generate faster and cheaper results than traditional focus groups, but also foster closer customer relationships. For example, Macy's quickly removed a metal toothbrush holder from its product line after receiving several complaints about it online (see Gogoi 2007). Companies like Dell are also learning that conversational marketing is less expensive and yields quicker results than focus groups. The computer maker operates a feedback site called IdeaStorm, where it allows customers to suggest and vote on improvements in its offerings.

Cookshack and many other companies operate online forums. Cookshack (forum.cookshack.com/groupee) invites customers to ask and answer questions about barbecue sauces, beef smokers, barbecue ovens, and cooking techniques. The community helps save money by freeing up customer-service personnel who used to answer such questions by phone or e-mail. The community also fosters customer loyalty.

With *enterprise feedback management*, companies are interested not only in collecting information, but also in the interaction between customers and company employees and in properly distributing customer feedback throughout the organization.

According to Gogoi (2007), retailers know that customers, especially the younger and more Net-savvy ones, want to be heard, and they also want to hear what others like them say. Increasingly, retailers are opening up their Web sites to customers, letting them post product reviews, ratings, and in some cases photos and videos. The result is that *customer reviews* are emerging as a prime place for online shoppers to visit.

Example 1: Del Monte. Del Monte, through its "I Love My Dog" program, gathers data from pet owners that can help shape its marketing decisions. Its private social network helps Del Monte make decisions about products, test-market campaigns, understand buying preferences, and generate discussions about new items and product changes.

Example 2: PETCO. PETCO operates approximately 800 pet supply stores in the United States. PETCO launched an external enterprise social network, mainly for customers, that included customer reviews as early as October 2005. PETCO noticed that customers who clicked on the highest customer-rated products were 49 percent more likely to buy something. PETCO also noticed that top customer-rated pet toys and other items draw more customers, even if the new customers weren't necessarily planning on buying them; people trust someone else's opinion that is independent of the manufacturer or retailer.

PETCO's experience is not unique. According to Gogoi (2007) and an eVoc Insights study, 47 percent of consumers consult reviews before making an online purchase, and 63 percent of shoppers are more likely to purchase from a site if it has ratings and reviews. Negative reviews not only help the retailer address a defect or poorly manufactured item, they also help decrease the number of returns. People are less likely to return an item due to personal expectation because reviews give realistic views of a product and its characteristics.

Customer Feedback with Twitter

An increasing number of companies are utilizing Twitter to solicit information from customers and interact with them.

Examples. Several examples can be found at business.twitter.com/twitter101. They include Dell (connecting with customers), JetBlue (learning about customers), Teusner Wines (gathering feedback, sharing information), and Pepsi (fast response time in dealing with complaints).

COMMERCIAL ACTIVITIES IN BUSINESS AND ENTERPRISE SOCIAL NETWORKS

Although advertising and sales are the major EC activities in public social networks, there are emerging possibilities for commercial activities in business-oriented networks such as LinkedIn and in enterprise social networks.

Recognizing the opportunities, many software vendors are developing Web tools and applications to support enterprise social networking. For example, IBM Lotus is encouraging its 5,000-plus solution providers who are working with Notes/Domino, Sametime, and other Lotus software to add Lotus Connections to their product lineups, building applications based on social networking technology.

Representative areas and examples of enterprise social networking follow.

Finding and Recruiting Workers

Most of the public social networks, especially the business-oriented ones, facilitate recruiting and job finding (see Hoover 2007). For example, recruiting is a major activity at LinkedIn (closing case of this chapter) and was the driver for the site's development. To be competitive, companies must look at the global market for talent, and they can use global social networking sites to find it. Large companies are using their in-house social networks to find in-house talent for vacant positions. For more on recruitment and job finding in social networks, see Chapter 3.

Management Activities and Support

Applications in this category are related to supporting managerial decision making based on analysis of data collected in social networks. Some typical examples include identifying key performers, locating experts and finding paths to access them, soliciting ideas and possible solutions to complex problems, and finding and analyzing candidates for management succession planning. For example, Deloitte Touche Tohmatsu set up a social network to assist its human resources managers in downsizing and regrouping teams. Hoover's has established a social network that uses Visible Path's technology to identify target business users for relationship building and to reach specific users. The Advances in Social Network Analysis and Mining conference on the use of data mining in social networks (July 2009 in Athens, Greece) has been dedicated to the topic.

Training

Several companies use enterprise social networking, and virtual worlds in particular, for training purposes. For example, Cisco is trying to use its virtual campus in Second Life for product training and executive briefings. IBM runs management and customer interaction training sessions in Second Life, too.

Knowledge Management and Expert Location

Applications in this category include activities such as knowledge discovery, creation, maintenance, sharing, transfer, and dissemination. An elaborate discussion on the role of discussion forums, blogs, and wikis for conversational knowledge management can be found in Wagner and Bolloju (2005). Other examples of these applications include expert discovery (see Chapter 6) and mapping communities of expertise.

Consider the following examples of social networking for KM and expert location:

▶ Innocentive (innocentive.com), a social network with over 150,000 participating scientists, specializes in solving science-related problems (for cash rewards).
▶ Northwestern Mutual Life created an internal social network where over 7,000 financial representatives share captured knowledge (using Awareness.com blogging software).
▶ Caterpillar created a knowledge network system for its employees, and it even markets the software to other companies.

Companies also are creating *retiree corporate social networks* to keep retirees connected with each other and with the organization. These people possess huge amounts of knowledge that can be tapped for productivity increases and problem solving (e.g., Alumni Connect from SelectMinds). With 64 million people retiring within the next few years (per the Conference Board), preserving their knowledge is critical.

Enhancing Collaboration

Collaboration in social networking is done both internally, among employees from different units working in virtual teams for example, and externally, when working with suppliers, customers, and other business partners. Collaboration is done mostly in forums and other types of groups and by using wikis and blogs. A list of blogging applications is provided in Section 2.6. For details on collaboration in social networks, see Chapter 6 and Coleman and Levine (2008).

Using Blogs and Wikis Inside the Enterprise

In Chapter 2, we provided some examples of blogs and wikis used within enterprises. For examples of how wikis are used within enterprises, see Online File W7.7. The use of these tools is expanding rapidly. Jefferies (2008) reports on a study that shows that 71 percent of the best-in-class companies use blogs and 64 percent use wikis for the following applications:

▶ Project collaboration and communication (63 percent)
▶ Process and procedure document (63 percent)
▶ FAQs (61 percent)
▶ E-learning and training (46 percent)
▶ Forums for new ideas (41 percent)
▶ Corporate-specific dynamic glossary and terminology (38 percent)
▶ Collaboration with customers (24 percent)

REVENUE-GENERATION STRATEGIES IN SOCIAL NETWORKS

The following are some interesting ways social networks generate revenue: (1) offer premium service to individuals for a monthly or per service fee, (2) partner with organizations that pay a monthly service fee, and (3) create affiliations with physical venues where members can meet (e.g., meetup.com). Physical venues, such as coffee shops, may pay a fee to be affiliated with the social network.

Exhibit 7.5 illustrates how Web 2.0 applications can generate revenue. It shows users' contributions and the relationships among people, advertising, and Web 2.0 tools, such as

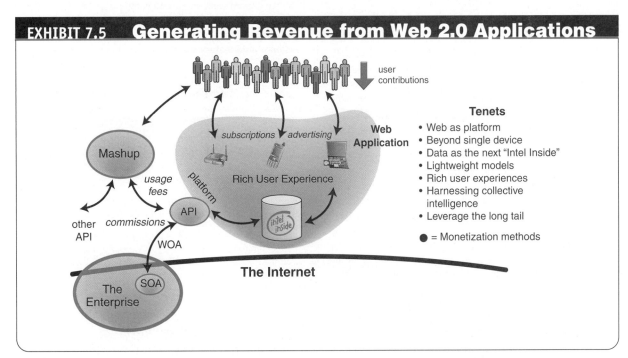

EXHIBIT 7.5 Generating Revenue from Web 2.0 Applications

Source: D. Hinchcliffe, *Web 2.0 Blog, web2.socialcomputingjournal.com*. Reprinted by permission from Dion Hinchcliffe.

mashups. The Web applications may generate revenue via subscription fees and advertisements. To learn more about how blogs can bring in big money, see Weber (2007).

Increased Revenue and Its Benefits

Web 2.0 tools can generate revenue growth, user growth, and increased resistance to competition in indirect ways, which, in turn, lead to increased subscriptions, advertising, and commission revenue.

The strategic use of online communities can increase revenue and profit. Case 7.1 describes some of the potential revenue sources created by EC in social networks.

RISKS AND LIMITATIONS WHEN INTERFACING WITH SOCIAL NETWORKS

Interfacing with social networks is not without risk. Aligning a product or company with sites where content is user-generated and not edited or filtered has its downsides.

CASE 7.1
EC Application
REVENUE SOURCES AT YOUTUBE

Some experts think that Google paid too much for YouTube, especially in light of its copyright-related legal problems (see Online File W7.4). However, Google may actually have gotten a bargain. Consider the following:

▶ **Two-minute YouTube clips were just the start.** As television comes to the Internet, dozens of companies are competing to become the networks of tomorrow. Whichever networks attract the most viewers will inevitably attract vast numbers of advertisers as well. YouTube's ad revenue in 2007 alone has been valued at $200 million by *eMarketer* and Citigroup. And wherever there's video programming, viewers will be seeing more video ads. One forecast from *eMarketer* predicts that overall video advertising on the Web (including video ads replacing banners on regular Web pages) will reach $4.6 billion in 2013, a sevenfold leap from the 2006 total of $410 million (Seeking Alpha 2009).

▶ **Brand-created entertainment content.** In 2005, Nike produced a pseudo-home video of soccer star Ronaldinho practicing while wearing his new Nike Gold shoes. In one week, the clip was downloaded 3.5 million times on YouTube (worldwide), providing Nike with tremendous exposure to its core, mostly young male, audience. As the younger generation moves away from traditional TV, it is shifting its attention to YouTube and similar offerings.

▶ **User-driven product advertising.** User-generated videos could be leveraged in a similar manner to product placement on TV. For example, although not intentional, a 17-year-old girl's use of Logitech's Webcam featured in a short clip on YouTube where she talks about the breakup with her boyfriend greatly contributed to awareness of Logitech's offerings. The product placement trend is also expanding across the blogosphere, with Nokia promoting its new smart phone through the 50 most influential bloggers in Belgium and establishing a blogger-relationship blog.

▶ **Multichannel word-of-mouth campaign.** When Chevrolet decided to combine its *Apprentice* Tahoe campaign with an online consumer-generated media (CGM) campaign, it did not anticipate the additional viral impact of YouTube. On the Chevrolet site, users could create their own customized video commercial, complete with text and background music. Environmentalists took the opportunity to produce spoof videos and published them on YouTube. However, the word-of-mouth advertising Chevrolet received on YouTube was ultimately beneficial to Chevrolet. The Chevrolet site generated 4 million page views, 400,000 unique visitors, and 22,000 ad submissions in just six months.

Sources: Compiled from Sahlin and Botello (2007) and Seeking Alpha (2009).

Questions

1. List the different advertising models on YouTube.
2. List the success factors from these cases.
3. How do users benefit from using YouTube?

Another risk is that the company needs to be willing to accept negative reviews and feedback. If a company has really positive customer relationships and strong feedback and is willing to have customers share the good, but possibly some bad, as well as the ugly, it is a good candidate for social networking. If, however, the company worries about what its customers would say, the product or business might not be ready for social networking.

Another key consideration is the 20–80 rule, which posits that a minority of individuals (20 percent) contribute most of the content (80 percent) to blogs, wikis, and similar tools. For example, approximately 1,000 of Wikipedia's millions of contributors write most of its content (see money.cnn.com/2007/02/21/magazines/business2/nextnet_ intro.biz2/index.htm). In an analysis of thousands of submissions over a three-week period on audience voting sites such as Digg and reddit, the *Wall Street Journal* reported that one-third of the stories that made it to Digg's homepage were submitted by 30 contributors (out of 900,000 registered members), and that one single person on Netscape, going by the online name "Stoner," was responsible for 13 percent of the top posts on that site. Such distribution may result in biases.

Finally, the use of Web 2.0 applications may present a security risk. In 2009, the top eight security risks included insufficient authentication controls, phishing, and information leakage (see readwriteweb.com/archives/top_8_web_20_security_threats.php). For a summary of risks in social networking, see Online File W7.8 and messagelabs.com/whitepaper/US_WP_SocialNetworking_Associate.pdf.

JUSTIFYING SOCIAL MEDIA AND NETWORKING

Many companies find it difficult to justify social media and networking because most of their benefits are intangible (e.g., positive word of mouth). If the costs of using such tools can be kept low and if risk can be contained, then a sophisticated ROI analysis many not be needed. However, a number of companies are developing metrics that can be used in cost-benefit analyses.

Example: Walmart's In-House Social Network. Although many companies have benefited significantly from enterprise social networking (e.g., Nike, Coca-Cola, and Sony), there have been some failures. For example, Walmart's enterprise networking effort was a complete failure.

For the largest retailer in the world, creating its own social network seemed to be natural and simple, but it was not. In 2007, Walmart launched a social network in order to bolster its image with younger consumers. The company hired professional actresses and actors to pose as teens on the site, but they were not convincing. Also, in an attempt to avoid future lawsuits, Walmart allowed parents to control page content. The young viewers were turned off. Because the number of visitors was so small, Walmart pulled down the site after a short period.

Section 7.6 ▶ REVIEW QUESTIONS

1. Why is there so much interest in EC via social communities?
2. How can a social network facilitate viral marketing?
3. How can social networks support shopping?
4. How is customer feedback solicited in social networks?
5. List some risks and limitations in enterprise social networking.
6. How do social networks generate revenue?

7.7 ENTERTAINMENT WEB 2.0 STYLE: FROM SOCIAL NETWORKS TO MARKETPLACES

The rich media capabilities of Web 2.0 technologies, the ability to engage millions of young people who are interested in online entertainment, the availability of innovative tools, and the creative and collaborative nature of Web 2.0 all facilitate entertainment. Web 2.0 tools also are aiding in the proliferation of on-demand entertainment. This section describes some of the entertainment-centered social networks as well as other issues related to Web 2.0 entertainment. Note that a major issue with such social networks is copyright violations; this topic will be discussed in more detail in Chapter 11.

ENTERTAINMENT AND SOCIAL NETWORKS

A large number of social networks and communities are fully or partially dedicated to entertainment. In fact, MySpace seems to be morphing into an entertainment portal. MySpace is the second most visited online video site after YouTube. It has a licensing agreement with Sony BMG and other large media companies that gives its members free access to streaming videos, music, and other entertainment in MySpace Music. The companies share in the ad revenue. MySpace is also offering free voice chat in collaboration with Skype.

The following are some additional examples of the use of Web 2.0 applications for entertainment.

Mixi

Mixi, Inc. (mixi.co.jp) is a popular invitation-only social networking service in Japan. The focus of mixi is on "community entertainment"; that is, meeting new people by way of common interests. Users can send and receive messages, write in a diary, read and comment on others' diaries, organize and join communities, and invite their friends to join. Mixi Station, a client program that detects songs being played in iTunes and Windows Media Player, uploads songs automatically to a communally accessible list in the "Music" section.

The word *mixi* is a combination of *mix* and *I*, referring to the idea that the user, "I," "mixes" with other users through the service. As of March 2009, the site had more than 12.4 million members and about 1 million small communities of friends and interests (en.wikipedia.org/wiki/Mixi).

Last.fm

Last.fm (last.fm) is an Internet radio station and music recommendation system that merged with its sister site, Audioscrobbler, in August 2005. In May 2007, CBS purchased Last.fm in order to extend its online reach. The system builds a detailed profile of each member's musical preferences. Based on this profile, Last.fm recommends artists similar to members' favorites and features their favorite artists and songs on a customizable Web page comprising the songs played on its stations selected via collaborative filtering (Chapter 4) or recorded by a Last.fm plug-in installed into its users' music-playing application.

Last.fm users can build their musical profiles in two ways: by listening to their personal music collection on a music player application with an Audioscrobbler plug-in or by listening to the Last.fm Internet radio service. Songs played are added to a log from which musical recommendations are calculated. Last.fm calls this automatic track logging *scrobbling*. The user's page also displays recently played tracks, allowing users to display them on blogs or as forum signatures.

Regular membership is free; premium membership is $3 per month. The site, which operates in 10 major languages, has won several Best Community awards.

Pandora

Similar to Last.fm, Pandora (pandora.com) is a site for music lovers. The site runs entirely within a Web browser (unlike Last.fm, which requires a plug-in) and relies on people to suggest new music. As users select and listen to songs on Pandora and give them a thumbs-up or thumbs-down, the site offers new songs that human music evaluators have determined to be similar in style. Users can search for a particular artist, song, or genre and Pandora will create an entire personalized "radio station" full of similar music.

eFans

EFans (efans.com) is a social network for sports fans, bringing together millions of fans from all over the world. The site features videos, sport news, blogs, and forums. It also offers event tickets and sports-related products for purchase.

Users can join networks based on teams and athletes, including Tiger Woods, FC Barcelona, Manchester United, Ronaldinho, the Boston Red Sox, and thousands more, including local teams. Users can create personal, team, and athlete pages; share photos; and upload videos from YouTube. Users can also get the latest news and live scores and post comments. Users can add to their content, similar to a wiki, making it a highly personalized, yet high-profile, interaction.

A new version of eFans includes many exciting features that may change the way sports fans connect on the Internet. For example, the new release has modules that unite fans who have the same favorite athlete or team.

For the Beijing Olympics, eFans hosted a special page devoted to the world's best sporting events. The summer games were covered by David Wallenchinsky, author of a series of *The Complete Book of the Olympics*, who contributed to eFans live from Beijing.

Internet Series and Movie Streaming

Internet series are similar to soap operas on TV. The number of Internet series is increasing, and some are already on DVD. Examples include *Broken Trail*, *Soup of the Day*, and *Floaters*.

Hulu (hulu.com) offers commercial-supported streaming video of TV shows and movies from NBC, Fox, and many other networks and studios. As of January 2009, Hulu videos were offered only to users in the United States. Hulu provides video in Flash video format, including many films and shows. In addition, some TV shows and movies are now offered in high definition.

Adult Entertainment in Virtual Worlds

The 3D capability of virtual worlds and the ease of manipulating avatars have opened the door to a variety of entertainment options, most notably adult entertainment. All major virtual worlds are full of adult entertainment features, including Second Life, specifically in redlightcenter.com.

MOBILE WEB 2.0 DEVICES FOR ENTERTAINMENT AND WORK

Several mobile devices have been designed with blogs, wikis, and other P2P services in mind. Here are some examples.

iPhone and Its Clones

The iPhone (from apple.com) was introduced in 2007. It is an all-in-one smart phone (see the following photo of the iPhone 3G). It is considered a disruptor in the cell

iPhone 3G

Source: Courtesy of Digital Trends. Used with permission.

phone market. Soon after the iPhone's release, Samsung announced a new smart phone, BlackBerry introduced the Storm, and Google launched the G1 Google phone. These smart phones are marketed by cell phone carriers such as AT&T and Verizon. The competition among these new smart phones is intense, and new capabilities appear frequently.

The iPhone is also a personal media player, offering all the capabilities of an iPod, with music and video playback, plus the benefits of a high-resolution widescreen display for watching movies and videos. It is a touchscreen smart phone with full-blown Internet communication capabilities; a quad-band, EDGE-capable mobile phone; and it has a brain (i.e., PAD capabilities), making it simple and easy to use. It also has a camera, a headset jack, and a built-in speaker. It also supports online multiplayer gaming.

The iPhone also has a sleep/wake button, and a proximity sensor turns off the screen when users hold the phone to their heads. It features automatic-orientation adjustment, switching between portrait and landscape modes on-the-fly. The iPhone boasts virtually no dedicated controls; instead, everything is driven using a new (patented) multitouch screen that Apple claims is far more accurate than previous touch-sensitive displays. For additional details, see apple.com/iphone and en.wikipedia.org/wiki/iphone.

The iPhone lets companies such as Apple and Google "merge without merging" by delivering Google services through Apple hardware.

Section 7.7 ▶ REVIEW QUESTIONS

1. Describe entertainment communities and provide an example.
2. Describe the online marketplaces for music.
3. What is an Internet series?
4. Describe the iPhone.

7.8 THE FUTURE: WEB 3.0 AND WEB 4.0

Web 2.0 is here, but not for long (Hempel 2009). What's next? The answer is referred to as **Web 3.0**, the future wave of Internet applications. Some of the characteristics of Web 3.0 are already in the making. Based on nontechnological success factors and technological factors and trends, there is general optimism about the future of the Web and EC.

WEB 3.0: WHAT'S NEXT?

Web 3.0 will not be just about shopping, entertainment, and search. Web 3.0 will deliver a new generation of business applications that will see business and social computing converge on the same fundamentals as on-demand architecture is converging with consumer applications today. Thus, Web 3.0 is just not merely of passing interest to those who work on enterprise EC. The Web 3.0 era could radically change individuals' career paths as well as the organizations where they work, and it may even revolutionize social networking (see Hempel 2009).

The next-generation Internet will not just be more portable and personal; it will also harness the power of people, making it even easier to zero in on precisely what you are looking for (see en.wikipedia.org/wiki/Web_3).

Web 3.0
A term used to describe the future of the World Wide Web. It consists of the creation of high-quality content and services produced by gifted individuals using Web 2.0 technology as an enabling platform.

Web 3.0 has the potential to usher in the following:

> ▶ Faster, far-flung connectivity; richer ways of interacting
> ▶ New Web Services that work entirely within a browser window
> ▶ More powerful search engines
> ▶ More clout for everyday people and more user-friendly application-creation capabilities
> ▶ New artificial intelligence applications
> ▶ 10 MB of bandwidth (instead of 1 MB in Web 2.0, on average)
> ▶ More uses of 3D tools
> ▶ Greater utilization of wireless and mobile social networks

Web 3.0 Structure

The topology of Web 3.0 can be divided into four distinct layers: *API services, aggregation services, application services,* and *serviced clients* (see Online File W7.9).

Web 3.0 and the Semantic Web

Semantic Web
An evolving extension of the Web in which Web content can be expressed not only in natural language, but also in a form that can be understood, interpreted, and used by intelligent computer software agents, permitting them to find, share, and integrate information more easily.

One of the major possible applications of Web 3.0 technologies is the **Semantic Web** (see en.wikipedia.org/wiki/Semantic_Web). The Semantic Web is an evolving extension of the Web in which Web content can be expressed not only in natural language, but also in a form that can be understood, interpreted, and used by intelligent computer software agents, permitting them to find, share, and integrate information more easily. The technology is derived from W3C director Tim Berners-Lee's vision of the Web as a universal medium for data, information, and knowledge exchange. At its core, the Semantic Web comprises a philosophy, a set of design principles, collaborative working groups, and a variety of enabling technologies.

A similar view about the role of the Semantic Web is expressed by Borland (2007), who believes that the role of the Semantic Web in Web 3.0 is certain, and coming soon. Borland believes that new Web 3.0 tools (some of which are already helping developers "stitch" together complex applications) will improve and automate database searches, help people choose vacation destinations, and sort through complicated financial data more efficiently.

Web 4.0
The Web generation after Web 3.0. It is still mostly an unknown entity. However, it is envisioned as being based on islands of intelligence and as being ubiquitous.

By 2010, a Semantic-Web browser may be available where users can display data, draw graphs, and so on. An example would be "friend-of-a-friend" networks, where individuals in online communities provide data in the form of links between themselves and friends. The Semantic Web could help to visualize such complex networks and organize them to enable a deeper understanding of such communities' structures. For more on Web 3.0 and the Semantic Web, see en.wikipedia.org/wiki/Web_3.

Web 4.0

Web 4.0 is the next Web generation after Web 3.0. It is still an unknown entity. However, Coleman and Levine (2008) envision it as being based on islands of intelligence and on being ubiquitous. Online File W7.10 depicts the relationship of Web 4.0 to Web 1.0, 2.0, and 3.0.

Future Threats

The following four trends may slow EC and Web 3.0 and even cripple the Internet:

1. **Security concerns.** Shoppers as well as users of e-banking and other services worry about online security. The Web needs to be made safer.

2. **Lack of Net neutrality.** If the big telecommunications companies are allowed to charge companies for a guarantee of faster access, critics fear that small innovative Web companies could be crowded out by the Microsofts and Googles that can afford to pay more.

3. **Copyright complaints.** The legal problems of YouTube, Wikipedia, and others may result in a loss of vital outlets of public opinion, creativity, and discourse.

4. **Choppy connectivity.** Upstream bandwidths are still constricted, making uploading of video files a time-consuming task. Usable mobile bandwidth still costs a lot, and some carriers impose limitations on how Web access can be employed.

Section 7.8 ▶ REVIEW QUESTIONS

1. What is Web 3.0, and how will it differ from Web 2.0?
2. Define Semantic Web.
3. List the major potential inhibitors of e-commerce and Web 3.0.
4. What is Web 4.0?

MANAGERIAL ISSUES

Some managerial issues related to this chapter are as follows.

1. **How will social networking impact businesses?** The impacts of social networking and the Internet can change the manner in which shoppers make decisions. The impact may be so strong that the entire manner in which companies do business will be changed, with significant impacts on procedures, people, organizational structure, management, and business processes. Strong impact will be felt in advertising, viral marketing, collaboration, and brand recognition.

2. **Should we explore Web 2.0 collaboration?** Consider whether your corporate culture is ready to experiment with collaboration tools and social networks. Work with your corporate-learning or organization-development department to find areas likely for experimentation.

3. **Do we need to sponsor a social network?** Although sponsoring a social network might sound like a good idea, it may not be simple to execute. Community members need services, which cost money to provide. The most difficult task is to find an existing community that matches your business. In many cases, the cost of a social network may be justified by its contribution to advertising. However, the social network service providers need to create various revenue models to maintain sustainable services. Creating revenue is the most challenging issue to social network service providers.

4. **How should we deal with Web 2.0 risks?** There are several possible risks, depending on the applications. The knowledge from unreliable participants may downgrade the credibility of knowledge from open sources. To protect the security of the open system, consult your internal security experts and get some outside legal advice. Use a consultant for large projects to examine and evaluate the risks.

5. **Should we have an in-house social network?** This is a debatable issue. Although most companies should probably opt to go into a successful public social network service, there are cases where an in-house service can be much more beneficial. Large companies may use both. It is probably most advantageous to build the knowledge management system using both internal sources and external sources.

SUMMARY

In this chapter, you learned about the following EC issues as they relate to the chapter's learning objectives.

1. **Web 2.0, social media, and disruptors.** Web 2.0 is about the innovative application of existing technologies. Web 2.0 has brought together the contributions of millions of people and has made their work, opinions, and identity matter. The consequences of the rapid growth of person-to-person computing, such as blogging, are currently hard to understand and difficult to estimate. User-created content is a major characteristic of Web 2.0, as is the emergence of social networking. One impact of Web 2.0 is the creation of industry disruptors.

2. **The structure and role of virtual communities.** Virtual communities create new types of business opportunities—people with similar interests that congregate at one Web site are a natural target for advertisers and marketers. Using chat rooms, members can exchange opinions about certain products and services. Of special interest are communities of transactions, whose interest is the promotion of commercial buying and selling. Virtual communities can foster customer loyalty, increase sales of vendors that sponsor communities, and facilitate customer feedback for improved service and business.

3. **Social network services.** These are very large Internet communities that enable the sharing of content, including text, videos, and photos, and promote online socialization and interaction. Hundreds of networks are popping up around the world, some of which are global, competing for advertising money.

4. **Representative social networking sites.** In addition to MySpace, we discussed YouTube, Facebook, Bebo, Orkut, Flickr, LinkedIn, and Hi5.

5. **Business-oriented social networks.** These communities concentrate on business issues both in one country and around the world (e.g., recruiting, finding business partners). Social marketplaces meld social networks and some aspects of business.

Notable business-oriented social networks are LinkedIn and Xing. Also, some companies own private social networks, whereas others conduct business in public social networks, such as in Facebook. Enterprise social networks are those owned and operated inside one company. Their members are usually employees and retirees. They are used mainly for collaboration, knowledge creation and preservation, training, and socialization. Many large companies have such networks (e.g., IBM, Wells Fargo).

6. **Social networks and e-commerce.** The major areas of interface are online shopping, online advertising, online market research, collaboration, and innovative revenue models. The major attraction is the volume of social networks, the possibility of viral marketing, and the hope that young people in the communities will be online buyers in the future.

7. **Web 2.0, social networking, and entertainment.** Rich media, user-created content, and groups and subgroups with common interests open many possibilities for a second generation of online entertainment. Add to this the wireless revolution and the increased capabilities in mobile devices to support Web 2.0 tools and social networking activities and you will discover a new and exciting world of online entertainment.

8. **Web 3.0 and Web 4.0.** Web 3.0, the next generation of the Web, will combine social and business computing. It will be more portable and personal, with powerful search engines, increased clout, and greater connectivity with the wireless environment and on-demand applications. Knowledge management will be one of its main pillars. The Semantic Web will play a major role in Web 3.0 applications. Web 4.0 is a futuristic Web that will be built on ubiquitous and intelligent systems. It will connect "islands" of intelligence from different sources.

KEY TERMS

Business network	269	Semantic Web	286	Viral blogging	274
Business social network	269	Social marketplace	273	Virtual (Internet) community	258
Disruptors	258	Social media	257	Web 2.0	255
Enterprise 2.0	272	Social network analysis (SNA)	262	Web 3.0	285
Mobile social networking	264	Social networking	261	Web 4.0	286

QUESTIONS FOR DISCUSSION BY INDIVIDUAL STUDENTS

1. How do business-oriented networks and enterprise social networks differ?

2. What are the major characteristics of Web 2.0? What are some of the advantages of Web 2.0 applications?

3. Discuss the use of virtual communities to do business on the Internet.

4. What are some of the risks companies may face if they decide to use public social networks?

5. Why are social marketplaces considered to be Web 2.0 applications?

6. How can marketers use social networks for viral marketing?

7. Discuss the commercial opportunities presented by public social networks.

8. Why are advertisers so interested in social networks?

9. What are the benefits of conversational marketing?

10. How can wikis be used to facilitate knowledge management?

11. Discuss the relationships among mobile devices, social networking, and EC.

12. Identify and discuss Facebook's revenue model.

TOPICS FOR CLASS DISCUSSION

1. Should companies build in-house social networks for external activities or use existing public social networks?

2. Social networks services, such as Visible Path, can provide social networking services for entire enterprises that are fairly secure. However, security may limit users' creativity and disrupt the business. Should a company use this service?

3. Some research suggests that the use of public social networks by employees can be good for a business, because employees develop relationships and share information, which increases productivity and innovation. Others say it is waste of time and ban the use of Facebook, YouTube, and other such sites. Discuss.

4. Some say that MySpace is turning into an entertainment center, whereas Facebook is becoming a communication center. Discuss.

5. Discuss the business value of social networking. As a start, read Tom Davenport's "Where's the Working in Social Networks" (blogs. harvard-business. org/ davenport/2007/10/wheres_the_working_ in_social_n.html) and Brett Bonfield's "Should Your Organization Use Social Networking Sites" (techsoup.org/ learningcenter/internet/page7935.cfm).

6. Discuss the opportunities that the faltering economy provides to social networking in assisting enterprises to overcome their problems.

INTERNET EXERCISES

1. Enter the Web site of a social network service (e.g., myspace.com or facebook.com). Build a homepage. Add a chat room and a message board to your site using the free tools provided. Describe the other capabilities available. Make at least five new friends.

2. Enter vivapets.com and dogster.com and compare their offerings.

3. Enter classmates.com, myspace.com, and linkedin.com and list their sources of revenue.

4. Enter xing.com and linkedin.com and compare their functionalities (capabilities). Also, enter ryze.com and view the video tutorial on networking. Compare Ryze's capabilities with those of LinkedIn.com. Write a report.

5. Enter chicstar.com. Why is it an online entertainment service? What are the benefits to viewers? Compare this site to starz.com.

6. Enter advertising.com. Find the innovative/scientific methods that are offered. Relate them to Web 2.0 and search.

7. Enter the paulgillin.com blog and find information related to enterprise applications of Web 2.0 technologies. Write a report.

8. Enter pandora.com. Find out how you can create and share music with friends. Why is this a Web 2.0 application?

9. Enter webkinz.com and compare its activities to that of facebook.com. Enter nielsen-online.com and find the average stay time on both social network sites.

10. Enter smartmobs.com. Go to blogroll. Find three blogs related to Web 2.0, and summarize their major features.

11. Enter mashable.com and review the latest news regarding social networks and network strategy. Right a report.

12. Access Hof's "My Virtual Life" (2008) at businessweek.com/print/magazine/content/ 06_18/b3982001.htm?chang=g1 and meet the seven residents in the slideshow. Prepare a table that shows the manner in which they make money, the required skills, and the reason they do it in Second Life.

13. Identify two virtual worlds (other than Second Life). Explore business opportunities there. Join as a member and write a report.

14. Enter secondlife.com and find the commercial activities of the following avatars: Fizik Baskerville, Craig Altman, Shaun Altman, FlipperPA Peregrine, and Anshe Chung. Describe briefly what they represent.

15. Enter businessinsider.com/alleyinsider/mobile and find the latest developments in iPhones and similar phones. Relate the developments to social networking. Write a report.

16. Enter en.wikipedia.org/wiki/Mixi and look at mixi's features that are similar to those offered by other social networks. Relate it to online entertainment.

17. Enter ning.com. Explore its capabilities and discuss how it is related to social network sites.

18. Enter yedda.com and explore its approach to knowledge sharing.

TEAM ASSIGNMENTS AND PROJECTS

1. Each group member selects a single-family house where he or she lives or where a friend lives. Next, enter zillow.com and find the value of a similar house in the neighborhood. Then, add improvements to adjust the value of the first house. Find out how to list the house for sale on Zillow and other sites (e.g., craigslist.org). Write a summary. Compare members' experiences.

2. Each group is assigned to a social network that has business activities on it (e.g., LinkedIn, Xing, Facebook, Second Life, etc.). Each group will then register with Hello TXT hellotxt.com to find out what is going on in the site with regard to recent business activities. Write a report and make a class presentation.

3. With Hello TXT, you log on to the site and enter your text message into the dashboard. You then select the sites you want to update with your new status message, and Hello TXT does the rest, reaching out to your various pages to add your new status message. It is a great centralized way to keep all your various profiles as up-to-date as possible, and it is designed to update your LinkedIn status by answering the question "What are you working on?"

4. The group signs in to secondlife.com and creates an avatar(s). Each member is assigned to explore a certain business area (e.g., virtual real estate, educational activities, diplomatic island). Make sure the avatar interacts with other people's avatars. Write a report.

5. Enter facebook.com and myspace.com and find out how 10 well-known corporations use the sites to conduct commercial activities (as per Sections 7.5 and 7.6). Also, compare the functionalities of the two sites.

Closing Case

LINKEDIN: THE BUSINESS-ORIENTED SOCIAL NETWORK

LinkedIn is a business-oriented social networking site mainly used for professional networking. As of May 2009, it had more than 40 million registered users spanning 200 industries around the world. LinkedIn can be used to find jobs, people, potential clients, service providers, subject experts, and other business opportunities.

A major purpose of LinkedIn is to allow registered users to maintain a list of contact details of people they know and trust in business (see *en.wikipedia.org/wiki/LinkedIn*). The people in each list are called *connections*. Users can invite anyone, whether they are a LinkedIn user or not, to become a connection. When people join, they create a profile that summarizes their professional accomplishments. The profile makes it possible to find and be found by former colleagues, clients, and partners.

A *contact network* consists of users' direct connections, each of their connections' connections (called second-degree connections), the connections

of second-degree connections (called third-degree connections), and so forth. The contact network makes it possible for a professional to gain an introduction to someone he or she wishes to know through a mutual, trusted contact. LinkedIn's officials are members and have hundreds of connections each (see Elad 2008 and *linkedin.com*).

The "gated-access approach," where contact with any professional requires either a preexisting relationship or the intervention of a contact of theirs, is intended to build trust among the service's users. LinkedIn participates in the EU Safe Harbor Privacy Framework.

The searchable LinkedIn groups feature allows users to establish new business relationships by joining alumni, industry, or professional, and other relevant, groups. It has close to 100,000 groups in its directory.

LinkedIn is especially useful in helping job seekers and employers find one another. Job seekers can list their résumés, search for open positions, check

Source: Courtesy of LinkedIn. Used with permission.

company profiles, and even review the profiles of hiring managers. Job seekers can also discover inside connections with existing contacts who can introduce them to a specific hiring manager. They can even see who has viewed their profiles.

Companies can use the site to post jobs and find and recruit employees, especially those who may not be actively searching for a new position.

As of January 2007, LinkedIn featured "LinkedIn Answers." As the name suggests, the service is similar to Answers.com or Yahoo! Answers. The service allows LinkedIn users to ask questions for the community to answer. "LinkedIn Answers" is free. The identity of the people asking and answering questions is known, so further communication is possible (see *linkedin.com/static?key=press_releases_011607*).

A mobile version of the site was launched in February 2008, which offers access to a reduced feature set over a mobile device. The mobile service is available in six languages: Chinese, English, French, German, Japanese, and Spanish.

In mid-2008, LinkedIn launched LinkedIn DirectAds as a form of sponsored advertising. It is similar to Google's AdWords. For a comparison with AdWords, see *targetinfolabs.com/online-ads/linkedin-directads-vs-google-adwords-ppc-a-comparison-test-for-best-value-for-money-lead-generation-round-1*.

LinkedIn has also joined forces with the financial news site CNBC. The deal integrates LinkedIn's

networking functionality into CNBC.com, allowing LinkedIn users to share and discuss financial and other news with their professional contacts. Community-generated content from LinkedIn, such as survey and poll results, will be broadcast on CNBC, and CNBC will provide LinkedIn with programming, articles, blogs, financial data, and video content. CNBC will be able to draw insights from LinkedIn's global user base to generate new types of business content for CNBC to broadcast.

The following are some useful resources on LinkedIn: *blog.linkedin.com*, *mylinkedinpower forum.com*, and *mylinksearch.com*.

Sources: Compiled from Elad (2008), *en.wikipedia.org/wiki/LinkedIn*, and *linkedin.com* (accessed May 2009).

Questions

1. Enter *linkedin.com* and explore. Why do you think the site is so successful?

2. What features are related to recruiting and job finding?

3. How does "LinkedIn Answers" work? Try to use it by posting a query. Report the results.

4. Why do you think President Obama created a page on LinkedIn while he was running for president?

ONLINE RESOURCES
Available at pearsonhighered.com/turban

Online Files

Comprehensive Educational Web Sites

informationweek.com/shared/printableArticleSrc.jhtml?articleID=202601956: "Growing Pains: Can Web 2.0 Evolve into an Enterprise Technology?"

cioinsight.com/c/a/Past-News/5-Reasons-to-Deploy-a-Corporate-Social-Network: "Five Reasons to Deploy a Corporate Social Network"

bloombergmarketing.blogs.com/Bloomberg_marketing: Diva Marketing Blog

blogs.zdnet.com/Hinchcliffe: Dion Hinchcliffe's Enterprise 2.0 blog

awarenessnetworks.com: Webinars on social media, Web 2.0, ROI, and marketing

newsgator.com/enterprise20/Oct2008: Webinar on social computing deployment

MOBILE COMPUTING AND COMMERCE

Content

Learning Objectives

Upon completion of this chapter, you will be able to:

1. Discuss the value-added attributes, benefits, and fundamental drivers of m-commerce.

2. Describe the mobile computing environment that supports m-commerce (devices, software, services).

3. Describe the four major types of wireless telecommunications networks.

4. Discuss m-commerce applications in finance.

5. Describe m-commerce applications in shopping, advertising, and provision of content.

6. Discuss the application of m-commerce within organizations and across the supply chain.

7. Describe consumer and personal applications of m-commerce.

8. Understand the technologies and potential application of location-based m-commerce.

9. Describe the major inhibitors and barriers of m-commerce.

THE BLOOMING OF FOOD LION

The Problem

Food Lion is a U.S. supermarket chain with approximately 1,300 stores in the Southeast and Mid-Atlantic states. Like other chains, Food Lion has found it increasingly difficult to compete on price against Walmart. Trying to seek an advantage against low-price competitors like Walmart, Food Lion decided to open a new, upscale chain called "Bloom" in 2004. From the beginning, Bloom stores focused on providing "a more hassle-free shopping experience" that would help consumers find products and check out quicker. This hassle-free experience rested on the creative use of "technology touch points" that improved the level of convenience for the shopper.

The Solution

At the heart of the shopping experience at Bloom are a variety of m-commerce technologies. For the moment, we define *m-commerce* as the ability to conduct commerce using a mobile device (e.g., a mobile or cell phone). Although Bloom utilizes a variety of information technologies, the following are critical to customer convenience:

- **Handheld scanners.** This handheld device (from Symbol Technologies) is a point-of-sale (POS) terminal that emulates the system used at checkout. The device is given to the customers. After picking an item from the shelf, the customer scans the item with the device, bags the item (in the cart), and continues shopping. The device shows the price of the item and the running total of all items bagged. Food Lion can also use the personal scanner (from Symbol Technologies) to send messages, such as special marketing offers, to customers while they are shopping. When they complete their shopping, customers hand the scanner to a store associate and settle the bill using whatever method they prefer. To deter shoplifting or cheating, customers are randomly picked to check whether items placed in the shopping cart have been scanned. Shoplifting has not been a serious problem.

- **Self-service produce scales.** These scales with specialized printers enable customers to create a bar-coded tag for vegetables, fruits, and other produce items that don't have price tags. Once the bar code is created, the item can be scanned like any other item in the store.

- **Information kiosks.** The meat and liquor departments provide kiosks that shoppers can use to scan items for nutritional and recipe information. The kiosks also enable shoppers to do party planning by generating shopping lists that indicate how much to buy based on the number of people expected to attend.

- **Wireless checkouts.** This is a mobile checkout POS terminal equipped with wheels that can be moved to any location in the store as well as outside (e.g., storefront for special sales). This adds flexibility and the ability to expedite checkout time. These devices can be added whenever checkout lines get long.

Results

Food Lion began the Bloom chain as an experiment with five stores. During the initial rollout, approximately 20 percent of regular Bloom shoppers used the handheld scanners. Based on their early success, the Bloom chain has expanded to 61 locations. The handheld scanners are available in 26 of these stores.

Overall, Bloom customers indicate that the scanners, and implicitly the associated technologies like the bar code printer, help them keep a running total against their budget and make it easier and faster to shop and check out. It also helps the company control costs, reduce prices, and increase revenue. Those customers who enjoy chatting with cashiers can still shop the old-fashioned way, but most customers, especially those in high-traffic locations, would rather use the scanners to save time.

Food Lion is not the only retailer experimenting with wireless devices. METRO Group is experimenting with in-store mobile devices at its Future Store in Rheinberg, Germany. At the Future Store, customers are provided with special mobile phones known as "Mobile Shopping Assistants (MSAs)." An MSA provides online access to product descriptions and pictures, pricing information, and store maps. It also enables a shopper to scan items as they are placed in the cart and to keep a running list and total cost of the items. At checkout, the MSA allows a shopper to "pay in passing" by using the MSAs to pass scanned data to a payment terminal. METRO has measured the reactions and satisfaction of Future Store shoppers. The results indicate that customers are more satisfied, customers visit the store more often, the percentage of new customers has increased, and customers spend more euros per month.

Sources: Compiled from Bonkoo (2007) and METRO (2008).

WHAT WE CAN LEARN . . .

From a retail perspective, the opening case illustrates that mobile devices have the potential to enhance the shopping experience for in-store customers and to increase the overall financial performance of retailers employing those technologies. This is only one example of the impact of emerging mobile and wireless technologies on commerce and electronic commerce (EC). In this chapter, we will explore a number of these emerging mobile and wireless technologies as well as their potential applications in the commercial arena.

8.1 MOBILE COMMERCE: ATTRIBUTES, BENEFITS, AND DRIVERS

Mobile commerce (m-commerce), also known as **m-business**, includes any business activity conducted over a wireless telecommunications network. This includes B2C and B2B commercial transactions as well as the transfer of information and services via wireless mobile devices. Like regular EC applications, m-commerce can be done via the Internet, via private communication lines, or over other computing networks. M-commerce is a natural extension of e-commerce. Mobile devices create an opportunity to deliver new services to existing customers and to attract new customers. However, the small screen size and reduced bandwidth of most mobile computing devices have limited consumer interest. So even though the mobile computing industry recognizes the potential for B2C m-commerce applications, the number of existing applications is still emerging, and consumer uptake has been slow. In this chapter, we consider some of the distinguishing attributes and key drivers of m-commerce, the technical underpinnings of m-commerce, and some of the major m-commerce applications. The overall landscape for m-commerce is summarized in Exhibit 8.1.

mobile commerce (m-commerce or m-business) Any business activity conducted over a wireless telecommunications network or from mobile devices.

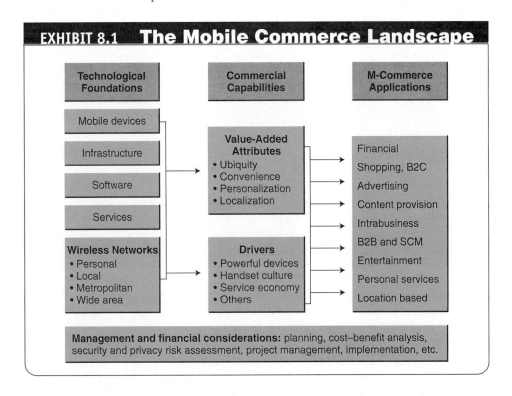

EXHIBIT 8.1 **The Mobile Commerce Landscape**

ATTRIBUTES OF M-COMMERCE

Generally speaking, many of the EC applications described in this book also apply to m-commerce. For example, online shopping, Internet banking, e-stock trading, e-entertainment, and online gambling are gaining popularity in wireless B2C. Auction sites are starting to use m-commerce (e.g., sending a text message alert when an auction is about to close), and wireless collaborative commerce in B2B EC is emerging. There are, however, some key attributes that offer the opportunity for development of new applications that are possible only in the mobile environment. These include:

▶ **Ubiquity.** *Ubiquity* means being available at any location at any time. A wireless mobile device such as a smart phone or tablet PC can deliver information when it is needed, regardless of the user's location (as long as Internet access is available). Ubiquity creates easier information access in a real-time environment, which is highly valued in today's business and competitive markets.

▶ **Convenience.** It is very convenient for users to operate in the wireless computing environment. Mobile computing devices are increasing in functionality and usability while remaining small. Unlike traditional computers, mobile devices are portable, can be set in a variety of monitoring modes, and most feature instant connectivity (i.e., no need to wait for the device to boot up). Mobile devices enable users to connect easily and quickly to the Internet, intranets, other mobile devices, and online databases.

▶ **Interactivity.** In comparison with the desktop computing environment, transactions, communications, and service provision are immediate and highly interactive in the mobile computing environment. Businesses in which customer support and delivery of services require a high level of interactivity with the customer are likely to find a high value-added component in mobile computing.

▶ **Personalization.** Mobile devices are truly personal computing devices. Whereas a computer in a home, library, or Internet café may be used by a number of people, mobile devices are almost always owned and operated by a single individual. This truly enables consumer personalization—the delivery of information, products, and services designed to meet the needs of individual consumers. For example, users planning a trip can be sent travel-related information for retrieval when and where they want.

▶ **Localization.** Knowing where a user is physically located at any particular moment is key to offering relevant mobile services in real time. Such services are known as location-based m-commerce (see Section 8.7). Localization may be general—for example, targeting everyone in a certain location (e.g., all shoppers at a shopping mall). Or, even better, it may be targeted so that users get messages that depend both on where they are and what their preferences are, thus combining personalization and localization.

Vendors and carriers can differentiate themselves in the competitive marketplace by offering new, exciting, and useful services based on these attributes. These value-adding attributes can be the basis for businesses to better deliver the value proposition they offer to customers.

DRIVERS OF M-COMMERCE

In addition to the value-added attributes just discussed, the development of m-commerce is being driven by the following technological, business, social, and economic factors:

- **Widespread availability of more powerful mobile devices.** By the end of 2008, worldwide mobile telephone subscriptions reached 4 billion—equivalent to over half the global population (ITU 2007). By 2011, the overall penetration is forecasted to be 75 percent. These devices are increasing in power, functionality, and features (e.g., color screens, GPS locators, Internet access) that support m-commerce. Thus, the potential mass market for conducting m-commerce has emerged.

- **The handset culture.** A closely related driver is the widespread use of cell phones among the 15- to 25-year-old age group. These users will constitute a major market of online buyers once they begin to make and spend reasonable amounts of money.

- **The service economy.** The transition from a manufacturing to a service-based economy is encouraging the development of mobile-based services, especially when customer service is a differentiator in highly competitive industries. Time-starved, but resource-rich, individuals will pay for mobile services that perform a range of tasks at their convenience (e.g., locating a restaurant or dry cleaner in close proximity to the user's position or mobile banking that allows users to pay bills online from their cell phones).

- **Vendor's push.** Both mobile communication network operators and manufacturers of mobile devices are advertising the many potential applications of m-commerce so that they can push new technologies, products, and services to buyers. The advertising expenditure by these companies to encourage businesses to "go mobile" or "mobilize your business" is huge. Also, the competition among vendors and products creates innovative applications.

- **The mobile workforce.** Some workers, such as salespeople and field service employees, have always worked away from an office. Increasingly, other sectors of the workforce also are "going mobile." This is being driven by social trends in the workplace such as telecommuting, employers' concerns about security, employees' desires for improved work–life balance, and a general questioning of where knowledge workers need to be located to conduct their work.

- **Increased mobility.** The most widely recognized benefit of increased mobility is the productive use of travel time. Workers who commute long distances, and especially executives who travel frequently, want to make more productive use of time they spend in public transportation vehicles or in airport lounges. Also, telecommuting is on the rise, enabled by the use of mobile devices.

- **Improved price/performance.** The price of wireless devices and of per-minute pricing of mobile services continues to decline even as available services and functionality are increasing. This is leading to improvements in the price/performance ratio, enticing new owners into the market and encouraging existing owners to increase consumption of services and to upgrade their handsets.

> **Improving bandwidth.** To properly conduct m-commerce, sufficient bandwidth is needed to transmit the desired information via text, picture, voice, video, or multimedia. Theoretically, the 3G communications technology supported by newer smart phones (e.g., the iPhone) is providing a data rate of up to 2 Mbps. Empirically, 3G transmission speeds are much slower, with actual rates somewhere between .1 and .5 Mbps. This is in comparison to standard Wi-Fi, which is close to 56 Mbps. Soon 3.5G and 4G will arrive with even better capabilities.

The drivers and attributes of m-commerce underlie most of the applications discussed in later sections of the chapter.

Section 8.1 ❱ REVIEW QUESTIONS

1. Briefly describe the five value-added attributes of m-commerce.
2. List and briefly describe eight major drivers of m-commerce.

8.2 COMPONENTS, TECHNICAL INFRASTRUCTURE, AND SERVICES OF MOBILE COMPUTING

In the traditional computing environment, users require a desktop computer and cabled connections to networks, servers, and peripheral devices such as printers. This situation has limited the use of computers to fixed locations and has created difficulties for people who either want or need to be connected anytime, anywhere. For instance, salespeople, field service employees, law enforcement agents, inspectors, utility workers, and executives who travel frequently can be more effective if they can use information technology while at their jobs in the field or in transit. A solution to this situation is **wireless mobile computing** (or just **mobile computing**), which enables a real-time connection between a mobile device and computing networks or to another computing device, anytime, anywhere. Mobile computing offers a computing environment suitable for workers who travel outside the boundaries of their workplace or for anyone on the move.

An extensive hardware and software infrastructure underlies mobile computing. First, there are the mobile devices (e.g., smart phones) that enable a user to connect to a mobile network. Next, there are those components (e.g., network access points) that support the wireless connection, as well as parts of the infrastructure (e.g., GPS locators) that support the delivery of services over the connection. Finally, there are those components that support m-commerce activities in the same way they support typical e-commerce activities. For example, a Web server, database server, and enterprise application server offer the same services to a wireless device as they do to a wired computer, with one significant exception. Certain characteristics of mobile devices—small screens, reduced memory, limited bandwidth, and restricted input capabilities—mean that hardware and software designers need to anticipate special requirements and design the system accordingly.

This section and the next briefly discuss the major components of the mobile computing infrastructure.

MOBILE DEVICES

A few years ago, a computer was basically a computer, a cell phone was basically a phone, and a personal digital assistant (PDA) was essentially a stand-alone personal information manager (calendar, contacts, calculator, and the like). Today, all of these devices are converging so that it is difficult from a functional perspective to tell them apart.

wireless mobile computing (mobile computing)
Computing that connects a mobile device to a network or another computing device, anytime, anywhere.

Mobile computers come in all shapes and sizes—laptops, thin-and-light notebooks, ultra portables, and ultra-mobile PCs (UMPCs). Most of these have the same basic capabilities (e.g., support for audio and video, e-mail, Internet browsers, and Wi-Fi connections) and run essentially the same operating systems (e.g., some form of Microsoft Windows). What distinguishes one type of mobile computer from another is its physical footprint. Thin notebooks weigh 4 to 6 pounds and have 14-inch displays. In comparison, ultra portables weigh less than 3 pounds and have smaller screens. Most of the major computer manufacturers (HP, Dell, ASUS, Toshiba, and Lenovo) produce thin notebooks and ultra portables. In contrast, few of the major computer makers currently produce UMPCs. Although UMPCs are also full-blown computers, they tend to have much smaller footprints—either no standard keyboard or much smaller keyboards, weigh between 1 and 2 pounds, and have much smaller screens (5 to 6 inches). Samsung, OQO, and ASUS are some of the manufacturers offering UMPCs.

Originally, a **personal digital assistant (PDA)**, also known as a *palmtop*, was a stand-alone handheld computer that provided access to a user's address book and calendar and supported calculation and desktop applications such as word processing and spreadsheets. Most of the original PDAs could also be synchronized with a user's desktop computer. This enabled a user to read e-mails offline. Over time, most PDAs have added support for wireless connectivity to the Internet through Wi-Fi. In this way, a PDA can be used to browse the Web and read and send e-mail in real time. Most PDAs also provide multimedia support for audio and video.

personal digital assistant (PDA)
A stand-alone handheld computer principally used for personal information management.

The leading producers of PDAs are Research In Motion (BlackBerry; rim.com), Palm, Inc. (palm.com) and Hewlett-Packard (hp.com). From a hardware perspective, most PDAs have small screens (2.5 to 4 inches), small memories (64 Mb of RAM; although by 2009 up to 256 Mb of RAM is available), either small keyboards with thumb wheels or a virtual keyboard on the screen, and expansion slots for memory cards (SD or compact flash) that offer additional storage or access to other applications. From a software perspective, most PDAs either run the Palm Operating System (OS) or Microsoft's Windows Mobile operating system.

Basically, a **smart phone** is a mobile phone with PDA-like or PC-like functionality, including e-mail, Web browsing, multimedia capabilities, address book, calendar, calculator, support for reading Word and PDF documents, a digital camera, and so forth. Unlike PDAs, there is a wide variety of smart phone manufacturers. There is also a wide variety of operating systems, including Symbian, Linux, Palm OS, Windows Mobile, Apple OS/X, and RIM BlackBerry. Like PDAs, smart phones have small screens, keyboards, memory, and storage.

smart phone
A mobile phone with PC-like capabilities.

Clearly, PDAs, smart phones, Internet appliances, and multimedia players appear to be converging toward the same endpoint—a small-footprint, handheld mobile device that combines all the capabilities of these devices in one package. The future of laptops, notebooks, and UMPCs is a little less clear, although these mobile computers will continue to support a broad span of capabilities in a shrinking footprint.

MOBILE COMPUTING SOFTWARE AND SERVICES

Although mobile devices such as cell phones and smart phones present a variety of software challenges, they also offer a number of software-enabled services that aren't found in the desktop or even mobile computer worlds. These services provide a foundation for many of the applications described later in the chapter. Included among these services are messaging, location-based, and voice-support services.

Messaging Services

Short message service (SMS), frequently referred to as *text messaging*, or simply *texting*, is a service that supports the transmittal of short text messages (up to 160 characters) between mobile phones on a cellular telephone network. The limited message length means users often use acronyms to convey the message in shorthand text. Examples include "how are you" becomes "how r u," and "great" becomes "gr8." Texting has been immensely popular in Asia and Europe for some time. In the United States, adoption of SMS has been slower than in other parts of the world, although usage has been growing at double-digit rates for the past few years.

Texting is getting more popular in the United States thanks to iPhone and Twitter. In 2008, the total global user base for SMS text messaging passed 3 billion. Today 76 percent of all mobile phone subscribers worldwide use SMS text messaging. More than half of Americans are active users of SMS text messaging catching up with average European SMS text messaging usage levels (Communities Dominate Brands 2009).

Multimedia messaging service (MMS) is the emerging generation of wireless messaging, delivering rich media, including video and audio, to mobile phones and other devices. MMS is an extension of SMS that was commercially introduced in 2002. It allows longer messages and utilizes a special protocol for displaying media content. MMS enables the convergence of mobile devices and personal computers because MMS messages can be sent between PCs, PDAs, and mobile phones that are MMS enabled.

Location-Based Services

Location-based services use the *global positioning system (GPS)* or other positioning techniques to find where customers and clients are located and deliver products and services to them based on the location in real time.

Voice-Support Services

The most natural mode of human communication is voice. Voice recognition and voice synthesizing in m-commerce applications offer advantages such as hands- and eyes-free operation, better operation in dirty or moving environments, faster input (people talk about two-and-a-half times faster than they type), and ease-of-use for disabled people. Most significantly, increased use of voice-support services exploits the built-in audio capabilities of many mobile devices and reduces their dependence on less-than-satisfactory input solutions, such as handwriting recognition, keypads, or virtual touch-screen keyboards.

Voice support applications such as **interactive voice response (IVR)** systems enable users to interact with a computerized system to request and receive information and to enter and change data using a telephone. These systems have been around since the 1980s but are becoming more functional and widespread as artificial intelligence and voice-recognition capabilities continue to improve.

The highest level of voice support services is a **voice portal**, a Web site with an audio interface that can be accessed through a telephone call. A visitor requests information by speaking, and the voice portal finds the information on the Web, translates it into a computer-generated voice reply, and provides the answer by voice. For example, tellme.com and bevocal.com allow callers to request information about weather, local restaurants, current traffic, and other handy information. IVR and voice portals are likely to become important ways of delivering m-commerce services over audio.

WIRELESS TELECOMMUNICATIONS NETWORKS

All mobile devices need to connect with a telecommunications network or with another device. How they do this depends on the purpose of the connection, the capabilities and location of the device, and what connection options are available at the time. Included among the various networks are (1) personal area networks for device-to-device connections up to 30 feet, (2) wireless local area networks for medium-range connections up to 300 feet, (3) wireless metropolitan networks for connections up to 30 miles, and (4) wireless wide area networks for connecting to a network with cellular phone coverage.

▶ **Personal area networks.** A personal area network (PAN) is suitable for mobile users who need to make very short-range device-to-device wireless connections within a small space, typically a single room. The most common way to establish a PAN is with Bluetooth. Bluetooth is a set of telecommunications standards that enables wireless devices to communicate with each other over short distances of up to 60 feet (20 meters). Bluetooth can be used to pair a number of different devices—wireless keyboards with tablet PCs, PDAs with computers for easy data synchronization, and digital cameras with printers. Bluetooth also can link more than two devices, as is done in connectBlue's operating-room control system (connectblue.se). Equipment that monitors a patient's heartbeat, ECG, respiration, and other vital signs can be linked via Bluetooth, eliminating obstructive and dangerous cables and increasing the portability of the equipment. For additional information, see bluetooth.com and bluetooth.org.

▶ **Wireless local area networks and Wi-Fi.** As its name implies, a wireless local area network (WLAN) is equivalent to a wired LAN, but without all the cables. Most WLANs run on a telecommunications standard known as *IEEE 802.11* (e.g., 802.11g) which is commonly called Wi-Fi (for wireless fidelity). Exhibit 8.2 outlines the processes and components underlying Wi-Fi. At the heart of a WLAN is a wireless access point that connects a wireless device to the desired network. The wireless device communicates with the access point by a wireless network card installed by the user or manufacturer of the device. In turn, the access point has a wired connection to the Internet in the same manner as a wired LAN cable. Most public hotspots located in airports, hotels, restaurants, and conference centers rely on Wi-Fi. Similarly, many home owners have installed Wi-Fi to enable Internet connectivity throughout their home without the need to retrofit the house with cables. Online File W8.1 describes the growing use of Wi-Fi by the traveling public.

▶ **Municipal Wi-Fi networks.** By using a large number of connected hotspots, one can create a wireless city. This is known as a *city-wide* or *municipal Wi-Fi network*. For example, on August 16, 2006, Google created a network of 380 access points posted on light poles throughout the city of Mountain View, California. Residents of Mountain View just had to choose the "GoogleWiFi" signal and sign into their Google accounts with their user ID and password to access the Web through the free Wi-Fi service. These networks also are known as *grid* or *mesh networks* (see Online File W8.2). Throughout the United States, there have been a number of municipal Wi-Fi projects. Most of these, like Philadelphia, Pennsylvania's "Wireless Philadelphia" project, have experienced cost and schedule overruns only to provide much less coverage than originally envisioned (*Philadelphia Inquirer* 2007).

personal area network (PAN)
A wireless telecommunications network for device-to-device connections within a very short range.

Bluetooth
A set of telecommunications standards that enables wireless devices to communicate with each other over short distances.

wireless local area network (WLAN)
A telecommunications network that enables users to make short-range wireless connections to the Internet or another network.

Wi-Fi (wireless fidelity)
The common name used to describe the IEEE 802.11 standard used on most WLANs.

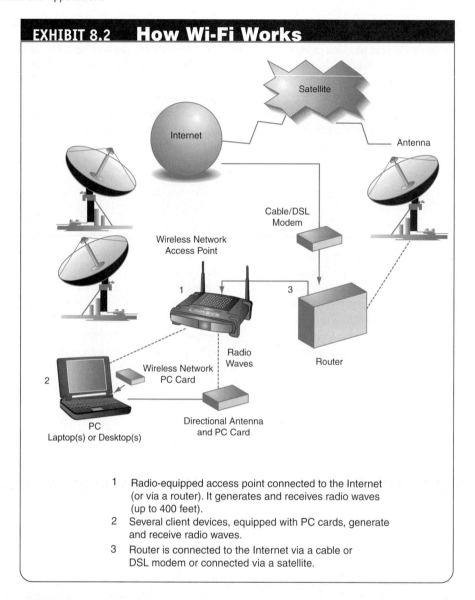

EXHIBIT 8.2   How Wi-Fi Works

1   Radio-equipped access point connected to the Internet
    (or via a router). It generates and receives radio waves
    (up to 400 feet).
2   Several client devices, equipped with PC cards, generate
    and receive radio waves.
3   Router is connected to the Internet via a cable or
    DSL modem or connected via a satellite.

WiMax

A wireless standard
(IEEE 802.16) for
making broadband
network connections
over a medium-size area
such as a city.

▶ **WiMax.** Instead of relying on a mesh or grid of multiple access points, like municipal Wi-Fi, **WiMax** (Worldwide Interoperability for Microwave Access) provides relatively fast (e.g., 70 Mbps) broadband access over a medium-sized area of up to 31 miles (50 kilometers). WiMax works somewhat like a cell phone. More specifically, WiMax coverage is divided into a series of overlapping areas called *cells*. Each of these cells provides broadband Internet coverage within a given geographical area. At the center of each cell is a tower with a base station that is connected to the Internet using high-speed lines. A tower broadcasts radio signals over a set radio frequency called a *spectrum*. Unlike Wi-Fi, the spectrum is restricted to companies who have licensed its usage (e.g., Sprint). This provides wider and more reliable coverage. Again, in order to access a WiMax network, a device (e.g., UMPC) requires a built-in or external card.

WiMax is gaining popularity in a number of municipal areas throughout the world. The WiMax Forum (wimaxforum.org) provides detailed information about WiMax capabilities and usage.

▶ **Wireless wide area networks.** A **wireless wide area network (WWAN)** offers the broadest wireless coverage. WWANs rely on the same network technologies as cell phones. This means that a user with a mobile computer and a WWAN card can access the Internet regionally, nationally, or even globally, depending on the coverage of the wireless service provider the user is accessing. WWANs can be distinguished by their speed (e.g., 2G versus 3G versus 4G networks), by the communication protocols they use (e.g., the time division multiple access [TDMA] protocol used in 2G networks versus the code division multiple access [CDMA] designed for 3G networks), and the cellular standards on which they are based (e.g., much of the world utilizes the Global System for Mobile Communications [GSM] and Personal Digital Cellular [PDC] in Japan). Exhibit 8.3 provides a summary of the differences among the various networks by speed (from 1G to 4G).

wireless wide area network (WWAN)
A telecommunications network that offers wireless coverage over a large geographical area, typically over a cellular phone network.

Information about WWANs can be found at the Web sites of the various service providers (e.g., sprint.com) and at the sites of various mobile or cellular associations (e.g., gsmworld.com).

Section 8.2 ▶ REVIEW QUESTIONS

1. Briefly describe some of the key differences and similarities among the major mobile devices.
2. Why is it difficult to develop software and services for mobile devices?

EXHIBIT 8.3 Four Generations of WWAN Technologies

WWAN Generation	Description
1G	This was the first generation of wireless technology. It was an analog-based technology in effect from 1979 to 1992 and was used exclusively for voice.
2G	This second generation of digital wireless technology is in widespread existence today. 2G is based on digital radio technology and is able to accommodate text messages (SMS).
2.5G	An interim technology based on new cell phone protocols such as GPRS (general packet radio service) and CDMA2000 (code division multiple access). This generation can communicate limited graphics, such as in picture text messages.
3G	The third generation of digital wireless technology supports rich media, such as video. 3G utilizes packet switching in the high 15 to 20 MHz range. 3G started in Japan in 2001, reached Europe in 2002, and the United States and much of Asia in 2003. As of 2004, the number of 3G-enabled devices was only a tiny fraction of the cell phone market. However, sales are projected to increase gradually as more 3G networks and applications become available.
3.5G	This generation is expected to be about seven times better than 3G. It promises data download speeds of 14 Mbps and upload speeds of up to 1.8 Mbps. This means major improvements in mobile voice telephony, video telephony, mobile TV, and other media.
4G	The next generation after 3.5G. The arrival of 4G, which will provide faster display of multimedia including video chat and mobile TV, is expected in 2010.

3. Briefly describe the types of messaging services offered for mobile devices.

4. What are the distinguishing features of PANs, WLANs, WiMax, and WWANs?

5. Define 3G. Why is it important for the adoption of mobile applications and services?

8.3 MOBILE FINANCIAL APPLICATIONS

Most mobile financial services are simply mobile versions of their wire line counterparts, but they have the potential to turn a mobile device—cellular phone or personal digital assistant—into a business tool, replacing bank branches, ATMs, and credit cards by letting a user conduct financial transactions with a mobile device, anytime, anywhere. These services fall into two broad categories: mobile banking and mobile payments.

MOBILE BANKING

Throughout Europe, the United States, and Asia, an increasing percentage of banks are offering mobile access to financial and account information. These banks enable their customers to use their mobile devices to check balances, conduct and monitor transactions, obtain other account information, transfer funds, locate branches or ATMs, and pay bills.

Most banks deploy these mobile services through a variety of channels, although the Internet and SMS are the most widely used. A blog written by Brandon McGee (brandonmcgee.blogspot.com) provides links to a number of banking Web sites throughout the world that provide these services. Take, for instance, the Chase Mobile services offered by J.P. Morgan Chase Bank. On the one hand, customers can access their accounts at (chase.com) via the browser on their smart phone in much the same way they would access their accounts from their desktop or laptop computers. On the other hand, customers can send Chase Mobile shorthand SMS text messages to inquire about their balances (BAL), payment due dates (DUE), or transaction histories (TRANS).

Historically, the uptake of mobile banking has been relatively low. This is beginning to change. Much of the change is being driven by the world economic crisis. Bank and financial service customers are utilizing their smart phones and cell phones to obtain up-to-the minute financial information and to perform up-to-the-minute transactions. MONILINK, the United Kingdom's mobile money network, which is used by most of the U.K. high-street banks, reported in October 2008 that customers had used the network for approximately 1 million transactions, a substantial increase over the previous months (*M2 Presswire* 2008). IMS Research, a global market research firm, recently forecast that the number of mobile banking users will reach approximately 1 billion in 2012 and that they will complete about 60 million transactions during that year (IMS Research 2008).

Similar patterns were revealed in a 2008 survey (*PaymentNews* 2008) of more than 1,000 cell phone users conducted on behalf of CheckFree (see checkfree.fiserv.com). Although only 23 percent of the survey respondents currently conduct financial activities over their cell phones, approximately 75 percent indicated that they would be interested in using their phones to check bank and credit card balances, receive and pay bills, transfer money between accounts, etc., if the services were made available. This represents a 50 percent increase over the percent expressing an interest in a survey conducted two years prior. Respondents cited anytime, anywhere access as the primary reasons for their interest.

MOBILE PAYMENTS

The term *mobile payment* refers to payment transactions initiated or confirmed using a person's cell phone or smart phone. These transactions include such things as point-of-sale (POS) purchases, transferring money to a person or business, or purchasing a product or service remotely. (Some are done by banks as described earlier.)

Mobile Proximity Payments

In the United States, mobile contactless payments have only been used in a handful of pilot projects. For instance, from January 2008 to May 2008 a select group of riders of the San Francisco Bay Area Rapid Transit (BART) were able to pay their fares using their mobile phones (*Wireless and Mobile News* 2008). These phones were outfitted with NFC-enabled chips. Likewise, NFC equipment was installed at the BART turnstiles. In this way, the riders simply tapped their phones on the NFC equipment to gain entrance through the turnstiles. The fare was then deducted via the phone from a prepaid account. These same riders could also use their phones to pay for meals at local Jack in the Box fast-food restaurants.

Although the BART pilot was deemed a success, it points to the "chicken–egg" problem that confronts most EC payment schemes. In simple terms, because the consumers' phones require specialized chips, the merchants (in this case BART) require specialized equipment to communicate with the chips. And, because specialized networks are also required to handle the payments, the chances against widespread adoption are substantial, if not overwhelming.

Outside the United States, adoption of mobile contactless payments has been a bit broader, especially in Japan. To date, approximately 20 million customers of NTT DOCOMO use mobile phones for debit card transactions. In the future, they will also use them as credit cards. Interestingly, taxis in Japan, Germany, and other countries are starting to install wireless systems for receiving payments.

Mobile Remote Payments

A number of initiatives have been launched to support mobile remote payments. These initiatives offer services that enable clients and consumers to use their mobile devices to pay their monthly bills, to shop on the Internet, to transfer funds to other individuals (P2P payments), and to "top off" their prepaid mobile accounts without having to purchase prepaid phone cards. Case 8.1 provides an example of how mobile remote payments are being used in developing countries like India to service loans to those on the economic margins of the country.

In the case of mobile bill payments, Internet shopping, P2P payments, and "topping off," the processes involved in executing a transaction are basically the same:

1. The payer initiating the payment sets up an account with a mobile payment service provider (MPSP).
2. To make a payment, the payer sends a text message or command to the MPSP that includes the dollar amount and the receiver's mobile phone number.
3. The MPSP receives the information and sends a message back to the payer, confirming the transaction and requesting his or her PIN.
4. The payer receives the request on his or her mobile device and enters a PIN.
5. When the MPSP receives the payer's PIN, money is transferred to the third party's account (credit card or bank account).
6. After the transaction occurs, the payment information is sent to the payer's mobile device.

CASE 8.1
EC Application
CLOSING THE DIGITAL DIVIDE WITH MOBILE MICROFINANCE

The term **digital divide** refers to the gap between people with effective access to digital and information technology and those without. The gap is both a symptom and product of the larger issues of poverty and inequality. In underdeveloped and developing countries, the divide has widened as more of everyday life has moved to the digital arena across the globe. This is especially true in the financial arena. Although many of these countries do not have money to implement wire line phone systems, they can afford WWANs. This provides the opportunity to utilize mobile devices to narrow the widening gap.

The vast majority of the inhabitants in developing countries such as India are "unbanked." Some estimates put the worldwide number of unbanked at 70 percent of the world's population. Basically, they lack access to some of the basic financial services needed to live their daily lives, much less lift them out of poverty. As a consequence, they often turn to local moneylenders who charge exorbitant interest rates (sometimes more than 10 percent per month) in order to handle personal emergencies, life-cycle needs (such as weddings and funerals), or to take advantage of investment opportunities (such as buying homes, land, or equipment).

The world of microfinance is aimed at addressing some of these needs. **Microfinance** refers to the provision of financial services to poor or low-income clients, including consumers and the self-employed. Microfinance is also a social movement predicated on the belief that access to a range of financial services will help lift the poor out of poverty. Obviously, financing can come from a variety of sources, both institutional and noninstitutional. However, the term *microfinance* is usually applied to formal financial institutions (such as banks).

A few years back, it was estimated that there were more than 3,000 financial institutions serving the needs of some 665 million poor clients. About a fourth of those serviced were classified as microfinance. In 2007, it was estimated that these institutions were providing more than

digital divide
Refers to the gap between people with effective access to digital and information technology and those without.

microfinance
Refers to the provision of financial services to poor or low-income clients, including consumers and the self-employed.

$25 billion in microfinance loans. Most of these individual loans were for amounts less than US$200.

Grameen Koota, one of these microfinance institutions, is located in Bangalore, India, and is part of a much larger financial institution, Grameen Bank. At the moment, it has more than 40,000 clients and a loan portfolio of more than US$20 million. In order to service its microfinance loans, it maintains a large staff of loan officers. One of the primary jobs of these loan officers is to attend weekly client meetings held within the local communities in order to collect repayments. This is a high-risk process, plagued by theft, fraud, and embezzlement.

Potentially, mobile banking and remote payments could be used to address some of the problems surrounding the collection of loans at Grameen Koota and other microfinance lending institutions. At least this is what Grameen Koota and the founders of start-up mChek, as well as mChek's financial backers at Draper Fisher Juvetson, believe.

Like the rest of India, cell phone use is growing rapidly among Grameen Koota's customers. In countries like India, China, and the Philippines, the penetration of cell phones even among the poor is skyrocketing. In part this is a result of rapidly declining costs of owning and using a cell phone. More than 1 billion people live in India; this is more than 17 percent of the world's population. More than 450 million of these people live in poverty—living on less than 25 rupees a day (a little more than 50 cents). It is estimated that midway through 2008, around 300 million Indians had cell phones. During the month of August, the number of cell phones grew by more than 9 million. At this rate, the number of cell phone owners in India will exceed 750 million by 2012. This makes India the fastest growing cell phone market in the world and the second largest market.

Even though most of the phones owned by the poor inhabitants in India have minimal functionality, they still offer SMS capabilities. These capabilities, in combination with mChek's software, will provide Grameen Koota with the mobile means to make loans and receive payments without the need to send loan officers into the local community. Recently, mChek got a boost when Bharti Airtel (India's leading provider of cell phones) decided to incorporate mChek's software directly into its SIM cards—the device inside a mobile phone that identifies the user and number.

CASE 8.1 *(continued)*

MChek is not the only Indian company focused on providing mobile microfinance capabilities. Obopay India (a branch of the U.S.-based Obopay) is also developing a microfinance mobile platform. Obopay is working with Grameen Solutions, one of the organizations created by Muhammad Yunus, who received the Nobel Peace Prize in 2006 along with Grameen Bank for his work with microcredit.

Sources: Compiled from Talbot (2008) and Mitra (2008).

Questions

1. What is microfinance?
2. What problem is Grameen Koota trying to solve by adopting mobile loans and payments?
3. How will mobile loans and payments work for organizations like Grameen Koota?

Similar sorts of steps are used to enable merchants or service providers the opportunity to conduct POS transactions without the need for special POS terminals. These payments have been labeled *mobile POS (mPOS)* transactions. With mPOS, the merchant utilizes a special mobile service to send a payment request from his or her mobile device to the customer's phone number. Once the request is received, the customer enters his or her PIN. At this point, the service sends a confirmation to both the merchant and the customer. The transactions are completed by debiting the customer's account and crediting the merchant's account. Even though the merchant is also charged transaction and communication costs by the service operator, the cost is substantially less than a POS credit card transaction. These services are aimed at small businesses and independent operators such as doctors, dentists, delivery companies, taxis, and plumbers.

Although a number of companies such as Obopay, PayPal Mobile, and TextPayMe offer mobile remote payment services, the worldwide uptake of these services has been minimal. Part of the problem is that few of the companies support a broad range of remote payment services. For instance, with PayPal Mobile, users can only check their PayPal balances, send money to other individuals, and make eBay purchases. Like any other electronic payment system without broader coverage and widely accepted payment methods and standards, most of these services are doomed to failure.

Section 8.3 ▶ REVIEW QUESTIONS

1. Describe some of the services provided by mobile banking.
2. Discuss proximity-based wireless payments. How have they been used in the transportation arena?
3. What are the basic processes used in handling mobile remote payments?

8.4 MOBILE MARKETING AND ADVERTISING

The ratio of mobile handsets to desktop and laptop computers is approximately two to one and growing. This represents a huge opportunity for online marketing and advertising. Not only has the opportunity been heightened by current economic conditions, but it has also been spurred by the higher response rates to mobile marketing campaigns when compared to more traditional or online campaigns.

MOBILE MARKETING CAMPAIGNS

According to a review of leading mobile marketing literature (Becker 2006), the analysis of 55 campaigns run by companies such as Coca-Cola and BMW, and interviews with

44 mobile marketing thought leaders, determined that there were basically four classes of online campaigns focused on one of four types of Internet campaign objectives. The classes included:

1. **Information.** Programs providing information about products, points of interest, news, weather, traffic, horoscopes, and related content.
2. **Entertainment.** Programs that "produce value to the customers" and provide amusement and emotional triggers through videos, music, games, personalization ringtones, wallpapers, and so forth.
3. **Raffles.** Programs that provide prizes such as digital content or physical goods.
4. **Coupons.** Programs that offer monetary incentives (like discounts), trial packages, or free services.

The major objectives of these classes fell into one of six categories:

1. **Building brand awareness.** Increase customers' ability to recognize and recall a brand in purchase and consumption situations.
2. **Changing brand image.** Change the perception of the brand by customers.
3. **Promoting sales.** Stimulate quicker or greater purchase of a product or service.
4. **Enhancing brand loyalty.** Increase consumers' commitment to repurchase the brand.
5. **Building customer databases.** Collect data about the mobile device, data network, or profiles of customers.
6. **Stimulating mobile word of mouth.** Encourage customers to pass ads from customer to customer via their mobile devices.

Obviously, these are the same types of campaigns and objectives underlying traditional marketing approaches. Currently, SMS and e-mails are the principal technologies used to deliver advertisements to cell phones. However, as more wireless bandwidth becomes available, content-rich advertising involving audio, pictures, and video clips will be generated for individual users with specific needs, interests, and inclinations.

Recent marketing campaigns conducted by high-end clothing retailers are indicative of the types of mobile campaigns.

Example: Dolce & Gabanna (D&G). In 2008, Dolce & Gabanna ran a mobile campaign on the Nokia Media Network. The goal of the campaign was to promote awareness of D&G's overall brand and their teen-focused fashion catalog. Part of the campaign involved a game called "Dee&Gee," which could be downloaded from the D&G mobile Web site. Once at the site, consumers could also view the D&G teen catalog and download D&G-branded wallpaper. The response to the D&G campaign was a 10 percent click-through rate (CTR). According to Nokia, this is typical. CTRs generally range from 2 percent to 20 percent. This may seem low, but it is consistently higher than similar online or traditional media ads. It is one of the main reasons for the growing interest in mobile advertising.

MOBILE MARKETING GUIDELINES

Although organizations such as the Direct Marketing Association have established codes of practice for Internet marketing, including the use of mobile media, most industry pundits agree that they are not well suited for the dynamic nature of mobile commerce. In response, the mobile media industry has established a set of guidelines and best practices for mobile advertising. The Global Code of Conduct from the Mobile

Marketing Association (MMA) (mmaglobal.com/codeofconduct.pdf) is indicative of the types of practices promoted by the industry. The basic principles of the code include:

> **Notice.** Informing users of the marketer's identity or products and services offered and the key terms and conditions that govern an interaction between the marketer and the user's mobile device.

> **Choice and consent.** Respecting the right of the user to control which mobile messages they receive by obtaining consent (opt-in) and implementing a simple termination (opt-out) process.

> **Customization and constraint.** Ensuring that collected user information is used to tailor communication to the interests of the recipient and is handled responsibly, sensitively, and in compliance with applicable law. Mobile messages should be limited to those requested by the user and provide value such as product and service enhancements, contests, requested information, entertainment, or discounts.

> **Security.** Implementing reasonable technical, administrative, and physical procedures to protect user information from unauthorized use, alteration, disclosure, distribution, or access.

> **Enforcement and accountability.** The MMA expects its members to comply with the MMA Privacy Code of Conduct and has incorporated the code into applicable MMA guidelines, including the U.S. Consumer Best Practice (CBP) guidelines. Until the code can be enforced effectively by a third-party enforcement organization, mobile marketers are expected to use evaluations of their practices to certify compliance with the code.

Section 8.4 ▶ REVIEW QUESTIONS

1. How are traditional media and mobile marketing campaigns alike?
2. What type of campaign was recently used by Dolce & Gabanna (D&G)? What were the underlying goals of the campaign?
3. Summarize the basic principles in the Global Code of Conduct from the Mobile Marketing Association.

8.5 MOBILE WORKFORCE SOLUTIONS

Although B2C m-commerce gets considerable publicity in the media, for most organizations the greatest short-term benefit from m-commerce is likely to come from intrabusiness applications aimed at supporting the mobile workforce who spend a substantial part of their workday away from corporate premises. Examples include members of sales teams, traveling executives, telecommuters, employees working in corporate yards or warehouses, and repair or installation employees who work at customers' sites or in the field. These individuals need access to the same office and work applications and data as their nonmobile counterparts. This section looks at the mobile devices and technologies that can be used to support mobile workers and the issues that arise in providing this support.

NEEDS OF THE MOBILE WORKFORCE

A **mobile worker** is usually defined as any employee who is away from their primary work space at least 10 hours a week or 25 percent of the time. Using this definition, IDC

mobile worker
Any employee who is away from his or her primary work space at least 10 hours a week or 25 percent of the time.

forecasts that by 2011 there will be approximately 1 billion mobile workers worldwide (*Business Wire* 2008). This will represent about a third of the total workforce. In the United States alone, they estimate that 75 percent of the workforce will be mobile by that year. This represents a major shift: In 2008, there were more than 150 million workers in the United States, of which approximately 50 million or one-third could be classified as mobile.

Even though the mobile workforce is growing more rapidly, workforce mobility is not a new phenomenon. What is new is the growing recognition within enterprises that a mobile workforce requires and can benefit from specialized mobile solutions and devices.

Toward this end, companies are providing a wide range of mobile devices, including BlackBerry's voice-enabled PDAs and Wi-Fi-enabled laptops, to a substantial percentage of their employees. The percentage of iPhones varies depending on the industry, as well as the company's size—the percentage is larger in IT and telecommunication firms and in small to midsize enterprises.

Benefits of Mobile Workforce Support

Like other IT investments, many enterprises cite enhanced productivity and reduced costs as the main reasons for the widespread deployment of mobile devices and applications within their organizations. Mobile solutions—devices and applications—provide mobile workers with real-time access to enterprise data and applications. This can reduce, for example, the time required in the field to process orders or to service customer requests. Mobile solutions can also automate existing paper and pen processes and workflows. This can ensure, for instance, that processes are completed in a uniform fashion with minimal data entry errors or data loss.

The specific benefits that accrue by deploying mobile solutions really depend on the segments of the mobile workforce toward which the solutions are aimed. Mobile workers can be divided into three segments: mobile professionals (such as senior executives and consultants), the mobile field force (such as field sales and service technicians), and mobile specialty workers (such as delivery personnel and construction workers). In the United States, these groups represent approximately 45 percent, 35 percent, and 20 percent, respectively. Clearly, the mobile solutions these groups need vary, as do the specific challenges the workers and their companies face in using and deploying these solutions.

Some of the solutions that are widely used by the three segments include the following:

▶ **Mobile office applications.** According to a worldwide survey of 375 top business executives conducted by the Intelligence Unit of *The Economist* magazine (*Economist* 2007), e-mail, calendaring, and keeping in touch with colleagues via messaging are the most popular mobile applications. Looking toward 2012, these applications are expected to maintain their popularity with a few minor changes. Executives feel that mobile voice-over-IP (VoIP) and videoconferencing will increase in importance. They also look toward greater use of mobile customer relationship management (CRM) by their sales and services teams. Finally, mobile collaboration is increasing, facilitated by microblogging (Twitter), blogging, and wikis.

▶ **Sales force automation (SFA).** Generally speaking, sales force automation (SFA) systems help guide and automatically record the various stages of the sales process. These stages run the gamut from managing contacts with customers and prospects, tracking sales leads, forecasting sales, and managing orders. Providing mobile access to a company's SFA system can help keep their mobile sales personnel better informed about new product launches, product information, pricing schedules, order status, manufacturing schedules, inventory levels, and delivery schedules. Sales staff can enter sales meetings with the most current and accurate information, perhaps even checking sales and product information during the meeting itself.

When it is time to close the deal, the salesperson can wirelessly check production schedules and inventory levels to confirm product availability and even specify a delivery date. This real-time available-to-promise/capacity-to-promise (ATP/CTP) capability reduces the potential for delayed or canceled sales. It also can mean more competitive and realistic offers to prospects and customers. Online File W8.3 provides a detailed example of the use of SFA at a major U.K. retail manufacturer.

▶ **Field force automation (FFA).** One group of inherently mobile employees are those involved in delivery and dispatch services, as well as services aimed at equipment and service repair, including transportation (e.g., delivery of food, oil, newspapers, and cargo; courier services; tow trucks; taxis), utilities (e.g., gas, electricity, phone, water), field services (e.g., computer, office equipment, home repair), health care (e.g., visiting nurses, doctors, social services), and security (e.g., patrols, alarm installation). FFA, also called *field service management (FSM)*, is designed to support this segment of the mobile workforce.

▶ **Mobile CRM (e-CRM).** E-CRM is discussed in detail in Online Appendix B. *CRM* is an industry term that encompasses methodologies and software that help an enterprise manage customer relationships in an organized fashion. Usually, an extensive database of customer information, including customer contact information, is at the center of a CRM system. In a CRM system, information is entered and accessed by a range of employees through the company, including sales, marketing, customer service, human resources, product engineering and manufacturing, and accounting and finance personnel.

Challenges of Mobile Workforce Support

Even though most enterprises recognize the need to provide mobile workers with specialized applications and devices, there are many nuts-and-bolts challenges involved in delivering mobile solutions to mobile workers. The challenges include issues from both the solution provider's and users' point of view:

▶ **Network coverage gaps and interruptions.** Imagine all the places where your cell phone doesn't work or works poorly—on the highway, in large buildings and warehouses, in hospitals and health care facilities, and in rural areas, to name just a few. Now imagine trying to do critical work in these locations. Not only do these dead spots cause interruptions, but they also result in poor performance for both devices and applications.

▶ **Internetwork roaming.** Cellular networks and devices are designed to support roaming from one cell or network to the next. As users roam or move from one cell or network to another, performance and latency issues can arise. Not only can roaming result in performance and latency issues, but it can also result in application crashes and can force users to reenter lost or corrupt data.

▶ **Mobile network and application performance.** As noted in Section 8.2, developing software and applications for mobile and wireless devices presents a variety of challenges. Many enterprise applications were only designed for desktops or laptops. Most either don't work or perform poorly on mobile devices unless redesigned.

▶ **Device and network management.** While mobile workers see the gaps, interruptions, and poor performance as major frustrations, the teams charged with planning and implementing these mobile solutions are more concerned with managing and securing network access to enterprise data and solutions. This can present a substantial challenge, especially if there are many disparate mobile devices.

▶ **Bandwidth management.** As the number of mobile workers and mobile solutions increases, so does network traffic. Unless the increases are well understood and planned for in a systematic fashion, there can be substantial contention for network bandwidth.

Section 8.5 ▶ REVIEW QUESTIONS

1. Describe the major segments of the mobile workforce. How quickly is this workforce growing?
2. What are some of the common benefits of mobile SFA, FFA, and CRM?
3. What are some of the challenges that companies incur when they try to implement solutions for mobile workforces?

8.6 MOBILE ENTERTAINMENT

There is some debate about what actually constitutes mobile entertainment and which of its segments falls under the rubric of m-commerce. For example, if you purchase a song on the Web and download it to your PC, then copy it to your MP3 player, is this a form of mobile entertainment? What if you copy it to your smart phone rather than an MP3 player? What if you buy it and download it directly from the Web to your smart phone? What if you buy it and download it from the Web directly to an iPod? What if the song was free? There are a lot of what ifs. By strict definition, **mobile entertainment** is any type of leisure activity that utilizes the wireless telecommunication networks, interacts with service providers, and usually incurs a fee upon usage. Given that it requires wireless telecommunications, the implication is that mobile entertainment involves devices that operate over these networks.

This section discusses some of the major types of mobile entertainment, including mobile music and video, mobile gaming, and mobile gambling. This discussion is preceded by a look at the mobile entertainment market in general.

mobile entertainment
Any type of leisure activity that utilizes wireless telecommunication networks, interacts with service providers, and incurs a cost upon usage.

GROWTH OF THE MOBILE ENTERTAINMENT MARKET

Based on research findings (Juniper Research 2008), it is estimated that the global market for mobile entertainment will jump from worldwide revenues of approximately $21 billion in 2008 to $65 billion in 2012.

As Exhibit 8.4 shows, mobile music is and will continue to be the largest segment, with approximately $10 billion in revenue in 2007 versus $18 billion in revenue in 2012. However, by 2012, mobile games will produce almost as much revenue as music.

Among the various regions of the world, China and the Far East will remain the largest regional market for mobile entertainment. For the period covered by the report, the revenues for this region will grow from $8.5 billion in 2007 to $21.3 billion in 2012.

To put these figures into context, PriceWaterhouseCoopers (2008) forecasts that the online and offline global entertainment and media industry as a whole will reach $2.2 trillion in 2012. Although it's hard to combine estimates from different sources, if we assume the various estimates are correct, mobile entertainment will be only 3 percent of the overall entertainment market (i.e., $65 billion versus $2.2 trillion). But the online segment is growing much faster than the offline one.

MOBILE MUSIC AND VIDEO

When you think of digital and mobile music and video, the first thing that comes to mind is Apple and iTunes. Apple is the clear leader in the digital distribution of music

EXHIBIT 8.4   Size and Growth of the Mobile Entertainment Market

Segment	2007 ($Billion)	2012 ($Billion)	Compound Annual Growth Rate
Infotainment	2	6	25 percent
User-Generated Content	0.5	6	64 percent
Mobile TV (broadcast)	2	43	67 percent
Mobile TV (streaming)	5	4.5	−1.7 percent
Music	10	18	12 percent
Games	5	16	26 percent
Adult	1	4	32 percent
Gambling	0.1	3	97 percent
Images	2.7	2.9	1.2 percent
Total	28.3	103	29.5 percent

Sources: Compiled from Juniper (2008) and eMarketer (2008).

and video. Since 2001, Apple has offered consumers the ability to download songs and videos from the Apple iTunes store. In August 2008, iTunes' customers had purchased and downloaded more than 5 billion songs (Apple 2008). Apple also announced in August 2008 that customers were downloading videos at the rate of 50,000 a day. At the end of 2007, Amazon.com, the largest online store, launched their Amazon MP3 and Amazon Video On Demand (originally called *unBox*) digital download services for music and video, respectively. Outside of market share, the major difference between Apple and Amazon.com is that the content downloaded from Amazon.com is not controlled by digital rights management (DRM) technologies, which restrict access, copying, or conversion of the downloaded material. Another major provider of music online is Walmart.com.

Although full-track songs and albums represent the major portion of the mobile music segment, there are three other components to this entertainment segment: ringtones, ringback tones, and streaming music and radio. Streaming music and radio represent a very small portion of the overall revenue. This is not the case for ringtones and ringback tones. Ringtones are the tones that play when someone calls you. Ringback tones are the tones that play when you call someone else. These tones come in many varieties.

MOBILE GAMES

A wide variety of mobile games have been developed to meet the needs and styles of different types of players. They can be classified in several ways:

- **Technology.** Embedded, SMS/MMS, Web browsing, J2ME, BREW, native OS
- **Number of players.** Soloplay or multiplay (from few to many)
- **Genre.** Action, logic/puzzle/skill, sports and racing, arcade, role playing, card and casino, movie, adult, and lifestyle

Several blogs provide information and discussion about the current state of the mobile gaming market, including various game offerings, as well as the technologies and platforms used to develop the games. One of the best is mobilegames.blogs.com.

The potential size and growth of the overall market explains the large number of companies involved in creating, distributing, and running mobile games. Some put the estimate of the number of game developers, aggregator-distributors, publishers, and portals at close to 2,000 enterprises. Many of these reside in the United States and Europe. Although the market is growing, especially in China and India, game publishers are facing some major hurdles such as lack of standards, different software and hardware, and cost. The coming generation of games requires advanced capabilities of the higher-end handsets and 3G networks. The adoption of these handsets and networks has not been as fast as originally anticipated. Finally, there was a belief that game advertising would generate revenues to offset the costs. The ad spending in mobile games has remained low.

To address these hurdles, some of the more established game publishers such as Sega Corporation, as well as many start-ups, are focusing attention on the Apple iPhone and similar devices.

MOBILE GAMBLING

Globally, online gambling is a well-entrenched segment of the overall gambling market. Regardless of the figures, mobile gambling is the fastest growing segment of mobile entertainment. The first online gambling site was established in August 1995. Today, there are thousands of gambling Web sites worldwide, including sports betting, casino games, and lotteries. Usually, online casino games require good graphics and high-speed connections. In contrast, the technical requirements for lotteries and sports betting are much less stringent. Even SMS can be used to play the lottery or place bets.

Unlike some of the other forms of mobile entertainment, the mobile gambling market has some unique hurdles. First, mobile gambling requires two-way financial transactions. Not only must bettors or gamblers have a way of paying for their online bets, but the online gambling establishment must also have a way of paying off the bettor or gambler if they win. Second, online gambling sites face major trust issues. Gamblers and bettors have to believe that the site is fair, that they have a chance of winning, and that they are not being ripped off. Finally, the legislative picture is very unclear. Most existing gambling legislation was passed prior to the advent of the Web and is outdated. Even if it isn't outdated, the legislative picture is like a patchwork quilt with some forms of gambling barred in certain territories but not in others.

From a legal standpoint, the United Kingdom has some of the least stringent regulations. This is one of the reasons that the United Kingdom is the largest market in terms of gross wagers, accounting for 52 percent of all wagers in 2007. In the future, the United Kingdom's overall percentage is likely to decline as the markets in other countries, such as China and the Far East, where online gambling is also legal, grow over the next five years. It is also one of the reasons that online gambling is not projected to grow much in the near term.

Some countries have attempted to prohibit online gambling altogether or to control the type of online gambling that takes place by making it illegal to operate an online gambling site or a particular type of online gambling site within their jurisdictions. This has simply created a business opportunity for other countries that have encouraged online gambling sites to operate within their borders and have licensed them to do so. For some reason, most of the countries taking advantage of this opportunity are small, frequently located on smaller islands. For example, Alderney, Antigua, Costa Rica, Gibraltar, and Malta are all popular hosting destinations for online gambling. Some of these, such as Alderney, Gibraltar, and Malta, have very strict licensing regulations so that only reputable, well-financed enterprises are awarded licenses. Others, such as

Antigua and Costa Rica, have less stringent licensing requirements, meaning that less reputable or underfinanced operations can obtain licenses. Overall, this simply means that even if a country eliminates online gambling sites within their borders, there are plenty of places for gamblers or bettors to place their wagers or bets.

Other countries have attempted to control online gambling by making it illegal either for the individual to gamble online, for the individual and the enterprise to use the "wire" for gambling activity, or for financial institutions to process gambling transactions. In the United States, for example, laws prohibit all three of these types of activities, although the laws don't necessarily apply uniformly across all the states.

Within the United States, some states have laws that ban gambling on the Internet outright, including Illinois, Indiana, Kentucky, Louisiana, Massachusetts, Michigan, Nevada, New Jersey, New York, Oregon, South Dakota, Washington, and Wisconsin. Additionally, attorneys general in Florida, Kansas, Minnesota, Oklahoma, and Texas have issued opinions that Internet gambling is illegal in their states. In the other states, online gambling is not directly prohibited, but it is controlled by federal statutes.

Section 8.6 ▶ REVIEW QUESTIONS

1. Briefly describe the growth patterns of the various segments of mobile entertainment.
2. Discuss the basic components of the mobile music market.
3. What are some of the key barriers to the growth of the mobile games market?
4. Discuss some of the key legal issues impeding the growth of mobile gambling.

8.7 LOCATION-BASED MOBILE COMMERCE

As noted earlier in this chapter, **location-based m-commerce (l-commerce)** refers to the use of GPS-enabled devices or similar technologies (e.g., triangulation of radio- or cell-based stations) to find where a customer or client is and advertise and sometimes deliver products and services based on the customer's location. Location-based services are attractive to both consumers and businesses alike. From a consumer's or business user's viewpoint, localization offers safety (emergency services can pinpoint the mobile device owner's exact location), convenience (a user can locate what is nearby without consulting a directory, pay phone, or map), and productivity (time can be optimized by determining points of interest within close proximity). From a business supplier's point of view, location-based m-commerce offers an opportunity to provide services that more quickly or precisely meet a customer's needs.

The services provided through location-based m-commerce focus on five key factors:

1. **Location.** Determining the basic position of a person or a thing (e.g., car or boat)
2. **Navigation.** Plotting a route from one location to another
3. **Tracking.** Monitoring the movement of a person or a thing (e.g., a package or vehicle)
4. **Mapping.** Creating maps of specific geographical locations
5. **Timing.** Determining the precise time at a specific location

The closing case describes how Walmart, in partnership with WeatherBug (weather.weatherbug.com) and Send Word Now (sendwordnow.com), has combined some of these services to ensure the safety of its customers, employees, and stores during weather emergencies.

location-based m-commerce (l-commerce)
Delivery of m-commerce transactions to individuals in a specific location, at a specific time.

L-COMMERCE INFRASTRUCTURE

L-commerce rests on an infrastructure made up of five basic components (Steiniger et al. 2006), which include the following:

▶ **Mobile devices.** These are tools used to request information. Location-based devices can be divided into two categories: single purpose or multipurpose. Single-purpose devices include such things as on-board navigation systems, toll boxes, transceivers, and GPS location devices. Multipurpose devices can be mobile phones, smart phones, PDAs, laptops, tablet PCs, and the like.

▶ **Communication network.** The network transfers user data and service requests from the mobile terminal to the service providers, and then the requested information is transferred back to the user.

▶ **Positioning component.** In order to process or service a user's request, the user's position has to be determined. This can be done either through a mobile network or by using a global positioning system (GPS).

▶ **Service or application provider.** Providers are responsible for servicing a user's request. Services can include such things as finding routes, searching yellow pages or other information sources based on the user's location, etc.

▶ **Data or content provider.** Service providers usually rely on geographic data or location-based information to service user requests. More often than not, the location data or information is maintained by a third party, not the service provider.

L-commerce is distinguished from general m-commerce by the positioning component and the geographical information systems on which the various location-based services or applications rest.

Positioning Component

network-based positioning
Relies on base stations to find the location of a mobile device sending a signal or sensed by the network.

terminal-based positioning
Calculating the location of a mobile device from signals sent by the device to base stations.

global positioning system (GPS)
A worldwide satellite-based tracking system that enables users to determine their position anywhere on the earth.

Usually, the positioning component of an l-commerce system is either network-based or terminal-based. **Network-based positioning** relies on base stations to find the location of a mobile device sending a signal or sensed by the network. For example, the location of a mobile phone can be determined by knowing the location of the nearest mobile phone antenna (base station). In **terminal-based positioning,** the device calculates the location from signals received from the base stations. For instance, this is how the well-known global positioning system (GPS) works.

The **global positioning system (GPS)** is based on a worldwide satellite tracking system that enables users to determine exact positions anywhere on the earth. GPS was developed by the U.S. Defense Department for military use, but its high value for civilian use was immediately recognized, and the technology was released into the civilian domain, originally for use by commercial airlines and ships. In recent years, GPS locators have become a part of the consumer electronics market and are used widely for business and recreation. Online File W8.4 provides an example of the use of GPS for tracking vehicles.

GPS is supported by 24 U.S. government satellites. Each satellite orbits the earth once every 12 hours on a precise path at an altitude of 10,900 miles. At any point in time, the exact position of each satellite is known, because the satellite broadcasts its position and a time signal from its onboard atomic clock, which is accurate to one-billionth of a second. Receivers on the ground also have accurate clocks that are synchronized with those of the satellites.

GPS locators may be stand-alone units or embedded into a mobile device. At any given time, a GPS locator can receive signals from at least six satellites. Using the fast speed of the satellite signals (186,272 miles, or 299,775 kilometers, per second; the speed of light), the system can determine the location (latitude and longitude) of any GPS locator, to within 50 feet (15 meters) by triangulation, using the distance from the GPS locator to three satellites to make the computation. A fourth satellite can also be used to determine elevation, although not to the same degree of accuracy as longitude or latitude. Advanced forms of GPS can pinpoint a location within a centimeter. GPS software then computes the latitude and longitude of the receiver. More information on how the GPS system works is available at trimble.com/gps.

In 1999, the European Union (EU) proposed the construction of an alternative global navigation satellite system called *Galileo*. Unlike the U.S. GPS, Galileo is a civilian system, not a military system. As envisioned, Galileo would consist of 30 satellites orbiting at a distance of 14,429 miles, or 23,222 kilometers, above the earth and would provide positioning to within about a meter. Although the European Union and European Space Agency agreed to fund the project in 2002, the project has been beset by budgetary problems. In April 2008, the EU transportation ministers of 27 countries reached an agreement on funding. Under this agreement, the system will supposedly be operational by 2013 (Parlamentul European 2008).

The newest development of l-commerce is known as **real-time location systems (RTLS)**, which are used to track and identify the location of objects in real time (see Malik 2009). Similar to RFID, these systems use readers to receive wireless signals from tags attached to items or people.

> **real-time location system (RTLS)**
> Systems used to track and identify the location of objects in real time.

Location-Based Data

Location-based services and l-commerce revolve around a series of location-based questions or queries. One way to categorize these questions is the following (Steiniger 2006):

▶ **Locating.** Where am I? Where is a specific object or person?
▶ **Navigating.** How do I get to a specific address, place, position, or person?
▶ **Searching.** Where is the nearest or most relevant object or person?
▶ **Identifying.** What, who, or how much is here or there?
▶ **Event checking.** What happens here or there?

Geocoding or *reverse geocoding* is often used to answer these questions. Geocoding translates geographical information (e.g., an address) into geographical coordinates (e.g., longitude and latitude). Reverse geocoding translates geographical coordinates into an associated textual location (e.g., street address). In addition to translating a person's position, location-based queries also rely on static information (e.g., points of interest and road networks), topical and temporal information (e.g., traffic information, weather forecasts, last-minute ticket deals), safety information (e.g., state of the roads or hiking trails, weather changes, emergency situations), and personal information (e.g., recommendations and ratings of places and events).

The data, information, and processes needed to service location-based queries are usually handled by a *geographical information system (GIS)*. A **geographical information system (GIS)** captures, stores, analyzes, manages, and presents data that refer to or is linked to a location. For example, suppose a person is using his or her mobile phone to ask an online directory service to provide a list of Italian restaurants that are close by. In order to service this query, the directory service would need access to a GIS containing information about local restaurants by geographical coordinates and type. As noted, location-based service providers usually rely on GISs provided by third parties.

> **geographical information system (GIS)**
> A computer system capable of integrating, storing, editing, analyzing, sharing, and displaying geographically referenced (spatial) information.

LOCATION-BASED SERVICES AND APPLICATIONS

Exhibit 8.5 provides an overview of the main categories of location-based services and applications.

The following examples illustrate some of the myriad of l-commerce services currently in operation:

Example: Navigation. One of the major problems in many cities is the lack of sufficient parking spaces. This is the situation in Paris, France, where as many as 20 to 25 percent of all vehicles may circulate the city, looking for a parking space at certain times of the day. This causes traffic jams and wastes gasoline. At the end of 2006, Orange, a large mobile telecommunications company, and its partners organized a system that allows drivers to quickly find empty parking spaces in nearby parking garages. Here is how it works: The 120 participating garages collect information electronically about open parking spaces. The information is updated over the Internet to a central server at Orange. Drivers contact the Orange server with their cell phones. Orange can determine the location of the driver either through the location of the antenna being used to make the cell phone call or, if the driver's phone is equipped with a GPS, through the coordinates provided by the GPS (*Taipei Times* 2006).

Example: Product Tracking. UltraEX, a U.S. West Coast company that specializes in same-day deliveries of items such as emergency blood supplies and computer parts, equips all of its vehicles with @Road's GPS receivers and wireless modems. In addition to giving dispatchers a big-picture view of the entire fleet, @Road helps UltraEX keep clients happy by letting them track the location and speed of their shipments on the Web in real time. This service shows customers a map of the last place the satellite detected the delivery vehicle and how fast it was traveling. Drivers use AT&T's Mobile Data Service to communicate with dispatch, and drivers who own their vehicles are unable to falsify mileage sheets because @Road reports exact mileage for each vehicle.

Example: Management. The Mexican company CEMEX is the third largest cement producer in the world. Concrete is mixed en route to construction sites and must be delivered within a certain time period or it will be unusable. Rather than waiting for orders, preparing delivery schedules, and then sending out the deliveries as most companies do, CEMEX has trucks fitted with GPS patrolling the roads at all times, waiting for orders; this allows the company to guarantee delivery within 20 minutes of the agreed-upon time. Real-time data on each truck's position are available not only to company managers but also to clients and suppliers, enabling them to plan their schedules to fit in with the next available truck. Digital maps help locate the customers and the trucks, allowing the use of shortcut routes.

EXHIBIT 8.5	Location-Based Applications and Services
Category	**Examples**
Advertising	Banners, advertising alerts
Billing	Road tolling, location-sensitive billing
Emergency	Emergency calls, automotive assistance
Games	Mobile games, geocaching
Information	Infotainment services, travel guides, travel planner, mobile yellow pages, shopping guides
Leisure	Buddy finder, instant messaging, social networking
Management	Facility, infrastructure, fleet, security, environmental
Navigation	Directions, indoor routing, car park guidance, traffic management
Tracking	People/vehicle tracking, product tracking

Sources: Compiled from Steiniger et al. (2006) and Zhou (2008).

Example: Leisure. Want to know where your friends are in real time? The mobile market is swarming with social networking start-ups in partnership with the cell phone behemoths who think they know the answer to the question. One of the start-ups is Loopt. Loopt has signed deals with many of the major mobile operators including Sprint Nextel, T-Mobile, Verizon, AT&T, and Boost. Loopt utilizes a cell phone's embedded GPS positioning to show users where friends are located and what they are doing via detailed, interactive maps on their mobile phones. Loopt helps friends connect on the fly and navigate their social lives by orienting them to people, places, and events.

BARRIERS TO LOCATION-BASED M-COMMERCE

What is holding back the widespread use of location-based m-commerce? Several factors come into play, including the following:

▶ **Lack of GPS in mobile phones.** In 2008, only about 15 percent of mobile phones were sold with GPS. This means that most of the mobile phones in existence lack the feature. Although it is possible to locate a mobile device with other means and GPS-enabled phones are increasing in popularity, this still inhibits the overall adoption of location-based services.

▶ **Accuracy of devices.** Some of the location technologies are not as accurate as people expect them to be. A good GPS provides a location that is accurate up to 50 feet (15 meters). Less expensive, but less accurate, locators can be used to find an approximate location within 1,640 feet (500 meters).

▶ **The cost-benefit justification.** For many potential users, the benefits of location-based services do not justify the cost of the devices or the inconvenience and time required to utilize the service. After all, many seem to feel that they can just as easily obtain information the old-fashioned way.

▶ **Limited network bandwidth.** Wireless bandwidth is currently limited; it will be improved as 3G technology spreads. As bandwidth improves, applications will improve, which will attract more customers.

▶ **Invasion of privacy.** When "always-on" cell phones are a reality, many people will be hesitant to have their whereabouts and movements tracked throughout the day, even if they have nothing to hide. This issue will be heightened when our cars, homes, appliances, and all sorts of other consumer goods are connected to the Internet and have a GPS device embedded in them.

Section 8.7 ▶ REVIEW QUESTIONS

1. Describe the key elements of the l-commerce infrastructure.
2. What is GPS? How does it work?
3. What are some of the basic questions addressed by location-based services?
4. How are location-based services being integrated with social networking?
5. What are some of the key barriers to l-commerce?

8.8 SECURITY AND OTHER IMPLEMENTATION ISSUES IN MOBILE COMMERCE

Despite the vast potential for mobile commerce to change the way many companies do business, several barriers are either slowing down the spread of m-commerce or leaving many m-commerce businesses and their customers disappointed or dissatisfied.

According to Betts (2008), the major barriers to enterprise mobile computing are security, performance, availability, difficulty integrating with in-house IT, and the inability to customize applications. In this section, we examine some of these barriers, starting with the issue of the security of mobile communications and mobile computing systems.

M-COMMERCE SECURITY ISSUES

In 2004, Cabir became the first known worm capable of spreading through mobile phones (Laudermilch 2006). The worm arrives in the phone's messaging in-box in the guise of a file named *caribe.sis*. When an unsuspecting recipient clicks on the file, the worm activates and is sent to other devices via Bluetooth. To date, the worm has not been launched on a widespread basis. The same is true for other malicious code, such as Brador and Redbrowser (Laudermilch 2006).

Most Internet-enabled cell phones in operation today have their operating systems and other functional software "burned" into the hardware. This makes them incapable of storing applications and, in turn, incapable of propagating a virus, worm, or other rogue program from one phone to another. However, as the capabilities of cellular phones increase and the functionality of PDAs and cell phones converge, the threat of attack from malicious code will certainly increase. Although m-commerce shares some of the same security issues as general e-commerce, there are some differences between the two.

The basic security goals of confidentiality, authentication, authorization, and integrity are just as important for m-commerce as they are for e-commerce but are more difficult to ensure (Chapter 9). Specifically, m-commerce transactions almost always pass through several networks, both wireless and wired. An appropriate level of security must be maintained on each network, in spite of the fact that interoperability among the various networks is difficult. Similarly, post-transactional security issues of auditing and nonrepudiation are more difficult because cell phones do not yet have the capability to store the digital equivalent of a receipt.

In general, many of the processes, procedures, and technologies used for e-commerce security and for general organizational computer security also apply to m-commerce security. Passwords, encryption, active tokens, and user education are cases in point. However, given the unique nature of mobile security, special security measures for m-commerce may also be required. For example, to prevent the theft of a mobile device, a user might carry a "wireless tether" that sounds a warning if a device is left behind or carried away. Wi-Fi networks have their own built-in security system known as *wired equivalent privacy (WEP)*, which is, as the name suggests, similar to encryption protocols used on wired networks. The approaches to m-commerce security are discussed in more detail in Online File W8.5.

TECHNOLOGICAL BARRIERS TO M-COMMERCE

When mobile users want to access the Internet, the *usability* of the site is critical to achieve the purpose of the visit and to increase user stickiness (the degree to which users remain at a site). However, current devices have limited usability, particularly with respect to pocket-size screens or data input devices. In addition, because of the limited storage capacity and information access speed of most smart phones and PDAs, it is often difficult or impossible to download large files to these devices.

Mobile visitors to a Web site are typically paying premium rates for Internet connections and are focused on a specific goal (e.g., conducting a stock trade). For visitors to find exactly what they are looking for easily and quickly, the navigation systems have to be fast and designed for mobile devices. Similarly, the information content needs to meet the user's needs. Other technical barriers related to mobile computing technology include limited battery life and transmission interference with home appliances. These barriers and others are listed in Exhibit 8.6.

EXHIBIT 8.6 Technical Limitations of Mobile Computing

Limitation	Description
Insufficient bandwidth	Sufficient bandwidth is necessary for widespread mobile computing, and it must be inexpensive. It will take a few years until 3G and WiMax are available in many places. Wi-Fi solves some of the problems for short-range connections.
Security standards	Universal standards are still under development. It may take three or more years for sufficient standards to be in place.
Power consumption	Batteries with long life are needed for mobile computing. Color screens and Wi-Fi consume more electricity, but new chips and emerging battery technologies are solving some of the power-consumption problems.
Transmission interferences	Weather and terrain, including tall buildings, can limit reception. Microwave ovens, cordless phones, and other devices on the free, but crowded, 2.4 GHz range interfere with Bluetooth and Wi-Fi 802.11b transmissions.
GPS accuracy	GPS may be inaccurate in a city with tall buildings, limiting the use of location-based m-commerce.
Potential health hazards	Potential health damage from cellular radio frequency emission is not known yet. Known health hazards include cell phone addiction, thumb-overuse syndrome, and accidents caused by people using cell phones while driving.
Human–computer interface	Screens and keyboards are too small, making mobile devices uncomfortable and difficult for many people to use.
Complexity	Too many optional add-ons (e.g., battery chargers, external keyboards, headsets, microphones, cradles) are available. Storing and using the optional add-ons can be a problem.

ETHICAL, LEGAL, AND HEALTH ISSUES IN M-COMMERCE

The increasing use of mobile devices in business and society raises new ethical, legal, and health issues that individuals, organizations, and society will have to resolve.

One workplace issue is the isolation that mobile devices can impose on a workforce. The introduction of desktop computing invoked a profound change on social interaction in the workplace, illustrated by the walled cubicles featured in Dilbert cartoons. Some workers had difficulty adjusting to this new environment and sought to replace face-to-face interactions with e-mail interactions, prompting organizational policies against the forwarding of nonbusiness-related e-mail and IM messages.

Equipping the workforce with mobile devices may have similar impacts. Field service employees dispatched remotely and who acquire replacement parts from third-party sources will visit "the office" only briefly at the start and end of each day, if at all. The result could be a reduction in organizational transparency, making it difficult for employees to know what other employees do, how the organization is evolving, and how they fit into it. These changes may have powerful implications for individuals and the organization for which they work. Whether the results are good or bad depends on how the change is managed.

The truly personal nature of the mobile device also raises ethical and legal issues in the workplace. Most employees have desktop computers both at home and at work, and separate business and personal work accordingly. However, it is not so easy to separate work and personal life on a cell phone, unless one is willing to carry two phones or two PDAs. And if an organization has the right to monitor e-mail communications on its own network, does it also have the right to monitor voice communications on a company-owned cell phone?

The widespread appearance of mobile devices in society has led to the need for cell phone etiquette, the creation of "cell free" zones in hospitals and airport lounges, and National Cell Phone Courtesy Month. For an insightful essay into the impact of cell phones in work and social spaces, see Australian Mobile Telecommunications Association (2008).

A widely publicized health issue is the potential, but not yet proven, health damage from cellular radio frequency emissions. Cell phone addiction also is a problem. A study by Seoul National University found that 30 percent of South Korean high school students reported addiction effects, such as feeling anxious when they did not have their phones with them. Many also displayed symptoms of repetitive stress injury from obsessive text messaging (Rosen 2006).

Other ethical, legal, and health issues include the ethics of monitoring staff movements based on GPS-enabled devices or vehicles, maintaining an appropriate work–life balance when work can be conducted anywhere at any time, and the preferred content of an organizational policy to govern the use and control of personal mobile computing devices in and out of the workplace.

Section 8.8 ▶ REVIEW QUESTIONS

1. How is m-commerce security similar to e-commerce security? How is it different?
2. Discuss the role that usability plays in the adoption of m-commerce.
3. Discuss a few of the technical limitations of m-commerce.
4. Describe the potential impact of mobile devices on the workplace.

MANAGERIAL ISSUES

Some managerial issues related to this chapter are as follows.

1. **What is your m-commerce strategy?** M-commerce is an amalgamation of three basic market segments: support for internal business processes; an extension of existing e-business services that touch customers, suppliers, and other partners; and extension of Web-based consumer services to a rapidly growing population of smart phone users. The key to success in the m-commerce world is to define your overall e-commerce and m-commerce business strategy, determine which segments are critical to the strategy and the order in which they need to be addressed, and which of the available mobile technologies will support the strategy and critical segments.

2. **What is your timetable?** Mobile technologies and applications are undergoing rapid change. It seems like every six months new technologies and opportunities emerge. In this accelerated environment, the challenge is to craft an m-commerce strategy that can take advantage of rapidly changing market conditions while at the same time ensuring that choice of mobile solutions and technologies is "future proof."

3. **Are there clear technical winners?** Among mobile devices, the answer is yes. The all-in-one devices, such as smart phones, have surged to the forefront of the mobile device market and will likely stay there. Among the other components of the mobile infrastructure (e.g., wireless networks such as WiMax, Wi-Fi, and 3G) the answer is no. There is still a confusing multiplicity of standards, devices, and supporting hardware. The key is to select a well-architected platform and infrastructure that can support in the near term a range of services while at the same time enabling adoption of future technologies as they emerge.

4. **Which applications should be implemented first?** Although there is something of a "cool factor" associated with various m-commerce applications,

especially location-based services, mobile applications must be judged like any other business technology—ROI, cost-benefit analysis, cost reductions, and efficiency. Toward these ends, many of the more mundane internal applications supporting the mobile workforce have resulted in the highest returns. Regardless, the application of mobile technology must be based on a realistic view of each situation to determine whether the technology is suitable or not. Recall that the m-commerce platform is the most preferred by younger generations. It is important to understand why Japan has a much higher penetration in m-commerce while other countries with the same level of mobile telecommunication infrastructure do not have a similar level of penetration.

SUMMARY

In this chapter, you learned about the following EC issues as they relate to the chapter's learning objectives.

1. **What is m-commerce, its value-added attributes, and fundamental drivers?** M-commerce is any business activity conducted over a wireless telecommunications network. M-commerce is a natural extension of e-commerce. M-commerce can help a business improve its value proposition to customers by utilizing its unique attributes: ubiquity, convenience, interactivity, personalization, and localization. Currently, m-commerce is being driven by large numbers of users of mobile devices; a developing "cell phone culture" among youth; demands from service-oriented customers; vendor marketing; declining prices; a mobile workforce; improved performance for the price; and increasing bandwidth.

2. **What is the mobile computing environment that supports m-commerce?** The mobile computing environment consists of two key elements: mobile devices and wireless networks. Although mobile computing devices vary in size and functionality, they are rapidly moving toward an all-in-one device that is rapidly overcoming some of the limitations associated with poor usability, such as small screen size, limited bandwidth, and restricted input capabilities. Even with their limitations, mobile devices offer a series of support services, principally SMS, voice, and location-based services, which differentiate m-commerce from e-commerce.

3. **Which networks support mobile devices?** Mobile devices connect in a wireless fashion to networks or other devices at a personal, local, metropolitan, or wide area level. Bluetooth (personal), cellular phone networks (WWAN), and wireless LANs (like Wi-Fi) are well-known technologies that are well established in the wireless marketplace. In contrast, municipal Wi-Fi and WiMax (metropolitan) are less well-known and are vying for a broader foothold in the wireless marketplace.

4. **Financial applications.** Many EC applications in the financial services industries (such as banking and electronic bill payment) can be conducted with wireless devices. Most mobile financial applications are simply mobile versions of their wire line counter parts that are conducted via SMS or the mobile Web. Mobile banking and mobile payments are good examples of this. Increasingly, banks throughout the world are enabling their customers to use mobile devices to check balances, monitor transactions, obtain account information, transfer funds, locate brands or ATMs, and sometimes pay bills. In the same vein, some companies are enabling their customers or clients to initiate or confirm payments via their cell phones or smart phones. These transactions are one of two types: mobile proximity payments or mobile remote payments. With mobile proximity payments, also known as "contactless" payments, a cell phone or smart phone is outfitted with a special chip that allows users to swipe their phones near a payment device (e.g., POS reader), much like a contactless smart card or credit card. With mobile remote payments, the mobile handset can be used to make person-to-person, person-to-business, and business-to-business payments just like they can be used to do mobile banking.

5. **Mobile marketing and advertising.** Like traditional and online media campaigns, mobile marketing and advertising campaigns fall into a variety of categories including information, entertainment, raffles, and coupons. Similarly, their objectives typically fall into one of six categories: building brand awareness, changing brand image, promoting sales, enhancing brand loyalty, building the customer base, and stimulating (mobile) word of mouth. The uptake of mobile marketing has been strong because the response is typically higher than with

more traditional or online campaigns. Although there are no strict guidelines for mobile advertising, the success of mobile advertising is linked to some basic principles, including notice, choice and consent, customization and constraint, security, and enforcement and accountability.

6. **Mobile workforce solutions.** Business applications such as mobile office applications, sales force automation (SFA), field force automation (FFA), mobile CRM, inventory management, and wireless job dispatch offer the best opportunities for high return on investment (ROI) for most organizations, at least in the short term. All of these applications are focused on supporting the mobile worker (someone who is away from his or her primary work space at least 10 hours a week or 25 percent of the time), although they are aimed at different segments of the mobile workforce (i.e., mobile professionals, mobile field force, and mobile specialty workers). Even though their potential ROI is high, their implementation faces a number of challenges, including interruptions and gaps in network coverage; problems caused by Internetwork roaming; performance problems created by slow mobile networks and applications; managing and securing mobile devices; and managing mobile network bandwidth.

7. **Mobile entertainment.** One of the fastest growing markets in m-commerce is mobile entertainment. Mobile entertainment encompasses mobile music, games, TV, gambling, adult services, and user-generated content and infotainment. Among

these, mobile music is the largest. Mobile gambling is one of the smallest, although it is the fastest growing in spite of the legal restrictions placed on it by various government bodies.

8. **Location-based commerce.** Location-based m-commerce (l-commerce) refers to the use of positioning devices, such as GPS, to find where a customer or client is and deliver products and services based on his or her location. The services provided by l-commerce companies tend to focus on one or more of the following factors: location, navigation, tracking, mapping, and timing. These services rest on five basic components: mobile devices, communication networks, positioning components, service and application providers, and data or content providers. Among these, the position and data components, especially geographical information (GIS), are critical. Although l-commerce has been widely hailed, several factors impede its widespread use, including the accuracy of the mobile devices, the cost of most applications in relation to the benefits, limited network bandwidth, and the potential invasion of privacy.

9. **Security and other implementation issues.** The mobile computing environment offers special challenges for security, including the need to secure transmission over open air and through multiple connecting networks. The biggest technological changes relate to the usability of devices. Finally, ethical, legal, and health issues can arise from the use of m-commerce, especially in the workplace.

KEY TERMS

Bluetooth	301	Mobile commerce		Real-time location	
Digital divide	306	(m-commerce)	295	systems (RTLS)	317
Geographical information		Mobile computing	298	Short message service (SMS)	300
system (GIS)	317	Mobile entertainment	312	Smart phone	299
Global positioning		Mobile worker	309	Terminal-based positioning	316
system (GPS)	316	Multimedia messaging		Voice portal	300
Interactive voice		service (MMS)	300	Wi-Fi (wireless fidelity)	301
response (IVR)	300	Network-based		WiMax	302
Location-based		positioning	316	Wireless local area network	
m-commerce		Personal area network		(WLAN)	301
(l-commerce)	315	(PAN)	301	Wireless mobile computing	298
M-business	295	Personal digital		Wireless wide area network	
Microfinance	306	assistant (PDA)	299	(WWAN)	303

QUESTIONS FOR DISCUSSION BY INDIVIDUAL STUDENTS

1. Discuss how m-commerce can expand the reach of EC.

2. Which of the m-commerce limitations listed in this chapter do you think will have the biggest near-term negative impact on the growth of m-commence? Which ones will be minimized within five years? Which ones will not?

3. Describe the ways in which Wi-Fi is affecting the use of cell phones for m-commerce.

4. WiMax, municipal Wi-Fi, and WWAN are all used to provide wide area access to the Internet. Which of these technologies is likely to survive into the future? Why or why not?

5. Discuss the factors that are critical to the overall growth of mobile banking and mobile payments.

6. Suppose you worked for a fashion retailer and were in charge of a new mobile advertising campaign designed to generate sales for a new clothing line. Describe the basic elements of your campaign and guidelines you would use to conduct it.

7. What is the relationship between mobile sales force automation, mobile field force automation, and mobile CRM?

8. Why are many of the more popular mobile gambling sites located on small island countries?

9. How are GPS and GIS related?

10. Location-based services can help a driver find his or her car or the closest gas station. However, some people view location-based services as an invasion of privacy. Discuss the pros and cons of location-based services.

TOPICS FOR CLASS DISCUSSION

1. Discuss how m-commerce can solve some of the problems of the digital divide (the gap within a country or between countries with respect to people's ability to access the Internet).

2. Discuss the potential benefits and drawbacks of conducting m-commerce on social networks.

INTERNET EXERCISES

1. Learn about smart phones by visiting vendors' sites such as Nokia, RIM, Apple, Motorola, and others. List the capabilities that the various devices from these vendors offer for supporting m-commerce. In the future, what sorts of new capabilities will be provided by smart phones?

2. Research the status of 3G and the future of 4G by visiting 3gnewsroom.co.uk (you can find information on 4G by searching for the term at the site). Prepare a report on the status of 3G and 4G based on your findings.

3. You've been asked to put together a directory of Wi-Fi hotspots in your local area. There are a number of sites, such as hotspot-locations.com, that offer search capabilities for finding hotpots in a given area. Construct a list of sites that offer this feature. Using these sites, create a directory for your area. Knowing what you do about the Wi-Fi sites in your area, which of the sites seems to produce the best list?

4. Download the white paper on location intelligence at pbinsight.com/files/resource-library/resource-files/BusinessObj_WP.pdf. Based on the white paper, discuss the role that location intelligence plays in retail, financial applications, insurance, government, and communications.

5. Most of the major social networking sites provide mobile capabilities. The same is true for newer start-ups like Loopt and GyPSii. Compare and contrast the types of social networking capabilities provided by the major sites and the start-ups.

6. Juniper Research has created a variety of white papers dealing with different segments of the mobile entertainment market (e.g., mobile games). Go to juniperresearch.com and download a white paper dealing with one of these segments. Use the white paper to develop a written summary of the market segment you selected—the size of the market, the major vendors, the factors encouraging and impeding its growth, and the future of the market segment.

7. Enter gpshopper.com. What sorts of products and services do they provide? One of their products is Slifter. Go to slifter.com and run the demo. Enter nearbynow.com. Compare the products and services they provide with those offered by GPShopper.

8. Find information about Google Maps for mobile devices. Also review the capabilities of Google SMS and other Google applications. Write a report on your findings.

9. Provide a general description of the EPC identification standard. What role do EPCglobal (epcglobalinc.org) and Auto-ID Labs (autoidlabs.org) play in this standard? EPCglobal has developed a set of policies for the use of EPCs. What are these policies and how are they enforced?

TEAM ASSIGNMENTS AND PROJECTS

1. Each team should examine a major vendor of mobile devices (Nokia, Kyocera, Motorola, Palm, BlackBerry, etc.). Each team will research the capabilities and prices of the devices offered by each company and then make a class presentation, the objective of which is to convince the rest of the class to buy that company's products.

2. Each team should explore the commercial applications of m-commerce in one of the following areas: financial services, including banking, stocks, and insurance; marketing and advertising; travel and transportation; human resources management; public services; and health care. Each team will present a report to the class based on their findings. (Start at mobiforum.org.)

3. Each team should take one of the following areas—homes, cars, appliances, or other consumer goods, such as clothing—and investigate how embedded microprocessors are currently being used and will be used in the future to support consumer-centric services. Each team will present a report to the class based on its findings.

Closing Case

WALMART TURNS TO MOBILE FOR WEATHER ALERTS

The Problem

The benefits of using weather information in the retail industry are numerous. Not only do retailers need to know the impact of weather on specific consumer demands at the store level and in turn on revenue and profitability, but they also need to ensure the safety and well-being of their customers, employees, and stores during weather emergencies. This is why larger retailers often have specialized staff devoted to monitoring weather forecasts and weather emergencies. A case in point is Walmart, the world's largest retailer.

Although the company would not reveal the dollar specifics, Jason Jackson, Walmart's director of emergency management, acknowledges that "weather is the greatest disruption point in Walmart's business." Until 2007, Walmart's emergency operation center monitored watches and warnings from the U.S. National Weather Service (NWS) and Storm Prediction Center, manually calling store managers to warn them of coming weather emergencies. For widespread and drawn out weather emergencies, like the 2005 hurricane season in the United States, it is difficult to keep up with the level of weather activity in specific locales. A manual system creates too much of a time lag between the time a potential emergency is detected in a given locale and the appropriate store managers are notified.

The Solution

In 2007, Walmart decided to institute an automated system that would deliver locally specific weather emergency information to its 3,800 stores across the United States. They selected the Smart Notification Weather Service. The service generates, authorizes, and delivers severe weather alerts to subscribers when severe weather (hurricanes, lightning, floods, wind gusts, tornadoes) is detected within their proximity. The service is a partnership between WeatherBug and Send Word Now.

The service utilizes information taken from WeatherBug's network of 8,000 tracking stations located throughout the United States, as well as information from the USPLN (United States Precision Lightning Network) and the NWS, to plot weather conditions within a 3-mile area. WeatherBug's stations update information every 2 seconds over the Internet and are far denser than the NWS's 1,200 stations, which are located mainly at major airports and provide updates every hour. The areas covered by the NWS are zip code–based and cover 5 miles to more than 30 miles in area.

The Send Word Now network matches standard or customized weather alerts to each subscriber's specific location (based on their GPS-based phone and weather profile). The service formats the appropriate alert to the supported devices and relays the alert to each individual. This provides greater accuracy and relevancy than previous alerting systems. A Java application on the user's mobile device lets the service provider know the user's location, and it can be enabled to receive more detailed information. In the case of Walmart, alerts are routed based on a store manager's location. The service also provides two-way messaging, so that local managers can send back a "message received" reply, and it generates an audit log that shows who received the message, when it was received, and on what device they acknowledged it.

The Results

In the summer of 2007, Walmart tested the service in 40 stores. They have since expanded it to 3,000 stores. For most subscribers, the cost of the system is $10 per month, although there is no information on how much Walmart spends per user. Overall, the automated system provided by the Smart Notification Weather Service is more precise, locally relevant, customized, and reliable than the manual system it replaced. With early warning about local conditions, managers have the information needed to make real-time decisions. As Walmart notes, the faster warning time enables maximum time for proper preparations, which minimizes safety issues and reduces the impact to the bottom line.

Sources: Compiled from McGee (2008) and Rash (2006).

Questions

1. Why was Walmart interested in instituting an automated weather alert system?

2. How does the Smart Notification Weather Service work? Why is it more precise, accurate, and relevant than the NWS tracking system?

3. What are the benefits of the Smart Notification Weather Service for Walmart?

ONLINE RESOURCES
available at pearsonhighered.com/turban

Online Files

W8.1 Wi-Fi and the Traveling Public

W8.2 Wi-Fi Mesh Networks, Google Talk, and Interoperability

W8.3 Application Case: Mobile Sales Solution Results in £1 Million Revenue Boost

W8.4 Application Case: NextBus: A Superb Customer Service

W8.5 Security Approaches for Mobile Computing

Comprehensive Educational Web Sites

ecommercetimes.com/perl/section/m-commerce
mobile-weblog.com/50226711/mobile_commerce.php
wimaxforum.org
brandonmcgee.blogspot.com
juniperresearch.com/shop/viewreports.php?category=
    70&pg=2

mobilegames.blog.com
trimble.com/gps
epcglobalinc.org/home
ipso-alliance.org

CHAPTER 9

E-COMMERCE SECURITY AND FRAUD PROTECTION

Content

Learning Objectives

Upon completion of this chapter, you will be able to:

1. Understand the importance and scope of security of information systems for EC.

2. Describe the major concepts and terminology of EC security.

3. Learn about the major EC security threats, vulnerabilities, and risks.

4. Understand phishing and its relationship to financial crimes.

5. Describe the information assurance security principles.

6. Identify and assess major technologies and methods for securing EC communications.

7. Describe the major technologies for protection of EC networks.

8. Describe various types of controls and special defense mechanisms.

9. Describe the role of business continuity and disaster recovery planning.

10. Discuss EC security enterprise-wide implementation issues.

11. Understand why it is not possible to stop computer crimes.

HOW SEATTLE'S HOSPITAL SURVIVED A BOT ATTACK

The Problem

On a cold Sunday afternoon, many calls reached the computer help desk at Seattle's Northwest Hospital and Medical Center. PCs were running slow, the hospital staff requested help, and documents wouldn't print. On Monday morning, as more employees came to work and logged onto their PCs, the problem spread. Finally, many PCs froze entirely.

By 10 A.M., all 50 people in the hospital's information technology (IT) department had been summoned, but their efforts made little difference. Strange things started happening. Operating-room doors stopped opening, and doctors' pagers wouldn't work. Even computers in the intensive care units were shut down.

Everybody was very frightened; hospital communications began to break down. What happened? Northwest was under attack by a *botnet,* a network of PCs infected with code that was controlled, in this case, by a 19-year-old Californian, Christopher Maxwell, and two juveniles. The trio exploited a flaw in Microsoft Windows that let them install pop-ups on the hospital's computers. As the bad code coursed through the network, the hospital's computers started turning into bots. These new bots, in turn, scanned the network, looking for new victims to infect, and the network become clogged with traffic. This kind of attack is known as a *zombie army* (Section 9.3), where computers are set up to attack other computers in the same or other organizations. Initially, Northwest's IT team tried to halt the attack by shutting off the hospital from the Internet. Even though the bots were now contained internally, they still infected PCs faster than the team could clean them.

The Solution

By Monday afternoon, the IT department had figured out which malware the bots were installing on the PCs and wrote a script, directing the PCs to remove the bad code. By Tuesday, Computer Associates—Northwest's antivirus vendor—figured out exactly which malware Maxwell had used to get into the network and wrote an antivirus program that blocked new code from coming in. The attack eventually harmed 150 out of 1,000 PCs—all of which had to have their hard drives wiped clean and their software reinstalled, at an estimated cost of $150,000.

The attack's aftermath lasted for weeks. As computers stopped working, hospital workers relied on *backup systems*— people and paper. Extra workers were brought in to help carry out tasks by hand. Lab results, for instance, were run by a person from the lab to the patients' bedsides on different floors. To save time, elective surgeries were postponed. Every day, department managers met several times to make sure the new security routines were holding and no patients were being endangered.

The Results

The hospital's network is now protected by CA's Pest Patrol, which blocks adware and spyware (Section 9.3), and Cisco MARS, an intrusion detection system (Section 9.3). The Windows flaw that the attacks slipped through has also been fixed.

Northwest wasn't Maxwell and crew's only prey. Among their other victims were the U.S. Department of Defense and

Colton Joint Unified School District in California, according to court papers. Maxwell pleaded guilty to conspiracy and intentionally causing damage to a protected computer. He was sentenced in August 2006 to 37 months in federal prison. He also was ordered to pay $115,000 to cover the hospital's direct expenses.

Sources: Compiled from Kawamoto (2006) and O'Hagan (2006).

WHAT WE CAN LEARN . . .

Information systems inside organizations can be attacked by criminals who may not even benefit financially from the attacks. This attack was done by using a virus hidden in pop-up ads. This is only one of the many methods used to attack information systems in organizations, disturbing their internal operations. Other attack methods interfere with online trading and other forms of e-commerce. In addition to criminal attacks, information systems may be attacked by natural disasters, human error, equipment malfunction, and more. In this chapter, we concentrate on e-commerce attacks and on the defense against them.

9.1   THE INFORMATION SECURITY PROBLEM

If you examine different lists of management concerns regarding the use of EC (and IT), the security issue is and has been among the top concerns. Security is considered to be the backbone of doing business over the Internet. Security-breaching incidents involving all types of organizations (including high-level, secure government agencies such as the CIA, FBI, and the military) appear on the news daily. Few organizations or individuals have not experienced some security breaches in their computerized systems. The damages of security breaches, including crimes, can be substantial and sometimes life-threatening, as was demonstrated in the opening case. Securing data, transactions, and privacy, and protecting people (buyers and sellers) is of utmost importance in conducting EC of any type.

In this chapter, we will provide an overview of the security problems and solutions as they are related to EC and IT. In this section, we look at the nature of the security problems, the magnitude of the problems, and the essential terminology and strategy used in dealing with these issues.

WHAT IS EC SECURITY?

Computer security refers to the protection of data, networks, computer programs, computer power, and other elements of computerized information systems (see en.wikipedia.org/wiki/Computer_security). It is a very broad concept due to the many methods of attack as well as the many modes of defense. The attacks and defense of computers can affect individuals, organization, countries, or the entire Web. Computer security aims to prevent or at least minimize the attacks. We classify computer security into two categories: *generic*, relating to any information system (e.g., encryption), and *EC-related*, such as buyers' protection. This chapter covers both, but it emphasizes the EC-related side. Attacks on EC Web sites, *identify theft* of both individuals and organizations, and a large variety of fraud schemes, such as phishing, are described in this chapter.

The Status of Computer Security in the United States

Several private and government organizations try to assess the status of computer security in the United States annually. Notable is the annual CSI report, which is described next.

No one really knows the true impact of online security breaches because, according to the Computer Security Institute (CSI, gocsi.com), only 27 percent of businesses report to legal authorities about computer intrusions. For the 2008 survey, known as the **CSI Computer Crime and Security Survey**, see Richardson (2008). This is an annual security survey of U.S. corporations and government agencies; financial, medical, and other institutions; and universities, conducted by the Computer Security Institute. Highlights from the 2008 Security Survey, which was based on responses from 520 participants, include the following five summary points:

CSI Computer Crime and Security Survey Annual security survey of U.S. corporations, government agencies, financial and medical institutions, and universities conducted by the Computer Security Institute.

> 1. **The most expensive computer security incidents were those involving financial fraud.** The average reported cost was close to $500,000 per respondent (for those who experienced financial fraud). The second-most expensive, on average, was dealing with "bot" computers within the organization's network (such as in the opening case), reported to cost an average of nearly $350,000 per respondent. The overall average annual loss reported was just under $300,000.

2. **Virus incidents occurred most frequently.** Virus incidents occurred at almost half (49 percent) of the respondents' organizations. Insider abuse of networks was second most frequently occurring, at 44 percent, followed by theft of laptops and other mobile devices (42 percent).

3. **Almost one in ten organizations reported experiencing a domain name system (DNS) incident.** These incidents were up 2 percent from 2007, and noteworthy, given the current focus on vulnerabilities in DNS.

4. **Twenty-seven percent of those surveyed responded positively to a question regarding "targeted attacks."** Respondents had detected at least one such attack, where "targeted attack" was defined as a malware attack aimed exclusively at the respondent's organization or at organizations within a small subset of the general business population.

5. **The vast majority of respondents said their organizations had a security policy.** Sixty-eight percent had policies, while 18 percent were developing a formal information security policy. Only 1 percent said they had no security policy.

Other Interesting Findings. Other findings in the report are:

▶ The budget for IT security is about 10 percent of the total IT budget (on average).

▶ Awareness training is about 3 percent of the total IT budget (on average).

▶ Forty percent of companies use ROI, 20 percent use NPV, and 20 percent use IRR (see Chapter 11) to justify security projects.

▶ About 40 percent outsource some computer security.

▶ About 43 percent experienced security incidents, usually less than 5 but not more than 10 each year.

▶ About half of the attacks are made by insiders.

▶ On average, the number of attacks is declining (50 percent decline over the last 10 years). The most frequent attacks (see Section 9.3) are shown with their occurrence frequency in Exhibit 9.1.

The average loss per respondent has been on the decline since 2001. Between 2003 and 2008, average loss was in the range of $168,000 to $526,000. The most commonly used defense technologies in 2008 are shown in Exhibit 9.2. Some of these are described in Sections 9.6 through 9.9.

This report indicates that despite the decline in the frequency of incidents and their severity, the security problems still persist.

National Security

Protection of the U.S. computer networks is in the hands of the Department of Homeland Security (DHS), which coordinates government policies for thwarting cyberthreats. It includes the following programs:

▶ **Cyber Security Preparedness and the National Cyber Alert System.** Computer users can stay up-to-date on cyberthreats through this program.

▶ **U.S.-CERT Operations.** Analyzes and combats cyberthreats and vulnerabilities.

▶ **National Cyber Response Coordination Group.** Comprising 13 federal agencies, it coordinates the federal response to incidents.

▶ **CyberCop Portal.** Coordination with law enforcement helps capture and convict those responsible for cyberattacks.

EXHIBIT 9.1   **Major Computer Attack Incidents in 2008**

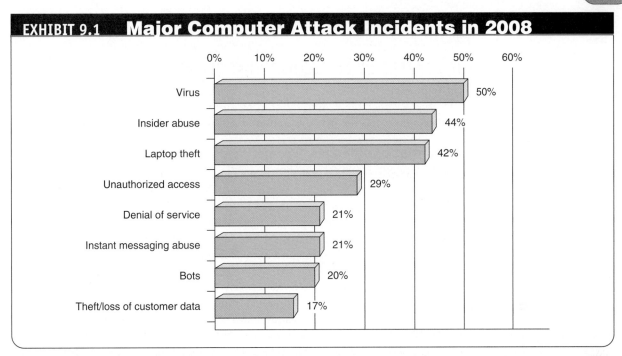

EXHIBIT 9.2   **Major Security Methods Used in 2008**

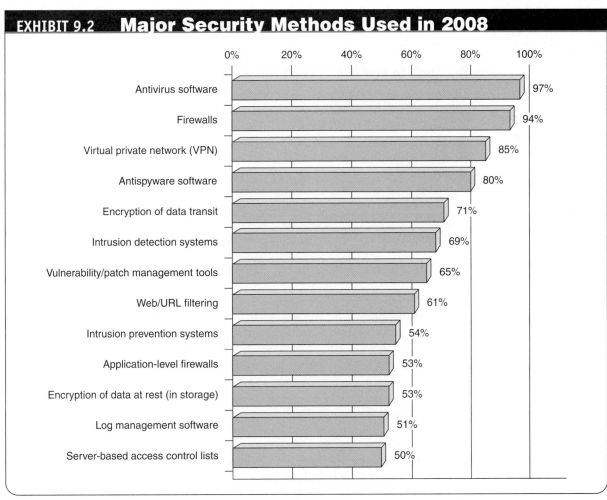

On February 9, 2009, President Obama ordered the DHS to review U.S. government cybersecurity plans.

THE DRIVERS OF EC SECURITY PROBLEMS

Security problems are the results of several drivers. Here, we describe four major ones: the Internet's vulnerable design, the shift to profit-induced crimes, the Internet underground economy, and the dynamic nature of EC systems and the role of insiders.

The Internet's Vulnerable Design

It is important to recognize that the Internet and its network protocols were never intended for use by untrustworthy people or criminals. They were designed to accommodate computer-to-computer communications in a closed and trusted community. However, the system evolved into an any-to-any means of communication in an open community. As you know, that community is global in scope, mostly unregulated, and out of control. Furthermore, the Internet was designed for maximum efficiency without regard for security or the integrity of a person sending a message or requesting access. Error checking to ensure that the message was sent and received correctly was important at that time but not user authentication or access control. The Internet is still a fundamentally insecure infrastructure.

Virtually every Internet application relies on the reliable operation of *domain name system* (DNS) services. The **domain name system (DNS)** translates (converts) domain names (e.g., pearson.com and fbi.gov) to their numeric IP addresses. An **IP address** is an address that identifies your computer on a network or Internet. The lack of source authentication and data integrity checking in DNS operations leaves nearly all Internet services vulnerable to attacks.

domain name system (DNS)
Translates (converts) domain names to their numeric IP addresses.

IP address
An address that uniquely identifies each computer connected to a network or the Internet.

The Shift to Profit-Induced Crimes

There is a clear shift in the nature of the operation of computer criminals (see Symantec 2008, 2009). In the early days of e-commerce, many hackers simply wanted to gain fame or notoriety by defacing Web sites or "gaining root," that is, root access to a network. The opening case illustrates a criminal who did not attack systems to make a profit. Today, criminals are profit-oriented, and there are many more of them. Most popular is the theft of personal information such as credit card numbers, bank accounts, and Internet IDs and passwords. According to Privacy Rights Clearinghouse, approximately 250 million records containing personally identifiable information were involved in security breaches in the three years between April 2005 and April 2008 (reported by Palgon 2008).

Examples. The following are some examples:

- On February 10, 2008, the U.S. Federal Aviation Administration admitted that someone hacked into its computers and accessed the names and social security numbers of 45,000 employees.
- In January 2008, T. Rowe Price began notifying 35,000 clients that their names and social security numbers might have been compromised. The breach stemmed from the December 2007 theft of computers from the offices of a third-party services provider, which was preparing tax forms on behalf of T. Rowe Price.
- In May 2009, hackers broke into some Facebook member accounts and sent messages to the members' friends, urging them to click on fake Web sites that look like the Facebook homepage. By doing so, they unwittingly gave their passwords to the hackers. The purpose was to spread spam advertisements or identity theft. This strategy is known as a *phishing attack* and will be described later in this chapter together with identity fraud.

▶ Cybercriminals launched an attack to extort money from StormPay, an online payment processing company. The attack shut down both of StormPay's data centers and its business for two days, causing financial losses and upsetting 3 million customers.

▶ Names, e-mail addresses, and phone numbers of an estimated 1.6 million jobseekers were accessed from Monster.com's résumé database in August 2007. Though widely described as a hacking, the data were actually accessed by attackers using legitimate user names and passwords, possibly stolen from professional recruiters or human resources personnel who were using Monster.com to look for job candidates.

Note that laptop computers are stolen for two reasons: selling the hardware and trying to find valuable data on the machine.

Intrusion access to corporate data occurred at discount retail conglomerate TJX (see Online File W9.1). A major driver of data theft and other crimes is the ability to profit from the theft. Stolen data are sold today in a huge illegal marketplace described next.

The Internet Underground Economy

The **Internet underground economy** refers to the e-markets for stolen information. Thousands of Web sites sell credit card numbers, social security numbers, other data such as numbers of bank accounts, social network IDs, passwords, and much more. Such credentials are sold for less than a dollar to several hundred dollars each to spammers or to criminals who are using them for illegal financial transactions such as transferring money to their accounts or paying with someone else's credit card. For example, in August 2008, the FBI arrested a Countrywide employee who stole more than 2 million customer records and sold them on the underground market. The Internet security company Symantec released a comprehensive report that provides statistical data about the Internet underground economy (Symantec 2008). The Symantec report provides information on how cybercriminals are getting organized in Russia and other countries. According to this report, about 30 percent of all the transactions in this market deal with stolen credit cards. The value of all unsold items is estimated to be $275 million, while the potential worth of just the credit cards and banking information for sale is $7 billion. Forty-one percent of the underground economy is in the United States, while 13 percent is in Romania. The report also covers the issue of software piracy, which is estimated to be more than $100 million annually. For highlights of the report, see Symantec (2008). Criminals use several methods to steal the information they sell. One popular method is *keystroke logging*.

Keystroke Logging. **Keystroke logging**, often called **keylogging**, is a method of capturing and recording user keystrokes. Such systems are also highly useful for both law enforcement and for law breaking—for instance, by providing a means to obtain passwords or encryption keys and thus bypassing other security measures. Keylogging methods are widely available on the Internet. For more information, see en.wikipedia.org/wiki/Keystroke_logging.

Internet underground economy
E-markets for stolen information made up of thousands of Web sites that sell credit card numbers, social security numbers, other data such as numbers of bank accounts, social network IDs, passwords, and much more.

keystroke logging (keylogging)
A method of capturing and recording user keystrokes.

The Dynamic Nature of EC Systems and the Role of Insiders

EC systems are changing all the time due to a stream of innovations. With changes often come security problems. In recent years, we have experienced many security problems in the new areas of social networks and wireless systems (some will be explored later in this chapter). Note also that almost half of the security problems are caused by insiders. New insiders are being added frequently and so are the threats they bring.

Example. An insider let two criminals into London's office of Sumitomo Mitsui Bank, where the criminals tampered with the computer system, gaining access to the asset holdings of companies such as Toshiba. Then they tried to steal hundreds of millions of dollars from the bank and its corporate customers. They attempted to electronically transfer $323 million from accounts in the bank to their own account. Fortunately the attempt failed. Otherwise it would have been the biggest theft of its kind (*Taipei Times* 2009).

WHY IS E-COMMERCE SECURITY STRATEGY NEEDED?

Computer security in its simplest form can be divided into three categories: *threats, defenses,* and *management.* As you will see in Sections 9.3 and 9.4, there are many potential threats. In general, we divide these threats into two categories: unintentional and intentional. The intentional threats are known as *cybercrimes* when they are performed on the Web. These change frequently as the criminals become more sophisticated.

The defense (Sections 9.5 through 9.10) is changing too and is improving in response to new attack methods and to new technological innovations. Yet, neither cybercrime nor cybercriminals can be stopped (see Section 9.10). Like in the physical world, Internet security systems cost money, sometimes a considerable amount. Therefore, one of management's tasks is to determine how much to invest in EC security. In addition, management is responsible to a variety of security programs across the enterprise. This requires a strategy.

The Computer Security Dilemma

Information security departments with big workloads and small budgets are not able to optimize their EC security program for efficiency. Endless worms, spyware, data piracy, and other crimes keep them working reactively rather than strategically; they address security concerns according to attackers' schedules instead of their own. As a result, their security costs and efforts from reacting to crises and paying for damages are greater than if they had an EC security strategy. This is the underlying reason why a comprehensive EC security is necessary.

Section 9.1 ▶ REVIEW QUESTIONS

1. Define computer security.
2. List the major findings of the CSI 2008 survey.
3. Describe the Internet vulnerability design.
4. Describe some profit-induced computer crimes.
5. Define the Internet underground economy.
6. Describe the dynamic nature of EC systems.
7. What makes EC security management so difficult? What is the dilemma?

9.2   BASIC E-COMMERCE SECURITY ISSUES AND LANDSCAPE

In order to better understand security problems, we need to understand some basic concepts in EC and IT security. We begin with some basic definitions, which constitute a vocabulary frequently used in dealing with security issues.

THE SECURITY BASIC TERMINOLOGY

In the opening case and in Section 9.1, we introduced some key concepts and security terms. We begin this section by introducing alphabetically the major terms needed to understand EC security issues:

- Business continuity plan
- Cybercrime
- Exposure
- Fraud
- Malware (malicious software)
- Phishing
- Risk
- Social engineering
- Spam
- Vulnerability
- Zombie

THE EC SECURITY BATTLEGROUND

In Section 9.1, we introduced some results of the CSI computer crime report. Notice the list of attack methods (Exhibit 9.1) and technologies to combat them (Exhibit 9.2). The essence of EC security can be viewed as a battleground between attacks and attackers, defense and defenders, and security requirements. This battleground includes the following components, as shown in Exhibit 9.3:

- The attacks, the attackers, and their strategies
- The items that are being attacked (the targets)
- The defenders and their methods and strategy

Threats and Attacks: Unintentional and Intentional

Information systems including EC are vulnerable to both unintentional and intentional threats.

Unintentional Threats. Unintentional threats fall into three major categories: human error, environmental hazards, and malfunctions in the computer system.

- **Human error.** Human error can occur in the design of the hardware or information system. It can also occur in programming, testing, data collection, data entry, authorization, and instructions. Errors can be a result of negligence or misunderstanding (for example, not changing passwords creates a security hole).

  Example 1. In November 2008, Jefferson County, West Virginia, released a site search engine that gave a new meaning to "open records." The engine exposed social security numbers and other personal information belonging to about 1.6 million citizens. It was a clear programming error made by a person.

- **Environmental hazards.** These include earthquakes, severe storms (e.g., hurricanes, blizzards, or sand), floods, power failures or strong fluctuations, fires (the most common hazard), explosions, radioactive fallout, and water-cooling system failures. Computer resources can also be damaged by side effects such as smoke and water.

---

business continuity plan
A plan that keeps the business running after a disaster occurs. Each function in the business should have a valid recovery capability plan.

cybercrime
Intentional crimes carried out on the Internet.

exposure
The estimated cost, loss, or damage that can result if a threat exploits a vulnerability.

fraud
Any business activity that uses deceitful practices or devices to deprive another of property or other rights.

malware (malicious software)
A generic term for malicious software.

phishing
A crimeware technique to steal the identity of a target company to get the identities of its customers.

risk
The probability that a vulnerability will be known and used.

social engineering
A type of nontechnical attack that uses some ruse to trick users into revealing information or performing an action that compromises a computer or network.

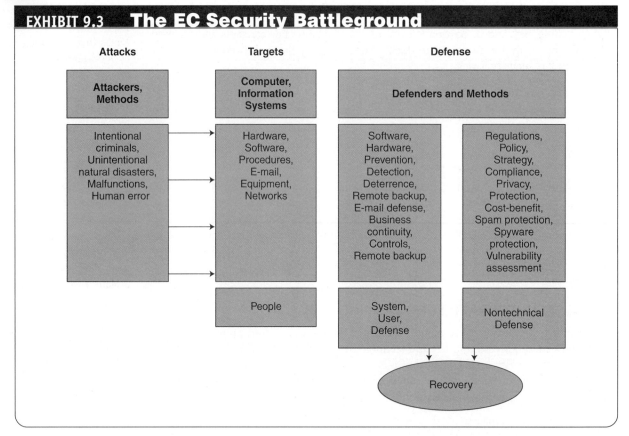

EXHIBIT 9.3 The EC Security Battleground

---

spam
The electronic equivalent of junk mail.

vulnerability
Weakness in software or other mechanism that threatens the confidentiality, integrity, or availability of an asset (recall the CIA model). It can be directly used by a hacker to gain access to a system or network.

zombies
Computers infected with malware that are under the control of a spammer, hacker, or other criminal.

▶ **Malfunctions in the computer system.** Defects can be the result of poor manufacturing, defective materials, and outdated or poorly maintained networks. Unintentional malfunctions can also happen for other reasons, ranging from lack of experience to inadequate testing.

Example 2. In January 2009, a glitch disabled thousands of Microsoft Zune personal music players. Users of certain blogs and social networking sites were unable to listen to music because it would not start properly. The problem occurred when the internal clock on the device moved automatically to January 1, but because 2008 had been a leap year and the programmers had forgotten about it, the glitch occurred.

Intentional Attacks and Crimes. Intentional attacks are done by criminals. Examples of intentional attacks include theft of data; inappropriate use of data (e.g., manipulating inputs); theft of laptops and equipment and /or programs; deliberate manipulation in handling, entering, processing, transferring, or programming data; vandalism or sabotage; malicious damage to computer resources; destruction from viruses and similar attacks; miscellaneous computer abuses; and Internet fraud.

Criminals and Social Engineering

Intentional crimes carried out on the Internet are called *cybercrimes*, which are done by **cybercriminals** (*criminals* for short) that include hackers and crackers. **Hacker** describes someone who gains unauthorized access to a computer system. A **cracker** is a *malicious hacker*, such as Maxwell, in the opening case, who may represent a serious problem for a corporation.

Hackers and crackers may implicate unsuspecting insiders in their crimes. In a strategy called *social engineering*, criminals trick unsuspecting insiders into giving them information or access that they should not have. Social engineering is a collection of tactics used to manipulate people into performing actions or divulging confidential information. Notorious hacker Kevin Mitnick, who served time in jail for hacking, used social engineering as his primary method to gain access to computer systems. One recent popular method is *scareware,* in which criminals persuade users to download malicious files disguised as security applications.

Vulnerable Areas Are Being Attacked

Any part of an information system can be attacked. PCs can be stolen or attacked by viruses and other malware. Users are subject to fraudulent identification. Databases can be attacked by unauthorized access, and data can be copied and stolen. Networks can be attacked, and information flow can be stopped or altered. Terminals, printers, and any other pieces of equipment can be damaged in many ways. Software and programs can be manipulated. Procedures and policies may be altered, and much more. Attacks are done on vulnerable areas.

Vulnerability. MITRE Corporation publishes a list of vulnerabilities called *common vulnerabilities and exposures (CVE)* (cve.mitre.org). In 2006, MITRE reported that four of the top five reported vulnerabilities were within Web applications. Vulnerabilities create *risk*, which is the probability that this weakness will be known and used. *Exposure* can result if a threat exploits a vulnerability.

Examples.   Three medical data breaches occurred in May 2008. Unauthorized peer-to-peer (P2P) file sharing led to a data breach at Walter Reed Army Medical Center that exposed the personal data of 1,000 patients. Patients at Staten Island University Hospital in New York were told that a computer with their medical records was stolen. Information on patients of the University of California San Francisco Medical Center was accidentally made accessible on the Internet.

Attacking E-Mail. One of the easiest places to attack is e-mail, since it travels via the unsecured Internet. One example is the ease with which Sarah Palin was hacked in March 2008. For a list of top attack areas, see Online File W9.2.

SECURITY SCENARIOS AND REQUIREMENTS IN E-COMMERCE

EC security involves more than just preventing and responding to cyberattacks and intrusion. Consider, for example, the situation in which users connect to a Web store to obtain some product literature. In return, the users are asked to "register," to fill out an electronic form providing information about themselves or their employers before receiving the literature. In this situation, what kinds of security issues arise?

From the user's perspective:

▶ How can the user know whether the Web server is owned and operated by a legitimate company?

▶ How does the user know that the Web page and form have not been compromised by spyware or other malicious code?

▶ How does the user know that an employee won't intercept and misuse the information?

cybercriminal
A person who intentionally carries out crimes over the Internet.

hacker
Someone who gains unauthorized access to a computer system.

cracker
A malicious hacker, such as Maxwell, in the opening case, who may represent a serious problem for a corporation.

From the company's perspective:

▶ How does the company know the user will not attempt to break into the Web server or alter the pages and content at the site?

▶ How does the company know that the user will not try to disrupt the server so that it is not available to others?

From both parties' perspectives:

▶ How do both parties know that the network connection is free from eavesdropping by a third party "listening" on the line?

▶ How do they know that the information sent back and forth between the server and the user's browser has not been altered?

Such questions illustrate the kinds of security issues that arise in an EC transaction. For transactions involving e-payments, additional types of security issues must be confronted.

EC Security Requirements

To protect EC transactions, we use the following set of requirements:

authentication
Process to verify (assure) the real identity of an individual, computer, computer program, or EC Web site.

authorization
Process of determining what the authenticated entity is allowed to access and what operations it is allowed to perform.

nonrepudiation
Assurance that online customers or trading partners cannot falsely deny (repudiate) their purchase or transaction.

▶ **Authentication.** Authentication is a process to verify (assure) the real identity of an entity, which could be an individual, software agent, computer program, or EC Web site. For transmissions, authentication verifies that the sender of the message is who the person or organization claims to be.

▶ **Authorization.** Authorization is the process of determining what an authenticated entity is allowed to access and what operations it is allowed to perform. Authorization of an entity occurs after authentication.

▶ **Auditing.** When a person or program accesses a Web site or queries a database, various pieces of information are recorded or logged into a file. The process of recording information about what was accessed, when, and by whom is known as *auditing*. Audits provide the means to reconstruct what specific actions have occurred and may help EC security investigators identify the person or program that performed unauthorized actions.

▶ **Availability.** Technologies such as load-balancing hardware and software help ensure availability.

▶ **Nonrepudiation.** Closely associated with authentication is nonrepudiation, which is the assurance that online customers or trading partners will not be able to falsely deny (repudiate) their purchase, transaction, or other obligation. Nonrepudiation involves several assurances, including providing:

  ▶ The sender of data with proof of delivery.

  ▶ The recipient (EC company) with proof of the sender's identity.

  ▶ Authentication and nonrepudiation are potential defenses against phishing and identity theft. To protect and ensure trust in EC transactions, *digital signatures*, or *digital certificates*, are often used to validate the sender and time stamp of the transaction so it cannot be later claimed that the transaction was unauthorized or invalid. A technical overview of digital signatures and certificates and how they provide verification is provided in Section 9.6. Unfortunately, phishers and spammers have devised ways to compromise certain digital signatures.

THE DEFENSE: DEFENDERS AND THEIR STRATEGY

Security should be everyone's business. However, in general, the information system department and vendors provide the technical side while management provides the administrative aspects. Such activities are done via security and strategy that users need to follow.

EC Defense Programs and Strategy

An **EC security strategy** consisting of multiple layers of defense is needed. Such a strategy views EC security as the process of deterring, preventing, and detecting unauthorized use of the organization's brand, identity, Web site, e-mail, information, or other assets and attempts to defraud the organization, its customers, and employees. **Deterring measures** refer to actions that will make criminals abandon their idea of attacking a specific system (e.g., the possibility of losing a job, for insiders). **Prevention measures** help stop unauthorized users (also known as *intruders*) from accessing any part of the EC system (e.g., by requiring a password). **Detection measures** help determine whether intruders attempted to break into the EC system; whether they were successful; and what they may have done.

Making sure that a shopping experience is safe and secure is a crucial part of improving the buyer experience. The ultimate goal of EC security is often referred to as **information assurance (IA)**. IA is the protection of information systems against unauthorized access to or modification of information whether in storage, processing, or in transit; protection against denial of service to authorized users; and those measures necessary to detect, document, and counter threats (see details in Section 9.5).

Defense Methods and Technologies

There are hundreds of defense methods, technologies, and vendors that can be classified in different ways. We introduce them in Sections 9.5 through 9.10.

Recovery

In security battles, there are winners and losers in single episodes, but no one can win the war. As discussed in Section 9.10, there are many reasons for this. On the other hand, after a security breach, organizations and individuals usually recover. Recovery is especially critical in cases of a disaster or a major attack. Organizations need to continue their business until the information systems are fully restored, and they need to restore them fast. This is done by using a *business continuity and disaster recovery plan* (Section 9.9).

Because of the complexity of EC and network security, this topic cannot be covered in a single chapter or even a book. Those readers interested in a more comprehensive discussion should see the *Pearson/Prentice Hall Security Series*.

Section 9.2 ▶ REVIEW QUESTIONS

1. List five major terms of EC security.
2. Describe the major unintentional security hazards.
3. List five examples of intentional EC security crimes.
4. Describe the security battleground, who participates, and how. What are the possible results?
5. Define hacker, cracker, and social engineering.

EC security strategy
A strategy that views EC security as the process of preventing and detecting unauthorized use of the organization's brand, identity, Web site, e-mail, information, or other asset and attempts to defraud the organization, its customers, and employees.

deterring measures
Actions that will make criminals abandon their idea of attacking a specific system (e.g., the possibility of losing a job for insiders).

prevention measures
Ways to help stop unauthorized users (also known as "intruders") from accessing any part of the EC system.

detection measures
Ways to determine whether intruders attempted to break into the EC system; whether they were successful; and what they may have done.

information assurance (IA)
The protection of information systems against unauthorized access to or modification of information whether in storage, processing, or transit, and against the denial of service to authorized users, including those measures necessary to detect, document, and counter such threats.

6. Define authentication and authorization requirements.
7. What is nonrepudiation?
8. Describe deterring, preventing, and detecting in EC security systems.

9.3 TECHNICAL ATTACK METHODS

Criminals use many methods to attack information systems and users. Here, we cover some major representative methods.

It's helpful to distinguish between two types of attacks—*technical* (which we discuss in this section) and *nontechnical*.

TECHNICAL AND NONTECHNICAL ATTACKS: AN OVERVIEW

Software and systems knowledge are used to perpetrate *technical attacks*. A computer virus is an example of a technical attack.

Nontechnical attacks are those in which a perpetrator uses some form of deception or persuasion to trick people into revealing information or performing actions that can compromise the security of a network. We include in these financial fraud, spam, *social engineering,* and *phishing.* The goals of social engineering are to gain unauthorized access to systems or information. Phishing attacks rely on social engineering.

Many attacks involve a combination of several methods, some of which can be technical and some nontechnical. For instance, an intruder may use an automated tool to post a message to an instant messaging service, offering the opportunity to download software of interest to the members (e.g., software for downloading music or videos) that includes a botnet. When an unsuspecting user downloads the software, the botnet automatically runs on his or her computer, enabling the intruder to turn the machine into a *zombie* to perpetrate a technical attack.

The Major Technical Attack Methods

Hackers often use several software tools readily and freely available over the Internet together with tutorials on how to use them in order to learn of vulnerabilities as well. Although some of the free tools require expertise, novice hackers can easily use many of the other tools. The major attack methods are described next.

MALICIOUS CODE: VIRUSES, WORMS, AND TROJAN HORSES

Malware (or *malicious software*) is software designed to infiltrate or damage a computer system without the owner's informed consent or even their knowledge. Malware is a general term used by computer professionals to mean a variety of forms of hostile, intrusive, or annoying software or program code.

Software is considered malware based on the perceived intent of the creator rather than any particular features. Malware includes computer viruses, worms, Trojan horses, most rootkits, spyware, dishonest adware, crimeware, and other malicious and unwanted software.

virus
A piece of software code that inserts itself into a host, including the operating systems, in order to propagate; it requires that its host program be run to activate it.

Viruses

A **virus** is a piece of software code that inserts itself into a host, including the operating systems; running its host program activates the virus. A virus has two components. First, it has a propagation mechanism by which it spreads. Second, it has a payload that refers to what the virus does once it is executed. Sometimes a particular event triggers the virus's execution. For instance, Michelangelo's birth date triggered the Michelangelo virus. On April 1, 2009, the entire world was waiting for a virus named Conficker C. Fortunately only limited attacks were reported. Some viruses simply infect and spread. Others do substantial damage (e.g., deleting files or corrupting the hard drive). The process of a virus attack is illustrated in Exhibit 9.4.

For tutorials and information about viruses, see microsoft.com/protect/computer/ basics/virus.mspx.

Worms. Unlike a virus, a **worm** can spread itself without any human intervention. Worms use networks to propagate and infect a computer or handheld device (e.g., cell phone) and can even spread via instant messages. Also, unlike viruses that generally are confined within a target computer, a worm's ability to self-propagate can degrade network performance. Worms consist of a set of common base elements: a warhead, a propagation engine, a payload, a target-selection algorithm, and a scanning engine. The *warhead* is the piece of code in a worm that exploits some known vulnerability. A huge number of worms have been spread all over the Internet (for example, as mentioned previously, the Conficker worm in April 2009).

In March 2009, the Koobface worm attacked Facebook and other social networks. It created bogus links that looked innocent, but when you clicked them, it gave hackers access to sensitive personal data.

Macro Virus. A **macro virus** or **macro worm** is executed when the application object that contains the macro is opened or a particular procedure is executed. Because worms spread much more rapidly than viruses, organizations need to proactively track new vulnerabilities and apply system patches as a defense against their spread.

worm
A software program that runs independently, consuming the resources of its host in order to maintain itself, that is capable of propagating a complete working version of itself onto another machine.

macro virus (macro worm)
A macro virus or macro worm is executed when the application object that contains the macro is opened or a particular procedure is executed.

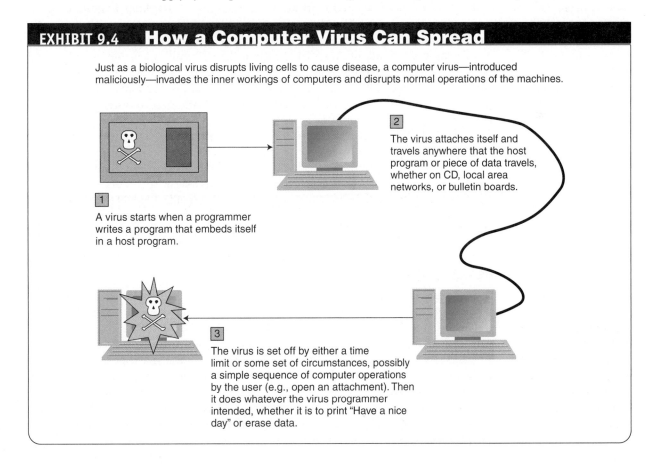

EXHIBIT 9.4   How a Computer Virus Can Spread

Just as a biological virus disrupts living cells to cause disease, a computer virus—introduced maliciously—invades the inner workings of computers and disrupts normal operations of the machines.

1 A virus starts when a programmer writes a program that embeds itself in a host program.

2 The virus attaches itself and travels anywhere that the host program or piece of data travels, whether on CD, local area networks, or bulletin boards.

3 The virus is set off by either a time limit or some set of circumstances, possibly a simple sequence of computer operations by the user (e.g., open an attachment). Then it does whatever the virus programmer intended, whether it is to print "Have a nice day" or erase data.

Trojan horse
A program that appears to have a useful function but that contains a hidden function that presents a security risk.

Trojan Horse. A **Trojan horse** is a program that appears to have a useful function but contains a hidden function that presents a security risk. The name is derived from the Trojan horse in Greek mythology. Legend has it that during the Trojan War the city of Troy was presented with a large wooden horse as a gift to the goddess Athena. The Trojans hauled the horse inside the city gates. During the night, Greek soldiers who were hiding in the hollow horse opened the gates of Troy and let in the Greek army. The army was able to take the city and win the war.

There are many variations of Trojan horse programs. The programs of interest are those that make it possible for someone else to access and control a person's computer over the Internet. This type of Trojan horse has two parts: a server and a client. The *server* is the program that runs on the computer under attack. The *client* program is the program used by the person perpetrating the attack. For example, the Girlfriend Trojan is a server program that arrives in the form of a file that looks like an interesting game or program. When the unsuspecting user runs the program, the user unknowingly installs the Trojan program. The installed program executes every time the user turns on the attacked computer. The server simply waits for the associated client program to send a command. This particular Trojan horse enables the perpetrator to capture user IDs and passwords, to display messages on the affected computer, to delete and upload files, and so on. Trojan threads are spread in many ways (e.g., under the guise of Verizon messages). Two examples follow:

Example 1. Spyware researchers at Webroot Software uncovered a stash of tens of thousands of stolen identities from 125 countries that they believe were collected by a new variant of a Trojan program the company named *Trojan-Phisher-Rebery* (Roberts 2006). The Rebery malicious software is an example of a **banking Trojan**, which is programmed to come to life when computer owners visit one of a number of online banking sites.

banking Trojan
A Trojan that comes to life when computer owners visit one of a number of online banking or e-commerce sites.

Example 2. Bank of America has more than 20 million customers online and processes more transactions online than it does in all of its physical banking centers. According to Gage (2006), Ahlo, a Miami wholesaler of ink and toner cartridges, sued the Bank of America for being responsible for an unauthorized transfer of more than $90,000 from Ahlo's account to a bank in Latvia. A Coreflood Trojan infected the company's PC. The Trojan was spread by a phishing attack—fraudulent e-mails that tricked bank customers into giving up their account information and infecting their computers with malware that logged keystrokes. (The bank does not discuss individual phishing attempts but posted information on its Web site, bofa.com/privacy/pdf/fin_security.pdf, to educate customers about online fraud.) Bank of America's battle against phishing shows how hard it is for businesses that have grown by acquiring companies with incompatible information systems to protect gullible and sometimes lazy or "can't happen to me" customers from cybercrime.

Denial of Service

denial of service (DoS) attack
An attack on a Web site in which an attacker uses specialized software to send a flood of data packets to the target computer with the aim of overloading its resources.

A **denial-of-service (DoS) attack** is an attack in which a large number of requests for service or access to a site bombard a system, which causes it to crash or become unable to respond in time. In a DoS attack, an attacker uses specialized software to send a flood of data packets to the target computer, with the aim of overloading its resources. Many attackers rely on software created by other hackers that is available over the Internet for free rather than developing it themselves. A common method is the use of *zombie PCs* to launch DoS attacks.

DoS attacks can be difficult to stop. Fortunately (or unfortunately), they are so commonplace that over the past few years, the security community has developed a series of steps for combating these costly attacks.

Web Server and Web Page Hijacking

Web servers and Web pages can be hijacked and configured to control or redirect unsuspecting users to scam or phishing sites. This exploit allows *any* Webmaster (including criminals) to have his or her own "virtual pages" rank for pages belonging to another Webmaster (e.g., a legitimate EC site). Successfully employed, this technique will allow the offending Webmaster ("the hijacker") to displace the pages of the "target" or victim Web site in the search engine result pages. This causes search engine traffic to the target Web site to vanish or redirects traffic to any other page of choice.

International organized crime syndicates, al-Qaida groups, and other cybercriminals steal hundreds of billions of dollars every year. Cybercrime is safer and easier than selling drugs, dealing in black market diamonds, or robbing banks. Online gambling offers easy fronts for international money laundering operations. And hack attacks are a key weapon of global jihad.

Botnets

A **botnet** is a huge number (as many as hundreds of thousands) of hijacked Internet computers that have been set up to forward traffic, including spam and viruses (recall the opening case), to other computers on the Internet. An infected computer is referred to as a *computer robot*, or *bot*. Botmasters, or bot herders, control botnets. The combined power of these coordinated networks of computers can scan for and compromise other computers and perpetrate DoS or other attacks. Botnets are used in scams, spams, and frauds. Botnets appear in different forms (e.g., see the opening case) and can be worms or viruses. Notable botnets include Srizbi, Cutwail, and Conficker.

botnet
A huge number (e.g., hundreds of thousands) of hijacked Internet computers that have been set up to forward traffic, including spam and viruses, to other computers on the Internet.

Example. At the beginning of 2004, the MyDoom.A e-mail virus infected several hundred thousand PCs around the world. Like many other e-mail viruses, this virus propagated by sending an official-looking e-mail message with a zip file attached. When the victim opened the zip file, the virus automatically found other e-mail addresses on the victim's computer and forwarded itself to those addresses. However, there was more to MyDoom than simple propagation. When the victim opened the zip file, the virus code also installed a program on the victim's machine that enabled the intruders to automatically launch a DoS attack. For more details see en.wikipedia.org/wiki/Mydoom.

Section 9.3 ▶ REVIEW QUESTIONS

1. Describe the difference between a nontechnical and a technical cyberattack.
2. What are the major forms of malicious code?
3. What factors account for the increase in malicious code?
4. What are some of the major trends in malicious code?
5. Define worm and Trojan horse.
6. How are DoS attacks perpetrated?
7. Describe botnet attacks.

9.4 PHISHING, FINANCIAL FRAUD, AND SPAM

As discussed in Section 9.1, there is a shift to profit-related Internet crimes. These crimes are conducted with the help of both technical methods, such as malicious code that can steal confidential information from your online bank account, and nontechnical methods, such as social engineering and phishing. Exhibit 9.5 illustrates how such cybercrimes are committed.

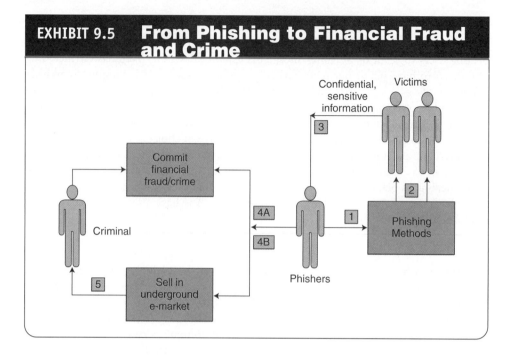

EXHIBIT 9.5   From Phishing to Financial Fraud and Crime

Phishers (or other criminals) obtain confidential information by methods ranging from social engineering to physical theft. The stolen information (e.g., credit card numbers, social security numbers) is used by thieves to commit financial fraud or is sold in the underground Internet marketplace to another set of criminals, who then use the information to conduct financial crime. In this section, we will describe how such systems work.

PHISHING

In the field of computer security, *phishing* is the criminal, fraudulent process of attempting to acquire confidential information such as user names, passwords, and credit card details by masquerading as a trustworthy entity such as a well-known bank, credit card company, large social network, or telecommunication company, in an electronic communication, usually via e-mail or IM. Phishing typically directs users to enter details at a fake Web site that looks and feels almost identical to the legitimate one. Even when using server authentication, it may require skill to detect that the Web site is fake.

Online shoppers and those conducting transactions electronically are attractive targets because they typically have higher incomes. Phishers, electronic shoplifters, con artists, and scammers stalk online shoppers because these cybercons want shoppers' confidential information—today's most valuable form of international currency.

Selling stolen information, like selling any stolen goods, can be profitable and unstoppable. In a 2006 survey, 21 percent of potential customers listed "too much risk of fraud, I don't trust online merchants" as their primary reason for not shopping online. Of the total fraud complaints reported to the FTC, Internet-related fraud complaints jumped from 1 percent in 1996 to 79 percent in 2008 (McMillan 2009b). Not only do concerns about cybercons stunt EC growth, but defending against these cons and compensating for damages also significantly increase the costs of conducting EC. As companies try to expand their e-business in countries where the legal systems are underdeveloped, opportunities for fraud expand with it.

Example. German phishers sent out messages pretending to come from a utility company that provides an electronic invoice as an Adobe PDF file. This social engineering trick worked. Many customers clicked the link to download an "important document," which contained a Trojan horse. The program gave the sender control of the infected machine. The Trojan monitored every Internet connection and keystroke, and reported passwords back to the Trojan's creator.

Sophisticated Phishing Methods

Phishing is a major provider of information used for financial fraud on the Internet. Exhibit 9.6 illustrates a typical phishing process called "drive-by downloads," a top Web threat (Symantec 2009). For other methods, see en.wikipedia.org/wiki/Phishing.

FRAUD ON THE INTERNET

Phishing is the first step that leads to fraud (recall Exhibit 9.5). An environment where buyers and sellers cannot see each other breeds fraud. Fraud is a problem for online retailers and customers alike. However, even though actual losses per incident are rising, the rate of those losses is flattening out. In other words, the threat actually may be lessening—somewhat. The loss for online fraud in the United States in 2008 averaged $300,000 (Richardson 2008). However, the percentage of revenues lost to fraud dropped to 1.4 percent in 2008, down from 1.6 percent in 2005. Since 2004, the percentage rate of revenue loss has declined. Since e-commerce sales continue to grow by about 20 percent a year, the overall dollar-loss amount showed a rise.

Online merchants reject roughly 4 percent of incoming orders because of suspicion of fraud. An estimated 1 percent of accepted orders turn out to be fraudulent. As an adjustment to a slowing economy, merchants shifted fraud-fighting priorities in 2008, dropping the unaccepted orders from 4.2 percent to 2.9 percent. Among online orders from outside the United States and Canada in 2006, 2.7 percent of the orders were

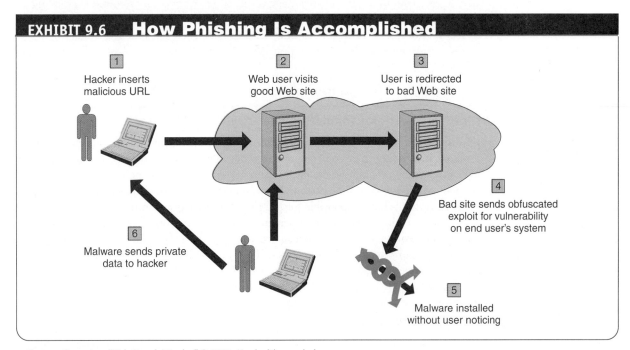

EXHIBIT 9.6   How Phishing Is Accomplished

1. Hacker inserts malicious URL
2. Web user visits good Web site
3. User is redirected to bad Web site
4. Bad site sends obfuscated exploit for vulnerability on end user's system
5. Malware installed without user noticing
6. Malware sends private data to hacker

Source: Symantec, "Web-Based Attacks," © 2009. Used with permission.

fraudulent. That rate is three times higher than the rate associated with orders from the United States and Canada (*Marketing Charts* 2009).

During the first few years of EC, many types of financial crime came to light, ranging from the online manipulation of stock prices to the creation of a virtual bank that disappeared together with the investors' deposits. Internet fraud has grown even faster than the Internet itself. The following examples demonstrate the scope of the problem. Also visit the Open Directory Project at dmoz.org/Society/Issues/Fraud/Internet for a comprehensive list of fraud resources.

Examples of Typical Online Fraud Attempts

▶ Phishing uses spam e-mails or pop-up messages to deceive victims into disclosing credit card numbers, bank account information, social security numbers, passwords, or other sensitive information. Typically, the e-mail or pop-up message claims to be from a business or organization that the recipient may deal with; for example, an ISP, bank, online payment service, or even a government agency.

▶ When one of the authors advertised online that he had a house to rent, several "doctors" and "nurses" from the United Kingdom and South America applied. They agreed to pay a premium for a short-term lease and said they would pay with a cashier's check. They asked if the author would accept checks for $6,000 to $10,000 and send them back the balance of $4,000 to $8,000. When advised that this would be fine, but that the difference would be returned only after their checks had cleared, none of the would-be renters followed up.

▶ Extortion rings in the United Kingdom and Russia pried hundreds of thousands of dollars from online sports betting Web sites. Any site refusing to pay protection fees was threatened with zombie computers using DoS attacks.

▶ Fake escrow sites take advantage of the inherent trust of escrow sites, stealing buyers' deposits. Dozens of fake escrow sites on the Internet have convincing names like "Honest-Escrow.net" and use ads such as "Worried about getting scammed in an Internet auction? Just use an escrow service like us."

More examples of Internet fraud are provided in Online File W9.3.

Identity Theft and Identify Fraud

identity theft
Fraud that involves stealing an identity of a person and then the use of that identity by someone pretending to be someone else in order to steal money or get other benefits.

Identity theft refers to stealing an identity of a person; that information is then used by someone pretending to be someone else in order to steal money or get other benefits. The term is relatively new and is actually a misnomer, since it is not inherently possible to steal an identity, only to use it. The person whose identity is used can suffer serious consequences when he or she is held responsible for the perpetrator's actions. In many countries, specific laws make it a crime to use another person's identity for personal gain. Identity theft is the number one concern of EC shoppers, according to the U.S. Federal Trade Commission (ftc.gov). According to 2008 statistics (CNNMoney 2009), identity fraud has affected 10 million Americans, who lost $48 billion (a 22 percent increase over 2007).

Identity theft is somewhat different from *identity fraud*, which is related to the unlawful usage of a "false identity" to commit fraud. Identity fraud activities include:

▶ Financial identity theft (using another's identity to obtain goods and services)
▶ Business/commercial identity theft (using another's business name to obtain credit)

▶ Criminal identity theft (posing as another when apprehended for a crime)

▶ Money laundering

Example. No one is immune from identity theft, even the sheriff of Merced County, California. On March 11, 2009, while the sheriff's deputies were searching the home of a woman accused of forging checks, they discovered on her computer the copied signature of their boss. Investigators said the woman lifted the sheriff's signature from a standard check given to departing inmates to reimburse them for pocket money confiscated during booking. She had uploaded the signature to a check-writing program. She used the checks to pay for services she received.

For additional information, see en.wikipedia.org/wiki/Identity_theft.

Other Financial Fraud

Stock fraud is a common area where swindlers are active. Other areas include the sale of bogus investments, phantom business opportunities, and other "get rich quick" schemes. In addition, foreign-currency-trading scams are increasing on the Internet because most online currency exchange shops are not licensed. For many examples of financial fraud, see Symantec (2009).

SPAM AND SPYWARE ATTACKS

E-mail spam, also known as *junk e-mail* or just *spam,* is a subset of spam that involves nearly identical messages sent to numerous recipients by e-mail. A common synonym for spam is *unsolicited bulk e-mail.* Over 90 percent of messages on corporate networks in April 2009 were e-mail spam. An estimated worldwide total of *62 trillion spam e-mails* were sent in 2008. Globally, annual spam energy use totals 33 billion kilowatt-hours (KWh). That's equivalent to the electricity used in *2.4 million homes in the United States,* with the same GHG emissions as 3.1 million passenger cars using 2 billion gallons of gasoline. (McMillan 2009a). E-mail spam has grown steadily since the early 1990s to several billion messages a day. Spam has frustrated, confused, and annoyed e-mail users. Laws against spam have been sporadically initiated. The total volume of spam (more than 100 billion e-mails per day as of April 2008) has leveled off slightly in recent years and is no longer growing exponentially. But the amount received by most e-mail users has decreased mostly because of better automatic filtering. Approximately 80 percent of all spam is sent by fewer than 200 spammers. Botnets, networks of virus-infected computers, and so forth are used to do it. Since the cost of the spam is borne mostly by the recipient, spam is effective e-mail advertising.

With antispam software and ISP spam filters defeating traditional e-mail spam, spamming tactics have mutated. Those mutations seek to ensure—by any means—a good shopper delivery rate. Spammers use sophisticated botnets and spam zombies to capture a large number of PCs that can generate and disseminate spam messages. Unsolicited junk advertisements are sent via all types of messaging media, including blogs, instant messages (IM), and cell phones. Spammers promote their gambling sites, prescription drugs, get-rich schemes, and the like (see Symantec 2009). There are also those who use spamming for facilitating crime (e.g., identity theft, money laundering, auction fraud).

E-mail addresses are collected from chat rooms, Web sites, newsgroups, and viruses that harvest users' address books. Much spam is sent to invalid e-mail addresses. ISPs have attempted to recover the cost of spam through lawsuits against spammers, although they have been mostly unsuccessful in collecting damages despite winning in court. An example of how spam is used for stock market fraud is provided in Case 9.1.

e-mail spam
A subset of spam that involves nearly identical messages sent to numerous recipients by e-mail.

CASE 9.1

EC Application

INTERNET STOCK FRAUD AIDED BY SPAM

A study reported by Lerer (2007) concluded that stock spam moves markets. The researchers found that the average investor who buys a stock during a spam promotion (campaign) and then sells after the campaign ends up losing about 5.5 percent of his or her investment. In contrast, the spammer who buys stock before the spam campaign and sells during the campaign makes a 5.79 percent return.

The federal government made headlines on March 8, 2007, by cracking down on dozens of penny stocks whose prices have been manipulated. The success of *Operation Spamalot*, conducted by the Securities and Exchange Commission (SEC), still will not end spam. There are two reasons spam won't go away: It works and it's profitable. Despite increased enforcement, warnings, and federal laws, spam is not only continuing but flourishing. And there's no reason to think the SEC will be able to do much to stop it.

Stock spam has gotten much worse in the last few years. Stock spam messages rose 120 percent during the six-month period ending March 2007. In total, stock-related messages make up about 20 percent of all e-mail spam. The SEC estimates that 100 million stock spam messages are sent each week.

Technology has increased spammers' ability to send junk e-mail. Spammers used to have to send all their

messages from one computer, making them easily blocked by spam filters. Today, spammers send their messages through botnets (linked networks of computers) that they control. With the extra bandwidth, they are sending billions of messages with promotional text embedded in image files—called *image spam*. Image spam looks identical to normal spam but sneaks by antispam programs that look only at text, not pictures or photos.

During 2006, global spam volume tripled. During a six-week period, Secure Computing Research saw a 50 percent increase in spam. Spam now accounts for nearly 90 percent of all e-mail. In that same time, the amount of image spam, which today accounts for 30 percent of all spam, tripled.

Sources: Compiled from Lerer (2007) and Secure Computing (2007).

Questions

1. Why might people buy the penny stocks promoted in an e-mail message from an unknown source?

2. Use the Internet (Google) to find what can be done to filter image spam.

Spyware

spyware
Software that gathers user information over an Internet connection without the user's knowledge.

Spyware is computer software that is installed surreptitiously on a personal computer to intercept or take partial control over the user's interaction with the computer, without the user's knowledge or consent. Although the term *spyware* suggests software that secretly monitors the user's behavior (Chapter 4), the functions of spyware extend well beyond simple monitoring. Spyware programs can collect various types of personal information, such as Internet surfing habits and tracking sites that you've visited therefore violating your privacy (see Chapter 11), but they can also interfere with user control of the computer in other ways, such as by installing additional (even malicious) software and redirecting Web browser activity. Spyware is known to change computer settings, resulting in slow surfing speeds and/or loss of Internet or functionality of other programs. In an attempt to increase the understanding of spyware, a more formal classification of its included software types is captured under the term *privacy-invasive software*. Although spyware is used mainly by advertisers, it may also be used by criminals.

SOCIAL NETWORKING MAKES SOCIAL ENGINEERING EASY

Social engineering tactics have been diversified. In the past, social engineers used cleverly worded e-mail and face-to-face conversations to get information to launch attacks. But now, social networking sites that contain goldmines of information are major targets for new attack methods. Social engineering tactics or scams that depended on user interaction to execute an attack against them rose dramatically in 2006. As more users take advantage of Web 2.0 applications like social networking sites, blogs, wikis, and RSS feeds, malware authors, identity thieves, and other criminals are going to exploit these users. With the rise of Web 2.0 and more social interaction on social networks sites, security experts warn of an increase in the incidence of hackers inserting malicious code into dynamically generated Web pages.

Despite all the social engineering incidents in 2006, it wasn't until the worm and phishing attack against MySpace in early December 2006 that the public recognized what some security experts are calling "the next big Internet threat." The attack forced MySpace to shut down thousands of user profile pages after a worm converted legitimate links to those that sent users to a phishing site. The phishing site attempted to obtain personal information, including MySpace user names and passwords. During 2008 and 2009, there were many breaches of security in social networks. For example, in March 2008, a Facebook security hole allowed actress Paris Hilton's private pictures to be leaked.

Social networking sites are creating a means for hackers and con artists to worm their way into the confidence of users, which leaves Internet users and businesses at a greater risk of attack, according to a study by Danish security firm CSIS.

Example. Dennis Rand, a security researcher at CSIS, created a fictitious entry on the LinkedIn network before inviting random and unknown users to LinkedIn to join his private network. By posing as an ex-employee of "targeted" firms, he was able to prompt real workers from these firms into establishing connections. Within a few weeks, Rand created a network of 1,340 trusted connections. In a research paper, Rand explains how information gleaned through this network might be used to harvest e-mail addresses to send messages containing links to malicious codes that are more likely to be accepted because they come from a "trusted" source (Rand 2007).

Because successful social engineering attacks depend, in effect, on the cooperation of the victims, stopping social engineering attacks also depends on the victims. Certain positions within an organization are clearly vulnerable, such as those with access to private and confidential information or those that interact with customers or vendors. In the AUP and employee training programs, all users should learn how to avoid becoming a victim of manipulation. Specific policies and procedures need to be developed for securing confidential information, guiding employee behavior with respect to confidential information, and taking the steps needed to respond to and report any social engineering breaches. Social networks are especially vulnerable to spam attacks.

Spam in Social Networks and in the Web 2.0 Environment

Social networks attracted spammers due to the large number of potential recipients and the less secured Internet platforms. Spammers like Facebook in particular despite the heavy fines imposed on them by the courts (see example p. 352). Another area is blogging.

Automated Blog Spam. Bloggers have found hundreds of automatically generated comments with links to herbal Viagra and gambling vendors on their pages. Software bots that trawl the Internet looking for suitable forms to fill in automatically generate the majority of blog spam. Blog owners can use tools to ensure that humans—and not an automated system—enter comments on their blogs.

Search Engine Spam and Splogs

Although content spam impacts media users, the greater concern to ethical e-commerce sites is **search engine spam**, which Yahoo! defines as "pages created deliberately to trick the search engine into offering inappropriate, redundant, or poor-quality search results." Those pages, called **spam sites**, use techniques that deliberately subvert a search engine's algorithms to artificially inflate the page's rankings. A similar tactic involves the use of **splogs** (short for *spam blog sites*), which are blogs created solely for marketing purposes.

search engine spam
Pages created deliberately to trick the search engine into offering inappropriate, redundant, or poor-quality search results.

spam site
Page that uses techniques that deliberately subvert a search engine's algorithms to artificially inflate the page's rankings.

splog
Short for *spam blog*. A site created solely for marketing purposes.

Spammers create hundreds of splogs that they link to the spammer's site to increase that site's search engine ranking. This method makes use of the fact that the number of links found determines a page's rank, as in Google's PageRank system, which calculates a page's position in search results by weighing the links to that page. For information on search engine algorithms and page rankings, see google.com/corporate/tech.html.

Sploggers work on the principle that once Web surfers arrive at their site, a few will click on one of the linked advertisements. Each of these clicks earns a few cents for the splogger. And because any one splogger can run thousands of splogs, the spam can be very profitable. (One splog partnership claimed $71,136.89 in earnings in the three months from August to October 2005.)

Examples. Some examples of spam attacks in social networks are:

- In January 2009, Facebook won $1.3 billion from spammers in Canada who falsely obtained log-in information for Facebook users and then sent spam to those users' friends, violating the CAN-SPAM Act. In 2008, MySpace was awarded $230 million in a similar case (in both cases, the companies were unable to collect).
- Twitter became a hot target for hackers who, in January 2009, hijacked the accounts of several high-profile users (now users are protected).
- Instant messaging in social networks was found to be very vulnerable to hackers and other cybercriminals.
- Hackers are posting content loaded with malicious software that is difficult to detect on YouTube, MySpace, and other social network sites. Other methods are frequently invented.
- Chat rooms harbor "fraud as a service" peddlers who use data-harvesting Trojans.
- VoIP is used extensively in social networks, yet it is vulnerable to many attacks (products such as VoIPguard can help).
- Blogs can be attacked by spammers fairly easily.
- Koobface and other worms targeted Facebook, as described earlier.

The discussion so far has concentrated on attacks. Defense mechanisms, including those related to spam and other unsolicited ads, are provided in Sections 9.6 through 9.10. First, let's examine what is involved in assuring information security.

Section 9.4 ▶ REVIEW QUESTIONS

1. Define phishing.
2. Describe the relationship of phishing to financial fraud.
3. Briefly describe some phishing tactics.
4. Describe spam and its methods.
5. Define splogs and explain how sploggers make money.
6. Why and how are social networks being attacked?

9.5 THE INFORMATION ASSURANCE MODEL AND DEFENSE STRATEGY

The *information assurance (IA) model* provides a framework for protection of information systems against unauthorized access to or modification of information that is stored, processed, or sent over a network. The importance of the IA model to EC is that it represents the processes for protecting information by insuring its confidentiality, integrity,

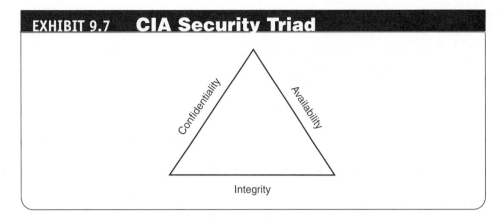

EXHIBIT 9.7   CIA Security Triad

Confidentiality

Availability

Integrity

and availability. This model is known as the **CIA security triad**, or simply the **CIA triad**, and is shown in Exhibit 9.7.

The model has three components that express the requirements for a secured information system: *confidentiality, integrity,* and *availability.*

CONFIDENTIALITY, INTEGRITY, AND AVAILABILITY

The success and security of EC can be measured by these components: confidentiality, integrity, and availability of information at the business Web site.

1. **Confidentiality** is the assurance of data privacy. The data or transmitted message is encrypted so that it is readable only by the person for whom it is intended. Encryption strength can vary. Depending on the strength of the encryption method, intruders or eavesdroppers might not be able to break the encryption to read the data or text.

2. **Integrity** is the assurance that data are accurate or that a message has not been altered. It means that stored data has not been modified without authorization; a message that was sent is the same message that was received. The integrity function detects and prevents the unauthorized creation, modification, or deletion of data or messages.

3. **Availability** is the assurance that access to data, the Web site, or other EC service is timely, available, reliable, and restricted to authorized users.

Three concepts related to the IA model are *authentication, authorization,* and *nonrepudiation.*

AUTHENTICATION, AUTHORIZATION, AND NONREPUDIATION

All the CIA functions depend on authentication. *Authentication* requires evidence in the form of credentials, which can take a variety of forms, including something known (e.g., a password), something possessed (e.g., a smart card), or something unique (e.g., a signature or fingerprint). *Authorization* requires comparing information about the person or program with access control information associated with the resource being accessed. *Nonrepudiation* is the concept of ensuring that a party in a dispute cannot repudiate or refute the validity of a statement or contract. Although this concept can be applied to any transaction, by far the most common application is in verification and trust of signatures. One nonrepudiation method is the use of a digital signature that makes it difficult for people to dispute that they were involved in an exchange.

CIA security triad (CIA triad)
Three security concepts important to information on the Internet: confidentiality, integrity, and availability.

confidentiality
Assurance of data privacy and accuracy. Keeping private or sensitive information from being disclosed to unauthorized individuals, entities, or processes.

integrity
Assurance that stored data has not been modified without authorization; a message that was sent is the same message as that which was received.

availability
Assurance that access to data, the Web site, or other EC data service is timely, available, reliable, and restricted to authorized users.

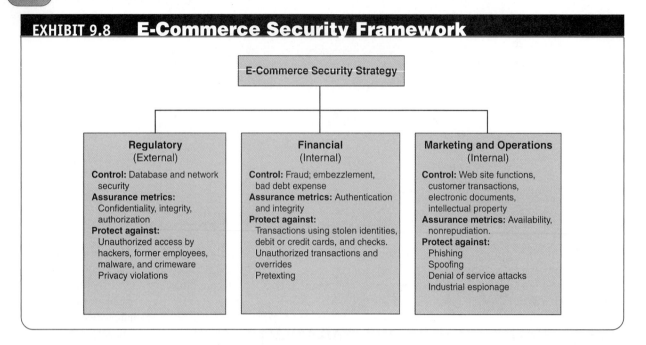

EXHIBIT 9.8   **E-Commerce Security Framework**

New or improved methods to ensure the confidentiality of credit card numbers, integrity of entire messages, authentication of the buyer and seller, and nonrepudiation of transactions are being developed as older ones become ineffective.

E-COMMERCE SECURITY STRATEGY

An EC security strategy needs to address the IA model and its components. In Exhibit 9.8, an EC security framework is presented that defines the high-level categories of assurance and their controls. The three major categories are regulatory, financial, and marketing and operations. Only the key areas are listed in the exhibit, but there is overlap in requirements in each category.

The following are the major objectives of defense strategies:

1. **Prevention and deterrence.** Properly designed controls may prevent errors from occurring, deter criminals from attacking the system, and better yet, deny access to unauthorized people. These are the most desirable controls.

2. **Detection.** Like a fire, the earlier an attack is detected, the easier it is to combat, and the less damage is done. Detection can be performed in many cases by using special diagnostic software, at a minimal cost.

3. **Containment (contain the damage).** This objective is to minimize or limit losses once a malfunction has occurred. It is also called *damage control*. This can be accomplished, for example, by including a *fault-tolerant system* that permits operation in a degraded mode until full recovery is made. If a fault-tolerant system does not exist, a quick (and possibly expensive) recovery must take place. Users want their systems back in operation as fast as possible.

4. **Recovery.** A recovery plan explains how to fix a damaged information system as quickly as possible. Replacing rather than repairing components is one route to fast recovery.

5. **Correction.** Correcting the causes of damaged systems can prevent the problem from occurring again.

6. **Awareness and compliance.** All organization members must be educated about the hazards and must comply with the security rules and regulations.

Treating EC Security as a Project

EC security programs have a life cycle, and throughout that life cycle the EC security requirements must be continuously evaluated and adjusted. An **EC security program** is the set of controls over security processes to protect organizational assets. The four high-level stages in the life cycle of an EC security program are:

1. Planning and organizing
2. Implementation
3. Operations and maintenance
4. Monitoring and evaluating

   For details, see Online File W9.4.

EC security programs
All the policies, procedures, documents, standards, hardware, software, training, and personnel that work together to protect information, the ability to conduct business, and other assets.

Section 9.5 ▶ REVIEW QUESTIONS

1. What is information assurance? List its major components.
2. Define confidentiality, integrity, and availability.
3. Describe the objectives and elements of EC strategy.

9.6 THE DEFENSE I: ACCESS CONTROL, ENCRYPTION, AND PKI

Most organizations rely on multiple technologies to secure their networks. These technologies can be divided into two major groups: those designed to secure communications across the network and those designed to protect the servers and clients on the network. This section considers the first of these technologies. The second group is the subject of Sections 9.7 and 9.8.

ACCESS CONTROL

Network security depends on access control. **Access control** determines who (person, program, or machine) can legitimately use a network resource and which resources he, she, or it can use. A resource can be anything—Web pages, text files, databases, applications, servers, printers, or any other information source or network component. Typically, access control lists define which users have access to which resources and what rights they have with respect to those resources (i.e., read, view, write, print, copy, delete, execute, modify, or move). Each resource needs to be considered separately, and the rights of particular users or categories of users (e.g., system administrators, northwest sales reps, product marketing department, trading partners, etc.) need to be established.

access control
Mechanism that determines who can legitimately use a network resource.

Access control involves authorization (having the right to access) and authentication, which is also called *user identification* (proving that the user is who he or she claims to be). Authentication methods include:

▶ Something only the user *knows*, such as a password.
▶ Something only the user *has*, for example, a smart card or a token.

> Something only the user *is*, such as a signature, voice, fingerprint, or retinal (eye) scan. It is implemented via *biometric controls*, which can be physical or behavioral.

Authentication and Passwords

After a user has been *identified*, the user must be *authenticated*. As noted earlier, authentication is the process of verifying that the user is who he or she claims to be. Verification usually is based on one or more characteristics that distinguish the individual from others. The distinguishing characteristics can be based on something one knows (e.g., passwords), something one has (e.g., a token), or something one possesses (e.g., fingerprint). Traditionally, authentication has been based on passwords. Passwords are notoriously insecure because people have a habit of writing them down in easy-to-find places, choosing values that are guessed easily, and willingly telling people their passwords when asked.

Biometric Systems

biometric control
An automated method for verifying the identity of a person based on physical or behavioral characteristics.

A **biometric control** is an automated method for verifying the identity of a person based on physical or behavioral characteristics.

Biometric systems can *identify* a person from a population of enrolled users by searching through a database for a match based on the person's biometric trait, or the system can *verify* a person's claimed identity by matching the individual's biometric trait against a previously stored version. Biometric verification is much simpler than biometric identification, and it is the process used in two-factor authentication (see Online File W9.5).

The most common biometrics are:

biometric systems
Authentication systems that identify a person by measurement of a biological characteristic, such as fingerprints, iris (eye) patterns, facial features, or voice.

> **Thumbprint or fingerprint.** Each time a user wants access, a thumb- or fingerprint (finger scan) is matched against a template containing the authorized person's fingerprint to identify him or her.
> **Retinal scan.** A match is attempted between the pattern of the blood vessels in the retina that is being scanned and a prestored picture of the retina.
> **Voice scan.** A match is attempted between the user's voice and the voice pattern stored on templates.
> **Signature.** Signatures are matched against the prestored authentic signature. This method can supplement a photo-card ID system.

Other biometrics are:

> Facial recognition
> Facial thermograph
> Hand geometry
> Hand veins
> Keystrokes
> Iris

For details and analysis, see en.wikipedia.org/wiki/Biometrics.

Biometric controls are now integrated into many e-business hardware and software products. Biometric controls do have some limitations: They are not accurate in certain cases, and some people see them as an invasion of privacy.

To implement a biometric authentication system, the physiological or behavioral characteristics of a participant must be scanned repeatedly under different settings. The scans are then averaged to produce a biometric template, or identifier. The template is stored in a database as a series of numbers that can range from a few bytes for hand geometry to several thousand bytes for facial recognition. When a person uses a biometric system, a live scan is conducted, and the scan is converted to a series of numbers that is then compared against the template stored in the database.

ENCRYPTION AND THE ONE-KEY (SYMMETRIC) SYSTEM

Encryption is the process of transforming or scrambling (encrypting) data in such a way that it is difficult, expensive, or time-consuming for an unauthorized person to unscramble (decrypt) it. All encryption has five basic parts (refer to Exhibit 9.9): *plaintext*, *ciphertext*, an *encryption algorithm*, the *key*, and *key space*. **Plaintext** is a human-readable text or message. **Ciphertext** is not human-readable because it has been encrypted. The **encryption algorithm** is the set of procedures or mathematical functions used to encrypt or decrypt a message. Typically, the algorithm is not the secret piece of the encryption process. The **key** (or **key value**) is the secret value used with the algorithm to transform the message. The **key space** is the large number of possible key values (keys) created by the algorithm to use when transforming messages.

Encryption is the foundation for two major security systems: the *symmetric systems*, with one secret key, and *asymmetric systems*, with two keys. The second method is the basis for the PKI system (described in the next section).

encryption
The process of scrambling (encrypting) a message in such a way that it is difficult, expensive, or time-consuming for an unauthorized person to unscramble (decrypt) it.

plaintext
An unencrypted message in human-readable form.

ciphertext
A plaintext message after it has been encrypted into a machine-readable form.

encryption algorithm
The mathematical formula used to encrypt the plaintext into the ciphertext, and vice versa.

EXHIBIT 9.9	Encryption Components	
Component	**Description**	**Example or Description**
Plaintext	The original message or document is created by the user, which is in human-readable form.	Credit card number 5342 8765 3652 9982.
Encryption algorithm	The set of procedures or mathematical functions to encrypt or decrypt a message. Typically, the algorithm is not the secret piece of the encryption process.	Add a number (the key) to each number in the card. If the resulting number is greater than 9, wrap around the number to the beginning (i.e., modulus arithmetic). For example, add 4 to each number so that 1 becomes 5, 9 becomes 3, etc.
Key or key value	The secret value used with the algorithm to transform the message.	The key dictates what parts (functions) of the algorithm will be used, in what order, and with what values.
Key space	The large number of possible key values (keys) created by the algorithm to use when transforming the message.	The larger the key space, the greater the number of possibilities for the key, which makes it harder for an attacker to discover the correct key.
Ciphertext	Message or document that has been encrypted into unreadable form.	The original 5342 8765 3652 9982 becomes 9786 2109 7096 3326.

key (key value)
The secret code used to encrypt and decrypt a message.

key space
The large number of possible key values (keys) created by the algorithm to use when transforming the message.

symmetric (private) key encryption
An encryption system that uses the same key to encrypt and decrypt the message.

Data Encryption Standard (DES)
The standard symmetric encryption algorithm supported by the NIST and used by U.S. government agencies until October 2000.

public key infrastructure (PKI)
A scheme for securing e-payments using public key encryption and various technical components.

public (asymmetric) key encryption
Method of encryption that uses a pair of matched keys—a public key to encrypt a message and a private key to decrypt it, or vice versa.

public key
Encryption code that is publicly available to anyone.

private key
Encryption code that is known only to its owner.

Symmetric (Private) Key Encryption

In a **symmetric (private) key encryption**, the same key is used to encrypt and decrypt the plaintext (see Exhibit 9.10). The sender and receiver of the text must share the same key without revealing it to anyone else—making it a so-called *private* system.

The **Data Encryption Standard (DES)** was at one time the standard symmetric encryption algorithm supported by U.S. government agencies. However, DES became too susceptible to attacks. In 2000, the National Institute of Standards and Technology (NIST) replaced DES with *Rijndael*, the new advanced encryption standard for encrypting sensitive but unclassified government data. Because the algorithms used to encrypt a message are well known, the confidentiality of a message depends on the key. It is possible to guess a key simply by having a computer try all the encryption combinations until the message is decrypted. High-speed and parallel processing computers can try millions of guesses in a second. This is why the length of the key (in bits) is the main factor in securing a message. If a key were 4 bits long (e.g., 1011), there would be only 16 possible combinations (i.e., 2 raised to the fourth power). However, a 64-bit encryption key would take 58.5 years to be broken at 10 million keys per second. That is 2 raised to the 64th power possible combinations!

PUBLIC KEY INFRASTRUCTURE (PKI)

Public key infrastructure (PKI) is a scheme for securing e-payments using public key encryption and various technical components. The symmetric one-key encryption requires the movement of a key from the writer of a message to its recipient. Imagine trying to use one-key encryption to buy something offered on a particular Web server. If the seller's key was distributed to thousands of buyers, then the key would not remain secret for long. If the transfer of the key is intercepted, the key may be stolen or changed. The solution was two keys, public and private, and additional features that create the PKI, which is very secure. In addition to the keys, PKI includes *digital signature*, hash digests (function), and digital certificate. Let's see how PKI works.

Public (Asymmetric) Key Encryption

Public (asymmetric) key encryption uses a pair of matched keys—a **public key** that is publicly available to anyone and a **private key** that is known only to its owner. If a message is encrypted with a public key, then the associated private key is required to decrypt

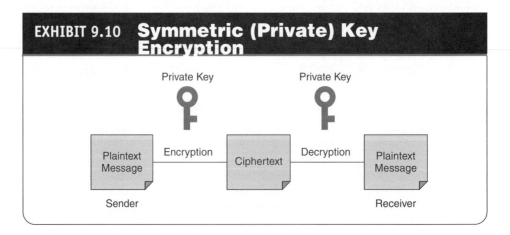

EXHIBIT 9.10   Symmetric (Private) Key Encryption

the message. If, for example, a person wanted to send a purchase order to a company and have the contents remain private, he or she would encrypt the message with the company's public key. When the company received the order, it would decrypt it with the associated private key, being the only one able to read it.

A most common public key encryption algorithm is RSA (rsa.com). RSA uses keys ranging in length from 512 bits to 1,024 bits. The main problem with public key encryption is speed. Symmetrical algorithms are significantly faster than asymmetrical key algorithms. Therefore, public key encryption cannot be used effectively to encrypt and decrypt large amounts of data. In practice, a combination of symmetric and asymmetric encryption is used to encrypt messages. Public key encryption is supplemented by digital signature and certificate authority.

The PKI Process: Digital Signatures and Certificate Authorities

Digital signatures or **digital certificates** are the electronic equivalent of personal signatures that cannot be forged. Digital signatures are based on public keys for authenticating the identity of the sender of a message or document. They also can ensure that the original content of an electronic message or document is unchanged. Digital signatures have additional benefits in the online world. They are portable, cannot be easily repudiated or imitated, and can be time-stamped. According to the U.S. Federal Electronic Signatures in Global and National Commerce Act of 2000, digital signatures in the United States have the same legal standing as a signature written in ink on paper.

Exhibit 9.11 illustrates how the PKI process works. Suppose a person wants to send a draft of a financial contract to a company with whom he or she plans to do business as an e-mail message. The sender wants to assure the company that the content of the draft has not been changed en route and that he or she really is the sender. To do so, the sender takes the following steps:

1. The sender creates the e-mail message with the contract in it.
2. Using special software, a mathematical computation called a **hash** function is applied to the message, which results in a special summary of the message, converted into a string of digits called a **message digest (MD)**.
3. The sender uses his or her private key to encrypt the hash. This is the sender's *digital signature.* No one else can replicate the sender's digital signature because it is based on the sender's private key, which no one else knows.
4. The sender encrypts both the original message and the digital signature using the recipient's public key. This couple forms the **digital envelope**.
5. The sender e-mails the digital envelope to the receiver.
6. Upon receipt, the receiver uses his or her private key to decrypt the contents of the digital envelope. This produces a copy of the message and the sender's digital signature. No one else can do it since there is only one copy of the private key.
7. The receiver uses the sender's public key to decrypt the digital signature, resulting in a copy of the original message digest.
8. Using the same hash function employed in step 2, the recipient then creates a message digest from the decrypted message.
9. The recipient then compares this digest with the original message digest.
10. If the two digests match, then the recipient concludes that the message is authentic.

digital signature or digital certificate
Validates the sender and time stamp of a transaction so it cannot be later claimed that the transaction was unauthorized or invalid.

hash
A mathematical computation that is applied to a message, using a private key, to encrypt the message.

message digest (MD)
A summary of a message, converted into a string of digits after the hash has been applied.

digital envelope
The combination of the encrypted original message and the digital signature, using the recipient's public key.

EXHIBIT 9.11 Digital Signatures

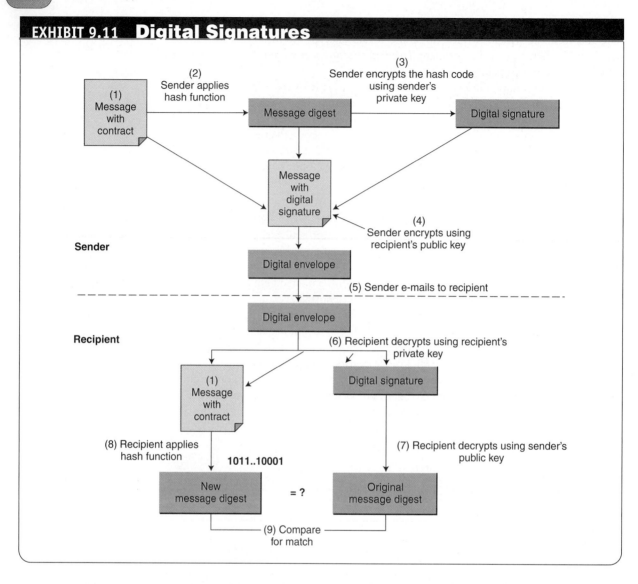

In this scenario, the company has evidence that the sender sent the e-mail because the sender is the only one with access to the private key. The recipient knows that the message has not been tampered with because if it had been, the two hashes would not have matched.

certificate authorities (CAs)

Third parties that issue digital certificates.

Certificate Authority. Third parties called **certificate authorities (CAs)** issue digital certificates. This is a certificate that contains things such as the holder's name, validity period, public key information, and a signed hash of the certificate data (i.e., hashed contents of the certificate signed with the CA's private key). There are different types of certificates, namely those used to authenticate Web sites (*site certificates*), individuals (*personal certificates*), and software companies (*software publisher certificates*).

There are many third-party CAs. VeriSign (verisign.com) is the best known of the CAs. VeriSign issues three classes of certificates: Class 1 verifies that an e-mail actually comes from the user's address. Class 2 checks the user's identity against a commercial credit database. Class 3 requires notarized documents. Companies such as Microsoft offer systems that enable companies to issue their own private, in-house certificates.

Secure Socket Layer (SSL): PKI Systems Are Further Secured with SSL—the Protocol for E-Commerce

If the average user had to figure out how to use encryption, digital certificates, digital signatures, and the like, there would be few secure transactions on the Web. Fortunately, Web browsers and Web servers handle many of these issues in a transparent fashion. Given that different companies, financial institutions, and governments in many countries are involved in e-commerce, it is necessary to have generally accepted protocols for securing e-commerce. One of the major protocols in use today is Secure Socket Layer (SSL), also known as Transport Layer Security (TLS).

The **Secure Socket Layer (SSL)** was invented by Netscape to use standard certificates for authentication and data encryption to ensure privacy or confidentiality. SSL became a de facto standard adopted by the browsers and servers provided by Microsoft and Netscape. In 1996, SSL was renamed **Transport Layer Security (TLS)**, but many people still use the SSL name. It is the major standard used for online credit card payments. SSL makes it possible to encrypt credit card numbers and other transmissions between a Web server and a Web browser. In the case of credit card transactions, there is more to making a purchase on the Web than simply passing an encrypted credit card number to a merchant.

In the next section, the focus is on the company's digital perimeter—the network.

Section 9.6 ▶ REVIEW QUESTIONS

1. Define access control.
2. What are the basic elements of an authentication system?
3. What is a passive token? An active token?
4. Define biometric systems and list five of their methods.
5. Describe the five basic components of encryption.
6. What are the key elements of PKI?
7. What are the basic differences between symmetric and asymmetric encryption?
8. What role does a certificate authority play?
9. What is the SSL protocol?

Secure Socket Layer (SSL)
Protocol that utilizes standard certificates for authentication and data encryption to ensure privacy or confidentiality.

Transport Layer Security (TLS)
As of 1996, another name for the SSL protocol.

9.7 THE DEFENSE II: SECURING E-COMMERCE NETWORKS

Several technologies exist that ensure that an organization's network boundaries are secure from cyberattack or intrusion and that if the organization's boundaries are compromised, the intrusion is detected quickly and combated. The selection and operation of these technologies should be based on certain design concepts, as described in Online File W9.6. The major components for protecting internal information flow inside organizations are described next.

FIREWALLS

Firewalls are barriers between a trusted network or PC and the untrustworthy Internet. Technically, it is a network node consisting of both hardware and software that isolates a private network from a public network. On the Internet, the data and requests sent from one computer to another are broken into segments called **packets**. Each packet contains the Internet address of the computer sending the data, as well as the Internet address of the computer receiving the data. Packets also contain other identifying information that

firewall
A single point between two or more networks where all traffic must pass (choke point); the device authenticates, controls, and logs all traffic.

packet
Segment of data sent from one computer to another on a network.

can distinguish one packet from another. A firewall examines all data packets that pass through it and then takes appropriate action—to allow or not to allow. Firewalls can be designed mainly to protect against remote log-in, access via backdoors, spam, and different types of malware (e.g., viruses or macros). For details, see Online File W9.7.

Personal Firewalls

The number of users with high-speed broadband (cable modem or digital subscriber lines [DSL]) Internet connections to their homes or small businesses has increased. These "always-on" connections are much more vulnerable to attack than simple dial-up connections. With these connections, the home owner or small business owner runs the risk of information being stolen or destroyed, of sensitive information (e.g., personal or business financial information) being stolen, and of the computer being used in a DoS attack against others.

personal firewall
A network node designed to protect an individual user's desktop system from the public network by monitoring all the traffic that passes through the computer's network interface card.

Personal firewalls protect desktop systems by monitoring all the traffic that passes through the computer's network interface card. They operate in one of two ways. With the first method, the owner can create filtering rules (much like packet filtering) that the firewall uses to permit or delete packets. With the other method, the firewall can learn, by asking the user questions, how it should handle particular traffic. For a detailed comparison of several of these products, see firewallguide.com/software.htm.

VIRTUAL PRIVATE NETWORKS (VPNS)

Suppose a company wants to establish a B2B application, providing suppliers, partners, and others access not only to data residing on its internal Web site, but also to data contained in other files (e.g., Word documents) or in legacy systems (e.g., large relational databases). Traditionally, communications with the company would have taken place over a private leased line or through a dial-up line to a bank of modems or a remote access server (RAS) that provided direct connections to the company's LAN. With a private line, the chances of a hacker eavesdropping on the communications between the companies would be minimal, but it is an expensive way to do business. A VPN allows a computer user to access a network via an IP address other than the one that actually connects the computer to the Internet. For details, see en.wikipedia.org/wiki/Virtual_private_network.

virtual private network (VPN)
A network that uses the public Internet to carry information but remains private by using encryption to scramble the communications, authentication to ensure that information has not been tampered with, and access control to verify the identity of anyone using the network.

The less expensive alternative would be to use a virtual private network. A **virtual private network (VPN)** uses the public Internet to carry information but remains private by using a combination of encryption to scramble the communications and authentication to ensure that the information has not been tampered with and comes from a legitimate source. A VPN verifies the identity of anyone using the network. In addition, a VPN can also support site-to-site communications between branch offices and corporate headquarters and the communications between mobile workers and their workplace.

VPNs can reduce communication costs dramatically. The costs are lower because VPN equipment is cheaper than other remote solutions; private leased lines are not needed to support remote access; remote users can use broadband connections rather than make long-distance calls to access an organization's private network; and a single access line can be used to support multiple purposes.

protocol tunneling
Method used to ensure confidentiality and integrity of data transmitted over the Internet by encrypting data packets, sending them in packets across the Internet, and decrypting them at the destination address.

The main technical challenge of a VPN is to ensure the confidentiality and integrity of the data transmitted over the Internet. This is where protocol tunneling comes into play. With **protocol tunneling**, data packets are first encrypted and then encapsulated into packets that can be transmitted across the Internet. A special host or router decrypts the packets at the destination address.

INTRUSION DETECTION SYSTEMS (IDSS)

Even if an organization has a well-formulated security policy and a number of security technologies in place, it still is vulnerable to attack. For example, most organizations have antivirus software, yet most are subjected to virus attacks. This is why an organization must continually watch for attempted, as well as actual, security breaches. This can be done by using intrusion detectors.

An **intrusion detection system (IDS)** is software and/or hardware designed to detect illegal attempts to access, manipulate, and/or disable computer systems through a network. An IDS cannot directly detect attacks within properly encrypted traffic.

An IDS is used to detect several types of malicious behaviors that can compromise the security and trust of a computer system. This includes network attacks against vulnerable services, data-driven attacks on applications, host-based attacks such as privilege escalation, unauthorized log-ins, access to sensitive files, and malware (viruses, Trojan horses, and worms).

The IDS checks files on a regular basis to see if the current signatures match the previous signatures. If the signatures do not match, security personnel are notified immediately. Some examples of commercial host-based systems are Symantec's Intruder Alert (symantec.com), Tripwire Security's Tripwire (tripwire.com), and McAfee's Entercept Desktop and Server Agents (mcafee.com).

A network-based IDS uses rules to analyze suspicious activity at the perimeter of a network or at key locations in the network. It usually consists of a monitor—a software package that scans the network—and software agents that reside on various host computers and feed information back to the monitor. This type of IDS examines network traffic (i.e., packets) for known patterns of attack and automatically notifies security personnel when specific events or event thresholds occur. A network-based IDS also can perform certain actions when an attack occurs.

intrusion detection system (IDS)
A special category of software that can monitor activity across a network or on a host computer, watch for suspicious activity, and take automated action based on what it sees.

HONEYNETS AND HONEYPOTS

Honeynets are another technology that can detect and analyze intrusions. A **honeynet** is a network of honeypots designed to attract hackers like honey attracts bees. In this case, the **honeypots** are information system resources—firewalls, routers, Web servers, database servers, files, and the like—that look like production systems but do no real work. The main difference between a honeypot and the real thing is that the activities on a honeypot come from intruders attempting to compromise the system. In this way, researchers watching the honeynet can gather information about why hackers attack, when they attack, how they attack, what they do after the system is compromised, and how they communicate with one another during and after the attack.

The Honeynet Project is a worldwide, not-for-profit research group of security professionals (see honeynet.org). The group focuses on raising awareness of security risks that confront any system connected to the Internet and teaching and informing the security community about better ways to secure and defend network resources. The project runs its own honeynets but makes no attempt to attract hackers. They simply connect the honeypots to the Internet and wait for attacks to occur.

Before a company deploys a honeynet, it needs to think about what it will do when it becomes the scene of a cybercrime or contains evidence of a crime and about the legal restrictions and ramifications of monitoring legal and illegal activity. Online File W9.8 discusses these issues. A similar technique is *penetration test* (or pen test).

honeynet
A network of honeypots.

honeypot
Production system (e.g., firewalls, routers, Web servers, database servers) that looks like it does real work, but that acts as a decoy and is watched to study how network intrusions occur.

Penetration Test

penetration test (pen test)
A method of evaluating the security of a computer system or a network by simulating an attack from a malicious source, (e.g., a cracker).

A **penetration test** (or **pen test**) is a method of evaluating the security of a computer system or a network by simulating an attack from a malicious source (e.g., a cracker). The process involves an active analysis of the system for any potential vulnerabilities and attacks. This analysis is carried out from the position of a potential attacker, and can involve active exploitation of security vulnerabilities. Any security issues that are found will be presented to the system owner, together with an assessment of their impact and often with a proposal for mitigation or a technical solution. The intent of a penetration test is to determine feasibility of an attack and the amount of business impact of a successful exploit, if discovered. It is a component of a full security audit. For details, see en.wikipedia.org/wiki/Penetration_test.

Section 9.7 ▶ REVIEW QUESTIONS

1. List the basic types of firewalls and briefly describe each.
2. What is a personal firewall?
3. How does a VPN work?
4. Briefly describe the major types of IDSs.
5. What is a honeynet? What is a honeypot?
6. Describe pen testing.

9.8 THE DEFENSE III: GENERAL CONTROLS AND OTHER DEFENSE MECHANISMS

general controls
Controls established to protect the system regardless of the specific application. For example, protecting hardware and controlling access to the data center are independent of the specific application.

application controls
Controls that are intended to protect specific applications.

The objective of IT security management practices is to defend all the components of an information system, specifically data, software applications, hardware, and networks. A defense strategy requires several controls, as shown in Exhibit 9.12. **General controls** are established to protect the system regardless of the specific application. For example, protecting hardware and controlling access to the data center are independent of the specific application. **Application controls** are safeguards that are intended to protect specific applications. In this and the following sections, we discuss the major types of these two groups of information systems controls.

GENERAL CONTROLS

The major categories of general controls are physical controls, access controls, data security controls, communication controls, administrative controls and other controls. A brief description of general controls are provided next.

Physical Controls

Physical security refers to the protection of computer facilities and resources. This includes protecting physical property such as computers, data centers, software, manuals, and networks. It provides protection against most natural hazards as well as against some human hazards. Appropriate physical security may include several controls, such as the following:

- Appropriate design of the data center. For example, the site should be noncombustible and waterproof.
- Shielding against electromagnetic fields.
- Good fire prevention, detection, and extinguishing systems, including sprinkler system, water pumps, and adequate drainage facilities.

EXHIBIT 9.12 Major Defense Controls

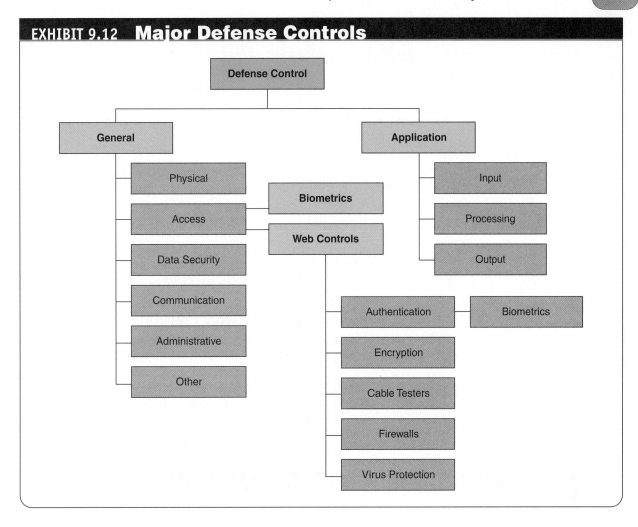

▶ Emergency power shutoff and backup batteries, which must be maintained in operational condition.

▶ Properly designed, maintained, and operated air-conditioning systems.

▶ Motion detector alarms that detect physical intrusion.

Network access control software is offered by all major security vendors (e.g., see symantec.com/business/network-access-control).

Administrative Controls

While the previously discussed general controls were technical in nature, administrative controls deal with issuing guidelines and monitoring compliance with the guidelines. Examples of such controls are shown in Exhibit 9.13.

APPLICATION CONTROLS

Sophisticated attacks are aimed at the application level, and many applications were not designed to withstand such attacks. For better survivability, information processing methodologies are being replaced with agent technology. **Intelligent agents**, also referred to as *softbots* or *knowbots*, are highly intelligent applications. The term generally

intelligent agents
Software applications that have some degree of reactivity, autonomy, and adaptability—as is needed in unpredictable attack situations. An agent is able to adapt itself based on changes occurring in its environment.

EXHIBIT 9.13 Representative Administrative Controls

- Appropriately selecting, training, and supervising employees, especially in accounting and information systems
- Fostering company loyalty
- Immediately revoking access privileges of dismissed, resigned, or transferred employees
- Requiring periodic modification of access controls (such as passwords)
- Developing programming and documentation standards (to make auditing easier and to use the standards as guides for employees)
- Insisting on security bonds or malfeasance insurance for key employees
- Instituting separation of duties, namely, dividing sensitive computer duties among as many employees as economically feasible in order to decrease the chance of intentional or unintentional damage
- Holding periodic random audits of the system

means applications that have some degree of reactivity, autonomy, and adaptability—as is needed in unpredictable attack situations. An agent is able to adapt itself based on changes occurring in its environment, as shown in Exhibit 9.14.

internal control environment
The work atmosphere that a company sets for its employees.

INTERNAL CONTROL AND COMPLIANCE MANAGEMENT

The **internal control environment** is the work atmosphere that a company sets for its employees. *Internal control (IC)* is a process designed to achieve (1) reliability of financial

EXHIBIT 9.14 Intelligent Agents

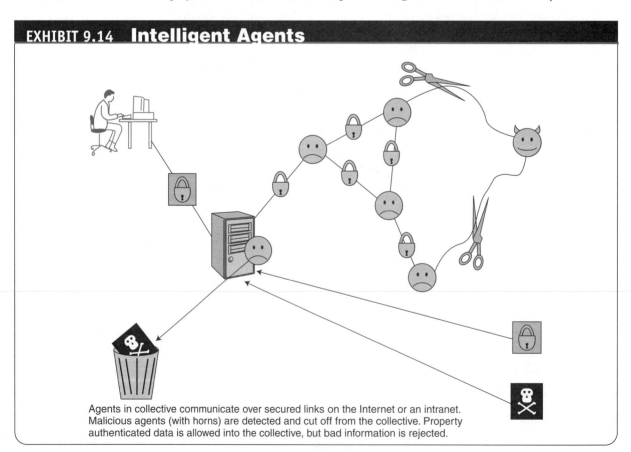

Agents in collective communicate over secured links on the Internet or an intranet. Malicious agents (with horns) are detected and cut off from the collective. Property authenticated data is allowed into the collective, but bad information is rejected.

Source: sandia.gov/media/NewsRel/NR2000/agent.htm. Courtesy of Sandia Labs.

reporting, (2) operational efficiency, (3) compliance with laws, (4) regulations and policies, and (5) safeguarding of assets.

PROTECTING AGAINST SPAM

Sending spam that disguises a sales pitch to look like a personal e-mail to bypass filters violates the U.S. Controlling the Assault of Non-Solicited Pornography and Marketing (CAN-SPAM) Act of 2003. However, many spammers hide their identity to escape detection by using hijacked PCs, or spam zombies, to send spam.

The **Controlling the Assault of Non-Solicited Pornography and Marketing Act**, or **CAN-SPAM Act**, makes it a crime to send commercial e-mail messages with false or misleading message headers or misleading subject lines. Other provisions of the law:

▶ Require marketers to identify their physical location by including their postal address in the text of the e-mail messages.

▶ Require an opt-out link in each message, which must also give recipients the option of telling senders to stop all segments of their marketing campaigns.

▶ Allow for suits to be brought by ISPs, state attorneys general, and the federal government.

▶ Carry penalties of up to $250 per spammed e-mail message, with a cap of $2 million, which can be tripled for aggravated violations. There is no cap on penalties for e-mail sent with false or deceptive headers.

▶ Carry other penalties—those found guilty of violating the law may face up to five years in prison.

(See spamlaws.com/federal/can-spam.shtml.)

Both legal and technological defenses are used to prevent or punish search engine and other forms of commercial spam. In one case, Verizon Wireless filed a lawsuit against the Florida-based travel agency Passport Holidays for violating federal and state laws by sending 98,000 unsolicited text messages to Verizon Wireless customers. Passport's messages encouraged recipients to call a toll-free number to claim a cruise to the Bahamas. In February 2006, a federal court judge granted Verizon Wireless's request for an injunction barring Passport Holidays from sending text message spam. Passport Holidays agreed to pay $10,000 to compensate Verizon Wireless. For more on protection against spam and spam blogs see Online File W9.9.

PROTECTING AGAINST POP-UP ADS

As discussed in Chapter 4, use of pop-ups and similar advertising programs is exploding. Sometimes it is even difficult to close these ads when they appear on the screen. Some of these ads may be part of a consumer's permission marketing agreement, but most are unsolicited. What can a user do about unsolicited pop-up ads? The following tools help stop pop-ups.

Tools for Stopping Pop-Ups. One way to avoid the potential danger lurking behind pop-up ads is to install software that will block pop-up ads and prevent them from appearing in the first place. Several software packages offer pop-up stoppers. Some are free (e.g., panicware.com and adscleaner.com); others are available for a fee. For a list of pop-up blocking software, visit snapfiles.com/Freeware/misctools/fwpopblock.html and netsecurity.about.com/od/popupadblocking/a/aafreepopup.htm.

Controlling the Assault of Non-Solicited Pornography and Marketing (CAN-SPAM) Act
Law that makes it a crime to send commercial e-mail messages with false or misleading message headers or misleading subject lines.

Many ISPs offer tools to stop pop-ups from appearing. The Mozilla Firefox Web browser does not allow pop-ups. Even the Google Toolbar will block pop-up ads. Microsoft offers pop-up blocking for its Internet Explorer browser.

However, adware or software that gets bundled with other popular applications like person-to-person file sharing is able to deliver the pop-up ads because they originate from the desktop, not the browser, and blocking tools do not govern them.

PROTECTION AGAINST PHISHING

Because there are many phishing attack methods, there are many defense methods as well. Illustrative examples are provided by Symantec (2009), ftc.gov, and en.wikipedia.org/wiki/Phishing. For analytical fraud protection, see sas.com/solutions/fraud/index.html.

PROTECTING AGAINST SPYWARE

In response to the emergence of spyware, a large variety of antispyware software exists. Running antispyware software has become a widely recognized element of computer security best practices for Microsoft Windows desktop computers. A number of jurisdictions have passed antispyware laws, which usually target any software that is surreptitiously installed to control a user's computer. The U.S. Federal Trade Commission (ftc.gov) has placed on the Internet a page of advice to consumers about how to lower the risk of spyware infection, including a list of "do's" and "don'ts." For an overview of consumer and seller protection in EC, see Online File W9.10.

Section 9.8 ❱ REVIEW QUESTIONS

1. What are general controls? List the various types.
2. List the various biometric controls. What are their functions?
3. Define access control.
4. Distinguish between application controls and internal controls.
5. How does one protect against spam? Against splogs?
6. How does one protect against pop-ups?

9.9 BUSINESS CONTINUITY, SECURITY AUDITING, AND RISK MANAGEMENT

A major building block in EC security for large companies or companies where EC plays a critical role (e.g., banks, airlines, stock brokerages, e-tailers) is to prepare for natural or man-made disasters. Disasters may occur without warning. The best defense is to be prepared. Therefore, an important element in any security system is the *business continuity plan*, mainly consisting of a disaster recovery plan. Such a plan outlines the process by which businesses should recover from a major disaster. Destruction of all (or most) of the computing facilities can cause significant damage. Therefore, it is difficult for many organizations to obtain insurance for their computers and information systems without showing a satisfactory disaster prevention and recovery plan. The comprehensiveness of a business recovery plan is shown in Exhibit 9.15.

EXHIBIT 9.15 Business Continuity Services

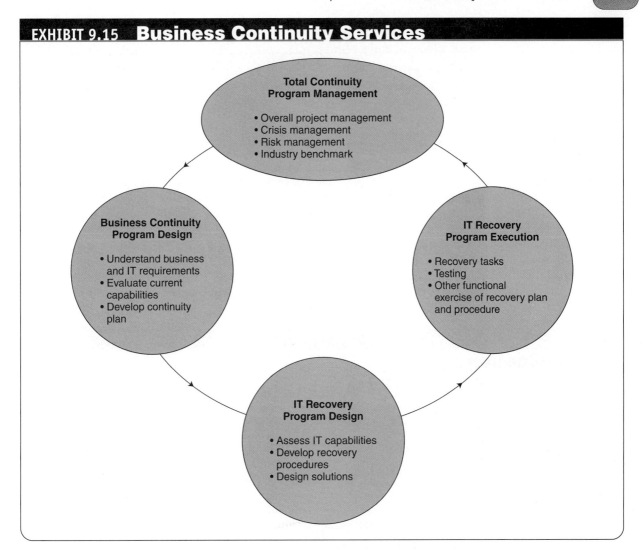

BUSINESS CONTINUITY AND DISASTER RECOVERY PLANNING

Disaster recovery is the chain of events linking the business continuity plan to protection and to recovery. The following are some key thoughts about the process:

▶ The purpose of a business continuity plan is to keep the business running after a disaster occurs. Each function in the business should have a valid recovery capability plan.

▶ Recovery planning is part of *asset protection*. Every organization should assign responsibility to management to identify and protect assets within their spheres of functional control.

▶ Planning should focus first on recovery from a total loss of all capabilities.

▶ Proof of capability usually involves some kind of what-if analysis that shows that the recovery plan is current.

> ▶ All critical applications must be identified and their recovery procedures addressed in the plan.
> ▶ The plan should be written so that it will be effective in case of disaster, not just in order to satisfy the auditors.
> ▶ The plan should be kept in a safe place; copies should be given to all key managers, or it should be available on the intranet. The plan should be audited periodically.

disaster avoidance
An approach oriented toward prevention. The idea is to minimize the chance of avoidable disasters (such as fire or other human-caused threats).

Disaster recovery planning can be very complex, and it may take several months to complete. Using special software, the planning job can be expedited. See Case 9.2 for a discussion of the importance of business continuity and the ability to recover from a disaster.

Disaster Avoidance. Disaster avoidance is an approach oriented toward *prevention*. The idea is to minimize the chance of avoidable disasters (such as fire or other human-caused threats). For example, many companies use a device called *uninterrupted power supply (UPS)*, which provides power in case of a power outage.

CASE 9.2
EC Application

BUSINESS CONTINUITY AND DISASTER RECOVERY

Ninety-three percent of companies that suffer a significant data loss go out of business within five years, according to Freeman Mendel, the chair of the FBI's 2006 InfraGard National Conference. Even though business continuity/ disaster recovery (BC/DR) is a business survival issue, many managers have dangerously viewed BC/DR as an IT security issue.

Disasters teach the best lessons for both IT managers and corporate executives who have not implemented BC/DR processes. The success or failure of those processes depends on IT, as the following case indicates.

The city of Houston, Texas, and Harris County swung into action by turning Reliant Park and the Houston Astrodome into a "temporary city" with a medical facility, pharmacy, post office, and town square to house more than 250,000 Hurricane Katrina evacuees. Coast Guard Lt. Commander Joseph J. Leonard headed up the operation, drawing on his knowledge of the National Incident Command System. As Leonard explained, ineffective communication between the command staff and those in New Orleans, who could have informed Houston authorities about the number and special needs of the evacuees, caused a serious problem. In addition, agencies and organizations with poor on-scene decision-making authority hampered and slowed efforts to get things done.

Now businesses in hurricane alleys, earthquake corridors, and major cities are deploying BC/DR plans supported with software tools that allow them to replicate, or back up, their mission-critical applications to sites away from their primary data centers. In case of a disaster, companies can transmit vital accounting, project management, or transactional systems and records to their disaster recovery facilities, limiting downtime and data loss despite an outage at the primary location.

Globally, regulators are increasingly paying closer attention to business continuity and recovery times, which are now measured in hours rather than days. The Australian Prudential Regulation Authority (APRA) released its prudential standard on business continuity in April 2005. APRA gave Australian firms only 12 months to fix their compliance gaps.

Sources: Compiled from Fagg (2006), *Fiber Optics Weekly* (2006), and *infragardconferences.com* (accessed November 2009).

Questions

1. Why might a company that had a significant data loss not be able to recover?

2. Why are regulators requiring that companies implement BC/DR plans?

A major related activity of business continuity is auditing. See Online File W9.11.

RISK-MANAGEMENT AND COST-BENEFIT ANALYSIS

It is usually not economical to prepare protection against every possible threat. Therefore, an IT security program must provide a process for assessing threats and deciding which ones to prepare for and which ones to ignore or provide only reduced protection.

Risk-Management Analysis

Risk-management analysis can be enhanced by the use of DSS software packages. A simplified computation is shown here:

$$\text{Expected loss} = P_1 \times P_2 \times L$$

where:

P_1 = probability of attack (estimate, based on judgment)
P_2 = probability of attack being successful (estimate, based on judgment)
L = loss occurring if attack is successful

Example:

$$P_1 = .02, P_2 = .10, L = \$1,000,000$$

Then, expected loss from this particular attack is:

$$P_1 \times P_2 \times L = 0.02 \times 0.1 \times \$1,000,000 = \$2,000$$

The amount of loss may depend on the duration of a system being out of operation. Therefore, some add duration to the analysis.

Ethical Issues

Implementing security programs raises several ethical issues. First, some people are against monitoring any individual's activities. Imposing certain controls is seen by some as a violation of freedom of speech or other civil rights. A Gartner Group study showed that even after the terrorist attacks of September 11, 2001, only 26 percent of Americans approved a national ID database. Using biometrics is considered by many a violation of privacy.

Handling the privacy versus security dilemma is tough. There are other ethical and legal obligations that may require companies to "invade the privacy" of employees and monitor their actions. In particular, IT security measures are needed to protect against loss, liability, and litigation. Losses are not just financial, but also include the loss of information, customers, trading partners, brand image, and ability to conduct business due to the actions of hackers, malware, or employees.

Section 9.9 ▶ REVIEW QUESTIONS

1. Why do organizations need a business continuity plan?
2. List three issues a business continuity plan should cover.
3. Identify two factors that influence a company's ability to recover from a disaster.
4. What types of devices are needed for disaster avoidance?
5. How can expected loss be calculated?
6. List two ethical issues associated with security programs.

9.10 IMPLEMENTING ENTERPRISE-WIDE E-COMMERCE SECURITY

Now that you have learned about both the threats and the defenses, we can discuss some implementation issues starting with the reason it is difficult, or even impossible, to stop computer crimes and information systems malfunction.

According to an *InformationWeek* survey (Fratto 2008), the major security challenges for corporations are:

▶ Managing the complexity of security (62 percent of respondents)
▶ Preventing data breaches from outside attackers (35 percent of respondents)
▶ Enforcing security policies (31 percent of respondents)

We will discuss these topics in this section.

SENIOR MANAGEMENT COMMITMENT AND SUPPORT

The success of an EC security strategy and program depends on the commitment and involvement of senior management. This is often called the "tone at the top." A genuine and well-communicated executive commitment about EC security and privacy measures is needed to convince users that insecure practices, risky or unethical methods, and mistakes due to ignorance will not be tolerated. Many forms of security are unpopular because they are inconvenient, restrictive, time-consuming, and expensive. Security practices tend not to be a priority unless they are mandatory and there are negative consequences for noncompliance.

Therefore, an EC security and privacy model for effective enterprise-wide security begins with senior management commitment and support, as shown in Exhibit 9.16. The model views EC security (as well as the broader IT security) as a combination of commitment and support, policies and training, procedures and enforcement, and tools executed as a continuous process.

EC SECURITY POLICIES AND TRAINING

The next step is to develop a general EC security policy, as well as policies that specify acceptable use of computers and networks, access control, enforcement, roles, and responsibilities. The policies need to be disseminated throughout the organization and necessary training provided to ensure that everyone is aware of and understands them. These policies are important because access control rules, access control lists, monitoring, and rules for firewalls and routers are derived from them. For example, to avoid violating privacy legislation when collecting confidential data, policies need to specify that customers:

▶ Know that data is being collected.
▶ Give permission, or "opt in," for data to be collected.

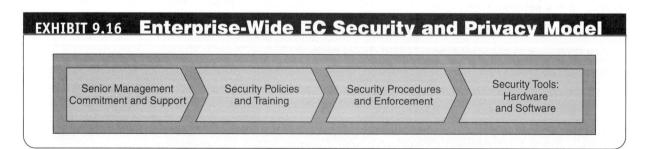

EXHIBIT 9.16 Enterprise-Wide EC Security and Privacy Model

Senior Management Commitment and Support → Security Policies and Training → Security Procedures and Enforcement → Security Tools: Hardware and Software

◗ Have some control over how the information is used.

◗ Know the data will be used in a reasonable and ethical manner.

The greater the understanding of how security issues directly impact production levels, customer and supplier relationships, revenue streams, and management's liability, the more security will be incorporated into business projects and proposals. It is essential to have a comprehensive and up-to-date **acceptable use policy (AUP)** that informs users of their responsibilities when using company networks, wireless devices, customer data, and so forth. To be effective, the AUP needs to define the responsibilities of every user by specifying both acceptable and unacceptable computer usage. Access to the company networks, databases, and e-mail should never be given to a user until after this process is completed.

EC SECURITY PROCEDURES AND ENFORCEMENT

EC security procedures require an evaluation of the digital and financial assets at risk—including cost and operational considerations. To calculate the proper level of protection, managers responsible for a digital asset need to assess its risk exposure.

Another assessment is the *business impact analysis.* **Business impact analysis (BIA)** is an exercise that determines the impact of losing the support of an EC resource to an organization; estimates how that loss may escalate over time; identifies the minimum resources needed to recover from the loss; and prioritizes the steps in the recovery of the processes and supporting systems. After estimating the risk exposure of digital assets, the organization should focus its resources on the risks that are the greatest.

INDUSTRY STANDARDS FOR CREDIT CARD PROTECTION (PCI DSS)

In addition to legal requirements and technical security measures, a unique industry standard was created in 2008 by industry members to protect their customers' and their members' brand images and revenues. It is called the *Payment Card Industry Data Security Standard (PCI DSS),* created by Visa, MasterCard, American Express, and Discover.

PCI is required for all members, merchants, or service providers that store, process, or transmit cardholder data. In short, PCI DSS requires merchants and card payment providers to make certain their Web applications are secure. If done correctly, it could actually help curb the number of Web-related security breaches. PCI DSS mandates that retailers ensure that Web-facing applications are protected against known attacks by applying either of the following two methods:

1. Have all custom supplication code reviewed for vulnerabilities by an application security firm.

2. Install an application layer firewall in front of Web-facing applications. Each application will have its own firewall to protect against intrusions and malware.

The purpose of the PCI DSS is to improve customers' trust in e-commerce, especially when it comes to online payments, and to increase the Web security of online merchants. To motivate companies to follow these standards, the penalties for noncompliance are severe. The card brands can fine the retailer, and increase transaction fees for each credit or debit card transaction. A finding of noncompliance can be the basis for lawsuits. For details, see en.wikipedia.org/wiki/Payment_Card_Industry_Data_ Security_Standard.

WHY IS IT DIFFICULT TO STOP INTERNET CRIME?

The following are the major reasons Internet crime is so difficult to stop.

acceptable use policy (AUP)
Policy that informs users of their responsibilities when using company networks, wireless devices, customer data, and so forth.

business impact analysis (BIA)
An exercise that determines the impact of losing the support of an EC resource to an organization and establishes the escalation of that loss over time, identifies the minimum resources needed to recover, and prioritizes the recovery of processes and supporting systems.

Making Shopping Inconvenient

Strong EC security makes online shopping inconvenient and is demanding on customers. The EC industry does not want to enforce safeguards that add friction to the profitable wheels of online commerce. It is possible, for example, to demand passwords or PINs for all credit card transactions, but that could discourage or prevent customers from completing their purchases. It is also possible to demand delivery only to the billing address for a credit card, but that would eliminate an important convenience for gift senders.

Lack of Cooperation from Credit Card Issuers

A second reason is the lack of cooperation from credit card issuers and local and especially foreign ISPs. If the source ISP would cooperate and suspend the hacker's access, it would be very difficult for hackers to do what they do. The hacker would not be able to hack from the comfort of home because that street address would be blacklisted by the ISP.

However, requiring stronger EC standards and information sharing by the credit card companies would not fix the problem. Many cybercriminals, especially ones that do not reside in a G8 nation, do not need to worry about prosecution from their government or even suspension from their ISP. (The Group of Eight [G8] is an international forum for the governments of Canada, France, Germany, Italy, Japan, Russia, the United Kingdom, and the United States.) This situation helps explain why a huge majority of the hackers (some estimate about 95 percent) reside in Turkey, China, Romania, or Brazil.

Shoppers' Negligence

The third reason pertains to customers. Online shoppers are to blame for not taking necessary precautions to avoid becoming a victim. Some shoppers rely too heavily on fraud protection provided by credit card issuers, ignoring the bigger risk of identity theft. Phishing is rampant because some people respond to it—making it profitable. Although phishing gets most of the media attention, users expose themselves to equally dangerous risks by using debit cards on online gambling sites or revealing themselves in online communities like MySpace, Facebook, and France's Skyblog.

Ignoring EC Security Best Practices

Computing Technology Industry Association (CompTIA)
Nonprofit trade group providing information security research and best practices.

The fourth reason is that many companies of all sizes fail to implement basic IT security management, such as best security practices, business continuity plans, and disaster recovery plans. In its fourth annual study on information security and the workforce released in 2008, the **Computing Technology Industry Association (CompTIA)**, a nonprofit trade group, said that the most widespread threats in the United States today stem from spyware, the lack of user awareness, and virus and worm attacks. Because of the known role of human error in information security breaches, 60 percent of the more than 2,000 government, IT, financial, and educational organizations surveyed worldwide had mandatory security training. Nearly 33 percent of all U.S. firms make certification required now, compared to only 25 percent in 2006 and 14 percent in 2005 (CompTIA 2008).

Design and Architecture Issues

A fifth reason arises from information systems (IS) design and security architecture issues. It is well known that preventing vulnerability during the EC design and preimplementation stage is far less expensive than mitigating problems later. The IS staff of a company needs to plan security from the design stage because simple mistakes, such as not ensuring that all traffic into and out of a network pass through a firewall, are often to blame for letting in hackers. If companies don't invest the resources needed to ensure that their applications are secure, they may as well forget about security elsewhere on the Web site. Security needs to be built into an EC site from the very beginning and also into the application level.

There's no doubt that Web applications are attackers' target of choice and that every component in an EC application is subject to some sort of security threat.

Lack of Due Care in Business Practices

The final reason is the lack of due care in business or hiring practices, outsourcing, and business partnerships. The **standard of due care** comes from the law and is also known as the "duty to exercise reasonable care." Due care in EC is care that a company is reasonably expected to take based on the risks affecting its EC business and online transactions. If managers ignore the standard of due care in business practices, hire criminals, outsource to fraudulent vendors, or partner with unsecured companies, they put their EC business and confidential data at risk, exposing themselves to legal problems. See Online File W9.12 for a discussion of the impacts on ChoicePoint for its negligence in not following reasonable information security and privacy practices. For a description of the PCI standard and requirements, see pcistandard.com.

standard of due care
Care that a company is reasonably expected to take based on the risks affecting its EC business and online transactions.

Section 9.10 ▶ REVIEW QUESTIONS

1. If senior management is not committed to EC security, how might that impact the e-business?
2. What is a benefit of using the risk exposure model for EC security planning?
3. Why should every company implement an acceptable use policy?
4. Why is training required?
5. List the six major reasons why it is difficult to stop computer crimes.

MANAGERIAL ISSUES

Some managerial issues related to this chapter are as follows.

1. **What is the EC security strategy of your company?** The security strategy of your company should be to deter, prevent, and detect the potential threats in conducting EC whether it is intentional or unintentional. Evaluating the threats, vulnerabilities, and risks of potential criminal attacks and their impacts on business operation is a manager's task. Developing the defense mechanism and disaster recovery plan should be shared throughout the organization. Designing the EC security plan as a part of the overall IT security plan is necessary. Educating senior management about the consequences of poor network security and the best practices in network risk management is essential to the development of a good strategy.

2. **Is the budget for IT security adequate?** To evaluate the adequacy of the IT security budget, it will be useful to compare yours with the national average. If the budget of your company is too low or too high, you will need to seriously review the reasons why. It is reported that the average IT security budget is about 10 percent of total IT budget, while awareness training is about 3 percent of total IT budget. Review whether the outsourcing plan for security expertise is adequately balanced with internal effort because about 40 percent of companies outsource some computer security.

3. **What steps should businesses follow in establishing a security plan?** Security risk management is an ongoing process involving three phases: asset identification, risk assessment, and implementation. By actively monitoring existing security policies and measures, companies can determine which are successful or unsuccessful and, in turn, which should be modified or eliminated. However, it also is important to monitor changes in business requirements, changes

in technology and the way it is used, and changes in the way people can attack the systems and networks. In this way, an organization can evolve its security policies and measures, ensuring that they continue to support the critical needs of the business.

4. **Should organizations be concerned with internal security threats?** Except for malware, breaches perpetrated by insiders are much more frequent than those perpetrated by outsiders. This is true for both B2C and B2B sites. Security policies and measures for EC sites need to address these insider threats. Pay special attention to the prevention of social engineering schemes that may allure insiders, and educate the new insiders about such threats.

5. **What is the key to establishing strong e-commerce security?** Most discussions about security focus on technology, with statements like "firewalls are mandatory" or "all transmissions should be encrypted." Although firewalls and encryption can be important technologies, no security solution is useful unless it solves a business problem and is adopted by customers. Determining your business requirements is the most important step in creating a security solution. Business requirements, in turn, determine your information requirements. Once you know your information requirements, you can begin to understand the value of those assets and the steps that you should take to secure those that are most valuable and vulnerable.

SUMMARY

In this chapter, you learned about the following EC issues as they relate to the chapter's learning objectives.

1. **The importance and scope of EC information security.** For EC to succeed, it must be secured. Unfortunately this is not an easy task due to many unintentional and intentional hazards. Security incidents and breaches interrupt EC transactions and increase the cost of doing business online. Internet design is vulnerable, and the temptation to commit computer crime is increasing with the increased applications and volume of EC. Criminals are expanding operations, creating an underground economy of stolen valuable information. A strategy is needed to handle the costly defense operation, which includes training, education, project management, and ability to enforce security policy. EC security will remain an evolving discipline because threats change, e-business needs change, and Web-based technologies to provide greater service change. An EC security strategy is needed to optimize EC security programs for efficiency and effectiveness. There are several reasons why. EC security costs and efforts from reacting to crises and paying for damages are greater than if organizations had an EC security strategy. The Internet is still a fundamentally insecure infrastructure. There are many criminals, and they are intent on stealing information for identity theft and fraud. Without a strategy, EC security is treated as a project instead of an ongoing, never-ending process.

2. **Basic EC security issues and perspectives.** The security issue can be viewed as a battleground between attackers and attack and defenders and defense. There are many variations on both sides and many possible collision scenarios. Owners of EC sites need to be concerned with multiple security issues: authentication, verifying the identity of the participants in a transaction; authorization, ensuring that a person or process has access rights to particular systems or data; auditing, being able to determine whether particular actions have been taken and by whom; confidentiality, ensuring that information is not disclosed to unauthorized individuals, systems, or processes; integrity, protecting data from being altered or destroyed; availability, ensuring that data and services are available when needed; and nonrepudiation, the ability to limit parties from refuting that a legitimate transaction took place.

3. **Threats, vulnerabilities, and attacks.** EC sites are exposed to a wide range of attacks. Attacks may be nontechnical (social engineering), in which a perpetrator tricks people into revealing information or performing actions that compromise network security. Or they may be technical, whereby software and systems expertise are used to attack the networks, database, or programs. DoS attacks bring operations to a halt by sending floods of data to target computers or to as many computers on the Internet as possible.

Malicious code attacks include viruses, worms, Trojan horses, or some combination of these. Over the past couple of years, various trends in malicious code have emerged, including an increase in the speed and volume of attacks; reduced time between the discovery of a vulnerability and the release of an attack to exploit the vulnerability; the growing use of bots to launch attacks; an increase in attacks on Web applications; and a shift to profit-motivated attacks.

4. **Phishing, financial crimes, and spam.** Phishing attempts to get valuable information from people by masquerading as a trustworthy entity. Personal information is extracted from people (stolen) and sold to criminals who use it to commit financial crimes such as transferring money to illegal accounts. One method of financial crime is to use e-mail spam in an attempt to influence the recipients.

5. **Information assurance.** The importance of the information assurance model to EC is that it represents the processes for protecting information by ensuring its confidentiality, integrity, and availability. Confidentiality is the assurance of data privacy. Integrity is the assurance that data is accurate or that a message has not been altered. Availability is the assurance that access to data, the Web site, or other EC data service is timely, available, reliable, and restricted to authorized users.

6. **Securing EC access and communications.** In EC, issues of trust are paramount. Trust starts with the authentication of the parties involved in a transaction; that is, identifying the parties in a transaction along with the actions they can perform. Authentication can be established with something one knows (e.g., a password), something one has (e.g., a token), or something one possesses (e.g., a fingerprint). Biometric systems can confirm a person's identity. Fingerprint scanners, iris scanners, facial recognition, and voice recognition are examples of biometric systems. Public key infrastructure (PKI), which is the cornerstone of secure e-payments, also can authenticate the parties in a transaction. PKI uses encryption (private and public) to ensure privacy and integrity and digital signatures to ensure authenticity and nonrepudiation. Digital signatures are themselves authenticated through a system of digital certificates issued by certificate authorities (CAs). For the average consumer and merchant, PKI is simplified because it is built into Web browsers and services. Such tools are secure because security is based on SSL (TSL) communication standards.

7. **Technologies for securing networks.** At EC sites, firewalls, VPNs, and IDSs have proven extremely useful. A firewall is a combination of hardware and software that isolates a private network from a public network. Firewalls are of two general types—packet-filtering routers or application-level proxies. A packet-filtering router uses a set of rules to determine which communication packets can move from the outside network to the inside network. An application-level proxy is a firewall that accepts requests from the outside and repackages a request before sending it to the inside network, thus, ensuring the security of the request. Individuals with broadband access need personal firewalls. VPNs are used generally to support secure site-to-site transmissions across the Internet between B2B partners or communications between a mobile and remote worker and a LAN at a central office. IDSs monitor activity across a network or on a host. The systems watch for suspicious activity and take automated actions whenever a security breach or attack occurs. In the same vein, some companies are installing honeynets and honeypots in an effort to gather information on intrusions and to analyze the types and methods of attacks being perpetrated.

8. **The different controls and special defense mechanisms.** The major controls are general (including physical, access controls, biometrics, administrative controls, application controls, and internal controls for compliance). In addition, there are controls against fraud and spam.

9. **Role of business continuity and disaster recovery planning.** Disaster recovery planning is an integral part of effective internal control and security management. Business continuity planning includes backup sites and a plan for what to do when disaster strikes. Such plans are required by insurance companies and some lenders. It is necessary to conduct drills that will ensure that people know what to do if disaster strikes.

10. **Enterprise-wide EC security.** EC and network security are inconvenient, expensive, tedious, and never-ending. A defensive in-depth model that views EC security as a combination of commitment, people, processes, and technology is essential. An effective program starts with senior management's commitment and budgeting support. This sets the tone that EC security is important to the organization. Other components are security policies and training. Security procedures must be defined with positive incentives for compliance and negative consequences

for violations. The last stage is the deployment of hardware and software tools based on the policies and procedures defined by the management team.

11. **Why is it impossible to stop computer crimes?**
Responsibility or blame for cybercrimes can be placed on criminals and victimized industries, users, and organizations. The EC industry does not want to enforce safeguards that add friction to the profitable wheels of online commerce. Credit card issuers try to avoid sharing leads on criminal activity with each other or law enforcement. Online shoppers fail to take necessary precautions to avoid becoming a victim. IS designs and security architectures are still incredibly vulnerable. Organizations fail to exercise due care in business or hiring practices, outsourcing, and business partnerships. Every EC business knows that the threats of bogus credit card purchases, data breaches, phishing, malware, and viruses never end—and that these threats must be addressed comprehensively and strategically.

KEY TERMS

QUESTIONS FOR DISCUSSION BY INDIVIDUAL STUDENTS

1. Consider how a hacker might trick people into giving him their user IDs and passwords to their Amazon.com accounts. What are some of the ways that a hacker might accomplish this? What crimes can be performed with such information?

2. B2C EC sites continue to experience DoS attacks. How are these attacks perpetrated? Why is it so difficult to safeguard against them? What are some of the things a site can do to mitigate such attacks?

3. All EC sites share common security threats and vulnerabilities. Do you think that B2C Web sites face different threats and vulnerabilities than B2B sites? Explain.

4. How are botnet identity theft attacks and Web site hijacks perpetrated? Why are they so dangerous to e-commerce?

5. Discuss some of the difficulties of eliminating online financial fraud.

6. Some companies prefer not to have disaster recovery plans. Under what circumstances does this make sense? Discuss.

7. Enter **idesia-biometrics.com** and look at its product. Discuss these benefits over other biometrics.

8. Enter **trendsecure.com** and find a tool called "hijack this." Try the free tool. Find an online forum that deals with it. Discuss the benefits and limitations.

TOPICS FOR CLASS DISCUSSION

1. Survey results on the incidence of cyberattacks paint a mixed picture; some surveys show increases, others show decreases. What factors could account for the differences in the reported results?

2. A business wants to share its customer account database with its trading partners and customers, while at the same time provide prospective buyers with access to marketing materials on its Web site. Assuming that the business is responsible for running all these network components, what types of security components (e.g., firewalls, VPNs, etc.) could be used to ensure that the partners and customers have access to the account information and others do not? What type of network configuration (e.g., bastion gateway server) will provide the appropriate security?

3. Why is it so difficult to fight computer criminals? What strategies can be implemented by financial institutions, airlines, and other heavy users of EC?

INTERNET EXERCISES

1. The National Vulnerability Database (NVD) is a comprehensive cybersecurity database that integrates all publicly available U.S. government vulnerability resources and provides references to industry resources. Visit **nvd.nist.gov** and review 10 of the recent CVE vulnerabilities. For each vulnerability, list its published date, CVSS severity, impact type, and the operating system or software with the vulnerability.

2. The Common Vulnerabilities and Exposures Board (**cve.mitre.org**) maintains a list of common security vulnerabilities. Review the list. How many different vulnerabilities are there? Based on the list, which computer system components appear to be most vulnerable to attack? What impact do these vulnerable components have on EC?

3. Your B2C site has been hacked with a new, innovative method. List two organizations where you would report this incident so that they can alert other sites. How do you do this, and what type of information do you have to provide?

4. Connect to the Internet. Determine the IP address of your computer by visiting at least two Web sites that provide that feature. You can use a search engine to locate Web sites or visit **ip-adress.com** or **whatismyipaddress.com**. What other information

does the search reveal about your connection? Based on this information, how could a company or hacker use that information?

5. Select a single type of physiological biometric system. Using a search engine, identify at least two commercial vendors offering these systems. Based on the information you found, what are the major features of the systems? Which of the systems would you select and why?

6. The National Strategy to Secure Cyberspace provides a series of actions and recommendations for each of its five national priorities. Search and download a copy of the strategy online. Selecting one of the priorities, discuss in detail the actions and recommendations for that priority.

7. The Symantec Annual Internet Security Threat Report provides details about the trends in attacks and vulnerabilities in Internet security. Obtain a

copy of the latest report and summarize the major findings of the report for both attacks and vulnerabilities.

8. Enter perimeterusa.com and look for a white paper titled "Top 9 Network Security Threats in 2009." Summarize these threats. Then look for a paper titled "The ABC's of Social Engineering." Summarize the suggested defense.

9. Enter security firm finjan.com and find examples of underground Internet activities in five different countries. Prepare a summary.

10. Enter identitytheft.info/breaches09.aspx and find the major identity security breaches in 2009.

11. Enter verisign.com and find information about PKI and encryption. Write a report.

12. Enter gfi.com/emailsecuritytest and similar sites. Write some guidelines for protecting your PC.

TEAM ASSIGNMENTS AND PROJECTS

1. Assign teams to report on the major spam and scam threats. Look at examples provided by ftc.gov, the Symantec report on the state of spam (2009), and white papers from IBM, VeriSign, and other security firms.

2. Several personal firewall products are available. A list of these products can be found at firewallguide.com/software.htm. Assign each team three products from the list. Each team should prepare a detailed review and comparison of each of the products they have been assigned.

3. Assign each team member a different B2C or B2B Web site. Have each team prepare a report

summarizing the site's security assets, threats, and vulnerabilities. Prepare a brief EC security strategy for the site.

4. Address the following topics in a class discussion:
   a. Some claim that the best strategy is to invest very little and only in proven technologies such as encryption and firewalls. Discuss.
   b. Can the underground Internet marketplace be controlled? Why or why not?
   c. Why is phishing so difficult to control? What can be done? Discuss.
   d. How secure is your e-mail?

Closing Case

UBS PAINEWEBBER'S BUSINESS OPERATIONS DEBILITATED BY MALICIOUS CODE

Employee (Allegedly) Planned to Crash All Computer Networks

In June 2006, a former systems administrator at UBS PaineWebber, Roger Duronio, 63, was charged with building, planting, and setting off a software

logic bomb designed to crash the network. His alleged motive was to get revenge for not being paid what he thought he was worth. He designed the logic bomb to delete all the files in the host server in the central data center and in every server in every U.S. branch office. Duronio was looking to make up for some of the cash he felt he had been denied. He wanted to take home $175,000 a year. He had a base salary of $125,000 and a potential annual bonus of $50,000, but the actual bonus was $35,000.

Duronio quit his job, went to a broker within hours, and bought stock options that would only pay out if the company's stock plunged within 11 days. By setting a short expiration date of 11 days instead of a year, the gain from any payout would be much greater. He tried to ensure a stock price crash by crippling the company's network to rock their financial stability. His "put" options expired worthless because the bank's national network did go down, but not UBS stock.

Discovering the Attack

In a federal court, UBS PaineWebber's IT manager Elvira Maria Rodriguez testified that on March 4, 2002, at 9:30 A.M. when the stock market opened for the day, she saw the words *cannot find* on her screen at the company's Escalation Center in Weehawken, New Jersey. She hit the enter key to see the message again, but her screen was frozen. Rodriguez was in charge of maintaining the stability of the servers in the company's branch offices.

When the company's servers went down that day in March 2002, about 17,000 brokers across the country were unable to make trades; the incident affected nearly 400 branch offices. Files were deleted. Backups went down within minutes of being run. Rodriguez, who had to clean up after the logic bomb, said, "How on earth were we going to bring them all back up? How was this going to affect the company? If I had a scale of 1 to 10, this would be a 10-plus."

The prosecutor, Assistant U.S. Attorney V. Grady O'Malley, told the jury: "It took hundreds of people, thousands of man hours and millions of dollars to correct." The system was offline for more than a day, and UBS PaineWebber (renamed *UBS Wealth Management USA* in 2003) spent about $3.1 million in assessing and restoring the network. The company did not report how much was lost in business downtime and disruption.

Tracking Down the Hacker

A computer forensics expert testified that Duronio's password and user account information were used to gain remote access to the areas where the malicious code was built inside the UBS network.

The U.S. Secret Service agent who had investigated the case found a hard copy of the logic bomb's source code on the defendant's bedroom dresser. A computer forensics investigator found electronic copies of the code on two of his four home computers.

Defense Blames UBS Security Holes

Chris Adams, Duronio's defense attorney, offered another scenario. Adams claimed that the code was planted by someone else to be a nuisance or prank. Adams also said the UBS system had many security holes and backdoors that gave easy access to attackers. Adams told the jury:

> UBS computer security had considerable holes. There are flaws in the system that compromise the ability to determine what is and isn't true. Does the ability to walk around in the system undetected and masquerade as someone else affect your ability to say what has happened?

He also claimed that UBS and @Stake, the first computer forensics company to work on the incident, withheld some information from the government and even destroyed some of the evidence. As for the stock options, Adams explained that they were neither risky bets nor part of a scheme, but rather a common investment practice.

Disaster Recovery Efforts

While trying to run a backup to get a main server up and functional, Rodriguez discovered that a line of code (MRM-r) was hanging up the system every time it ran. She renamed the command to hide it from the system and rebooted the server. This action stopped the server from deleting anything else. After testing to confirm the fix, backup tapes brought up the remaining 2,000 servers, and the line of code was deleted from each one. Restoring each server took from 30 minutes to 2 hours unless there was a complication. In those cases, restoration took up to 6 hours. UBS called in 200 IBM technicians to all the branch offices to expedite the recovery.

Many of the servers were down a day and a half, but some servers in remote locations were down for weeks. The incident impacted all the brokers who were denied access to critical applications because the servers were down.

Minimizing Residual Damages

UBS asked the judge to bar the public from Duronio's trial to avoid "serious embarrassment" and "serious injury" to the bank and its clients and possibly reveal sensitive information about the UBS network and operations. UBS argued that documents it had provided to the court could help a criminal hack into the bank's computer systems to destroy critical business information or to uncover confidential client information.

Duronio faced federal charges, including mail fraud, securities fraud, and computer sabotage, which carry sentences of up to 30 years in jail, $1 million in fines, and restitution for recovery costs.

Sources: Compiled from Gaudin (2006) and Whitman (2006).

Questions

1. What "red flags" might have indicated that Duronio was a disgruntled employee? Would any of those red flags also indicate that he would sabotage the network for revenge?

2. How could this disaster have been prevented? What policies, procedures, or technology could have prevented such an attack by an employee with full network access?

3. Did UBS have a disaster recovery plan in place for an enterprise-wide network crash?

4. Do you agree with the defense lawyer's argument that anyone could have planted the logic bomb because UBS's computer security had considerable holes?

5. Given the breadth of known vulnerabilities, what sort of impact will any set of security standards have on the rise in cyberattacks?

ONLINE RESOURCES
available at pearsonhighered.com/turban

Online Files

W9.1 Application Case: Hackers Profit from TJX's Corporate Data

W9.2 Top Cybersecurity Areas in 2008

W9.3 Examples of Internet Fraud

W9.4 Life Cycle of an EC Security Program

W9.5 Application Case: The Eyes Have It

W9.6 Basic Security Design Concepts

W9.7 What Firewalls Can Protect

W9.8 Application Case: Honeynets and the Law

W9.9 Protecting Against Spam and Splogs

W9.10 Consumer and Seller Protection for Online Fraud

W9.11 Auditing Information Systems

W9.12 Application Case: Impacts of ChoicePoint's Negligence in Information Security

Comprehensive Educational Web Sites

nvd.nist.gov: A comprehensive cybersecurity database.

itworld.com/security: Comprehensive collection of papers on security.

spamlaws.com: News, cases, legal information, and much more; spam, scams, security.

technet.microsoft.com/en-us/security/default.aspx: Comprehensive collection of papers on security.

eseminarslive.com: Webinars, events, news on security.

verisignsecured.com: A major security vendor; tutorials.

thebci.org: Business Continuity Institute.

drj.com: Disaster recovery journal.

webbuyersguide.com/resource/rllibrary.aspx?sitename=webbuyersguide: Look for security topics.

csrc.nist.gov: Computer Security Resource Center.

technologyevaluation.com: White papers, etc.; look for security.

ic3.gov/crimeschemes.aspx: A comprehensive list of Internet crime schemes and how to deal with them.

cbintel.com/auctionfraudreport.htm: A comprehensive list of Internet auction fraud statistics.

ELECTRONIC COMMERCE PAYMENT SYSTEMS

Content

Learning Objectives

Upon completion of this chapter, you will be able to:

1. Understand the shifts that are occurring with regard to online payments.

2. Discuss the players and processes involved in using credit cards online.

3. Discuss the different categories and potential uses of smart cards.

4. Discuss various online alternatives to credit card payments and identify under what circumstances they are best used.

5. Describe the situations where e-micropayments are used and the alternative ways for handling these situations.

6. Describe the processes and parties involved in e-checking.

PAY-PER-VIEW PAGES: THE NEXT ITUNES

The Problem

The e-book market is heating up. In February 2009, Amazon.com released the second version of its popular Kindle e-book reader. This was followed in March 2009 with the release of an iPhone application for reading content purchased on Amazon.com's Kindle Web site and then in May 2009 with the announcement of the Kindle DX with its larger nine-inch display format. Around the same time, the Canadian book retailer Indigo Books & Music Inc. launched a Web site, Shortcovers.com, for people who read books and articles online or on mobile devices. The service focuses on providing "bite-sized chunks" of about 5,000 words such as individual chapters, short stories, blogs, magazines, newspaper articles, and pieces written and uploaded by users. Free and paid content can be viewed online or transferred to mobile devices using mobile apps that are distributed through iTunes and the Shortcovers Web site.

For the most part, e-books are sold as "exact digital replicas" of their print counterparts. In other words, e-books are not sold a page or chapter at a time. Instead, the buyer has to purchase the whole book. This is the way the Kindle online store works. Also, it is the way that the Shortcovers site works. For most of the books in its online catalog, Shortcovers provides the first chapter for free, sells the next two chapters for 99 cents, or offers the entire e-book at a discount of up to half the publisher's list price. This works fine for works of fiction. Most fiction readers are primarily interested in purchasing the entire book, not individual pages or chapters. This isn't the case for nonfiction readers. Plenty of nonfiction readers do not need nor want the complete works. For example:

- A reader is traveling to Rome, Italy, on his or her next vacation and only wants a couple of chapters from Fodor's holiday travel guide to Italy, not the whole guide.

- A software programmer faces a perplexing problem and discovers a solution in a particular chapter of a well-known programming book. The book sells for $80, but the programmer only needs 5 pages from the 600-page edition.

- A professor wants to assign his or her students a series of chapters from a list of textbooks. Without violating copyright laws or requiring the students to spend a small fortune purchasing the texts, this really isn't feasible.

A few years ago, Amazon.com and Random House tried to remedy this problem. Amazon.com announced a plan called "Amazon Pages" that would allow readers to purchase parts of books online. The plan never came to fruition. Instead, they released the Kindle and opened the Kindle online store. Similarly, in February 2008, Random House began testing the idea of selling individual chapters online for $2.99. To date, the first, and only, title offered is Chip and Dan Heath's *Made to Stick*.

Selling books online—either hardcopy or electronic—is straightforward. Selling pages, chapters, or any other sections of a book or journal online for under $5 is another story. The barrier is not technical, it is financial. In the online world, the vast majority of consumers use credit cards to make purchases. The financial institutions issuing credit cards charge a fixed percentage for each credit card purchase, as well as a fixed fee. For a purchase under $5, it is difficult for a vendor to break even. It is the same problem faced by merchants in the offline world. Fortunately, the credit card companies, as well as electronic payment companies, such as PayPal, are well aware of the issues associated with small-value purchases and have begun to address the problem.

The Solution

Purchases under $5 are called *micropayments*. In the offline world, these small purchases have been made with cash because credit card companies charge merchants too much in fees to make the transactions profitable. Cash does not work in the online world. In the online world, virtually every attempt to disintermediate cash and credit cards has failed. Yet, ample evidence suggests that consumers are willing to use their credit cards for micropayments.

In the online world, Apple's iTunes has clearly been a success. Originally, iTunes sold individual songs for $0.99. At MacWorld 2009, Apple announced a multitier pricing scheme for iTunes: $0.69, $0.99, or $1.29, depending on a song's age and popularity. Apple also announced that it had sold over 6 billion songs.

Apple has overcome the costs associated with credit and debit card fees by having consumers set up accounts. The purchases of single items are aggregated until the total purchase amount makes it cost-effective to submit the payment to the credit or debit card issuer. Systems that aggregate purchases are also called "closed-loop" systems. The credit card companies are not enamored with these systems and prohibit merchants from aggregating purchases directly. However, they are currently reconsidering their stance because more and more consumers want to use their cards for small purchases (Mitchell 2007).

The credit and debit card companies, as well as e-payment vendors (e.g., PayPal), are well aware of the difficulties associated with using cards for online micropayments. In response, they have lowered their fees in an effort to entice online (and offline) vendors to permit credit and debit card micropayments. Even with the new fee structure, purchases of less than $2 are still cost-prohibitive for the average merchant. Small-value payments are much less prohibitive for larger vendors, whose large card-purchase volume enables them to negotiate with the card issuers for even smaller fees.

The Results

To date, companies such as Amazon.com and Random House have been unsuccessful with their pay-per-page or chapter plans. Clearly, Amazon.com is in a position to negotiate for smaller credit card fees. Like iTunes, it also has the ability to aggregate purchases for individual buyers. However, Random House does not sell directly to the public. Instead, it relies on other vendors, such as Amazon.com, to do the selling for them. Even with a viable micropayment system, there is no guarantee that pay-per-page or pay-per-chapter systems will interest consumers, especially given the usual restrictions placed on purchases of this sort.

Consider, for a moment, a few of the restrictions Random House has placed on its viewing programs:

- Books will be available for full indexing, search, and display.
- No downloading, printing, or copying will be permitted.
- Encryption and security measures must be applied to ensure protection of the digital content and compliance with the prescribed usage rules and territorial limitations.

In essence, the only thing the purchaser can do is view the page or chapter online. This is much more onerous than the restrictions placed on music or video downloads, which at least permit the purchaser to copy the content to their PCs or multimedia players. Unless these restrictions are loosened or eliminated, they will likely lead to the long-run failure of the Random House effort and other similar ones.

Sources: *CBCNews* (2009) and Mitchell (2007).

WHAT WE CAN LEARN . . .

The overwhelming majority of B2C purchases are paid for by credit card. For merchants, the costs of servicing card payments are high. Transaction costs, potential chargeback fees for fraudulent transactions, and the costs of creating and administering a secure EC site for handling card payments are steep. Over the years, a number of less costly e-payment alternatives to credit cards have been proposed. Digital Cash, PayMe.com, Bank One's eMoneyMail, Flooz, Beenz, Wells Fargo's and eBay's Billpoint, and Yahoo!'s PayDirect are examples of alternatives that failed to gain a critical mass of users and subsequently folded. For a variety of reasons, PayPal is one of the few alternatives to credit cards that has succeeded against significant odds. The same can be said for the world of B2B e-payments. Implementing linkages between order-taking and payment systems also can be helpful in improving order fulfillment (see Online File W10.1). Although a number of diverse payment methods have been proposed, few have survived. This chapter discusses various e-payment methods for B2C and B2B and the underlying reasons why some have been adopted and others have not.

10.1   THE PAYMENT REVOLUTION

Today, we are in the midst of a worldwide payment revolution, with cards and electronic payments taking the place of cash and checks. The tipping point of the revolution occurred in 2003. In that year, the combined use of credit and debit cards for in-store payments for the first time exceeded the combined use of cash and checks. By 2005, debit and credit cards accounted for 55 percent of in-store payments, with cash and checks making up the rest (Simon 2007). The growth in the use of plastic is attributable to the substantial growth in the use of debit cards and the decline in the use of cash. In recent years, debit card use has been spurred by a change in the U.S. Electronic Funds Transfer Act, which eliminated the requirement for merchants to issue receipts for debit purchases of $15 or less.

Similar trends have occurred in noncash payments of recurring bills. In 2001, over 75 percent of all recurring bills were paid by paper-based methods (e.g., paper checks), whereas less than 25 percent of these payments were made electronically. Now, the percent of recurring bills paid electronically hovers around 50 percent.

For decades people have been talking about the cashless society. Although the demise of cash and checks is certainly not imminent, many individuals can live without checks and nearly without cash. In the online B2C world, they already do. Throughout the world, the overwhelming majority of online purchases are made with credit cards, although there are some countries where other payment methods prevail. For instance, consumers in Germany prefer to pay with either direct debit or bank cards, whereas those in China rely on debit cards.

For online B2C merchants, the implications of these trends are straightforward. In most countries, it is hard to run an online business without supporting credit card payments, despite the costs. It also is becoming increasingly important to support payments by debit card. Eventually, the volume of debit card payments may surpass credit card payments in the online world, as they have for offline purchases. For merchants who are interested in international markets, there is a need to support a variety of e-payment mechanisms, including bank transfers, COD, electronic checks, private-label cards, gift cards, instant credit, and other noncard payment systems, such as PayPal. Merchants who offer multiple payment types have lower shopping cart abandonment rates and higher order conversion, on average, resulting in increased revenues.

The short history of e-payments is littered with the remains of companies that have attempted to introduce nontraditional payment systems. It takes years for any payment system to gain widespread acceptance. For example, credit cards were introduced in the 1950s but did not reach widespread use until the 1980s. A crucial element in the success of any e-payment method is the "chicken-and-egg" problem: How do you get sellers to adopt a method when there are few buyers using it? And, how do you get buyers to adopt a method when there are few sellers using it? A number of factors come into play in determining whether a particular method of e-payment achieves critical mass. Some of the crucial factors include the following:

Independence. Some forms of e-payment require specialized software or hardware to make the payment. Almost all forms of e-payment require the seller or merchant to install specialized software to receive and authorize a payment. Those e-payment methods that require the payer to install specialized components are less likely to succeed.

Interoperability and Portability. All forms of EC run on specialized systems that are interlinked with other enterprise systems and applications. An e-payment method must mesh with these existing systems and applications and be supported by standard computing platforms.

Security. How safe is the transfer? What are the consequences of the transfer being compromised? Again, if the risk for the payer is higher than the risk for the payee, then the payer is not likely to accept the method.

Anonymity. Unlike credit cards and checks, if a buyer uses cash, there is no way to trace the cash back to the buyer. Some buyers want their identities and purchase patterns to remain anonymous. To succeed, special payment methods, such as e-cash, have to maintain anonymity.

Divisibility. Most sellers accept credit cards only for purchases within a minimum and maximum range. If the cost of the item is too small—only a few dollars—a credit card will not do. In addition, a credit card will not work if an item or set of items costs too much (e.g., an airline company purchasing a new airplane). Any method that can address the lower or higher end of the price continuum or that can span one of the extremes and the middle has a chance of being widely accepted.

Ease of Use. For B2C e-payments, credit cards are the standard due to their ease of use. For B2B payments, the question is whether the online e-payment methods can supplant the existing offline methods of procurement.

Transaction Fees. When a credit card is used for payment, the merchant pays a transaction fee of up to 3 percent of the item's purchase price (above a minimum fixed fee). These fees make it prohibitive to support smaller purchases with credit cards, which leaves room for alternative forms of payment.

International Support. EC is a worldwide phenomenon. A payment method must be easily adapted to local buying patterns and international requirements before it can be widely adopted.

Regulations. A number of international, federal, and state regulations govern all payment methods. Even when an existing institution or association (e.g., Visa) introduces a new payment method, it faces a number of stringent regulatory hurdles. PayPal, for instance, had to contend with a number of lawsuits brought by state attorneys general that claimed that PayPal was violating state banking regulations.

Section 10.1 ▶ REVIEW QUESTIONS

1. Describe the trends that are occurring in cash and noncash payments in the United States.
2. What types of e-payments should B2C merchants support?
3. What is the "chicken-and-egg" problem in e-payments?
4. Describe the factors that are critical for an e-payment method to achieve critical mass.

10.2 USING PAYMENT CARDS ONLINE

Payment cards are electronic cards that contain information that can be used for payment purposes. They come in three forms:

payment card
Electronic card that contains information that can be used for payment purposes.

▶ **Credit cards.** A credit card provides the holder with credit to make purchases up to a limit fixed by the card issuer. Credit cards rarely have an annual fee. Instead, holders are charged high interest rates—the annual percentage rate—on their average daily unpaid balances. Visa, MasterCard, and Europay are the predominant credit cards.

▶ **Charge cards.** The balance on a charge card is supposed to be paid in full upon receipt of the monthly statement. Technically, holders of a charge card receive a loan for 30 to 45 days equal to the balance of their statement. Such cards usually have annual fees. American Express's Green Card is the leading charge card, followed by the Diner's Club card.

▶ **Debit cards.** With a debit card, the money for a purchased item comes directly out of the holder's checking account (called a demand-deposit account). The actual transfer of funds from the holder's account to the merchant's takes place within one to two days. MasterCard, Visa, and Europay are the predominant debit cards.

PROCESSING CARDS ONLINE

authorization

Determines whether a buyer's card is active and whether the customer has sufficient funds.

settlement

Transferring money from the buyer's to the merchant's account.

The processing of card payments has two major phases: authorization and settlement. **Authorization** determines whether a buyer's card is active and whether the customer has sufficient available credit line or funds. **Settlement** involves the transfer of money from the buyer's to the merchant's account. The way in which these phases actually are performed varies somewhat depending on the type of payment card. It also varies by the configuration of the system used by the merchant to process payments.

There are three basic configurations for processing online payments. The EC merchant may:

▶ **Own the payment software.** A merchant can purchase a payment-processing module and integrate it with its other EC software. This module communicates with a payment gateway run by an acquiring bank or another third party.

▶ **Use a point of sale system (POS) operated by an acquirer.** Merchants can redirect cardholders to a POS run by an acquirer. The POS handles the complete payment process and directs the cardholder back to the merchant site once payment is complete. In this case, the merchant system only deals with order information. In this configuration, it is important to find an acquirer that handles multiple cards and payment instruments. If not, the merchant will need to connect with a multitude of acquirers.

▶ **Use a POS operated by a payment service provider.** Merchants can rely on servers operated by third parties known as **payment service providers (PSPs)**. In this case, the PSP connects with the appropriate acquirers. PSPs must be registered with the various card associations they support.

payment service provider (PSP)

A third-party service connecting a merchant's EC system to the appropriate acquiring bank or financial institution. PSPs must be registered with the various card associations they support.

For a given type of payment card and processing system, the processes and participants are essentially the same for offline (card present) and online (card not present) purchases. Exhibit 10.1 compares the steps involved in making a credit card purchase both online and offline. As the exhibit demonstrates, there is very little difference between the two.

Based on the processes outlined in Exhibit 10.1, the key participants in processing card payments online include the following:

▶ **Acquiring bank.** Offers a special account called an *Internet Merchant Account* that enables card authorization and payment processing.

▶ **Credit card association.** The financial institution providing card services to banks (e.g., Visa and MasterCard).

▶ **Customer.** The individual possessing the card.

▶ **Issuing bank.** The financial institution that provides the customer with a card.

▶ **Merchant.** A company that sells products or services.

▶ **Payment processing service.** The service that provides connectivity among merchants, customers, and financial networks, which enables authorization and payments. Usually these services are operated by companies such as CyberSource (cybersource.com).

▶ **Processor.** The data center that processes card transactions and settles funds to merchants.

FRAUDULENT CARD TRANSACTIONS

Although the processes used for authorizing and settling card payments offline and online are very similar, there is one substantial difference between the two. In the online world,

EXHIBIT 10.1 Credit Card Purchases: Online Versus Offline

Online Purchase	Offline Purchase
1. The *customer* decides to purchase a CD on the Web, adding it to the electronic shopping cart and going to the check-out page to enter his or her credit card information.	1. The *customer* selects a CD to purchase, takes it to the checkout counter, and hands his or her credit card to the sales clerk.
2. The *merchant* site receives the customer's information and sends the transaction information to its *payment processing service (PPS)*.	2. The *sales clerk* swipes the card and transfers transaction information to a *point-of-sale (POS)* terminal.
3. The PPS routes information to the *processor* (a large data center for processing transactions and settling funds to the merchant).	3. The POS terminal routes information to the *processor* via a dial-up connection.
4. The processor sends information to the *issuing bank* of the customer's credit card.	4. The processor transmits the credit card data and sales amount with a request for authorization of the sale to the *issuing bank* of the customer's credit card.
5. The issuing bank sends the transaction to the processor, either authorizing the payment or not.	5. If the cardholder has enough credit in his or her account to cover the sale, the issuing bank authorizes the transaction and generates an authorization code; if not, the sale is declined.
6. The processor routes the transaction result to the PPS.	6. The processor sends the transaction code back through the processor to the POS.
7. The PPS passes the results to the merchant.	7. The POS shows the outcome to the merchant.
8. The merchant accepts or rejects the transaction.	8. The merchant tells the customer the outcome of the transaction.

Sources: Courtesy of Visa International Service Association, PayPal (2004), and Lamond and Whitman (1996).

merchants are held liable for fraudulent transactions. In addition to the lost merchandise and shipping charges, merchants who accept fraudulent transactions can incur additional fees and penalties imposed by the card associations. However, these are not the only costs. There also are the costs associated with combating fraudulent transactions. These include the costs of tools and systems to review orders, the costs of manually reviewing orders, and the revenue that is lost from rejecting orders that are valid. In their 10th annual survey of fraudulent online card transactions, CyberSource (2009) indicated that managing online fraud continues to be a significant and growing problem for online merchants of all sizes.

For the past nine years, CyberSource has sponsored a survey to address the detection, prevention, and management of fraud perpetrated against online merchants. CyberSource's 2008 survey of 400 merchants documented the following trends (CyberSource 2009):

▶ Although the percentage of online revenues lost per merchant has declined slightly since 2004, the total dollars lost to fraud increased substantially, from $1.9 billion in 2003 to $4.0 billion in 2008. The rise was attributable to the increase in the amount of business that was being done online, which grew by 20 percent or more annually over the same time period.

▶ In 2008, merchants estimated that an average of 1.1 percent of their orders were fraudulent. This represented a slight decline from the previous year. The fraudulent orders resulted in merchants' crediting the real cardholder's account (a chargeback). The median value of these fraudulent orders was $200, which was 67 percent higher than the average value of valid orders.

▶ Fifty-two percent of the merchants surveyed accepted international orders outside the United States and Canada. These orders represented 17 percent of the sales for these merchants. The fraud rate for these orders was approximately 4 percent, or more than 3.5 times higher than the fraud rate for domestic orders.

▶ Certain merchants were more susceptible to fraud than others. This was due to a number of factors: the merchant's visibility on the Web, the steps the merchant had taken to combat fraud, the ease with which the merchant's products could be sold on the open market, and the merchant's size. Larger firms were less susceptible to fraud than smaller firms.

▶ Although overall security expenditures for online fraud detection remained the same from 2006 to 2007, the amount spent on manual review of orders increased over 30 percent, or by about $100 million. As the number of online orders continues to increase, this is not a viable long-term strategy for merchants.

In addition to tracking cyberfraud trends, the CyberSource surveys also have monitored the steps taken by merchants to combat fraud. In 2008, merchants used more tools than in the past to combat fraud. In 2008, the median number of tools used by merchants was 4.7, compared with 3 in 2003. Merchants are also spending more to combat fraud. The median amount spent to combat fraud in 2008 was 0.2 percent of online revenues. Most of the money was spent on review staff (51 percent), followed by third-party tools and services (25 percent) and internally developed tools (24 percent). The key tools used in combating fraud were:

Address Verification System (AVS)
Detects fraud by comparing the address entered on a Web page with the address information on file with the cardholder's issuing bank.

▶ **Address verification.** Approximately 80 percent of all merchants use the **Address Verification System (AVS)**, which compares the address entered on a Web page with the address information on file with the cardholder's issuing bank. This method results in a number of false positives, meaning that the merchant may reject a valid order. Cardholders often have new addresses or simply make mistakes in inputting numeric street addresses or zip codes. AVS is only available in the United States and Canada.

▶ **Manual review.** Over 80 percent of all merchants use the manual review method, which relies on staff to manually review suspicious orders. For small merchants with a small volume of orders, this is a reasonable method. For larger merchants, this method does not scale well, is expensive, and impacts customer satisfaction. In spite of these limitations, the percentage of merchants using this method is increasing, along with the percentage of items being reviewed. In 2008, the number of orders being reviewed was one in three, versus one in four in 2003.

▶ **Fraud screens and automated decision models.** Larger merchants (those generating over $25 million in revenue) often use fraud screens and automated decision models. These tools are based on automated rules that determine whether a transaction should be accepted, rejected, or suspended. A key element of this method is the ability of the merchant to easily change the rules to reflect changing trends in the fraud being perpetrated against the company.

card verification number (CVN)
Detects fraud by comparing the verification number printed on the signature strip on the back of the card with the information on file with the cardholder's issuing bank.

▶ **Card verification number (CVN).** Approximately 75 percent of all merchants use the **card verification number (CVN)** method, which compares the verification number printed on the signature strip on the back of the card with the information on file with the cardholder's issuing bank. However, if a fraudster possesses a stolen card, the number is in plain view.

▶ **Card association payer authentication services.** In the last couple of years, the card associations have developed a new set of payer identification services (e.g., Verified by Visa and MasterCard SecureCode). These services require cardholders to register with the systems and merchants to adopt and support both the existing systems and the new systems. In 2004, it was estimated that over 55 percent of merchants would be using this method by 2005. In reality, only 25 percent of merchants in the 2008 survey indicated that they had adopted this method.

▶ **Negative lists.** Thirty-eight percent of all merchants use negative lists. A negative list is a file that includes a customer's information (IP address, name, shipping/billing address, contact numbers, etc.) and the status of that customer. A customer's transaction is matched against this file and flagged if the customer is a known problem.

The overall impact of these tools is that merchants are rejecting a significant number of orders due to suspicion of fraud. In 2003, the average number of rejected orders was more than three for every fraudulent order accepted. This represented a rejection rate of 4 percent. The problem with rejection rates is that a number of the rejected orders are valid, resulting in lost revenue.

Section 10.2 ▶ REVIEW QUESTIONS

1. Describe the three types of payment cards.
2. What options does a merchant have in setting up an e-payment system?
3. List the major participants in processing cards online.
4. What costs does an online merchant incur if it submits a fraudulent card transaction?
5. Describe the major trends in fraudulent orders perpetrated against online merchants.
6. What steps are often taken by online merchants to combat fraudulent orders?

10.3 SMART CARDS

Outside North America, smart cards often are used in place of or in addition to traditional credit and debit cards. They also are used widely to support nonretail and nonfinancial applications. A smart card looks like a plastic payment card, but it is distinguished by the presence of an embedded microchip (see Exhibit 10.2). The embedded chip may be a microprocessor combined with a memory chip or just a memory chip with

smart card
An electronic card containing an embedded microchip that enables predefined operations or the addition, deletion, or manipulation of information on the card.

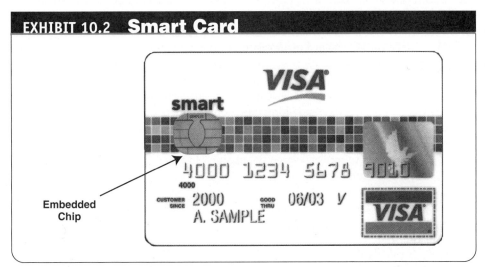

EXHIBIT 10.2   Smart Card

Source: Courtesy of Visa International Service Association.

nonprogrammable logic. Information on a microprocessor card can be added, deleted, or otherwise manipulated; a memory-chip card is usually a "read-only" card, similar to a credit card. Although the microprocessor is capable of running programs like a computer does, it is not a stand-alone computer. The programs and data must be downloaded from and activated by some other device (such as an ATM machine).

TYPES OF SMART CARDS

There are two distinct types of smart cards. The first type is a **contact card**, which is activated when it is inserted into a smart card reader. The second type of card is a **contactless (proximity) card**, meaning that the card only has to be within a certain proximity of a smart card reader to process a transaction. *Hybrid cards* combine both types of cards into one.

Contact smart cards have a small gold plate about one-half inch in diameter on the front. When the card is inserted into the smart card reader, the plate makes electronic contact and data are passed to and from the chip. Contact cards can have electronically programmable, read-only memory (EPROM) or electronically erasable, programmable, read-only memory (EEPROM). EPROM cards can never be erased. Instead, data are written to the available space on the card. When the card is full, it is discarded. EEPROM cards are erasable and modifiable. They can be used until they wear out or malfunction. Most contact cards are EEPROM.

In addition to the chip, a contactless card has an embedded antenna. Data and applications are passed to and from the card through the card's antenna to another antenna attached to a smart card reader or other device. Contactless cards are used for those applications in which the data must be processed very quickly (e.g., mass transit applications, such as paying bus or train fares) or when contact is difficult (e.g., security-entering mechanisms to buildings). Proximity cards usually work at short range, just a few inches. For some applications, such as payments at highway toll booths, the cards can operate at considerable distances.

With *hybrid* and *dual-interface* smart cards, the two types of card interfaces are merged into one. A hybrid smart card has two separate chips embedded in the card: contact and contactless. In contrast, a dual-interface, or combi, smart card has a single chip that supports both types of interfaces. The benefit of either card is that it eliminates the need to carry multiple cards to support the various smart card readers and applications.

With both types of cards, smart card readers are crucial to the operation of the system. Technically speaking, a smart card reader is actually a read/write device. The primary purpose of the **smart card reader** is to act as a mediator between the card and the host system that stores application data and processes transactions. Just as there are two basic types of cards, there are two types of smart card readers—*contact* and *proximity*—which match the particular type of card. Smart card readers can be transparent, requiring a host device to operate, or stand alone, functioning independently. Smart card readers are a key element in determining the overall cost of a smart card application. Although the cost of a single reader is usually low, the cost can be quite high when hundreds or thousands are needed to service a large population of users (e.g., all the passengers traveling on a metropolitan mass transit system).

Like computers, smart cards have an underlying operating system. A **smart card operating system** handles file management, security, input/output (I/O), and command execution and provides an application programming interface (API). Originally, smart card operating systems were designed to run on the specific chip embedded in the card. Today, smart cards are moving toward multiple and open application operating systems such as MULTOS (multos.com) and Java Card (java.sun.com/products/javacard). These operating systems enable new applications to be added during the life of the card.

contact card
A smart card containing a small gold plate on the face that when inserted in a smart card reader makes contact and passes data to and from the embedded microchip.

contactless (proximity) card
A smart card with an embedded antenna, by means of which data and applications are passed to and from a card reader unit or other device without contact between the card and the card reader.

smart card reader
Activates and reads the contents of the chip on a smart card, usually passing the information on to a host system.

smart card operating system
Special system that handles file management, security, input/output (I/O), and command execution and provides an application programming interface (API) for a smart card.

APPLICATIONS OF SMART CARDS

The worldwide use of smart cards is growing rapidly. Globally, an estimated 4 billion smart cards were shipped in 2008. This represented an 18 percent increase over the 3.3 billion cards shipped in 2007 (*Card Technology* 2007). The largest demand for smart cards continues to come from the Asia-Pacific region. The growth in smart card usage, which is somewhere between 20 and 30 percent per annum, is being driven by a variety of financial, transit, mobile phone, health care, and government applications. A general discussion of these applications can be found at the GlobalPlatform Web site (globalplatform.org). Within EC, smart cards are used in place of standard credit cards for general retail purchases and for transit fares.

Retail Purchases

The credit card associations and financial institutions are transitioning their traditional credit and debit cards to multiapplication smart cards. Of the 4 billion cards shipped in 2008, approximately 600 million were banking (credit and debit) smart cards. In many parts of the world, smart cards have reached mass-market adoption rates. This is especially true in Europe, where all bank cards are slated to be smart cards with strong authentication and digital signature capabilities by 2010.

In 2000, the European Commission established an initiative known as the Single Europe Payment Area (SEPA), encompassing 31 European countries. To bring this initiative to fruition, all the EU banks agreed to use the same basic bank card standard, enabling the use of credit and debit cards throughout the EU. The standard, EMV, is named after the three card associations that developed it (Europay, MasterCard, and Visa). It is based on smart cards with a microprocessor chip. The chip is capable of storing not only financial information, but other applications as well, such as strong authentication and digital signatures. The 31 countries have agreed to shift all their magnetic strip cards to EMV smart cards by December 2010. To date, over 50 percent of the cards have been migrated.

One benefit of smart cards versus standard cards is that they are more secure. Because they are often used to store more valuable or sensitive information (e.g., cash or medical records), smart cards often are secured against theft, fraud, or misuse. If someone steals a standard payment card, the number on the card is clearly visible, as is the owner's signature and security code. Although it may be hard to forge the signature, in many situations only the number (and security code) is required to make a purchase. The only protection cardholders have is that there usually are limits on how much they will be held liable for (e.g., in the United States it is $50). If someone steals a stored-value card (or the owner loses it), the original owner is out of luck.

However, if someone steals a smart card, the thief is usually out of luck (with the major exception of contactless, or "wave and go," cards used for retail purchases). Some smart cards show account numbers, but others do not. Before the card can be used, the holder may be required to enter a PIN that is matched with the card. Theoretically, it is possible to "hack" into a smart card. Most cards, however, now store information in encrypted form. The smart cards can also encrypt and decrypt data that is downloaded or read from the card. Because of these factors, the possibility of hacking into a smart card is classified as a "class 3" attack, which means that the cost of compromising the card far exceeds the benefits.

The other benefit of smart cards versus standard payment cards is that they can be extended with other payment services. In the retail arena, many of these services are aimed at those establishments where payments are usually made in cash and speed and convenience are important. This includes convenience stores, gas stations, fast-food or quick-service restaurants, and cinemas. Contactless payments exemplify this sort of value-added service.

A few years ago, the card associations began piloting contactless payment systems in retail operations where speed and convenience are crucial. All these systems utilize the existing POS and magnetic strip payment infrastructure used with traditional credit and debit cards. The only difference is that a special contactless smart card reader is required. To make a purchase, a cardholder simply waves his or her card near the terminal, and the terminal reads the financial information on the card. Data supplied by Bank of America supports the contention that contactless credit cards speed things along. The data indicate, for example, that the average contactless fast-food restaurant transaction takes 12.5 seconds, versus 26.7 seconds for the traditional credit card swipe and 33.7 seconds for cash.

In spite of their convenience, the overall uptake of contactless payment cards has been slow. MasterCard's PayPass (mastercard.com/aboutourcards/paypass.html) is a case in point. MasterCard PayPass is an EMV-compatible card that supports both magnetic strip and contactless payments. The card was introduced in 2003 in a market trial conducted in Orlando, Florida, with J.P. Morgan Chase, Citibank, and MBNA. The trial involved more than 16,000 cardholders and more than 60 retailers. The introduction of PayPass served as a catalyst to increase card usage and loyalty in the Orlando area. During the trial, MasterCard experienced an 18 percent active rate for previously inactive accounts. MasterCard also saw a 23 percent increase in transaction value, a 28 percent increase in total weekly spending, and a 12 percent month-over-month increase in transaction volumes at participating merchants.

Based on the success of this trial, as well as MasterCard survey data indicating that a substantial majority of consumers would be willing to use a contactless card if it were provided, MasterCard began a wider rollout of PayPass in 2005. Today, MasterCard PayPass can be used in over 20 countries and is accepted by more than 80,000 merchants worldwide. In spite of this rollout, to date, only a small fraction of financial institutions have issued the PayPass card. The same fate has also befallen Visa's payWave and American Express' ExpressPay. Worldwide, less than 10 percent of the banking smart cards issued in 2008 were contactless payment cards. Again, it is the same "chicken and egg" problem encountered by any new payment system.

Transit Fares

In major U.S. cities, commuters often have to drive to a parking lot, board a train, and then change to one or more subways or buses to arrive at work. If the whole trip requires a combination of cash and multiple types of tickets, this can be a major hassle. For those commuters who have a choice, the inconvenience plays a role in discouraging the use of public transportation. To eliminate the inconvenience, most major transit operators in the United States are implementing smart card fare-ticketing systems. In addition, the U.S. federal government provides incentives to employers to subsidize the use of public transportation by their employees. In the United States, the transit systems in Washington, DC; Baltimore; San Francisco; Oakland; Los Angeles; Chicago; San Diego; Seattle; Minneapolis; Houston; Boston; Philadelphia; Atlanta; and the New York/New Jersey area have all instituted smart card payment systems. Two of the largest implementations to date, Washington, DC's SmarTrip card and Boston's MBTA Charlie Card, have issued over 2.5 million and 1.4 million cards, respectively. The result will be the introduction of an estimated 15 million contactless smart cards and over 20,000 payment processing devices (Smart Card Alliance 2006).

Metropolitan transit operators are moving away from multiple, nonintegrated fare systems to systems that require only a single contactless card regardless of how many modes of transportation or how many transportation agencies or companies are involved. The SmarTrip program run by the Washington Metropolitan Area Transit Authority (WMATA) in the District of Columbia exemplifies this movement (wmata.com/fares/smartrip/). In 1999, WMATA was the first transportation system in the United States to employ smart cards. SmarTrip is a permanent, contactless, rechargeable fare card that can hold up to $300 in fare value. The card can be used with 17 different transit systems, including WMATA-operated parking lots, the Metrorail, Metrobuses, and other regional rail services. SmarTrip handles the complexities associated with the various systems, including zone-based and time-based fares, volume discounts, and bus-to-train and bus-to-bus transfers. To date, close to half a million SmarTrip cards have been issued, and more than one-third of Metrorail riders use the cards regularly.

The U.S. smart card transit programs are modeled after those used in Asia. Case 10.1 describes one of these—the TaiwanMoney Card—and Online File W10.2 discusses another Asian implementation. Like their Asian counterparts, some U.S. transit operators are looking to partner with retailers and financial institutions to combine their transit cards with payment cards to purchase goods and services such as snacks, bridge tolls, parking fees, or food in restaurants or grocery stores located near the transit stations.

In addition to handling transit fares, smart cards and other e-payment systems are being used for other transportation applications. For instance, Philadelphia has retooled all its 14,500 parking meters to accept payment from prepaid smart cards issued by the Philadelphia Parking Authority (philapark.org). Similarly, many of the major toll roads in the United States and elsewhere accept electronic payments rendered by devices called transponders that operate much like contactless smart cards.

CASE 10.1
EC Application
TAIWANMONEY CARD

In October 2005, the Kaohsiung City Government (KCG) in Taiwan began, as part of its e-City initiative, the Smart Transport Card Project. Similar to other municipalities in Asia, KCG was interested in utilizing smart card technology to enable contactless payments throughout its transport system. Unlike other municipalities, however, KCG was not interested in introducing a specialized transport card. Typically, transport cards are purchased from a transport authority, and their primary function is to pay transport fares. Occasionally, they can be used at other venues. For example, the Hong Kong metro card known as the Octopus Card can be used at fast-food restaurants and convenience stores. Instead, KCG decided to partner with MasterCard to produce a single card that could be used for both retail and transport payments. In this way, KCG could avoid many of the problems associated with issuing the cards, managing the overall payment systems, and

instituting specialized legislation dictating how the cards could be used.

The card, which is produced by MasterCard for KCG, is called the TaiwanMoney Card. Technically, the card was MasterCard's first OneSMART PayPass Chip Combi Card. The card complies with the EMV standard, making it the first EMV-based card to support transport payments. Although KCG is the owner of the Smart Transport Card Project, the cards are marketed, issued, and serviced by Cathay United Bank, E. Sun Bank, and Bank of Kaohsiung.

The KCG system, which is operated by Mondex Taiwan, supports two types of cards. There are *stand-alone cards* for children and nonlocal and nonbanked customers that are used for single trips. The second card is *Payment Plus*. This type of card is for existing MasterCard holders and new account customers. It is a dual-branded MasterCard

(*continued*)

CASE 10.1   (continued)

credit card or debit card that can be used for both transportation and shopping.

In order for the transportation system to support the cards, contactless TaiwanMoney Card readers had to be installed on all buses. In order for retailers to support the cards, their POS terminals had to be upgraded to accept the TaiwanMoney or MasterCard PayPass contactless cards.

By the end of 2005, there were approximately 100,000 cardholders using the TaiwanMoney Cards to pay fares on buses running in Kaohsiung and six other cities in southern Taiwan. They were also using the cards to make purchases at 5,000 convenience stores, supermarkets, and other retail outlets in the region.

Following the success of the 2005 pilot project, a full-scale rollout of the TaiwanMoney card was initiated

in 2007. Because the card is essentially a MasterCard PayPass card, it can be used anywhere PayPass can be used.

Sources: Chen (2008), Hendry (2007), and Tan (2007).

Questions

1. What is the TaiwanMoney Card?
2. Why did KCG decide to use a smart money card for its transportation system rather than a specialized transportation card?
3. What change was required for the PayPass card to work with KCG's metro system?

Section 10.3 ▶ REVIEW QUESTIONS

1. What is a smart card? Contact card? Contactless card?
2. What is a smart card operating system?
3. Describe the use of smart cards in metropolitan transportation systems.

10.4   STORED-VALUE CARDS

stored-value card
A card that has monetary value loaded onto it and that is usually rechargeable.

What looks like a credit or debit card, acts like a credit or debit card, but isn't a credit or debit card? The answer is a **stored-value card**. As the name implies, the monetary value of a stored-value card is preloaded on the card. From a physical and technical standpoint, a stored-value card is indistinguishable from a regular credit or debit card. It is plastic and has a magnetic strip on the back, although it may not have the cardholder's name printed on it. The magnetic strip stores the monetary value of the card. This distinguishes a stored-value card from a smart card. With smart cards, the chip stores the value. Consumers can use stored-value cards to make purchases, offline or online, in the same way that they use credit and debit cards—relying on the same networks, encrypted communications, and electronic banking protocols. What is different about a stored-value card is that anyone can obtain one without regard to prior financial standing or having an existing bank account as collateral.

Stored-value cards come in two varieties: *closed loop* and *open loop*. Closed-loop, or single-purpose, cards are issued by a specific merchant or merchant group (e.g., a shopping mall) and can only be used to make purchases from that merchant or merchant group. Mall cards, store cards, gift cards, and prepaid telephone cards are all examples of closed-loop cards. Gift cards represent a strong growth area, especially in the United States. Until 2008, spending on gift cards was growing at a rapid rate. In 2008, spending retreated to 2006 levels. For example, during the 2008 holiday season, gift card spending in the United States fell 6 percent, from a high of $26 billion in 2007 to $24.9 billion. The average spent per card dropped from approximately $156 to $147 during that time. The 2008 figures were slightly above the 2006 figures.

In contrast, an open-loop, or multipurpose, card can be used to make debit transactions at a variety of retailers. Open-loop cards also can be used for other purposes, such as receiving direct deposits or withdrawing cash from ATM machines. Financial institutions with card-association branding, such as Visa or MasterCard, issue some open-loop cards. They can be used anywhere that the branded cards are accepted. Payroll cards, government benefit cards, and prepaid debit cards are all examples of open-loop cards.

Stored-value cards may be acquired in a variety of ways. Employers or government agencies may issue them as payroll cards or benefit cards in lieu of checks or direct deposits. Merchants or merchant groups sell and load gift cards. Various financial institutions and nonfinancial outlets sell preloaded cards by telephone, online, or in person. Cash, bank wire transfers, money orders, cashiers' checks, other credit cards, or direct payroll or government deposits fund preloaded cards.

Stored-value cards have been and continue to be marketed heavily to the "unbanked" and "overextended." Approximately 100 million adults in the United States do not have credit cards or bank accounts—people with low incomes, young adults, seniors, immigrants, minorities, and others. Among those with credit cards, 40 percent are running close to their credit limits. The expectation is that these groups will be major users of prepaid cards in the future.

For example, individuals in the United States transferred over $12 billion to individuals in Mexico. Instead of sending money orders or cash, programs like the EasySend card from Branch Banking and Trust (BB&T) provide a secure alternative to transferring money to relatives and friends. With the EasySend program, an individual establishes a banking account, deposits money in the account, and mails the EasySend card to a relative or friend, who can then withdraw the cash from an ATM machine. When it was introduced in 2004, EasySend was focused primarily on the Hispanic community. Today, it is used by immigrant populations all over the world.

In a slightly different vein, the MasterCard MuchMusic and Visa Buxx cards, which are described in detail in Online File W10.3, provide young people with a prepaid, preloaded card alternative to credit cards or cash. Among other things, these alternatives provide a relatively risk-free way to teach kids fiscal responsibility.

Employers who are using payroll cards as an extension of their direct deposit programs are driving the growth of the prepaid, preloaded card market. Like direct deposit, payroll cards can reduce administrative overhead substantially. Payroll cards are especially useful to companies in the health care and retail sectors and other industries where the workforce is part time or transient and less likely to have bank accounts.

Section 10.4 ▶ REVIEW QUESTIONS

1. What is a closed-loop stored-value card? What is an open-loop card?
2. Identify the major markets for stored-value cards.

10.5 E-MICROPAYMENTS

Consider the following online shopping scenarios:

▶ A customer goes to an online music store and purchases a single song that costs $0.99.

▶ A person goes online to a leading newspaper or news journal (such as *Forbes* or *BusinessWeek*) and purchases (downloads) a copy of an archived news article for $1.50.

▶ A person goes to an online gaming company, selects a game, and plays it for 30 minutes. The person owes the company $3.00 for the playing time.

▶ A person goes to a Web site selling digital images and clip art. The person purchases a couple of images at a cost of $0.80.

These are all examples of **e-micropayments**, which are small online payments, usually under $5. From the viewpoint of many vendors, credit and debit cards do not work well for

e-micropayments
Small online payments, typically under $10.

such small payments. Vendors who accept credit cards typically must pay a minimum transaction fee that ranges from $0.25 to $0.35, plus 2 to 3 percent of the purchase price. The same is true for debit cards, where the fixed transaction fees are larger even though there are no percentage charges. These fees are relatively insignificant for card purchases over $5, but can be cost-prohibitive for smaller transactions. Even if the transaction costs were less onerous, a substantial percentage of micropayment purchases are made by individuals younger than 18, many of whom do not have credit or debit cards.

Regardless of the vendor's point of view, there is substantial evidence, at least in the offline world, that consumers are willing to use their credit or debit cards for purchases under $5. A random sample telephone survey conducted in 2006 by Ipsos Insight and Peppercoin, an e-micropayment company that was acquired by Chockstone in 2007, examined consumers' spending habits for low-priced items. Based on the survey, more than 67 million Americans had used their credit cards in the 30 days prior to the survey to purchase items priced at $5 or less. For the most part, these purchases were made at convenience stores, quick-service restaurants, and coffee shops or were for subway or other transportation tolls.

In the online world, the evidence suggests that consumers are interested in making small-value purchases, but the tie to credit or debit card payments is less direct. For example, in 2008 Apple's iTunes music store celebrated its 5 billionth download. A substantial percentage of these were downloads of single songs at $0.99 a piece. Although most of iTunes' customers paid for these downloads with a credit or debit card, the payments were not on a per-transaction basis. Instead, iTunes customers set up accounts and Apple then aggregated multiple purchases before charging a user's credit or debit card. Other areas where consumers have shown a willingness to purchase items under $5 are cell phone ringtones and ringback tones and online games. The market for ringtones and ringback tones is in the billions of dollars. The download of both types of tones is charged to the consumer's cell phone bill. Similarly, the market for online games is in the billions of dollars. Like songs and tones, the download of a game is usually charged to the consumer's account, which is, in turn, paid by a credit or debit card.

As far back as 2000, a number of companies have attempted to address the perceived market opportunity by providing e-micropayment solutions that circumvent the fees associated with credit and debit cards. For the most part, the history of these companies is one of unfulfilled promises and outright failure. DigiCash, First Virtual, Cybercoin, Millicent, and Internet Dollar are some of the e-micropayment companies that went bankrupt during the dot-com crash. A number of factors played a role in their demise, including the fact that early users of the Internet thought that digital content should be free.

More recently, Bitpass declared on January 2007 that it was going out of business. As late as fall 2006, Bitpass launched a digital wallet service that enabled consumers to store online downloads of digital content and the payment method used to fund their accounts (i.e., credit cards, PayPal, or Automated Clearing House debits). Bitpass succeeded in partnering with a large number of smaller vendors, as well as a number of larger companies, such as Disney Online and ABC, Inc. However, it purposely focused on the sale of digital content rather than branching out into other markets. Its narrow focus was probably a major factor in its demise.

Currently, there are five basic micropayment models that do not depend solely or directly on credit or debit cards and that have enjoyed some amount of success. Some of these are better suited for offline payments than online payments, although there is nothing that precludes the application of any of the models to the online world. The models include the following (D'Agostino 2006):

- **Aggregation.** Payments from a single consumer are batched together and processed only after a certain time period has expired (20 business days) or a certain monetary threshold (e.g., $10) is reached. This is the model used by Apple's iTunes. This model is well suited for vendors with a lot of repeat business.

▶ **Direct payment.** Micropayments are added to a monthly bill for existing services, such as a phone bill. This is the model used by the cellular companies for ringtone downloads. The payment service provider PaymentOne (paymentone.com) provides a network and e-commerce platform that enable consumers to add purchases of any size to their phone bills. A similar service is offered by Paymo (paymo.com) in 39 countries around the world.

▶ **Stored value.** Up-front payments are made to a debit account, and then purchases are deducted as they are made. Offline vendors (e.g., Starbucks) often use this model, and music-download services use variants of this model.

▶ **Subscriptions.** A single payment covers access to content for a defined period of time. Online gaming companies often use this model, and a number of online newspapers and journals (e.g., *Wall Street Journal*) also use it.

▶ **À la carte.** Vendors process purchases as they occur and rely on the volume of purchases to negotiate lower credit and debit card processing fees. The Golden Tee Golf video game uses this model, and quick-service restaurants (QSRs) such as McDonald's and Wendy's also use it.

In the past few years, micropayments have come to represent a growth opportunity for credit card companies, because credit cards are being used increasingly as a substitute for cash. In response, both Visa and MasterCard have lowered their fees, especially for vendors such as McDonald's with high transaction volumes. In August 2005, PayPal also entered the micropayment market when it announced a new alternative fee structure of 5 percent plus $0.05 per transaction. This is in contrast to its standard fees of 1.9 to 2.9 percent plus $0.30 per transaction. If a PayPal vendor is being charged at a rate of 1.9 percent plus $0.30, then the alternative fee of 5 percent plus $0.05 will be cheaper for any item that costs $7 or less (you can do the math). It is $12 or less for 2.9 percent plus the $0.30 rate. Overall, the movement of the credit card companies and PayPal into the micropayment market does not bode well for those companies that provide specialized software and services for e-micropayments. In the long run, the credit card companies and PayPal will dominate this market. One exception, which is discussed in this chapter's closing case, is the online social gaming world. Here, there are a number of new micropayment entrants focused solely on social networks, not the broader micropayment market.

Section 10.5 ▶ REVIEW QUESTIONS

1. What is a micropayment?
2. List some of the situations where e-micropayments can be used.
3. Outside of using credit or debit cards, what are some of the alternative ways that an online merchant can handle micropayments?

10.6 E-CHECKING

As noted in Section 10.1, in the United States paper checks are the only payment instrument that is being used less frequently now than five years ago (Simon 2007). In contrast, e-check usage is growing rapidly. In 2007, the use of online e-checks grew by 27 percent over the previous year, reaching 1.74 billion transactions. Based on a CyberSource survey (2008) of Web merchants, this percentage will continue to grow. Web merchants hope that e-checks will raise sales by reaching consumers who do not have credit cards or who are unwilling to provide credit card numbers online. According to CyberSource, online merchants that implement e-checks experience a 3 to 8 percent increase in sales, on average.

An **e-check** is the electronic version or representation of a paper check. E-checks contain the same information as a paper check, can be used wherever paper checks are used, and

e-check
A legally valid electronic version or representation of a paper check.

are based on the same legal framework. An e-check works essentially the same way a paper check works, but in pure electronic form with fewer manual steps. With an online e-check purchase, the buyer simply provides the merchant with his or her account number, the nine-digit bank ABA routing number, the bank account type, the name on the bank account, and the transaction amount. The account number and routing number are found at the bottom of the check in the magnetic ink character recognition (MICR) numbers and characters.

E-checks rely on current business and banking practices and can be used by any business that has a checking account, including small and midsize businesses that may not be able to afford other forms of electronic payments (e.g., credit and debit cards). E-checks or their equivalents also can be used with in-person purchases. In this case, the merchant takes a paper check from the buyer at the point of purchase, uses the MICR information and the check number to complete the transaction, and then voids and returns the check to the buyer (see Case 10.2 for a complete description of the process).

CASE 10.2
EC Application
TO POP OR BOC: DIGITAL CHECKS IN THE OFFLINE WORLD

The use of e-checks is growing in the online world. Paradoxically, the same is true in the offline world, although it is occurring at a slower rate. First, evidence suggests that the use of a special NACHA system known as Purchase Order Processing (POP) is on the uptake. Second, another NACHA system, Back-Office Order Conversion (BOC), went into effect in March 2007. With both systems, merchants convert checks written by consumers into the equivalent of e-checks and process them as ACH debits. The difference between the two systems is whether the check is converted at the POS by a cashier or converted after the sale by other staff in the back office.

The traditional processes used in handling paper checks written by consumers to make purchases in a store involve a number of steps and intermediaries (as many as 28). At a minimum, the checks taken by cashiers are collected periodically throughout the day. After collection, back-office personnel process them. Once this is done, an armored car usually takes them from the store and delivers them to the store's bank. The store's bank processes them and sends them to a clearinghouse. From the clearinghouse, they move to the customer's bank. Not only is this time consuming, but it is also costly. Statistics show that it costs companies $1.25 to $1.55 to handle a paper check. This is in comparison to the administrative costs for an e-check, which can be as low as $0.10 per transaction. Based on these figures, any company stands to save a substantial amount of

money by streamlining these traditional processes. This is where POP and BOC come into play.

The Gap, Walmart, and Old Navy are some of the companies that have instituted POP. With POP, consumer checks are converted to ACH transactions at the time of the sale. When a customer writes a check for a purchase at a POS device, an MICR reader scans the check to capture the check details. The reader either keys or inserts the payment amount and the payee name at the time of purchase. At this point, the customer signs a written authorization. The cashier then voids the check and returns it to the customer with a signed receipt. Eligible transactions pass through the ACH system, and a record of payment appears on the customer's bank statement.

POP has a number of benefits:

▶ Back-office and check-handling costs are substantially reduced.
▶ Consumer payments are received more quickly.
▶ Availability of funds is improved.
▶ Notification of insufficient funds happens sooner.

Although POP saves money, it also has a number of costs including:

▶ It requires specialized readers for each checkout counter.
▶ Cashiers need special training to convert the checks to ACH transactions at the POS.
▶ The authorization process can be cumbersome and confusing to consumers.
▶ It slows the purchase process.

(continued)

CASE 10.2   (continued)

For these reasons, some critics suggest that BOC is a better alternative for the average merchant.

With BOC, the customer experience is similar to the traditional process. The customer writes a check for a purchase. The clerk either accepts or rejects the check after the merchant's verification service or guarantee provider verifies it. This process does not require explicit customer authorization to convert the check to an electronic form. Once the checks are collected and moved to the back office, they are scanned into an ACH file and processed electronically. In this way, a merchant only needs one or two scanners and a few personnel to handle the process.

Kohl's, a well-known clothing retailer, began implementing BOC in September 2008. Its implementation is based on an outsourced solution called SPIN from Solutran (*solutran.com*). The solution eliminates all manual check deposits. Solutran provides the facilities required to convert a check to a form of electronic settlement, to create and maintain images of the check, to generate an electronic deposit file, and to submit it to a financial institute. None of these processes require specialized equipment at the POS. The solution eventually will be rolled out across all of Kohl's 957 locations.

Sources: *Business Wire* (2008) and Robb (2007).

Questions

1. What does POC stand for, and how does it work?
2. What does BOC stand for, and how does it work?
3. What are the advantages and disadvantages of POC?

Most businesses rely on third-party software to handle e-check payments. Fiserv (fiserv.com), Chase Paymentech (paymentech.com), and Authorize.Net (authorize.net) are some of the major vendors of software and systems that enable an online merchant to accept and process electronic checks directly from a Web site. For the most part, these software offerings work in the same way regardless of the vendor.

The system shown in Exhibit 10.3 is based on Authorize.Net and is typical of the underlying processes used to support e-checks. Basically, it is a seven-step process. First,

EXHIBIT 10.3   Processing E-Checks with Authorize.Net

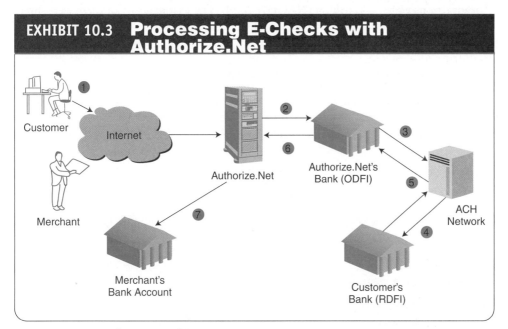

Source: Authorize.Net®. "eCheck.Net® Operating Procedures and Users Guide," October 28, 2004. *Authorize.net/files/echecknetuserguide.pdf*. Copyright 2004. Authorize.Net and eCheck.Net are registered trademarks of Lightbridge, Inc.

the merchant receives written or electronic authorization from a customer to charge his or her bank account (step 1). Next, the merchant securely transmits the transaction information to the Authorize.Net Payment Gateway server (step 2). The transaction is accepted or rejected based on criteria defined by the Payment Gateway. If accepted, Authorize.Net formats the transaction information and sends it as an ACH transaction to its bank (called the Originating Depository Financial Institution, or ODFI) with the rest of the transactions received that day (step 3). The ODFI receives transaction information and passes it to the ACH Network for settlement. The Automated Clearing House (ACH) Network uses the bank account information provided with the transaction to determine the bank that holds the customer's account (which is known as the Receiving Depository Financial Institution, or RDFI) (step 4). The ACH Network instructs the RDFI to charge or refund the customer's account (the customer is the receiver). The RDFI passes funds from the customer's account to the ACH Network (step 5). The ACH Network relays the funds to the ODFI (Authorize.Net's bank). The ODFI passes any returns to Authorize.Net (step 6). After the funds' holding period, Authorize.Net initiates a separate ACH transaction to deposit the e-check proceeds into the merchant's bank account (step 7).

Automated Clearing House (ACH) Network A nationwide batch-oriented electronic funds transfer system that provides for the interbank clearing of electronic payments for participating financial institutions.

As Exhibit 10.3 illustrates, the processing of e-checks in the United States relies quite heavily on the **Automated Clearing House (ACH) Network**. The ACH Network is a nationwide batch-oriented electronic funds transfer (EFT) system that provides for the interbank clearing of electronic payments for participating financial institutions. The Federal Reserve and Electronic Payments Network act as ACH operators, which transmit and receive ACH payment entries. ACH entries are of two sorts: credit and debit. An ACH credit entry credits a receiver's account. For example, when a consumer pays a bill sent by a company, the company is the receiver whose account is credited. In contrast, a debit entry debits a receiver's account. For instance, if a consumer preauthorizes a payment to a company, then the consumer is the receiver whose account is debited. In 2008, the ACH Network handled an estimated 15 billion transactions worth $30 trillion (NACHA 2009). The vast majority of these were direct payment and deposit entries (e.g., direct-deposit payroll). Only 2.1 billion of these entries were Web-based ones, although this represented a 20 percent increase from 2007 to 2008.

E-check processing provides a number of benefits:

▶ It reduces the merchant's administrative costs by providing faster and less paper-intensive collection of funds.

▶ It improves the efficiency of the deposit process for merchants and financial institutions.

▶ It speeds the checkout process for consumers.

▶ It provides consumers with more information about their purchases on their account statements.

▶ It reduces the float period and the number of checks that bounce because of nonsufficient funds (NSFs).

Section 10.6 ▶ REVIEW QUESTIONS

1. What is an e-check?
2. Briefly describe how third-party e-check payment systems work.
3. What is the ACH?
4. List the benefits of e-checking.

MANAGERIAL ISSUES

Some managerial issues related to this chapter are as follows.

1. **What payment methods should your B2C site support?** The majority of B2C trades are paid by credit card (about 60 percent). EFT is the next most popular payment method (about 30 percent). Most B2C sites use more than one payment gateway to support customers' preferred payment methods. Companies that only accept credit cards rule out a number of potential segments of buyers (e.g., teenagers, non-U.S. customers, and customers who cannot or do not want to use credit cards online). EFT, e-checks, stored-value cards, and PayPal are some possible alternatives to credit cards. The e-check is not used at all in Asia, because it is not an efficient method in the electronic era; thus, selecting a globally acceptable payment method is important for the globalization of EC.

2. **What e-micropayment strategy should your e-marketplace support?** If your EC site deals with items priced less than $10, credit cards are not a viable solution. Many digital-content products cost less than $1. For small-value products, e-micropayments should be supported. Fees may be taken from a prepaid account that is tied to a buyer's bank account or credit card, or the fee may be charged to the buyer's cell phone bill. The use of stored-value smart cards on the Internet has emerged, but has not widely penetrated because buyers need to install the card reader/writer. Your company should support multiple options so that customers can choose their preferred payment method.

3. **What payment methods should the C2C marketplace support?** In C2C sites like eBay, an e-mail payment method such as PayPal is popular. An alternative secure payment service is the escrow service. A buyer pays the e-market operator, and the e-market operator pays the seller once the delivery is confirmed by the buyer. The Internet Auction Corporation site, the leading auctioneer in Korea, which was acquired by eBay, supports an escrow service for the payment of successful bids. The reason it provides the service is because PayPal restricts Korean customers from making purchases with PayPal. However, PayPal does allow Koreans to receive payment for goods they have sold. The bottom line is that it is important to understand popular payment methods in particular markets.

4. **Should we outsource our payment gateway service?** It takes time, skill, money, software, and hardware to integrate the payment systems of all the parties involved in processing any sort of e-payment. For this reason, even a business that runs its own EC site outsources the e-payment service. Many third-party vendors provide payment gateways designed to handle the interactions among the various financial institutions that operate in the background of an e-payment system. Also, if a Web site is hosted by a third party (e.g., Yahoo! Store), an e-payment service will be provided.

5. **How secure are e-payments?** Security and fraud continue to be major issues in making and accepting e-payments of all kinds. This is especially true with regard to the use of credit cards for online purchases. B2C merchants are employing a wide variety of tools (e.g., address verification and other authentication services) to combat fraudulent orders. These and other measures that are employed to ensure the security of e-payments have to be part of a broader security scheme that weighs risks against issues such as the ease of use and the fit within the overall business context.

6. **What is the required security to use Internet banking?** EFT is one of the primary methods of electronic payment, thus Internet banking is one of the most important entities for EC. In Korea, digital certificates based on public key infrastructure are required for all financial transactions; thus, virtually all Internet bank users have digital certificates. Today, most certificates are stored on PCs. However, certificates are increasingly being stored in smart cards or cell phone chips. In addition, two-factor authentication is required for bank account access in many countries; so other authentication schemes have been developed to complement password-authentication measures.

SUMMARY

In this chapter, you learned about the following EC issues as they relate to the chapter's learning objectives.

1. **Payment revolution.** Cash and checks are no longer kings. Debit and credit cards now rule—both online and offline. This means that online B2C businesses need to support debit and credit card purchases. In international markets outside of Western Europe, buyers often favor other forms of e-payment (e.g., bank transfers). With the exception of PayPal, virtually all the alternatives to charge cards have failed. None have gained enough traction to overcome the "chicken and egg" problem. Their failure to gain critical mass has resulted from the confluence of a variety of factors (e.g., they required specialized hardware or setup, or they failed to mesh with existing systems).

2. **Using payment cards online.** The processing of online card payments is essentially the same as it is for brick-and-mortar stores and involves essentially the same players and the same systems—banks, card associations, payment processing services, and the like. This is one of the reasons why payment cards predominate in the online world. The major difference is that the rate of fraudulent orders is much higher online. Surveys, such as those conducted annually by CyberSource, indicate that merchants have adopted a wide variety of methods over the past few years to combat fraudulent orders, including address verification, manual review, fraud screens and decision models, card verification numbers, card association authentication services, and negative files. In the same vein, some consumers have turned to virtual or single-use credit cards to avoid using their actual credit card numbers online.

3. **Smart cards.** Smart cards look like credit cards but contain embedded chips for manipulating data and have large memory capacity. Cards that contain microprocessor chips can be programmed to handle a wide variety of tasks. Other cards have memory chips to which data can be written and from which data can be read. Most memory cards are disposable, but others—smart cards—can hold large amounts of data and are rechargeable. Smart cards have been and will be used for a number of purposes, including contactless retail payments, paying for mass transit services, identifying cardholders for government services, securing physical and network access, and storing health care data and verifying eligibility for health care and other government services. Given the sensitive nature of much of the data on smart cards, public key encryption and other cryptographic techniques are used to secure their contents.

4. **Stored-value cards.** A stored-value card is similar in appearance to a credit or debit card. The monetary value of a stored-value card is housed in a magnetic strip on the back of the card. Closed-loop stored-value cards are issued for a single purpose by a specific merchant (e.g., a Starbucks gift card). In contrast, open-loop stored-value cards are more like standard credit or debit cards and can be used for multiple purposes (e.g., a payroll card). Those segments of the population without credit cards or bank accounts—people with low incomes, young adults, seniors, and minorities—are spurring the substantial growth of stored-value cards. Specialized cards, such as EasySend, make it simple for immigrant populations to transfer funds to family members in other countries. Similarly, specialized cards, such as MasterCard's MuchMusic, provide teens and preteens with prepaid debit cards that function like standard credit or debit cards while helping parents monitor and maintain control over spending patterns.

5. **E-micropayments.** When an item or service being sold online costs less than $5, credit cards are too costly for sellers. A number of other e-payment systems have been introduced to handle these micropayment situations. For the most part, they have failed. Yet, ample evidence indicates that consumers are interested in using their credit and debit cards for small-value online purchases (e.g., songs on iTunes, online games, and ringtone sales). In response, a number of newer micropayment models, such as aggregated purchases, have been developed to reduce the fees associated with credit and debit cards.

6. **E-checking.** E-checks are the electronic equivalent of paper checks. They are handled in much the same way as paper checks and rely quite heavily on the ACH Network. E-checks offer a number of benefits, including speedier processing, reduced administrative costs, more efficient deposits, reduced float period, and fewer "bounced" checks. These factors have resulted in the rapid growth of e-check usage. The rapid growth is also being spurred by the use of e-checks for in-store purchases. Purchase Order Processing (POP) and Back-Office Order Conversion (BOC) are two systems, established by the NACHA, that enable retailers to convert paper checks used for in-store purchases to ACH debits (i.e., e-checks) without the need to process the checks using traditional procedures.

KEY TERMS

QUESTIONS FOR DISCUSSION BY INDIVIDUAL STUDENTS

1. Paymo recently introduced a system enabling buyers to charge their purchases to their cell phone accounts. Do you think Paymo's system will succeed? What factors will play a major role in its success or failure?

2. A textbook publisher is interested in selling individual book chapters on the Web. What types of e-payment methods would you recommend to the publisher? What sorts of problems will the publisher encounter with the recommended methods?

3. Recently, a merchant who accepts online credit card payments has experienced a wave of fraudulent orders. What steps should the merchant take to combat the fraud?

4. A retail clothing manufacturer is considering e-payments for both its suppliers and its buyers. What sort of e-payment method should it use to pay for office supplies? How should it pay suppliers of raw materials? How should its customers—both domestic and international clothing retailers—pay?

5. A metropolitan area wants to provide riders of its public transportation system with the ability to pay transit fares, as well as make retail purchases, using a single contactless smart card. What sorts of problems will it encounter in setting up the system, and what types of problems will the riders encounter in using the cards?

TOPICS FOR CLASS DISCUSSION

1. Apple's iTunes clearly dominates the online music business. In the long run, which company has the best chance of dominating the e-book business, Google, Amazon.com, or one of the other sellers like Barnes & Noble? Explain.

2. If you were running an online retail store would you permit purchases with e-checks? Why or why not?

3. Why is the marketplace for electronic payment systems so volatile? Is there a need for some other form of electronic payment?

4. Besides e-books and online music, what are some of the other places where e-micropayments could be used?

INTERNET EXERCISES

1. Use various online sources to research the dispute involving the Authors' Guild, various book publishers (e.g., Penguin), and Google over Google's Book Search Library Project. Describe some of the details of the settlement that was reached among these parties.

2. A number of years ago, eBay offered a payment system called Billpoint. It was a head-to-head competitor with PayPal. Use online sources to research why PayPal succeeded and Billpoint failed. Write a report based on your findings.

3. Select a major retail B2C merchant in the United States and one outside of North America. Detail the similarities and differences in the e-payment systems they offer. According to CyberSource's "Insider's Guide to ePayment Management" (cybersource.com/cgi-bin/pages/prep.cgi?page=/promo/InsidersGuide2008/index.html), what other payment systems could the sites offer?

4. Download "Transit and Contactless Financial Payment: New Opportunities for Collaboration and Convergence" from smartcardalliance.org//pages/publications-transit-financial. What are the key requirements for an automated fare-collection system? Based on the report, what type of payment system did the Utah Transit Authority (UTA) pilot?

What factors helped determine the type of system to be piloted? How did the pilot work? What was the role of contactless payment in the UTA system (if any)?

5. Kohl's utilizes Solutran's SPIN for its BOC system. So does Walgreens. Based on information provided at Solutran's Web site (solutran.com) and information found in online articles about the system, what sorts of capabilities and benefits does the system provide? What is unique about the system?

6. Go to nacha.org. What is NACHA? What is its role? What is the ACH? Who are the key participants in an ACH e-payment?

TEAM ASSIGNMENTS AND PROJECTS

1. Select some B2C sites that cater to teens and others that cater to older consumers. Have team members visit these sites. What types of e-payment methods do they provide? Do the methods used differ based on the target market? What other types of e-payment would you recommend for the various sites and why?

2. Write a report comparing smart card applications in two or more European and/or Asian countries. In the report, discuss whether those applications would succeed in North America.

3. Have one team represent MasterCard PayPass and another represent Visa payWave. The task of each team is to convince a company that its product is superior.

4. Have each team member interview three to five people who have made a purchase or sold an item via an online auction. Find out how they paid. What security and privacy concerns did they have regarding the payment? Is there an ideal payment method?

Closing Case

FREEMIUMS IN THE SOCIAL GAMING WORLD

Social games played on sites like Facebook and MySpace are the hottest part of the game industry. The market for social games has been dominated by three companies: Zynga (*zynga.com*), Playdom (*playdom.com*), and Playfish (*playfish.com*). In November 2009, Electronic Arts (*ea.com*) acquired Playfish for $300 million in cash and stock and guaranteed another $100 million in bonus payouts if certain milestones were met by 2012. A short time later in December 2009, Digital Sky

Technologies (*dst-global.com*), a Russian firm with offices in Moscow and London, bought a $180 million stake in Zynga. Based on this investment, as well as other investments in the firm, many financial analysts put Zynga's market share worth somewhere between $1.5 and $3.0 billion.

To the casual observer, these valuations seem astounding. It is the case that social games are simpler than the average video game and take much less time to play. It is also the case that they have expanded the game audience beyond traditional video gamers who tend to be young males. Yet, from an economic standpoint, the major difference between social games and video games is that the former are free. If players don't have to pay, where does the return on investment (ROI) for companies like Electronic Arts and investors like DST come from? The answer lies in micropayments.

The Solution

In 2007 Facebook launched a platform that enabled software developers to create applications for the site. Currently, the site has tens of thousands of applications. Similarly, MySpace, which relies on Google's OpenSocial platform, has 4,500 applications available to users. Today the most popular application category for both of these social networks is social gaming. On Facebook, for example, there are nine games that have more than 12 million active players per month. This is more than the number of monthly players for *World of Warcraft*, the most popular online game. Of course, they pay to play. Among the top 10 most popular social games on Facebook, Zynga has three offerings—*Farmville, Mafia Wars*, and *Café Word*—with a combined audience of over 105 active players per month, while Playfish has two offerings—*Pet Society* and *Restaurant City*—which has 60 million active users per month.

If it doesn't cost anything to play a social game, then how does the game company make its money. One way is with advertising. Either continually or at various times during the game, ads can be displayed. Just as the advertising firms do with the search engine companies or other Web sites, the game companies can either be paid for "impressions" or "clicks." Historically, advertising revenues have been very low for all kinds of applications on Facebook, MySpace, or any of the other social networks. It is especially true for social games because advertising firms like to pay when a user clicks on an advertisement rather than paying for simply displaying the advertisement. Obviously, clicking on an advertisement while the game is in progress is disrupting to the flow of the game.

Increasingly, application developers of all sorts are turning toward a new model, which has been called "freemium" in the United States. The "freemium" has its roots in Asia and is built on the concept of providing a service for free and charging either for virtual goods or premium features. For example, in China the most popular instant messenger service is Tencent's QQ. Tencent is not a household name, except in Asia. Tencent has a market cap of $80 billion and its QQ offering controls over 85 percent of the market with more than 330 million users. In 2007, the company generated

$523 million in revenue—that's four times as much as Facebook, in a country where the average monthly wage is less than $20—with operating profits of $224 million. Only 13 percent of the revenue came from ads. Two-thirds came from Internet services like games and digital goods: "gifts" such as virtual flowers, background music for users' profiles, and virtual pets. Some of the most popular items involve QQShow which is like Yahoo! Avatars. However, unlike Yahoo! Avatars, QQ avatars can be customized and personalized for a price. You can buy new clothes, hairstyles, accessories, and backgrounds. QQ users can also create a living space for their avatars, furnishing it with digital plants, couches, and the like. All of this can be done for a few RMBs here and a few RMBs there. RMB stands for renminbi, the Chinese currency, which is equal to about US$.15. Pretty soon all of those RMBs add up to millions of dollars.

In the case of social games, the freemium model is built on the notion of giving away the games but charging players a small amount for virtual goods that enhance the game experience. One example is *Mob Wars*, a Facebook application in which players rise through the ranks of a gangster organization by committing crimes and fighting other players. *Mob Wars* costs nothing to play. Players are given a certain amount of virtual currency to spend on recruiting and equipping their mobs. To earn more, you have to perform certain tasks—or sidestep the process by paying with real money instead. According to TechCrunch, *Mob Wars* is generating $1 million per month from these microtransactions.

An open question is: how are these microtransactions handled? It's the same micropayment issue that was raised in the opening case of the chapter. However, in this instance there a number of start-ups that have arisen to address the issue, such as Spare Change (*sparechangeinc.com*), Zong (*zong.com*), and PayByCash (*paybycash.com*).

Among these, Spare Change seems to have the most traction. Spare Change, which was recently bought by PlaySpan (*store.playspan.com*), is used by the developers of *Mob Wars* and 700 other Facebook, MySpace, and Bebo applications. It takes three lines of code to add the Spare Change micropayment system to an application. Spare Change is processing $2.5 million micropayments per month, which is approximately $30 million a year. The Spare Change system handles payments as low as $.10. In order to use the system, a player needs to register and tie his or her account to a credit card, a PayPal account, a Spare Change account, or a mobile phone bill. Once registered, the player is given a PIN number that can be used to purchase the virtual goods or services. Spare Change charges 8 percent for each transaction, which is much cheaper than the credit card companies or PayPal.

Results

At this point, it is difficult to tell what will happen to the companies developing social games and the companies developing the micropayment systems designed to support the games. It appears that they both have substantial momentum. But, we've seen this pattern before only to have the various companies meet their demise, especially the companies selling the micropayment systems. For the micropayment companies, one potential threat is the social networking companies themselves. A couple of years back, both Facebook and MySpace were working on payment systems for their application development platforms. Over time, both these efforts faded into the background. Even if the social networks eventually provide their own systems, it does not mean that they will capture the market. Remember what happened to eBay in its battle with PayPal. Of course, while it lost the battle, it also won the war when it purchased PayPal.

Sources: May (2009), TechCrunch (2009), and ZeroDegrees (2009).

Questions

1. What does the term *freemium* refer to? Give some examples.
2. On the social networks, why is it difficult to generate revenue through advertising? Why is it particularly hard for social games?
3. How does the Zong system differ from the Spare Change system?
4. What is the long-term prognosis for companies like Zong and Spare Change?

ONLINE RESOURCES
available at pearsonhighered.com/turban

Online Files

W10.1   Order Fulfillment and Logistics—an Overview
W10.2   Application Case: Hong Kong's Octopus Card
W10.3   Application Case: Stored-Value Cards: Tapping the Teen and Preteen Markets

Comprehensive Educational Web Sites

afponline.org: Association for Financial Professionals Web site.

cardtechnology.com: Source for news about smart cards and such related payment and identification technologies as biometrics, PKI, mobile commerce, physical access control, and computer network security. Keep track of upcoming smart card conferences and find smart card vendors.

cybersource.com: CyberSource is focused on services that optimize business results through active management of the payment process from payment acceptance and order screening, through reconciliation and payment security.

globalplatform.org: Driven by its member organizations, with cross-industry representation from all continents, GlobalPlatform is the worldwide leader in smart card infrastructure development.

nacha.org: NACHA—Electronic Payments Association.

paymentsnews.com: Web site maintained by Glenbrook Partners. For many years, the payments professionals at Glenbrook have monitored the news of the day across the wide-ranging field of electronic payments. Using a number of techniques, Glenbrook Partners continuously scans for news stories that are of interest to payment professionals.

smartcardalliance.org: The Smart Card Alliance is a nonprofit, multi-industry association working to stimulate the understanding, adoption, use, and widespread application of smart card technology.

EC STRATEGY AND IMPLEMENTATION: JUSTIFICATION, GLOBALIZATION, SMEs, AND REGULATORY AND ETHICAL ISSUES

Content

Learning Objectives

Upon completion of this chapter, you will be able to:

1. Describe the strategic planning process.

2. Describe the purpose and content of a business plan in e-commerce.

3. Describe EC strategy implementation including the use of metrics.

4. Describe the need for justifying EC investments, how it is done, and how metrics are used to determine justification.

5. Understand the difficulties in measuring and justifying EC investments.

6. Evaluate the issues involved in global EC.

7. Analyze the impact of EC on SMEs.

8. Understand the foundations for legal and ethical issues in EC.

9. Explain privacy, free speech, and defamation and their challenges.

10. Discuss the challenges caused by spam, splogs, and pop-ups.

11. Describe the importance of green EC and the major issues of concern.

12. Describe the anticipated future of EC.

TRAVELOCITY'S SUCCESSFUL E-STRATEGY

The Problem

Travelocity (*travelocity.com*) was the first online travel company (owned by American Airlines and Sabre). Its initial strategy was to concentrate on airline ticketing and some hotel booking and to sell advertisements on its Web site. This business model worked very well initially, making the company the leading online travel service. However, this business model became ineffective when the airlines reduced, and then eliminated, travel agents' commissions and when competitors entered the market.

Expedia became the market leader, and by 2002 it pulled in nearly five times more revenue than Travelocity. The losses in market share resulted in mounting financial losses.

The Solution

Guided by rigorous study of customer behavior, the company developed a new strategy. Specifically, instead of focusing on airline tickets, Travelocity moved to selling customized packages, including more hotel rooms and car rentals. Instead of being a commission-based intermediary, it started to buy blocks of airline tickets and hotel rooms (discounted wholesale) and sold them to individual customers in customized "merchant travel" packages. Another strategy was to create a fast and effective search engine for finding the lowest prices for its customers.

To better understand customer behavior and to set performance standards for its e-strategy, the company used business analysis done by the operations research department of Sabre Holding, Travelocity's parent company. The

study identified a need for better customer service. This became a top priority.

Improving the performance of the overall system meant setting performance goals for each of the subsystems and then improving them by using several software packages. Quantitative targets and goals formed the basis for the whole system. Once these were set, the planning focused on how to achieve them. The performance standards were related to a mathematical model of how customers choose between travel options, based on the perceived value of each option. Different customers prioritize criteria such as price or departure time differently, and Travelocity is trying to provide their needs. For example, cost-conscious travelers receive e-mails about price drops of more than 20 percent (from or to their favorite destinations). This program, known as "Good Day to Buy," is a major CRM activity.

The Results

By the first quarter of 2006, revenue grew to almost half of Expedia's (versus 20 percent in 2002), about 300 percent above its performance in 2002. The acquisition of *Lastminute.com*, a strategic acquisition completed in 2005, contributed to part of this growth.

Travelocity made the following progress on three performance metrics:

- **Brand impact index.** This gauges the image people have of the company. Travelocity moved from sixth place in 2004 to third in 2005.
- **Conversion impact index.** This measures the conversion from browsing to shopper. Travelocity

showed a 55 percent improvement, placing it in first place in the industry in 2005 versus second place in 2004.

- **Customer satisfaction from the Web site.** Travelocity was second place in 2005 versus fourth in 2004. (Only 6 percent of customers said they could not find the lowest fares on the site in 2005 versus 18 percent in 2004.)

Overall, Travelocity is turning itself around from a loser to a winner. It trimmed losses from $100 million in 2003 to $2.8 million in 2005.

Sources: Compiled from Carr (2006) and Gagnon et al. (2002).

WHAT WE CAN LEARN . . .

Proper strategy can help companies survive and excel. For pure-play companies, it may be even more important to be able to change strategies quickly. Strategies are based on *performance indexes*, which are used as targets as well as measures of success. Once performance targets are set, including quantitative measures, improvement plans can be initiated; then the strategy can be implemented. Later progress can be assessed. These are the basic steps in EC strategy, which is the first subject of this chapter. The chapter also presents the related topics of EC investment justification, global EC, and EC in SMEs. Then, success factors are presented. Next, regulatory and ethical issues are discussed. The chapter concludes with a discussion of green EC followed by some predictions about the future of EC.

11.1 STRATEGY, PLANNING, AND IMPLEMENTATION OF ELECTRONIC COMMERCE

An organizational **strategy** is a broad-based formula for how a business is going to accomplish its mission, what its goals should be, and what plans and policies it will need to accomplish these goals. An EC strategy addresses fundamental questions about the current position of a company and its future directions:

▶ What is the long-term direction of our organization?

▶ What is the overall plan for deploying our organization's resources?

▶ What trade-offs are necessary? What resources will we need to share?

▶ What is our unique positioning vis-à-vis the competitors?

▶ How do we achieve sustainable competitive advantage over rivals in order to ensure lasting profitability?

strategy
A broad-based formula for how a business is going to accomplish its mission, what its goals should be, and what plans and policies will be needed to carry out those goals.

STRATEGY AND THE WEB ENVIRONMENT

Strategy is more than deciding what a company should do next. Strategy also is about making tough decisions about what not to do. Strategic positioning is making decisions about trade-offs, recognizing that a company must abandon or not pursue some products, services, and activities in order to excel at others. How are these trade-offs determined? Not merely with a focus on growth and increases in revenue, but also on profitability and increases in shareholder value over the long run. How is this profitability and economic value determined? By establishing a unique value proposition and the configuration of a tailored value chain that enables a company to offer unique value to its customers. Therefore, strategy has been, and remains, focused on questions about organizational fit, trade-offs, profitability, and value (Porter 2001).

Any contemporary strategy-setting process must include the Internet. Strategy guru Michael Porter (2001) argues that a coherent organizational strategy that includes the Internet is more important than ever before: "Many have argued that the Internet renders strategy obsolete. In reality, the opposite is true . . . it is more important than ever for companies to distinguish themselves through strategy. The winners will be those that view the Internet as a complement to, not a cannibal of, traditional ways of competing" (p. 63).

Porter's Competitive Forces Model and Strategies

Porter's competitive forces model has been used to develop strategies for companies to increase their competitive edge. It also demonstrates how IT and EC can enhance competitiveness.

The model recognizes five major forces that could endanger a company's position in a given industry. Other forces, such as those cited in Chapter 1, including the impact of government, affect all companies in the industry, and therefore may have less impact on the relative success of a company within its industry. Although the details of the model differ from one industry to another, its general structure is universal. The five major forces in an industry that affect the degree of competition and, ultimately, the degree of profitability are:

1. Threat of entry of new competitors
2. Bargaining power of suppliers
3. Bargaining power of customers or buyers
4. Threat of substitute products or services
5. Rivalry among existing firms in the industry

The strength of each force is determined by the industry's structure. Existing companies in an industry need to protect themselves against the forces; alternatively, they can use the forces to improve their position or to challenge the leaders in the industry. The relationships are shown in Exhibit 11.1. You can find the definitions and details in Porter (1980).

While implementing Porter's model, companies can identify the forces that influence competitive advantage in their marketplace and then develop a strategy. Porter (1985) proposed three such strategies: cost leadership, differentiation, and niche strategies.

In Online File W11.1, we first list Porter's three classical strategies, plus nine other general strategies, for dealing with competitive advantage. Each of these strategies can be enhanced by EC, as shown throughout the book.

The Impact of the Internet

Porter (2001) has identified several ways that the Internet impacts each of the five forces of competitiveness—bargaining power of consumers and suppliers, threats from

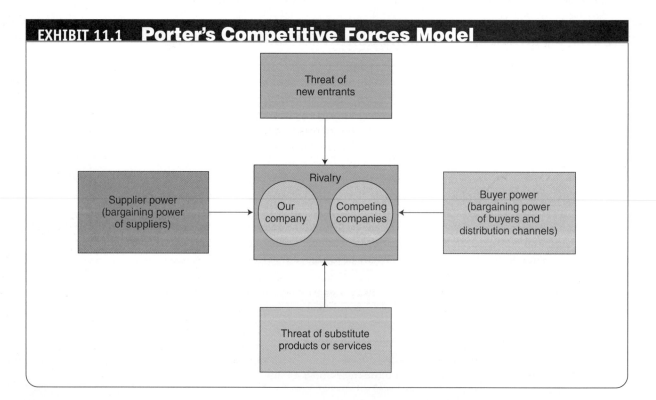

EXHIBIT 11.1   Porter's Competitive Forces Model

substitutes and new entrants, and rivalry among existing competitors—that were originally described in one of his seminal works on strategy (Porter 1980). The majority of impacts are negative, reflecting Porter's view that "The great paradox of the Internet is that its very benefits—making information widely available; reducing the difficulty of purchasing, marketing, and distribution; allowing buyers and sellers to find and transact business with one another more easily—also make it more difficult for companies to capture those benefits as profits" (Porter 2001, p. 66).

The impact of the Internet on strategic competitiveness and long-term profitability will differ from industry to industry. Accordingly, many businesses are taking a focused look at the impact of the Internet and EC on their future. For these firms, an **e-commerce strategy**, or **e-strategy**, is the formulation and execution of a vision of how a new or existing company intends to do business electronically. The process of building an e-strategy is described next.

THE STRATEGIC PLANNING PROCESS

A strategy is important, but the process of developing a strategy can be even more important. Strategy development will differ depending on the type of strategy, the implementation method, the size of the firm, and the approach that is taken. Nevertheless, any strategic planning process has four major phases, as shown in Exhibit 11.2. The major phases of the strategic planning process, and some identifiable activities and outcomes associated with each phase, are discussed briefly in this chapter. Note that the process is cyclical and continuous.

Strategy Initiation

In the **strategy initiation** phase, the organization examines itself and its environment. The principal activities include setting the organization's mission and goals, examining

e-commerce strategy (e-strategy)
The formulation and execution of a vision of how a new or existing company intends to do business electronically.

strategy initiation
The initial phase of strategic planning in which the organization examines itself and its environment.

EXHIBIT 11.2 The Strategic Planning Process

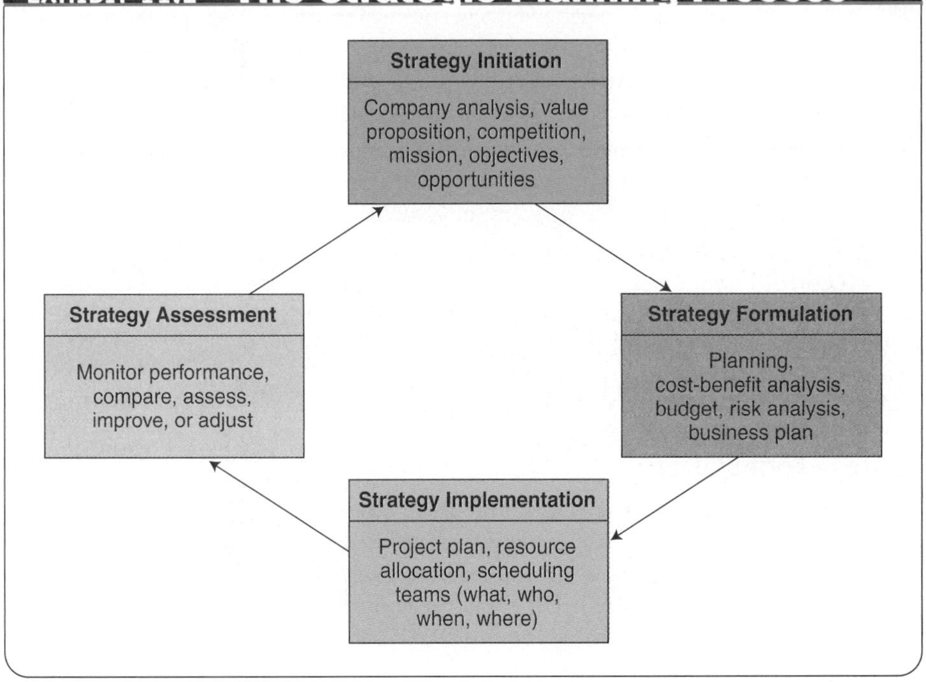

organizational strengths and weaknesses, assessing environmental factors impacting the business, and conducting a competitor analysis. As emphasized throughout this chapter, this includes an examination of the potential contribution that the Internet and other emerging technologies can make to the business.

Specific outcomes from this phase include:

value proposition
The benefit that a company's products or services provide to a company and its customers.

> **Company analysis and value proposition.** The *company analysis* includes the vision, mission, value proposition, goals, capabilities, constraints, strengths, and weaknesses of the company. Questions typically asked in a company analysis are: What business are we really in? Who are our future customers? Do our mission statement and our goals adequately describe our intended future? What opportunities, and threats, do our business and our industry face? One key outcome from this analysis should be a clear statement of the company's **value proposition**—the benefit that a company's products or services provide to a company and its customers. Value proposition is actually a statement that summarizes the customer segment, competitor target, and the core differentiation of one's product from the offering of competitors. It describes the value added by the company (or the e-commerce projects), and usually is included in the business plan. It is only by knowing what benefits a business is providing to customers that chief-level executives can truly understand "what business they are in" and who their potential competitors are. For example, Amazon.com recognizes that it is not just in the book-selling business, but that it also is in the information-about-books business. Amazon.com's strategists know this is where customers find value in shopping at Amazon.com and where a great deal of Amazon.com's competitive advantage lies. So Amazon.com has introduced new services such as "search inside the book" to deliver on that value proposition to its customers.
>
> **Core competencies.** A core competency refers to the unique combination of the resources and experiences of a particular firm. It takes time to build these core competencies, and they can be difficult to imitate. For example, Google's core competency is its expertise in information search technology, and eBay's core competency is in conducting online auctions. A company is using its core competency to deliver a product or service. Google's products are AdWords and AdSense, and Intel produces chips.
>
> **Forecasts.** Forecasting means identifying business, technological, political, economic, and other relevant trends that are currently affecting the business or that have the potential to do so in the future.
>
> **Competitor (industry) analysis.** Competitor analysis involves scanning the business environment to collect and interpret relevant information about direct competitors, indirect competitors, and potential competitors. Several methodologies are available to conduct such an analysis, including a strengths, weaknesses, opportunities, and threats (SWOT) analysis, and competitor analysis grid.

Strategy Formulation

strategy formulation
The development of strategies to exploit opportunities and manage threats in the business environment in light of corporate strengths and weaknesses.

Strategy formulation is the development of strategies to exploit opportunities and manage threats in the business environment in light of corporate strengths and weaknesses. In an EC strategy, the end result is likely to be a list of EC applications or projects to be implemented. For tools for conducting strategy, see Online File W11.2.

Specific activities and outcomes from this phase include:

▶ **Business opportunities.** If the strategy initiation has been done well, a number of scenarios for future development of the business will be obvious. How well these scenarios fit with the future direction of the company are assessed. Similarly, the first phase may also have identified some current activities that are no longer relevant to the company's future and are candidates for divestiture, outsourcing, or elimination.

▶ **Cost-benefit analysis.** Each proposed opportunity must be assessed in terms of the potential costs and benefits to the company in light of its mission and goals. These costs and benefits may be financial or nonfinancial, tangible or intangible, or short-term or long-term. More information about conducting a cost-benefit analysis is included in Section 11.2. A major part of such analysis is measuring profits on the Web (see Online File W11.3).

▶ **Risk analysis, assessment, and management.** The risks of each proposed EC initiative (project) must be analyzed and assessed. If a significant risk is evident, then a risk management plan is required. Of particular importance in an EC strategy are business risk factors such as transition risk and partner risk.

▶ **Business plan.** Many of the outcomes from these first two phases—goals, competitor analysis, strategic opportunities, risk analysis, and more—come together in a business plan. Every business—large or small, new or old, successful or not—needs a *business plan* to acquire funding and to ensure that a realistic approach is being taken to implement the business strategy. A business plan for EC is presented in the next section.

Strategy Implementation

In this phase, the emphasis shifts from "what do we do?" to "how do we do it?" In the  phase, detailed, short-term plans are developed for carrying out the projects agreed on in strategy formulation. Specifically, decision makers evaluate options, establish specific milestones, allocate resources, and manage the projects.

Specific activities and outcomes from this phase include:

▶ **Project planning.** Inevitably, strategy implementation is executed through an EC project or a series of projects. Project planning includes setting specific project objectives, creating a project schedule with milestones, and setting measurable performance targets. Normally, a project plan would be set for each project and application.

▶ **Resource allocation.** Organizational resources are those owned, available to, or controlled by a company. They can be human, financial, technological, managerial, or knowledge based. This phase includes business process outsourcing (BPO) consideration and use.

▶ **Project management.** This is the process of making the selected applications and projects a reality—hiring staff; purchasing equipment; licensing, purchasing, or writing software; contracting vendors; and so on.

Strategy Assessment

Just as soon as implementation is complete, assessment begins. **Strategy assessment** is the continuous evaluation of progress toward the organization's strategic goals, resulting in corrective action and, if necessary, strategy reformulation. In strategy assessment, specific measures called *metrics* assess the progress of the strategy. In some cases, data gathered in the first phase can be used as baseline data to assess the strategy's effectiveness. If not, this information will have to be gathered. For large EC projects, business performance management tools can be employed (see oracle.com/hyperion).

strategy implementation
The development of detailed, short-term plans for carrying out the projects agreed on in strategy formulation.

strategy assessment
The continuous evaluation of progress toward the organization's strategic goals, resulting in corrective action and, if necessary, strategy reformulation.

What happens with the results from strategy assessment? As shown in Exhibit 11.2 (p. 413), the strategic planning process starts over again, immediately. Note that a cyclical approach is required—a strategic planning process that requires constant reassessment of today's strategy while preparing a new strategy for tomorrow.

A major organizational restructuring and transformation was the reason for the development of a new strategic plan for InternetNZ, as Case 11.1 describes.

CASE 11.1
EC Application
STRATEGIC PLANNING AT INTERNETNZ

InternetNZ is not only an Internet-based business; its business is the Internet. An incorporated, nonprofit organization, InternetNZ describes itself as "the guardian of the Internet for New Zealand," and its primary business activity is management of the .nz country code top-level domain (ccTLD).

After a somewhat turbulent transition from its predecessor organization, the Internet Society of New Zealand, in early 2004 InternetNZ embarked on a comprehensive strategic-planning exercise. The result of that exercise, *InternetNZ Strategic Plan: 2004–2007*, is a model of content that should be in every strategic plan.

▶ **Environment analysis.** In addition to describing trends that affect the global Internet and the Internet in New Zealand, a PEST analysis (political, economic, social, and technological) lists factors in the political, economic, and social environment that affect the conduct of InternetNZ's business. For example: "No large pro-censorship lobby in NZ" (political), "Increasing dependence on the Internet for information" (social), and "The Internet bridges NZ's geographical disadvantage" (economic).

▶ **Vision statement.** Sixteen visionary goals (e.g., "Benefits of the Internet have been extended to all New Zealanders") follow a vision statement for 2007 ("The Internet, open and uncapturable, offering high performance and unfettered access for all").

▶ **Mission statement.** "To protect and promote the Internet in New Zealand" captures many of the characteristics—visionary, realistic, easily understood, short and concise—of a good mission statement.

▶ **SWOT analysis.** A SWOT analysis lists 13 strengths (e.g., "Committed, involved, clever volunteers," "Has created a best practice model for .nz ccTLD"), 13 weaknesses (e.g., "Perception of InternetNZ as mainly 'geeks' or 'techies,'" "Lack of internal resources to respond to rapidly changing environment"), 14 opportunities (e.g., "A leader in the fight against spam," "Help insure widespread broadband access"), and 11 threats (e.g., "Unnecessary government intervention or regulation," "Low level of

SWOT analysis
A methodology that surveys external opportunities and threats and relates them to internal strengths and weaknesses.

membership, hence, providing little funding and vulnerable to take over").

▶ **Core values.** Six core values—openness, transparency, ethical behavior, neutrality, supportive, commitment—are identified and described briefly.

▶ **Goal statements.** Eight strategies (e.g., management of .nz ccTLD, advocacy and representation to government, promote the Internet, support Internet innovation and technical leadership) are listed. For each strategy, one to eight goals are listed, and it clearly identifies the InternetNZ committee held accountable for achievement of the strategy. The 2004–2007 InternetNZ business plan identifies a goal statement of purpose, projected outcomes, and specific examples for execution of the goal for each goal.

▶ **Business plan.** Separate from, but an integral part of the *InternetNZ Strategic Plan: 2004–2007*, is the *InternetNZ Business Plan: 2004–2007*. This document lists, describes, and prioritizes the specific activities that are necessary to achieve the goals, with associated income and expenses, also available in both the *InternetNZ Strategic Plan: 2008–2009* and the *InternetNZ Business Plan: 2007–2009*.

The InternetNZ Council adopted the strategic plan and the business plan at its April 2004 meeting, and both plans are in the process of being implemented.

Finally, Keith Davidson, who was appointed as executive director of the company in 2005, said that the continued fulfillment of InternetNZ's strategic plan is his major focus as director. This plan outlines steps for InternetNZ's management of the .nz ccTLD advocacy to the government, support for industry best practice and self-regulation, protection and promotion of the Internet, as well as NZ representation globally.

Sources: Compiled from InternetNZ (2006) and Auckland (2005).

Questions

1. Why would a nonprofit organization, such as InternetNZ, need a strategic plan or a business plan?
2. What is the difference between a vision statement and a mission statement?

BUSINESS PLANNING IN E-COMMERCE

One almost inevitable outcome of strategy setting is a business plan. A **business plan** is a written document that identifies the company's goals and outlines how the company intends to achieve the goals. Exhibit 11.3 shows a typical, nondetailed outline of a business plan. This outline follows the Online Tutorial's outline.

Business Plan Fundamentals

Business plans are written for a variety of purposes. The customary reason why a business needs a business plan is to acquire funding. Entrepreneurs in start-up companies use business plans to get funding from investors, such as a venture capitalist or a bank. An existing company may write a business plan to get funding from a bank, the financial markets, or a prospective business partner.

A second reason to write a business plan is to acquire nonfinancial resources. A prospective landlord, equipment supplier, or ASP may want to see a viable business plan before entering into a contract. Similarly, a business plan can be useful for recruiting senior management. Any person truly capable of leading a medium-sized or large business will want to see an organization's business plan before accepting the position.

Another purpose for writing a business plan is to obtain a realistic approach to the business. The process of writing the plan forces the business owner to think ahead, set achievable goals, seek out and analyze competitors, figure out how to reach target markets, anticipate problems, and compare projected revenue streams against realistic expense statements. As with strategy setting, the process, not the plan itself, increases the likelihood that the business will be a success.

business plan
A written document that identifies a company's goals and outlines how the company intends to achieve the goals and at what cost.

EXHIBIT 11.3 **Outline of a Business Plan**

Executive Summary: The executive summary is a synopsis of the key points of the entire business plan. Its purpose is to explain the fundamentals of the business in a way that both informs and excites the reader.

Business Description: The business description describes the nature and purpose of the business and includes the firm's mission statement, goals, value proposition, and a description of the products and services it provides. The purpose of the business description is to objectively explain and justify the business idea in a positive and enthusiastic manner.

Operations Plan: The operations section of the business plan describes the inputs, processes, procedures, and activities required to create what products the business will sell or what services it will deliver.

Financial Plan: The financial plan estimates the monetary resources and flows that will be required to carry out the business plan. The financial plan also indicates when and by how much the business intends to be profitable. Finally, the financial statements (e.g., balance sheet, cash flow statement) tell a lot about the entrepreneur in terms of business commitment and financial wherewithal to make the business a profitable success.

Marketing Plan: The central part of the marketing plan is the market analysis, which defines the firm's target markets and analyzes how the organization will position its products or services to arouse and fulfill the needs of the target markets in order to maximize sales. Other aspects of the marketing plan include pricing strategy, promotion plan, distribution plan, and a demand forecast.

Competitor Analysis: The competitor analysis (a) outlines the competitive strengths and weaknesses of rivals in the industry and (b) reveals the firm's competitive position in the market space.

A realistic approach also means that sometimes the most successful outcome of writing a business plan is a decision not to proceed. Researching and writing a plan can reveal the realities of tough competition, a too-small target market, or an income and expense statement that is awash in red ink. Many owners of failed start-ups would have saved considerable time, money, and heartbreak if they had created a proper business plan.

When do you create a business plan? The most obvious time is when a new business is seeking start-up funds and other resources. However, a business plan may also be required if an existing company is planning to create a separate division, reengineer or restructure the existing company, or launch the company in a new direction. A plan also is required when the existing plan is reaching its use-by date. If the original plan set forth a three-year plan and the business just celebrated its second birthday, it is time to write a new plan.

Several software packages are available for the creation of business plans (e.g., see bplans.com and planware.org).

BUSINESS CASE

business case

A business plan for a new initiative or large, new project inside an existing organization.

A distinctive type of business plan is the *business case*. As described in the previous section, a business plan is used often when launching a new business. A **business case** is a business plan for a new initiative or large, new project *inside an existing organization*. Its purpose is the same as with a business plan—to justify a specific investment of funds—but the audience is the company's board of directors and senior management, not an external funding agency. The business case helps clarify how the organization will use its resources by identifying the strategic justification ("Where are we going?"), technical justification ("How will we get there?"), operational justification ("When will we get there?"), and financial justification ("Why will we win?"). Examples of EC initiatives that may require a business case include the launch or major revision of a Web site, implementation of an e-procurement project, or deploying a CRM system.

The content of a business case is similar to that of a business plan. One difference is that the business plan concentrates on the viability of a company, whereas a business case assesses both viability of the project and the fit of the initiative with the firm's mission and goals. A business case also will almost certainly have more operational detail and a justification that it is the best way for the organization to use its resources to accomplish the desired strategy. The Online Tutorial highlights other differences between a business plan and a business case.

With a firm foundation of organizational strategy and business planning in place, we now turn our attention to e-commerce strategy.

E-COMMERCE STRATEGY: CONCEPTS AND OVERVIEW

What is the role of the Internet in organizational strategy? Strategy setting begins with the business strategy—determining an organization's vision, mission statement, and overall goals (see Exhibit 11.4). Then the information systems (IS) strategy is set, primarily by determining *what* information and associated information systems are required to carry out the business strategy. The information and communications technology (ICT) strategy is decided based on *how* to deliver the information and information systems via technology. The EC strategy is a derivative of both the IS strategy and the ICT strategy. The solid downward pointing arrows in Exhibit 11.4 depict the top-down portion of the process. The broken lines indicate possible bottom-up activities, which mean that lower-level strategies cause adjustments in higher-level strategies.

The Internet impacts all levels of organizational strategy setting, and it is shown by the boxes in Exhibit 11.4. Business strategists need to consider the Internet's role in creating or

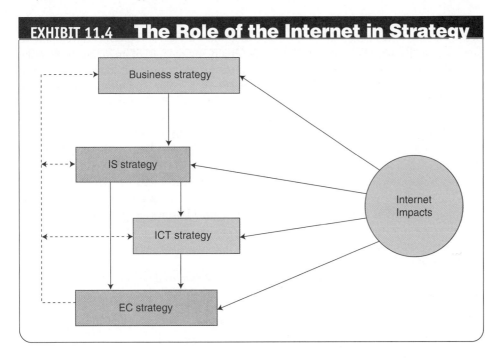

EXHIBIT 11.4   The Role of the Internet in Strategy

innovating products, in product and service delivery, in supplier and customer relationships, and in assessing the impact on competition in the marketplace. Generally, strategic planners need to view the Internet as a complement to traditional ways of marketing and competing, not as a source of competitive advantage in and of itself. Information systems strategists need to consider the Internet as a tool for collecting information and distributing it to where it is required. ICT planners will need to plan the integration of the Internet-based technologies into the existing and future ICT infrastructure. Thinking about and planning for the Internet should be subsumed into each of the four strategy levels.

Using the process previously mentioned, businesses continue to evolve their own e-commerce strategies, defined as the formulation and execution of a vision of how a new or existing company intends to do business electronically. The following section explains in detail one of the most important aspects of e-strategy: The justification of an EC start-up and EC projects.

Strategy in the Web 2.0 Environment and in Social Networking

A 2007 study conducted by McKinsey & Company found that 75 percent of respondents (executives from global companies) plan to maintain or increase investments in Web 2.0 technologies in coming years (reported by Miller 2007).

Miller (2007) suggests that companies should start small so that they can observe how people react to the tools, learn how to manage the process, and develop a social system. For instance, companies can start with a small internal project that addresses a real business problem around knowledge sharing. They can also start in one department by providing blogs to employees to share ideas around a particular project, such as customer development in sales, competitive analysis in marketing, and so forth. After the companies complete the internal "beta" project, they can expand the effort to include other Enterprise 2.0 tools, as well as to bring other departments onboard and even move outside the organization to involve customers, partners, and suppliers. For example, Dell first launched internal blogs before creating IdeaStorm, which is offered to external customers.

Marketers are increasingly using social networking tools in a wide range of activities, including advertising, public relations, customer service, and product development. For example, Brewtopia (brewtopia.com.au) initially invited 140 of its friends to describe their ideal beer. Within weeks, more than 10,000 people from over 20 countries joined the community and voted for their favorite beer's style, color, and alcohol content; the shape of the bottle; and the color printed on the label. In 2007, the company offered a platform for its customers to collaboratively create their own beers.

Although there are a number of successful examples, there is a lack of well-established Web 2.0 strategies. One attempt is that of Shenkan and Sichel (2007) who suggest a top-down approach for marketers: Start with a conceptual map that links a company's brand, industry, and customer characteristics with its core marketing activities that could benefit from the social network. Adopting this approach, companies can establish priorities, identify the most relevant initiatives, evaluate their potential business impact, and invest more heavily in the most promising ones. For example, marketers in industries where R&D is a competitive differentiator should focus on getting consumers involved in the product-development process.

Siteworx (2008) proposes an "outside-in" perspective in developing social networking strategies. Its four-part methodology includes the following steps:

 ▶ Collect and analyze assumptions about the target audience and business objectives.
 ▶ Validate assumptions through research, analysis, and testing.
 ▶ Examine the current IT infrastructure and make key decisions regarding whether to upgrade the existing technology or build or buy a solution.
 ▶ Plan the initiative.

A comprehensive guide to Web 2.0 strategy is provided by Shuen (2008). A strategic guide for m-commerce in social networks is provided by SmartPhone.com (2009). For a guide on how to develop a business-aligned social media and social networking strategy, see ddmcd.com/managing-technology/how-to-develop-a-business-aligned-social-media-social-networ.html.

Section 11.1 ▶ REVIEW QUESTIONS

1. What is strategy?
2. Describe the strategic planning process.
3. Describe the four phases of strategic planning.
4. What is a business plan?
5. What is a business case? How is it different from a business plan?
6. Describe the process of deriving an EC strategy.
7. Describe issues in using Web 2.0 and social networks in EC strategy.

11.2 JUSTIFICATION AND COST-BENEFIT ANALYSIS

Companies need to justify their EC investments as part of strategy formulation for a number of different reasons, but most face an uphill battle to address this new accountability, as demonstrated by the following statistics from Peppard and Ward (2005):

 ▶ Sixty-five percent of companies lack the knowledge or tools to do ROI calculations.
 ▶ Seventy-five percent have no formal processes or budgets in place for measuring ROI.
 ▶ Sixty-eight percent do not measure how projects coincide with promised benefits six months after completion.

At the same time, demand for expanding or initiating e-business projects remains strong. In order to achieve the optimal level of investment, CIOs will need to effectively communicate the value of proposed EC projects in order to gain approval.

OTHER REASONS WHY EC JUSTIFICATION IS NEEDED

The following are some additional reasons for conducting EC justification:

▶ Companies now realize that EC is not necessarily the solution to all problems. Therefore, EC projects must *compete for funding and resources* with other internal and external projects. Analysis is needed to determine when funding of an EC project is appropriate.

▶ Some large companies, and many public organizations, mandate a formal evaluation of requests for funding.

▶ Companies need to assess the success of EC projects after completion and later on a periodic basis.

▶ The success of EC projects may be assessed in order to pay bonuses to those involved with the project.

▶ When there is pressure from top management.

▶ When there is a large amount of money involved.

▶ When weak business conditions exist.

Justification forces EC and IT into better alignment with the corporate business strategy. Also, justification increases the credibility of EC projects.

EC INVESTMENT CATEGORIES AND BENEFITS

Before we look at how to justify EC investments, let's examine the nature of such investments. One basic way to categorize different EC investments is to distinguish between investment in infrastructure and investment in specific EC applications.

The IT *infrastructure* provides the foundation for EC applications in the enterprise. The IT infrastructure includes intranets, extranets, data centers, data warehouses, and knowledge bases, and many applications throughout the enterprise share the infrastructure. Infrastructure investments are made for the long term.

EC applications are specific systems and programs for achieving certain objectives; for example, taking a customer order online or providing e-CRM. The number of EC applications can be large. They may be in one functional department, or several departments may share them, which makes evaluation of their costs and benefits more complex.

The basic reasons that companies invest in IT and EC are to improve business processes, lower costs, increase productivity, increase customer satisfaction and retention, increase revenue, reduce time to market, and increase market share.

HOW IS AN EC INVESTMENT JUSTIFIED?

Justifying an EC investment means comparing the costs of each project against its benefits in what is known as a **cost-benefit analysis**. To conduct such an analysis, it is necessary to define and measure the relevant EC benefits and costs. Cost-benefit analysis is frequently assessed by *return on investment (ROI)*, which is also the name of a specific method for evaluating investments.

A number of different methods measure the *business value* of EC and IT investments. Traditional methods that support such analyses are net present value (NPV) and ROI (see Online File W11.4).

cost-benefit analysis
A comparison of the costs of a project against the benefits.

The cost-benefit analysis and the business value are part of the business case. Several vendors provide templates, tools, guidelines, and more for preparing the business case for specific areas. For example, Business Case (businesscase.com) provides a Business Case Resource Kit.

WHAT NEEDS TO BE JUSTIFIED? WHEN SHOULD JUSTIFICATION TAKE PLACE?

Not all EC investments need to be formally justified. In some cases, a simple one-page qualitative justification will do. The following are cases where formal evaluation may not be needed:

▶ When the value of the investment is relatively small for the organization
▶ When the relevant data are not available, are inaccurate, or are too volatile
▶ When the EC project is mandated—it must be done regardless of the costs and benefits involved

However, even when formal analysis is not required, an organization should have at least some qualitative analysis to explain the logic of investing in the EC project.

USING METRICS IN EC JUSTIFICATION

metric
A specific, measurable standard against which actual performance is compared.

A **metric** is a specific, measurable standard against which actual performance is compared. Metrics are used to describe costs, benefits, or the ratio between them. They are used not only for justification, but also for other economic activities (e.g., to compare employee performance in order to reward specific employees). Metrics can produce very positive results in organizations by driving behavior in a number of ways. Metrics can:

▶ Define the value proposition of business models.
▶ Communicate a business strategy to the workforce through performance targets.
▶ Increase accountability when metrics are linked with performance-appraisal programs.
▶ Align the objectives of individuals, departments, and divisions to the enterprise's strategic objectives.
▶ Track the performance of EC systems, including usage, types of visitors, page visits, conversion rate, and so on.
▶ Assess the health of companies by using tools such as balanced scorecards and performance dashboards.

EC metrics can be tangible or intangible; see Exhibit 11.5 for examples.

Metrics, Measurements, and Key Performance Indicators

Metrics need to be defined properly with a clear way to measure them. For example, *revenue growth* can be measured in total dollars, in percentage change over time, or in percentage growth as compared to the entire industry. *Cost avoidance*, for example, can be achieved in many ways, one of which may be "decrease obsolete stock write-offs as percentage of revenue." Defining the specific measures is critical; otherwise, what the metrics actually measure may be open to interpretation.

key performance indicators (KPIs)
The quantitative expression of critically important metrics.

The *balanced scorecard method* uses customer metrics, financial metrics, internal business processes metrics, and learning and growth metrics. Metrics are related to the organization's goals, objectives, vision, and plans. **Key performance indicators (KPIs)**, which are the quantitative expression of critically important metrics (known as *critical*

EXHIBIT 11.5　Sample EC Metrics for Various Entities of Users

EC User	Tangible Metrics	Intangible Metrics
Buyer (B2C)	• Cost/price of the product • Time in executing the transaction • Number of available alternatives	• Ease of use of EC • Convenience in purchasing • Information availability • Reliability of the transaction • Privacy of personal data
Seller (B2C)	• Profit per customer • Conversion rate of visitors • Customer retention rate • Inventory costs • Profit per item sold • Market share	• Customer satisfaction • Customer loyalty • Transaction security
Net-enhanced organization (B2B)	• From design to market (time) • Cash-to-cash cycle • Percentage of orders delivered on time or early • Profit per item sold	• Flexibility in changing purchase orders • Ability to sustain unplanned production increase • Risk reduction • Improved quality of products/ services
Government (G2C)	• Reduction in cost of transactions • Reduction in licensing fees • Increase in participation in government programs • Lower tax rates	• Citizen satisfaction • Reelection of candidates • Choice of interacting with elected officials • Promoting democratic principles • Disseminating more information quickly

Examples of Security-Related Metrics

- More than one-third of consumers use the same password for online banking as they do for other online activities.
- The number of different brands targeted by phishing scams in one year.
- The percentage of consumers who say they are less likely to respond to an e-mail from their bank because of phishing threats.
- The percentage of the infrastructures of large industries that are likely to be hit by cyberattacks.
- The percentage of consumers of financial products who say phishing has turned them away from Web transactions.
- Consumers are slightly more likely to receive permission-based e-mails from online merchants than other retail businesses.
- Two-thirds of computers have spyware on them.
- Spam messages are at least 70 percent shorter than legitimate e-mails.
- EBay tops the list of online destinations on Black Friday (the day after Thanksgiving).

Sources: Compiled from *cio.com/topic/1381/Metrics* (accessed March 2010), Borenstein et al. (2005), and from Sardar et al. (2003).

*success factor*s), frequently measure metrics that deal directly with performance (e.g., sales, profits). Frequently, one metric has several KPIs. Examples of metrics were provided in Online File W11.3.

Any organization, private or public, can use metrics. Let's look at an example. In Australia, the government of Victoria (vic.gov.au) is one of the leaders in exploiting the Internet to provide a one-stop service center called "Do It Online." In the United States,

MyCalifornia (ca.gov) offers many services for the citizens of California. In either case, the metric of "travel and wait time" for the citizens who would otherwise have to visit a physical office justifies offering the service of renewing driver's licenses.

We limit our discussion here mostly to individual EC projects or initiatives. EC projects deal mostly with the automation of business processes, and, as such, they can be viewed as *capital investment* decisions.

Now that we understand the need for conducting EC justification and the use of metrics, let's see why EC justification is so difficult to accomplish.

Section 11.2 ❯ REVIEW QUESTIONS

1. List some of the reasons for justifying an EC investment.
2. Describe the risks of not conducting an EC justification study.
3. Describe how an EC investment is justified.
4. List the major EC investment categories.
5. When is justification of EC investments unnecessary?
6. What are metrics? What benefits do they offer?

11.3 DIFFICULTIES IN MEASURING AND JUSTIFYING E-COMMERCE INVESTMENTS AND SUCCESS

Justifying EC (and IT) projects can be a complex and, therefore, difficult process. Let's see why.

THE EC JUSTIFICATION PROCESS

The EC justification process varies depending on the situation and the methods used. However, in its extreme, it can be very complex, as shown by Misra (2006) who identified five areas that must be considered in the justification of IT projects, as shown in Exhibit 11.6. In this section, we also discuss intangibles and tangibles.

We will see later in this section that one major difficulty with EC justification is measuring intangible benefits and costs. Next, we provide other difficulties in conducting justifications.

DIFFICULTIES IN MEASURING PRODUCTIVITY AND PERFORMANCE GAINS

One of the major benefits of using EC is increased productivity. However, productivity increases may be difficult to measure for a number of different reasons as listed next.

Data and Analysis Issues

Data, or the analysis of the data, may hide productivity gains. Why is this so? For manufacturing, it is fairly easy to measure outputs and inputs. For example, Toyota produces motor vehicles—a relatively well-defined product—that show gradual quality changes over time. It is not difficult to identify the inputs used to produce these vehicles with reasonable accuracy. However, in service industries, such as finance or health care delivery, it is more difficult to define what the products are, how they change in quality, and how they may be related to corresponding benefits and costs.

For example, banks now use EC to handle a large portion of deposits and withdrawal transactions through ATMs. The ability to withdraw cash from ATMs 24/7 is a substantial benefit for customers compared with the limited hours of the physical branch. But, what is the value of this to the bank in comparison with the associated

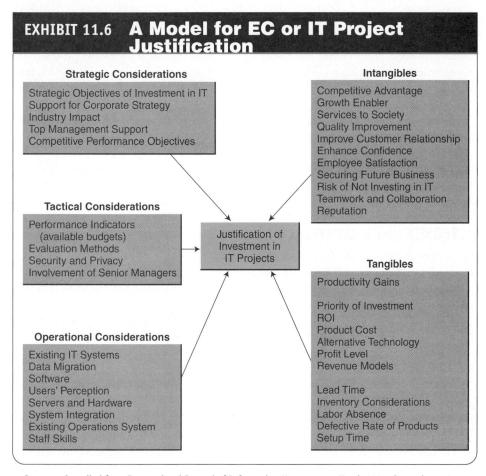

EXHIBIT 11.6 A Model for EC or IT Project Justification

Strategic Considerations
Strategic Objectives of Investment in IT
Support for Corporate Strategy
Industry Impact
Top Management Support
Competitive Performance Objectives

Intangibles
Competitive Advantage
Growth Enabler
Services to Society
Quality Improvement
Improve Customer Relationship
Enhance Confidence
Employee Satisfaction
Securing Future Business
Risk of Not Investing in IT
Teamwork and Collaboration
Reputation

Tactical Considerations
Performance Indicators
 (available budgets)
Evaluation Methods
Security and Privacy
Involvement of Senior Managers

Justification of Investment in IT Projects

Tangibles
Productivity Gains

Priority of Investment
ROI
Product Cost
Alternative Technology
Profit Level
Revenue Models

Lead Time
Inventory Considerations
Labor Absence
Defective Rate of Products
Setup Time

Operational Considerations
Existing IT Systems
Data Migration
Software
Users' Perception
Servers and Hardware
System Integration
Existing Operations System
Staff Skills

Sources: Compiled from *International Journal of Information Management,* March 2001, Gunasekaran A., P. Love, F. Rahimi, and R. Miele. "A Model for Investment Justification in Information Technology Projects," © 2006, with permission from Elsevier, and R. Misra, "Evolution of the Philosophy of Investments in IT Projects," *Issues in Informing Sciences and Information Technology,* Vol. 3, 2006.

costs? If the incremental value exceeds the incremental costs, then it represents a productivity gain; otherwise the productivity impact is negative.

EC Productivity Gains May Be Offset by Losses in Other Areas
Another possible difficulty is that EC gains in certain areas of the company may be offset by losses in other areas. For example, increased online sales may decrease offline sales. Or, consider the situation where an organization installs a new EC system that makes it possible to increase output per employee; if the organization reduces its production staff but has to increase its IT staff, the productivity gains from EC could be small, or even negative.

Incorrectly Defining What Is Measured
The results of any investment justification depend on what is actually measured. For example, to assess the benefits of EC investment, one should usually look at productivity improvement in the area where the EC project was installed. However, a productivity increase may not necessarily be a profitable improvement (e.g., due to losses in other areas). The problem of definitions can be overcome by using appropriate metrics and key performance indicators.

Other Difficulties

Other performance measurement difficulties also have been noted. A number of researchers have pointed out, for example, that time lags may throw off productivity measurements (Misra 2006). Many EC investments, especially those in e-CRM, take five to six years to show significant positive results, but many studies do not wait that long to measure productivity changes.

Furthermore, changes in organizational performance may occur years after installing an EC application. Thus, proper evaluation must be done over the entire life cycle of the system. This requires forecasting, which may be difficult. In EC, it is even more difficult, because investors often require that risky and fast-changing EC systems pay for themselves within three years. For difficulties in measuring intangible costs and benefits, see Online File W11.5.

DETERMINING E-COMMERCE SUCCESS

The success factors of EC depend on the industry, the sellers and buyers, and the products sold. Furthermore, the ability of sellers to create economic value for consumers will determine EC success. When deciding to sell online, looking at the major factors that determine the impact of EC can evaluate the potential for success.

E-market success factors can be divided into the following four categories: product, industry, seller, and consumer characteristics.

Product Characteristics

Digitized products, such as software, documents, music, and videos, are particularly well suited for e-markets because they can be distributed to customers electronically, resulting in instant delivery and very low distribution costs. Digitization also decreases the amount of time involved in the order-taking cycle because automation can be introduced to help customers search for, select, and pay for a product, anyplace and anytime, without the intervention of a sales or technical person. Finally, product updates can be communicated to customers rapidly.

A product's *price* may also be an important determinant of its success. The higher the product price, the greater the level of risk involved in the market transaction between buyers and sellers who are geographically separated and who may have never dealt with each other before.

Another product characteristic is the cost and speed of *product customization*. Millions of consumers configure computers, cars, toys, clothes, and services to their liking, and if sellers can fulfill such requests at a reasonable cost and in a short amount of time, they can assure success (e.g., Dell). Finally, computers, electronic products, consumer products, and even cars can be sold online because consumers know exactly what they are buying. The more product information that is available, the easier it is to sell. The use of multimedia and product tutorials (e.g., see bluenile.com) can dramatically facilitate product description.

Another aspect of a product's characteristics is *cross-selling* and *up-selling*. EC enables efficient and effective cross-selling and up-selling of many (but not all) products and services.

Industry Characteristics

Electronic markets are most useful when they are able to match buyers and sellers directly. However, some industries require transaction brokers. E-markets affect these industries less than those that do not require brokers. Stockbrokers, insurance agents, and travel agents may provide needed services, but in some cases software may reduce the need for these brokers. This is particularly true as intelligent systems become more available to assist consumers.

Other important industry characteristics include the following: Who are the major players (corporations) in the industry? How many companies in the industry are well managed? How strong is the competition, including foreign companies?

Seller Characteristics

Electronic markets reduce *search costs*, allowing consumers to find sellers that offer lower prices, better service, or both. As in the case of the motion picture industry, this may reduce profit margins for sellers that compete in e-markets, but it may increase the number of transactions that take place (i.e., people watching more movies). However, if sellers are unwilling to participate in this environment, it may reduce the impact of e-markets. In highly competitive industries with low barriers to entry, sellers may not have a choice but to join in; if they do not, online customers' searches will lead them to an online competitor's distribution channel.

Consumer Characteristics

Consumers can be classified as impulse, patient, or analytical. Electronic markets may have little impact on industries in which impulse buyers make a sizable percentage of purchases. Because e-markets require a certain degree of effort and preparation on the part of the consumer, e-markets are more conducive to consumers who do some comparisons before buying (i.e., the patient and analytical buyers). Mobile devices are changing this situation because real-time information is available now while shoppers are in physical stores.

Analytical buyers can use the Internet to evaluate a wide range of information before deciding on what and where to buy. In contrast, *m-commerce*, and especially *l-commerce*, which provides and even customizes services based on a customer's location, are banking on impulse buyers—on the customer's being in the right place at the right time.

Section 11.3 ▶ REVIEW QUESTIONS

1. List the major difficulties in measuring costs, benefits, and success of EC.
2. Describe product characteristics in EC.
3. What are industry characteristics in EC?
4. What are seller characteristics in EC?
5. What are consumer characteristics in EC?

11.4 GLOBAL E-COMMERCE

Global electronic activities have existed for more than 25 years, mainly EFT and EDI in support of B2B and other repetitive, standardized financial transactions. However, these activities required expensive and inflexible private telecommunications lines and, therefore, were limited mostly to large corporations. The emergence of the Internet and technologies such as extranets and XML has resulted in an inexpensive and flexible infrastructure that can greatly facilitate global trade.

A global electronic marketplace is an attractive thrust for an EC strategy. "Going global" means access to larger markets, mobility (e.g., to minimize taxes), and flexibility to employ workers anywhere. However, going global is a complex and strategic decision process due to a multiplicity of issues. Geographic distance is one of the most obvious dimensions of conducting business globally, but frequently it is not the most important dimension. Instead cultural, political, legal, administrative, and economic dimensions are equally likely to threaten a firm's international ambitions. This section briefly examines the opportunities, problems, and solutions for companies taking e-commerce to a global level.

BENEFITS AND EXTENT OF OPERATIONS

The major advantage of EC is the ability to do business at any time, from anywhere, and at a reasonable cost. These also are the drivers behind global EC, and there have been some incredible success stories in this area. For example:

▶ EBay conducts auctions in hundreds of countries worldwide.

▶ Alibaba.com (Chapter 5) provides B2B trading services to hundreds of thousands of companies in hundreds of countries.

▶ Amazon.com sells books and hundreds of other items to individuals and organizations in over 200 countries.

▶ Small companies, such as ZD Wines (zdwines.com), sell to hundreds of customers worldwide. Hot Hot Hot! (hothothot.com) reported its first international trade only after it went online; within three years, global sales accounted for 25 percent of its total sales. By 2009, the company had over 10,000 hits per day (up from 500 in 1997), and its annual growth rate was over 125 percent, selling to customers in 45 countries.

▶ Major corporations, such as GE and Boeing, have reported an increasing number of out-of-the-country vendors participating in their electronic RFQs. These electronic bids have resulted in a 10 to 15 percent cost reduction and an over 50 percent reduction in cycle time.

▶ Many international corporations considerably increased their success in recruiting employees for foreign locations when they used online recruiting (see xing.com and linkedin.com).

BARRIERS TO GLOBAL EC

Despite the benefits and opportunities offered by globalization, there are many barriers to global EC. Some of these barriers face any EC venture but become more difficult when international impacts are considered. These barriers include authentication of buyers and sellers (Chapter 10), generating and retaining trust (Chapter 4), order fulfillment and delivery (Online Appendix A), security (Chapter 9), and domain names. Others are unique to global EC. We will use the culture, administration, geography, economics (CAGE) distance framework proposed by Ghemawat (2001) to identify areas in which natural or human-made barriers hinder global EC. Each of the four factors represents a different type of distance (difference) between two companies.

Cultural Issues and Language Translation

The Internet is a multifaceted marketplace made up of users from many cultures. The multicultural nature of global EC is important because cultural attributes determine how people interact with companies, agencies, and each other based on social norms, local standards, religious beliefs, and language. Doing business globally requires *cultural marketing*, a strategy for meeting the needs of a culturally diverse population.

Cultural and related differences include language, spelling differences (e.g., American versus British spelling), information formatting (e.g., dates can be mm/dd/yy or dd/mm/yy), graphics and icons (e.g., mailbox shapes differ from country to country), measurement standards (e.g., metric versus imperial system), the use of color (e.g., white is a funeral color in some countries), protection of intellectual property (e.g., Chinese tolerance of copyright infringement has Confucian roots), time standards (e.g., local time zones versus Greenwich Mean Time), and information requests (e.g., requiring a zip code in an order form can lead to abandoned shopping carts in countries without postal codes).

Solutions for overcoming cultural barriers begin with an awareness of the cultural identities and differences in the target markets. Different sites may need to be created for different cultural groups, taking into account site design elements, pricing and payment infrastructures, currency conversion, customer support, and language translation. One solution involves language translation by machine.

Machine Translation of Web Pages

Language translation is one of the most obvious and most important aspects of maintaining global Web sites. The primary problems with language translation are speed and cost. It may take a human translator a week to translate a medium-sized Web site into another language. For large sites, the cost can be up to $500,000, depending on the complexity of the site and languages of translation and it may take a long time. A good translator needs to pay attention to cultural issues. Some companies address the cost and time problems by translating their Web pages into different languages through so-called *machine translators* (a list of these translator programs is available in Online File W11.6). However, machine translation is only about 70 to 75 percent accurate (Florencia 2009), which is why many companies use native-language, in-country translators to review and revise the results from machine translation software. For an organization that is successfully using machine translation, see Online File W11.6.

Transclick (transclick.com) provides real-time machine translation of e-mails, SMS, text messages, and instant messaging over computers, smart phones, and mobile PDAs in 16 different languages.

For more on machine translation, see en.wikipedia.org/wiki/Machine_Translation. Note that some social networks use volunteers to translate their pages. In some cases, thousands of volunteers sign up to translate an entire site into their native language and accomplish it in less than two weeks.

Administrative and Legal Issues

One of the most contentious areas of global EC is the resolution of international legal issues. A number of national governments and international organizations are working together to find ways to avoid uncoordinated actions and encourage uniform legal standards.

International trade organizations, such as the World Trade Organization (WTO) and the Asia-Pacific Economic Cooperation (APEC) forum, have working groups that are attempting to reduce EC trade barriers in areas such as pricing regulations, customs, import/export restrictions, tax issues, and product specification regulations.

Geographic Issues and Localization

The geographic issues of shipping goods and services across international borders are well known. Barriers posed by geography differ based on the transportation infrastructure between and within countries and the type of product or service being delivered. For example, geographic distance is almost irrelevant with online software sales.

Many companies use different names, colors, sizes, and packaging for their overseas products and services. This practice is referred to as *localization*. In order to maximize the benefits of global information systems, the localization approach should also be used in the design and operation of the supporting information systems. For example, many Web sites offer different language or currency options, as well as special content.

Europcar (europcar.com), for example, offers portals in 160 countries, each with an option for 1 of 10 languages. For more on localization, see en.wikipedia.org/wiki/Localization.

Economic and Financial Issues

Economic and financial issues encompassing global EC include government tariffs, customs, and taxation. In areas subject to government regulation, tax and regulatory agencies have attempted to apply the rules used in traditional commerce to electronic commerce, with considerable success. Exceptions include areas such as international tariff duties and taxation. Software shipped in a box would be taxed for duties and tariffs when it arrives in the country. However, software downloaded online relies on self-reporting and voluntary payment of tax by the purchaser, something that does not happen very often.

A key financial barrier to global EC is electronic payment systems. To sell effectively online, EC firms must have flexible payment methods that match the ways different groups of people pay for their online purchases. Although credit cards are used widely in the United States, many European and Asian customers prefer to complete online transactions with offline payments. Even within the category of offline payments, companies must offer different options depending on the country. For example, French consumers prefer to pay with a check, Swiss consumers expect an invoice by mail, Germans commonly pay for products only upon delivery, and Swedes are accustomed to paying online with debit cards.

Pricing is another economic issue. A vendor may want to price the same product at different prices in different countries in consideration of local prices and competition. However, if a company has one Web site, differential pricing will be difficult or impossible. Similarly, what currency will be used for pricing? What currency will be used for payment?

BREAKING DOWN THE BARRIERS TO GLOBAL EC

A number of international organizations and experts have offered suggestions on how to break down the barriers to global EC. Some of these suggestions include the following:

- **Be strategic.** Identify a starting point and lay out a globalization strategy. Remember that Web globalization is a business-building process. Consider what languages and countries it makes sense for the company to target, and how the company will support the site for each target audience.
- **Know your audience.** Carefully consider the target audience. Be fully informed of the cultural preferences and legal issues that matter to customers in a particular part of the world.
- **Localize.** As much as is practical and necessary, offer Web sites in national languages; offer different sites in different countries (e.g., "Yahoo! Japan" is at yahoo.co.jp); price products in local currencies; and base terms, conditions, and business practices on local laws and cultural practices.
- **Think globally, act consistently.** An international company with country Web sites managed by local offices must make sure that areas such as brand management, pricing, corporate information, and content management are consistent with company strategy.
- **Value the human touch.** Trust the translation of the Web site content only to human translators, not machine translation programs. Involve language and technical editors in the quality assurance process. One slight mistranslation or one out-of-place graphic may turn off customers forever.

▶ **Clarify, document, explain.** Pricing, privacy policies, shipping restrictions, contact information, and business practices should be well documented and located on the Web site and visible to the customer. To help protect against foreign litigation, identify the company's location and the jurisdiction for all contract or sales disputes.

▶ **Offer services that reduce barriers.** It is not feasible to offer prices and payments in all currencies, so link to a currency exchange service (e.g., xe.com) for the customer's convenience. In B2B e-commerce, be prepared to integrate the EC transaction with the buyer's accounting/finance internal information systems.

We close our discussion of global e-commerce with an example of a company's expansion into the international market in Case 11.2.

CASE 11.2
EC Application
PIERRE LANG EXPANDS INTO EASTERN EUROPE

Pierre Lang Europe (*pierrelang.com*) sells designer jewelry throughout Western Europe. Its traditional business model was to sell earrings, pendants, necklaces, and other jewelry through the firm's 5,500 sales representatives. When Pierre Lang decided to expand into Eastern Europe, the firm decided it needed to change this business model and the underlying information systems and business processes.

The company knew it was losing business because it was unable to keep track of customers and it did not have direct contact with them. If sales representatives left the company for any reason, they would take their customers with them. Pierre Lang Europe wanted more than sales from its customers; it wanted customer relationships for follow-on sales and customer support.

Like many companies expanding globally, Pierre Lang also anticipated that this expansion could double its revenues and order volume. The company needed better information about its finances, improved control of its order process, and a system that could handle the multiple legal and language requirements of doing business in many different countries.

Lang selected mySAP after evaluating several competing solutions. Installation began in July 2003; early rollout projects were in place by November; and financial and controlling capabilities went live in all company locations in January 2004.

Today, Pierre Lang uses country-specific versions of mySAP to handle invoicing, tax, language, and fiscal issues. France, for example, has unique requirements for tracking the import and export of gold and silver. "Lots of small things like that have to be considered because they're vital for Pierre Lang. It has to work perfectly in every country, so they have to know whom they will charge what, and do that automatically," says Rudolf Windisch, one of Pierre Lang's consulting partners on this project. "They also have to deal with all the tax issues, which vary

considerably from one country to another. There are no homogeneous tax systems in Europe."

Pierre Lang expects to increase the accuracy of its information and eliminate the need for manual transfers of tax data to develop reports. Executives also anticipate decreased inventory costs through improved material disposition as well as better information about sales efforts and costs that will lead to improved forecasting and planning.

As noted in this chapter, expanding regionally or globally can have a dramatic impact on a company's bottom line but only if it is prepared to deal with the heterogeneous legal and financial systems in different countries. Pierre Lang knew this and met the challenge.

To safeguard its multinational enterprise network, the company uses an integrated network security platform (from *fortinet.com*). The system protects both the headquarters in Vienna and 65 sales offices throughout Europe. The centrally managed system protects every remote user. The system is updated in real time.

Sources: SAP AG (2004), *sap.com* (accessed November 2009), and *Fortinet.com* (2005).

Questions

1. Why was it necessary for Pierre Lang to look at fundamental changes in its business model and information systems?

2. What have been the results of implementing mySAP at Pierre Lang?

3. Why is security so important to the company and how is it protected?

4. Enter *fortinet.com* and examine the capabilities of its FortiGate products.

Section 11.4 ▶ REVIEW QUESTIONS

1. Describe globalization in EC and the advantages it presents.
2. Describe the major barriers to global EC.
3. What can companies do to overcome the barriers to global EC?

11.5 E-COMMERCE IN SMALL AND MEDIUM-SIZED ENTERPRISES

Some of the first companies to take advantage of Web-based electronic commerce were SMEs. Whereas most of the larger, established, tradition-bound companies hesitated, SMEs moved onto the Web because they realized there were opportunities in marketing, business expansion, business launches, cost cutting, and tighter partner alliances. Some examples of small companies that have embraced EC are hothothot.com and philaprintshop.com.

SMEs consider the Internet to be a valuable business tool. According to a 2008 survey by Register.com (Palotie 2008), 41 percent of small businesses expect more than one-quarter of their annual sales to come from the Internet; 70 percent of the respondents expected sales to grow even in the economic downturn. And it isn't only online sales that are being used to measure success. Most of the respondents planned to enhance their Web site's design, search engine optimization, and e-mail marketing in order to stay in touch with customers and reach potential customers. However, many SMEs have found it difficult to formulate or implement an EC strategy, mainly because of low use of EC and IT by customers and suppliers, lack of knowledge or IT expertise in the SME, and limited awareness of the opportunities and risks. Exhibit 11.7 provides a more complete list of major advantages and disadvantages of EC for SMEs. For critical success factors for SMEs, see Online File W11.7.

When analyzing e-commerce for SMEs, one should distinguish between B2C, which may be simple, and B2B, which may be complex when the SME is a supplier to a large company.

SUPPORTING SMES

SMEs have a variety of support options. Almost every developed country in the world has a government agency devoted to helping SMEs become more aware of and able to participate in electronic commerce (e.g., sba.gov, business.gov.au).

Vendors realized the opportunity represented by thousands of businesses going online, and many have set up a variety of service centers that typically offer a combination of free information and fee-based support. Examples are IBM's Small Business Center (ibm.com/businesscenter) and Microsoft's Small Business Center (microsoft.com/smallbusiness/hub.mspx). Professional associations, Web resource services (e.g., smallbusiness.yahoo.com), and small businesses that are in the business of helping other small businesses go online sponsor other small business support centers.

Section 11.5 ▶ REVIEW QUESTIONS

1. What are the advantages or benefits of EC for small businesses?
2. What are the disadvantages or risks of EC for small businesses?
3. What are the CSFs for small businesses online? (Hint: See Online File W11.7.)
4. How can one support EC in a small company?

EXHIBIT 11.7 **Advantages and Disadvantages of EC for Small and Medium-Sized Businesses**	
Advantages/Benefits	**Disadvantages/Risks**
<ul><li>Inexpensive sources of information (search engines).</li><li>Inexpensive ways of advertising and conducting market research. Banner exchanges, newsletters, chat rooms, and so on are nearly zero-cost ways to reach customers.</li><li>Competitor analysis is easier. A Scandinavian study found that Finnish firms rated competitor analysis third in their use of the Internet, after information search and marketing.</li><li>Inexpensive ways to build (or rent) a storefront. Creating and maintaining a Web site is relatively easy and cheap.</li><li>SMEs are less locked into legacy technologies and existing relationships with traditional retail channels.</li><li>Image and public recognition can be generated quickly. A Web presence makes it easier for a small business to compete against larger firms.</li><li>An opportunity to reach worldwide customers. No other medium is as efficient at global marketing, sales, and customer support.</li><li>Other advantages for SMEs include increased speed of customer payments, closer ties with business partners, reduced errors in information transfer, lower operating costs, and other benefits that apply to all businesses.</li></ul>	<ul><li>Lack of financial resources to fully exploit the Web. A transactional Web site may entail relatively high up-front, fixed costs in terms of cash flow for an SME.</li><li>Lack of technical staff or insufficient expertise in legal issues, advertising, etc. These human resources may be unavailable or prohibitively expensive to an SME.</li><li>Less risk tolerance than a large company. If initial sales are low or the unexpected happens, the typical SME does not have a large reserve of resources to fall back on.</li><li>When the product is not suitable or difficult for online sales (e.g., experiential products such as clothes or beauty products; perishable products, such as certain foods), the Web opportunity is not as great.</li><li>Reduced personal contact with customers represents the dilution of what is normally a strong point for a small business.</li><li>Inability to afford entry to or purchase enough volume to take advantage of digital exchanges.</li></ul>

11.6 INTELLECTUAL PROPERTY AND OTHER REGULATORY ISSUES

A large number of ethical legal and regulatory issues may be involved in EC implementation. They are covered in Sections 11.6 through 11.8.

LAWS ARE SUBJECT TO INTERPRETATION

Keep in mind that *many* laws and regulations are broadly and sometimes vaguely written and, therefore, only provide outlines to guide public policy.

Specific disputes (such as the legality of spam) cannot be resolved by simply referring to relevant laws for two reasons. First, the scope of a law (i.e., whether it applies to a specific situation) needs to be interpreted by looking at lawmakers' intent. Second, laws may conflict with each other. For example, how companies use information collected from customers via their Web sites is subject to privacy laws. One privacy law may prohibit a company from sharing customers' social security numbers with business partners, whereas a homeland security law may require revealing the identity of customers. (Banks with CRM programs often encounter these legal conflicts). Another example of legal conflict is the debate between free speech and protection of children from offensive content (see Section 11.7). An example of different interpretations in different countries is illustrated in Case 11.3.

CASE 11.3
EC Application
IS EBAY A STORE OR A BULLETIN BOARD?

Let's look at two 2008 court decisions testing eBay's liability for counterfeit merchandise sold by its users. Courts in the United States and France reached opposite conclusions on nearly identical facts, demonstrating just how fractured and confused the developing law of Internet commerce can be.

The luxury jeweler Tiffany & Co. sued eBay for refusing to comply with its demands to eliminate the sale of fake Tiffany merchandise on eBay. Citing eBay's multimillion-dollar program to control the sale of fakes, as well as extensive tools provided to Tiffany and other brands to identify and report suspicious listings, the judge ruled in favor of eBay in 2008. "It is the trademark owner's burden to police its mark," he concluded. (A similar decision was made in Belgium in May 2009.)

The Paris Commercial Court reached the opposite conclusion a week earlier, and ordered eBay to pay more than $60 million in damages to a European jeweler. A particularly disturbing feature of the French case is that some of the merchandise was not alleged to be counterfeit, but was simply being sold or resold without permission from the jeweler.

Both decisions are being appealed. EBay has lost similar cases in Europe. In the United States, an American software trade association has threatened to sue eBay over allowing unauthorized or unlicensed software sales.

The difficulty here is that the legal system does not define what an electronic marketplace is. Also, eBay never takes possession of the goods that are sold through its Web site. Thus, eBay argues that it is simply a host for classified ads, like a newspaper. The truth is that electronic markets are something new and are not covered properly by the legal system.

Sources: Compiled from Downes (2008) and Arden-Besunder and Sherwin (2009).

Questions

1. In your opinion is eBay a store or an electronic board? Why?

2. Can such conflicting court decisions happen in the same country? Why or why not?

3. Why is it said that a corporate strategy can help an EC vendor?

4. Some say that the jewelers are suing eBay because it interferes with their illegal price-fixing practices. Comment on this issue.

PERSONAL AND PROPERTY RIGHTS

In a legal system, the government produces a set of rules and regulations and has the power to enforce them, as shown in the legal framework in Exhibit 11.8.

Rights are divided into two categories: personal rights and property rights. Generally, the interests of *life* and *liberty* fall into the personal rights category. *Property* interests are in the category of property rights. Internet business Web sites, proprietary systems, and customer lists are examples of property.

Owners of property, including intellectual property, are entitled to:

▶ Control of the use of the property.
▶ The right to any benefit from the property.
▶ The right to transfer or sell the property.
▶ The right to exclude others from the property

civil litigation
An adversarial proceeding in which a party (the plaintiff) sues another party (the defendant) to get compensation for a wrong committed by the defendant.

Referring to Exhibit 11.8, it is clear that an online business has the legal right to prevent spammers or other businesses from interfering with or harming the benefits (profits) from its EC site—and can file lawsuits against them. Lawsuits are one type of **civil litigation**, which is an adversarial proceeding in which a party (the plaintiff) sues another party (the defendant) to get compensation for a wrong committed by the defendant. For example, the entertainment industry has the right to its intellectual

EXHIBIT 11.8 Legal Framework for Understanding Law, Rights, and Duties

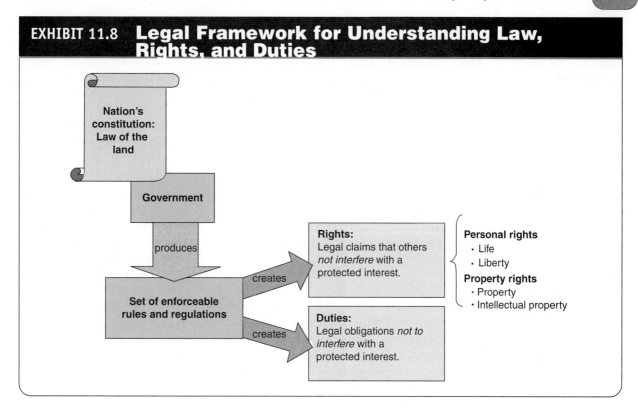

property (IP) and can file lawsuits (civil charges) against online businesses, such as YouTube and MySpace, for any interference with the ability to profit from its IP or for profiting from the recording industry's property without authorization and compensation. In contrast, law enforcement or a public official brings criminal litigation. The next section discusses criminal and civil laws further. You will also learn the terminology needed to understand legal issues.

Regulatory Compliance in EC

In general, compliance means conforming to a specification or policy, standard, or law that has been clearly defined. Corporate scandals, such as the financial crisis in 2008–2009 or the Enron case in 2001, have highlighted the need for stronger compliance regulations for publicly listed companies. One of the most significant regulations in this context is the Sarbanes-Oxley Act, which defines significantly tighter personal responsibility of corporate top management for the accuracy of reported financial statements.

Regulatory compliance refers to systems or departments in an organization whose job is to ensure that personnel are aware of and take steps to comply with relevant laws, standards, policies, and regulations. These laws can have criminal or civil penalties. Unfortunately, the definition of what constitutes an effective compliance plan has been elusive.

A single point of access to government services and information concerning business compliance with government regulations is available at business.gov.

To help with compliance, one can use EC software, especially with compliance data. **Compliance data** is defined as all data belonging or pertaining to an enterprise or included in the law, which can be used for the purpose of implementing or validating compliance. Compliance software is available from all major software companies (e.g., Oracle, IBM, EMC, and Computer Associates).

regulatory compliance
Systems or departments in an organization whose job is to ensure that personnel are aware of and take steps to comply with relevant laws, standards, policies, and regulations.

compliance data
All data belonging or pertaining to an enterprise included in the law, which can be used for the purpose of implementing or validating compliance.

INTELLECTUAL PROPERTY LAW (A CIVIL LAW)

intellectual property
Creations of the mind, such as inventions, literary and artistic works, and symbols, names, images, and designs, used in commerce.

Intellectual property is a creation of the mind, such as inventions, literary and artistic works, and symbols, names, images, and designs, used in commerce. Intellectual property law is the area of the law that includes copyright law, patent law, trademark law, trade secret law, and other branches of related law, such as licensing and unfair competition. See Online File W11.8 for intellectual property Web sites.

Another perspective is that intellectual property law is concerned with the legal regulation of mental products (e.g., performing arts, video games), including creativity.

Copyright

copyright
An exclusive right of the author or creator of a book, movie, musical composition, or other artistic property to print, copy, sell, license, distribute, transform to another medium, translate, record, perform, or otherwise use.

A **copyright** is an exclusive right of the author or creator of a book, movie, musical composition, or other artistic property to print, copy, sell, license, distribute, transform to another medium, translate, record, perform, or otherwise use. In the United States, as soon as a work is created and in a tangible form such as through writing or recording, the work automatically has federal copyright protection. A copyright does not last forever; it is good for a fixed number of years after the death of the author or creator (e.g., 50 in the United Kingdom). In the United States, copyright was extended to 70 years after the death of the author by the *1998 Sonny Bono Copyright Extension Act.* After the copyright expires, the work reverts to the public domain. The legal term for the use of the work without permission or contracting for payment of a royalty is **infringement**. Numerous high-profile lawsuits have been filed for EC copyright infringement. For more on copyrights, see en.wikipedia.org/wiki/Wikipedia:Copyrights.

infringement
Use of the work without permission or contracting for payment of a royalty.

To protect its interests, the Recording Industry Association of America (RIAA), the recording industry's trade group, uses lawsuits to stamp out rampant music piracy on university campuses. RIAA launched a lawsuit-settlement Web site (p2plawsuits.com; no longer live) and sent a mass mailing to college and university presidents across the United States asking for their cooperation in its ongoing war against file sharing. RIAA sought compensation from university students for losses that it alleged were caused by copyright infringement. In February 2007, RIAA announced that it would give 400 college students at 13 universities suspected of illegally pirating music online the option to reach discounted settlements before being sued for greater damages for copyright infringement. In 2008, RIAA changed its tactics and instituted a "three-strike" plan. The plan calls for RIAA to tell Internet service providers who they believe are sharing copyrighted material. The ISPs cooperate by agreeing to send an e-mail warning; the second time, sending a letter; and the third time Internet access is cut off.

Universal Music Group, the world's largest music company, filed a lawsuit against MySpace for copyright infringement of thousands of artists' work. French media giant Vivendi owns Universal, and it filed the lawsuit at the U.S. District Court of California. Universal estimated maximum damages for each copyrighted work at $150,000. YouTube avoided a similar lawsuit by reaching a licensing agreement with Universal Music.

Digital Rights Management (DRM)

digital rights management (DRM)
An umbrella term for any of several arrangements that allow a vendor of content in electronic form to control the material and restrict its usage.

Digital rights management (DRM) is an umbrella term for any of several arrangements that allow a vendor of content in electronic form to control the material and restrict its usage. These arrangements are really technology-based protection measures. Typically, the content is a copyrighted digital work to which the vendor holds rights.

In the past, when content was analog in nature, it was easier to buy a new copy of a copyrighted work on a physical medium (e.g., paper, film, tape) than to produce such a copy independently. The quality of most copies often was inferior. Digital technologies make it possible to produce a high-quality duplicate of any digital recording with minimal effort. The Internet virtually has eliminated the need for a physical medium to transfer a work, which has led to the use of DRM systems for protection.

However, DRM systems may restrict the *fair use* of material by individuals. In law, **fair use** refers to the use of copyrighted material for noncommercial purposes. Several DRM technologies were developed without regard for privacy protection. Many systems require the user to reveal his or her identity and rights to access protected content. Upon authentication of identity and rights to the content, the user can access the content (see epic.org/privacy/drm). For more on DRM, see en.wikipedia.org/wiki/Digital_rights_management.

fair use
The use of copyrighted material for noncommercial purposes.

Patents

A **patent** is a document that grants the holder exclusive rights to an invention for a fixed number of years (e.g., 17 years in the United States and 20 years in the United Kingdom). Patents serve to protect tangible technological inventions, especially in traditional industrial areas. They are not designed to protect artistic or literary creativity. Patents confer monopoly rights to an idea or an invention, regardless of how it may be expressed. An invention may be in the form of a physical device or a method or process for making a physical device. Similar to a patent is a **trademark** which is a symbol businesses use to identify their goods and services; government registration of the trademark confers exclusive legal right to its use.

Certain patents granted in the United States deviate from established practices in Europe. For example, Amazon.com successfully obtained a U.S. patent on its *1-Click* ordering procedure. Using this patent, Amazon.com sued Barnes & Noble in 1999 and in 2000, alleging that its rival had copied its patented technology. Barnes & Noble was enjoined by the courts from using the procedure. Similarly, in 1999 Priceline.com filed a suit against Expedia.com alleging that Expedia was using Priceline's patented reverse-auction business model. The suit was settled in 2001 when Expedia.com agreed to pay Priceline.com royalties for use of the model. However, in Europe and many Asian, African, and South American countries, it is almost impossible to obtain patents on business methods or computer processes.

patent
A document that grants the holder exclusive rights to an invention for a fixed number of years.

trademark
A symbol used by businesses to identify their goods and services; government registration of the trademark confers exclusive legal right to its use.

Section 11.6 ▶ REVIEW QUESTIONS

1. Why is the law subject to interpretation?
2. Define personal and property rights.
3. Define intellectual property.
4. Define copyright.
5. Define civil law.
6. Define DRM. Describe one potential impact on privacy.
7. Define patents and relate them to EC.

11.7 ETHICS IN E-COMMERCE

Ethics describes how individuals choose to interact with one another. It is the branch of philosophy that deals with what is considered to be right and wrong. Ethics define the nature of duties that people owe themselves and one another. One duty is to not intrude on a person's **privacy**, which is the right to be left alone and free of unreasonable personal intrusions.

ethics
The branch of philosophy that deals with what is considered to be right and wrong.

privacy
The right to be left alone and free of unreasonable personal intrusions.

ETHICAL PRINCIPALS AND GUIDELINES

Law embodies ethical principles, but the two are not the same. Acts that are generally considered unethical may not be illegal. Lying to a friend may be unethical, but it is not illegal. Conversely, the law is not simply the coding of ethical norms, nor are all ethical codes incorporated into public law.

A common agreement in a society as to what is right and wrong determines ethics, but they are not subject to legal sanctions except when they overlap with activities that also are illegal. Online File W11.9 shows a framework for ethical issues. An example of one ethical issue is the Facebook fiasco of 2009.

Example: Who Owns User-Generated Content at Facebook?

In February 2009, Facebook casually slipped into its terms of service an updated clause that users must sign before joining, announcing that users give Facebook an irrevocable, perpetual, nonexclusive, transferable, fully paid, worldwide license to use, retain, and display content posted to the site. In other words, anything you upload to Facebook can be used by Facebook in any way it deems fit, forever, no matter what you do later. Consumer watchdog groups and privacy experts immediately cried foul.

The objective of this change was to enable Facebook to sell customer data to marketers: Facebook needed more revenue sources. As a result, Facebook pointed out that the company wouldn't use information in a way that goes against the privacy settings outlined by users. Facebook also claimed that the new policy was consistent with how other services (like e-mail) work. However, legal and privacy experts say that Facebook is giving itself wider latitude in how it can use content than several other companies that rely on user-generated content. Retaining rights to content after the user has left is unprecedented for a social media site.

Facebook did not do a good enough job of communicating the changes to the terms of service, privacy experts say. Rather than asking users to agree to the new terms, or even sending an e-mail alert to all users, the company quietly added this line to its terms: "Your continued use of the Facebook Service after any such changes constitutes your acceptance of the new terms." That may not be good business practice, but is it unethical?

BUSINESS ETHICS

business ethics

A form of applied ethics that examines ethical principles and moral or ethical problems that arise in a business environment.

Business ethics is a form of applied ethics that examines ethical principles and moral or ethical problems that arise in a business environment.

Business ethics defines how a company integrates the core values of honesty, trust, respect, and fairness into its policies and practices—and complies with legal standards and regulations. The scope of business ethics has expanded to encompass a company's actions with regard not only to how it treats employees and obeys laws but to the nature and quality of the relationships with shareholders, customers, business partners, suppliers, the community, the environment, and even future generations, as well. European companies especially have embraced this expanded definition of ethics. Under recent clarifications of the U.S. Federal Sentencing Guidelines (ussc.gov/guidelin.htm), companies with credible ethics programs, as opposed to merely *paper* programs such as that of Enron Corp., may reduce penalties or avoid prosecution for crimes committed by managers or employees.

Because of the worldwide scope and universal accessibility of the Internet, there are serious questions as to which ethical rules and laws apply in EC. These questions involve an appreciation of the law that is constantly changing. Lawsuits and criminal charges are very disruptive, expensive, and may damage customer relations. The best strategy is to avoid behaviors that expose the company to these types of risks.

EXHIBIT 11.9   Safeguards to Minimize Exposure to Risk of Criminal or Civil Charges

1. Does the Web site clearly post shipment policies and guarantees? Can the company fulfill those policies and guarantees? Does the Web site explain what happens in case of a missed deadline? Does it comply with Federal Trade Commission (FTC) rules?
2. Does the Web site clearly articulate procedures for customers to follow when returning gifts or seeking a refund for services not received?
3. Has the company checked backgrounds before entering agreements with third-party vendors and supply chain partners? Do those agreements with vendors and partners indemnify (i.e., protect) the company against their failure to deliver goods or process transactions on time and correctly?
4. If a third-party ISP or Web-hosting service is used, are there safeguards if the site crashes, is infected by malware, or if bandwidth is insufficient to meet all of your customers' needs?
5. Is there sufficient customer support staff, and are they knowledgeable and adequately trained to process inquiries from customers?

Businesspeople engaging in e-commerce need guidelines as to what behaviors are reasonable and what risks are foreseeable under a given set of circumstances. Based on what you have read, it is clear that the two major risks are a criminal charge or lawsuit (civil charge). Exhibit 11.9 lists examples of safeguards to minimize exposure to those risks.

EC ETHICAL ISSUES

There are many EC- and Internet-related ethical issues. Examples of ethical issues discussed elsewhere in this book are channel conflict (Chapter 3), pricing conflict (Chapter 3), disintermediation (Chapters 2, 3, and 5), and trust (Chapter 4). Two additional EC-related ethical issues are nonwork-related use of the Internet and codes of ethics.

Nonwork-Related Use of the Internet

A majority of employees use e-mail and surf the Web for nonwork-related purposes. The use of company property for e-mail and Internet use creates risk and wastes time. The degree of risk depends on the extent to which the company has implemented policies and procedures to prevent and detect illegal uses. For example, companies may be held liable for their employees' use of e-mail to harass another employee, participate in illegal gambling, or distribute child pornography.

Codes of Ethics

A practical and necessary approach to limiting nonwork-related Internet surfing is an Internet acceptable use policy (AUP) to which all employees must conform. It includes EC, social networks, and any IT-related topics. Without a formal AUP, it is much more difficult to enforce acceptable and eliminate unacceptable behaviors and punish violators. Whenever a user signs on to the corporate network, the user should see a reminder of the AUP and be notified that online activities are monitored. Such notification should be a part of a code of ethics.

Corporate *codes of ethics* state the rules and expected behaviors and actions. Typically, the ethics code should address the use of offensive content and graphics, as well as proprietary information. It should encourage employees to think about who should and who should not have access to information before they post it on the Web site. The code should specify whether the company allows employees to set up their own Web pages on

EXHIBIT 11.10 Corporate Web Policy Guidelines

- Issue written AUP guidelines about employee use of the Internet and communication systems including e-mail and instant messaging.
- Make it clear to employees that they cannot use copyrighted or trademarked material without permission.
- Post disclaimers concerning content, such as sample code, that the company does not support.
- Post disclaimers of responsibility concerning content of online forums and chat sessions.
- Make sure that Web content and activity comply with the laws in other countries, such as those governing contests and privacy.
- Make sure that the company's Web content policy is consistent with other company policies.
- Appoint someone to monitor Internet legal and liability issues and have that person report to a senior executive or legal counsel.
- Have attorneys with cyberlaw expertise review Web content to make sure that there is nothing unethical or illegal on the company's Web site, and that all required statements and disclaimers are properly included.

the company intranet and state policies regarding private e-mail usage and nonwork-related surfing during working hours. A company should formulate a general idea of the role it wants Web sites to play in the workplace. This should guide the company in developing an AUP and provide employees with a rationale for that policy. Finally, do not be surprised if the code of ethics looks a lot like simple rules of etiquette; it should. Exhibit 11.10 lists several useful guidelines for a corporate Web policy. For a list of Web site quality guidelines, see Online File W11.10. For ethics case studies, see harpercollege.edu/~tmorris/ekin/home.htm.

Section 11.7 ▶ REVIEW QUESTIONS

1. What does business ethics define?
2. Give an example of an EC activity that is unethical but not illegal.
3. Identify an employee activity that exposes a company to legal risk.
4. List the major issues that a code of ethics should include.

11.8 PRIVACY, VIOLATION AND PROTECTION, AND THE CONFLICT WITH FREE SPEECH

The explosion in online communications technologies has created complex new ethical dilemmas for businesses. As transaction costs for processing, storing, and transmitting data dropped dramatically and sophisticated tracking and monitoring software became widespread, concerns rose around online consumer privacy, free speech, and defamation. For example, there is an increasing risk of personal privacy invasion from compromising photos that digital cameras or cell phones capture, particularly when they are posted on the Internet. Related to this is the possible misuse of personal information, whether public or private.

PRIVACY RIGHTS AND PROTECTION

Privacy means different things to different people. In general, privacy is the right to be left alone and the right to be free of unreasonable personal intrusions. (For other definitions of privacy, see the Privacy Rights Clearinghouse at privacyrights.org.) Privacy has long been a legal, ethical, and social issue in most countries.

Today, virtually all U.S. states and the federal government, either by statute or by common law, recognize the right to privacy. The definition of privacy can be interpreted quite broadly. However, the following two rules have been followed fairly closely in past U.S. court decisions: (1) The right of privacy is not absolute. Privacy must be balanced against the needs of society. (2) The public's right to know is superior to the individual's right of privacy. These two rules show why it is sometimes difficult to determine and enforce privacy regulations.

Section 5 of the Federal Trade Commission Act prohibits unfair or deceptive practices and gives the Federal Trade Commission (FTC; a regulatory agency) authority to take action against companies whose lax security practices could expose the personal financial information of customers to theft or loss; it also protects privacy. For explanation of the act, see ftc.gov/privacy/privacyinitiatives/promises.html. Those practices extend to privacy, free speech, and defamation if the company does not fulfill its duty to protect the rights of others.

Opt-In and Opt-Out

To some extent, privacy concerns have been overshadowed by post–September 11 terrorism efforts, but consumers still expect and demand that companies behave as responsible custodians of their personal data. One way to manage this issue is *opt-in* and *opt-out* information practices. **Opt-out** is a business practice that gives consumers the opportunity to refuse to share information about themselves. Offering opt-out is a good customer practice, but it is difficult to opt out in some industries either because consumer demand for opt-out is low or the value of the customer information is high. In contrast, **opt-in** is based on the principle that information sharing should not occur unless customers affirmatively allow it or request it.

opt-out
Business practice that gives consumers the opportunity to refuse sharing information about themselves.

opt-in
Agreement that requires computer users to take specific steps to allow the collection of personal information.

FREE SPEECH ONLINE VERSUS PRIVACY PROTECTION

As with all rights, the right of free speech is not unlimited. Free speech does not mean any speech. Some of the traditional restrictions on what may be freely said or published are defamation laws (including privacy violation), contempt of court, and national security. For example, it is illegal to scream "fire" in a crowded theater or make bomb threats in an airport. Free speech often clashes with privacy, protection of children, indecency, and so forth.

Free Speech Online Versus Child Protection Debate

The conflict over free speech versus child protection erupted after the **Children's Internet Protection Act (CIPA)** was signed into law in December 2000. CIPA mandated the use of filtering technologies in schools and libraries that received certain types of U.S. federal funding. CIPA was immediately challenged in court, so it did not go into effect at that time.

Opponents of the law relied on earlier court cases (that is, a legal precedent), saying that government-imposed limitations on the public's right to freely read and learn at public libraries violated the free speech protections of the First Amendment. An example of child protection versus privacy can be seen in Online File W11.11.

Children's Internet Protection Act (CIPA)
U.S. law that mandates the use of filtering technologies in schools and libraries that receive certain types of federal funding.

THE PRICE OF PROTECTING AN INDIVIDUAL'S PRIVACY

In the past, the complexity of collecting, sorting, filing, and accessing information manually from several different government agencies was a built-in protection against misuse of private information. It was simply too expensive, cumbersome, and complex to invade a person's privacy. The Internet, in combination with large-scale databases, eliminated those barriers.

The inherent power in systems that can access vast amounts of data can be used for the good of society. For example, by matching records with the aid of a computer, it is possible to eliminate or reduce fraud, crime, government mismanagement, tax evasion, welfare fraud, employment of illegal aliens, and so on. The question is: What price must every individual pay in terms of loss of privacy so that the government can better apprehend these types of criminals? A related issue is the control of content in classified ads as described in the following Craigslist example.

Example: Sheriff Sues Craigslist to Curb Prostitution

The sheriff of Cook County, Illinois, filed a federal lawsuit in March 2009, alleging that Craigslist has become the top provider of prostitution services in the United States and claiming that missing children, runaways, abused women, and women trafficked in from foreign countries are routinely forced to have sex with strangers because they're being pimped on Craigslist.

The sheriff wanted Craigslist to shut down the erotic services category of its Web site and to compensate his department for the cost of prosecuting Web site–related prostitution cases. But Web free speech advocates say that existing laws insulate Craigslist from any illegal activities related to its ads, and they predict a quick defeat for the sheriff's legal efforts.

In May 2009, Craigslist decided to eliminate its "erotic services" category and screen all submissions to a new "adult services" section, and there will be manual checks of all submissions before they are posted.

HOW INFORMATION ABOUT INDIVIDUALS IS COLLECTED

The Internet offers a number of opportunities to collect private information about individuals. Exhibit 11.11 lists several ways that the Internet can be used to find information about an individual; the last three are the most common ways of gathering information on the Internet.

Web Site Registration

Virtually all B2C sites, marketing Web sites, online magazines, vendors, government sites, and social networks ask visitors to fill out registration forms. During the process, individuals voluntarily provide their names, addresses, phone numbers, e-mail addresses, hobbies and likes or dislikes, and other personal information to participate, receive a download, win a lottery, or receive some other item in exchange. There are few restraints

---

EXHIBIT 11.11 How to Use the Internet to Find Information

- By reading an individual's blogs or newsgroup postings
- By looking up an individual's name and identity in an Internet directory
- By reading an individual's e-mail, IM, or text messages
- By monitoring and conducting surveillance on employees
- By wiretapping wire line and wireless communication lines
- By asking an individual to complete a registration form on a Web site
- By recording an individual's actions as they navigate the Web with a browser, usually using cookies
- By using spyware, keystroke loggers, and similar methods

on the ways in which the site can use this information. The site might use it to improve customer service. Or the site could just as easily sell the information to another company, which could use it in an inappropriate or intrusive manner.

Internet users are skeptical of the necessity of giving such information to online businesses. Most people dislike registering at Web sites they visit; 15 percent refuse to register at all. Many do not trust companies not to share their personal information.

Cookies

Another way that a Web site can gather information about an individual is by using cookies. As described in Chapter 4, a cookie contains data that are passed back and forth between a Web site and an end user's browser as the user navigates the site. Cookies enable sites to keep track of users without having to constantly ask the users to identify themselves. Web bugs and spyware, described in Section 4.2, are similar to cookies.

Originally, cookies were designed to help with personalization and market research, as described in Chapter 4. However, cookies also can invade an individual's privacy. Cookies allow Web sites to collect detailed information about a user's preferences, interests, and surfing patterns. The personal profiles created by cookies often are more accurate than self-registration, because users have a tendency to falsify information in a registration form.

Although the ethics of the use of cookies are still being debated, concerns about cookies reached a pinnacle in 1997 at the U.S. FTC hearings on online privacy. Following those hearings, Netscape and Microsoft introduced options enabling users to block cookies. Since that time, the uproar has subsided because most users accept cookies rather than fight them. The problem with deleting or disabling cookies is that the user will have to keep reentering information and, in some instances, may be blocked from viewing particular pages.

RFID's Threat to Privacy

As mentioned in earlier chapters, privacy advocates fear that the information stored on RFID tags or collected with them may be used to violate an individual's privacy. To protect the individual, RSA Security and others are developing locking technologies that will protect consumers from being tracked after buying products with RFID tags. Several states (e.g., California) are considering legislation to protect customers from a loss of privacy due to the tags.

Privacy of Employees

In addition to customers' privacy, there is the issue of employees' privacy. Many employers monitor their employees' e-mail and Web activities. In addition to wasting time online, employees may disclose trade secrets and possibly make employers liable for defamation based on what they do on the corporate Web site. In response to these concerns, most companies monitor their employees' communications.

Another privacy concern stems from the "underground Internet" of private online communities called **darknets** that are only open to those who belong to the private network.

darknets
Private online community that is only open to those who belong to it.

PRIVACY ISSUES IN WEB 2.0 TOOLS AND SOCIAL NETWORKS

The explosion of social networks raises some special issues in privacy and free speech. Here are a few examples.

Presence, Location, and Privacy

Presence in the social networking world is becoming popular. For example, Facebook added instant messaging (IM) to its Web site, enabling users to know when friends are online. IBM Lotus also supports presence capabilities tied into "Connections," while Microsoft offers similar capabilities with SharePoint. The iPhone E2.0 Impact includes two applications, Loopt and Whrrl, which enable users to see both the real-time presence and the location of others by leveraging iPhone's built-in location awareness capabilities.

What happens when LinkedIn, Facebook, or MySpace provides the ability for a GPS-enabled mobile device or iPhone to dynamically share its location status with others? Will, or how will, businesses begin to take advantage of these same capabilities to build applications to enable tracking of field sales and support personnel by leveraging the location status capabilities already present in their mobile devices? What are the privacy implications? Who will be held responsible or legally liable for unforeseen harm resulting from so much awareness and connectivity?

Free Speech via Wikis and Social Networks

Free speech and privacy rights collide in a world populated by anonymous critics and cyber-bullies. But the attacks are not always from competitors or others outside the company.

Companies victimized by online gossip and rumors have legal recourse, but against whom? What if the identity of the sender or poster is unknown? What if the sender or poster is in another country? Who is responsible for restricting troublesome content?

PRIVACY PROTECTION USING ETHICAL PRINCIPLES

The ethical principles commonly applied to the collection and use of personal information also apply to information collected in e-commerce. These principles include the following:

▷ **Notice or awareness.** Consumers must be given notice of an entity's information practices prior to the collection of personal information. Consumers must be able to make informed decisions about the type and extent of their disclosures based on the intentions of the party collecting the information.

▷ **Choice or consent.** Consumers must be made aware of their options as to how their personal information may be used, as well as any potential secondary uses of the information. Consent may be granted through opt-in clauses.

▷ **Access or participation.** Consumers must be able to access their personal information and challenge the validity of the data.

▷ **Integrity or security.** Consumers must be assured that their personal data are secure and accurate. It is necessary for those collecting the data to take whatever precautions are required to ensure that they protect data from loss, unauthorized access or alteration, destruction, and fraudulent use, and to take reasonable steps to gain information from reputable and reliable sources. This principle has been extended to digital property.

▷ **Enforcement or redress.** A method of enforcement and remedy must be available. Otherwise, there is no real deterrent or enforceability for privacy issues.

P3P Privacy Platform

Platform for Privacy Preferences Project (P3P)
A protocol allowing Web sites to declare their intended use of information they collect about browsing users.

The **Platform for Privacy Preferences Project (P3P)** is a protocol allowing Web sites to declare their intended use of information they collect about browsing users. It is designed to give users more control of their personal information when browsing by communicating a Web site's privacy policies to its users, allowing them to compare the policies to their preferences or to other standards.

P3P is a mechanism that helps to express a Web site's data management practices. P3P manages information through privacy policies. When a Web site uses P3P, it sets up a set of policies that allows it to state its intended uses of personal information that may be gathered from its site's visitors.

The Purpose of P3P. As the Web became an acceptable medium in which to sell products and services, electronic commerce Web sites tried to collect more information about the people who purchased their merchandise. Some companies used controversial practices such as tracker cookies to ascertain the users' demographic information and buying habits, using this information to provide specifically targeted advertisements. Users who saw this as an invasion of privacy would sometimes turn off the cookies or use proxy servers to keep their personal information secure. P3P is designed to give users more precise control over this kind of information. The main goal of P3P is to increase user trust and confidence in the Web through technical empowerment.

When users decide to use P3P, they set their own policies and state what personal information they will allow to be seen by the sites that they visit. For implementation details, see w3.org/P3P/details.html.

THE USA PATRIOT ACT

The **USA PATRIOT Act** (officially, Uniting and Strengthening America by Providing Appropriate Tools to Intercept and Obstruct Terrorism) was passed in October 2001, in the aftermath of the September 11 terrorist attacks. Its intent is to give law enforcement agencies broader range in their efforts to protect the public. The American Civil Liberties Union (ACLU), the Electronic Freedom Foundation (EFF), and other organizations have grave concerns, including (1) expanded surveillance with reduced checks and balances, (2) overbreadth with a lack of focus on terrorism, and (3) rules that would allow U.S. foreign intelligence agencies to more easily spy on Americans.

On March 9, 2007, the U.S. Department of Justice (DOJ) said that the FBI had improperly used provisions of the USA PATRIOT Act to obtain thousands of telephone, business, and financial records without prior judicial approval. The report is available at justice.gov/oig/special/index.htm. The result of this report may restrain some of the parts of the act that allowed expanded surveillance in the following areas:

USA PATRIOT Act Uniting and Strengthening America by Providing Appropriate Tools to Intercept and Obstruct Terrorism Act passed in October 2001, in the aftermath of the September 11 terrorist attacks. Its intent is to give law enforcement agencies broader range in their efforts to protect the public.

- E-mail and Internet searches
- Nationwide roving wiretaps
- Requirement that ISPs hand over more user information
- Expanded scope of surveillance based on new definitions of terrorism
- Government spying on suspected computer trespassers with no need for a court order
- Wiretaps for suspected violations of the Computer Fraud and Abuse Act
- Dramatic increases in the scope and penalties of the Computer Fraud and Abuse Act
- General expansion of Foreign Intelligence Surveillance Act (FISA) authority
- Increased information sharing between domestic law enforcement and intelligence
- FISA detours around federal domestic surveillance limitations; domestic surveillance detours around FISA limitations

For more details, see en.wikipedia.org/wiki/USA_PATRIOT_Act.

Section 11.8 ❱ REVIEW QUESTIONS

1. Define privacy and describe some privacy rights.
2. How is privacy colliding with free speech?
3. List some of the ways that the Internet can collect information about individuals.
4. What are cookies and what do they have to do with online privacy?
5. Describe theP3P privacy platform.
6. List four common ethical principles related to the gathering of personal information.
7. How has the USA PATRIOT Act expanded the government's reach?

11.9 EC AND GREEN COMPUTING

Before concluding this book, we discuss one more important topic, the relationship of EC and the environment. We mentioned this topic briefly in Chapter 1. The fact is that successful EC companies such as Google, Akamai, Amazon.com, and eBay operate with hundreds of thousands of servers. These servers are housed in data centers and if not properly controlled, can cause major environmental problems.

OPERATING GREENER BUSINESSES AND ECOFRIENDLY DATA CENTERS

green computing
The study and practice of ecofriendly computing resources; is now a key concern of businesses in all industries—not just environmental organizations.

green IT
Green IT begins with manufacturers producing environmentally friendly products and encouraging IT departments to consider more friendly options like virtualization, power management, and proper recycling habits.

In this section, we focus on how EC is *going green* by adopting environmentally friendly practices. Enterprises are trying to reduce energy costs and increase the use of recyclable materials. **Green computing** is the study and practice of ecofriendly computing resources (e.g., see en.wikipedia.org/wiki/Green_computing).

Organizations and individuals are looking at potential improvements and savings that can be made in the EC and IT industry. These efforts are known as **Green IT**. A major area is energy use in data centers (a *data center* is a facility used to house computer systems and associated components, such as storage).

Data center servers are known to be both power hungry and heat generating. In addition, PC monitors consume about 80 to 100 billion kilowatt hours of electricity every year in the United States alone. (Therefore PCs should be turned off when not in use.) Additionally, the manufacturing process of PCs generates CO_2 (carbon dioxide) that damages the atmosphere. Finally, discarded PCs and other computer equipment cause waste disposal problems. An important issue is how to recycle old equipment and whose responsibility (the manufacturers? the users?) it is to take care of the problem. One solution is *green software*, which refers to software products that help companies save energy or comply with EPA requirements.

How to Operate Greener Businesses, Data Centers, and Supply Chains

In the United States, data centers consume about 20 to 30 billion kilowatt hours per year, and the number of servers is growing at 50 percent every three years. EC is supported in many cases by data centers. Data centers worldwide account for about 2 percent of all energy consumption. Virtualization software can combine multiple computing jobs onto fewer computers to cut energy use significantly. Standardized designs for data centers can enhance efficiency and benefits. IBM has developed data centers that use a modular design to cut energy consumption in half, compared with existing data centers (LaMonica 2009).

According to the Gartner Group, 80 percent of the world's data centers are constrained by heat, space, and power requirements. In addition to the demand on processing capability to satisfy the growth of the business, there is enormous demand on power consumption and space requirements for computing platforms. Data center configurations are no longer based on one dimension (e.g., price or performance)—meaning that factors other than affordability or performance must be considered. The equation is much more complicated. Gartner predicted that by 2008, 50 percent of current data centers would have insufficient power and cooling capacity to meet the demands of high-density equipment that traditionally accounted for less than 10 percent of an overall IT budget; demand could soon account for more than half. All of these factors must be taken into consideration when deciding on the design of a data center (reported by Sun Microsystems 2007).

An enterprise can cut energy costs in half, double space efficiency, and increase server utilization levels to as high as 85 percent. Gaining these efficiencies requires dealing with these four issues: the desktop, data center computing power, data center power/cooling, and data center storage. For more details on green computing, see Online File W11.12.

Example 1. Wells Fargo is a large financial institution that offers a wide range of services, including consumer and corporate banking, insurance, investments, and mortgages. The company is data-dependent and known for its ecofriendliness. In 2007, with the increase in energy costs, the company decided to go "green" in its two new data centers. The two new facilities have more than 8,000 servers that consume considerable power and generate heat. Data centers must ensure security and availability of their services, and when they are planned from scratch, they can be energy efficient with low power consumption.

Several energy-saving features were introduced, including water-based economizers that regulate energy usage and cool the physical environment, a computer-controlled central fan system for cooling the floors, direct air to cool specific hot spaces, and semiconductor chips that automatically shut off power until it is needed. With increasing volumes of data, Wells Fargo constantly expands and renovates its data centers, taking environmental concerns into consideration. The company experimented with a solar system for making hot water, with motion-detector lights, and with variable-speed fans.

Example 2. Monsanto, Inc., a large global provider of agriculture products with 2008 revenues of $11 billion, is building an energy-efficient data center that supports analysis of its worldwide operations. Two factors driving investment in the new center were the 50 percent annual growth in data usage and high cooling costs for the old data center. The new energy-efficient center houses 900 servers and uses air for cooling rather than water. Another feature is the exterior glass shield that deflects 90 percent of the sun's heat.

Both companies have their data centers certified by the Leadership in Energy and Environmental Design (LEED) of the U.S. Green Building Council. In both Wells Fargo and Monsanto, virtualization technologies increase the speed of data processing.

Global Green Regulations

Global regulations also are influencing green business practices. Sustainability regulations such as RoHS (rohs.eu and rohs.gov.uk) in the European Union (EU) will increasingly impact how supply chains function regardless of location. The RoHS directive stands for "the restriction of the use of certain hazardous substances in electrical and electronic equipment." For example, EU member states ensured that beginning in July 2006, new electrical and electronic equipment put on the market would not contain any of six banned substances—lead, mercury, cadmium, hexavalent chromium, polybrominated biphenyls (PBB), and polybrominated diphenyl ethers (PBDE)—in quantities exceeding maximum concentration values. Moreover, China has passed its own RoHS legislation.

Similar legislation is developing elsewhere. For example, California's Electronic Waste Recycling Act (EWRA) prohibits the sale of electronic devices banned by the EU's RoHS, including CRTs, LCDs, and other products that contain the four heavy metals restricted by RoHS. In addition, many states have enacted mercury and PBDE bans, and several are considering bills similar to EWRA. For example, Seattle has issued many regulations related to eliminating paper-based manuals and mandating recycling.

Ecofriendly practices reduce costs and improve public relations in the long run. Not surprisingly, demand for green computers is on the rise. A tool to help companies find such hardware is the Electronic Product Environmental Assessment Tool (EPEAT).

Electronic Product Environmental Assessment Tool

Electronic Product Environmental Assessment Tool (EPEAT)

A searchable database of computer hardware that meets a strict set of environmental criteria.

Maintained by the Green Electronics Council (GEC), the **Electronic Product Environmental Assessment Tool (EPEAT)** is a searchable database of computer hardware that meets a strict set of environmental criteria. Among other criteria, products registered with EPEAT comply with the U.S. government's Energy Star 4.0 rating (see energystar.gov); have reduced levels of cadmium, lead, and mercury; and are easier to upgrade and recycle. Energy Star–qualified products use less energy. Depending on how many criteria they meet, products receive a gold, silver, or bronze certification rating. Worldwide purchases of EPEAT-registered desktops, notebooks, and monitors result in the following environmental benefits when compared to conventional products: Reduces use of primary materials; reduces use of toxic materials; eliminates use of mercury; and avoids the disposal of tons of hazardous waste. EPEAT-registered products must meet 23 mandatory environmental criteria. There are an additional 28 optional criteria used to determine whether products earn EPEAT Bronze, Silver, or Gold recognition. In June 2007, HP and Dell registered the first EPEAT Gold products. As of January 2009, there were 30 manufacturers with 1,053 EPEAT-registered products listed on the EPEAT Product Registry Web page epeat.net/Search.aspx (for more details see epa.gov/oppt/ar/2007-2009/working/epeat.htm).

Section 11.9 ▶ REVIEW QUESTIONS

1. Define green computing. Why is it so important?
2. Describe the problems related to green computing, particularly in regard to data centers.
3. Describe some solutions to green computing.
4. What is the purpose of global green regulations?

11.10 THE FUTURE OF ELECTRONIC COMMERCE

Generally speaking, the consensus is that the future of EC is bright. EC will become an increasingly important method of reaching customers, providing services, and improving operations of organizations. Also, EC facilitates collaboration and people-to-people interactions. Analysts differ in their predictions about the anticipated growth rate of EC and how long it will take for it to become a substantial portion of the economy, as well as in the identification of industry segments that will grow the fastest. However, there is general optimism about the future of EC. Companies such as Amazon.com, eBay, and Newegg.com are growing very rapidly.

INTEGRATING THE MARKETPLACE WITH THE MARKETSPACE

Throughout this book, we have commented on the relationship between the physical marketplace and the marketspace. We have pointed out conflicts in certain areas, as well as successful applications and cooperation. The fact is that from the point of view of the consumer, as well as of most organizations, these two entities exist, and will continue to exist, together.

Probably the most noticeable integration of the two concepts is in the click-and-mortar organization. For the foreseeable future, the click-and-mortar organization will be the most prevalent model (e.g., see Sears.com and Walmart.com), although it may take different shapes and formats. Some organizations will use EC as just another selling channel, as most large retailers do today. Others will use EC for only some products and services, selling other products and services the conventional way (e.g., LEGO). As experience is gained on how to excel at such a strategy, more organizations, private and public, will move to this dual mode of operation.

A major problem with the click-and-mortar approach is how the two outlets can cooperate in planning, advertising, logistics, resource allocation, and so on, and how the strategic plans of the marketspace and marketplace can align. Another major issue is the potential conflict with existing distribution channels (i.e., wholesalers, retailers).

Another area of coexistence is in many B2C ordering systems, where customers have the option to order the new way or the old way. For example, consumers can bank both online and offline. People can trade stocks via the computer, by placing a call to their broker, or just by walking into a brokerage firm and talking to a trader. In the areas of B2B and G2B, the option to choose the old way or the new way may not be available much longer; some organizations may discontinue the old-economy option as the number of offline users declines below a certain threshold. However, in most B2C activities, the option will remain, at least for the foreseeable future.

In conclusion, many people believe that the impact of EC on our lives will be as much as, and possibly more profound than, that of the Industrial Revolution. No other phenomenon since the Industrial Revolution has been classified in this category. It is our hope that this book will help you move successfully into this exciting and challenging digital revolution.

SOCIAL NETWORKS

There has been an explosive growth of mobile social networks. The explosion of wireless Web 2.0 services and companies enables many social communities to be based on mobile phones and other portable wireless devices. This extends the reach of social interaction to millions of people who don't have regular or easy access to computers. For example, MySpace can be accessed via Cingular's (now AT&T) mobile system. At a minimum, existing members who use PCs will supplement their activities with wireless devices. In the fourth quarter of 2008 alone, 23 percent (2 million) of people in the United Kingdom visited social networks over their handsets. In the United States, 19 percent (10.6 million) people did so. This was an increase over 2007 of 249 percent in the United Kingdom and 156 percent in the United States (Nielsen 2009).

FUTURE TRENDS

The following four trends may slow EC and Web 2.0, and even cripple the Internet:

- **Security concern.** Both shoppers and users of e-banking and other services worry about online security. The Web needs to be made safer.
- **Lack of Net neutrality.** If the big telecom companies are allowed to charge companies for a guarantee of faster access, critics fear that small innovative Web companies could be crowded out by the Microsofts and Googles that can afford to pay more.

▶ **Copyright complaints.** The legal problems of YouTube, Wikipedia, and others may result in a loss of vital outlets of public opinion, creativity, and discourse.

▶ **Choppy connectivity.** Upstream bandwidths are still constricted, making uploading of video files a time-consuming task. Usable mobile bandwidth still costs a lot, and some carriers impose limitations on how Web access can be employed.

Section 11.10 ▶ REVIEW QUESTIONS

1. Discuss the integration of marketplaces and marketspaces.
2. Describe mobile social networks.
3. List the major potential inhibitors of e-commerce.

MANAGERIAL ISSUES

Some managerial issues related to this chapter are as follows.

1. **What is the strategic value of EC to the organization?** Management needs to understand how EC can improve marketing and promotions, customer service, and sales. More significant, the greatest potential of EC is realized when management views EC from a strategic perspective, not merely as a technological advancement.

2. **Who determines EC strategy?** Strategy is ultimately the responsibility of senior management. But participation in setting an e-commerce strategy is something that should happen at all levels and in all areas of the organization. It frequently is said that "soon all business will be e-business." If this is true, then planning this evolutionary process must include marketing, operations, information technology, and all other areas of the business.

3. **What are the benefits and risks of EC?** Strategic moves have to be carefully weighed against potential risks. Identifying CSFs for EC and doing a cost-benefit analysis should not be neglected. Benefits often are hard to quantify, especially because gains tend to be strategic. In such an analysis, risks should be addressed with contingency planning (deciding what to do if problems arise).

4. **What metrics should we use?** The use of metrics is very popular, but the problem is that one must compare "apples with apples." Companies first must choose appropriate metrics for the situation and then exercise caution in deriving conclusions whenever gaps between the metrics and actual performance exist.

5. **How do we measure the value of EC investment?** EC investments must be measured against their contribution to business objectives. Such investments will involve direct and indirect costs as well as benefits. The impact of EC on integrating existing processes and systems must not be ignored. Furthermore, EC must create value for all participants, support or improve existing processes, and supplement rather than replace the human element of transactions. The measurement of EC value should occur against the backdrop of metrics that define business performance and success.

6. **How can we go global?** Going global is a very appealing proposition, but it may be difficult to do, especially on a large scale. In B2B, one may create collaborative projects with partners in other countries.

7. **Can we learn to love smallness?** Small can be beautiful to some; to others it may be ugly. Competing on commodity-type products with the big guys is very difficult, and even more so in cyberspace. Finding a niche market is advisable, but it will usually be limited in scope. More opportunity exists in providing specialized support services than in selling goods and services.

8. **What legal and ethical issues should be of major concern to an EC enterprise?** Key issues to consider include the following: (1) What type of proprietary information should we allow and disallow on our site? (2) Who will have access to information that visitors post to our site? (3) Do the content and activities on our site comply with laws in other countries? (4) What disclaimers do we need

to post on our Web site? (5) Are we using trade-marked or copyrighted materials without permission? Regardless of the specific issues, an attorney should periodically review the content on the site, and someone should be responsible for monitoring legal and liability issues.

9. **What are the most critical ethical issues?** Negative or defamatory articles published about people, companies, or products on Web sites or blogs can lead to charges of libel—and libel can stretch across countries. Issues of privacy, ethics,

and legal exposure may seem tangential to running a business, but ignoring them puts the company at risk of fines, customer anger, and disruption of the operation of an organization. Privacy protection is a necessary investment.

10. **How shall we approach EC green computing?** EC is related to green IT. So, first you need to study the issues of green IT and their solutions. The data center is a major problem in green IT and should be investigated first. Dealing with old equipment and recycling is another area.

SUMMARY

In this chapter, you learned about the following EC issues as they relate to the chapter's learning objectives.

1. **The EC strategic process.** Considering e-commerce in strategy development does not radically change the process, but it does impact the outcome. Move-to-the-Net firms must approach the process differently than born-on-the-Net firms, but both types of firms must recognize the way electronic technologies, such as the Internet, make a difference. Because of the comprehensiveness of EC, formal strategic planning is a must.

2. **Writing a business plan and a business case.** A business plan is an essential outcome of a strategic planning process. Writing the business plan may produce more significant outcomes than the plan itself. The purpose of the plan is to describe the operation of the business, and its content includes revenue sources, business partners, and trading procedures.

3. **The need for EC justification.** Like any other investment, EC investment (unless it is small) needs to be justified. Many start-up EC companies have failed because of no, or incorrect, justification. In its simplest form, justification looks at revenue minus all relevant costs. Analysis is done by defining metrics related to organizational goals.

4. **The difficulties in justifying EC investment.** The nature of EC makes it difficult to justify due to the presence of many intangible costs and benefits. In addition, the relationship between investment and results may be complex, extending over several years. Also, several projects may share both costs

and benefits, and several areas may feel the impacts (sometimes negative).

5. **Issues in global EC.** Going global with EC can be done quickly and with a relatively small investment. However, businesses must deal with a number of different issues in the cultural, administrative, geographic, legal, and economic dimensions of global trading.

6. **Small businesses and EC.** Depending on the circumstances, innovative small companies have a tremendous opportunity to adopt EC with little cost and to expand rapidly. Being in a niche market provides the best chance for small business success, and a variety of Web-based resources are available that small business owners can use to help ensure success.

7. **Understanding the foundation for legal and ethical issues.** Laws and regulations are broadly written and can only provide outlines to guide public policy. Ethics also are generally defined. Simply referring to relevant laws or philosophical principles cannot resolve specific legal disputes or ethical dilemmas. Law and ethics provide systems for social control and achieving the greater good. As with all systems, the formation of laws is a dynamic process that responds to ever-changing conditions. The nature of law is dynamic so that it can be responsive to new threats to individual rights or failures to perform one's duties. The Net not only offers freedom of speech, but also widens opportunities for irresponsible activity.

8. **Privacy, free speech, and intellectual property and their challenges.** B2C companies depend on customer information to improve products and services and use CRM. Registration and cookies are two of the ways used to collect this information. The key privacy issues are who controls this information and how private it should remain. Strict privacy laws have been passed recently that carry harsh penalties for any negligence that exposes personal or confidential data. Debate continues about censorship on the Internet. Proponents of censorship feel that it is up to the government and various ISPs and Web sites to control inappropriate or offensive content. Others oppose any form of censorship; they believe that control is up to the individual. In the United States, most legal attempts to censor content on the Internet have been found unconstitutional. The debate is not likely to be resolved.

9. **Green EC.** EC requires large data centers that waste energy and create warm environments. Other environmental concerns are also caused by the use of EC. There are several ways to make EC greener, including working from home (telecommuting).

10. **The future of EC.** EC will continue to expand fairly rapidly for a number of reasons. To begin with, its infrastructure is becoming better and less expensive with time. Consumers will become more experienced and will try different products and services and tell their friends about them. Security, privacy protection, and trust will be much higher, and more support services will simplify the transaction process. Legal issues will be formally legislated and clarified, and more products and services will be online at reduced prices. The fastest growing area is B2B EC. Company-centric systems (especially e-procurement) and auctions will also continue to spread rapidly. The development of exchanges and other many-to-many e-marketplaces will be much slower. Wireless technologies (especially Wi-Fi) will facilitate EC. Finally, and most important, is the increased rate of innovation with new business models and applications appearing constantly. Finally, Web 2.0 and social networks will play a major role in EC.

KEY TERMS

Business case	418	Electronic Product		Patent	437
Business ethics	438	Environmental Assessment		Platform for Privacy Preferences	
Business plan	417	Tool (EPEAT)	448	Project (P3P)	444
Children's Internet Protection		Ethics	437	Privacy	437
Act (CIPA)	441	Fair use	437	Regulatory compliance	435
Civil litigation	434	Green computing	446	Strategy	411
Compliance data	435	Green IT	446	Strategy assessment	415
Copyright	436	Infringement	436	Strategy formulation	414
Cost-benefit analysis	421	Intellectual property	436	Strategy implementation	415
Darknets	443	Key performance indicators		Strategy initiation	413
Digital rights management		(KPIs)	422	SWOT analysis	416
(DRM)	436	Metric	422	Trademark	437
E-commerce strategy		Opt-in	441	USA PATRIOT Act	445
(e-strategy)	413	Opt-out	441	Value proposition	414

QUESTIONS FOR DISCUSSION BY INDIVIDUAL STUDENTS

1. How would you identify competitors for a small business that wants to launch an EC project?

2. How would you apply Porter's five forces and Internet impacts to the Internet search engine industry?

3. Why must e-businesses consider strategic planning to be a cyclical process?

4. Discuss how writing an e-business plan differs from writing a traditional business plan. (See the Online Tutorial.) Discuss the pros and cons of going global with a physical product.

5. Find some SME EC success stories and identify the common elements in them.

6. Enter businesscase.com and find material on ROI analysis. Discuss how ROI is related to a business case.

7. What are some of the things that EC Web sites can do to ensure the safeguarding of personal information?

8. Discuss the insufficient protection of opt-in and opt-out options. Which method do you prefer?

TOPICS FOR CLASS DISCUSSION

1. A company is planning a wireless-based CRM system. Almost all the benefits are intangible. How can you justify the project to top management?

2. Privacy is the right to be left alone and free of unreasonable personal intrusions. What are some intrusions that you consider to be "unreasonable"?

3. Discuss what the RIAA hopes to achieve by using lawsuits (civil law) against college students for copyright infringement.

4. Many hospitals, health maintenance organizations, and federal agencies are converting, or plan to convert, all patient medical records from paper to electronic storage (using imaging technology). Once completed, electronic storage will enable quick access to most records. However, the availability of these records in a database and on networks or smart cards may allow people, some of whom are unauthorized, to view another person's private medical data. To protect privacy fully may cost too much money or may considerably slow the speed of access to the records. What policies could health care administrators use to prevent unauthorized access? Discuss.

INTERNET EXERCISES

1. Enter digitalenterprise.org and go to Web analytics. One of the most global companies online is Amazon.com (amazon.com). Find stories about its global strategies and activities (perform a Google search and check out the press releases on the selected sites you find). What are the three most important lessons you learned?

2. Visit website101.com and find some of the EC opportunities available to small businesses. Also, visit the Web site of the Small Business Administration (SBA) office in your area. Summarize some EC-related topics for SMEs.

3. Find out how Web sites such as tradecard.com facilitate the conduct of international trade over the Internet. Prepare a report based on your findings.

4. Use a currency conversion table (e.g., xe.com/ucc) to find out the exchange rate of US$100 with the currencies of Brazil, Canada, China, India, Sweden, the European Union, and South Africa.

5. Conduct research on small businesses and their use of the Internet for EC. Visit sites such as microsoft.com/smallbusiness/hub.mspx and uschamber.com. Also, enter google.com or yahoo.com and type "small businesses + electronic commerce." Use your findings to write a report on current small business EC issues.

6. Enter businesscase.com and review its products.

7. Enter languageweaver.com and find its language translation product. Write a report.

8. Enter alinean.com and find information that explains Alinean's approach to measuring return on IT. You can download two free e-books from the site that relate to this chapter. Summarize your findings in a report.

9. Enter nucleusresearch.com. Go to "Research," search for the file titled "Market Scorecard: Hosted CRM" for a review of hosted CRM vendors. Summarize your findings in a report. (Note: Use Google to find this information.)

10. Go to google.com and search for articles dealing with the ROI of RFID. List the key issues in measuring the ROI of RFID.

11. Enter citrix.com, sharkfinesse.com, and search marketing.yahoo.com/calculator/roi.php. Review their calculators. Write a report.

12. You want to set up an ethical blog. Review "A Bloggers' Code of Ethics" at cyberjournalist.net/news/000215.php. Make a list of the top 10 ethical issues for blogging.

13. Use google.com to prepare a list of industry and trade organizations involved in various computer privacy initiatives. One of these groups is the World Wide Web Consortium (W3C). Describe its Privacy Preferences Project (w3.org/tr/2001/wd-p3p-20010928).

14. Download freeware from junkbuster.com and learn how to prohibit unsolicited e-mail. Describe how your privacy is protected.

TEAM ASSIGNMENTS AND PROJECTS

1. Have three teams represent the following units of one click-and-mortar company: (1) an offline division, (2) an online division, and (3) top management. Each team member represents a different functional area within the division. The teams will develop a strategy in a specific industry (a group of three teams will represent a company in one industry). Teams will present their strategies to the class.

2. The relationship between manufacturers and their distributors regarding sales on the Web can be very strained. Direct sales may cut into the distributors' business. Review some of the strategies available to handle such channel conflicts. Each team member should be assigned to a company in a different industry. Study the strategies, compare and contrast them, and derive a proposed generic strategy.

3. Each team must find the latest information on one global EC issue (e.g., cultural, administrative, geographic, economic). Each team will prepare a report based on its findings.

4. Survey google.com to find out about EC efforts in different countries. Assign a country or two to each team. Relate the developments to each country's level of economic development and to its culture.

5. Compare the services provided by Yahoo!, Microsoft, and Website Pros Inc. to SMEs in the e-commerce area. Each team member should take one company and make a presentation.

6. Enter whatis.techtarget.com or similar resource sites. Read about spam and splogs. Find out how spam and splog filters work (also see ironport.com and other vendors). Prepare a report and class presentation.

Closing Case

WHY IS DISNEY FUNDING CHINESE PIRATES?

Disney's funding arm, Steamboat Ventures, invested $10 million in a popular Chinese video- and file-sharing site called 56.com. The site had 33 million registered members in 2009. Note that the words for "56" in Chinese sound similar to "I'm Happy."

The Problem

In May 2008, The Walt Disney Company released its animated film *WALL-E*; the film was released on DVD in November 2008. However, immediately after the movie release in May, the robot love story was available for free on the Chinese video site *56.com*. In other words, Disney is funding a Chinese site that bootlegs it own work.

The problem is that pirated movies are difficult to detect because they appear under different names. Although 56.com managed to remove some of the full-length bootlegged copies, many others remain. The 56.com site is often referred to as a Chinese version of YouTube. But unlike YouTube, 56.com and similar sites like Tudou and Youku don't impose 10-minute limits on uploaded videos. And that makes them a haven for illegally uploaded videos, including full-length movies and TV episodes.

If 56.com were in any country but China, we'd expect the Recording Industry Association of America (RIAA) and similar organizations to put pressure on the company to remove copyrighted materials. But China doesn't have a very strong record of enforcing Western copyright laws.

The Solution

One reason that Disney invested in 56.com was that it hoped that Steamboat Ventures, as a major investor, would influence 56.com to take action against copyright violators. In other words, Steamboat Ventures is trying to help 56.com curb pirated videos.

In the United States, you can take legal action against companies such as 56.com. For example, media giant Viacom is suing YouTube for $1 billion. However, that is not an option (yet) in China. At best, the Chinese government will provide a warning to violators.

The Results

Although 56.com is still facilitating free movies, video games, and the like, Disney seems not to be too concerned with these actions. Its investment provides the company a channel of distribution for its products that may provide a strategic advantage to Disney in China. In March 2009, Disney allowed YouTube to run short videos as well as full episodes of its ABC (a television station) and ESPN (Internet and television sports channel) networks under an ad-revenue sharing arrangement.

Sources: Compiled from McBride and Chao (2008) and *en.wikipedia.org/wiki/56.com* (accessed December 2009).

Questions

1. Why is it difficult to stop pirated copyrighted material from showing up on the Internet?
2. Why aren't copyright laws useful in this situation?
3. Why has Disney invested in *56.com*?
4. Why isn't Disney fighting with *56.com*?
5. Identify the legal issues in this case.

ONLINE RESOURCES
available at pearsonhighered.com/turban

Online Files

W11.1   Strategies for Competitive Advantage
W11.2   Strategic Planning Tools
W11.3   Application Case: Measuring Profit on the Web
W11.4   Traditional Methods for Evaluating EC Investments
W11.5   Difficulties in Measuring Intangible Costs and Benefits
W11.6   Automatic Translation of Web Pages
W11.7   Critical Success Factors for SMEs
W11.8   Intellectual Property Web Sites—International Sites
W11.9   Framework for Ethical Issues
W11.10   Web Site Quality Guidelines
W11.11   Application Case: Protection Pitted Against Privacy
W11.12   How to Go Green in a Data Center and the Related Supply Chain

Comprehensive Educational Web Sites

sba.gov/smallbusinessplanner: Business plan advice.
entrepreneur.com: Information on starting a business.
onlinebusiness.about.com: A guide for beginners.
nucleusresearch.com: Metrics, ROI.
roi-calc.com: Calculators, metrics.
baselinemag.com: Calculators, metrics.
strassmann.com: ROI, justification, metrics.
privacy.org: A comprehensive source of privacy information.
itworld.com/green-it: A comprehensive source for IT-related issues, including green EC and IT.
digitaldivide.net: A comprehensive collection of related material.
greenit.net: A comprehensive collection of related material.

CHAPTER

12

Part 7: Applications and Site Development

LAUNCHING A SUCCESSFUL ONLINE BUSINESS AND EC PROJECTS

Learning Objectives

Upon completion of this chapter, you will be able to:

1. Understand the fundamental requirements for initiating an online business.
2. Describe the process of initiating and funding a start-up e-business or large e-project.
3. Understand the process of adding EC initiatives to an existing business.
4. Describe the issues and methods of transforming an organization into an e-business.
5. Describe the process of acquiring Web sites and evaluating building versus hosting options.
6. Understand the importance of providing and managing content and describe how to accomplish this.
7. Evaluate Web sites on design criteria, such as appearance, navigation, consistency, and performance.
8. Understand the process of building a Webstore.
9. Discuss the major steps in developing an EC system.
10. Describe the major EC development strategies and list their major advantages and disadvantages.
11. List the various EC application development methods along with their benefits and limitations.
12. Describe the criteria used in selecting software vendors and packages.

Content

Opening Case: Vodafone Essar of India

12.1 Getting into E-Commerce and Starting a New Online Business

12.2 Adding E-Commerce Initiatives or Transforming to an E-Business

12.3 Building or Acquiring a Web Site

12.4 Web Site Hosting and Obtaining a Domain Name

12.5 Content Creation, Delivery, and Management

12.6 Web Site Design

12.7 A Five-Step Approach to Developing an E-Commerce System

12.8 Development Strategies for E-Commerce Major Applications

12.9 Vendor and Software Selection

Managerial Issues

Closing Case: Developing a Web 2.0 Platform to Enable Innovative Market Research at Del Monte

A complete version of this chapter is available on the textbook's Web site.

REFERENCES

CHAPTER 1

Alter, A. "My Virtual Summer Job." SmallBiz.com, May 21. 2008. smsmallbiz.com/profiles/My_Virtual_Summer_Job.html (accessed March 2009).

Amit, R., and C. Zott. "Value Creation in E-Business." *Strategic Management Journal*, 22, no. 6 (2001).

Blakely, L. "Making Their Point." *Business 2.0*, April 23, 2007.

Burger, A. K. "The Olympics, Part 2: Gold-Medal Network Performance." *E-Commerce Times*, August 16, 2008. ecommercetimes.com/story/64180.html?wlc=1222501114 (accessed March 2009).

Burns, E. "U.S. Wireless Subscriptions Surge Past 250 Million." Clickz.com, November 27, 2007. clickz.com/showPage.html?page=3627705 (accessed March 2009).

De Jonge, A. *Social Networks Around the World*. North Charleston, SC: Booksurge Publications, 2008.

Drucker, P. *Managing in the Next Society*. New York: Truman Talley Books, 2002.

Farivar, C. "New Ways to Pay." *Business 2.0*, July 1, 2004.

Fass, A. "TheirSpace.com." *Forbes*, May 6, 2006. forbes.com/forbes/2006/0508/122.html (accessed March 2009).

FKI Logistex. "Zappos.com." 2007. fkilogistex.com/_pdf/case-studies/Zappos_CS.pdf (accessed July 2009).

Harmony Hollow Software. "What Are the Barriers of Implementing E-Commerce Solutions?" 2006. harmonyhollow.net/webmaster-resources/ecommerce/15604.php (accessed March 2009).

Harrington, R. "The Transformer" (an e-mail interview with *Baseline's* editor-in-chief, J. McCormic). *Baseline,* April 2006.

Hupfer, R., et al. *MySpace for Dummies.* Hoboken, NJ: Wiley Publishers, Inc., 2007.

IBM. "IBM Global CEO Study: The Enterprise of the Future." IBM special study, 2008.

IDC. "IDC Finds More of the World's Population Connecting to the Internet in New Ways and Embracing Web 2.0 Activities." June 25, 2008. idc.com/getdoc.jsp? containerId=prUS21303808 (accessed July 2009).

InformationWeek. "Some Beijing Olympics Fireworks Faked." August 11, 2008a. informationweek.com/news/personal_tech/TV_theater/showArticle.jhtml?articleID=210002310 (accessed March 2009).

InformationWeek. "YouTube to Broadcast Beijing Olympics, But Not in the U.S." August 5, 2008b. informationweek.com/news/personal_tech/TV_theater/showArticle.jhtml?articleID=209903442 (accessed November 2008).

IT Strategy. "IT's Role in the Beijing Olympics." August 28, 2008. **itstrategyblog.com/it%E2%80%99s-role-in-beijing-olympics** (accessed March 2009).

Jones, S., and S. Fox. "Generations Online in 2009." *PewResearch.org*, January 8, 2009. **pewresearch.org/pubs/1093/generations-online** (accessed July 2009).

Joyner, A. *The eBay Billionaire's Club.* Hoboken, NJ: Wiley Publications, 2007.

Khosrow-Pour, M. (Ed.). *Encyclopedia of E-Commerce, E-Government, and Mobile Commerce.* Hershey, PA: Idea Group Reference, 2006.

Loebbecke, C. "RFID in the Retail Supply Chain." In Khosrow-Pour, M. (Ed.). *Encyclopedia of E-Commerce, E-Government, and Mobile Commerce.* Hershey, PA: Idea Group Reference, 2006.

Logistics Online. "FKI Logistex 'Wows' Zappos.com with New Automated Order Fulfillment Center." March 23, 2008. **logisticsonline.com/article.mvc/FKI-Logistex-Wows-Zapposcom-With-New-Automate-0002l** (accessed July 2009).

MacDonald, K. *One Red Paperclip: Or How an Ordinary Man Achieved His Dream with the Help of a Simple Office Supply.* New York: Three Rivers Press, 2007.

Magnier, M. "Beijing Olympics Visitors to Come Under Widespread Surveillance." *Los Angeles Times,* August 7, 2008.

McGee, M. K. "Chiefs of the Year: Internet Call to Arms." *InformationWeek,* November 27, 2000.

Mockler, R. J., D. G. Dologite, and M. E. Gartenfeld. "B2B E-Business." In Khosrow-Pour, M. (Ed.). *Encyclopedia of E-Commerce, E-Government, and Mobile Commerce.* Hershey, PA: Idea Group Reference, 2006.

Needle, D. "Huffington: Obama Not Elected Without Internet." **Internetnews.com**, November 7, 2008. **internetnews.com/webcontent/article.php/3783741/Huffington+Obama+Not+Elected+Without+Internet.htm** (accessed April 2009).

O'Reilly, T. "What Is Web 2.0?" *OReillynet.com*, September 30, 2005. **oreillynet.com/pub/a/oreilly/tim/news/2005/09/30/what-is-web-20.html** (accessed March 2008).

Plunkett, J.W. *Plunkett's E-Commerce and Internet Business Almanac 2006.* Houston, TX: Plunkett Research, Ltd., February 2006.

Prahalad, C. K., and M. S. Krishnan. *The New Age of Innovation.* New York: McGraw-Hill, 2008.

Rappa, M. "Business Models on the Web." *Digitalenterprise. org*, 2008. **digitalenterprise.org/models/models.html** (accessed March 2009).

Reda, S. "Godiva.com's Story Parallels Dynamic Growth of E-Commerce." *Stores,* February 2004.

Rymaszewski, M., et al. *Second Life: The Official Guide.* Indianapolis, IN: Wiley Publishers, Inc., 2008.

Schonfeld, E. "ComScore: Internet Population Passes One Billion; Top 15 Countries." **Techcrunch.com**, January 23, 2009. **techcrunch.com/2009/01/23/comscore-internet-population-passes-one-billion-top-15-countries** (accessed July 2009).

Sellers, P. "MySpace Cowboys." *Fortune,* September 4, 2006.

Strategic Direction. "DotCom Boom and Bust: The Secrets of E-Commerce Failure and Success." February 2005.

Taft, D. K. "NBC Olympic Coverage Shines as Silverlight Proving Ground." *e-Week,* August 13, 2008.

Taylor, B. "Why Zappos Pays New Employees to Quit— and You Should Too." *Harvard Business Publishing*, May 19, 2008. **blogs.harvardbusiness.org/taylor/2008/05/why_zappos_pays_new_employees.html** (accessed July 2009).

Todé, C. "E-Commerce Is Flat as a Percentage of Total Retail Sales." *DMNews*, February 2, 2009. **dmnews.com/E-commerce-is-flat-as-a-percentage-of-total-retail-sales/article/126725** (accessed July 2009).

Van Toorn, C., D. Bunker, K. Yee, and S. Smith. "The Barriers to the Adoption of E-Commerce by Micro Businesses, Small Businesses and Medium Enterprises." *Sixth International Conference on Knowledge, Culture, and Change in Organisations,* Prato, Tuscany, Italy, July 11–14, 2006.

Vise, D. A., and M. Malseed. *The Google Story.* New York: Delacorte Press, 2006.

Wall Street Journal. "Zappos CEO Posts Letter to Staff." July 22, 2009. **blogs.wsj.com/digits/2009/07/22/zappos-ceos-letter-to-staff** (accessed October 2009).

CHAPTER 2

Bakos, Y. "The Emerging Role of Electronic Marketplaces on the Internet." *Communications of the ACM* (August 1998).

Clark, K. "Discover the Best of Craigslist." *L'Atelier*, March 10, 2009. **atelier-us.com/internet-usage/article/discover-the-best-of-craigslis** (accessed August 2009).

Copeland, M. V. "The Big Guns' Next Target: eBay." *CNNMoney.com*, January 31, 2006. **money.cnn.com/magazines/business2/business2_archive/2006/01/01/8368106/index.htm** (accessed August 2009).

Copeland, V. M., and K. Kelleher, "The New New Careers," *Business 2.0*, May 2007.

Cox, J. L., E. R. Martinez, and K. B. Quinlan. "Blogs on the Corporation: Managing the Risk, Reaping the Benefits," *Journal of Business Strategy*, 29, no. 3 (2008).

Edgar Online. "Growth of Online Commerce and Online Auction Market." March 17, 2006. **sec.edgar-online.com/2006/03/17/0001047469-06-003660/Section9.asp** (no longer available online).

E-Market Services. "Why Use E-Markets?" *E-marketservices. com*, 2006. **emarketservices.com/start/Knowledge/eMarket-Basics/Why-use-eMarkets/index.html** (accessed August 2009).

Farber, D. "2009: The Year of Enterprise Social Networks." *ZDNet*, February 14, 2008. **blogs.zdnet.com/BTL/?p=7997** (accessed August 2009).

Flynn, N. *Blog Rules: A Business Guide to Managing Policy, Public Relations, and Legal Issues*. Saranac Lake, NY: AMACOM, 2006.

Hinchcliffe, D. "Profitably Running an Online Business in the Web 2.0 Era," *SOA Web Services Journal*, November 29, 2006. web2.wsj2.com (accessed August 2009).

Hof, R. D. "My Virtual Life," *BusinessWeek*, May 1, 2008.

Joyner, A. *The eBay Billionaires Club*, Hoboken, NJ: Wiley, 2007.

Li, E. Y., and T. C. Du (Eds.). *Advances in Electronic Business*, Volume 1. Hershey, PA: Idea Group Publishing, 2005.

Liedtke, M. "Study: Craigslist Revenue to Climb 23% to $100 Million." *Physorg.com*, June 10, 2009. physorg.com/news163824409.html (accessed August 2009).

Linden, M. "State of the Economy." *SecondLife.com*, April 9, 2009. blogs.secondlife.com/community/features/blog/tags/lindex (accessed August 2009).

Martin, R. "The Right Search Tool." *InformationWeek*, September 29, 2008.

Naughton, J. "Web Sites That Changed the World." *IndiaStudyChannel.com*, August 14, 2006. indiastudychannel.com/resources/10578-Websites-that-changed-world.aspx (accessed August 2009).

Nerille, J. "X-treme Web 2.0," *Optimize Magazine*, January 2007.

Nissanoff, D. *Future Shop: How the New Auction Culture Will Revolutionize the Way We Buy, Sell, and Get Things We Really Want*. New York: The Penguin Press, 2006.

O'Buyonge, A. A., and L. Chen. "E-Health Dot-Coms' Critical Success Factors." In M. Khosrow-Pour (Ed.). *Encyclopedia of E-Commerce, E-Government, and Mobile Commerce*. Hershey, PA: Idea Group Reference, 2006.

Robbins, S., and M. Bell. *Second Life for Dummies*. Hoboken, NJ: Wiley, 2008.

Rosedale, P. "Alter Egos." *Forbes*, May 7, 2007.

Roush, W. "Second Earth." *Technology Review*, July/August 2007.

Rymaszewski, M., et al. *Second Life: The Official Guide*, 2nd ed. Indianapolis, IN: Wiley, 2008.

Saarinen, T., M. Tinnild, and A. Tseng (Eds.). *Managing Business in a Multi-Channel World: Success Factors for E-Business*. Hershey, PA: Idea Group, Inc., 2006.

Sloan, P., and P. Kaihla. "Blogging for Dollars." *Business 2.0*, September 2006.

Terdiman, D., *The Entrepreneur's Guide to Second Life*, Indianapolis, IN: Wiley, 2008.

Turban, E., et al. *Business Intelligence: A Managerial Approach*, 2nd ed. Upper Saddle River, NJ: Prentice Hall, 2011.

Weber, S. *eBay 101: Selling on eBay for Part Time or Full Time Income*. Falls Church, VA: Web Books, 2008.

Weblogs, Inc. "The Social Software Weblog," 2007. socialsoftware.weblogsinc.com (accessed August 2009).

CHAPTER 3

Acharya, R. N., A. Kagan, and S. R. Lingam. "Online Banking Applications and Community Bank Performance." *International Journal of Bank Marketing* (October 2008).

Ahorre.com. "2009 Real Estate Internet Marketing." January 2009. ahorre.com/dinero/internet/marketing/2009_real_estate_internet_marketing (accessed September 2009).

AlexFrankel.com. "Personality Tests." January 15, 2008. alexfrankel.com/blog/?p=8 (accessed September 2009).

Baranzelli, M. F. "Growing Revenue in Internet Gambling." *Online Casino Extra*, November 18, 2008. onlinecasino-extra.com/zcasino_news_1811.html (accessed February 2009).

Baseline. "E-Commerce's New Dimension." November 30, 2007. baselinemag.com/c/a/Projects-Supply-Chain/Ecommerces-New-Dimension (accessed September 2009).

Biz Report. "Toys Made in China off Christmas Shopping Lists." *BizReport.com*, November 14, 2007. bizreport.com/2007/11/toys_made_in_china_off_christmas_shopping_lists.html (accessed February 2009).

Bowers, T. "Hiring Manager: Step Away from the Facebook!" September 10, 2008. blogs.techrepublic.com.com/career/?p=398 (accessed September 2009).

Bowling, B. "Lawrence County Joins Tax Movement Against Online Hotel Businesses." *Tribune Review*, September 9, 2009.

Brown, K. "Social Media Marketing: B2C Success Stories." *SlideShare.net*, April 2009. slideshare.net/pixelpointpress/social-media-marketing-b2c-success-stories-1251538 (accessed September 2009).

Butcher, M. "WAYN Said to Be Close to Sale. The Price? $200m. The Buyer? AOL." *Tech Crunch*, January 16, 2008. uk.techcrunch.com/2008/01/16/wayn-said-to-be-close-to-sale-the-price-200m-the-buyer-aol (accessed February 2009).

Cash Edge. "Cash Edge Survey Confirms Consumer Demand for Value Added Online Banking Services." *News Blaze*, October 12, 2006. newsblaze.com/story/2006101206005100005.pz/topstory.html (accessed February 2009).

Competeinc. "Compete Releases Top 25 Retail Web Sites for July 2009." August 27, 2009. competeinc.com/news_events/pressReleases/23 (accessed September 2009).

Dignan, L. "Retail Stinks, but Amazon Doesn't; E-Tailer Delivers Strong Fourth Quarter." *ZDNet*, January 29, 2009. blogs.zdnet.com/BTL/?p=11928 (accessed February 2009).

Fisher, A. "30 Best Web Sites for Job Hunters." *Fortune Magazine*, May 9, 2008. money.cnn.com/2008/05/07/news/economy/best.websites.fortune/index.htm (accessed February 2009).

Ha, S., and L. Stoel. "Consumer E-Shopping Acceptance: Antecedents in a Technology Acceptance Model." *Journal of Business Research* (In press, 2009).

Internet Retailer. "60% of Internet Users Shop Online, Make 36 Purchases a Year, Study Says." 2009a. **internetretailer. com/internet/marketing-conference/46151-60-internet-users-shop-online-making-36-purchases-year-study-says.html** (accessed September 2009).

Internet Retailer. "Facts About the Internet's Top 500 E-Tailers." 2009b. **internetretailer.com/top500/facts.asp** (accessed September 2009).

Internet Retailer. "Wal-Mart's New In-Store Pick-Up Service Might Not Be Fast, But It's Free." March 6, 2007. **internetretailer.com/dailyNews.asp?id=2164** (accessed February 2009).

Javelin Strategy and Research. "2009 Online Banking and Bill Payment Forecast: Active Users Grow While Bill Pay Overtakes Biller Direct." 2009. **javelinstrategy.com/ lp/onlinebankingbillpayLP.html** (accessed September 2009).

Jupiter Research. "Online Dating in 2007." *Market Research*, February 2, 2007. **marketresearch.com/product/display. asp?productid=1601597&SID=25013955-446132061-468369822&curr=USD&kw=Online%09dating&view= abs** (accessed May 2009).

Keegan, V. "Zopa Shows Banks How to Do It Right." *The Guardian*, November 13, 2008. **guardian.co. uk/technology/ 2008/nov/13/zopa-credit-crunch** (accessed September 2009).

Kuchment, A., and K. Springen. "The Tangled Web of Porn in the Office." *Newsweek*, November 29, 2008. **newsweek.com/id/171279** (accessed February 2009).

Kwon, W. S., and S. J. Lennon. "What Induces Online Loyalty? Online Versus Offline Brand Images." *Journal of Business Research* (In Press, 2009).

Maestri, N. "Walmart.com Offers 'Thousands' of Wiis from Monday." *Reuters*, December 7, 2008. **reuters.com/ article/technologyNews/idUSTRE4B608520081207** (accessed February 2009).

McDougall, P. "Web Lets Insurers Cut Costs, Improve Service." *InformationWeek*, September 17, 2007.

McElroy, J. "An Intriguing Build-to-Order Concept." *Autoline*, June 11, 2009. **autolinedetroit.tv/journal/? p=4395** (accessed September 2009).

Mulpuru, S., C. Johnson, B. McGowan, and W. Scott. "U.S. eCommerce Forecast: 2008 to 2012." Forrester Research, January 18, 2008. **forrester.com/Research/Document/ Excerpt/0,7211,41592,00.html** (accessed February 2009).

PriceWaterhouseCoopers. "Global Entertainment & Media to Reach $2.2T in 2012, Driven by Digital, Mobile." *Marketing Charts*, June 20, 2008. **marketingcharts. com/television/global-entertainment-media-toreach-22t-in-2012-driven-by-digital-mobile-5012** (accessed September 2009).

Prindle, C. "The Next Wave of E-Tail: Considered Commerce." *E-Commerce Times*, June 23, 2009. **ecommercetimes.com/ story/67349.html?wlc=1253210603** (accessed September 2009).

Realtors Magazine. "Market Research by Industry." *Realtors Magazine*, 2009. **realtor.org/wps/wcm/connect/ 752953004bbaa1ca950bdff09f174b6c/Research+Book. pdf?MOD=AJPERES&CACHEID=752953004bbaa1 ca950bdff09f174b6c** (accessed May 2009).

Reuters. "Amazon Net Profit Doubles, Helped by Asset Sale." July 23, 2008. **reuters.com/article/pressReleases Molt/ idUSWNAB207520080723** (accessed February 2009).

Stokes, J. "The Matrix, but with Money: The World of High-Speed Trading." ARS Technica, July 27, 2009. **arstechnica.com/tech-policy/news/2009/07/-it-sounds-like-something.ars** (accessed September 2009).

Taipei Times. "Online Group Buying—A Great Way to Save Money." March 26, 2009. **taipeitimes.com/ News/lang/archives/2009/03/26/2003439407** (accessed September 2009).

Weiner, M. (2006) "The 5-Day Car: Ordered on Monday—Delivered on Friday." *Ilipt.org*, February 28, 2006. **fraunhofer.de/fhg/Images/magazine_2-2006 _28_tcm6-64704.pdf** (accessed February 2009).

Workplace.gov.au. "A Job Seekers Guide to Jobsearch." 2009. **workplace.gov.au/NR/rdonlyres/F1CE1A17-0AEC-4630-8351-CCD24CA15247/0/GuidetoAJS_final.pdf** (accessed September 2009).

CHAPTER 4

Angel, G. "The Art and Science of Choosing Net Marketing Channels." *E-Commerce Times*, September 21, 2006. **ecommercetimes.com/story/53141.html** (accessed November 2007).

Anke, J., and D. Sundaram. "Personalization Techniques and Their Application," in Khosrow-Pour (2006).

Bosman, J. "Hey, Kid, You Want to Buy a Toyota Scion?" *New York Times*, June 14, 2006. **nytimes.com/2006/06/14/ business/media/14adco.html?_r=2&oref=slogin&oref=sl ogin** (accessed April 2008).

Buckley, N. "E-Route to Whiter Smile." *Financial Times*, August 26, 2002.

Cant, M. C., et al. *Marketing Management*. South Africa: Juta Academic, 2009.

Chan, S. *Strategic Management of e-Business*, 2nd ed. Chichester, UK: John Wiley & Sons, 2005.

Cheung, C. M. K., and M. K. O. Lee. "The Asymmetric Impact of Website Attribute Performance on User Satisfaction: An Empirical Study." *Proceedings of Hawaii International Conference on System Sciences*, Big Island, Hawaii, January 2005.

Collier, J. E., and C. C. Bienstock. "How Do Customers Judge Quality in an E-Tailer?" *MIT Sloan Management Review* 48, no. 1 (2006).

Computer Industry Almanac. "Worldwide Internet Users Top 1 Billion in 2005. USA Reach Nearly 200M Internet Users." January 4, 2006. **c-i-a.com/pr0106. htm** (accessed January 2008).

eMarketer. "Social Network Ad Space: Sorry, Sold Out!" November 3, 2006.

Faught, K. S., K. W. Green Jr., and D. Whitten. "Doing Survey Research on the Internet." *Journal of Computer Information Systems* 44, no. 3 (2004).

Floh, A., and H. Treiblmaier. "What Keeps the E-Banking Customer Loyal? A Multigroup Analysis of the Moderating Role of Consumer Characteristics on ELoyalty in the Financial Service Industry." *Journal of Electronic Commerce Research* 7, no. 2 (2006).

Flynn, L. J. "Like This? You'll Hate That. (Not All Web Recommendations Are Welcome)." *New York Times*, January 23, 2006.

Gao, Y., M. Koufaris, and R. H. Ducoffe. "Negative Effects of Advertising Techniques in Electronic Commerce," in Khosrow-Pour, 2006.

Gregg, D. G., and S. Walczak. "Adaptive Web Information Extraction." *Communications of the ACM* (2006).

Hallerman, D. "The Death of Mass Marketing, *iMediaConnection*, June 16, 2006. **imediaconnection. com/content/10063.asp** (accessed November 2007).

Hodgin, R. "YouTube Growing with 20 Hours of New Video Content per Minute." *Geek.com*, May 22, 2009. **geek .com/articles/news/youtube-growing-at-20-hours-of-new-video-content-per-minute-20090522** (accessed September 2009).

Hoffman, L. J., K. Lawson-Jenkins, and J. Blum. "An Expanded Trust Model." *Communications of the ACM* (July 2006).

Jeanson, B., and J. Ingham. "Consumer Trust in E-Commerce," in Khosrow-Pour (2006).

Khosrow-Pour, M. (Ed.). *Encyclopedia of E-Commerce, E-Government, and Mobile Commerce.* Hershey, PA: Idea Group Reference, 2006.

Lee, M., and E. Turban. "Trust in B2C Electronic Commerce: A Proposed Research Model and Its Application." *International Journal of Electronic Commerce,* 6, no. 1 (2001).

Marketing Charts. "Social Network Ad Spend Doesn't Yet Match Hype." May 19, 2008. **marketingcharts.com/interactive/social-network-ad-spend-doesnt-yet-match-hype-4637** (accessed March 2009).

MarketingVox.com. "Automakers Look to Create Own Broadband Channels." July 10, 2007a. **marketingvox. com/archives/2007/07/10/automakers-look-to-create-own-broadband-channels** (accessed April 2008).

MarketingVox.com. "Scion Joins Fourth—Yes, Fourth—Virtual World." August 16, 2007b. **marketingvox.com/scion-joins-fourth-yes-fourth-virtual-world-032282** (accessed April 2008).

MarketingVox.com. "Scion's Online Strategy Favors Niche over Reach." July 5, 2007c. **marketingvox.com/scions-online-strategy-favors-niche-over-reach-031136** (accessed April 2008).

marketleap.com/report/ml_report_24.htm (accessed November 2007).

McKinsey Quarterly. "How Businesses Are Using Web 2.0: A McKinsey Global Survey." March 2007. **mckinseyquarterly.com/How_businesses_are_using_ Web_20_A_McKinsey_Global_Survey_1913** (accessed March 2009).

MediaBuyerPlanner.com. "Toyota Targets Kids, Hopes to Influence Parents." June 14, 2006. **mediabuyerplanner. com/2006/06/14/toyota_targets_kids_hopes_to** (accessed April 2008).

Netflix.com. "Netflix and USA Weekend Partner on 'Netflix Movie Picks' Promotion." September 13, 2006. **netflix.com/ MediaCenter?id=5363** (accessed November 2007).

NewMedia TrendWatch. "eCommerce." February 19, 2009. **newmediatrendwatch.com/world-overview/101-ecommerce** (accessed March 2009).

O'Keefe, R. M., and T. McEachern. "Web-Based Customer Decision Support System." *Communications of the ACM* (March 1998).

Ploof, R. "Johnson & Johnson Does New Media: A Case Study." *Ronamok.com*, June 15, 2009. **ronamok.com/ ebooks/jnj_case_study.pdf** (accessed September 2009).

Pons, A. P. "Biometric Marketing: Targeting the Online Consumer." *Communications of the ACM* (August 2006).

Reuters. "U.S. Web Video Ads Seen Up to $4.3 Billion in 2011: Study." July 25, 2007. **reuters.com/article/ InternetNews/idUSN2544002420070725?feedType= RSS** (accessed March 2009).

RightNow.com. "Procter & Gamble Applies Right Now to Deliver Superior Consumer Experience." August 30, 2006. **rightnow.com/news/article.php?id=7072** (accessed November 2007).

Rodgers, Z. "Scion Goes Urban, Eschewing Big Reach Buys." *Clickz.com*, July 3, 2007. **clickz.com/showPage. html?page=3626318** (accessed March 2009).

Sanders, T. "Extortionists Behind Million Dollar DoS Attack." *Computing*, January 19, 2006. **computing.co.k/ vnunet/news/2148849/cyber-criminalstarget-pixel** (accessed November 2007).

Sutel, S. "As Internet Ad Market Grows, Advertisers Want Better Audience Measures." *Savanna Morning News*, December 25, 2007.

Tode, C. "Survey: E-Commerce Leads in Customer Satisfaction." *DMNews*, February 21, 2006.

Turban, E., et al. *Business Intelligence: A Managerial Approach*, 2nd ed. Upper Saddle River, NJ: Prentice Hall, 2011.

Weber, S. *Plug Your Business!* Falls Church, VA: Weber Books, 2007.

Yeo, A. Y. C., and K. M. Chiam. "E-Customer Loyalty," in Khosrow-Pour (2006).

Yoon, S. J., and J. H. Kim. "Is the Internet More Effective Than Traditional Media? Factors Affecting the Choice of Media." *Journal of Advertising Research* (November–December 2001).

webMethods. "WebMethods Helps Power WWRE's Global Data Synchronization Solution." WWRE Success Story, 2005. accessmylibrary.com/coms2/summary_0286-24312890_ITM?email=ecommerce2008@gmail.com &library= (accessed May 2009).

CHAPTER 5

Chandler, C. "China's Web King." *Fortune*, November 23, 2007.

eMarketer."B2B Marketing on Social Networks: Engaging the Business Audience." August 2008. emarketer.com/Report.aspx?code=emarketer_2000516 (accessed February 2009).

Endica. "Delivering a Consistent and Intuitive Online Catalog." 2008. Download at endeca.com/resource-center-case-studies.htm (accessed August 2009).

Fortune. "E-Procurement: Unleashing Corporate Purchasing Power." 2000.

Full Tilt. "Brady Goes Full Tilt to Streamline E-Catalog Production." 2004. managingautomation.com/sponsors/fulltilt/gold_brady_cs.pdf (accessed August 2009).

IDC. "IDC Finds More of the World's Population Connecting to the Internet in New Ways and Embracing Web 2.0 Activities." IDC press release, June 25, 2008. idc.com/getdoc.jsp% 3Bjsessionid=YM12N2YZKZ03UCQJAFICFGAKBEAUMIWD?containerId=prUS21303808 (accessed May 2009).

iMarketKorea. "iMarketKorea Enters into Strategic Business Cooperation Agreement with Sumitomo Corporation Japan." January 25, 2006. imarketkorea.co.kr/en_HD/menu_05001-19view.jsp (accessed May 2009).

Lee, Z., and D. S. Lee. "Transition from a Buyer's Agent to a Procurement Service Provider in B2B iMarketKorea." In J. K. Lee, et al., *Premier E-Business Cases from Asia.* Singapore: Prentice Hall and Pearson Education South Asia, 2007.

Lucas, H. C. *Information Technology: Strategic Decision Making for Managers.* Hoboken, NJ: John Wiley and Sons, 2005.

MasterCard. "MasterCard Corporate Purchasing Card." *Mastercard.com*, 2009. mastercard.com/us/business/en/middlemarket/cardprograms/purchasing_card.html (accessed May 2009).

OCG. "Online Auction for Pharmaceutical Supplies Helps Portsmouth Hospitals NHS." 2004. ogc.gov.uk/documents/Portsmouth_Hospitals.pdf (accessed May 2009).

Spagnuolo, J. "Is the B2B Marketplace Utilizing Online Video, Social Networking, and Wikis?" November 13, 2008. newmedia.org/articles/43/1/Is-the-B2B-Marketplace-Utilizing-Online-Video-Social-Networks—Wikis/Page1.html (accessed May 2009).

CHAPTER 6

Baumgarten, J., and M. Chui. "E-Government 2.0." *McKinsey Quarterly*, Summer 2009.

Bjelland, O. M., and R. C. Wood. "An Inside View of IBM's Innovation Jam." *MIT Sloan Management Review* (Fall 2008).

Boehle, S. "Caterpillar's Knowledge Network." *Management Smart.com*, October 16, 2007. managesmarter. com/msg/content_display/training/e3iff0e5ee8955eaff00d02da7d36a 5b662 (accessed September 2009).

Chan, S. C. H., and E. W. Ngai. "A Qualitative Study of IT Adoption: How Ten Organizations Adopted Web-Based Training." *Information Systems Journal* (June 6, 2007).

Chu, K. C., and Q. Lam. "Using an E-Book for Learning." In M. Khosrow-Pour (Ed.). *Encyclopedia of E-Commerce, E-Government, and Mobile Commerce.* Hershey, PA: Idea Group Reference, 2006.

D'Agostino, D. "Expertise Management: Who Knows About This?" *CIO Insight*, July 1, 2004.

Epstein, J. "Electronic Voting." *Computer*, August 2007.

Garud, R., and A. Kumaraswamy. "Vicious and Virtuous Circles in the Management of Knowledge: The Case of Infosys Technologies." *MIS Quarterly* (March 1, 2005).

Gibson, R., and C. Brown. "Electronic Voting as the Key to Ballot Reform." In M. Khosrow-Pour (Ed.). *Encyclopedia of E-Commerce, E-Government, and Mobile Commerce.* Hershey, PA: Idea Group Reference, 2006.

Glynn, C. E. "Building a Learning Infrastructure." *Training and Development,* January 2008.

Government Technology. "Don't Block Web 2.0 Access, Says Gartner." May 10, 2008. govtech.com/gt/271948 (accessed September 2009).

Henriksen, H. Z. "Fad or Investment in the Future: An Analysis of the Demand of E-Services in Danish Municipalities." *Electronic Journal of E-Government,* 4, no. 1 (2006).

Holsapple, C. W. (Ed.). *Handbook on Knowledge Management.* Heidelberg, Germany: Springer Computer Science, 2003.

Huang, W., Y. Chen, and K. L. Wang. "E-Government Development and Implementation." In M. Khosrow-Pour (Ed.). *Encyclopedia of E-Commerce, E-Government, and Mobile Commerce.* Hershey, PA: Idea Group Reference, 2006.

Hyperion. "Federal Government—Additional Details." 2007. hyperion.com/solutions/federal_division/legislation_summaries.cfm (no longer available online).

Keen, J. "Politicians' Campaigns Invade MySpace." *USA Today*, October 17, 2006.

Kumar, N., and Q. Peng. "Strategic Alliances in E-Government Procurement." *International Journal of Electronic Business*, 4, no. 2 (2006).

Lagorio, C. "The Ultimate Distance Learning." *New York Times News Service*, published in *Taipei Times*, January 7, 2007.

Lee, S. M., X. Tan, and S. Trimi. "Current Practices of Leading E-Government Countries." *Communications of the ACM*, 48, no. 10 (October 2005).

Mark, R. "Election 2.0." *eWeek*, November 12, 2007.

Massey, L. L., and D. W. Taylor, "Out of the Cubicle and into the Field: Mobility Matters in Extending Public Service Delivery." A white paper from BlackBerry Inc. and the center for Digital Government at Republic Inc., 2007.

Morrison, M. "Learner E-Learning: The University of Toyota Case." *Training* (January 2008).

Neal, L. "Predictions for 2007." *eLearn Magazine*, January 12, 2007. elearnmag.org/subpage.cfm?article=42-1&section=articles (accessed March 2009).

New Zealand E-Government. "Networking Government in New Zealand: Agency Initiatives." 2008a. e.govt.nz/resources/research/progress/agency-initiatives/chapter9.html (accessed September 2009).

New Zealand E-Government. "Networking Government in New Zealand: Web 2.0 Networking Tools." 2008b e.govt.nz/resources/research/progress/agency-initiatives/chapter6.html (accessed September 2009).

Perenson, M. J. "Hands-On with Amazon's Kindle 2." *PCWorld.com*, February 9, 2009. pcworld.com/article/159193/handson_with_the_amazon_kindle_2.html (accessed September 2009).

Robbins, S., and M. Bell. *Second Life for Dummies*. Hoboken, NJ: Wiley, 2008.

Roberts, B. "Hard-Facts About Self Skills E-Learning." *HR Magazine*, January 2008.

Shark, A., and S. Toporkoff. *Beyond e-Government and e-Democracy: A Global Perspective*. Scotts Valley, CA: BookSurge Publishing, 2008.

Swisher, J. R., S. H. Jacobson, J. B. Jun, and O. Balci. "Modeling and Analyzing a Physician Clinic Environment Using Discrete-Event (Visual) Simulation." *Computers and Operations Research* (February 2001).

Trimi, S., and H. Sheng. "Emerging Trends in M-Government." *Communications of the ACM* (May 2008).

U.S. Department of Housing and Urban Development. *FY 2008 Performance and Accountability Report*. November 2008. hud.gov/offices/cfo/reports/hudpar-fy2008.pdf (accessed March 2009).

U.S. Government. *E-Government Strategy*. Office of the President of the United States, Special Report, 2003. whitehouse.gov/omb/egov/2003egov_strat.pdf (no longer available online).

Wagner, E. "Delivering on the Promise of E-Learning." Adobe Systems, Inc., San Jose, CA. white paper #95010203, May 2008.

West, E. "Rapid E-learning." Adobe Systems, Inc., San Jose, California, white paper, 2007.

CHAPTER 7

Abram, C., and L. Pearlman. *Facebook for Dummies*. Hoboken, NJ: Wiley 2008.

Ankeny, J. "Mobile Social Networkers to Top 600 Million Worldwide by 2013." FierceMobileContent. com, November 13, 2009. fiercemobilecontent.com/story/mobile-social-networkers-top-600-million-world-wide-2013/2009-11-13 (accessed March 2010).

Blodget, H. "Who the Hell Writes Wikipedia, Anyway?" *Silicon Alley Insider*, January 3, 2009. alleyinsider.com/2009/1/who-the-hell-writes-wikipedia-anyway (accessed March 2009).

Borland, J. "A Smarter Web." *Technology Review*, March–April 2007.

Coleman, D., and S. Levine, *Collaboration 2.0*. Cupertino, CA: Happy About Info, 2008.

Elad, J. *LinkedIn for Dummies*. Hoboken, NJ: Wiley, 2008.

Farrell, N. "Microsoft Rumbled over Wikipedia Edits." *The Inquirer*, January 24, 2007. theinquirer.net/ gb/inquirer/news/2007/01/24/microsoft-rumbled-over-wikipedia-edits (accessed March 2009).

Gogoi, P. "Retailers Take a Tip from MySpace." *BusinessWeek Online*, February 13, 2007. businessweek.mobi/detail.j sp?key=6158&rc=sb&p=4&pv=1 (accessed March 2009).

Grossman, L. "Time Person of the Year—YOU, Power to People." *Time*, December 25, 2006–January 1, 2007.

Hempel, J. "Web 2.0 Is So Over, Welcome to Web 3.0." *Fortune*, January 8, 2009.

Hof, R. D. "My Virtual Life." *BusinessWeek*, May 1, 2008.

Hoover, J. N. "Enterprise 2.0." *InformationWeek*, February 26, 2007.

Jefferies, A. "Sales 2.0: Getting Social About Selling." *CRM Buyer*, October 30, 2008.

Kafka, P. "Blue Sky." *Forbes*, February 12, 2007.

Kolakowski, N. "7 Things Needed for an Enterprise Social Network." *eWeek*, March 12, 2009. eweek.com/c/a/Messaging-and-Collaboration/7-Things-Needed-for-an-Enterprise-Social-Network-245891 (accessed September 2009).

Megna, M. "Bust or Boon? Calculate Blog ROI." *E-Commerce Guide*, February 8, 2007. ecommerce-guide.com/solutions/article.php/3658776 (accessed March 2009).

Murray-Buechner, M. "25 Sites We Can't Live Without." *Time*, August 3, 2006.

Sahlin, D., and C. Botello. *YouTube for Dummies.* Hoboken, NJ: Wiley, 2007.

Schonfeld, E., and C. Morrison. "The Next Disruptors." *Business 2.0,* August 22, 2007. money.cnn.com/magazines/business2/business2_archive/2007/09/01/100169862/index.htm (accessed November 2009).

Seeking Alpha. "eMarketer Top 10 Predictions for 2009." January 9, 2009. seekingalpha.com/article/114028-emarketer-top-10-predictions-for-2009 (accessed March 2009).

Wagner, C., and N. Bolloju. "Supporting Knowledge Management in Organizations with Conversational Technologies: Discussion Forums, Weblogs, and Wikis." *Journal of Database Management,* 16, no. 2 (2005).

Weber, S. *Plug Your Business.* Falls Church, VA: Weber Books, 2007.

CHAPTER 8

Apple. "iTunes Store Tops over Five Billion Songs Sold: Apple Renting and Selling over 50,000 Movies Per Day." June 19, 2008. apple.com/pr/library/2008/06/19itunes.html (accessed November 2009).

Australian Mobile Telecommunications Association. "The Impact of the Mobile Phone on Work/Life Balance." March 2008. apo.org.au/research/impact-mobile-phone-worklife-balance-final-report (accessed November 2009).

Becker, M. "Academic Review: Mobile Marketing Framework Overview." *Mobile Marketing,* 2006. mmaglobal.com/articles/academic-review-mobile-marketing-framework-overview (accessed November 2009).

Betts, M. "Cloud Computing: Gauging the Benefits, Barriers, Hype, and Reality." *ComputerWorld.com,* October 6, 2008. blogs.computerworld.com/cloud_computing_benefits_barriers_and_hype (accessed November 2009).

Bonkoo, T. "Grocery Stores Providing a New Way of Shopping to Customers: Handheld Device Allows Customer to Forgo Long Line." *Associated Content Media,* January 18, 2007. associatedcontent.com/article/284899/grocery_stores_providing_a_new_way.html (accessed November 2009).

Business Wire. "IDC Predicts the Number of Worldwide Mobile Workers to Reach 1 Billion by 2011." January 15, 2008. findarticles.com/p/articles/mi_m0EIN/is_2008_Jan_15/ai_n24230213 (accessed November 2009).

Communities Dominate Brands. "3 Billion Use SMS, What Does That Mean?" March 6, 2009. communities-dominate.blogs.com/brands/2009/03/3-billion-use-sms-what-does-that-mean.html (accessed November 2009).

Economist. "Business in Motion: Managing the Mobile Workforce." *Economist Intelligence Unit,* 2007. graphics.eiu.com/ebf/PDFs/Business_in_motion_April%202007_FINAL.pdf (accessed November 2009).

eMarketer. "Mobile Video and Television: Ads Wait for a Clearer Picture." August 2008. emarketer.com/Reports/All/Emarketer_2000507.aspx (accessed March 2010).

IMS Research. "900M Users for Mobile Banking and Payment Services in 2012." May 29, 2008. imsresearch.com/press_release_details.html&press_id=486 (accessed November 2009).

ITU. "ICT Statistics Newslog—Worldwide Mobile Cellular Subscribers to Reach 4 Billion Mark Late 2008." September 29, 2008. itu.int/ITU-D/ict/newslog/Worldwide+Mobile+Cellular+Subscribers+To+Reach+4+Billion+Mark+Late+2008.aspx (accessed November 2009).

Juniper Research. "Mobile—Let Me Entertain You." 2008. wirelessmobile-jobsboard.com/pdf/Mobile_Entertainment_∼_White_Paper.pdf (accessed November 2009).

Laudermilch, N. "Will Cell Phones Be Responsible for the Next Internet Worm?" *InformIT,* April 28, 2006. informit.com/articles/article.aspx?p=465449 (accessed November 2009).

M2 Presswire. "MONILINK: MONILINK Reaches One Million Account Enquiries Per Month." November 11, 2008. ip-pbx.tmcnet.com/news/2008/11/11/3778246.htm (accessed November 2009).

Malik, A. *RTLS for Dummies.* Hoboken, NJ: John Wiley and Sons, 2009.

METRO. "METRO Group and Real- Open the Store of the Future." May 2008. metro-link.com/metro-link/html/en/15449208/index.html (accessed November 2009).

Mitra, S. "Mobile Microfinance." *Forbes,* June 6, 2008. forbes.com/home/2008/06/05/mitra-mobile-microfinance-tech-wire-cx_sm_0606mitra.htm (accessed November 2009).

Parlamentul European. "Getting Galileo into Orbit by 2013." April 16, 2008. europarl.europa.eu/sides/getDoc.do?language=EN&type=IM-PRESS&reference=20080414BKG26528 (accessed November 2009).

PaymentNews. "Fiserv Survey Finds Increased Consumer Interest in Mobile Banking." September 2008. paymentsnews.com/2008/09/fiserv-survey-f.html (accessed November 2009).

Philadelphia Inquirer. "It's Getting There: Wi-Fi Baby Steps." December 17, 2007. philly.com/inquirer/opinion/20071217_Editorial___Its_Getting_There.html?adString=inq.news/opinion;!category=opinion;&randomOrd=020408041722 (no longer available online).

PriceWaterhouseCoopers. "Global Entertainment & Media to Reach $2.2T in 2012, Driven by Digital, Mobile." *Marketing Charts,* June 20, 2008. marketingcharts.com/television/global-entertainment-media-to-reach-22t-in-2012-driven-by-digital-mobile-5012 (accessed November 2009).

Rash, W. "WeatherBug, Send Word Now Create Emergency Weather Service." June 12, 2006. eweek.com/c/a/Mobile-and-Wireless/WeatherBug-Send-Word-Now-Create-Emergency-Weather-Service (accessed November 2009).

Rosen, C. "Our Cell Phones, Ourselves." *The New Atlantis,* May 29, 2006. thenewatlantis.com/publications/our-cell-phones-ourselves (accessed November 2009).

Steiniger, S., M. Neun, and A. Edwardes. "Foundation of Location-Based Services." 2006. geo.unizh.ch/publications/cartouche/lbs_lecturenotes_steinigeretal2006.pdf (accessed November 2009).

Taipei Times. "New GPS Parking Hits the Spot for Paris." November 21, 2006. taipeitimes.com/News/world/archives/2006/11/21/2003337287 (no longer available online).

Talbot, D. "Upwardly Mobile." Technology Review, November–December 2008. technologyreview.com/business/21533 (accessed November 2009).

Wireless and Mobile News. "NFC Mobile Phone Trial on SF BART in Jack in the Box Successful." October 7, 2008. wirelessandmobilenews.com/2008/10/nfc_mobile_phone_trial_on_sf_b.html (accessed November 2009).

Zhou, J. Providing Location Services in the Ubiquitous Computing Era. Saarbrucken, Germany: VDM Verlag Publishing, 2008.

CHAPTER 9

CNNMoney. "Identity Theft Hits Record 10M Americans." February 9, 2009. money.cnn.com/2009/02/09/news/newsmakers/identity_theft.reut/index.htm? postversion=2009020907 (no longer available online).

CompTIA. "Trends in Information Security: A CompTIA Analysis of IT Security and the Workforce." 2008. informationweek.com/whitepaper/government/ecurity/trends-in-information-security-a-comptia-analysi-wp1223489141665;jsessionid= L3YEJVF2MUVWVQE1GHRSKH4ATMY32JVN (accessed November 2009).

Fagg, S. "Continuity for the People." Risk Management Magazine, March 2006.

Fiber Optics Weekly. "Telstra Uses NetEx Gear." January 13, 2006.

Fratto, M. "Secure What Matters." InformationWeek, December 1, 2008.

Gage, D. "Bank of America Seeks Anti-Fraud Anodyne." Baseline, May 10, 2006. baselinemag.com/article2/0,11040,1962470,00.asp (accessed November 2009).

Gaudin, S. "Nightmare on Wall Street: Prosecution Witness Describes 'Chaos' in UBS PaineWebber Attack." Information Week, June 6, 2006. informationweek.com/story/showArticle.jhtml?articleID=188702216 (accessed March 2009).

Kawamoto, D. "California Man Pleads Guilty to Bot Attack." CNET News, May 5, 2006. news.cnet.com/California-man-pleads-guilty-to-bot-attack/2100-7348_3-6069238.html (accessed November 2009).

Lerer, L. "Why the SEC Can't Stop Spam." Forbes, March 8, 2007. forbes.com/2007/03/08/sec-spam-stock-tech-security-cx_ll_0308spam.html (accessed November 2009).

Marketing Charts. "Fraudsters Filch $4B Online; Record Losses for U.S. E-Commerce." 2009. marketingcharts.com/interactive/fraudsters-filch-4b-online-record-losses-for-us-e-commerce-7144/cybersource-order-reject-rates-online-segment-fall-2008jpg (accessed November 2009).

McMillan, R. "90 Percent of E-Mail Is Spam, Symantec Says." PCWorld, May 26, 2009. pcworld.com/article/ 165533/90_percent_of_email_is_spam_symantec_says.html (accessed November 2009).

McMillan, R. "FBI: Internet Fraud Complaints Up 33 Percent in 2008." IDG News, March 30, 2009. networkworld.com/news/2009/033009-fbi-internet-fraud-complaints-up.html?page=1 (accessed November 2009).

O'Hagan, M. "Three Accused of Inducing Ill Effects on Computers at Local Hospital." Seattle Times, February 22, 2006. seattletimes.nwsource.com/html/localnews/2002798414_botnet11m.html (accessed November 2009).

Palgon, G. "Simple Steps to Data Security." Security Management, June 2008.

Rand, D. "Threats When Using Online Social Networks." CSIS Security Group, May 16, 2007. (csis.dk/dk/forside/LinkedIn.pdf (accessed November 2009).

Richardson, R. "2008 CSI Computer Crime and Security Survey." Computer Security Institute, 2008. i.zdnet.com/blogs/csisurvey2008.pdf (accessed November 2009).

Roberts, P. F. "Webroot Uncovers Thousands of Stolen Identities." InfoWorld, May 8, 2006. infoworld.com/article/06/05/09/78139_HNTrojanrebery_1.html (accessed November 2009).

Secure Computing. "How to Protect Your Company and Employees from Image Spam." securecomputing.com/image_spam_WP.cfm (accessed November 2009).

Symantec. Symantec Report on the Underground Economy: July 07–June 08. Symantec Corp., November 2008, Report #14525717.

Symantec. Web-Based Attacks. White paper #20016955, February 2009.

Taipei Times. "Two Convicted for Theft." March 6, 2009. taipeitimes.com/News/world/archives/2009/03/06/2003437699 (accessed November 2009).

Whitman, J. "UBS Wants to Bar Public at Tech 'Bomb' Trial." New York Post, June 6, 2006. tmronline.com/A55951/tmrarticles.nsf/b02380a2f0e146ca862569240078f070/0b601788814bab1486257186007a9056!OpenDocument (accessed November 2009).

CHAPTER 10

Business Wire. "Kohl's Successfully Implements Back-Office Conversion with Solutran." September 9, 2008. allbusiness.com/company-activities-management/operations-back/11553648-1.html (accessed December 2009).

Card Technology. "Eurosmart: 2008 Shipments to Approach 4 Billion." November 13, 2007. cardtechnology.com/article.html?id=200711130Q64SQXC (accessed December 2009).

CBCNews. "Indigo Books Targets E-Book Market Chapter by Chapter." March 2, 2009. cbc.ca/arts/books/ story/2009/03/02/tech-shortcovers.html (accessed December 2009).

Chen, J. "KCG Ticketing Project in Southern Taiwan." March 2008. multos.com/downloads/10-years/taiwanmoneycard.pdf (accessed December 2009).

CyberSource. "10th Annual Online Fraud Report." 2009. forms.cybersource.com/forms/FraudReport2009NACYBSwww020309 (accessed December 2009).

CyberSource. "Insider's Guide to ePayment Management." 2008. cybersource.com/cgi-bin/pages/prep.cgi?page=/promo/InsidersGuide2008/index.html (accessed December 2009).

D'Agostino, D. "Pennies from Heaven." *CIO Insight*, January 2006. cioinsight.com/c/a/Trends/In-ECommerce-Small-is-the-New-Big/ (accessed December 2009).

Hendry, M. *Multi-Application Smart Cards: Technology and Applications.* Cambridge, UK: Cambridge University Press, 2007.

Lamond, K., and D. Whitman. "Credit Card Transactions: Real World and Online." *VirtualSchool.edu*, 1996. virtualschool.edu/mon/ElectronicProperty/klamond/credit_card.htm (accessed March 2010).

May, T. "The Nanopayment Plan." *.Netmag*, July 2009. sparechange.s3.amazonaws.com/homepage/NET190.f_nano.pdf (accessed December 2009).

Mitchell, D. "In Online World, Pocket Change Is Not Easily Spent." *New York Times*, August 27, 2007. nytimes.com/2007/08/27/technology/27micro.html (accessed December 2009).

NACHA. "ACH Transaction Volume Grew in 4th Quarter Despite Tough Economy." NACHA press release. February 11, 2009. nacha.org/docs/News%20Release%20Q4%202008%20ACH%20Volume.pdf (accessed December 2009).

PayPal. "Business Guide to Online Payment Processing." 2004, Available at paypal.com/us/cgi-bin/webscr? cmd=_pp-promo-thanks&CID= MG5SFTRF463JMJS6 (accessed March 2010).

Robb, S. "The Benefits of Back-Office Conversion." *gtnews.com*, February 19, 2007. gtnews.com/article/6638.cfm (accessed December 2009).

Simon, J. "Paper to Plastic: Checks and Cash Losing to Debit and Credit." October 3, 2007. creditcards.com/credit-card-paper-vs-plastic.php (accessed December 2009).

Smart Card Alliance. "Transit and Contactless Financial Payments: New Opportunities for Collaboration and Convergence." October 2006. smartcardalliance.org/pages/publications-transit-financial (accessed December 2009).

Tan, G. "MasterCard Announces the Full-Scale Roll-Out of the Internationally Recognized TaiwanMoney Card." MasterCard press release, June 1, 2007. mastercard.com/us/company/en/newsroom/pr_taiwanmoney-card.html (accessed December 2009).

TechCrunch. "Spare Change on Track to Process $30 Million in Micropayments." December 2009. sparechange.s3.amazonaws.com/homepage/Spare_Change_On_Track_To_Process_$30_Million_In_Micropayments.pdf (accessed December 2009).

ZeroDegrees. "QQ: Master of the Micropayment." December 2009. zerosocialmedia.com/2009/08/qq-master-of-the-micropayment/ (accessed December 2009).

CHAPTER 11

Arden-Besunder, A., and L. J. Sherwin. "Who Should Monitor Online Counterfeiters?" *New York Law Journal* (March 18, 2009).

Auckland, J. S. "Davidson Appointed InternetNZ Executive Director." *Computerworld*, May 31, 2005. computerworld.co.nz/news.nsf/0/C77829204EE51915CC257011006C7F51?OpenDocument&pub=Computer world (accessed November 2009).

Borenstein, D., P. Betencourt, and R. Baptista. "A Multi-Criteria Model for the Justification of IT Investments." *INFOR*, February 2005.

Carr, D. F. "Changing Course amid Turbulence." *Baseline*, September 2006.

Downes, L. "eBay and the Legal Problems with Online Marketplaces." *CIO Insight*, August 13, 2008.

Florencia, M. "Top Four Online Translation Services." MakeUseOf.com, April 4, 2009. makeuseof.com/tag/online-machine-translation-services-is-there-a-good-one (accessed November 2009).

Fortinet.com. "Pierre Lang Jewelers Safeguards Multi-National Enterprise Network," March 30, 2005. fortinet.com/news/pr/2005/pr033005.html (accessed November 2009).

Gagnon, D., S. Lee, F. Ramirez, S. Ravikumar, and J. Santiago. "Consumer Power and the Internet." *MIT Sloan School of Management*, June 11, 2002. mitsloan.mit.edu/50th/pdf/consumerpowerpaper.pdf (accessed November 2009).

Ghemawat, P. "Distance Still Matters: The Hard Reality of Global Expansion." *Harvard Business Review* (September 2001).

InternetNZ. "InternetNZ Strategic Plan: 2006." February 23, 2006. internetnz.net.nz/reports/plans/archive/2006/2006-03-04-strategicplan/?searchterm=nz (accessed November 2009).

McBride, S., and L. Chao. "Disney Battles Pirates at China Affiliate." *Wall Street Journal-Asia*, November 24, 2008.

Miller, R. "Enterprise 2.0: Definition and Solutions." CIO.com, July 12, 2007. cio.com/article/123550/Enterprise_2.0_Definition_and_Solutions (accessed November 2009).

Misra, R. "Evolution of the Philosophy of Investments in IT Projects." *Issues in Informing Sciences and Information Technology* 3 (2006).

Nielsen. "Global Faces and Networked Places: A Nielsen Report on Social Networking's New Global Footprint." March 2009. Downloadable at en-us.nielsen.com/main/insights/reports (accessed November 2009).

Palotie, L. "Small Firms Upbeat About Online Sales." *Inc.*, May 22, 2008. inc.com/news/articles/2008/05/web.html (accessed November 2009).

Peppard, J., and J. Ward, "Unlocking Sustained Business Value from IT Investments," *California Management Review* (Fall 2005).

Porter, M. E. *Competitive Advantage: Creating and Sustaining Superior Performance.* New York: The Free Press, 1985.

Porter, M. E. *Competitive Strategy: Techniques for Analyzing Industries and Competitors.* New York: The Free Press, 1980.

Porter, M. E. "Strategy and the Internet." *Harvard Business Review* (March 2001).

SAP AG. "Pierre Lang Europe." 2004. Downloadable at sap.com/demos/pdfs/CS_Pierre_Lang.pdf (accessed November 2009).

Sardar, M., N. Islam, and K. B. Oh. *Applied Financial Econometrics in E-Commerce.* Amsterdam: Elsevier Science Publishing Company, 2003.

Shenkan, A. G., and Sichel, B. "Marketing with User-Generated Content." *McKinsey Quarterly*, November 2007.

Shuen, A. *Web 2.0: A Strategy Guide: Business Thinking and Strategies Behind Successful Web 2.0 Implementations.* Sebastopol, CA: O'Reilly, 2008.

Siteworx, Inc. "Developing a Social Networking Strategy: A Strategic Approach to Applying Social Media to Sales, Marketing, and Operations." 2008. siteworx.com/static/docs/webinar/SiteworxSocialNetworking.pdf (accessed November 2009).

SmartPhone.com. "E-Guide: A Strategic Approach to Enabling Mobile Business Applications." Sponsored by BlackBerry. Downloadable at smartphone. searchmobilecomputing.com/document; 95219/computer-phone-research.htm (accessed November 2009).

GLOSSARY

acceptable use policy (AUP) Policy that informs users of their responsibilities when using company networks, wireless devices, customer data, and so forth.

acceptance testing Determining whether a Web site meets the original business objectives and vision.

access control Mechanism that determines who can legitimately use a network resource.

ad management Methodology and software that enable organizations to perform a variety of activities involved in Web advertising (e.g., tracking viewers, rotating ads).

ad views The number of times users call up a page that has a banner on it during a specific period; known as impressions or page views.

Address Verification System (AVS) Detects fraud by comparing the address entered on a Web page with the address information on file with the cardholder's issuing bank.

affiliate marketing A marketing arrangement by which an organization refers consumers to the selling company's Web site.

angel investor A wealthy individual who contributes personal funds and possibly expertise at the earliest stage of business development.

application controls Controls that are intended to protect specific applications.

attractors Web site features that attract and interact with visitors in the target stakeholder group.

auction A competitive process in which a seller solicits consecutive bids from buyers (forward auctions) or a buyer solicits bids from sellers (backward auctions). Prices are determined dynamically by the bids.

audit An important part of any control system. Auditing can be viewed as an additional layer of controls or safeguards. It is considered as a deterrent to criminal actions especially for insiders.

authentication Process to verify (assure) the real identity of an individual, computer, computer program, or EC Web site.

authorization Determines whether a buyer's card is active and the customer has sufficient funds.

Automated Clearing House (ACH) Network A nationwide batch-oriented electronic funds transfer system that provides for the interbank clearing of electronic payments for participating financial institutions.

autoresponders Automated e-mail reply systems (text files returned via e-mail) that provide answers to commonly asked questions.

availability Assurance that access to data, the Web site, or other EC data service is timely, available, reliable, and restricted to authorized users.

avatars Animated computer characters that exhibit human-like movements and behaviors.

B2B portals Information portals for businesses.

back end The activities that support online order fulfillment, inventory management, purchasing from suppliers, payment processing, packaging, and delivery.

balanced scorecard A management tool that assesses organizational progress toward strategic goals by measuring performance in a number of different areas.

banking Trojan A Trojan that comes to life when computer owners visit one of a number of online banking or e-commerce sites.

banner On a Web page, a graphic advertising display linked to the advertiser's Web page.

bartering The exchange of goods and services.

bartering exchange An intermediary that links parties in a barter; a company submits its surplus to the exchange and receives points of credit, which can be used to buy the items that the company needs from other exchange participants.

behavioral targeting The use of information collected on an individual's Internet-browsing behavior to select which advertisements to display to that individual.

biometric control An automated method for verifying the identity of a person based on physical or behavioral characteristics.

biometric systems Authentication systems that identify a person by measurement of a biological characteristic, such as fingerprints, iris (eye) patterns, facial features, or voice.

biometrics An individual's unique physical or behavioral characteristics that can be used to identify an individual precisely (e.g., fingerprints).

blog A personal Web site that is open to the public to read and to interact with; dedicated to specific topics or issues.

Bluetooth A set of telecommunications standards that enables wireless devices to communicate with each other over short distances.

botnet A huge number (e.g., hundreds of thousands) of hijacked Internet computers that have been set up to forward traffic, including spam and viruses, to other computers on the Internet.

brick-and-mortar (old economy) organizations Old-economy organizations (corporations) that perform their primary business offline, selling physical products by means of physical agents.

brick-and-mortar (old economy) retailers Retailers who do business in the non-Internet, physical world in traditional brick-and-mortar stores.

build-to-order (pull system) A manufacturing process that starts with an order (usually customized). Once the order is paid for, the vendor starts to fulfill it.

bullwhip effect Erratic shifts in order up and down supply chains.

business case A document that justifies the investment of internal, organizational resources in a specific application or project.

business continuity plan A plan that keeps the business running after a disaster occurs. Each function in the business should have a valid recovery capability plan.

business ethics A form of applied ethics that examines ethical principles and moral or ethical problems that arise in a business environment.

business impact analysis (BIA) An exercise that determines the impact of losing the support of an EC resource to an organization and establishes the escalation of that loss over time, identifies the minimum resources needed to recover, and prioritizes the recovery of processes and supporting systems.

business intelligence Activities that not only collect and process data, but also make possible analysis that results in useful—intelligent—solutions to business problems.

business model A method of doing business by which a company can generate revenue to sustain itself.

business network A group of people who have some kind of commercial relationship; for example, sellers and buyers, buyers among themselves, buyers and suppliers, and colleagues and other colleagues.

business plan A written document that identifies a company's goals and outlines how the company intends to achieve the goals and at what cost.

business process management (BPM) Method for business restructuring that combines workflow systems and redesign methods; covers three process categories—people-to-people, systems-to-systems, and systems-to-people interactions.

business social network A social network whose primary objective is to facilitate business connections and activities.

business-oriented networks Social networks whose primary objective is to facilitate business.

business-to-business (B2B) E-commerce model in which all of the participants are businesses or other organizations.

business-to-business e-commerce (B2B EC) Transactions between businesses conducted electronically over the Internet, extranets, intranets, or private networks; also known as eB2B (electronic B2B) or just B2B.

business-to-business-to-consumer (B2B2C) E-commerce model in which a business provides some product or service to a client business that maintains its own customers.

business-to-consumer (B2C) E-commerce model in which businesses sell to individual shoppers.

business-to-employees (B2E) E-commerce model in which an organization delivers services, information, or products to its individual employees.

button A small banner that is linked to a Web site. It can contain downloadable software.

buy-side e-marketplace A corporate-based acquisition site that uses reverse auctions, negotiations, group purchasing, or any other e-procurement method.

Captcha tool Completely Automated Public Turing test to tell Computers and Humans Apart, which uses a verification test on comment pages to stop scripts from posting automatically.

card verification number (CVN) Detects fraud by comparing the verification number printed on the signature strip on the back of the card with the information on file with the cardholder's issuing bank.

certificate authorities (CAs) Third parties that issue digital certificates.

channel conflict Situation in which an online marketing channel upsets the traditional channels due to real or perceived damage from competition.

chatterbots Animation characters that can talk (chat).

Children's Internet Protection Act (CIPA) U.S. law that mandates the use of filtering technologies in schools and libraries that receive certain types of federal funding.

CIA security triad (CIA triad) Three security concepts important to information on the Internet: confidentiality, integrity, and availability.

ciphertext A plaintext message after it has been encrypted into a machine-readable form.

civil litigation An adversarial proceeding in which a party (the plaintiff) sues another party (the defendant) to get compensation for a wrong committed by the defendant.

click (click-through or ad click) A count made each time a visitor clicks on an advertising banner to access the advertiser's Web site.

click-and-mortar (click-and-brick) organizations Organizations that conduct some e-commerce activities, usually as an additional marketing channel.

click-and-mortar retailers Brick-and-mortar retailers that offer a transactional Web site from which to conduct business.

click-through rate The percentage of visitors who are exposed to a banner ad and click on it.

click-through ratio The ratio between the number of clicks on a banner ad and the number of times it is seen by viewers; measures the success of a banner in attracting visitors to click on the ad

clickstream behavior Customer movements on the Internet.

clickstream data Data that occur inside the Web environment; they provide a trail of the user's activities (the user's clickstream behavior) in the Web site.

collaboration hub The central point of control for an e-market. A single c-hub, representing one e-market owner, can host multiple collaboration spaces (c-spaces) in which trading partners use c-enablers to exchange data with the c-hub.

collaborative commerce (c-commerce) The use of digital technologies that enable companies to collaboratively plan, design, develop, manage, and research products, services, and innovative EC applications.

collaborative filtering A market research and personalization method that uses customer data to predict, based on formulas derived from behavioral sciences, what other products or services a customer may enjoy; predictions can be extended to other customers with similar profiles.

collaborative planning A business practice that combines the business knowledge and forecasts of multiple players along a supply chain to improve the planning and fulfillment of customer demand.

collaborative planning, forecasting, and replenishment (CPFR) Project in which suppliers and retailers collaborate in their planning and demand forecasting to optimize flow of materials along the supply chain.

collaborative Web site A site that allows business partners to collaborate.

company-centric EC E-commerce that focuses on a single company's buying needs (many-to-one, or buy-side) or selling needs (one-to-many, or sell-side).

competitor analysis grid A strategic planning tool that highlights points of differentiation between competitors and the target firm.

compliance data All data belonging or pertaining to an enterprise included in the law, which can be used for the purpose of implementing or validating compliance.

Computer Fraud and Abuse Act (CFAA) Major computer crime law to protect government computers and other Internet-connected computers.

Computing Technology Industry Association (CompTIA) Nonprofit trade group providing information security research and best practices.

confidentiality Assurance of data privacy and accuracy. Keeping private or sensitive information from being disclosed to unauthorized individuals, entities, or processes.

considered commerce Conducting e-commerce where the online channel of a business is integrated with the physical retail business as opposed to being a separate channel.

consortium trading exchange (CTE) An exchange formed and operated by a group of major companies in an industry to provide industry-wide transaction services.

consumer-to-business (C2B) E-commerce model in which individuals use the Internet to sell products or services to organizations or individuals who seek sellers to bid on products or services they need.

consumer-to-consumer (C2C) E-commerce model in which consumers sell directly to other consumers.

contact card A smart card containing a small gold plate on the face that when inserted in a smart card reader makes contact and passes data to and from the embedded microchip.

contactless (proximity) card A smart card with an embedded antenna, by means of which data and applications are passed to and from a card reader unit or other device without contact between the card and the card reader.

content The text, images, sound, and video that make up a Web page.

content management The process of adding, revising, and removing content from a Web site to keep content fresh, accurate, compelling, and credible.

Controlling the Assault of Non-Solicited Pornography and Marketing (CAN-SPAM) Act Law that makes it a crime to send commercial e-mail messages with false or misleading message headers or misleading subject lines.

conversion rate The percentage of clickers who actually make a purchase.

cookie A data file that is placed on a user's hard drive by a remote Web server, frequently without disclosure or the user's consent, that collects information about the user's activities at a site.

copyright An exclusive right of the author or creator of a book, movie, musical composition, or other artistic property to print, copy, sell, license, distribute, transform to another medium, translate, record, perform, or otherwise use.

corporate portal A major gateway through which employees, business partners, and the public can enter a corporate Web site.

cost-benefit analysis A comparison of the costs of a project against the benefits.

CPM (cost per thousand impressions) The fee an advertiser pays for each 1,000 times a page with a banner ad is shown.

cracker A malicious hacker who may represent a serious problem for a corporation.

CRM analytics Applying business analytic techniques and business intelligence such as data mining and online analytic processing to CRM applications.

cross-selling Offering similar or complementary products and services to increase sales.

CSI Computer Crime and Security Survey Annual security survey of U.S. corporations, government agencies, financial and medical institutions, and universities conducted by the Computer Security Institute.

customer interaction center (CIC) A comprehensive service entity in which EC vendors address customer service issues communicated through various contact channels.

customer relationship management (CRM) A customer service approach that focuses on building long-term and sustainable customer relationships that add value both for the customer and the selling company.

customization Creation of a product or service according to the buyer's specifications.

cybercrime Intentional crimes carried out on the Internet.

cybercriminal A person who intentionally carries out crimes over the Internet.

darknets Private online community that is only open to those who belong to it.

Data Encryption Standard (DES) The standard symmetric encryption algorithm supported by the NIST and used by U.S. government agencies until October 2000.

data mart A small data warehouse designed for a strategic business unit (SBU) or department.

data mining The process of searching a large database to discover previously unknown patterns; automates the process of finding predictive information.

data warehouse (DW) A single, server-based data repository that allows centralized analysis, security, and control over data.

denial of service (DoS) attack An attack on a Web site in which an attacker uses specialized software to send a flood of data packets to the target computer with the aim of overloading its resources.

desktop purchasing Direct purchasing from internal marketplaces without the approval of supervisors and without the intervention of a procurement department.

desktop search Search tools that search the contents of a user's or organization's computer files, rather than searching the Internet. The emphasis is on finding all the information that is available on the user's PC, including Web browser histories, e-mail archives, and word-processed documents, as well as in all internal files and databases.

detection measures Ways to determine whether intruders attempted to break into the EC system; whether they were successful; and what they may have done.

deterring measures Actions that will make criminals abandon their idea of attacking a specific system (e.g., the possibility of losing a job for insiders).

differentiation Providing a product or service that is unique.

digital divide Refers to the gap between people with effective access to digital and information technology and those without.

digital economy An economy that is based on digital technologies, including digital communication networks, computers, software, and other related information technologies; also called the Internet economy, the new economy, or the Web economy.

digital enterprise A new business model that uses IT in a fundamental way to accomplish one or more of three basic objectives: reach and engage customers more effectively, boost employee productivity, and improve operating efficiency. It uses converged communication and computing technology in a way that improves business processes.

digital envelope The combination of the encrypted original message and the digital signature, using the recipient's public key.

digital products Goods that can be transformed to digital format and delivered over the Internet.

digital rights management (DRM) An umbrella term for any of several arrangements that allow a vendor of content in electronic form to control the material and restrict its usage.

digital signature or digital certificate Validates the sender and time stamp of a transaction so it cannot be later claimed that the transaction was unauthorized or invalid.

direct marketing Broadly, marketing that takes place without intermediaries between manufacturers and buyers; in the context of this book, marketing done online between any seller and buyer.

direct materials Materials used in the production of a product (e.g., steel in a car or paper in a book).

disaster avoidance An approach oriented toward prevention. The idea is to minimize the chance of avoidable disasters (such as fire or other human-caused threats).

disintermediation The removal of organizations or business process layers responsible for certain intermediary steps in a given supply chain.

disruptors Companies that introduce a significant change in their industries, thus causing a disruption in normal business operations.

distance learning Formal education that takes place off campus, usually, but not always, through online resources.

domain name A name-based address that identifies an Internet-connected server. Usually it refers to the portion of the address to the left of .com and .org, etc.

Domain Name System (DNS) A hierarchical naming system for computers, services, or any resource participating in the Internet; it is like a directory that translates (converts) domain names to their numeric IP addresses..

double auction An auction in which multiple buyers and their bidding prices are matched with multiple sellers and their asking prices, considering the quantities on both sides.

dynamic pricing Prices that change based on supply and demand relationships at any given time.

dynamic Web content Content that must be kept up-to-date.

e-bartering (electronic bartering) Bartering conducted online, usually in a bartering exchange.

e-book A book in digital form that can be read on a computer screen or on a special device.

e-business A broader definition of EC that includes not just the buying and selling of goods and services, but also servicing customers, collaborating with business partners, and conducting electronic transactions within an organization.

e-check A legally valid electronic version or representation of a paper check.

e-commerce (EC) risk The likelihood that a negative outcome will occur in the course of developing and operating an electronic commerce strategy.

e-commerce strategy (e-strategy) The formulation and execution of a vision of how a new or existing company intends to do business electronically.

e-distributor An e-commerce intermediary that connects manufacturers with business buyers (customers) by aggregating the catalogs of many manufacturers in one place—the intermediary's Web site.

e-government E-commerce model in which a government entity buys or provides goods, services, or information to businesses or individual citizens.

e-grocer A grocer that takes orders online and provides deliveries on a daily or other regular schedule or within a very short period of time.

e-learning The online delivery of information for purposes of education, training, or knowledge management.

e-loyalty Customer loyalty to an e-tailer or loyalty programs delivered online or supported electronically.

e-mail spam A subset of spam that involves nearly identical messages sent to numerous recipients by e-mail.

e-mall (online mall) An online shopping center where many online stores are located.

e-marketplace An online market, usually B2B, in which buyers and sellers exchange goods or services; the three types of e-marketplaces are private, public, and consortia.

e-micropayments Small online payments, typically under $10.

e-newsletter A collection of short, informative articles sent at regular intervals by e-mail to individuals who have an interest in the newsletter's topic.

e-procurement The electronic acquisition of goods and services for organizations. E-procurement supports the purchase of both direct and indirect materials and employs several Web-based functions such as online catalogs, contracts, purchase orders, and shipping notices.

e-sourcing The process and tools that electronically enable any activity in the sourcing process, such as quotation/tender submittance and response, e-auctions, online negotiations, and spending analyses.

e-supply chain A supply chain that is managed electronically, usually with Web technologies.

e-supply chain management (e-SCM) The collaborative use of technology to improve the operations of supply chain activities as well as the management of supply chains.

e-tailers Retailers who sell over the Internet.

e-tailing Online retailing, usually B2C.

EC architecture A plan for organizing the underlying infrastructure and applications of a site.

EC security programs All the policies, procedures, documents, standards, hardware, software, training, and personnel that work together to protect information, the ability to conduct business, and other assets.

EC security strategy A strategy that views EC security as the process of preventing and detecting unauthorized use of the organization's brand, identity, Web site, e-mail, information, or other asset and attempts to defraud the organization, its customers, and employees.

electronic (online) banking or e-banking Various banking activities conducted from home or the road using an Internet connection; also known as cyberbanking, virtual banking, online banking, and home banking.

electronic auctions (e-auctions) Auctions conducted online.

electronic catalogs (e-catalogs) The presentation of product information in an electronic form; the backbone of most e-selling sites.

electronic commerce (EC) The process of buying, selling, or exchanging products, services, or information via computer.

electronic CRM (e-CRM) Customer relationship management conducted electronically.

electronic market (e-marketplace) An online marketplace where buyers and sellers meet to exchange goods, services, money, or information.

Electronic Product Environmental Assessment Tool (EPEAT) A searchable database of computer hardware that meets a strict set of environmental criteria.

electronic retailing (e-tailing) Retailing conducted online, over the Internet.

electronic shopping cart An order-processing technology that allows customers to accumulate items they wish to buy while they continue to shop.

electronic signature A generic, technology-neutral term that refers to the various methods by which one can "sign" an electronic record.

encryption The process of scrambling (encrypting) a message in such a way that it is difficult, expensive, or time-consuming for an unauthorized person to unscramble (decrypt) it.

encryption algorithm The mathematical formula used to encrypt the plaintext into the ciphertext, and vice versa.

Enterprise 2.0 Technologies and business practices that free the workforce from the constraints of legacy communication and productivity tools such as e-mail. Provides business managers with access to the right information at the right time through a Web of interconnected applications, services, and devices.

enterprise application integration (EAI) Class of software that integrates large systems.

enterprise search The practice of identifying and enabling specific content across the enterprise to be indexed, searched, and displayed to authorized users.

ethics The branch of philosophy that deals with what is considered to be right and wrong.

exchanges (trading communities or trading exchanges) Many-to-many e-marketplaces, usually owned and run by a third party or a consortium, in which many buyers and many sellers meet electronically to trade with each other.

expert location systems (ELS) Interactive computerized systems that help employees find and connect with colleagues who have expertise required for specific problems—whether they are across the country or across the room—in order to solve specific, critical business problems in seconds.

exposure The estimated cost, loss, or damage that can result if a threat exploits a vulnerability.

extranet A network that uses a virtual private network to link intranets in different locations over the Internet; an "extended intranet."

fair use The use of copyrighted material for noncommercial purposes.

FAQ page A Web page that lists questions that are frequently asked by customers and the answers to those questions.

firewall A single point between two or more networks where all traffic must pass (choke point); the device authenticates, controls, and logs all traffic.

folksonomy (collaborative tagging, social classification, social indexing, social tagging) The practice and method of collaboratively creating, classifying, and managing tags to annotate and categorize content.

forward auction An auction in which a seller entertains bids from buyers. Bidders increase price sequentially.

fraud Any business activity that uses deceitful practices or devices to deprive another of property or other rights.

front end The portion of an e-seller's business processes through which customers interact, including the seller's portal, electronic catalogs, a shopping cart, a search engine, and a payment gateway.

general controls Controls established to protect the system regardless of the specific application. For example, protecting hardware and controlling access to the data center are independent of the specific application.

geographical information system (GIS) A computer system capable of integrating, storing, editing, analyzing, sharing, and displaying geographically referenced (spatial) information.

global positioning system (GPS) A worldwide satellite-based tracking system that enables users to determine their position anywhere on the earth.

government-to-business (G2B) E-government category that includes interactions between governments and businesses (government selling to businesses and providing them with services and businesses selling products and services to the government).

government-to-citizens (G2C) E-government category that includes all the interactions between a government and its citizens.

government-to-employees (G2E) E-government category that includes activities and services between government units and their employees.

government-to-government (G2G) E-government category that includes activities within government units and those between governments.

green computing The study and practice of ecofriendly computing resources; is now a key concern of businesses in all industries—not just environmental organizations.

green IT Green IT begins with manufacturers producing environmentally friendly products and encouraging IT departments to consider more friendly options like virtualization, power management, and proper recycling habits.

group purchasing The aggregation of orders from several buyers into volume purchases so that better prices can be negotiated.

hacker Someone who gains unauthorized access to a computer system.

hash A mathematical computation that is applied to a message, using a private key, to encrypt the message.

hit A request for data from a Web page or file.

honeynet A network of honeypots.

honeypot Production system (e.g., firewalls, routers, Web servers, database servers) that looks like it does real work, but that acts as a decoy and is watched to study how network intrusions occur.

horizontal marketplaces Markets that concentrate on a service, material, or a product that is used in all types of industries (e.g., office supplies, PCs).

identity theft Fraud that involves stealing an identity of a person and then the use of that identity by someone pretending to be someone else in order to steal money or get other benefits.

incubator A company, university, or nonprofit organization that supports businesses in their initial stages of development.

indirect materials Materials used to support production (e.g., office supplies or lightbulbs).

infomediaries Electronic intermediaries that provide and/or control information flow in cyberspace, often aggregating information and selling it to others.

information architecture How the site and its Web pages are organized, labeled, and navigated to support browsing and searching throughout the Web site.

information assurance (IA) The protection of information systems against unauthorized access to or modification of information whether in storage, processing, or transit, and against the denial of service to authorized users, including those measures necessary to detect, document, and counter such threats.

information visibility The process of sharing critical data required to manage the flow of products, services, and information in real time between suppliers and customers along the supply chain.

informational Web site A Web site that does little more than provide information about the business and its products and services.

infringement Use of the work without permission or contracting for payment of a royalty.

insourcing In-house development of applications.

integration testing Testing the combination of application modules acting in concert.

integrity Assurance that stored data has not been modified without authorization; a message that was sent is the same message as that which was received.

intellectual property Creations of the mind, such as inventions, literary and artistic works, and symbols, names, images, and designs, used in commerce.

intelligent agents Software applications that have some degree of reactivity, autonomy, and adaptability—as is needed in unpredictable attack situations. An agent is able to adapt itself based on changes occurring in its environment.

interactive marketing Online marketing, facilitated by the Internet, by which marketers and advertisers can interact directly with customers, and consumers can interact with advertisers/vendors.

interactive voice response (IVR) A voice system that enables users to request and receive information and to enter and change data through a telephone to a computerized system.

interactive Web site A Web site that provides opportunities for the customers and the business to communicate and share information.

intermediary A third party that operates between sellers and buyers.

internal control environment The work atmosphere that a company sets for its employees.

internal procurement marketplace The aggregated catalogs of all approved suppliers combined into a single internal electronic catalog.

Internet radio A Web site that provides music, talk, and other entertainment, both live and stored, from a variety of radio stations.

Internet underground economy E-markets for stolen information made up of thousands of Web sites that sell credit card numbers, social security numbers, other data such as numbers of bank accounts, social network IDs, passwords, and much more.

interoperability Connecting people, data, and diverse systems; the term can be defined in a technical way or in a broad way, taking into account social, political, and organizational factors.

intrabusiness EC E-commerce category that includes all internal organizational activities that involve the exchange of goods, services, or information among various units and individuals in an organization.

intranet An internal corporate or government network that uses Internet tools, such as Web browsers, and Internet protocols.

intrusion detection system (IDS) A special category of software that can monitor activity across a network or on a host computer, watch for suspicious activity, and take automated action based on what it sees.

IP address An address that uniquely identifies each computer connected to a network or the Internet.

ISP hosting service A hosting service that provides an independent, stand-alone Web site for small and medium-sized businesses.

key (key value) The secret code used to encrypt and decrypt a message.

key performance indicators (KPIs) The quantitative expression of critically important metrics.

key space The large number of possible key values (keys) created by the algorithm to use when transforming the message.

keystroke logging (keylogging) A method of capturing and recording user keystrokes.

keyword banners Banner ads that appear when a predetermined word is queried from a search engine.

knowledge discovery in databases (KDD)/knowledge discovery (KD) The process of extracting useful knowledge from volumes of data.

knowledge management (KM) The process of capturing or creating knowledge, storing it, updating it constantly, disseminating it, and using it whenever necessary.

localization The process of converting media products developed in one environment (e.g., country) to a form culturally and linguistically acceptable in countries outside the original target market.

location-based m-commerce (l-commerce) Delivery of m-commerce transactions to individuals in a specific location, at a specific time.

macro virus (macro worm) A macro virus or macro worm is executed when the application object that contains the macro is opened or a particular procedure is executed.

maintenance, repair, and operation (MRO) Indirect materials used in activities that support production.

malware (malicious software) A generic term for malicious software.

market segmentation The process of dividing a consumer market into logical groups for conducting marketing research and analyzing personal information.

marketspace A marketplace in which sellers and buyers exchange goods and services for money (or for other goods and services), but do so electronically.

mass customization A method that enables manufacturers to create specific products for each customer based on the customer's exact needs.

maverick buying Unplanned purchases of items needed quickly, often at non-prenegotiated higher prices.

merchant brokering Deciding from whom (from what merchant) to buy products.

message digest (MD) A summary of a message, converted into a string of digits after the hash has been applied.

metadata Data about data, including software programs about data, rules for organizing data, and data summaries.

metric A specific, measurable standard against which actual performance is compared.

microblogging A form of blogging that allows users to write messages (usually up to 140 characters) and publish them, either to be viewed by anyone or by a restricted group that can be chosen by the user. These messages can be submitted by a variety of means, including text messaging, instant messaging, e-mail, MP3, or just on the Web.

microfinance Refers to the provision of financial services to poor or low-income clients, including consumers and the self-employed.

mobile advertising (m-advertising) Ads sent to and presented on mobile devices.

mobile commerce (m-commerce or m-business) Any business activity conducted over a wireless telecommunications network or from mobile devices.

mobile entertainment Any type of leisure activity that utilizes wireless telecommunication networks, interacts with service providers, and incurs a cost upon usage.

mobile government (m-government) The wireless implementation of e-government mostly to citizens but also to businesses.

mobile portal A portal accessible via a mobile device.

mobile social networking Members converse and connect with one another using cell phones or other mobile devices.

mobile worker Any employee who is away from his or her primary work space at least 10 hours a week or 25 percent of the time.

multichannel business model A business model where a company sells in multiple marketing channels simultaneously (e.g., both physical and online stores).

multimedia messaging service (MMS) The emerging generation of wireless messaging; MMS is able to deliver rich media.

name-your-own-price model Auction model in which a would-be buyer specifies the price (and other terms) he or she is willing to pay to any willing and able seller. It is a C2B model that was pioneered by Priceline.com.

network-based positioning Relies on base stations to find the location of a mobile device sending a signal or sensed by the network.

nonrepudiation Assurance that online customers or trading partners cannot falsely deny (repudiate) their purchase or transaction.

on-demand CRM CRM hosted by an ASP or other vendor on the vendor's premise; in contrast to the traditional practice of buying the software and using it on-premise.

on-demand delivery service Express delivery made fairly quickly after an online order is received.

online analytical processing (OLAP) End-user analytical activities, such as DSS modeling using spreadsheets and graphics, that are done online.

online intermediary An online third party that brokers a transaction online between a buyer and a seller; may be virtual or click-and-mortar.

operational data store A database for use in transaction processing (operational) systems that uses data warehouse concepts to provide clean data.

opt-in Agreement that requires computer users to take specific steps to allow the collection of personal information.

opt-out Business practice that gives consumers the opportunity to refuse sharing information about themselves.

outsourcing A method of transferring the management and/or day-to-day execution of an entire business function to a third-party service provider.

packet Segment of data sent from one computer to another on a network.

page An HTML (Hypertext Markup Language) document that may contain text, images, and other online elements, such as Java applets and multimedia files. It can be generated statically or dynamically.

partner relationship management (PRM) Business strategy that focuses on providing comprehensive quality service to business partners.

patent A document that grants the holder exclusive rights to an invention for a fixed number of years.

payment card Electronic card that contains information that can be used for payment purposes.

payment service provider (PSP) A third-party service connecting a merchant's EC system to the appropriate acquiring bank or financial institution. PSPs must be registered with the various card associations they support.

penetration test (pen test) A method of evaluating the security of a computer system or a network by simulating an attack from a malicious source, (e.g., a cracker).

permission advertising (permission marketing) Advertising (marketing) strategy in which customers agree to accept advertising and marketing materials (known as "opt-in").

person-to-person lending Lending done between individuals circumventing the bank's traditional role in this process.

personal area network (PAN) A wireless telecommunications network for device-to-device connections within a very short range.

personal digital assistant (PDA) A stand-alone handheld computer principally used for personal information management.

personal firewall A network node designed to protect an individual user's desktop system from the public network by monitoring all the traffic that passes through the computer's network interface card.

personalization The tailoring of services, products, and advertising content with individual consumers and their specific preferences.

personalized content Web content that matches the needs and expectations of the individual visitor.

phishing A crimeware technique to steal the identity of a target company to get the identities of its customers.

plaintext An unencrypted message in human-readable form.

Platform for Privacy Preferences Project (P3P) A protocol allowing Web sites to declare their intended use of information they collect about browsing users.

pop-up ad An ad that appears in a separate window before, after, or during Internet surfing or when reading e-mail.

pop-up under ad An ad that appears underneath the current browser window, so when the user closes the active window the ad is still on the screen.

prevention measures Ways to help stop unauthorized users (also known as "intruders") from accessing any part of the EC system.

privacy The right to be left alone and free of unreasonable personal intrusions.

private key Encryption code that is known only to its owner.

procurement The process made up of a range of activities by which an organization obtains or gains access to the resources (materials, skills, capabilities, facilities) it requires to undertake its core business activities.

procurement management The planning, organizing, and coordinating of all the activities related to purchasing goods and services needed to accomplish the organization's mission.

product brokering Deciding what product to buy.

protocol tunneling Method used to ensure confidentiality and integrity of data transmitted over the Internet by encrypting data packets, sending them in packets across the Internet, and decrypting them at the destination address.

public (asymmetric) key encryption Method of encryption that uses a pair of matched keys—a public key to encrypt a message and a private key to decrypt it, or vice versa.

public e-marketplaces Third-party exchanges open to all interested parties (sellers and buyers).

public key Encryption code that is publicly available to anyone.

public key infrastructure (PKI) A scheme for securing e-payments using public key encryption and various technical components.

random banners Banner ads that appear at random, not as the result of the user's action.

real-time location system (RTLS) Systems used to track and identify the location of objects in real time.

referral economy The effect upon sales of consumers receiving a referral or recommendation from other consumers.

regulatory compliance Systems or departments in an organization whose job is to ensure that personnel are aware of and take steps to comply with relevant laws, standards, policies, and regulations.

reintermediation The process whereby intermediaries (either new ones or those that had been disintermediated) take on new intermediary roles.

request for proposal (RFP) Notice sent to potential vendors inviting them to submit a proposal describing their software package and how it would meet the company's needs.

request for quote (RFQ) The "invitation" to participate in a tendering (bidding) system.

reusability The likelihood a segment of source code can be used again to add new functionalities with slight or no modification.

reverse auction (bidding or tendering system) Auction in which the buyer places an item for bid (tender) on a request for quote (RFQ) system, potential suppliers bid on the job, with the price reducing sequentially, and the lowest bid wins; primarily a B2B or G2B mechanism.

risk The probability that a vulnerability will be known and used.

ROI calculator Calculator that uses metrics and formulas to compute ROI.

sales force automation (SFA) Software that automates the tasks performed by salespeople in the field, such as data collection and its transmission.

scalability How big a system can grow in various dimensions to provide more service; measured by total number of users, number of simultaneous users, or transaction volume.

scenario planning A strategic planning methodology that generates plausible alternative futures to help decision makers identify actions that can be taken today to ensure success in the future.

search engine A computer program that can access databases of Internet resources, search for specific information or key words, and report the results.

search engine optimization (SEO) The craft of increasing site rank on search engines; the optimizer uses the ranking algorithm of the search engine (which may be different for different search engines) and best search phases, and tailors the ad accordingly.

search engine spam Pages created deliberately to trick the search engine into offering inappropriate, redundant, or poor-quality search results.

Secure Socket Layer (SSL) Protocol that utilizes standard certificates for authentication and data encryption to ensure privacy or confidentiality.

self-hosting When a business acquires the hardware, software, staff, and dedicated telecommunications services necessary to set up and manage its own Web site.

sell-side e-marketplace A Web-based marketplace in which one company sells to many business buyers from e-catalogs or auctions, frequently over an extranet.

Semantic Web An evolving extension of the Web in which Web content can be expressed not only in natural language, but also in a form that can be understood, interpreted, and used by intelligent computer software agents, permitting them to find, share, and integrate information more easily.

service-level agreement (SLA) A formal agreement regarding the division of work between a company and a vendor.

settlement Transferring money from the buyer's to the merchant's account.

shopping portals Gateways to e-storefronts and e-malls; may be comprehensive or niche oriented.

shopping robots (shopping agents or shopbots) Tools that scout the Web on behalf of consumers who specify search criteria.

short message service (SMS) A service that supports the sending and receiving of short text messages on mobile phones.

site navigation Aids that help visitors find the information they need quickly and easily.

smart card An electronic card containing an embedded microchip that enables predefined operations or the addition, deletion, or manipulation of information on the card.

smart card operating system Special system that handles file management, security, input/output (I/O), and command execution and provides an application programming interface (API) for a smart card.

smart card reader Activates and reads the contents of the chip on a smart card, usually passing the information on to a host system.

smart phone A mobile phone with PC-like capabilities.

social bookmarking Web service for sharing Internet bookmarks. The sites are a popular way to store, classify, share, and search links through the practice of folksonomy techniques on the Internet and intranets.

social computing An approach aimed at making the human–computer interface more natural.

social engineering A type of nontechnical attack that uses some ruse to trick users into revealing information or performing an action that compromises a computer or network.

social marketplace The term is derived from the combination of *social networking* and *marketplace.* An online community that harnesses the power of one's social networks for the introduction, buying, and selling of products, services, and resources, including one's own creations. Also may refer to a structure that resembles a social network but is focused on individual members.

social media The online platforms and tools that people use to share opinions, experiences, insights, perceptions, and various media, including photos, videos, and music, with each other.

social network A category of Internet applications that help connect friends, business partners, or individuals with specific interests by providing free services such as photos presentation, e-mail, blogging, and so on using a variety of tools.

social network advertising Online advertising that focuses on social networking sites.

social network analysis (SNA) The mapping and measuring of relationships and information flows among people, groups, organizations, computers, and other information- or knowledge-processing entities. The nodes in the network are the people and groups, whereas the links show relationships or flows between the nodes. SNAs provide both visual and a quantitative analysis of relationships.

social network service (SNS) A service that builds online communities by providing an online space for people to build free homepages and that provides basic communication and support tools for conducting different activities in the social network.

social networking Social networks and activities conducted in social networks. It also includes activities conducted using Web 2.0 (e.g., wikis, microblogs) not within social networks.

spam The electronic equivalent of junk mail.

spam site Page that uses techniques that deliberately subvert a search engine's algorithms to artificially inflate the page's rankings.

spamming Using e-mail to send unwanted ads (sometimes floods of ads).

splog Short for *spam blog.* A site created solely for marketing purposes.

spot buying The purchase of goods and services as they are needed, usually at prevailing market prices.

spyware Software that gathers user information over an Internet connection without the user's knowledge.

standard of due care Care that a company is reasonably expected to take based on the risks affecting its EC business and online transactions.

stickiness Characteristic that influences the average length of time a visitor stays in a site.

storebuilder service A hosting service that provides disk space and services to help small and microbusinesses build a Web site quickly and cheaply.

stored-value card A card that has monetary value loaded onto it and that is usually rechargeable.

strategic (systematic) sourcing Purchases involving long-term contracts that usually are based on private negotiations between sellers and buyers.

strategy A broad-based formula for how a business is going to accomplish its mission, what its goals should be, and what plans and policies will be needed to carry out those goals.

strategy assessment The continuous evaluation of progress toward the organization's strategic goals, resulting in corrective action and, if necessary, strategy reformulation.

strategy formulation The development of strategies to exploit opportunities and manage threats in the business environment in light of corporate strengths and weaknesses.

strategy implementation The development of detailed, short-term plans for carrying out the projects agreed on in strategy formulation.

strategy initiation The initial phase of strategic planning in which the organization examines itself and its environment.

supplier relationship management (SRM) A comprehensive approach to managing an enterprise's interactions with the organizations that supply the goods and services it uses.

supply chain The flow of materials, information, money, and services from raw material suppliers through factories and warehouses to the end customers.

supply chain management (SCM) A complex process that requires the coordination of many activities so that the shipment of goods and services from supplier right through to customer is done efficiently and effectively for all parties concerned. SCM aims to minimize inventory levels, optimize production and increase throughput, decrease manufacturing time, optimize logistics and distribution, streamline order fulfillment, and overall reduce the costs associated with these activities.

SWOT analysis A methodology that surveys external opportunities and threats and relates them to internal strengths and weaknesses.

symmetric (private) key encryption An encryption system that uses the same key to encrypt and decrypt the message.

syndication The sale of the same good (e.g., digital content) to many customers, who then integrate it with other offerings and resell it or give it away free.

tag A nonhierarchical keyword or term assigned to a piece of information (such as an Internet bookmark, digital image, video clip, or any computer document).

tendering (bidding) system Model in which a buyer requests would-be sellers to submit bids; the lowest bidder wins.

terminal-based positioning Calculating the location of a mobile device from signals sent by the device to base stations.

text mining The application of data mining to nonstructured or less-structured text files.

total benefits of ownership (TBO) Benefits of ownership that include both tangible and intangible benefits.

total cost of ownership (TCO) A formula for calculating the cost of owning, operating, and controlling an IT system.

trademark A symbol used by businesses to identify their goods and services; government registration of the trademark confers exclusive legal right to its use.

transaction log A record of user activities at a company's Web site.

transactional Web site A Web site that sells products and services.

Transport Layer Security (TLS) As of 1996, another name for the SSL protocol.

Trojan horse A program that appears to have a useful function but that contains a hidden function that presents a security risk.

trust The psychological status of willingness to depend on another person or organization.

turnkey approach Ready to use without further assembly or testing; supplied in a state that is ready to turn on and operate.

tweets Text-based posts up to 140 characters in length posted to Twitter.

Twitter A free microblogging service that allows its users to send and read other users' updates.

unique visits A count of the number of visitors entering a site, regardless of how many pages are viewed per visit.

unit testing Testing application software modules one at a time.

up-selling Offering an upgraded version of the product in order to boost sales and profit.

USA PATRIOT Act Uniting and Strengthening America by Providing Appropriate Tools to Intercept and Obstruct Terrorism Act passed in October 2001, in the aftermath of the September 11 terrorist attacks. Its intent is to give law enforcement agencies broader range in their efforts to protect the public.

usability (of Web site) The quality and usefulness of the user's experience when interacting with the Web site.

usability testing Testing the quality of the user's experience when interacting with a Web site.

user profile The requirements, preferences, behaviors, and demographic traits of a particular customer.

value proposition The benefit that a company's products or services provide to a company and its customers.

vendor-managed inventory (VMI) The practice of retailers' making suppliers responsible for determining when to order and how much to order.

venture capital (VC) Money invested in a business by an individual, a group of individuals (venture capitalists), or a funding company in exchange for equity in the business.

vertical marketplaces Markets that deal with one industry or industry segment (e.g., steel, chemicals).

viral blogging Viral (word-of-mouth) marketing done by bloggers.

viral marketing Word-of-mouth method by which customers promote a product or service by telling others about it.

virtual (Internet) community A group of people with similar interests who interact with one another using the Internet.

virtual (pure-play) e-tailers Firms that sell directly to consumers over the Internet without maintaining a physical sales channel.

virtual (pure-play) organizations Organizations that conduct their business activities solely online.

virtual private network (VPN) A network that uses the public Internet to carry information but remains private by using encryption to scramble the communications, authentication to ensure that information has not been tampered with, and access control to verify the identity of anyone using the network.

virtual university An online university from which students take classes from home or other offsite locations, usually via the Internet.

virtual world A user-defined world in which people can interact, play, and do business. The most publicized virtual world is Second Life.

virus A piece of software code that inserts itself into a host, including the operating systems, in order to propagate; it requires that its host program be run to activate it.

visibility The knowledge about where materials and parts are at any given time, which helps solve problems such as delay, combining shipments, and more.

visit A series of requests during one navigation of a Web site; a pause of a certain length of time ends a visit.

vlog (or video blog) A blog with video content.

voice commerce (v-commerce) An umbrella term for the use of speech recognition to allow voice-activated services including Internet browsing and e-mail retrieval.

voice portal A Web site with an audio interface that can be accessed through a telephone call.

vortals B2B portals that focus on a single industry or industry segment; "vertical portals."

vulnerability Weakness in software or other mechanism that threatens the confidentiality, integrity, or availability of an asset (recall the CIA model). It can be directly used by a hacker to gain access to a system or network.

Web 2.0 The second generation of Internet-based services that lets people collaborate and share information online in new ways, such as social networking sites, wikis, communication tools, and folksonomies.

Web 3.0 A term used to describe the future of the World Wide Web. It consists of the creation of high-quality content and services produced by gifted individuals using Web 2.0 technology as an enabling platform.

Web 4.0 The Web generation after Web 3.0. It is still mostly an unknown entity. However, it is envisioned as being based on islands of intelligence and as being ubiquitous.

Web bugs Tiny graphics files embedded in e-mail messages and in Web sites that transmit information about users and their movements to a Web server.

Web hosting service A dedicated Web site hosting company that offers a wide range of hosting services and functionality to businesses of all sizes.

Web mining The application of data mining techniques to discover meaningful patterns, profiles, and trends from both the content and usage of Web sites. Also extracting information from Web documents and Web usage.

Web portal A single point of access, through a Web browser, to critical business information located inside and outside (via Internet) an organization.

Web self-service Activities conducted by users on the Web to find answers to their questions (e.g., tracking) or for product configuration.

Web video analytics A way of measuring what viewers do when they watch an online video.

Webcasting A free Internet news service that broadcasts personalized news and information, including seminars, in categories selected by the user.

Webstore (storefront) A single company's Web site where products or services are sold and usually has an online shopping cart associated with it. Many Webstores target a specific industry and find their own unique corner of the market.

Wi-Fi (wireless fidelity) The common name used to describe the IEEE 802.11 standard used on most WLANs.

wiki (wikilog) A blog that allows everyone to participate as a peer; anyone may add, delete, or change content.

WiMax A wireless standard (IEEE 802.16) for making broadband network connections over a medium-size area such as a city.

wireless local area network (WLAN) A telecommunications network that enables users to make short-range wireless connections to the Internet or another network.

wireless mobile computing (mobile computing) Computing that connects a mobile device to a network or another computing device, anytime, anywhere.

wireless wide area network (WWAN) A telecommunications network that offers wireless coverage over a large geographical area, typically over a cellular phone network.

worm A software program that runs independently, consuming the resources of its host in order to maintain itself, that is capable of propagating a complete working version of itself onto another machine.

zombies Computers infected with malware that are under the control of a spammer, hacker, or other criminal.

Index

Note: Page numbers with W indicates Online Files; E indicates Exhibit; A indicates Appendix A; and B indicates Appendix B.

3G communications technology 298